The
Reflective Woman

Fifth Edition

COLLEGE *of* ST. CATHERINE

Development of The Reflective Woman *was supported in part by grants from the National Endowment for the Humanities and the Bush Foundation.*

Copley Custom Publishing Group
Acton, Massachusetts 01720

Editors

Nancy J. Peterson-Anderson
CSC Alumna

Gabrielle F. Civil
Assistant Professor, English

Donna Hauer
Director, Multicultural Programs and Services

Kathleen Heinlen
Associate Director, O'Neill Center

Suzanne Hendricks
Director, Core Curriculum
Professor, Family, Consumer, and Nutritional Sciences

Anita T. Ho
Assistant Professor, Philosophy

With significant contributions from St. Kate's faculty, staff and students.

Contents

Preface to the TRW Reader

Welcome to the College of St. Catherine, and to our liberal arts core curriculum. The Reflective Woman course will be your introduction to what we do here at the college—how we see ourselves, what we think about, what we hope for. Every St. Kate's undergraduate takes this course, and nearly every department, program or office at the college is involved in it. Faculty members from each discipline teach "TRW," joined by some Student Affairs and administrative staff—even deans! Librarians, Sisters of St. Joseph, alumnae, technicians and support staff pitch in. It is truly a St. Kate's course, both unique to our college and central to our work.

And that work is, as our mission statement declares, "educating women to lead and influence." Our model of education is active. Together we read, study, research, connect, assess, write, discuss and reflect. We take each other seriously. As faculty, we challenge you to "claim an education," as Adrienne Rich writes in her essay in this text.

In this course we also engage our college traditions from Catholicism and the liberal arts. Catholic intellectual tradition holds thinking and studying in highest regard, next to service, prayer and ritual, as ways to draw nearer to God. In fact, the saint we are named for, St. Catherine of Alexandria, was a noted scholar and is called "the student's saint." From our Catholic roots comes our attention to art, music and literature in TRW. As Lawrence Cunningham points out in his essay in this reader, "Catholicism as a historical tradition is unthinkable apart from its churches, paintings, sculptures, works of literature, musical compositions, and finely crafted items of religious and liturgical usage." Finally, as you will see in the last unit of TRW and throughout your senior-level core course, Global Search for Justice, we build on a more recent Catholic tradition of social justice teachings that comes to us from our founders, the Sisters of St. Joseph of Carondelet.

The Sisters were determined that theirs would be a liberal arts college, one that encouraged students always to be thinkers and scholars as well as teachers, health care workers, lawyers and judges, scientists, artists, social workers and professional women of every sort. And so it has been. In 1937, only 32 years after its founding, St. Catherine's became the first Catholic college with a Phi Beta Kappa chapter, the highest recognition for liberal arts education. The liberal arts tradition provides the questions and concerns of this course. Organized into four units, "Composing a Life," "Experiencing Art and the Aesthetic," "Searching for Truths," and "Working toward Community and Justice," TRW explores key liberal arts concepts through readings, journal reflections, videos, projects and discussions.

Composing a Life

This first unit prompts us to examine how we actively construct our own lives. Together, we look closely at our own life choices and simultaneously think more broadly about the major life choices of contemporary women in a diverse culture. By considering other lives, and other assessments of "the good life," we aim to find paradigms to challenge our own choices.

Here we also set the tone for the course, building the classroom community, and clarifying what it means to get a St. Kate's education. So we begin with readings about our community. These include the Leadership Statement, excerpts from the history of the college, an examination of our mission and, for many instructors, the video "Hillary's Class." Some ideas you might consider in this unit include: choice and values; acquisitiveness, materialism, and simplicity; the role of education in "a good life"; education as an integrating experience beyond preparation for employment; learning as a process; the notion that you can "have it all"; living within multiple identities; and how culture and race, gender and sexuality, class and language contribute to who you are.

Experiencing Art and the Aesthetic

In this unit we invite you to join the American cultural conversation about art: What is art? Who decides if it's good or bad? On what do we base our judgements? Each of us has, in some fashion, entertained these questions—in our choice of music, movies or clothes, even in our enjoyment of nature.

If you haven't already encountered the traditional concepts and works of Western art that are an essential part of liberal arts education, this unit should serve as a lively introduction. However, we also want you to enjoy reflective conversations about aesthetic experiences of all sorts—the types of conversations we're enjoying in the global culture of the new millennium. So this unit also examines non-Western art. Together we will explore how the production of art and artistic values parallels the production of other values, how it is a matter of cultural consensus as well as personal choice.

Some ideas you might encounter include: the purpose of difficult art, the search for language to talk about what you like and why you like it, the concept of canon and its critiques, the role of art in our lives, the ways fiction can reveal truth, and how art can be a community endeavor.

Searching for Truths

The primary goal of "Searching for Truths" is to improve your skills as a critical thinker. We will ask, "What is truth and how do we recognize it?" But we will ask those questions from different angles—philosophical, theological and scientific. We will also approach them in a practical way, in the context of library research. In other words, how do you distinguish between reliable and not-so-reliable sources, especially in an internet search?

By way of the "Structured Controversy" project, you will also have the chance to increase your capacity for reflective judgment on matters of fact and conflicting ideas, and to connect that capacity to your educational, ethical, aesthetic and spiritual experiences. In the end, this unit aims to help you clarify the relationship between self-knowledge and academic learning.

Some skills you might engage in this unit include how to: learn collaboratively; structure an argument; question objectivity; sift through perceived truths; develop an opinion from knowledge, not just habit; agree to disagree; recognize stakeholders and claims to power in arguments; and argue not to "win," but to listen, learn and understand.

Working toward Community and Justice

The readings in this final unit bid us to consider the larger contexts in which we live our lives. Returning to the concept of life choices, we will reflect on how we can connect in rich and useful ways to the rest of our social and natural world.

"Working toward Community and Justice" also opens the discussion of the central questions of the Global Search for Justice course. We hope these same questions underscore all of our work at St. Kate's—questions such as: Who are our neighbors? What is our responsibility to them and to the communities we share? How have our communities affected who we are? How has prejudice or racism affected our lives in the U.S.? What is justice? What role does art play in social change? And how can we work to make the world a better place?

As you reach the end of these readings, we hope you will have found new ways to question, to problem-solve, to think and write, and to be reflective. The TRW faculty is committed to interdisciplinary learning—that means we aim to benefit as much from our work with each other and from our interactions with you as we do from our own fields of expertise. This same interdisciplinary enterprise is at the heart of liberal arts learning. The skills you gain at St. Kate's will transcend your discipline and allow you to be a more creative, thoughtful leader in whatever field you enter.

This eclectic collection of readings affirms that philosophy. We know we speak for most of us when we say that we teach this course because the course keeps teaching us. With this fifth edition of the text come new readings to challenge and engage us.

The faculty, staff and students who put together each of the earlier editions of the reader deserve recognition and thanks. They include members of the Core Committee and the TRW Subcommittee, and, among others, Helen Humeston (Information Management and Library and Information Science), Shanan Wexler (Theater), Cecilia Konchar Farr (English and Women's Studies), Sharon Doherty (Women's Studies), Tracy Meade (O'Neill Center), William Myers (Philosophy), Tom West (Theology), Geri Chavis (English), Ann Maloney (Philosophy), Dale McGowan (Music), Carol Pavlish (Nursing), and Brian Fogarty (Sociology), the founding Director of the Core Curriculum. Each edition of the text builds on the creativity and insights of the editions preceding it. This fifth edition is no exception.

So as you begin your education at the College of St. Catherine, join us in answering the poet Mary Oliver's challenge, a challenge for reflective women: "What is it you plan to do with your one wild and precious life?"

We can't wait to hear what we have to tell each other. Welcome to TRW.

Suzanne Hendricks,
Director of Core Curriculum and
Cecilia Konchar Farr,
Former Director of Core Curriculum,
for the Core Committee
and the TRW faculty
June 2002

Composing a Life

Joan Mitchell, CSJ (b. 1940), received a B.A. from CSC in 1962 and a M.A. in English from the University of Iowa. She taught high school English and religion, and also worked as a writer and editor. She is a former member of the CSC Board of Trustees.

All Women Can Be: The Spirit of the Sisters of St. Joseph

Joan Mitchell, CSJ

I feel a personal passion for St. Catherine's because I found my life here in my undergraduate years 1958–1962. My four years were a journey of empowerment. I came undereducated and afraid; I left able to write, think, and perform. I also found a community of women, the Sisters of St. Joseph of Carondelet, with whom to invest my life in service.

Empowering is what Sisters of St. Joseph have been about from their beginning in 1650. Pre-revolutionary France had terrible social and economic inequalities. With wealth concentrated in the church and nobility the country suffered much the same chronic problems as Third World countries today. The desperate needs of the people at the bottom gave birth to *apostolic* orders, whose cloisters became the streets, whose prayer became the works of mercy.

Among their ministries the first sisters helped young women forced to support themselves through prostitution to learn lacemaking and become self-supporting. Many marriageable young men had gone to the New World, leaving many young women without the possibility of marriage. The sisters gave these women at the bottom of society a stepping stone to their own place in its economic life beyond the social norm of their day.

The College of St. Catherine has educated and empowered most of the present members of the Sisters of St. Joseph of the St. Paul Province. Most sisters attended St. Catherine as beleaguered teachers coming on Saturday mornings or during the hot days of summer sessions, to finish degrees on the twenty-year plan. Many attended in the days before the Second Vatican Council, when we were forbidden to talk to the other students and cut off from the community life of the college. Many sisters have returned to St. Catherine's to do graduate work, for example, in the Master of Arts in Organizational Leadership, theology, and spirituality, and their work has nurtured the community.

2

However, norms for women also affected us. Our community educated many women to the doctoral level but never in medicine, nor did we train our own women in advanced theology degrees until after Vatican II. Sister Rosalie Ryan led that small revolution toward the college theology department of today. In her research and writing she is one of the pioneering women bible scholars who have recovered the importance of women among Jesus's disciples, those women who follow and serve him and are with him from the beginning in Galilee but whose presence was lost to us in the scant two and three verses the gospel gives to their presence.

The Sisters of St. Joseph College Consortium, which has twelve member colleges, funded a study of their mission and image, surveying 480 people, twenty-five on this campus, four of them sisters. Sister Karen Kennelly, formerly academic dean on the St. Paul Campus and now president of Mount St. Mary's in Los Angeles, chairs this consortium. Their study reports five distinctive characteristics of these colleges, which include St. Catherine:

1) Hospitality and caring community
2) Concern for all without distinction
3) Addressing the needs of the time
4) Striving for excellence in all endeavors
5) Making a difference in local and world community

These same characteristics reach back to our beginnings as a community. Our houses were to be hubs of hospitality, caring, and outreach to our neighbors. The first foundation of the Sisters of St. Joseph was a secret society. It lasted only two years. This was a small group of pious women who wanted to help others. The Jesuit Father Medaille, who articulated the spirituality of these women, describes the community as a "little design," called by the name of St. Joseph, a model of hidden service, like the self-emptying humility of Jesus hidden in the tabernacle among the people. What lasted of this first foundation is its identity with Joseph, of whom little is known but his care for Mary and Jesus. From this name we take an ethic of *charity to the dear neighbor without distinction.*

To address the needs of the time was why the community of St. Joseph began anew in 1650 in LePuy, France, with the support of Bishop de Maupas, in a hospital. The first sisters formed a hub from which the spokes of the wheel of ministry went out. Our first constitutions directed the sisters to "divide the city into various sections, and either by visiting the sick personally or through the lay associates of the congregation . . . make every effort to learn what disorders prevail in each quarter so that they may remedy them either by their own efforts or by the intermediary of those who have some power over the person engaged in these disorders."

Striving for excellence is an ethic at the heart of St. Catherine. Seventeenth-century piety used the word *zeal* and the concept of *the more* to express this value that we know so well from the history of the St. Paul campus where Mother Antonia sent six young sisters to study in European universities. They became the living endowment of the college's early years. We know this quality well, too, from the history of the Minneapolis campus where the faculty practically had to teach in the stairwells as second and third year nursing students contended for space with the first class of the junior college Sister Ann Joachim founded.

The *more* is an ethic of liberation that envisioned the sisters being all women could be and envisioned people at the bottom of society empowered to be all they could be. At our general chapter as a congregation in 1993 we asked ourselves again, "What more is being asked of us now in our commitment to justice?" You see the clear common roots of the two campuses in these characteristics:

- Hospitality and caring
- Concern for the dear neighbor without distinction
- Addressing the needs of the time
- Striving for excellence

They add up to making a difference.

Sometimes when I hear people talk about *the sisters*, I sense they are not talking about me or sisters today but about women farther back, perhaps those who founded St. Catherine's or those who formed the academic community in the past. I share reverence for these sisters, but I suspect they seem wise and foresighted rather than dangerous and single-minded because they are safely dead. We laud Mother Antonia today but would we have sided with her when she put up Mendel Hall to stop Prior from going through the St. Paul Campus? Where beyond the status quo would her passion for excellence and education for women lead her today? Perhaps where it has led our 1989 general chapter, which declared, "We support the exercise of the gifts of all the baptized for ministry." And what more? Conflict, conversation, argument—these are creative processes.

George Arbunckle, a cultural anthropologist, Marist priest, and New Zealander, says the Catholic Church missed the modern era. At the Council of Trent, which met twenty-five times between 1546 and 1563, the Church responded to the Protestant Reformation by effectively freezing itself in a medieval time warp that lasted until the Second Vatican Council 402 years later.

In the Church's fixed self-understanding prior to Vatican II, sisters' permanent vowed commitment gave them a special, privileged place in the structure of the Church, lower than the clergy but higher than the faithful laity. The Second Vatical Council radically flattened these hierarchical gradations by stressing the common call to holiness all Christians share, none more than others, by reason of the baptism.

Thirty years ago we sisters lived our higher spiritual vocation by being set apart from lay people. Today we are part of the ordinary life of the human community rather than apart from it. We understand ourselves not only as a community of vowed members but a vast inclusive network of relationships with colleagues in ministry, former members, families, and friends. We share life, prayer, ministry, and companionship with consociates who link themselves with us through interest and shared charism rather than vows.

There are positives in missing the modern era. Catholic consciousness remains very shaped by the communal experience that antedates the Enlightenment focus on individual subjectivity. Books such as *Habits of the Heart* call for church to become the glue of fragmented postmodern society. Catholic tradition and sisters' experience in creating community together have something to offer the civic community toward this need, not in going backward to a community that buries the individual but forward to communities of mutuality and interdependence. In fact, in Latin America a base-community movement has arisen reinventing Christian community at the grassroots level. This movement is spreading here in the U.S., too.

The Second Vatican Council called Christians to serve the poor and make a difference in this world. "The joys and the hopes, the griefs and the anxieties of the people of this age, especially those who are poor or are in any way afflicted, those too are the joys and hopes, the griefs and anxieties of the followers of Christ," it said (*Pastoral Constitution on the Church in the Modern World, #1*). Our ministries as a community have radically broadened in response to this call. Our history in this century had been one of participating in the building of the Catholic school system in this country and the Catholic health care system. Things were gained in this national endeavor—immigrant Catholics were educated and assimilated into the American culture. This era also made us semi-cloistered in our convents and limited to staffing schools and hospitals. Since Vatican II we have rediscovered we are an order founded to serve on the streets and form partnerships with lay people. We were founded to "divide the city in various sections."

At first, this emphasis strained relations between people who moved out of their classroom to give direct service to the poor and those who stayed in institutions such as the college. Now thirty years later, we see very clearly the importance of higher education in people's journey out of poverty, welfare, and hunger. I'll bet anyone who heard the student from the Minneapolis campus with the six children and the disabled husband who spoke one year at our Student/Board of Trustees Dialog still remembers her and the difference her education was making for all of them. I remember Anita Pampusch remarking at the tenth anniversary of Weekend College that those who established educational policies in large corporations probably did not have in mind educating the numbers of women in secretarial work who took advantage of these programs to earn bachelors' degrees.

The Sisters of St. Joseph have profoundly changed in the last thirty years and we want you to know who we are today. We continue to have sisters on the college faculty and staff, but fewer than in the past. In the past thirty years sisters have developed new ministries that offer sites for volunteer work, internships, and mentoring programs. Sisters are actively involved with Peace House, where Rose Tillemans welcomes and shares lunch and prayer with street people in a community of respect right next to the Dairy Queen near Franklin and Portland. Down Portland is St. Joseph House, which Char Madigan helped start and so many keep going as a place that welcomes battered women and nurtures clients as staff members. HOPE, Homes on Portland Enterprises, has refurbished former crack houses on the same block. At Incarnation House sisters helped found and staff this place for women with young children; at Ascension Place, women are struggling out of addictions. Sisters are teaching in literacy programs in the Frogtown area and at the Administration Center and Carondelet Center next door. In these new ministries as in our earliest ministries we partner with lay people.

Few people in the Church have changed more than sisters as a group. We were readied to respond to the needs of the time by good educations. We have roared through modern consciousness into the postmodern. Today we pursue our own talents and gifts in ministry rather than getting educated to fill a waiting position. Today we are working out new forms of governance that build vision from the bottom up by hearing into words all our voices.

The Second Vatican Council was part of the social change and challenge of the 1960's that also revived the women's movement. This movement began in the last century among Quaker and Unitarian women who joined the cause for abolition and moved on to women's suffrage. In the last twenty years Catholic women have taken their place in the movement, especially in the theological fields.

Elisabeth Schussler Fiorenza has put feminist methodologies to work retrieving the importance of women in the bible, theorizing that the first Christian communities formed a discipleship of equals and aiming to make the scriptures no longer tablets of stone but bread to nourish women and men today.

Rosemary Radford Ruether, pioneer Catholic woman historian, godmothers younger feminists. She insists women rape victims in her classes can relate to Jesus because of his experience of violence. He is Christ and Christa. Mary Daly's prodigious research chronicles violence to women in many cultures and creates new language for women's experience. Elizabeth Johnson is a Sister of St. Joseph of Brentwood and professor at Fordham who suggests, in her book *She Who Is* that we no longer neglect the feminine imagery of God as Spirit and recognize the imminent presence of God as Spirit cogiven with all life. Hispanic sisters have formed Las Hermanas to further the struggle for liberation among Hispanic women. The Black Sisters Conference has contributed its own voices— Toinette Eugene, Jamie Phelps, Thea Bowman.

Catholic women and men stand at a threshold today. People ask sisters, "How can you stay in the Catholic Church? It's so patriarchal. How can you let the pope tell you what to do?" How can one care about educating men and women for interdependency and community and stay in the church? I should point out that these are not only women's questions. St. Catherine honored Bishop Raymond Lucker for his support of women during the debates about the women's pastoral.

At the last board retreat I attended we had to draw an image of St. Catherine. I found myself drawing the stacks of books in the library and beside them the big doors of the chapel. I drew the shelves open but put a lock on the chapel. How does a Catholic college educate women to be all they can be when the church does not welcome their gifts for ministry?

Withdrawing from the church is the easiest answer. It's the answer of preference among Catholics in their twenties. It's not mine. It's not a lot of people's. As a Sister of St. Joseph I am a publicly committed woman of the church. I say, "We are the Church. This is our home. We won't be put out." More than that, women have always belonged here. Scripture gives us evidence of women disciples, apostles, deacons, prophets. Church history tells us Hilda of Whitby and Brigid of Ireland were abbesses of double monasteries of men and women. Shawn Madigan's research identifies women mystics in every age.

What do the Sisters of St. Joseph ask and offer this college toward the future? We are here today asking for dialog. We have to offer our struggle to change since Vatican II and a long history as an alternative Christian community within the Church. Feminist and other liberation theologies locate authority in the voices of the oppressed struggling for justice. These liberation theologies call us to speak the truth of our experience and to make room for others through listening them into speech.

A cultural anthropologist looks at the current movement to restore the pre-Vatican II Catholic Church and says that it's surprising the backlash isn't worse because the social upheaval and chaos have been so profound. This is the restoration church. On the other side, another kind of church is taking form in small Christian communities of lay men and women who break open the word together, do justice together, seek equality together. This is the emergent church.

The restoration church says the conversation is over. The emergent church says we must begin a conversation that includes everyone and invites all to speak for themselves as their most fundamental act of being human. We are asking for dialog and engagement in improvising a useful future.

Pope John Paul II's statement on Catholic education, *Ex Corde Ecclesiae*, has renewed conversation about what Catholic means in the missions of institutions of higher learning. In *America*, for May 28, 1994, Father Joseph Feeney of St. Joseph University in Philadelphia asks familiar questions: "While Jesuit colleges do and should welcome students of all faiths and no faith, has a diverse student body clouded institutional vision? How is Jesuit education defined? As liberal-arts based? Humanistic? Christian humanistic? Faith and justice based? How to link campus ministry and classroom? How to cherish diversity and build community?"

The Sisters of St. Joseph who came to the United States in 1836 from France to New Orleans, up the Mississippi to St. Louis, to the town of Carondelet just south of St. Louis, came to do what had to be done in the New World. In 1851 sisters came upstream to St. Paul to teach Indians, but they wound up founding the first hospital in the state, St. Joseph's, because a cholera epidemic demanded their school become a hospital. They improvised a useful future.

Sister Rita Steinhagen is a legend among the sisters for all she has initiated as a result of Father Harry Bury taking her to the streets of Cedar Riverside, where she began hearing people's needs and started a Free Store, the West Bank Clinic, the Bridge for runaway kids, and with Char Madigan St. Joseph House for Battered Women. Rita and Char taught us to listen to the needs of the dear neighbor without distinction as the confraternities of mercy had done in France in the beginning.

At our last all-community gathering Sister Marian Louwaige brought to the eucharistic table a piece of Belgian lace. She saw in its airy pattern a symbol of room for all in the design of the community and its future. Sister Sharon Howell brought to the altar a piece of kinte clothe, a tightly woven African cloth. She saw in the weave a symbol of the solidarity in which we must stand together. What we really ask of you is to continue the lacemaking with us, to weave a future that continues to reintegrate those who have least with those who have most, that makes of the threads of our lives a pattern of grace that is both open to all and tight enough not to come undone, or fray, but last as an intricacy where sisters cared and joined hands with lasting friends in entwining circles of learning and care, love and service.

A 1936 graduate of CSC with majors in History, Latin and English, Rosalie Ryan, CSJ, Ph.D., began her tenure at CSC in 1948 as Professor of English. She later served as Admissions Director and Academic Dean and retired in 1985 from the Theology Department. She is Professor Emeritus of Theology.

John Christine Wolkerstorfer, CSJ, earned a B.A. at CSC in 1961 and went on to earn a Ph.D. from the University of Minnesota. She was a Professor of American History at CSC, with special interests in oral history and in the U.S. Civil War. She retired in 1997.

from More than a Dream
Eighty-five Years at the College of St. Catherine

Rosalie Ryan, CSJ and John Christine Wolkerstorfer, CSJ

Chapter One: A Vision of Excellence

Early in 1905, a bulletin announced that a new Catholic college for women would introduce "the third epoch in the development of the educational work of the Sisters of St. Joseph in the Northwest. In 1851 they opened the first Catholic elementary school . . . some years later they built St. Joseph's Academy, the first preparatory school; and finally they founded St. Catherine's . . . the purpose of those in charge is to make this college the best and highest school of its kind in the Northwest." Twenty-seven sisters had already begun to fulfill this vision in a single building on isolated farmland west of St. Paul.

The College of St. Catherine opened to students in January 1905, but the project had been long in the making. Archbishop John Ireland had begun to plan for the college in the early 1890s, helping his sister Ellen—Mother Seraphine Ireland—acquire 110 acres of land at the comer of Randolph and Cleveland avenues. A financial panic in 1893 postponed the project, and ten years passed before the work continued. Not everyone greeted plans for the new college with enthusiasm. Institutions for the higher education of women had not found favor in the United States in the late 1800s. Women's education was carried on chiefly by "female seminaries," which gave courses in "domestic training": needlework, manners, and a host of other topics intended to prepare a woman for her place in the home. Toward the end of the century, individual women began asking for more, and the heads of some colleges moved towards providing education in literature and the sciences to prepare women for teaching and other professions. George Schmidt wrote of what this entailed in *The Liberal Arts College: A Chapter in American Cultural History*: "To reach the college level . . . it would be necessary to slough off the many fashionable and vocational scraps of knowledge and concentrate on the solid subjects which sharpened the understanding and disciplined the mind. This meant the higher reaches of Latin, Greek, mathematics, mental and moral philosophy." Efforts to create greater intellectual challenge for women often met with shock, alarm, or derision. "Such an experience," said one critic, "can only be hardening and deforming." Another said, "This borders on the vulgar."

Historian Thomas Woody wrote that the Reverend John Todd, a Protestant minister, absolutely denounced the idea: "As for training young ladies through a long intellectual course, as we do young men, it can never be done. They will die in the process . . . The poor thing has her brain crowded with history, grammar, arithmetic, geography, natural history, chemistry . . . metaphysics, French, often German, Latin, perhaps Greek. . . . She must be on the strain all the school hours, study in the evening till her eyes ache, her brain whirls, her spine yields and gives way, and she comes through the process of education enervated, feeble, without courage or vigor, elasticity or strength."

The naysayers deterred neither the sisters nor Archbishop Ireland, who had already given material as well as moral support. In 1900 he had signed over to the sisters the rights to his book, *The Church and Modern Society*, which they peddled from door to door, selling 20,000 copies and raising $60,000 for the college building fund. In 1902, Hugh Derham, a wealthy farmer from Rosemount, asked the archbishop to name a special charity. Ireland suggested he support the effort toward a new Catholic liberal arts college for women. Derham donated $20,000 toward the erection of the first building and $5,000 for a scholarship. Later, Mother Seraphine said of the gift: "It may not seem very large . . . but it gave us courage to go on. He well deserved to have Derham Hall named for him."

Because of problems with construction, the school, scheduled to open in September 1904, was not ready for occupancy until the end of that year. On December 26, 1904, twenty-seven sisters walked a mile in a snowstorm from St. Joseph's Academy in downtown St. Paul to board the Grand Avenue streetcar at Seven Corners. They got off the bus at Cleveland Avenue, then walked another mile south to Randolph Avenue. The elements did not discourage their excitement over the new building. Sister Bridget Bohan later reminisced that on December 27 Archbishop Ireland came out with a team of horses. With him were Mother Seraphine and Sister Celestine Howard. Promptly at 7:00 A.M., the archbishop offered the first Mass. Then he blessed the rooms of Derham Hall: "They had lanterns to light their way around the house . . . a cat followed . . . Sister Jarlath [Noonan] said that Sister Eulalia [Dress] brought the cat from the academy in a bag . . . The cat went into all the rooms as they were being blessed. Whenever the archbishop shook the holy water, the cat went up to receive . . . Finally he said, 'What's that doing here?'" Because of the continuing snow, the three guests left after breakfast. A few days later the boarding students from St. Joseph's Academy arrived to become students of Derham Hall.

The sisters had started from scratch in furnishing the new school, and they sometimes came up short. According to Sister Bridget: "We had about ninety boarders, and when their trunks came out with everything, we had sheets enough for about forty-eight or fifty beds . . . And this was the Christmas holidays. Sister Hyacinth [Werden] said, 'I don't know what to do.' 'Well,' I said, 'give us some money, and we'll do the buying.' Sister Edith [Hogan] and I went over to Minneapolis, and you couldn't get sheets ready-made. You had to buy the bolt of unbleached muslin . . . We rented [sewing] machines and Sister Antonia [McHugh] and I sat at those machines from dawn to dark, and Sister Monica [Berghs] made up the sheets. And the boarders took them without being laundered. They made nothing of it . . . Unbleached, oh, it was unspeakable!" Neverthe-less, the school shortly offered an "academic" (college preparatory) course, music, art, and domestic arts. In September 1905, college courses formally began, with seven students registered as freshmen.

The challenge of building enrollment engaged the sisters from the start. Brochures extolled the beauty of the campus, and, later, paid advertise-ments in the *Catholic Bulletin* lured prospective students. The first printed materials read: "On this spot Nature has poured her beauty with a prodi-gal hand. To the west of the college is the Mississippi, just recovering from its dash over the Falls [of St. Anthony]; further still to the west, the laughing waters of Minnehaha make constant melody, and on all sides alternating stretches of unkempt forest and billowy greensward complete the beauty of the scene."

Later notices stressed the healthfulness of the site. In 1906: "No school in the United States for the education of young ladies is more favorably sit-uated . . . in regard to the healthfulness and sanitation . . . The drainage and plumbing are as nearly perfect as can be found anywhere." Another ad read: "In the construction of the college building the comfort and safety of its inmates were taken into consideration . . . The wide corridors which extend through the whole length of the building afford space for recreation and exercise in inclement weather." And in 1907, signed by Charles Meade, physician for the college: "The site is exceptionally healthful, and the extensive grounds afford ample opportunity for free outdoor life and exercise in the bracing Minnesota air." Would such claims refute accusations of the likes of the Reverend Todd?

The earliest catalog stated plainly the college's objectives:

- to give the students a liberal education to train and develop all their powers simultaneously
- to train Catholic "girls" to be solidly virtuous and religious—to teach all, irrespective of their denominational differences, to respect, appreciate, and encourage religion and Christian morality.

Despite the publicity, enrollment grew slowly, and for the first six years the College of St. Catherine was really a small high school with just a handful of "specials" doing postsecondary work. Most students wishing to continue beyond the sophomore year transferred to the University of Minnesota. Finally in 1911, two students who had completed the sophomore year, Gertrude Malloy and Marguerite McCusker (Testor), returned as juniors. They remained to graduate in 1913. . . . That year Sisters Frances Clare Bardon, Margaret Kerby, and Antonia McHugh filed a certificate of incorporation for the College of St. Catherine to promote letters, sciences, and the arts through the care, protection, housing, and instruction of students in subjects including the practice of religion.

The next year, at the insistence of Archbishop Ireland, Sister Antonia McHugh was appointed the first dean (chief administrative officer). Building a great college for women was the object of her unceasing labor for the next twenty-four years.

Fit for Pioneer Work

Sister Antonia's background fitted her for pioneering work. She was born Anna McHugh in Omaha in 1873 of an itinerant frontier family. Her father, Patrick McHugh, after several moves in the Dakotas, settled in Langdon, North Dakota, to serve as mayor, postmaster, and bank director. He was elected a commissioner of Cavalier County, then to the territorial legislature for three terms and to the North Dakota legislature for four. Patrick McHugh often took young Anna with him on his business and political travels in the territory.

When she was twelve years old, Anna's father took her to St. Joseph's Academy in St. Paul to study and prepare for her first Holy Communion. During the next three years, she attended St. Mary's Academy in Winnipeg, which was closer to home. Sister Mary Joseph Calasenz, SNJM, remembered Anna McHugh from her days in high school: "She was remarkable in her practical piety, application to study, and generosity. Her outspokenness was proverbial among her companions; her frankness was of a nature to abash those who were not lovers of the truth." Said Sister Teresa Toomey: "During the whole of her life as an educator,

Sister Antonia showed herself to be a true daughter of pioneers, alert, eager, undaunted by difficulties, and bold in her dreams of what Catholic schools in the Northwest could mean for both the Church and the nation she loved."

In 1890 Anna entered the novitiate of the Sisters of St. Joseph in St. Paul, then began teaching third and fourth grades at St. Joseph's Academy. She was among the first group of sisters at the new college. There she threw herself into a routine of cleaning and housekeeping, teaching, supervising resident students, and attending daily prayers. She continued her education with classes at the University of Chicago in summer and correspondence courses during the school year. . . Sister Antonia attended four successive seminars beginning in 1905, with a full year of study arranged for 1908. By December of that year, she had a bachelor's degree in philosophy and education. In 1909 she received a master's degree in history. . . .

Sister Antonia had returned from studies in Chicago to teach at the College of St. Catherine with characteristic enthusiasm. Her classes in history were filled with love of the classical age of Greece and Rome. For study of the Middle Ages she had collected hundreds of pictures of cathedrals and castles. She had spent much time in the study of geology and geography, so the map of Europe became familiar to her students. Her knowledge of music and art was extensive.

Sister Antonia sprinkled her teaching with dozens of maxims and phrases. When she said, "energize yourself," the student moved. She considered some responses "clear as mud" or "windy." Outside of class she might comment that "things for sale are in windows" or "only horses hang their heads" or "she who would be a woman must avoid mediocrity." From Room 12, she impartially handed out apples and advice. Her classroom was a place where young women found out what was the matter with them even when they didn't want to know. But there was also talk about books and stars and music and pictures. The seriousness of a particular conference with a student could be gauged by whether the door to Room 12 was open or closed.

In these ways Sister Antonia impressed students deeply: "I certainly knew, from the minute I set my foot here, that she was the most important one on the campus. She was the one I loved most, respected most, feared most, and she certainly was running things," said Sister Marie Philip Haley '21.

Spreading the News

When Sister Antonia became dean in 1914, eighteen students were enrolled in the college, but the sisters were determined to attract more. News items, articles, and full-page advertisements in the *Catholic Bulletin* helped make the public aware of the college's facilities: "Come to the College of St. Catherine. Don't put it off. Decide now. If you need financial help, write to us. We will do all we can. Many students earn their way through college. A college education is worth a big sacrifice. Come." On June 3, 1916, pictures first graced an ad. Around the same time, the college began placing ads in the St. Paul *Pioneer Press* and St. Paul *Dispatch* and publishing more and better brochures. The start of a regular run of the no-fare "dinky" from Snelling to Cleveland on Randolph in 1916 supported recruitment for day students, too. Earlier, the nearest streetcar lines were a mile east and north, on Snelling and Grand Avenues. . . .

Students in area elementary and secondary schools were advised by their teachers of opportunities at the college. Family members, friends, and acquaintances of students spoke highly of it. Sometimes a parish priest recommended a student, and alumnae visitors also spread the news. In response to laws passed in Minnesota and North Dakota requiring all teachers in elementary and high schools to meet requirements for state certification, Sister Antonia assisted the sisters in her congregation as well as those of others. She received letters from sisters in all parts of the country, asking for help in evaluating credits and meeting the new requirements, usually including a bachelor's degree. She gave advice and education, tuition-free at the college, in the hope that the recipients would send future students to their alma mater. In 1921–22, for example, five Sisters of the Holy Names from Vancouver, two Missionary Sisters of the Most Holy Trinity from Alabama, and two Sisters of St. Joseph from Crookston, Minnesota, registered at the college.

These strategies all helped toward increasing enrollment from 30 students in 1914 to 218 in 1920. But the most direct recruiting method—the personal visit—met with the most success. Genevieve Lamb (Oberly) recalled that every year the sisters stayed at her grandmother's home while visiting her hometown of Michigan, North Dakota. A teenager of fourteen or fifteen, she was called upon to drive a surrey carrying the sisters and their lunches to neighboring towns such as Crary. Obtaining the names of Catholic girls from the parish priest, the sisters then visited them in their homes. With no Catholic college in the state, North Dakota was a rich field for recruitment, and enrollment from the area increased from one in 1911 to thirty-one in 1919.

The sisters traveled to Minnesota towns, branching out to Wisconsin and Montana. They went to and from the coast on the Northern Pacific and

Great Northern railways on passes granted by the railroads on the assumption that students would come back as paying fares. Each pair of sisters carried fifty dollars in cash to cover six weeks' travel expenses. They stopped in every fair-sized town along the way, staying without cost in convents or hospitals and in the homes of students or alumnae. They visited the homes of those who had inquired about the college or who were known as prospective recruits by students or alumnae from the town. Difficulties were compensated for by their success at bringing in registrants and the chance to see the West—including Yellowstone and Glacier parks, as arranged by alumnae or parents of students.

The college took a step forward in recruiting techniques in 1924–25 with the production of a movie on campus life called *A Day at St. Catherine's*. Its plot centered on the adventures of a new student. Athletic events (including a field day and a tennis tournament), music classes, the dedication of the chapel, and a commencement procession were shown. Two years later, the college announced the availability of honor tuition scholarships in Catholic high schools throughout Minnesota and surrounding states. This strategy, coupled with a student service program initiated in 1922, helped to increase enrollment even during the economic depression of the 1930s.

Sister Antonia clearly was not interested in enrollment for enrollment's sake, however, and she carefully planned for every facet of college development. Sister Teresa remembered that she labored, usually in several areas at once, to carry through this fourfold program:

1. to obtain national and international recognition for the scholastic work
2. to offer to the sisters of the college the opportunity for a wide cultural background and for professional education at outstanding American and European centers of learning
3. to work out a schedule of study and activity ensuring education at once religious, humanistic, and professional
4. to secure funding for the erection of new buildings, the maintenance of an adequate library, and the establishment of an endowment fund.

Official Recognition

Between 1916 and 1920, the college was accredited by the North Central Association of Colleges, the National Educational Association, the National Catholic Educational Association, and the Association of American Colleges. . . . Accreditation by the North Central Association of Colleges had been particularly complicated, since the financial organization of public universities and colleges differed from that of private colleges, especially Catholic ones. During the winter of 1915–16, the college prepared a self-study and was visited by an accrediting team from the association. The sticking point was the matter of endowment. The college had very little, most of its resources being invested in buildings and faculty development. Sister Antonia worked to convince team members that the contributed services of the sisters constituted a considerable endowment. Team member Charles Judd, a friend from the University of Chicago, seemed to understand the concept, for he wrote in his North Central report: "These teachers do not receive any pay and have no private contracts with the institution but are under the general control of the orders to which they belong. Many of the institutions undoubtedly receive in this way services that represent a large endowment."

But the larger commission did not at first accept the concept. Judd wrote to Sister Antonia: "The committee . . . is not including the name of your institution on the tentative list . . . on the grounds set forth in this report." She replied immediately, on March 18, 1916: "I note with complete satisfaction your just appreciation of the endowment question for Catholic schools. . . . With this matter settled in our favor, I am at a loss to know why our name is not included on your approved list, as I know we more than meet every other standard recommended by the Association."

The committee evidently reversed itself; the Spring 1916 *Ariston* crowed: "On Saturday, March 25, the announcement was made to us that our college had been placed upon its list of schools accredited by the North Central Association of Colleges." That year college recruitment ads replaced the line "accredited by the Minnesota State Board of Public Instruction and by several prominent universities" with "the only college for women in the Northwest belonging to the North Central Association, which places it educationally on a par with Vassar, Wellesley, and Smith."

Professional Educators

Indeed, the teaching services of the sisters constituted an extraordinary endowment. Sister Antonia had given high priority to the professional and cultural education of the faculty. The teaching sisters were to be as well educated as their equals at other colleges and universities. To Sister Antonia, that meant attending and receiving degrees at great universities in the United States as well as travel and study abroad, and the process had begun before the college opened. Sisters Hyacinth, who taught German, and Bridget, who taught music, had studied in France and Germany in 1903. Sister Antonia had begun her correspondence course at the University of Chicago, unheard of for Catholic sisters at the time. But with the cooperation of the superiors of the Sisters of St. Joseph, Sister Antonia sent many young sisters for further study as soon as they left the novitiate, conveniently constructed just east of the college in 1912. As they finished their graduate work, these sisters became the core of the St. Catherine faculty. Sometimes they started teaching before finishing their studies, working on dissertations in their free hours or while sitting up to check in residents returning from concerts and other events.

Sister Agnes Rita Lingl reflected: "To the horror of some people, sometimes bishops, Sister Antonia sent the sisters out to many non-Catholic or rather secular universities. . . . We studied at the University of Chicago, and [when the university] wanted to start a three-year master's program, they picked out a number of colleges—I think only thirty-seven across the country—St. Catherine's was the Catholic representative . . . the sisters from other communities were all being sent to the Catholic University or to Notre Dame."

●   ●   ●

With the well-educated sisters donating their teaching services, the college had little need for full-time lay teachers. The earliest years saw a succession of part-time teachers for subjects such as piano and violin, voice and elocution. Sister Antonia brought in competent part-time instructors from the University of Minnesota, St. Thomas and the St. Paul Seminary for areas in which the sisters were not yet prepared to teach. . . . George Klasse from the Minneapolis Symphony Orchestra also taught part-time. . . .

Among the most loved teachers from the University of Minnesota was author and scholar Mary Ellen Chase. She taught English at the college for three school years beginning in 1929 and for three additional summers. She devoted a chapter in her book *A Goodly Fellowship* to the college and the friends she made there, saying: "I have never seen happier people, or funnier for that matter, than the nuns at St. Catherine's. Many of them were Irish by inheritance, some by birth, and their sense of humor was inimitable. I have never known so much laughter elsewhere or such good, rich cause for it. I like the thought, which I learned first at St. Catherine's, that those virtues resulting in sainthood are, first of all, simplicity and joy in the Lord rather than meekness, humility, patience, and other less attractive forms of holiness. Knowledge of the saints was not encouraged in my Maine upbringing; but in the years since then I have had a great good time in reading of some of them, and they have added immeasurably to my enjoyment of life.

"St. Catherine's, so far as I know, never looked upon me as either a heretic or a heathen. I shared, in so far as my 'heresy' allowed me, in its life, from which I gained blessings immeasurable. I liked the peace of its chapel, the quiet of its garden, the friendliness and fun of its nuns, the good manners of its students. I liked the shuffling off of a hundred trivialities, the release of which seemed not only possible but inevitable within its gates . . . I liked the single-mindedness . . . the sense that religion was not something to be seized upon in uneasy moments, but natural, like one's hands and feet, and waiting only to be discovered.". . .

Religious, Humanistic, and Professional

. . . Sociology and social work curricula . . . developed remarkably in the 1920s and 1930s. The College Bulletin announced: "The new part that women must take in solving social problems makes it imperative that the department of social and political science furnish a standard of judgment, and include courses like 'Racial Backgrounds and Americanization'." To help meet the need for specially trained workers in the field of social service and to encourage students to become interested in social work, the department listed four senior courses in applied sociology, later called "social case work." The dean's report for June 1932 announced the addition of an organized course in social service work, leading to a social service major. The course consisted of one quarter of social psychology, one of social psychiatry, and one of supervised field work.

Interest in the social sciences on campus reflected the growing involvement of women in fields of social service in the United States. . . . Sister Marie Philip, later reflecting on social work experiences of students in the 1920s, said that a social worker named Ruby Boughman was teaching at the college during that period. She took students to visit a street along the Mississippi River called "The Levee": "There was something like a frame schoolhouse—just one room, as I can remember. And you would go in there and there would be . . . just the nicest Italian chefs and bakers—all men. The women didn't go out at night. . . . We were trying to teach them. Of course, we knew nothing about teaching English to foreigners—absolutely nothing. . . . But I remember those nights, the warmth of them and the gratitude of those men. . . . We kind of prepared them for Americanization. For citizenship papers you need to know a little civics. And we felt perfectly safe. Nobody worried about us walking from Seventh Street to the Levee and back."

New emphasis was also placed on educating teachers for preschool children. Particularly gifted in teaching young children, Sister Ann Harvey, who had earned a master's degree in childhood education at Columbia in 1930, took over the nursery school opened by Ruby Blackhurst in 1929, continuing until her retirement in 1974. Over the years she taught several thousand children, some of whom became prominent St. Paul professionals.

• • •

Of Buildings, Bucks, and Books

Increased enrollment and expanding programs necessitated buildings in addition to Derham Hall, and Sister Antonia had embarked on a large-scale construction program. With friends from the University of Chicago and elsewhere, Sister Antonia set out for New York more than once to submit proposals for new buildings to various funding institutions.

When Sister Antonia was appointed dean in 1914, work on a second major building for the college had already begun. With the Derham Hall dormitories filled to overflowing, some provision had to be made for housing. The November 12, 1912, *Catholic Bulletin* commented: "The excavation of the new building to be added to St. Catherine's College is about completed and work on the basement walls has begun. It will have a frontage of 198 feet on Randolph Street, near Prior, and will have a depth of 173 feet. It will be a brick building of reenforced concrete, and will have four stories and a basement." In the fall of 1914, College Hall (at first called simply "the other building"), for housing college students and college facilities, was opened. The central section of the first story was designated Music Hall, East Hall housed the art department, the west wing—Science Hall—housed home economics and science. The residence corridors could accommodate 250 students. Jeanne d'Arc Auditorium, an extension, soon welcomed students, teachers, and speakers, as well as music department concerts and dramatic productions.

Ecstatic about its lovely new building, members of the St. Catherine community watched the beginnings of war on the other side of the world. Sentiment was strong against U.S. involvement both across the country and on campus until, after some provocation, Congress voted to help France fight Germany, on April 2, 1917. Then, much of the discussion on campus turned towards how best to serve. The Summer 1917 *Ariston* included an editorial called "College Women and War" as well as poems such as "War Hymn to Mary" and "Flag of Peace." A later editorial countered a suggestion that the college close so students could work for the war effort. After all, well-trained minds would be needed to put the world back together: To continue school, pray for peace, and join the Red Cross effort seemed the better course.

The college stayed open. Sister Eleanore Michel worked to retain the teaching of German and build the department despite the growing regulation of German texts by the Minnesota Commission of Public Safety. Students variously put on war benefits or continued antiwar efforts, expressing their positions in poems and editorials. And though not all students and faculty members agreed on American involvement in the war, almost everyone on campus became involved in knitting or making dressings for the St. Paul Red Cross, setting up the Derham Hall dining room every Friday afternoon for the purpose. All were happy to hear "The Great War is Over" ringing through the hall at midday on Friday, November 8, 1918. A bit prematurely, Sister Antonia gave the rest of the day off, but on the following Monday, the armistice was signed.

Despite suggestions that college students go to work, the war had in fact brought enrollment up. On December 14, 1918, the *Catholic Bulletin* noted that "twenty music rooms have been converted into dormitories and thirty single rooms have been transformed into double rooms. The intention of young women to prepare themselves to fill positions of men who have gone to the front is thought to be one of the reasons for breaking all records." Sister Antonia was ready. To make her vision concrete, she had drawn up a complete building and landscape plan. The next step would be a building for the music department, to be named for the patron of music, St. Cecilia. She set out on one of several visits to George Vincent at the Rockefeller Foundation, returning from New York with the promise of financial help and advice to establish a board of trustees.

On January 27, 1919, the Board of Trustees of the College of St. Catherine met for the first time, in the "Alumnae Parlour" of College Hall. . . . The twelve-member board was to hold and invest endowment funds and to approve mortgages, indebtedness, purchase and sale of property, and the erection of buildings. . . . They appointed a committee to plan an endowment campaign to raise $200,000 as a match for a $100,000 grant from the Rockefeller Foundation and planned to entertain Wallace Buttrick, president of the foundation's General Education Board. At the next two meetings, they agreed with Buttrick on the terms of the grant, including that it not be used for theological instruction, and approved plans for the new music hall. . . . In the fall of 1921, Caecilian Hall opened with studios for the faculty, practice rooms for students, and a recital hall for performances.

The first college homecoming, sponsored by the St. Catherine Alumna Association in June 1923, marked the twentieth anniversary of the laying of the college cornerstone. . . . Also in 1923, the entire campus was enclosed by a wrought-iron fence with elaborate gates, and planning was initiated for a separate chapel. It would be large, Romanesque, and beautiful—from the high bell tower to the tiled roof and tile facing on interior walls and pillars. H. A. Sullwold was chosen as architect and Paul Steenberg as contractor. Sullwold was sent to Europe to visit Spanish and French medieval cathedrals so he would understand what the chapel should look like. He visited the Church of St. Trophime at Arles, France, which Sister Antonia had admired in 1922. She told him that with a few adaptations, the chapel at the college must follow suit.

Work on the chapel progressed rapidly, with many conferences among Sister Antonia, the architect, and the contractor. When the workers laying concrete for the floor were unable to finish before Thanksgiving of 1923, Sister Antonia promised to provide Thanksgiving dinner if they would work through the holiday to finish. And so they did. On another occasion, when the tile company did not want to work on Saturday, contractor Paul Steenberg persuaded the carpentry foreman and bricklayer foremen to lay tiles themselves. Sister Antonia was so pleased she gave each of them a box of cigars. Years later, Steenberg wrote: "I was much pleased with doing this chapel for many reasons. First, it was a place to worship God. It was a beautiful chapel, and I believe I had satisfied Sister Antonia's wish, which I was told could not be done. [She] was a woman who knew what she wanted and was pleased when she got a real job."

On October 7, 1924, the chapel was complete, and it was dedicated on the feast of Our Lady of Victory, for whom it was named. Three days earlier, the *Catholic Bulletin* had given fourteen pages almost exclusively to the college and its new chapel. Archbishop Dowling reportedly said: "Sister Antonia asked to build a chapel, but she built a cathedral." Sister Lioba, an enthusiastic observer, wrote to Sister Ste. Helene at Oxford University in England: "That great day dawned . . . summer sun, summer warmth, summer green on all sides—and through this loveliness of combined beauty there passed from College Hall to the Chapel of Our Lady of Victory, the procession of dedication—the Archbishop in Cappa Magna, monsignori in such a blaze of glory that it communicated itself to the entire line, priests to the number of at least seventy, the college student body, and people world without end . . . Father [Francis] Missia and the seminarians sang the litany all the way down the aisle, and the reverence of students and congregation can never be forgotten.

"Father [Aloysius] Ziskowsky presided in the sanctuary and his prowess in the church service kept things moving with both grace and precision, but with no sign of obtrusiveness . . . Some of the college girls were ushers in the true sense of the word, for they seated a throng which must have numbered 1,000. All the pews were full with six in a pew besides hundreds of chairs. Mr. [Leopold] Bruenner's Mass was divine—parts of it like the Agnus Dei really inspired—and never did Anna [Goulet] play nor the sisters sing as on last Tuesday. The seminarians sang the gradual and the proper of the Mass in Gregorian chant and the change from their voices to the choir was most affecting . . . there is no telling when [Anna] will again come down to foot locomotion." Sister Anna had first use of what the *Catholic Bulletin* described as: "a fine, three-manual organ . . . That this organ might thoroughly harmonize with the beautiful new building, the Reuter Organ Company sent their experts to St. Paul to go over the plans and details of the building with the architects . . . It . . . has character, one that is admirably well fitted for concert purposes as well as for chapel services."

With the dedication complete, faculty and staff helped move the library from Derham Hall to the ground floor of the new chapel. A new closed stack system meant that student assistants in large numbers paged books to waiting patrons. The library science department, at first called the "School of Library Science," moved there, too. Beginning in 1918 with a nine-credit course in school librarianship, the program had quickly grown. . . . In 1926 a principal sequence, distributed over the junior and senior years and leading to a bachelor's degree in library science, was offered.

• • •

In the meantime, Sister Antonia had attended to the construction of a new building for the sciences. A second grant of $100,000 from the Rockefeller Foundation in 1926 made possible the erection of Mendel Hall, named for the great Austrian biologist and discoverer of the laws of heredity. The *Catholic Bulletin* noted upon its opening in September 1927: "Mendel Hall is to be used exclusively by the science departments. It is a five-story building of variegated red and terra cotta brick . . . The building is divided by a tower, the center of which is ninety-four feet from the east end . . . The new hall was designed to hold approximately fifteen laboratories, as well as lecture rooms, study hall, and faculty office." But Mendel Hall soon accommodated the art department, the education department, and a Montessori child care facility as well. . . .

In 1929, the Rockefeller Foundation granted $300,000 to help develop the health program at the college. The new building, at first known as the Health Center and later as Fontbonne Hall, particularly was to provide space for training in basic sciences for nurses and in physical education for teachers. Sister Antonia, in the president's report for 1931–32, stated that the new Health Center, open that year, "embodies the complete realization . . . of the health unit in our expansion program." The burgeoning library school also moved to the Health Center. The new office for the department chair, a laboratory room for technical processes, and a large classroom there meant more room for the crowded library beneath the chapel.

Praise with Pots and Pans . . .

The care and maintenance of six buildings and the hundreds of students filling them demanded much of the nonteaching staff of the college. Among those working behind the scenes was Sister Georgia Morrisson, beloved friend and counselor of students living in Whitby Hall. She had greeted the first students arriving from St. Joseph's Academy in 1905. Among other responsibilities, she had charge of the laundry, which at that time meant washing all the students' clothes. Sister Georgia assigned each sister, including faculty members, a part of the laundry work according to her own estimate of the other's intelligence. When a task was not well done, she might say: "And you with your Ph.D.!"

●   ●   ●

Well known among students, too, were several Sisters of St. Joseph who had come to America from Ireland as lay missionaries. (The United States was considered mission territory until 1921.) The Irish sisters—Odelia Murphy, Jarlath Noonan, Candida Gallahue, Elerius Hennessy, and others—provided a warm, loving atmosphere, consoling many a homesick freshman with an extra cookie or piece of cake. Magdalen (later Sister Marie David) Schimanski, a student in the late 1930s, remembered: "Sister Odelia . . . used to provide our work-a-day spreads on a summer evening because we always stayed during summers and vacations . . . the painters, the electricians would have to work in the buildings, so we would move every month to a different building . . . I was very fond of all those kitchen sisters from Ireland: Sister Candida, Elerius, Jarlath. I remember them standing in the chapel—it would be the grand entrance to the chapel overlooking the Dew Drop. They'd be looking at the sunset there. I could almost draw them from memory—those silhouettes of those great big women. There was something beautiful about their peacefulness and their joy and the way they were friendly to us students."

Another admirer, Mary Ellen Chase, wrote in *A Goodly Fellowship*: "They praised the Lord with pots and pans as cymbals and harps and with good food. I used to go into their huge kitchen below the chapel cloister and talk with them as they beat, stirred, and kneaded. The four of them were ample women of great good humor. They wore large gray aprons over their black habits and usually had a touch of flour somewhere on their black veils. As they bustled about in their convent garb intent upon the means of existence, they somehow connected the religious life with the ageless, and surely religious, necessity of daily bread."

●   ●   ●

And Beyond

Sister Antonia oversaw the construction of five college buildings from 1914 to 1932, but her vision for the students reached beyond buildings, beyond campus, beyond city and nation. To her mind, one could not be fully educated without travel in Europe. She emphasized that basic to preparation for travel was intensive study of the appropriate language: "I am quite sure of this, that encouragement should be given to our young people in schools to acquire a language sense. They should be encouraged to learn at least one or two modern languages which they could use with facility—other than our mother tongue.

Many times I have had parents ask me, 'What is the good of learning French or German? Our daughter will not speak these languages here in America.' True, there is rare occasion for their use, but let us hope that most of our boys and girls will have a chance to visit the countries where these languages are spoken. Certainly it makes for cultural background in every way."

If students could not get to other countries, she found a way to bring other countries to them. One way to accomplish that was to offer scholarships to international students. Several students from Canada and one from Mexico had attended the college earlier, but the first European students were Lucienne and Angele Petit, at the college from 1918 to 1920. Emerging from the postwar devastation of France, they had had little preparation for the United States. Sister Mona Riley recalled: "I can remember them sitting with babushkas over their heads, not knowing any English, but they turned out beautifully. Lucienne finished at one of the universities—I think it was Columbia—and then she taught at Adelphi College on Long Island."

After these first two students from France, a steady stream of students—from Puerto Rico, Panama, Peru, and Brazil, from Germany, Hungary, Italy, Spain, Greece, the Philippines, Iraq, Israel, and Japan—registered at the college. In the 1970s and 1980s many students came from Africa—Kenya, Tanzania, Nigeria—and from the Orient—Japan, China, Malaysia, and Pakistan. . . . Sister Antonia also encouraged international-mindedness by inviting teachers from other countries as native speakers to help students improve their language skills.

•   •   •

Students unable to travel abroad learned much from international students and teachers on campus, as well as from other visitors and events of the day. In the vanguard of American women preparing for new participation in the world, they were independent in spirit and sometimes broke college rules designed to limit "radical behavior." Lucy Sanschagrin '25 (later Sister Marie Ursule), for instance, was almost expelled for bobbing her hair, and Mary O'Brien '27 (Sister Antonine's sister) was accused of "suffragetteism" for carrying a swagger stick. There seems to have been little activity related to women's suffrage (most students were not old enough to vote), but after women's right to vote was ratified in

1919, mock presidential elections were held. The first, apparently in response to the election of Calvin Coolidge, was described in the 1924 student yearbook: "Not to be outstripped by any other independent women in America, we of the College of St. Catherine decided to use our privilege of franchise and held our own election. It was with much agitation and anxiety that the girls gathered at eleven o'clock on a certain Wednesday morning in the auditorium. After several days electioneering the students met ready to assert their opinions and support their candidates. In fact, the meeting resembled a Republican caucus."

Then interest in social and political events grew, and with faculty members returning from study in other lands, the discussion of world issues flourished. . . . A *Wheel* editorial on April 12, 1935, discussed a speaker at the Woman's Club of Minneapolis: "Dame Rachel Crowdy, head of the humanitarian committee of the League of Nations, was scheduled to speak on 'Women in International Affairs.' She was astonished when told of her topic and said, 'I could not speak for five minutes on *women* in international affairs. There are none.' We, who are vitally interested in international peace, will some day answer Dame Crowdy's challenge and give her ample opportunity."

Some students combined artistic, entertainment and economic activities to good effect. Proceeds from a grassroots attempt to produce plays on campus were donated to a fund for a new elevator in Derham Hall in the early 1920s, for example. . . . Among the more formal musical and dramatic productions was *The Messiah*, presented by the Choral Club and assisted by the men of the St. Paul Municipal Chorus. On March 2, 1926, the *Lantern* (a weekly published by the sophomores for one year only) mentioned Austrian composer and pianist Percy Grainger's visit and the two programs he gave in Jeanne d'Arc Auditorium. Inspired by Edvard Grieg, he had collected English and Irish folksongs and arranged them for concert use. Sister Antonia's voice rang forth: "This event is one of the greatest privileges which are given to the students, probably a privilege which to some may not again be granted . . . It is your duty, girls, to let the public know of his coming and invite them."

• • •

Despite her many responsibilities, Sister Antonia kept in touch with the students, making sure the world of each was expanded through cultural activities outside the classroom. Sister Ann Harvey recalled: "Someone sent Mother Antonia four tickets to the symphony, and the seats were very good. She asked me if I wanted one and I said 'Yes,' because I was a poor little girl and did not have any money . . . a telephone call came from Mother Antonia about twenty minutes after she gave me the ticket, to please come to her office because she wanted to tell me what to wear, and how to look. She told me to wear a hat and bring my purse and wear gloves . . . In true Sister-Antonia-fashion, she waited up for us after the symphony and got our enthusiastic ideas on the music. It was my first symphony, and I thought I was in heaven."

According to Sister Antonia, the accumulation of knowledge was not the sole purpose of a college education. Character training or "the building of a life" was most often the subject of her assembly talks. Sister Marie Philip noted: "Wednesday after Wednesday she lashed us into a fairly homogeneous student group. She drove at practice, at homely virtues— honesty, cleanliness, industry, dependableness, a nice consideration for others. Who could ever forget her urging us to chisel our characters, to accomplish hard things, to be women of good sense? She taught us that the ideal of sound and strong Catholic womanhood is big, simple, noble, and practicable."

Mary Ellen Chase wrote in *A Goodly Fellowship:* " Sister Antonia went at the realization of St. Catherine's College with everything she had in her . . . *Laborare est orare* was sound doctrine to her . . . She saw architects and remade their plans; she sat on stone heaps and inspired workmen. She laid out grounds and planted trees . . . She had read widely and seemingly she had forgotten nothing that she had ever read. She was the best of teachers . . . Her feverish activity made her not only apparently omnipresent, but completely master of every scene and situation as well . . . In the chapel she could be intent upon her own devotions and aware of any lack of devotion in her girls . . . She was a handsome woman with an alert, eager face and a fine carriage. When she swept down the corridors of her college in her black habit on her way to the chapel, or the garden or the kitchen or the powerhouse, everyone upon her swift approach straightened head and shoulders."

In 1936, Sister Antonia became ill, suffering several strokes. In 1937 she resigned because of increasing disability, to live quietly in Whitby 106. Friends and alumnae still visited, and the honors poured in as before: President Herbert Hoover invited her to the White House Conference on Child Health and Protection. Pope Pius XI awarded her the *Pro Ecclesia et Pontifice* medal. She was elected president of the Association of Minnesota Colleges and awarded an honorary degree of Doctor of Laws by the University of Minnesota.

Sister Antonia McHugh died quietly on October 11, 1944. The Spring 1927 *Ariston* had written of her: "Sister Antonia succeeded in building up not only the physical plant but the curriculum and the faculty as well . . . Our development in every line is due to her farsightedness, her zeal in furthering the course of Catholic education in America. Under her wise guidance, courses of study have been organized and the college standardized until it is now recognized by the highest authorities. All the best in American universities, all the advantages, all the benefits of foreign travel, have been utilized . . . in the preparation of superior teachers."

Five years after her death, *Ariston* was still paying her tribute: "Always to her St. Catherine's has been a great college. Even when it was only a dream. Never just a building on a hill, it was a growing family of buildings: Caecilian, Mendel, the Health Center, the Chapel. All these she planned, built, and peopled in her mind long before the architects were ever summoned. The pews of Our Lady of Victory Chapel were filled with girls in cap and gown when the old chapel on fourth Derham was still adequate to the college needs. It is that vision for the future, that aspiration for excellence, and the creative power to convert vision into reality that has distinguished Mother Antonia's work." That vision of excellence was her legacy.

Into the Nineties

. . . The College of St. Catherine Leadership Statement:

The College of St. Catherine is committed to the development of effective, ethical leaders. Through study, practice, and life experience, individuals have opportunities to enrich the knowledge, refine the skills, and clarify the attitudes essential for responsible action. In varied roles and settings, the College of St. Catherine leader:

- lives a commitment to the values of justice and caring
- acts from a strong self-concept
- thinks critically and creatively
- communicates and interacts effectively within groups
- takes risks willingly
- exercises power appropriately
- articulates a positive sense of direction
- and evokes hope.

American poet, essayist, feminist activist and speaker, Adrienne Rich (b. 1929) has been the recipient of a MacArthur Fellowship and the National Book Award. Her current works include a book of essays, Arts of the Possible: Essays and Conversations *(2001), and the collection of poems,* Fox: Poems 1998–2000 *(2001). In 1999, she was elected Chancellor of the Academy of American Poets. Rich lives in northern California.*

Claiming an Education

Adrienne Rich

For this convocation, I planned to separate my remarks into two parts: some thoughts about you, the women students here, and some thoughts about us who teach in a women's college. But ultimately, those two parts are indivisible. If university education means anything beyond the processing of human beings into expected roles, through credit hours, tests, and grades (and I believe that in a women's college especially it *might* mean much more), it implies an ethical and intellectual contract between teacher and student. This contract must remain intuitive, dynamic, unwritten, but we must turn to it again and again if learning is to be reclaimed from the depersonalizing and cheapening pressures of the present day academic scene.

The first thing I want to say to you who are students, is that you cannot afford to think of being here to *receive* an education; you will do much better to think of yourselves as being here to *claim* one. One of the dictionary definitions of the verb "to claim" is: *to take as the rightful owner; to assert in the face of possible contradiction.* "To receive" is *to come into possession of; to act as receptacle or container for; to accept as authoritative or true.* The difference is that between acting and being acted-upon, and for women it can literally mean the difference between life and death.

One of the devastating weaknesses of university learning, of the store of knowledge and opinion that has been handed down through academic training, has been its almost total erasure of women's experience and thought from the curriculum, and its exclusion of women as members of the academic community. Today, with increasing numbers of women students in nearly every branch of higher learning, we still see very few women in the upper levels of faculty and administration in most institutions. Douglass College itself is a women's college in a university administered overwhelmingly by men, who in turn are answerable to the state legislature, again composed predominantly of men. But the most significant fact for you is that what you learn here, the very texts you read, the lectures you hear, the way your studies are divided into categories and

29

fragmented one from the other—all this reflects to a very large degree, neither objective reality, nor an accurate picture of the past, nor a group of rigorously tested observations about human behavior. What you can learn here (and I mean not only at Douglass but any college in any university) is how *men* have perceived and organized their experience, their history, their ideas of social relationships, good and evil, sickness and health, etc. When you read or hear about "great issues," "major texts," "the mainstream of Western thought," you are hearing about what men, above all white men, in their male subjectivity have decided is important.

Black and other minority peoples have for some time recognized that their racial and ethnic experience was not accounted for in the studies broadly labeled human; and that even the sciences can be racist. For many reasons, it has been more difficult for women to comprehend our exclusion, and to realize that even the sciences can be sexist. For one thing, it is only within the last hundred years that higher education has grudgingly been opened up to women at all, even to white, middle-class women. And many of us have found ourselves poring eagerly over books with titles like: *The Descent of Man; Man and His Symbols; Irrational Man; The Phenomenon of Man; The Future of Man; Man and the Machine; From Man to Man; May Man Prevail?; Man, Science and Society;* or *One-Dimensional Man*—books pretending to describe a "human" reality that does not include over one-half the human species.

Less than a decade ago, with the rebirth of a feminist movement in this country, women students and teachers in a number of universities began to demand and set up women's studies courses—to *claim* a woman-directed education. And, despite the inevitable accusations of "unscholarly," "group therapy," "faddism," etc., despite backlash and budget cuts, women's studies are still growing, offering to more and more women a new intellectual grasp on their lives, new understanding of our history, a fresh vision of the human experience, and also a critical basis for evaluating what they hear and read in other courses, and in the society at large.

But my talk is not really about women's studies, much as I believe in their scholarly, scientific, and human necessity. While I think that any Douglass student has everything to gain by investigating and enrolling in women's studies courses, I want to suggest that there is a more essential experience that you owe yourselves, one which courses in women's studies can greatly enrich, but which finally depends on you, in all your interactions with yourself and your world. This is the experience of *taking responsibility toward yourselves*. Our upbringing as women has so often told us that this should come second to our relationships and responsibilities to other people. We have been offered ethical models of the self-denying wife and mother; intellectual models of the brilliant but slapdash dilettante who never commits herself to anything the whole way, or the intelligent woman who denies her intelligence in order to seem more "feminine," or who sits in passive silence even when she disagrees inwardly with everything that is being said around her.

Responsibility to yourself means refusing to let others do your thinking, talking, and naming for you; it means learning to respect and use your own brains and instincts; hence, grappling with hard work. It means that you do not treat your body as a commodity with which to purchase superficial intimacy or economic security; for our bodies and minds are inseparable in this life, and when we allow our bodies to be treated as objects, our minds are in mortal danger. It means insisting that those to whom you give your friendship and love are able to respect your mind. It means being able to say, with Charlotte Bronte's *Jane Eyre*: "I have an inward treasure born with me, which can keep me alive if all the extraneous delights should be withheld or offered only at a price I cannot afford to give."

Responsibility to yourself means that you don't fall for shallow and easy solutions—predigested books and ideas, weekend encounters guaranteed to change your life, taking "gut" courses instead of ones you know will challenge you, bluffing at school and life instead of doing solid work, marrying early as an escape from real decisions, getting pregnant as an evasion of already existing problems. It means that you refuse to sell your talents and aspirations short, simply to avoid conflict and confrontation. And this, in turn, means resisting the forces in society which say that women should be nice, play safe, have low professional expectations, drown in love and forget about work, live through others, and stay in the places assigned to us. It means that we insist on a life of meaningful work, insist that work be as meaningful as love and friendship in our lives. It means, therefore, the courage to be "different"; not to be continuously available to others when we need time for ourselves and our work; to be able to demand of others— parents, friends, roommates, teachers, lovers, husbands, children—that they respect our sense of purpose and our integrity as persons. Women everywhere are finding the courage to do this, more and more, and we are finding that courage both in our study of women in the past who possessed it, and in each other as we look to other women for comradeship, community, and challenge. The difference between a life lived actively, and a life of passive drifting and dispersal of energies, is an immense difference. Once we begin to feel committed to our lives, responsible to ourselves, we can never again be satisfied with the old, passive way.

Now comes the second part of the contract. I believe that in a women's college you have the right to expect your faculty to take you seriously. The education of women has been a matter of debate for centuries, and old, negative attitudes about women's role, women's ability to think and take leadership, are still rife both in and outside the university. Many male professors (and I don't mean only at Douglass) still feel that teaching in a women's college is a second-rate career. Many tend to eroticize their women students—to treat them as sexual objects—instead of demanding the best of their minds. (At Yale a legal suit [*Alexander v. Yale*] has been brought against the university by a group of women students demanding a stated policy against sexual advances toward female students by male professors.) Many teachers, both men and women, trained in the male-centered tradition, are still handing the ideas and texts of that tradition on to students without teaching them to criticize its anti-woman attitudes, its omission of women as part of the species. Too often, all of us fail to teach the most important thing, which is that clear thinking, active discussion, and excellent writing are all necessary for intellectual freedom, and that these require *hard work*. Sometimes, perhaps in discouragement with a culture which is both anti-intellectual and anti-woman, we may resign ourselves to low expectations for our students before we have given them half a chance to become more thoughtful, expressive human beings. We need to take to heart the words of Elizabeth Barrett Browning, a poet, a thinking woman, and a feminist, who wrote in 1845 of her impatience with studies which cultivate a "passive recipiency" in the mind, and asserted that "women want to be made to *think actively*: their apprehension is quicker than that of men, but their defect lies for the most part in the logical faculty and in the higher mental activities." Note that she implies a defect which can be remedied by intellectual training; *not* an inborn lack of ability.

I have said that the contract on the student's part involves that you demand to be taken seriously so that you can also go on taking yourself seriously. This means seeking out criticism, recognizing that the most affirming thing anyone can do for you is demand that you push yourself further, show you the range of what you can do. It means rejecting attitudes of "take-it-easy," "why-be-so-serious," "why-worry-you'll-probably-get-married-anyway." It means assuming your share of responsibility for what happens in the classroom, because that affects the quality of your daily life here. It means that the student sees herself engaged *with* her teachers in an active, ongoing struggle for a real education. But for her to do this, her teachers must be committed to the belief that women's minds and experience are intrinsically valuable and indispensable to any civilization worthy of the name; that there is no more exhilarating and intellectually fertile place in the academic world today than a women's college—*if* both students and teachers in large enough numbers are trying to fulfill this contract. The contract is really a pledge of mutual seriousness about women, about language, ideas, methods, and values. It is our shared commitment toward a world in which the inborn potentialities of so many women's minds will no longer be wasted, raveled-away, paralyzed, or denied.

Kari Smalkoski is a faculty member in the Liberal Arts and Sciences Department at the Minneapolis campus of the College of St. Catherine.

Notes on Hunger

Kari Smalkoski

A given place becomes our temporary home, and yet we preserve a sufficient distance to feel its strangeness, not perceived by those who live there permanently.

—Czeslaw Milosz

Dear E.,

I've felt severed my entire life, literally, as if a part of me was cut off or more appropriately, taken away. I'm missing this entire part of myself that is Korean. People ask when it was I realized I was adopted and I tell them I always knew.

A friend of mine, also an adopted Korean, is learning Korean so she can meet other Koreans in an attempt to reclaim what it is she's lost. I've known other Korean adoptees who have tried this but it's been more than frustrating for them. Most Korean nationals they've encountered don't accept them and neither do many Korean Americans. They look down on us and consider us charity cases. Perhaps my resentment for you all those times we argue about Asian American identity issues is not because I disagree with you (I disagree with you on many points, but that's another letter), but because I am envious that you have in your family, in your life, something I will never possess or know, no matter how hard I try, no matter what it is I do, in my own. I often feel you take this for granted because you can.

There was a time, not so long ago, that I didn't know any Asians and I went out of my way not to be associated with them. Now, I know many Asians, particularly Asian Americans, a few who have become friends, like you. Even so, I can't help but feel I'm living a huge lie when I'm with them because they see me as them and I am not and can never be. I don't know if it's more an issue of not feeling accepted by Asians or still thinking of myself as so different from them. I don't look in the mirror anymore and see my mother and sister with their Eastern European features staring back at me. However, it does still get confusing when Asians assume I am just like them and whites shy away from me—act awkward in my presence because they think of me as completely different from them.

Have I ever mentioned anything to you about my first year of college? I was seventeen years old, idealistic and, most importantly, still thought I was a white girl. There was a woman who worked behind the cafeteria counter at the dorms who asked for our student IDs before every meal so she could check our name off a list. I took an instant liking to her because it was my first time away from home and she reminded me of a mother and I missed my own mother terribly. Over a month later, I noticed she wasn't asking for anybody's ID besides mine and one day she said quite innocently to me, "I still have to see *your* ID because your name just doesn't match your face." I recall walking very matter of factly to my dorm room, locking the door behind me and crying the rest of the day. I'll never forget how it felt to hear that—to realize that it was true.—Mia.

Dear M.—

I have more than one confession to make to you. Do you recall when it was I first saw you? You were sitting in that cafe, way back in November. I spent most of the evening trying to decide if I was interested in you because you were the only other Asian in the place and if I would have still been interested if I would have seen you at a predominately Asian place, like a Chinese restaurant. When I saw you sitting in Dr. Harrison's class, I felt an immediate paradox. I remembered you instantly, only I was quite aware that you and I stood out somehow. I've always fit in, or at least, I've always thought I have. It was the first time I felt like I didn't.

Most of my life I have believed that any Asian woman would be glad to date a guy like me. I apologize for sounding arrogant, which you accuse me of being all the time anyway, but, it's true. My mother believes this about me as well. She always identified much more with being an "American" than my father who still identifies strongly with being Chinese, even though he is third generation. When I learned you were an adopted Korean, you intrigued me even more. In my mind, I transformed you into a sort of oddity: not white but not Asian. I'm not saying I saw you as Amerasian or anything like that. Perhaps I saw you as a white woman in disguise. A friend of mine in college once commented that adopted Korean women were the ideal because they were actually white women who looked Asian. Perfect to bring home to an Asian mother and father!

I've never sensed you wished you had been born a white woman, although I've never sensed you're thrilled being who you are. Perhaps, like me, you believe that if you had been born white, your life somehow would have been less complicated. You wouldn't have to think so much all the time about every goddamn thing that's happening to you. You wouldn't always have to read into everything and everyone all the time. Being adopted Korean is complicated. If a white guy or any other guy of another race (besides Asian) is attracted to you, you have to second guess his intentions. You have to figure out if he has an Asian woman thing because maybe *he* doesn't even realize he does. If he's white, it becomes more confusing to you because you still see yourself as a white person, in a lot of ways. If you are attracted to some white guy and he isn't attracted to you, you have to figure out if your race has something to do with it. In my high school, Asian American women were either completely rejected by guys, particularly white guys, because they *were* Asian, or, completely obsessed over because they were.

Now, if an Asian guy is attracted to you, you have to get over the idea of it feeling inter-racial somehow, realizing that he sees you as an Asian woman and that he sees you as he sees himself. Still, he knows he can't just bring you home to meet his mom and pop, particularly if he's Korean. We both know what the "real" Koreans think about adopted Koreans. It isn't pretty.

You say I grew up believing I was really a white person, that I am in complete denial about who I am and where I come from. I disagree with you. It is true, I haven't given these issues much thought until we met, but with me it has been an entirely different experience. My family is Chinese American. I grew up with the culture, the language, the food—and unlike you, it matched my face. You once said I am the only person you know who likes eating the kind of Chinese food that *Chinese* really eat, not that white people eat. I'd never thought about it like that before. Eating things that you can't even stand to look at always seemed normal to me like turkey and stuffing were to you at Christmas.

Perhaps my Dear M., you think of me as a mild version of one of those born again Asian Americans that the politically conscious Asian Americans keep discussing. What does it mean to be a politically conscious Asian American? I find the criteria preposterous. When I was growing up, we were the only Asian American family in our neighborhood in Connecticut. My father was colleagues with many of the men on our block and so we never had any trouble, that is, nobody said anything to us or seemed to have a problem with us being there. I went to predominately white schools with kids who came from old money, real blue blood families, WASP types and I seemed to fit in fine. Although, I never had any serious relationships in high school and looking back on it now, I suppose I could say it was because I was Asian, or more specifically, not WASP, but I was never ostracized, at least I don't think I was.

Early in our friendship you accused my race as being 'invisible' to people and quite honestly, I did not know what you were implying. I decided I'd finally met my match, that there was someone else walking around the world taking themselves much too seriously and thinking about things too much. I suppose, like anyone, I wished to fit in and I did. I never had trouble fitting in. I wasn't teased like you, wasn't called *chink* and *gook* and *jap* every day. I don't think people understand the severity of what that can do to a kid who eventually turns into an adult. People don't realize how it gets internalized, how it's carried around inside of you, eating away at you your entire life.

Look, perhaps what this all boils down to is that I put unfair expectations on you because you are Asian. But then maybe, ideally, it has nothing to do with us being Asian at all, maybe it just has to do with us. But can it ever have to do with us, without us acknowledging our race? Can we ever just have the luxury of simply being Mia and Elliot? You know, that girl from Minneapolis and that guy from Connecticut? *Not* the adopted Korean woman or the Chinese American guy? It's funny, I thought I knew everything about this Asian American thing before I met you.—E.

Dear E.—

I ran into an old friend, Charles, the other day. We decided to have coffee and after sitting across from him for a few minutes, it became apparent to me that we had nothing to say to one another. There was a time when we were extremely close friends, the best of friends. There never seemed enough time for us to say everything we wanted. We met five years ago as sophomores in college. He was my father's wet dream, my mother's idea of marrying well, my grandmother's idea of good sperm for offspring and a product of East Coast society and the good ol' boys network. *Good stock* as my father calls Charles, spent his developing years at the fine boarding school called *Andover*, moved to Minnesota when his father, also a CEO and coincidentally a member of the same country club as my father, was permanently relocated, had been the president of his fraternity in college and is presently in his first year in medical school—not because he worked hard or is even smart for that matter, but because his father is friends with the Vice Chancellor.

"You know what a man really wants in a woman when you ask him to describe his favorite car, just like you know what a woman wants in a man when you ask her to describe her ideal house," was what Charles said to me over coffee, breaking a ten minute bantering called *small talk*. I changed the subject quickly, although I could tell he wanted to put his theory to test. I told him I thought I'd seen him walking down the street the other day. "Could have been. I'm white, male and in my twenties, it happens all the time," he said defensively.

I said to him, "the same could be said for me, you know, Asian American, female in her twenties." I watched his face go noticeably blank. It was the first time he'd ever heard me refer to myself as Asian American and the closest we'd ever come to discussing the fine subject of race, particularly mine. "I've had my fair share of people who come up to me and start talking really slow, like they know I can't speak English—the whole time they think I'm someone else. It's *so* bizarre," I said.

Charles appeared baffled. He crossed his arms and said, "I take it for granted, not having to worry about people making assumptions like that." Only, he hadn't said it as if a light bulb had come on in his head, rather, his tone was full of arrogance and sarcasm. There was a tone in his voice that said, *I'm really sick of all this multicultural, diversity shit, so could you just shut up please?* "Maybe I actually learned something in those waste of my time diversity seminars they forced us to go to in college," he laughed to himself and then said, "nah, I didn't."

A navy blue Land Rover is Charles' ideal car and in twenty minutes I found myself describing his ideal woman. Afterwards, I described my ideal house at which he took the liberty of describing my ideal man. What struck me about his preposterous theory was that when describing his ideal woman, I described myself with the physical attributes of women who look very much like my mother and sister and most of my friends. When describing my ideal man, he described himself, my father, brother and every man who would never consider me at all (including Asian men who claim they do not find Asian women attractive) and who would never describe me as their ideal. This was only a week ago. This scares the shit out of me.

I guess I've always known why Charles and I never had anything more than friendship, why it was he kept such a calculated distance and why, sadly, I entertained thoughts of him being what I wished to include in my long term plans; sadly, realizing as girls do, that they cannot marry their fathers; sadly, realizing I still wanted to end up with mine, as much as I hate and resent and love him as eldest daughters often do. I am, as far as I know, the only person of Asian descent my father has ever known. I am the only person of Asian descent anyone in my family or their friends, have ever personally known. I, the Korean adoptee, have insight that many Asians do not, which is truly no blessing or curse. It's simply the way it is.—M.

Dear E.

Vladimir's good friend, Yurri, from his hometown in Russia, is staying with Vladimir for a week. Ever since he got off the plane, Vladimir has been speaking Russian non-stop. I can't tell you what it's been like since it's the first time I've ever heard Vladimir speak Russian. It is also the first time I've understood the intimate connection Vladimir and I have shared from the beginning. I've always known he's experienced an immeasurable loss, similar to mine and I can't explain it the way I want to, not even in words—particularly not in words.

When Vladimir speaks Russian there's this almost secretive tone in his voice, this fluidness in language, an expressiveness I've never heard before. It has nothing to do with language, rather, it's a confidence and comfort I've never witnessed in him before. There are times when we are trying to communicate and we get stuck. He cannot say what he wants to and cannot understand what I'm trying to convey on a deeper level. But I've always trusted that he understands somehow, because he has this depth to him that has nothing to do with what he says.

There's a new aura about him since Yurri arrived. It is a similar feeling that adopted adults experience when they find their birth parents and meet them for the first time: the missing link has finally been found. Last week they went to a baseball game and asked me to come along. I didn't go because they were going with a group of Russian guys and their Russian girlfriends and I felt Vladimir needed time alone with them. Vladimir needs to spend time with his Russian friends without me. And yet, there's this part of me that feels deeply left out, more so than say, my sister Maddy would ever feel. I know this is due to my hunger for a culture that is everything I've never had or known.—Mia.

My dear Mia,

You are angry with me for the assumptions I made about Vladimir over the phone last week and I know I deserve your silence. However, this letter is not a feeble attempt to ask for your forgiveness. In all truth, I have many more confessions to make, things I've wanted to confess for some time.

Before moving to Minnesota, a Korean American colleague of mine at Yale had informed me that all Asians in Minnesota were Hmong and Vietnamese refugees and boat people who were uneducated, on welfare and spoke no English. It didn't hit me until after settling here, that he had actually been warning me that I may be mistaken for one of them. And of course, it really hit me while standing across from you in Dr. Harrison's office, that early on I had made similar presumptions about you that a naive white person or a naive Asian American, might make.

I realize now this and other events led to my unusual harshness with you in regards to your relationship with Vladimir. I have been much harder on you than I would be with a white woman—even a white woman who is dating an Asian guy. All those same expectations Asians have of you for "looking" the part, I've subconsciously had of you all along. I used to want to say, particularly when I first was getting to know you, "stop thinking like a white woman!" I am glad I never did, but I doubt it would have been half as bad as some of the judgments I've since made about you and about your and Vladimir's relationship. Even when something appears to be cut and dry, it never can be, can it?

I could not understand the camaraderie you shared with Vladimir from the beginning, because he's Russian Jewish born and bred because his family's immigration to this country was one of exile; how it is you and he share an immeasurable loss in language and culture, amongst other things. I couldn't understand it because I didn't want to. I didn't want to accept the notion that someone with an Asian face like yours could grow up identifying much more with being Polish, even *if* your father was a Polish immigrant and you grew up immersed in the culture. I couldn't accept how it was for many years, you identified more with the writing of someone such as Czeslaw Milosz rather than Maxine Hong Kingston.

I spent the night at Kelly's and at three in the morning woke because I'd just come up with this brilliant line for a poem I'm working on. I tried to wake her so I could share the line before I forgot it but she just mumbled something incomprehensible and turned over. I shook her again and she looked at the clock and said, "Elliot, it's three in the morning, I have to be at work at seven-thirty, can't this wait?! I mean really, it's just a stupid poem!" By then, I'd already forgotten the line and I'm uncertain now what bothers me most, that I forgot it or that I couldn't share it with my girlfriend or even more significantly that she couldn't see the value in why I had woke her. It's not that I expected her to understand the line or even like it. What I wanted her to understand was why it was important to me and I guess I wanted *that* to be important to her.

How I miss you, Mia. Please come back.—E.

Sonja D. Curry-Johnson was born September 15, 1968 in Needham, Mass. She graduated from Tuskegee University with a B.A. in English. She currently lives in Virginia with her husband, David, and two children, David III and Imani, and works on "the great American novel" between diaper changes.

Weaving an Identity Tapestry

Sonja D. Curry-Johnson

The Negro is a sort of a seventh son, born with a veil, and gifted with second-sight in this American world—a world which yields him no true self-consciousness, but only lets him see himself through the revelation of the other world. It is a peculiar sensation, this double-consciousness, this sense of always looking at one's self through the eyes of others, of measuring one's soul by the tape of a world that looks on in amused contempt and pity. One ever feels his twoness—an American, a Negro: two souls, two thoughts, two unreconciled strivings; two warring ideals in one dark body, whose dogged strength alone keeps it from being torn asunder.[1]

—W. E. B. Du Bois

These words, written in 1903, eloquently capture the duality that was and still is the African American experience. Yet as much as every African American has felt the "two unreconciled strivings," it seems to me that Dr. Du Bois' description applies more to black men than black women. Could Du Bois ever imagine the multiplicity that defines the existence of the contemporary African American woman? Could he fathom the dilemma of being both inwardly and outwardly torn among many factions in the quest to become a complete woman? As an African American, I feel the duality. But I suffer from more than duality. As an educated, married, monogamous, feminist, Christian, African American mother, I suffer from an acute case of multiplicity.

Each identity defines me; each is responsible for elements of my character, from each I derive some sustenance for my soul. But they do not peacefully coexist within me any more than the duality does in the lives of black men. These elements are in constant conflict, questioning my loyalties, my convictions, my love. How can you love, honor and cherish your husband, yet keep your last name and high personal aspirations? admonishes my Christian ethic, critical of my feminist dogma. How can you subscribe to a faith that was once used to enslave your people? demands my African American heritage, inspired by the heady themes of black nationalism, suspicious of anything without marked African origins. Why do you buy into the male-dominated media myth of feminine beauty? cries my feminist credo, condemning my quest for a "better" body and lamenting my trivial affinity for high fashion. At times one voice can pull stronger than the others; yet, as I struggle to find my place in the world, I am always aware of each presence.

In spite of my inner turmoil, I am not in need of psychotherapy, nor am I wandering through my life constantly confused, nor do I lack self-confidence. But in my dark hours, and frankly I have many, these voices of multiplicity rant and rail against each other; most often it is many voices struggling with my feminist voice. For self-preservation's sake, I desperately try to blend them together harmoniously like one cooks a soup or weaves a tapestry. My efforts, however, sometimes seem to be in vain, because as it is in the world around me, there is always sediment left in the bottom of the pot or a loose thread dangling at the seam.

But surely I am not the only woman, African American or otherwise, caught up in this dilemma. Once we decide to raise and carry the feminist banner, we may feel some sort of loss as we abandon traditional ways of thinking and living. Like it or not, our society forces us to make sacrifices in many aspects of our lives if we assert our feminist beliefs. For example, whether we are raised Islamic, Baptist, Catholic, Jewish or Mormon, we may miss something when we reject, for the sake of our own integrity, the religion of our parents solely because of the positions women hold (or don't hold) within its doctrine. Must we now be without spiritual guidance because the people within our religions are afraid to change? If the purpose of organized religion is to touch as many souls as possible, I believe that purpose is undermined when sanctioned hypocrisy alienates women, who make up a significant portion of the congregations. Similarly undermined are the noble crusades of the movements dedicated to the advancement of those under siege in a racist society, when they allow this same pervasive hypocrisy to taint their inner workings. If we are part of a maligned and disenfranchised minority, and we object to devoting all our energies to the uplift of the males in our group, our priorities are suspect. We deserve to have a place as women and as feminists within our religious institutions, social change movements or any other group that means something to us. We should be able to bring our whole selves to the table.

As long as we can't be our full selves, we will feel a need to hide parts of ourselves. In order to get a job or get ahead in her career, for example, a woman may feel a need to repress those aspects of herself that she fears will cause her to appear too "feminine." This same type of phenomenon is found in minorities trying not to appear too "ethnic," even to the point of changing their surnames. In either case, I find the results tragic and abhorrent, yet

I myself fell victim to this syndrome when I allowed my pregnancy to derail my confidence while looking for a job.

Even though I knew full well that there are laws specifically prohibiting discrimination on the basis of pregnancy, I felt that the first thing a prospective employer would see was not my résumé but my ample abdomen, and that he (or maybe even she) would summarily dismiss me in his mind. I imagined all the possible excuses that would be used to put me off: that my familial responsibilities would not allow me to give my all to a job, or that I would be too distracted by home ties to give my undivided attention to my work, or that I would take a lot of time off for children's illnesses and appointments. So I never even attempted to set up one measly interview. I still don't know what infuriates me more, the fact that I allowed myself to be cowed, or the fact that, unfortunately, a lot of my fears were probably well-founded.

Rest assured, these issues would have never come up for my husband if he had been the one job-hunting, although he, too, was expecting this child; he just wasn't carrying it. And so I pose the question: Is it necessary that we sacrifice a good career because of society's expectation that a proper wife and mother is chained to her family, condemned to live out a nightmare of domestic martyrdom? Conversely, must we let go of our dreams of marriage and family because workplaces refuse to accommodate women—or men—who are committed to their families? When we consider ourselves intelligent, competent and confident, we answer these questions with a resounding "No," but deep within ourselves these answers can sometimes ring hollow. Simply put, theory and practice often yield very different outcomes. In reality, when a woman is committed to asserting herself as a valuable, independent member of society, unwilling to be ignored, disrespected or dominated, she can find herself thwarted by the inflexibility of societal expectations.

I believe that children should, whenever possible, be nurtured and raised at home with a parent until they enter elementary school. But why does that parent always have to be the mother? Women are expected to stay at home, but then often find it difficult to reenter the workforce. Meanwhile, most fathers are trapped in the workplace because if they ask for the time to really help raise their children, it could mean a death warrant for their careers. Until these destructive attitudes change, women will face impossible choices, and men will remain cut off from their children.

I believe I was born a feminist, because I can't remember a specific point in my life when I can say I was "enlightened." I read Betty Friedan's *The Feminine Mystique* in high school, but it didn't bring me to a dramatic revelation. In my mind Friedan was only stating a logical fact that should be obvious to any logical being: Men and women are equals and should be treated as equals. Indeed, for me the revelation was that the society I was living in did not truly believe that women and men were equal creations. Somehow women came out on the losing end of things simply because we are able to give birth. I was incredulous that we were being penalized for ensuring the continuance of human existence, and I was floored when I realized that many women structured their lives around this ignorant train of thought. The idea of being trivialized because of my gender infuriated me almost as much as being marginalized because of my race. I remember feeling quite strongly that the administrators at the single-sex prep school I attended were bent on our finding not career goals and colleges but husbands with secure futures, and I begged my friends not to fall into this limiting mental trap. I constantly warned my classmates about the subtle messages that lurked behind the well-meaning faculty's lectures, counseling and advice. Some of my classmates shared my concern, but I was puzzled and angered when others seemed calm in the face of this sinister plot to turn us into smiling domestic sponges who would lay our lives at the feet of the false idol of some antiquated view of "family values." Only when I recognized that the deep religious undertones of the school (a religion that I did not share) were largely responsible for my friends' apathy did it start to dawn on me just what kind of conflicts would face me if I continued to openly declare myself a feminist.

I was and am a deeply religious person, and although my Baptist church has no official catechism, most sermons and lectures make it clear that women can best do their part in the advancement of the Word by being good wives and mothers and by not using our feminine wiles to tempt upstanding men to sin. Women are not encouraged to preach the doctrine unless we do it in a demure manner, such as singing in the choir, rather than the dramatic, largely male performances in the pulpit. If I were not convinced that God had actually touched my soul, and if I had not felt from an early age that basic Christian doctrines and legends are true, I would have separated from the church. But as it is, I know, because of the spiritual connection I have with God, that these patriarchal influences are of man, not God, and in time, the universal truth will be revealed to all in an event that has been promised to be the "great equalizer." I still attend church and observe traditional holidays, and I frequently challenge those who have the audacity to question my commitment to Christianity.

In college, conflicts did not lessen, but rather grew, both around me and within me. Here I had to decide what meant more to me, the attention and admiration of men, or my integrity as an independent woman. Unfortunately, there were times when my willingness to find and keep a boyfriend outweighed my desire to live my life honestly as my own person. During these times, I often placed the needs of the relationship over my own. It took a few years and a few broken relationships for me to reassess the importance of romantic love and to realize that there was no fantasy that was worth my denying any part of my identity. I decided not to become involved with a man unless I was sure he was the type of person that would not only accept my feminist ideals but also support my execution of them in my personal and professional lives. That type of man, in my mind, was a rare bird indeed. No sooner had I resigned myself to a life without romance, than I met such a bird and, in perhaps the least-debated decision of my life, married him.

Of course, marriage and the raising of a family have presented their own problems, but most of the discord can be attributed to the adjustments any two people must make when they decide to share living space on a long-term basis. Within our family it is clear that Mom and Dad are partners, and neither is concerned about who is wearing trousers. Finances, discipline and in fact all major and minor decisions in the household are handled jointly.

Outside of the family hub, however, are the old familiar rumblings. Because of the traditional facade of our relationship, friends and family tend to comment on what they assume is my abandonment of my feminist beliefs. At this time in our lives, my husband is working outside the home while I stay at home with our son and daughter, a joint decision arrived at after consideration of financial, geographical and time-frame conditions. My high school friends tease me constantly, amused at the firebrand feminist turned "little mother." They conveniently forget that my husband was the primary caregiver for our son when he was first born, enabling me to finish the first semester of my last year of school with peace of mind. They also fail to recall that when my husband had to relocate because of his military career and I could not immediately join him because I was still in school, I single-handedly cared for the baby while finishing my last undergraduate semester in a blaze of grade-point glory. They don't hear my husband urging me to get into a graduate program and to finish the "Great American Novel" I've been working on for eons.

Strangers who ask me about my career often frown at my glib descriptions of life as a domestic engineer. They usually don't bother to examine me a bit closer and would rather cluck about the "waste" of my college education. Nor do they care that their comments stir guilt, doubt and fear within me about my decision. Will this time away from professional activity rob me of my talent, instincts, competence? If I am as smart as I once thought I was, am I wasting precious time as the world revolves quite well without my being in the thick of things? Am I too concerned with making my family's laundry brighter and softer, my kitchen floors shiny and disinfected, my meals healthy and exciting? Maybe, but when I cannot pull myself out of the vortex of the fear of becoming June Cleaver, my husband becomes a mirror that reflects the image I'm afraid of losing. She's still there, the "firebrand" feminist, the independent, self-assured woman who is doing something just as important as running a company or educating the masses: raising sensitive, moral, self-aware children. Soon the career will evolve, the advanced degree will be obtained and I will truly have it all.

These days, as our threat to the old order increases, stereotypes about feminists seem to be more and more negative. Even among women peers, I find myself defending my feminist identity. I challenge them with three questions: Do you believe women should earn equal salaries for equal jobs? Do you believe women should defend other women if the need arises? Do you believe a woman should have the right to choose if and when she wants to raise a family? When they answer yes, I tell them simply, "You, too, are a feminist."

I am tired of feeling as though I must sacrifice parts of myself, and so I fight daily to meld my life into a celebration of womanhood, Christianity and the African American experience. What helps me most in the struggle to achieve inner harmony is my understanding that to call oneself a feminist need not be to offer oneself up as a martyr for the "cause," as many may think it must be. It is to celebrate and explore all that is woman, not to defame or emasculate all that is man. When a woman insists upon being treated as a living, thinking human being, while also standing up for the rights of all her sisters, how can this be interpreted as threatening by anyone but the most ignorant of people?

I now know that it is not necessary to shun marriage and family. Instead we must redefine these concepts and break the narrow traditional encasings of a mother, a father, a wife and a husband. We can make the roles fit our own identity instead of deriving our identity from these labels.

I suspect many of my sisters, women of all races, feel the same way I do about the concept of multiplicity and how it drives our lives, but we tend to try to manage one element at a time; to address the entire package can be overwhelming. Maybe multiplicity is like Du Bois' duality, in the sense that we can create a cohesive whole by nurturing and addressing each force within us singularly. We must hold on to the hope that in our quest to successfully merge the many forces that affect us so deeply, we will become stronger and more adroit. All the aspects of our identities can be sources of strength within ourselves and sources of understanding among us. Women can make sure that as long as we are leaning on each other, we are also protecting and celebrating one another. I like to think that if enough of us subscribe to this theory, maybe the wars within us will cease and we can forge a definition of what it means to be a woman that incorporates our whole selves.

Note

[1] W. E. B. Du Bois, *The Souls of Black Folk* (New York: Bantam, 1989), p. 3.

Amy Tan is the author of many works for children and adults, including the award-winning novels The Joy Luck Club *(1989) and* The Bonesetter's Daughter *(2000). Ms. Tan was born in Oakland in 1952 to parents who emigrated to the U.S. from China in the late 1940s. She earned her B.A. from San Jose State University. Ms. Tan worked with disabled children, as editor for a medical journal, and as a technical writer before beginning her career as a writer. She and her husband live in San Francisco and New York.*

Mother Tongue

Amy Tan

I am not a scholar of English or literature. I cannot give you much more than personal opinions on the English language and its variations in this country or others.

I am a writer. And by that definition, I am someone who has always loved language. I am fascinated by language in daily life. I spend a great deal of my time thinking about the power of language—the way it can evoke an emotion, a visual image, a complex idea, or a simple truth. Language is the tool of my trade. And I use them all—all the Englishes I grew up with.

Recently, I was made keenly aware of the different Englishes I do use. I was giving a talk to a large group of people, the same talk I had already given to half a dozen other groups. The nature of the talk was about my writing, my life, and my book, *The Joy Luck Club*. The talk was going along well enough, until I remembered one major difference that made the whole talk sound wrong. My mother was in the room. And it was perhaps the first time she had heard me give a lengthy speech, using the kind of English I have never used with her. I was saying things like, "The intersection of memory upon imagination" and "There is an aspect of my fiction that relates to thus-and-thus"—a speech filled with carefully wrought grammatical phrases, burdened, it suddenly seemed to me, with nominalized forms, past perfect tenses, conditional phrases, all the forms of standard English that I had learned in school and through books, the forms of English I did not use at home with my mother.

Just last week, I was walking down the street with my mother, and I again found myself conscious of the English I was using, and the English I do use with her. We were talking about the price of new and used furniture and I heard myself saying this: "Not waste money that way." My husband was with us as well, and he didn't notice any switch in my English. And then I realized why. It's because over the twenty years we've been together I've often used that same kind of English with him, and sometimes he even uses it with me. It has become our language of intimacy, a different sort of English that relates to family talk, the language I grew up with.

So you'll have some idea of what this family talk I heard sounds like, I'll quote what my mother said during a recent conversation which I videotaped and then transcribed. During this conversation, my mother was talking about a political gangster in Shanghai who had the same last name as her family's, Du, and how the gangster in his early years wanted to be adopted by her family, which was rich by comparison. Later, the gangster became more powerful, far richer than my mother's family, and one day showed up at my mother's wedding to pay his respects. Here's what she said in part:

"Du Yusong having business like fruit stand. Like off the street kind. He is Du like Du Zong—but not Tsung-ming Island people. The local people call putong, the river east side, he belong to that side local people. That man want to ask Du Zong father take him in like become own family. Du Zong father wasn't look down on him, but didn't take seriously, until that man big like become a mafia. Now important person, very hard to inviting him. Chinese way, came only to show respect, don't stay for dinner. Respect for making big celebration, he shows up. Mean gives lots of respect. Chinese custom. Chinese social life that way. If too important won't have to stay too long. He come to my wedding. I didn't see, I heard it. I gone to boy's side, they have YMCA dinner. Chinese age I was nineteen."

You should know that my mother's expressive command of English belies how much she actually understands. She reads the *Forbes* report, listens to *Wall Street Week*, converses daily with her stockbroker, reads all of Shirley MacLaine's books with ease—all kinds of things I can't begin to understand. Yet some of my friends tell me they understand 50 percent of what my mother says. Some say they understand 80 to 90 percent. Some say they understand none of it, as if she were speaking pure Chinese. But to me, my mother's English is perfectly clear, perfectly natural. It's my mother tongue. Her language, as I hear it, is vivid, direct, full of observation and imagery. That was the language that helped shape the way I saw things, expressed things, made sense of the world.

Lately, I've been giving more thought to the kind of English my mother speaks. Like others, I have described it to people as "broken" or "fractured" English. But I wince when I say that. It has always bothered me that I can think of no way to describe it other than "broken," as if it were damaged and needed to be fixed, as if it lacked a certain wholeness and soundness. I've heard other terms used, "limited English," for example.

But they seem just as bad, as if everything is limited, including people's perceptions of the limited English speaker.

I know this for a fact, because when I was growing up, my mother's "limited" English limited *my* perception of her. I was ashamed of her English. I believed that her English reflected the quality of what she had to say. That is, because she expressed them imperfectly her thoughts were imperfect. And I had plenty of empirical evidence to support me: the fact that people in department stores, at banks, and at restaurants did not take her seriously, did not give her good service, pretended not to understand her, or even acted as if they did not hear her.

My mother has long realized the limitations of her English as well. When I was fifteen, she used to have me call people on the phone to pretend I was she. In this guise, I was forced to ask for information or even to complain and yell at people who had been rude to her. One time it was a call to her stockbroker in New York. She had cashed out her small portfolio and it just so happened we were going to go to New York the next week, our very first trip outside California. I had to get on the phone and say in an adolescent voice that was not very convincing, "This is Mrs. Tan."

And my mother was standing in the back whispering loudly, "Why he don't send me check, already two weeks late. So mad he lie to me, losing me money."

And then I said in perfect English, "Yes, I'm getting rather concerned. You had agreed to send the check two weeks ago, but it hasn't arrived."

Then she began to talk more loudly. "What he want, I come to New York tell him front of his boss, you cheating me?" And I was trying to calm her down, make her be quiet, while telling the stockbroker, "I can't tolerate any more excuses. If I don't receive the check immediately, I am going to have to speak to your manager when I'm in New York next week." And sure enough, the following week there we were in front of this astonished stockbroker, and I was sitting there red-faced and quiet, and my mother, the real Mrs. Tan, was shouting at his boss in her impeccable broken English.

We used a similar routine just five days ago, for a situation that was far less humorous. My mother had gone to the hospital for an appointment, to find out about a benign brain tumor a CAT scan had revealed a month ago. She said she had spoken very good English, her best English, no mistakes. Still, she said, the hospital did not apologize when they said they had lost the CAT scan and she had come for nothing. She said they did not seem to have any sympathy when she told them she was anxious to know the exact diagnosis, since her husband and son had both died of brain tumors. She said they would not give her any more information until the next time and she would have to make another appointment for that. So she said she would not leave until the doctor called her daughter. She wouldn't budge. And when the doctor finally called her daughter, me, who spoke in perfect English—lo and behold—we had assurances the CAT scan would be found, promises that a conference call on Monday would be held, and apologies for any suffering my mother had gone through for a most regrettable mistake.

I think my mother's English almost had an effect on limiting my possibilities in life as well. Sociologists and linguists probably will tell you that a person's developing language skills are more influenced by peers. But I do think that the language spoken in the family, especially in immigrant families which are more insular, plays a large role in shaping the language of the child. And I believe that it affected my results on achievement tests, IQ tests, and the SAT. While my English skills were never judged as poor, compared to math, English could not be considered my strong suit. In grade school I did moderately well, getting perhaps B's, sometimes B-pluses, in English and scoring perhaps in the sixtieth or seventieth percentile on achievement tests. But those scores were not good enough to override the opinion that my true abilities lay in math and science, because in those areas I achieved A's and scored in the ninetieth percentile or higher.

This was understandable. Math is precise; there is only one correct answer. Whereas, for me at least, the answers on English tests were always a judgment call, a matter of opinion and personal experience. Those tests were constructed around items like fill-in-the-blank sentence completion, such as, "Even though Tom was ____, Mary thought he was ____." And the correct answer always seemed to be the most bland combinations of thoughts, for example, "Even though Tom was shy, Mary thought he was charming," with the grammatical structure "even though" limiting the correct answer to some sort of semantic opposites, so you wouldn't get answers like, "Even though Tom was foolish, Mary thought he was ridiculous." Well, according to my mother, there were very few limitations as to what Tom could have been and what Mary might have thought of him. So I never did well on tests like that.

The same was true with word analogies, pairs of words in which you were supposed to find some sort of logical, semantic relationship—for example, "*Sunset* is to *nightfall* as ____ is to ____." And here you would be presented with a list of four possible pairs, one of which showed the same kind of relationship: *red* is to *stoplight*, *bus* is to *arrival*, *chills* is to *fever*, *yawn* is to *boring*. Well, I could never think that way. I knew what the tests were asking, but I could not block out of my mind the images already created by the first pair, "*sunset* is to *nightfall*"—and I would see a burst of colors against a darkening sky, the moon rising, the lowering of a curtain of stars. And all the other pairs of words—red, bus, stoplight, boring—just threw up a mass of confusing images, making it impossible for me to sort out something as logical as saying: "A sunset precedes nightfall" is the same as "a chill precedes a fever." The only way I would have gotten that answer right would have been to imagine an associative situation, for example, my being disobedient and staying out past sunset, catching a chill at night, which turns into feverish pneumonia as punishment, which indeed did happen to me.

I have been thinking about all this lately, about my mother's English, about achievement tests. Because lately I've been asked, as a writer, why there are not more Asian Americans represented in American literature. Why are there few Asian Americans enrolled in creative writing programs? Why do so many Chinese students go into engineering? Well, these are broad sociological questions I can't begin to answer. But I have noticed in surveys—in fact, just last week—that Asian students, as a whole, always do significantly better on math achievement tests than in English. And this makes me think that there are other Asian-American students whose English spoken in the home might also be described as "broken" or "limited." And perhaps they also have teachers who are steering them away from writing and into math and science, which is what happened to me.

Fortunately, I happen to be rebellious in nature and enjoy the challenge of disproving assumptions made about me. I became an English major my first year in college, after being enrolled as pre-med. I started writing nonfiction as a freelancer the week after I was told by my former boss that writing was my worst skill and I should hone my talents toward account management.

But it wasn't until 1985 that I finally began to write fiction. And at first I wrote using what I thought to be wittily crafted sentences, sentences that would finally prove I had mastery over the English language. Here's an example from the first draft of a story that later made its way into *The Joy Luck Club*, but without this line: "That was my mental quandary in its nascent state." A terrible line, which I can barely pronounce.

Fortunately, for reasons I won't get into today, I later decided I should envision a reader for the stories I would write. And the reader I decided upon was my mother, because these were stories about mothers. So with this reader in mind—and in fact she did read my early drafts—I began to write stories using all the Englishes I grew up with: the English I spoke to my mother, which for lack of a better term might be described as "simple"; the English she used with me, which for lack of a better term might be described as "broken"; my translation of her Chinese, which could certainly be described as "watered down"; and what I imagined to be her translation of her Chinese if she could speak in perfect English, her internal language, and for that I sought to preserve the essence, but neither an English nor a Chinese structure. I wanted to capture what language ability tests can never reveal: her intent, her passion, her imagery, the rhythms of her speech and the nature of her thoughts.

Apart from what any critic had to say about my writing, I knew I had succeeded where it counted when my mother finished reading my book and gave me her verdict: "So easy to read."

Currently serving a year in AmeriCorps working with the Youth Volunteer Corps, Alia Ganaposki is interested in developing projects that incorporate storytelling with social justice and peace issues. Previously she edited features for a computer trade magazine in London and worked as a receptionist in a mental hospital.

Being Poor

A Look Inside This Secret Society

Alia Ganaposki

The good thing about being poor in college is you can hide it; you can pass as middle class as long as you hang out with people who think thrift store chic is a lifestyle choice and not a lifestyle necessity. Poverty is a secret club. In our rich, by-the-bootstraps society, being poor is a mortal sin and a blight on you and your family. So if you can pass, you do. Because of this secrecy and shame I don't think those who live in a land of plenty understand the real levels of poverty that exist on college campuses.

It wasn't until my final year of high school that I outed myself as poor. I had sat silently through a Friday afternoon economics class in my rural town, where my peers denounced welfare and kept talking about the inner-city-black-single-mother-welfare-cheat problem. By the end, tears were running down my face. In polite words edged with aggrieved righteousness and patronizing philanthropy, my classmates were attacking both my mother and my right to exist.

The next Monday, I walked into class, gripping a speech I had spent all weekend polishing. In the speech, I pointed out that poverty was not an urban, racial, or faraway problem. It was about not having money, about needing money in order to buy groceries, Christmas trees, and everything they took for granted. When they attacked welfare mothers, they were attacking my mother. I went on for several angry pages, and when I was done, there was silence. After class, many people came up to me, shocked that I wasn't like them and embarrassed that they had been called out on politically incorrect assumptions voiced in front of the "minority" they were attacking. Tentatively, they assured me that they didn't mean me, but some of them apologized and even seemed to alter their worldview a fraction.

During my senior year of high school I stopped feeling the need to protect myself by pretending I fit in economically with my peer group. By the time I got to college, I wasn't ashamed and felt I could take advantage of a new, student-formed Low Income Student Alliance (LISA). I was so excited to meet other people who might understand what it was like to send my mother an allowance from my wages rather than the other way around, who would laugh knowingly when I told the story about her response to the pamphlet I received during orientation on the expensive college medical plan: "Well, honey, don't get sick."

We shared stories—about roommates who didn't understand that we couldn't take our dirty laundry home to Mom during holidays, because she didn't have a washer and dryer—and frustrations—like how our small liberal arts college had canceled need-blind admissions during my freshman year and what further damage that would do to the already skewed representation of economic class on campus.

It was wrong and it made us angry—but between our part-time jobs and academic schedules, we didn't have time or energy to pursue it. In fact, LISA eventually ceased to exist because we weren't able to fit it into our lives. But there were people who understood and tried to help. One person I am particularly grateful to was a resident of the African Heritage House, who mentioned a grant for needy students who had to spend the winter term at school. There were posters up all over her house but none anywhere else on campus. My high school experience rushed back to me. The white liberal establishment wanted to help, but they had already decided who needed their help and in what manner. Needy person equals black person. She knew that poverty is color-blind. I did get the grant, though the department secretary informed me, when I asked about the allowance, that it was "for people who really needed it." But if I hadn't received the grant, I would not have been able to fulfill my winter term requirement on campus. I couldn't afford to do it anywhere else, and so I would have failed to meet the college's requirements and been kicked out.

In my final two years at college, I became a residential coordinator, responsible for the care and nurture of a floor of students in a dorm. I made it loudly clear from the beginning that I was poor, so that later, quietly, people who needed to could come to me and ask for help of the kind that LISA had given me. One of my residents in particular came to me often. I pointed her to all the sympathetic people in high places I knew, but in the end it wasn't enough. She had to leave college when the money she expected didn't come through, and the college couldn't bend anymore. I grieved for my personal loss, as she had been one of my charges and I felt that I had failed her—but I grieved more for this college that traded on its historically liberal reputation and yet couldn't understand that, yes, some people really were that poor. The college had become truly need-blind—it couldn't see need at all.

When the establishment finally did recognize me as being poor—in my fourth and final year—it was in the form of a mysterious invitation to go to the student support center. I had been getting excellent grades while holding down two part-time jobs, teaching classes on storytelling, and being a member of a busy campuswide committee. Why would I need support? I arrived and was greeted by a slightly patronizing woman who told me she was there for me because my file indicated my family was poor. And that was all. Despite all my achievements both academic and personal, I had a scarlet letter—a green dollar sign, even—hanging around my neck. The powers that be had suddenly decided I needed special help. Granted, perhaps some students did, and I shouldn't bash this attempt at recognizing low-income needs. But we didn't need counseling or coaching or support. What we needed was money. That didn't make us stupid; it didn't even make us less academically prepared. By my fourth year, it was a damn sight late for that kind of support, anyway. I politely declined her offer and rushed to my next class. Despite experiences like these, I loved my alma mater and got a lot out of my college years, and I know it could have been far worse elsewhere.

For example, when I was choosing a college, at that time when first impressions are crucial, one big-name college dropped off my top five list immediately after I received its standard financial aid form. One of the first blank spaces was for the needy student to list all the cars (plural!) her family owned and what model and make they were. The question led me to believe that the base level of poverty that this university anticipated in its applicants was so far above mine that it would be impossible for me to fit in. Forget diversity, inclusion, support. If this school assumed students needed financial aid if their family could afford only two cars, I couldn't see how I—with my family's single automobile—could navigate its hallowed halls.

On the other hand, we low-income students had a different view of those same halls, which allowed us to escape the stereotypical ivory tower trip. Although some students never left campus during their four years unless they needed a pack of cigarettes, I and the low-income students I knew tried much harder to interact with the town because we had more in common with that world than the world of our more privileged classmates.

Some volunteered in the schools; some worked at the stores. As part of my student aid package, I worked at a local museum and met wonderful old women and bustling old men, struggling but cheerful moms, and school trips by the busload. My college experience was much richer and more real because my friendships were not limited to people aged eighteen to twenty-one. Some of my most cherished, vivid memories of that time—and greatest learning experiences—happened far away from those hallowed halls of learning. My low-income friends were proof that students' political passion had not died out. We just took it out of the classroom and integrated it into our lives.

People are fond of saying, "Give a man a fish and feed him for a day. Teach him how to fish and feed him for a lifetime." This looks very good on a poster. But when the man is too hungry to concentrate on what his well-fed teacher thinks he should know, it just sounds gross.

There are many reasons people are poor, and when all the sources of poverty are understood and eradicated, it will be a great day for humanity. Until then, ask your low-income students what they need, and believe them when they tell you. Ask them what they know and what they want to learn. Maybe they will show you a new way to fish and change your worldview a fraction.

Kristina Anderson graduated from the College of St. Catherine in 2000 with a B.A. in English and philosophy. She is from Rochester, Minnesota.

Where I Belong

Kristina Anderson

I didn't even know what a lesbian was until I was twelve or thirteen. As I began to connect the word and its meaning with what I was feeling as a young adolescent, my world collapsed around me. Like many people in junior high and high school, the only references I heard to homosexuality were negative. "Dyke," "fag," "homo," and "fairy" were just a few of the hurtful words hurled at anyone a little different. I hid quietly, trying to blend into the crowd of ordinariness, hoping that no one could tell I might be a lesbian. I grasped early on that my confused sexual feelings must never be revealed, for I knew that homosexuality was not acceptable. In desperation and fear, I made an ultimatum with myself: if I discovered I truly was a lesbian, I would end my life. It sounded simple enough, and in many senses it comforted me to know that I could escape from what I perceived to be an unforgivable evil. I was certain that no one could live happily or productively as a lesbian, and if that turned out to be who I was, I had no choice but to die.

With time and the positive influence of others I reluctantly began to observe and even speak about my sexual orientation. I was still very much confused and filled with guilt and shame. Nonetheless, the more I dared to speak the more I came to understand that what I was feeling was not evil. The ultimatum I had made began to fade in my mind as I gained more confidence in myself. As high school came to end, I knew I needed to find a college where I could openly discover myself in an environment that was both supportive and challenging.

I thought that by attending a women's college I would find the freedom to be myself, to be open about my sexual orientation. The College of St. Catherine was an immediate first choice because of its urban location, beautiful campus, and women-centered educational philosophy. I imagined St. Kate's to be a place where women, regardless of sexual orientation, were encouraged in their goals and dreams. The first day I arrived on campus St. Kate's seemed to be all I had imagined. As my family and I pulled into the parking lot of the dorm I was to live in, two women stood on the sidewalk holding hands. They appeared relaxed in their affection for one another, laughing and smiling. I stared at them from the window of the car, trying not to visibly display my excitement. "This is it!" I thought. These two women are being open about who they are, right in front of the first year dorm on moving in day. I felt a small sense of hope and excitement as I moved into the dorm, knowing I was not alone.

Within a few days I began to wonder if the lesbians I had seen on the sidewalk were not lesbians at all, or rather the only two such women who existed at St. Kate's. The first year dorm in which I resided was a stifling atmosphere of heterosexuality. I was inundated by glossy pictures of scantily clad male figures each time I entered the bathroom. It wasn't that I cared that many of the other residents enjoyed having male company while brushing their teeth, but rather that many women never considered the possibility that some of us were not attracted to men. Talk in the hallways and dorm rooms was not much better. Many of the women had boyfriends back home or were pursuing males they had met at parties. I began to feel resentful at the very sight of a woman and her boyfriend being able to express their affection for one another in the halls and lounges of the dorm.

One day after becoming exasperated by the hetero-ness on my floor, I decided to try a little experiment. If the bathroom had been claimed as heterosexual territory, then I was going to claim the walls of the elevator as a more woman friendly environment. I carefully searched through magazines that did not promote sexualized waifs and found pictures of strong, intelligent, beautiful women. There was nothing about these women that made them look dyke-ish; they were just women, sexual orientation undefined. I made several trips to the elevator throughout the day to check on the condition of the pictures taped to the walls. No more than four or five hours had passed before I found them torn from the walls, violently I imagined, and discarded in a crumpled heap on the floor. I did try again, cutting out more pictures and taping them up, just as determined as before. I was rewarded with the same results. I had expected this reaction from the beginning, but even so there still existed within me the tiniest bit of hope that no one would care. If we had to look at handsome men all the while brushing our teeth, could we not look at beautiful women while riding the elevator? You certainly do not have to be a lesbian to think women are beautiful. But somebody did not understand this. Someone was offended, perhaps disgusted, or maybe even frightened by their own reaction to the pictures.

The silence among my classmates was unnerving, as if I were walking around with some hideous malfunction that everyone pretended did not exist out of politeness. Some of the people around me were aware of my sexual orientation because I had found the courage to tell them, yet for whatever reason the subject was taboo. People rarely spoke about it directly to me, but rumors circulated freely. It was a strange feeling that people who knew nothing about me knew I was a lesbian. It didn't make much of a difference to them that I was active in campus groups striving for social justice, involved in campus ministry, that I loved outdoor activities, enjoyed writing poetry, or that my favorite thing to do on the weekends was watch movies. For some, none of these commonly shared activities made any difference because my sexual orientation was all they knew of me, perhaps all they allowed themselves to know. There was a certain group of students on campus, I discovered, who were deeply opposed to homosexuality. Someone within this group told me in confidence that I had been identified as a lesbian among these students; they had been informed not to have any contact with me. I was deeply hurt by this, and in many ways still am, because I have always been overly sensitive to the opinions of others. I try very hard to be liked by everyone. I am especially bothered when people do not like me before they truly know me. I felt ashamed any time I encountered these people around campus because I could only imagine what they were thinking of me (what I imagined them to be thinking were the same horrible things I had thought of my own self for so long). I am certain they held within their minds a negative notion of lesbianism and applied this to me. I wanted desperately to speak with them and let them know that lesbianism is only one part of my identity. And yet, I never really did. I stayed in my comfortable corner, as did they. This benefited neither of us. I was too frightened and intimidated to share other parts of myself with them, as were they to receive from me. I do not think it is my duty to prove to others that there is nothing wrong with homosexuality, but if no one takes the initiative to educate others about our common differences, divisions will remain. If I had been more comfortable with my own sexual orientation, perhaps I could have attempted to dispel the fears and myths this group had.

Even among some of my friends, people I should have felt comfortable and safe with, lesbianism was a topic rarely discussed. I *wanted* to talk about it. I wanted to know what people felt and thought. I wanted to tell people how excited and scared and confused and thrilled I was at the process of accepting a part of myself I had detested for so long. I wanted to share with my friends the amazing music, literature, poetry, films, and art that the lgbt (lesbian, gay, bisexual, transgender) community produced. Yet as long as my friends appeared accepting of my sexual orientation, few of them felt it necessary to ever discuss the matter or become involved in active support. I recall an incident in which I was telling one of my friends about an Indigo Girls concert that attracted protesters because of the musicians' sexual orientation. I was angry and discouraged by yet another attack on homosexuality. I went to my friend looking for some encouragement. Instead, she curtly replied, "Is that all you ever talk about?!?" It took all my energy not to scream at her and say, "I listen to you talk about your guy problems every night! Why is it that any time

I mention anything having to do with lesbianism, which is not often, I am suddenly talking about it all the time?" She never questioned talking about guys and everything heterosexual because this was a privilege she took for granted. If I was a lesbian that was fine with her, as long as I did not talk about it.

One of my greatest struggles in dealing with my sexual orientation was how to do so in the academic arena. While there are many important aspects of college life, academics was always my top priority. I worked hard to receive good grades. I yearned for a student/professor relationship in which I could drop in during office hours and chat in depth about class discussions and related issues. Yet, I was fearful my emerging sexual orientation might jeopardize my grade or a relationship with a professor. I was a chameleon of sorts, changing attitudes and interests with each professor I met. I quickly found myself in conflict with one of the professors I greatly respected and admired. I took a few of her classes and found myself passionate about the subject matter she presented. However, I was distracted from this passion by the language she used in lectures and class discussions. I can excuse heterosexist language once, maybe twice, but when a professor's class examples continually ask a classroom of women to imagine a situation in which they are with their boyfriend or husband, I cannot relate. "Imagine you are on your honeymoon with your husband," she might say, creating a pleasant heterosexual scene that related in some way to the topic we were studying. Even if I could have imagined my honeymoon with an imaginary husband, I did not want to. Why did I have to pretend I was someone I was not, even in a class example?

It may seem trivial that professors ignore or refuse to acknowledge the possibility that some of their students may not be heterosexual, but it never felt trivial to me. If you have ever been the minority in a room of people praised and given attention to because of the color of their skin, religious beliefs, political affiliations, race, educational background, ability level, socioeconomic status, gender, age, or sexual orientation, you are familiar with the feeling of invisibleness. I felt invisible to this professor each time she excluded me from class examples by using heterosexist language, knowing full well I was not heterosexual. I was not asking her, or anyone else, to accept my sexual orientation, simply to acknowledge it. I wanted to be seen and spoken to as a whole person. I did not want parts of my identity to be ignored. There is nothing more painful or life threatening than being invisible because of your mere creation.

It came as a great relief, a secret celebration, each time I found supportive students and professors in my classes. I always looked for professors' doors that were decorated with a sign or symbol indicating they were an ally of the lgbt community. Those signs were a friendly sight when walking down a hallway of dismally blank doors that showed no indication my whole self was welcome. Certainly many professors who do not display lgbt support are themselves supportive, but it is often difficult to discern this. I listened for subtle clues in class lectures that signaled to me a professor was okay with homosexuality. I remember the first time I was sitting in a class and the professor used the word "significant other" in place of boyfriend. My heart burst out of my chest upon hearing these two simple words. Finally, at last, my entire being had been acknowledged. My invisibleness was beginning to melt away and the silence had been broken.

As I had yet to feel accepted in the residence halls, I reached outside of the dorm life and my straight friends to find what I thought I was looking for. I suppose it is like anyone who does not feel welcome in a community and turns elsewhere to find what it is they need. I met other lesbians on campus and tried to bring myself to be like them. Many of the women were what I considered to be very "out," both in appearance and attitude. Some were the stereotypical dyke in appearance with hair cut short and masculine attire. Some had freedom rings in their ears or eyebrows and others wore jewelry emblazoned with the black triangle, all symbols of pride in their sexual orientation. Some talked freely about their girlfriends, others questioned their like for women and even the necessity for labeling sexual orientation. They all appeared to have a confidence in themselves that allowed them to talk about their sexual orientation and say such words as "dyke" and "lesbian" in a positive, almost righteous way. I seemed to come in on the middle of this ongoing conversation because I could not yet utter such words, nor did I feel comfortable in the presence of those who could. I wanted to be "out," but I also wanted to be me. I felt as if these two identities were in conflict, especially since I was still figuring out who I was.

I knew I was a white girl who grew up in a middle class Christian family of rather conservative values. I knew the things I was hearing among the lesbians I met, and even the things I was feeling, were not in line with what I had been taught to believe. But somehow I wanted to embrace these things. I cut my hair short in the middle of the winter and began wearing a black triangle in my ear. I tried to be more assertive in counteracting the heterosexist language in classes, among my friends, and in the dorms. I thought that if I forced this upon myself it would eventually feel natural. There were times, however, when I didn't have the energy to notice the heterosexism, when I took my earring out around certain people, or when I didn't even correct people if they asked if I had a boyfriend. I was finding that I didn't feel like I belonged among the lesbians on our campus either. I questioned where I belonged.

It never occurred to me during my first years at St. Kate's that I did not have to give up my values, hobbies, taste in music, spiritual and religious beliefs, etc., etc. to be a lesbian. I was so concerned with being a "real" lesbian that everything I valued and held to be true slipped away. I thought you had to look a certain way, act a certain way, dress a certain way, be a certain way to be a lesbian. As I tried to do all these things, I began to realize what little investment I had in myself. I simply wanted to fit in with a certain crowd, and if that meant being dishonest with myself, then I was willing to do this. However, I became increasingly unhappy as everything familiar and comforting was discarded for new ways of doing things. It wasn't that the new way was wrong or bad, it was simply different, and it wasn't always me. I do not know exactly what it was, perhaps the enormous amount of energy it took to be someone I was not, that made me realize I did not have to be a certain way to be a lesbian. I can be a lesbian who likes classical music, goes to church, reads literature, and goes fishing. As I again embraced those things that were important to me, while integrating some of my new interests, I became more confident among my lesbian and straight peers alike. First and foremost I discovered I am who I am, my sexual orientation is simply another element of my identity.

As time progressed, I began to create a place for myself at St. Kate's. I experimented with who I was and how I was going to portray myself to the world. I failed many times at this, made many mistakes, but always I found the courage and support to try again. I discovered I did not have to be like any other lesbian at St. Kate's, or any other lesbian in the world, to be a lesbian. I could be a self-described lesbian. I realized I could be a successful student, as well as an "out" lesbian. While this has never been easy, it has come to be less painful then pretending to be someone I am not. St. Kate's became what I made it: an environment in which to grow, discover, change, and voice opinions. This certainly did not come without great struggle and effort, but what St. Kate's offers, if you dare to find it, is a place to form definitions of who you are and find, meaning in yourself, others, and the world.

Sucheng Chan is a professor of Asian American Studies at the University of California, Santa Barbara, and teaches courses in immigration history and contemporary community issues. She earned her Ph.D. from the University of California, Berkeley, and is the author of several books, including Hmong Means Free: Life in Laos and America *(1994) and* The Bittersweet Soil: The Chinese in California Agriculture, 1860–1910 *(1986).*

You're Short, Besides!

Sucheng Chan

When asked to write about being a physically handicapped Asian American woman, I considered it an insult. After all, my accomplishments are many, yet I was not asked to write about any of them. Is being handicapped the most salient feature about me? The fact that it might be in the eyes of others made me decide to write the essay as requested. I realized that the way I think about myself may differ considerably from the way others perceive me. And maybe that's what being physically handicapped is all about.

I was stricken simultaneously with pneumonia and polio at the age of four. Uncertain whether I had polio of the lungs, seven of the eight doctors who attended me—all practitioners of Western medicine—told my parents they should not feel optimistic about my survival. A Chinese fortune teller my mother consulted also gave a grim prognosis, but for an entirely different reason: I had been stricken because my name was offensive to the gods. My grandmother had named me "grandchild of wisdom," a name that the fortune teller said was too presumptuous for a girl. So he advised my parents to change my name to "chaste virgin." All these pessimistic predictions notwithstanding, I hung onto life, if only by a thread. For three years, my body was periodically pierced with electric shocks as the muscles of my legs atrophied. Before my illness, I had been an active, rambunctious, precocious, and very curious child. Being confined to bed was thus a mental agony as great as my physical pain. Living in war-torn China, I received little medical attention; physical therapy was unheard of. But I was determined to walk. So one day, when I was six or seven, I instructed my mother to set up two rows of chairs to face each other so that I could use them as I would parallel bars. I attempted to walk by holding my body up and moving it forward with my arms while dragging my legs along behind. Each time I fell, my mother gasped, but I badgered her until she let me try again. After four nonambulatory years, I finally walked once more by pressing my hands against my thighs so my knees wouldn't buckle.

My father had been away from home during most of those years because of the war. When he returned, I had to confront the guilt he felt about my condition. In many East Asian cultures, there is a strong folk belief that a person's physical state in this life is a reflection of how morally or sinfully he or she lived in previous lives. Furthermore, because of the tendency to view the family as a single unit, it is believed that the fate of one member can be caused by the behavior of another. Some of my father's relatives told him that my illness had doubtless been caused by the wild carousing he did in his youth. A well-meaning but somewhat simple man, my father believed them.

Throughout my childhood, he sometimes apologized to me for having to suffer retribution for his former bad behavior. This upset me; it was bad enough that I had to deal with the anguish of not being able to walk, but to have to assuage his guilt as well was a real burden! In other ways, my father was very good to me. He took me out often, carrying me on his shoulders or back, to give me fresh air and sunshine. He did this until I was too large and heavy for him to carry. And ever since I can remember, he has told me that I am pretty.

After getting over her anxieties about my constant falls, my mother decided to send me to school. I had already learned to read some words of Chinese at the age of three by asking my parents to teach me the sounds and meaning of various characters in the daily newspaper. But between the ages of four and eight, I received no education since just staying alive was a full-time job. Much to her chagrin, my mother found no school in Shanghai, where we lived at the time, which would accept me as a student. Finally, as a last resort, she approached the American School, which agreed to enroll me only if my family kept an *amah* (a servant who takes care of children) by my side at all times. The tuition at the school was twenty U.S. dollars per month—a huge sum of money during those years of runaway inflation in China—and payable only in U.S. dollars. My family afforded the high cost of tuition and the expense of employing a full-time *amah* for less than a year.

We left China as the Communist forces swept across the country in victory. We found an apartment in Hong Kong across the street from a school run by Seventh-Day Adventists. By that time I could walk a little, so the principal was persuaded to accept me. An *amah* now had to take care of me only during recess when my classmates might easily knock me over as they ran about the playground.

After a year and a half in Hong Kong, we moved to Malaysia, where my father's family had lived for four generations. There I learned to swim in the lovely warm waters of the tropics and fell in love with the sea. On land I was a cripple; in the ocean I could move with the grace of a fish. I liked the freedom of being in the water so much that many years later, when I was a graduate student in Hawaii, I became greatly enamored with a man just because he called me a "Polynesian water nymph."

As my overall health improved, my mother became less anxious about all aspects of my life. She did everything possible to enable me to lead as normal a life as possible. I remember how once some of her colleagues in the high school where she taught criticized her for letting me wear short skirts. They felt my legs should not be exposed to public view. My mother's response was, "All girls her age wear short skirts, so why shouldn't she?"

The years in Malaysia were the happiest of my childhood, even though I was constantly fending off children who ran after me calling, "*Baikah! Baikah!*" ("Cripple! Cripple!" in the Hokkien dialect commonly spoken in Malaysia). The taunts of children mattered little because I was a star pupil. I won one award after another for general scholarship as well as for art and public speaking. Whenever the school had important visitors my teacher always called on me to recite in front of the class.

A significant event that marked me indelibly occurred when I was twelve. That year my school held a music recital and I was one of the students chosen to play the piano. I managed to get up the steps to the stage without any problem, but as I walked across the stage, I fell. Out of the audience, a voice said loudly and clearly, "Ayah! A *baikah* shouldn't be allowed to perform in public." I got up before anyone could get on stage to help me and, with tears streaming uncontrollably down my face, I rushed to the piano and began to play. Beethoven's "Für Elise" had never been played so fiendishly fast before or since, but I managed to finish the whole piece. That I managed to do so made me feel really strong. I never again feared ridicule.

In later years I was reminded of this experience from time to time. During my fourth year as an assistant professor at the University of California at Berkeley, I won a distinguished teaching award. Some weeks later I ran into a former professor who congratulated me enthusiastically. But I said to him, "You know what? I became a distinguished teacher by *limping* across the stage of Dwinelle 155!" (Dwinelle 155 is a large, cold, classroom that most colleagues of mine hate to teach in.) I was rude not because I lacked graciousness but because this man, who had told me that my dissertation was the finest piece of work he had read in fifteen years, had nevertheless advised me to eschew a teaching career.

"Why?" I asked.

"Your leg . . ." he responded.

"What about my leg?" I said, puzzled.

"Well, how would you feel standing in front of a large lecture class?"

"If it makes any difference, I want you to know I've won a number of speech contests in my life, and I am not the least bit self-conscious about speaking in front of large audiences. . . . Look, why don't you write me a letter of recommendation to tell people how brilliant I am, and let *me* worry about my leg!"

This incident is worth recounting only because it illustrates a dilemma that handicapped persons face frequently: those who care about us sometimes get so protective that they unwittingly limit our growth. This former professor of mine had been one of my greatest supporters for two decades. Time after time, he had written glowing letters of recommendation on my behalf. He had spoken as he did because he thought he had my best interests at heart; he thought that if I got a desk job rather than one that required me to be a visible, public person, I would be spared the misery of being stared at.

Americans, for the most part, do not believe as Asians do that physically handicapped persons are morally flawed. But they are equally inept at interacting with those of us who are not able-bodied. Cultural differences in the perception and treatment of handicapped people are most clearly expressed by adults. Children, regardless of where they are, tend to be openly curious about people who do not look "normal." Adults in Asia have no hesitation in asking visibly handicapped people what is wrong with them, often expressing their sympathy with looks of pity, whereas adults in the United States try desperately to be polite by pretending not to notice.

One interesting response I often elicited from people in Asia but have never encountered in America is the attempt to link my physical condition to the state of my soul. Many a time while living and traveling in Asia people would ask me what religion I belonged to. I would tell them that my mother is a devout Buddhist, that my father was baptized a Catholic but has never practiced Catholicism, and that I am an agnostic. Upon hearing this, people would try strenuously to convert me to their religion so that whichever God they believed in could bless me. If I would only attend this church or that temple regularly, they urged, I would surely get cured. Catholics and Buddhists alike have pressed religious medallions into my palm, telling me if I would wear these, the relevant deity or saint would make me well. Once while visiting the tomb of Muhammad Ali Jinnah in Karachi, Pakistan, an old Muslim, after finishing his evening prayers, spotted me, gestured toward my legs, raised his arms heavenward, and began a new round of prayers, apparently on my behalf.

In the United States adults who try to act "civilized" toward handicapped people by pretending they don't notice anything unusual sometimes end up ignoring handicapped people completely. In the first few months I lived in this country, I was struck by the fact that whenever children asked me what was the matter with my leg, their adult companions would hurriedly shush them up, furtively look at me, mumble apologies, and rush their children away. After a few months of such encounters, I decided it was my responsibility to educate these people. So I would say to the flustered adults, "It's okay, let the kid ask." Turning to the child, I would say, "When I was a little girl, no bigger than you are, I became sick with something called polio. The muscles of my leg shrank up and I couldn't walk very well. You're much luckier than I am because now you can get a vaccine to make sure you never get my disease. So don't cry when your mommy takes you to get a polio vaccine, okay?" Some adults and their little companions I talked to this way were glad to be rescued from embarrassment; others thought I was strange.

Americans have another way of covering up their uneasiness: they become jovially patronizing. Sometimes when people spot my crutch, they ask if I've had a skiing accident. When I answer that unfortunately it is something less glamorous than that they say, "I bet you *could* ski if you put your mind to it!" Alternately, at parties where people dance, men who ask me to dance with them get almost belligerent when I decline their invitation. They say, "Of course you can dance if you *want* to!" Some have given me pep talks about how if I would only develop the right mental attitude, I would have more fun in life.

Different cultural attitudes toward handicapped persons came out clearly during my wedding. My father-in-law, as solid a representative of middle America as could be found, had no qualms about objecting to the marriage on racial grounds, but he could bring himself to comment on my handicap only indirectly. He wondered why his son, who had dated numerous high school and college beauty queens, couldn't marry one of them instead of me. My mother-in-law, a devout Christian, did not share her husband's prejudices, but she worried aloud about whether I could have children. Some Chinese friends of my parents, on the other hand, said that I was lucky to have found such a noble man, one who would marry me despite my handicap. I, for my part, appeared in church in a white lace wedding dress I had designed and made myself—a miniskirt!

How Asian Americans treat me with respect to my handicap tells me a great deal about their degree of acculturation. Recent immigrants behave just like Asians in Asia; those who have been here longer or who grew up in the United States behave more like their white counterparts. I have not encountered any distinctly Asian American pattern of response. What makes the experience of Asian American handicapped people unique is the duality of responses we elicit.

Regardless of racial or cultural background, most handicapped people have to learn to find a balance between the desire to attain physical independence and the need to take care of ourselves by not overtaxing our bodies. In my case, I've had to learn to accept the fact that leading an active life has its price. Between the ages of eight and eighteen, I walked without using crutches or braces but the effort caused my right leg to become badly misaligned. Soon after I came to the United States, I had a series of operations to straighten out the bones of my right leg; afterwards though my leg looked straighter and presumably better, I could no longer walk on my own. Initially my doctors fitted me with a brace, but I found wearing one cumbersome and soon gave it up. I could move around much more easily—and more important, faster—by using one crutch. One orthopedist after another warned me that using a single crutch was a bad practice. They were right. Over the years my spine developed a double-S curve and for the last twenty years I have suffered from severe, chronic back pains, which neither conventional physical therapy nor a lighter work load can eliminate.

The only thing that helps my backaches is a good massage, but the soothing effect lasts no more than a day or two. Massages are expensive, especially when one needs them three times a week. So I found a job that pays better, but at which I have to work longer hours, consequently increasing the physical strain on my body—a sort of vicious circle. When I was in my thirties, my doctors told me that if I kept leading the strenuous life I did, I would be in a wheelchair by the time I was forty. They were right on target: I bought myself a wheelchair when I was forty-one. But being the incorrigible character that I am, I use it only when I am *not* in a hurry!

It is a good thing, however, that I am too busy to think much about my handicap or my backaches because pain can physically debilitate as well as cause depression. And there are days when my spirits get rather low. What has helped me is realizing that being handicapped is akin to growing old at an accelerated rate. The contradiction I experience is that often my mind races along as though I'm only twenty while my body feels about sixty. But fifteen or twenty years hence, unlike my peers who will have to cope with aging for the first time, I shall be full of cheer because I will have already fought, and I hope won, that battle long ago.

Beyond learning how to be physically independent and, for some of us, living with chronic pain or other kinds of discomfort, the most difficult thing a handicapped person has to deal with, especially during puberty and early adulthood, is relating to potential sexual partners. Because American culture places so much emphasis on physical attractiveness, a person with a shriveled limb, or a tilt to the head, or the inability to speak clearly, experiences great uncertainty—indeed trauma—when interacting with someone to whom he or she is attracted. My problem was that I was not only physically handicapped, small, and short, but worse, I also wore glasses and was smarter than all the boys I knew! Alas, an insurmountable combination. Yet somehow I have managed to have intimate relationships, all of them with extraordinary men. Not surprisingly, there have also been countless men who broke my heart—men who enjoyed my company "as a friend," but who never found the courage to date or make love with me, although I am sure my experience in this regard is no different from that of many able-bodied persons.

The day came when my backaches got in the way of having an active sex life. Surprisingly that development was liberating because I stopped worrying about being attractive to men. No matter how headstrong I had been, I, like most women of my generation, had had the desire to be alluring to men ingrained into me. And that longing had always worked like a brake on my behavior. When what men think of me ceased to be compelling, I gained greater freedom to be myself.

I've often wondered if I would have been a different person had I not been physically handicapped. I really don't know, though there is no question that being handicapped has marked me. But at the same time I usually do not *feel* handicapped—and consequently, I do not *act* handicapped. People are therefore less likely to treat me as a handicapped person. There is no doubt, however, that the lives of my parents, sister, husband, other family members, and some close friends have been affected by my physical condition. They have had to learn not to hide me away at home, not to feel embarrassed by how I look or react to people who say silly things to me, and not to resent me for the extra demands my condition makes on them. Perhaps the hardest thing for those who live with handicapped people is to know when and how to offer help. There are no guidelines applicable to all situations. My advice is, when in doubt, ask, but ask in a way that does not smack of pity or embarrassment. Most important, please don't talk to us as though we are children.

So, has being physically handicapped been a handicap? It all depends on one's attitude. Some years ago, I told a friend that I had once said to an affirmative action compliance officer (somewhat sardonically since I do not believe in the head count approach to affirmative action) that the institution which employs me is triply lucky because it can count me as non-white, female and handicapped. He responded, "Why don't you tell them to count you four times? . . . Remember, you're short, besides!"

A widely published African-American poet, Lucille Clifton was born in Depew, NY, in 1936. Her poems generally focus on racial issues or on the strength that women draw upon during adversity, and many have been translated into other languages, including Norwegian, Hebrew, and Japanese. Her work also includes several children's books (the "Everett Anderson" series). Clifton is currently Distinguished Professor of the Humanities at St. Mary's College of Maryland.

homage to my hips

Lucille Clifton

these hips are big hips.
they need space to
move around in.
they don't fit into little
petty places. these hips
are free hips.
they don't like to be held back.
these hips have never been enslaved,
they go where they want to go
they do what they want to do.
these hips are mighty hips.
these hips are magic hips.
i have known them
to put a spell on a man and
spin him like a top!

what the mirror said

Lucille Clifton

listen,
you a wonder.
you a city
of a woman.
you got a geography
of your own.
listen,
somebody need a map
to understand you.
somebody need directions
to move around you.
listen,
woman,
you not a noplace
anonymous
girl;
mister with his hands on you
he got his hands on
some
damn
body!

Raymond Carver (1938–1988) is credited as being one of a handful of contemporary writers who revived the dying short story genre. In addition to short stories, he authored several novels, poems, and essays. He received two Pulitzer Prize nominations for fiction: for Cathedral *in 1985 and for* Where I'm Calling From: New and Selected Stories *in 1989.*

Cathedral

Raymond Carver

This blind man, an old friend of my wife's, he was on his way to spend the night. His wife had died. So he was visiting the dead wife's relatives in Connecticut. He called my wife from his in-laws'. Arrangements were made. He would come by train, a five-hour trip, and my wife would meet him at the station. She hadn't seen him since she worked for him one summer in Seattle ten years ago. But she and the blind man had kept in touch. They made tapes and mailed them back and forth. I wasn't enthusiastic about his visit. He was no one I knew. And his being blind bothered me. My idea of blindness came from the movies. In movies, the blind moved slowly and never laughed. Sometimes they were led by seeing-eye dogs. A blind man in my house was not something I looked forward to.

That summer in Seattle she had needed a job. She didn't have any money. The man she was going to marry at the end of the summer was in officer's training school. He didn't have any money, either. But she was in love with the guy, and he was in love with her, etc. She'd seen something in the paper: Help Wanted—Reading for Blind Man, and a telephone number. She phoned and went over, was hired on the spot. She'd worked with this blind man all summer. She read stuff to him, case studies, reports, that sort of thing. She helped him organize his little office in the county social service department. They'd become good friends, my wife and the blind man. How do I know these things? She told me. And she told me something else. On her last day in the office, the blind man asked if he could touch her face. She agreed to this. She told me he ran his fingers over every part of her face, her nose—even her neck! She never forgot it. She even tried to write a poem about it. She was always writing a poem. She wrote a poem or two every year, usually after something really important had happened to her.

When we first started going out together, she showed me the poem. In the poem she recalled his fingers and the way they had moved around over her face. In the poem she talked about what she had felt at the time, about what went through her mind as he touched her nose and lips. I can recall I didn't think much of the poem. Of course I didn't tell her that. Maybe I just don't understand poetry. I admit it's not the first thing I reach for when I pick up something to read.

Anyway, this man who'd first enjoyed her favors, the officer-to-be, he'd been her childhood sweetheart. So okay. I'm saying that at the end of the summer she let the blind man run his hands over her face, said good-bye to him, married her childhood etc., who was now a commissioned officer, and she moved away from Seattle. But they'd kept in touch, she and the blind man. She made the first contact after a year or so. She called him up one night from an Air Force base in Alabama. She wanted to talk. They talked. He asked her to send him a tape and tell him about her life. She did this. She sent the tape. On the tape she told the blind man about her husband and about their life together in the military. She told the blind man she loved her husband but she didn't like it where they lived and she didn't like it that he was a part of the military-industrial complex. She told the blind man she'd written a poem and he was in it. She told him that she was writing a poem about what it was like to be an Air Force officer's wife in the Deep South. The poem wasn't finished yet. She was still writing it. The blind man made a tape. He sent her the tape. She made a tape. This went on for years. My wife's officer was posted to one base and then another. She sent tapes from Moody AFB, McGuire, McConnell, and finally Travis, near Sacramento, where one night she got to feeling lonely and cut off from people she kept losing in that moving-around life. She balked, couldn't go it another step. She went in and swallowed all the pills and capsules in the medicine cabinet and washed them down with a bottle of gin. Then she got into a hot bath and passed out.

But instead of dying she got sick. She threw up. Her officer—Why should he have a name? He was the childhood sweetheart, and what more does he want?—came home from a training mission, found her, and called the ambulance. In time, she put it on the tape and sent the tape to the blind man. Over the years she put all kinds of stuff on tapes and sent the tapes off lickety-split. Next to writing a poem every year, I think it was her chief means of recreation. On one tape she told the blind man she'd decided to live away from her officer for a time. On another tape she told him about her divorce. She and I began going out, and of course she told her blind man about this. She told him everything, so it seemed to me. Once she asked me if I'd like to hear the latest tape from the blind man. This was a year ago. I was on the tape, she said. So I said okay, I'd listen to it. I got us drinks and we settled down in the living room. We made ready to listen. First she inserted the tape into the player and adjusted a couple of dials. Then she pushed a lever. The tape squeaked and someone began to talk in this loud voice. She lowered the volume. After a few minutes of harmless chitchat, I heard my own name rasped out by this stranger, this man I didn't even know! And then this: "From all you've said about him,

I can only conclude—" But we were interrupted, a knock at the door, something, and we didn't get back to the tape. Maybe it was just as well. I'd heard enough, anyway.

Now this same blind stranger was coming to sleep in my house.

"Maybe I could take him bowling," I said to my wife. She was at the draining board doing scalloped potatoes. She put down the knife she was using on the onion and turned around.

"If you love me," she said, "you can do this for me. If you don't love me, okay. But if you had a friend, any friend, and the friend came to visit, I'd make him feel comfortable." She wiped her hands with the dish towel.

"I don't have any blind friends," I said.

"You don't have *any* friends," she said. "Period. Besides," she said, "god-damnit, his wife's just died! Don't you understand that? The man's lost his wife!"

I didn't answer. She'd told me a little about the blind man's wife. The wife's name was Beulah. Beulah! That's a name for a colored woman.

"Was his wife a Negro?" I asked.

"Are you crazy?" my wife said. "Have you just flipped or something?" She picked up the onion. I saw it hit the floor, then roll under the stove. "What's wrong with you?" she said. "Are you drunk?"

"I'm just asking," I said.

Right then my wife filled me in with more detail than I cared to know. I made a drink and sat at the kitchen table to listen. Pieces of the story began to fall into place.

Beulah had gone to work for the blind man the summer after my wife had stopped working for him. Pretty soon Beulah and the blind man had themselves a church wedding. It was a little wedding—who'd be anxious to attend such a wedding in the first place?—just the two of them, and the minister and the minister's wife. But it was a church wedding just the same. What Beulah had wanted, he'd said. But even then Beulah must have been carrying cancer in her lymph glands. After they had been inseparable for eight years—my wife's word, *inseparable*—Beulah's health went into a rapid decline. She died in a Seattle hospital room, the blind man sitting beside the bed and holding on to her hand. They'd married, lived and worked together, slept together—had sex, sure—and then the blind man buried her. All this without his having ever seen what the goddamned woman looked like. It was beyond my understanding. Hearing this, I felt sorry for the blind man for a minute. And then I found myself thinking what a pitiful life this woman must have led. Imagine a woman who could never see herself reflected in the eyes of her loved one. A woman who could go on day after day and never receive the smallest compliment from her beloved. A woman whose husband would never read the expression on her face, be it misery or something better. Someone who could wear make-up or not—what difference to him? She could, if she wanted, wear green eye shadow around one eye, a straight pin in her nostril, yellow slacks and burgundy pumps, no matter. And then to slip off into death, the blind man's hand on her hand, his blind eyes streaming tears—I'm imagining now—her last thought maybe this: that her beloved never knew what she looked like, and she on an express to the grave. Robert was left with a small insurance policy and half of a twenty-peso Mexican coin. The other half of the coin went into the box with her. Pathetic.

So when the time rolled around, my wife went to the rail station. With nothing to do but wait—and sure, I blamed him for that—I was having a drink and watching TV when I heard the car pull into the drive. I got up from the sofa with my drink and went to the window to have a look.

I saw my wife laughing as she parked the car. I saw her get out of the car and shut the door. She was still wearing a smile. Just amazing. She went around to the other side of the car to where the blind man was already starting to get out. This blind man, feature this, he was wearing a full beard! A beard on a blind man! Too much, I say. The blind man reached into the back seat and dragged out a suitcase. My wife took his arm, shut the car door, and, talking all the way, moved him down the drive and then up the steps to the front porch. I turned off the TV. I finished my drink, rinsed the glass, dried my hands. Then I went to the door.

My wife said, "I want you to meet Robert. Robert, this is my husband. I've told you all about him." She closed the porch screen. She was beaming. She had this blind man by his coat sleeve.

The blind man let go of his suitcase and up came his hand.

I took it. He squeezed hard, held my hand, and then he let it go.

"I feel like we've already met," he boomed.

"Likewise," I said. I didn't know what else to say. Then I said, "Welcome. I've heard a lot about you." We began to move then, a little group, from the porch into the living room, my wife guiding him by the arm. He carried his suitcase in his other hand. My wife said things like, "To your left here, Robert. That's right. Now watch it, there's a chair. That's it. Sit down right here. This is the sofa. We just bought this sofa two weeks ago."

I started to say something about the old sofa. I'd liked that old sofa. But I didn't say anything. Then I wanted to say something else, small talk, about the scenic Hudson River. How going *to* New York, sit on the right-hand side of the train, and coming *from* New York, the left-hand side.

"Did you have a good train ride?" I said. "Which side of the train did you sit on, by the way?"

"What a question, which side!" my wife said. "What's it matter which side?" she said.

"I just asked," I said.

"Right side," the blind man said. "For the sun. Until this morning," the blind man said, "I hadn't been on a train in nearly forty years. Not since I was a kid. With my folks. That's been a long time. I'd nearly forgotten that sensation. I have winter in my beard now," he said. "So I've been told, anyway. Do I look distinguished, my dear?" he said to my wife.

"You look distinguished, Robert," she said. "Robert," she said.

"Robert, it's just so good to see you." My wife finally took her eyes off the blind man and looked at me.

I had the distinct feeling she didn't like what she saw. I shrugged.

I've never met or personally known anyone who was blind. This blind man was late forties, a heavyset, balding man with stooped shoulders, as if he carried a great weight there. He wore brown slacks, brown cordovan shoes, a light brown shirt, a tie, a sports coat. Spiffy. He also had this full beard. But he didn't carry a cane and he didn't wear dark glasses. I'd always thought dark glasses were a must for the blind. Fact was, I wished he had a pair. At first glance, his eyes looked like anyone else's eyes. But if you looked close there was something different about them. Too much white in the iris, for one thing, and the pupils seemed to move around in the sockets without his knowing it or being able to control it. Creepy. As I stared at his face, I saw the left pupil turn in toward his nose, while the other made a futile effort to keep in one place. But it was only an effort, for that eye was on the roam without his knowing it or wanting it to be.

I said, "Let me get you a drink. What's your pleasure? We have a little of everything. It's one of our pastimes."

"Bub, I'm a Scotch man myself," he said fast enough, in this big voice.

"Right," I said. Bub! "Sure you are. I knew it."

He let his fingers touch his suitcase, which was sitting alongside the sofa. He was taking his bearings. I didn't blame him for that.

"I'll move that up to your room," my wife said.

"No, that's fine," he said loudly. "It can go up when I go up."

"A little water with the Scotch?" I said.

"Very little," he said.

"I knew it," I said.

He said, "Just a tad. The Irish actor, Barry Fitzgerald? I'm like that fellow. When I drink water, Fitzgerald said, I drink water. When I drink whiskey, I drink whiskey." My wife laughed. The blind man brought his hand up under his beard. He lifted his beard slowly and let it drop.

I did the drinks, three big glasses of Scotch with a splash of water in each. Then we made ourselves comfortable and talked about Robert's travels. First the long flight from the West Coast to Connecticut, we covered that. Then from Connecticut up here by train. We had another drink concerning that leg of the trip.

I remembered having read somewhere that the blind didn't smoke because, speculation had it, they couldn't see the smoke they exhaled. I thought I knew that much and that much only about blind people. But this blind man smoked his cigarette down to the nubbin and then lit another one. This blind man filled his ashtray and my wife emptied it.

When we sat down to the table for dinner we had another drink. My wife heaped Robert's plate with cube steak, scalloped potatoes, green beans. I buttered him up two slices of bread. I said, "Here's bread and butter for you." I swallowed some of my drink. "Now let us pray," I said, and the blind man lowered his head. My wife looked at me, her mouth agape. "Pray the phone won't ring and the food doesn't get cold," I said.

We dug in. We ate everything there was to eat on the table. We ate like there was no tomorrow. We didn't talk. We ate. We scarfed. We grazed that table. We were into serious eating. The blind man had right away located his foods, he knew just where everything was on his plate. I watched with admiration as he used his knife and fork on the meat. He'd cut two pieces of meat, fork the meat into his mouth, and then go all out for the scalloped potatoes, the beans next, and then he'd tear off a hunk of buttered bread and eat that. He'd follow this up with a big drink of milk. It didn't seem to bother him to use his fingers once in a while, either. He used his bread to scoop beans.

We finished everything, including half of a strawberry pie. For a few moments we sat as if stunned. Sweat beaded on our faces. Finally, we got up from the table and left the dirty plates. We didn't look back. We took ourselves into the living room and sank into our places again. Robert and my wife sat on the sofa. I took the big chair. We had us two or three more drinks while they talked about the major things that had transpired for them in the past ten years. For the most part, I just listened. Now and then I joined in. I didn't want him to think I'd left the room, and I didn't want her to think I was feeling left out. They talked of things that had happened to them—to them!—these past ten years. I waited in vain to hear my name on my wife's sweet lips: "And then my dear husband came into my life"—something like that. But I heard nothing of the sort. More talk of Robert. Robert had done a little of everything, it seemed, a regular blind jack-of-all-trades. But most recently he and his wife had had an Amway distributorship, from which, I gathered, they'd earned their living, such as it was. The blind man was also a ham radio operator. He talked in his loud voice about conversations he'd had with fellow operators in Guam, the Philippines, Alaska, even Tahiti. He said he'd have a lot of friends there if he ever wanted to go visit those places. From time to time he'd turn his blind face toward me, put his hand under his beard, ask me something. How long had I been at my present position? (Three years.) Did I like my work? (I didn't.) Was I going to stay with it? (What were the options?)

Finally, when I thought he was beginning to run down, I got up and turned on the TV.

My wife looked at me with irritation. She was heading toward a boil. Then she looked at the blind man and said, "Robert, do you have a TV?"

The blind man said, "My dear, I have two TVs. I have a color set and a black-and-white thing, an old relic. It's funny, but if I turn the TV on, and I'm always turning it on, I turn the color set on. Always. It's funny."

I didn't know what to say to that. I had absolutely nothing to say about that. No opinion. So I watched the news program and tried to listen to what the announcer was saying.

"This is a color TV," the blind man said. "Don't ask me how, but I can tell."

"We traded up a while ago," I said.

The blind man had another taste of his drink. He lifted his beard, sniffed it, and let it fall. He leaned forward on the sofa. He positioned his ashtray on the coffee table, then put the lighter to his cigarette. He leaned back on the sofa and crossed his legs at the ankles.

My wife covered her mouth, and then she yawned. She stretched. She said, "I think I'll go upstairs and put on my robe. I think I'll change into something else. Robert, you make yourself comfortable," she said.

"I'm comfortable," the blind man said.

"I want you to feel comfortable in this house," she said.

"I am comfortable," the blind man said.

After she'd left the room, he and I listened to the weather report and then to the sports roundup. My wife had been gone so long I didn't know if she was going to come back. I thought she might gone to bed. I wished she'd come back downstairs. I didn't want to be left alone with a blind man. I asked him if he wanted another drink, and he said sure. Then I asked if he wanted to smoke dope with me. I said I'd just rolled a number. I hadn't, but I planned to do so in about two shakes.

"I'll try some with you," he said.

"Damn right," I said. "That's the stuff."

I got our drinks and sat down on the sofa with him. Then I rolled us two fat numbers. I lit one and passed it. I brought it to his fingers. He took it and inhaled.

"Hold it as long as you can," I said. I could tell he didn't know the first thing.

My wife came back downstairs wearing her robe and pink slippers. "What do I smell?" she said.

"We thought we'd have us some cannabis," I said.

My wife gave me a purely savage look. Then she looked at him and said, "Robert, I didn't know you smoked."

He said, "I do now, my dear. First time for everything," he said. "But I don't feel anything yet."

"This stuff is pretty mellow," I said. "This stuff is mild. It's dope you can reason with. It doesn't mess you up."

"Not much it doesn't, bub," he said, and laughed.

My wife sat on the sofa between the blind man and me. I passed her the number. She took it and inhaled and then passed it back to me. "Which way is this going?" she said. Then she said, "I shouldn't be smoking this. I can hardly keep my eyes open as it is. That dinner did me in. I shouldn't have eaten so much."

"It was the strawberry pie," the blind man said. "That's what did it," he said, and he laughed his big laugh. Then he shook his head.

"There's more strawberry pie," I said.

"Do you want some more, Robert?" my wife asked.

"Maybe in a little while," he said.

We gave our attention to the TV. My wife yawned again. She said, "Your bed is made up when you feel like going to bed, Robert. I know you must have had a long day. When you're ready to go to bed, say so." She pulled his arm. "Robert?"

He came to and said, "I've had a real nice time. This beats tapes, doesn't it?"

I said, "Coming at you," and I put the number between his fingers. He inhaled, held the smoke, and then let it go. It was like he'd been doing it since he was nine years old.

"Thanks, bub," he said. "But I think this is all for me. I think I'm beginning to feel it," he said. He held the burning roach out for my wife.

"Same here," she said. "Ditto. Me too." She took the roach and passed it to me. "I may just sit here for a while between you two guys with my eyes closed. But don't let me bother you, okay? Either one of you. If it bothers you, say so. Otherwise, I may just sit here with my eyes closed until you're ready to go to bed," she said. "Your bed's made up, Robert, when you're ready. It's right next to our room at the top of the stairs. We'll show you up when you're ready. You wake me up now, you guys, if I fall asleep." She said that and then she closed her eyes and went to sleep.

The news program ended. I got up and turned the channel. I sat back down on the sofa. I wished my wife hadn't pooped out. Her head lay across the back of the sofa, her mouth open. She'd turned so that her robe had slipped away from her legs, exposing a juicy thigh. I reached to draw her robe over the thigh, and it was then I glanced at the blind man. What the hell! I flipped the robe open again.

"You say when you want some strawberry pie," I said.

"I will," he said.

I said, "Are you tired? Do you want me to take you up to your bed? Are you ready to hit the hay?"

"Not yet," he said. "No, I'll stay up with you, bub. If that's all right. I'll stay up until you're ready to turn in. We haven't had a chance to talk. Know what I mean? I feel like me and her monopolized the evening." He lifted his beard and he let it fall. He picked up his cigarettes and his lighter.

"That's all right," I said. Then I said, "I'm glad for the company." And I guess I was. Every night I smoked dope and stayed up as long as I could before I fell asleep. My wife and I hardly ever went to bed at the same time. When I did go to sleep, I had these dreams. Sometimes I'd wake up from one of them, the heart going crazy.

Something about the Church and the Middle Ages, narrated by an Englishman, was on the TV. Not your run-of-the-mill TV fare. I wanted to watch something else. I turned to the other channels.

But there was nothing on them, either. So I turned back to the first channel and apologized.

"Bub, it's all right," he said. "It's fine with me. Whatever you want to watch is okay. I'm always learning something. Learning never ends. It won't hurt me to learn something tonight. I got ears," he said.

We didn't say anything for a time. He was leaning forward with his head turned at me, while his right ear was aimed in the direction of the set. Very disconcerting. Now and then his eyelids drooped and then they snapped open again. Now and then he put his fingers into his beard and tugged, as if thinking about something he was hearing on the television.

On the screen a group of men wearing cowls was being set upon and tormented by men dressed in skeleton costumes and men dressed as devils. The men dressed as devils wore devil masks, horns, and long tails. This pageant was part of a procession. The Englishman said it all took place in Málaga Spain, once a year. I tried to explain to the blind man what was happening.

"Skeletons," he said. "I know about skeletons," he said, and he nodded.

The TV showed Chartres Cathedral. Then there was a long slow look at Sainte-Chapelle. Finally the picture switched to Notre-Dame, with its flying buttresses, its spires reaching toward clouds. The camera pulled away to show the whole of the cathedral rising above the skyline.

There were times when the Englishman who was telling the thing would shut up, would simply let the camera move around over the cathedrals. Or else the camera would tour the countryside, men in fields walking behind oxen. I waited as long as I could. Then I felt I had to say something. I said, "They're showing the outside of this cathedral now. Gargoyles. Little statues carved to look like monsters. Now I guess they're in

Italy. Yeah, they're in Italy. There's fresco paintings on the walls of this one church."

"What's fresco painting, bub?" he asked, and he sipped from his drink.

I reached for my glass. But it was empty. I tried to remember what I could remember about frescoes. "You're asking me what are frescoes?" I said. "That's a good question. I don't know."

The camera moved to a cathedral outside Lisbon, Portugal. The differences in the Portuguese cathedral compared with the French and Italian were not that great. But they were there. Mostly the interior stuff. Then something occurred to me and I said, "Something has occurred to me. Do you have an idea what a cathedral is? What they look like, that is? Do you follow me? If somebody says *cathedral* to you, do you have any notion what they're talking about? Do you know the difference between that and a Baptist church, say? Or that and a mosque, or synagogue?"

He let the smoke issue from his mouth. "I know they took hundreds of workers fifty or a hundred years to build," he said. "I just heard the man say that, of course. I know generations of the same families worked on a cathedral. I heard him say that, too. The men who began their life's work on them, they never lived to see the completion of their work. In that wise, bub, they're no different from the rest of us, right?" He laughed. Then his eyelids drooped again. His head nodded. He seemed to be snoozing. Maybe he was imagining himself in Portugal. The TV was showing another cathedral now. This one was in Germany. The Englishman's voice droned on. "Cathedrals," the blind man said. He sat up and rolled his head back and forth. "If you want the truth, bub, that's about all I know. What I just said. What I heard him say. But maybe you could describe one to me? I wish you'd do it. I'd like that. If you want to know, I really don't have a good idea."

I stared hard at the shot of the cathedral on the TV. It held a minute. Then it was gone, and the view was of the inside with rows of benches and high windows. How could I even begin to describe it? But say my life depended on it. Say my life was being threatened by an insane Turkish bey.

They took the camera outside again. I stared some more at the cathedral before the picture flipped off into the countryside. There was no use. I turned to the blind man and said, "To begin with, they're very tall. Very, very tall." I was looking around the room for clues. I tried again. "They reach way up. Up and up. Toward the sky. They soar. They're like poetry, that's what they're like. They're so big, some of them, they have to have these supports. To help hold them up, so to speak. These supports are called buttresses. They remind me of viaducts for some reason. But maybe you don't know viaducts, either? Sometimes the cathedrals have devils and such carved into the front. Sometimes great lords and ladies. Don't ask me why this is," I said. He was nodding. The whole upper part of his body seemed to be moving back and forth. "I'm not doing so good, am I?" I said.

He stopped nodding and leaned forward on the edge of the sofa. As he listened to me, he was running his fingers through his beard. I wasn't getting through to him though, I could see that. But he waited for me to go on just the same. He nodded, as if trying to encourage me. I tried to think what else I could say. "They're really big. They're massive. They're built of stone. Marble, too, sometimes. In those old days, when they built cathedrals, men aspired to be close to God. In those days God was an important part of everyone's life. This was reflected in their cathedral building. I'm sorry," I said, "but it looks like that's the best I can do for you. I'm just no good at it."

"That's all right, bub," he said. "Hey, listen. I hope you don't mind my asking you. Can I ask you something? Let me ask you a simple question, yes or no. I'm just curious and there's no offense. You're my host. But let me ask if you are in any way religious? You don't mind my asking?"

I shook my head. He couldn't see that, though. A wink is the same as a nod to a blind man. "I guess I'm agnostic or something. No, the fact is, I don't believe in it. Anything. Sometimes it's hard. You know what I'm saying?"

"Sure, I do," he said.

"Right," I said.

The Englishman was still holding forth. My wife sighed in her sleep. She drew a long breath and continued with her sleep.

"You'll have to forgive me," I said. "But I can't tell you what a cathedral looks like. It just isn't in me to do it. I can't do any more than I've done." The blind man sat very still, his head down, as he listened to me. "The truth is, cathedrals don't mean anything special to me. Nothing. Cathedrals. They're something to look at on late-night TV. That's all they are."

It was then he cleared his throat, He brought something up. He took a handkerchief from his back pocket. In a minute he said, "I get it, bub. It's okay. It happens. Don't worry about it," he said. "Hey, listen to me. Will you do me a favor? I got an idea. Why don't you find us some heavy paper? And a pen. We'll do something. An experiment. Sure, you can do it. You can. We'll draw one together. Get us a pen and some heavy paper. Go on, bub, get the stuff," he said.

So I went upstairs. My legs felt like they didn't have any strength in them. They felt like they did sometimes after I'd run a couple miles. In my wife's room I looked around. I found some ballpoints in a little basket on her table. And then I tried to think where to look for the kind of paper he was talking about.

Downstairs, in the kitchen, I found a shopping bag with onion skins in the bottom of the bag. I emptied the bag and shook it. I brought it into the living room and sat down with it near his legs. I moved some things, smoothed the wrinkles from the bag, spread it out on the coffee table. The blind man got down from the sofa and sat next to me on the carpet.

He ran his fingers over the paper. He went up and down the sides of the paper and the edges, top and bottom. He fingered the corners. "All right," he said. "All right. Let's do her."

He found my hand, the hand with the pen. He closed his hand over my hand. "Go ahead, bub, draw," he said. "Draw. You'll see. I'll follow along with you. It'll be all right. Just begin now, like I'm telling you. You'll see. Draw," he said.

So I began. First I drew a box that resembled a house. It could have been the house I lived in. Then I put a roof on the house. At either end of the roof I drew spires. Crazy.

"Swell," he said. "Terrific. You're doing fine," he said. "Never thought anything like this could happen in your lifetime, did you? Well, it's a strange life, bub, we all know that. Go on now. Keep it up."

I put in windows with arches. I drew flying buttresses. I hung great doors. I couldn't stop. The TV station went off the air. I put down the pen and closed and opened my fingers. The blind man felt around over the paper. He moved the tips of his fingers slowly over the paper, over what I'd drawn, and he nodded. "Doing fine," he said.

I took up the pen, and he found my hand once more. I kept at it. I'm no artist. But I kept drawing just the same.

My wife opened her eyes and gazed at us. She sat up on the sofa, her robe hanging open. She said, "What are you doing? What in the world are you doing?"

I didn't answer her. The blind man said, "We're drawing a cathedral, dear. Me and him are working on something important. Press hard now," he said to me. "That's right. That's good," he said. "Sure. You got it, bub. I can tell. You didn't think you could. But you can, can't you? You're cooking with Crisco now. You'll see. Know what I'm saying? We're going to have us something here in a minute. How's the old arm?" he said. "Put some people in there now. What's a church without people, bub?"

"What's going on?" my wife said. "Robert, what are you doing? What's going on?"

"It's all right," he said to her. "Close your eyes now, bub," he said.

I did that. I closed them just like he said.

"Are they closed?" he said, "Don't fudge."

"They're closed," I said.

"Keep them that way," he said. He said, "Don't stop now." So we kept on with it. His fingers rode my fingers as my hand went over the rough paper. It was like nothing else in my life up to now.

In a minute he said, "I think that's enough. I think you got the idea," he said. "Take a look. What do you think?"

But I had my eyes closed. I thought I'd keep them closed a little longer. I thought it was something I ought not to forget.

"Well?" he said. "Are you looking?"

My eyes were still closed. I was in my house and I knew that. But I didn't feel inside anything.

"It's really something," I said.

Experiencing Art and the Aesthetic

Brian E. Fogarty came of age during the turbulent '60s amid the Cold War, Beat-lemania, and Vietnam. Born to a solidly working-class family, his college education opened a world of ideas and interests that had previously been unknown or unappreciated. Fogarty earned the Ph.D. in Sociology at Purdue University and has taught at Saint Louis University and Briar Cliff College before coming to St. Kate's in 1989. He is author of War, Peace, and the Social Order *(2000).*

Art Matters

Brian E. Fogarty

The study of the arts is not new to any of us. We have taken "art class" since kindergarten, starting with finger painting and flower-pressing activities, and gradually gaining artistic sophistication through our school years. But one thing has remained consistent throughout our academic experience with art: for most of us, it has always been a less serious, non-academic class. Art class is fun; a break from books and tests. It's a chance for self-expression, unfettered by too much thinking or scholarly principles. In fact, one might argue that art is the course taken least seriously by students and school authorities alike. Even physical education classes involve a certain amount of exertion at least, and the importance placed in American society on fitness and competition is surely reflected in the authority of the PE coach. By the time we are in high school, only art retains its playful, non-serious status among our classes.

It's no wonder, then, that by the time we enter college, we might question the importance of art to the serious education we seek. Although our previous experience of the arts has been a break from the more serious routine of learning things, at least that education was free for most of us. We could afford the luxury of dabbling in something we had no real need to learn about, and besides, our younger years were less serious anyway. Today the stakes are higher: as college students we are motivated to learn something useful; we may even have specific career goals in mind—and college is expensive. In the end, it seems worthwhile to ask: why should we commit this kind of money and effort to something that seems recreational? Why *learn* about the arts?

I'd like to make the case that learning about the arts and about aesthetics in general is as important and as worthwhile as the learning you'll do about biology or literature or political science. Nor do I mean that it is important in some unspecified, vague way, perhaps because it will make you a better citizen, or because it will enrich your middle age when the pursuits of youth become less interesting. On the contrary, the study of aesthetics will make you a more skilled, more perceptive student right away, and it will make you a better qualified graduate. Whether you aspire to become a business executive, nurse, physicist, sociologist, or something else, the study of aesthetics will better qualify you for a career, and it will help that career advance more rapidly than it otherwise would. In short, *art matters*, and the study of art matters is an important part of serious higher education.

I don't mean to suggest that thinking a little about aesthetic values in *The Reflective Woman* or taking a course in art history or jewelry design will turn you from an intellectual ugly duckling into a magnificent swan. No single course or body of knowledge does that. I do believe, though, that learning about the arts is at least as useful as learning any other body of knowledge; say, chemistry or history or accounting. Here are some reasons why.

1. Art is another form of communication. We know that college work (and, by the way, the work of most professions as well) involves communicating ideas to people and understanding communications from others, usually through writing or speaking. And many of the ideas we deal with are fairly mundane ones. Ordinary words, in the form of essays, research reports, memos, and letters are usually good enough communications devices in these instances. But what happens when you need to express some subtle and complex idea about love, or faith, or freedom, or oppression? How many pages would it take for your essay to describe a strong feeling or passion about one of these ideas? At some point, you might depart from prose and write a poem, or perhaps words would simply fail altogether.

Yet music, film, painting, dance, even architecture—all the arts are exactly geared to expressing those very ideas and values that words fail to express. We are often "left speechless" by a work of art or music for precisely that reason—the work expresses something for which words are inadequate. After all, if words could be used to describe the ideas conveyed, we wouldn't need the art in the first place.

This is hardly a twentieth-century discovery, by the way. I once heard a lecture by an expert on Chartres cathedral, in which he demonstrated how its stained-glass windows were used to express the metaphorical subtleties of holy scripture. Each main window, it turns out, is actually a pair of windows: one side tells a New Testament story, while the other side shows the Old Testament parallel to it. The "language" of the images is capable of expressing the thematic similarities and contrasts between the two sources far more subtly and more efficiently than words could do—and this was just as well, since almost no one could read in the thirteenth century anyway. What an irony that the lowest serf of the middle ages may have understood the Bible in a more subtle way than we literate moderns do!

Art also has the advantage of speaking "below the surface" of conscious-ness. One doesn't always have to be trying to "read" a piece of art in order for it to communicate to us. For example, the U.S. Capitol building probably expresses both majesty and democracy, even to the casual visi-tor, better than reams of written material or lofty speeches. Try imagining a modern steel-and-glass capitol instead, or a gothic one, or a square one of red brick, and the impact of architecture becomes clear. And speaking of Washington, doesn't the starkness of the Vietnam memorial speak as clearly about the legacy of that war than all the heroic statuary we see commemorating World War II?

The trouble is, art is by nature subtle and it requires some effort to under-stand. Thus, our previous non-serious training in the arts—not only in school but throughout our experience—encourages us to reject a lot of difficult art, because it doesn't give pleasure right away, or sometimes not at all. This has a serious implication for our intellectual and professional development: that to reject "difficult" art in favor of what we like and are comfortable with is to reject a message. It's a little like deciding to read at only a fifth-grade level because all the stories are easy, happy ones. And this, of course, is nothing more than opting for ignorance. Shouldn't the task of higher education be to discourage this?

People are trying to communicate with us; to tell us things we can't understand any other way. They are artists, musicians, dancers, play-writes, poets, architects. And in fact, the more complex and subtle the idea being communicated, the more "difficult" the art is. The ability to participate in this sort of communication may not be very important to those in careers that don't involve subtleties. But people who make deci-sions for a living, who work at non-routine and complex jobs, are at a serious disadvantage if they haven't developed the skill to get something from a poem or painting or dance.

2. Art provides an analytical workout. I was a teenager in the summer of 1964 when the "British invasion" of rock music arrived on American shores. Literally dozens of recordings would be released by these new English groups every week. I remember a promotional contest that my local radio station ran at the time: they would play a new release from one of the new groups, and you would have to guess whether or not it was the Beatles. Sometimes it was, but often it was the Dave Clark Five, or Jerry and the Pacemakers or the Zombies or somebody else. Since nobody had heard the new release before, there was an interesting ana-lytical task involved: you had to develop some concepts for determining whether the new song had the *sound* of the Beatles, or whether it was some other group. What made up the Beatles' sound? Were there certain characteristics of the melodies, or the lyrics, or the arrangements, that made them Beatles songs? I became very good at this by the end of the summer—though I can't put into words what rules or concepts or theories I used to distinguish the Beatles from the others.

A few years later I found myself in a large college lecture hall, trying to do the same thing with Beethoven and Mozart. As a matter of fact, the "game" hadn't changed much: the final exam consisted of listening to short recorded musical passages; we'd have to write down the composer's name for each one. Now, the hard way to approach this was to try to memorize which composer went with which recording. They were all on reserve at the library and we were to spend our evenings there drumming into our brains various tricks for linking them together ("It's a bird, it's a plane, it's a Mozart," sung to the tune of the Mozart piece that would be on the quiz, was one device). The smart students figured out the better tactic: to try to develop some analytic concepts for distinguishing Beethoven's sound from Mozart's—and Stravinsky's, Prokofiev's and Britten's and all the others.

The funny things is, while I had become adept at distinguishing very readily the Stones from the Beatles, I had great difficulty distinguishing the various symphonic composers from one another. And this was remarkable, since I'm sure that Beethoven's music was in its day considered as great a departure from Mozart as Pearl Jam is from Frank Sinatra. But to an eighteen-year-old whose experience had included little of this, it all sounded the same—the way that, say, traditional Japanese music still does to my unschooled ear.

The study of aesthetics thus affords us an opportunity to exercise our analytical powers in ways that are not always tapped by other academic work, and this is probably a worthwhile thing in itself. But still, what reason do we have to believe this exercise to be beneficial in a pragmatic way? Put bluntly, how will it make one a better physical therapist, or lawyer, or insurance underwriter? The answer is that these same analytical skills are the ones that professional people put to use every day. They are the mental faculties by which we make subtle decisions based on scanty information. The care of a patient, the handling of a personnel dispute, the tone of a memo, the design of a lesson plan—they all involve reading the subtle cues of a situation, forming categories and concepts, and applying them to a decision. They are the kind of skills that people might say "can't be taught" but rather are innate or acquired through long experience. People who possess these skills are simply considered "smart" people. But the fact is, they *can* be taught—you can learn them through study of the arts.

3. Art expresses political realities that must be reckoned with. The arts have a curious and ambivalent character regarding politics and morals.

On the one hand, the arts tend to be at the forefront of avant-garde thinking, and seem to endorse and celebrate new lifestyles, challenge traditional values, and elevate the bohemian to the artistic elite. But on the other hand, the arts also express the traditions of a society, not only in what is portrayed but in who portrays it. A walk through your local art museum or a visit to Orchestra Hall will make the point: even in the 1990's, there is a stunning overrepresentation of Europeans and men among the painters, composers, and performers. This is not simply to say that there is a conspiracy of white men at the "top" of the art world, although many will make that point persuasively. Rather, these biases of representation show us something more fundamental about our culture: that the dominance of one race and one gender runs deep in American society. I'd say, in fact, that they show precisely that this dominance is *not* a matter of the conspiracy of a few, but rather a deeply-rooted element of our national character. Frankly, this is much more difficult to swallow than a simplistic conspiracy theory, but it fits better with the facts.

At the same time, we often see in a typical visit to the museum a special exhibit of "Emerging African-American Artists" or "Women of the Arts and Crafts Movement," or "Caribbean Carnival Costume," each giving voice and exposure to a heretofore neglected cultural tradition. And this tells us something, too: that these groups are emerging, gaining force and recognition within the artistic community, finding their way into the public consciousness. Such exhibits were not so common fifty years ago, and it is a measure of social change that we see them in established museums and galleries today.

And it's not only the authorship of the arts that conveys political and social realities. The content of the paintings, photographs, and music also tells us something. How are women represented in 19th-century painting? Are they action figures, suffering saints, sex objects? What does Puccini's opera *Madama Butterfly* say about encounters between the industrialized world and the traditional one? Or about encounters between men and women? Or about Western stereotypes of Asians?

What is considered "acceptable" art in a certain place in a certain time tells us much about the values and ideals of the society that produced it—keeping in mind that art is a production not just of the artist but of the publishers, critics, and viewing or listening public as well. In the 1930's the Nazi regime banned "degenerate" art—that is, modern, Jewish, or politically critical art—allowing only heroic and representational works to be publicly displayed. It's easy for us today to see how wrong that was. But what's our own reaction to gay literature, or anti-American films, or avant-garde music? What does art and our response to it say about us as a people?

All of this aside, we must still address the question of how understanding the political and social realities we learn from art can help us in the "real" world. The answer, of course, is that the real world is full of the very people we've been talking about! Our workplaces are made up of people of different races, genders, sexual identities, political stripes. Even looking at it from a strictly pragmatic standpoint, is it good for our careers to remain ignorant of how things look and sound and feel to our colleagues, clients, patients, students, customers?

4. Art is a window to culture. We are told incessantly that we now live in a global society, and that we shall have to understand the values and beliefs of other cultures in order to be successful in our lives. This may not seem very relevant to us today, because American culture seems so pervasive throughout the world. But this won't last forever. There will come a time when Americans will have to compete in that global marketplace—and not only for resources and markets, but also in terms of language and ideas and values and traditions. What then? We shall have to understand deeply the meanings things have for people of other cultures—what ideals are important, what constitutes beauty, what is considered the best way to live. Our study of aesthetics will help us perceive these diverse points of view, especially if our studies include diverse aesthetic traditions.

But perhaps more important, the arts connect one deeply to one's *own* culture, and that is a fundamental human need. My total immersion in rock music as a teenager was the main way that I *was* a teenager. And we all take on and proclaim our cultural identity all the time through attending concerts, buying records, going to movies, buying clothes, and many other aesthetic activities. My aesthetic choices are a part of who I am— that is, my identification with a community—and it helps both to make me who I am and to communicate it to others. When those medieval serfs looked up at the impossibly soaring and airy space of Chartres cathedral and read the stained-glass windows, they must have felt a profound sense of belonging to something, and of understanding their own identity. These feelings cannot be imparted by words—they require forms of understanding that lie underneath the verbal realm we usually operate in. They require artistic expression and perception.

In the end, the study of aesthetics is the study of the meanings and ideas that make up one's own community, and to understand and appreciate the arts is to understand that community more deeply. I believe one reason many people—and not just students—chafe at understanding the arts is that much of the art we are shown seems to represent a community other than our own. We have already seen that this is true to some extent for people of color, women, and others who are underrepresented or under-appreciated overall in American society. But this hardly argues for a rejection of the study of art, for a retreat to ignorance. In fact, one could argue that this inequity alone justifies a serious effort to learn about the aesthetic dimension of life, simply because it reflects so well the position of various cultural groups in a society.

But curiously, there is a strong tendency even among Euro-Americans to reject learning about their own aesthetic traditions. There is a feeling that the art found in the museums and in the texts is of some other community than one's own, and that it is "shoved down the throats" of students by their professors. I know I experienced it as a younger man; I had to be dragged kicking and screaming to Picasso and Mozart by my professors too. In a sense, they really did represent a community foreign to me; one that I had little interest in and no claim to. But the fact is, so did all the other things I learned in college—the literature, the biology, the math, the philosophy, the political science. They were *all* part of a different world than the one I had inhabited until then: the world of the educated person. To incorporate that knowledge and to study those ideas would be to enter that community—and it would mean changing who I was.

Most of us like ourselves just fine the way we are, and I think the prospect of change in one's identity is a large part of the resistance to learning about the arts. It's more comfortable to hold on to one's own tastes and resist the new because in doing so we can remain our old familiar selves. In fact, this resistance to change tells us all by itself how important the arts are—they help us define and know ourselves. It's difficult to open up to new aesthetic tastes. In fact, we are more willing to explore new ideas about science or politics or ethics or even religion than we are to explore new aesthetic preferences, because they are in some ways more fundamental to our identity.

But do we come to college to stay the way we are? Isn't this supposed to be a period of exploration and growth? I believe that college is meant to be a life-changing experience; that we are supposed to emerge from our education with a somewhat different identity than the one we entered with. Any less wouldn't be worth the expense. Frankly, I am a different person than the one I was when I entered college, and I don't regret it. Nor have I really had to give anything up; for example, I never did lose my taste for rock music of the 60's and 70's. I've simply gained new interests that I didn't have then. In fact, "It's a bird, it's a plane, it's a Mozart" (Symphony No. 40) is a particular favorite.

Maya Lin is best known as the artist whose winning design for the Vietnam Veterans Memorial in Washington, DC, was submitted when she was only a college senior at Yale University. She combines her heritage as a Chinese-American with culturally diverse sources such as works by American earthworks artists of the 1960s and 1970s and Japanese gardens to create her sculptures and other architectural projects. Born in Ohio in 1959, Lin currently lives in New York and Colorado.

On Making

Maya Lin

I begin by imagining an artwork verbally. I try to describe in writing what the project is, what it is trying to do. I need to understand the artwork without giving it a specific materiality or solid form.

I try not to find the form too soon. Instead, I try to think about it as an idea without a shape.

Most of my art and architectural works are commissioned for a specific site by a specific individual or group. And with these commissioned works I have often started with a written description of what I think the work is about or what its purpose should be. When making these works, I spend much time researching the site—not just the physical aspects of the site but the cultural context of it as well: who will use the site, the history of the place, the nature of the people who live there. I spend the first few months researching a multitude of facts, history, and materials, not knowing if anything I am studying will be of use to me in the artwork.

Sometimes, as with the memorials, I see a very specific and clearly defined purpose to the project. With the *Vietnam Veterans Memorial*, I needed to ask myself the question "What is the purpose of a war memorial at the close of the twentieth century?" My question led me to a study of war memorials, from the earliest funereal stelae to the monuments of the great world wars. I felt that the design should focus on the individuals who died and not on the politics surrounding that war. I sought a design that would bring the viewer to an honest acceptance of the deaths of those individuals.

For the *Civil Rights Memorial*, the sponsor, the Southern Poverty Law Center, felt the need for such a memorial but left it to me to define what such a memorial would specifically entail. I had to ask myself what its purpose should be. As I began to learn more about the civil rights movement, I was surprised at how little I knew about the history surrounding the struggle for racial equality. I decided early on that a memorial to civil rights had to evoke the history of that period. Just listing the names of those killed in the movement would not give a visitor a true idea of what that struggle for equality had been about. I felt the goal of the memorial would be to present a brief idea of what that time period had been about (as a teaching tool), so that the struggles and sacrifices would not be forgotten.

For both these memorials, my research and study led me in the general direction I wanted to take before I had visited the sites, and when I did visit the sites, the idea that I brought with me helped me to imagine almost instantly the form each memorial would take. In both instances, I waited until I knew my direction partly because I was afraid that if I saw the site too soon, I might react to it in a more formal way and imagine a design onto which I would then have to force a function.

At other times, as with most of my outdoor artworks, the project takes its purpose or shape from a combination of my research of the site and my aesthetic interests. The *Wave Field*, which is sited at an aerospace engineering building at the University of Michigan, is based on an image I found while researching the mechanics of flight, whereas in *Reading a Garden*, a sculpture for the Cleveland Public Library, I had been waiting for a library as a site so that I could collaborate with a writer to create a garden of words.

For most of the works, I make an initial visit to a site, put it somewhere in the back of my mind, then return to my studio and start researching the project. I never know what I am looking for at this point and I never try to focus too directly or self-consciously on the search for an idea for the artwork. The research, in fact, is more about my curiosity about a new subject, such as flight dynamics or computer technology. Perhaps this is because of my academic background, or perhaps I just miss school. In any case, each project allows me to learn about a new subject.

But I rarely arrive at an idea by consciously sitting down at a desk and trying to figure out what I want to do. Once I start thinking about a project, though, it doesn't really leave my focus until I have come up with an idea.

I cannot force a design; I do not see this process as being under my conscious control. It is a process of percolation, with the form eventually finding its way to the surface.

Sometimes the idea takes initial shape as an essay. *10 Degrees North* began as an essay on balancing and mobiles. *Reading a Garden* began as a collaborative essay between a poet and a sculptor. Or it can start as a sketch with text, as in the very first sketches for the *Women's Table*. But most of the time my artworks begin as models.

I will make a model of a work without trying to draw it or plan how to make the model; they are made instantaneously. Sometimes I just wake up and without really thinking make a model—as with the *Women's Table* or *Eclipsed Time*, this "automatic act" takes place after many months of letting the project sit in my head.

I think with my hands.

These models, which I also refer to as sketches, have a clue or thread that will give me an understanding of what I am trying to do. Yet to most who are used to looking at models as finished miniature representations of actual work, they are sometimes indecipherable. But I am blind without these models.

I never fully realized how atypical this reliance on three-dimensional modeling was to my training as an architect until quite recently—most architects are trained to design in drawings. Yet I have always relied on the making of models to see and create my work; drawings for anything other than plans are harder for me to see or, more importantly, to feel what a space or place is.

I was never drawn to two-dimensional processes but always to three-dimensional arts: sculpture, metalsmithing, anything I could physically work with my hands. Growing up near Ohio University, where my father was a ceramicist and the dean of fine arts, I was able to experiment with most arts and crafts mediums before I left high school.

Watching my father pull a pot from a mound of clay, seeing the immediacy of making a form—without plans, drawings, blueprints—has had a profound impact on my creative process.

I do not think that we can fully understand how one makes a specific mark upon a page—at some point one has to trust one's eye, one's intuition. I do not think that that implies a lack of rational thought. I just think that one cannot understand why one makes a specific move, that the creative act is a combination of conscious and subconscious thoughts that cannot or should not be deciphered.

My creative process balances analytic study, based very much on research, with, in the end, a purely intuited gesture. It is almost as if after months of thinking I shut that part of my brain down and allow the nonverbal side to react. It is this balance between the analytical and the intuitive, or between the left side and the right side of the brain, that is so much a part of these works.

The phrase that some people have used to describe my process is that I lay an "egg." It is a rather strange metaphor, but an accurate one. My idea appears very quickly and is fully formed when it arrives. I do not work and rework the idea. And in looking at the final work, I think it is most successful when it captures the spirit of those first sketches or models.

But no matter how often I have gone through this process, I am never sure when I am going to find the form. Or, more accurately, when the form is going to find me.

The fact that these works are almost always commissioned, rather than made in the studio, requires that I present the design to others at an early stage. In order to get them built, I must go through a fairly public process. I have always relied on writing a description of the artwork or architectural work because I feel writing is the best way to convey what the project will be. It allows me to describe not just the physicality of the works but how one will experience the works. These essays become an integral part of each piece, helping to define for me what each work is. I consider them verbal sketches—like the models or drawings—and they are invaluable to me. I do not see the artwork as something that can be described in image alone, just as I feel the finished work cannot be understood from a single picture. Instead the experience of the work is critical to its understanding, and writing is the clearest form in which to capture what the work is about. I use the essays to clarify and distill the intentions of the work.

The essays for the Rockefeller Foundation's *10 Degrees North* and for *Sounding Stones* are not finished texts but sketches that give me a sense of what I am searching for. Defining the work in words sets the concept that I will follow throughout the development of the idea—the words are my guide.

The development of the design and its realization is a long, drawn-out process. Depending upon the complexity of the work, and how integrated the project is with existing architecture, this process can take years. The difficulty in translating idea into reality varies considerably from artwork to artwork. There are always technical problems to be worked out—getting the water in the *Civil Rights Memorial* to flow upside down or designing the clock mechanism for *Eclipsed Time*—but these problems did not pose a real difficulty for me (though my technical consultants might disagree). The challenge, for me, is not technical but emotional: the attempt to capture the essence of the idea that is so much a part of the original model. The *Wave Field* existed first as a photograph and then as a small model. I tried to stay close to the power of the original photos and models, but as the scale of the models increased, they began to lose the fluidity and poetry of those first images. I found it was impossible to predict or model or visualize its final shape until we actually built it; the piece literally changed, becoming too stiff with every increase in scale. I finally realized that I would not understand it or be able to predict if the form would work until I built it at its actual scale. After months of analyzing the form of a water wave—how it begins and ends—I just had to go out into the field and shape it.

Creating these works is never simply a process of replication. If the end result looks identical to the smaller-scale versions, then something has failed in the development. Architecture that looks like a blown-up version of its scale model has lost something in its translation. Obviously, the process of building architecture does not allow for as much spontaneity in the actual construction—nor would I want it to—but in those works as well, the early conceptual models have a presence that I try not to lose as the design develops.

No matter how many iterations—research, sketches, models—precede it, I am trying to capture that instantaneous act of making in the final piece, much the same way those first models or sketches convey a certain character or feeling. Perhaps it marks the presence of the human hand or the free-form creative act—something we are familiar with in smaller works, such as paintings or small-scaled sculptures, but is difficult to capture in the larger scale—when the method to construct these larger works involves teams of people, blueprints, engineered documents . . .

The last thing that I make about each work is its name. I don't feel the piece is complete until I have named it, yet I cannot even begin to think about its name until I have seen it finished.

There are always clues in the writings I have already made and in the drawings about the works. I need to return to the original text descriptions to find the clues. Each work always gives a descriptive clue to what it is.

Sometimes, as in *Sounding Stones*, the working title becomes the name, but only at the last minute. The piece changed, transformed into a fountain, and I saw it as something else. But then when I experienced the piece, its earlier name fit it; as I heard the echoes of the city noises and the water traveling through the drilled holes, I returned to its earlier name.

Other names . . . *Water Tables, 10 Degrees North, A Shift in the Stream, Phases of the Moon, The Earth is (not) Flat; Longitude, Equator, Latitude, Stones, Avalanche, Craters.* Whether large scale or small, these artworks and their names all speak of place, geography, naturally occurring phenomena, the environment.

I see the name as its final shape. And once it has its name, it's on its own. I have moved on both mentally and emotionally from it.

Gary Witherspoon, Ph.D., is an anthropologist who studies Navajo art, language, religion and culture. He is a Professor in American Indian Studies at the University of Washington in Seattle, WA.

from Navajo Aesthetics

Gary Witherspoon

In the Western world, where mind has been separated from body, where man has been extracted from nature, where affect has been divorced from "fact," where the quest for and focus upon the manipulation and accumulation of things has led man to exploit rather than to respect and admire the earth and her web of life, it is not surprising that art would be divorced from the more practical affairs of business and government and the more serious matters of science, philosophy, and theology. In the Navajo world, however, art is not divorced from everyday life, for the creation of beauty and the incorporation of oneself in beauty represent the highest attainment and ultimate destiny of man. *Hózhó* expresses the Navajo concept of beauty or beautiful conditions. But beauty is not separated from good, from health, from happiness, or from harmony. Beauty—*hózhó*—is the combination of all these conditions. It is not an abstractable quality of things or a fragment of experience; it is the normal pattern of nature and the most desirable form of experience.

For the Navajo, beauty is not so much in the eye of the beholder as it is in the mind of its creator and in the creator's relationship to the created (that is, the transformed or the organized). The Navajo does not look for beauty; he generates it within himself and projects it onto the universe. The Navajo says *shit hózhó* "with me there is beauty," *shii' hózhó* "in me there is beauty," and *shaa hózhó* "from me beauty radiates." Beauty is not "out there" in things to be perceived by the perceptive and appreciative viewer; it is a creation of thought. The Navajo experience beauty primarily through expression and creation, not through perception and preservation. Beauty is not so much a perceptual experience as it is a conceptual one.

In the Western world beauty as a quality of things to be perceived is, in essence, static; that is, it is something to be observed and preserved. To the Navajo, however, beauty is an essential condition of man's life and is dynamic. It is not in things so much as it is in the dynamic relationships among things and between man and things. Man experiences beauty by creating it. For the Anglo observer of Navajo sandpaintings, it has always been a source of some bewilderment and frustration that the Navajo "destroy" these sandpaintings in less time than they take to create them. To avoid this overt destruction of beauty and to preserve its artistic value, the Anglo observer always want to take a photograph of the sandpainting, but the Navajo sees no sense and some danger in that. To the Navajo the artistic or aesthetic value of the sandpainting is found in its creation, not in its preservation. Its ritual value is in its symbolic or representational power and in its use as a vehicle of conception. Once it has served that purpose, it no longer has any ritual value.

Navajos take little interest in the display or preservation of their works of art, with the exception of silver and turquoise jewelry. They readily sell them to non-Indians who are looking for beauty in things. Traditionally, they put their works of art to practical use in their daily activities. Now it is more practical to sell them for money and buy stainless steel pots and other more durable but less artistic things. This practice offends the purist's view of aesthetics, but it is, in fact, not a depreciation of aesthetic value at all. It is simply based on the idea that beauty is a dynamic experience in conception and expression, not a static quality of things to be perceived and preserved.

With regard to the two different views of art contrasted above, it is not surprising that Navajo society is one of artists (art creators) while Anglo society consists primarily of nonartists who view art (art consumers). The Navajo find it incomprehensible that we have more art critics than we have artists, and more art collectors than we have art creators. Nearly all Navajos are artists and spend a large part of their time in artistic creation. All Navajos are singers, and most Navajos have composed many songs. Traditionally, over 90 percent of all adult women wove rugs and today, despite limited opportunities to learn this art, a majority of Navajo women over thirty still weave. A large number of Navajo men are skilled at silver work and sandpainting. Some women still make pottery and beautifully designed baskets. Teachers in Navajo schools find that nearly all Navajo students take a special interest in and have an unusual proficiency in the graphic arts. Navajos are also very eloquent and often poetic in their use of language.

In white society it is the exceptional and abnormal person that becomes an artist. The artist is usually associated with marginality and nonconformity with regard to the mainstream of society. From this marginal position the artist dedicates himself almost solely to his artistic creations. The nonartist among the Navajo is a rarity. Moreover, Navajo artists integrate their artistic endeavors into their other activities. Living is not a way of art for them, but art is a way of living.

Navajo artistic interests and talents are enhanced by, if not derived from, the emphasis on the creative nature of thought and the compulsive power of speech. Art is a nondiscursive form of expression, but it involves many of the same processes of symbolic transformation that are found in discursive symbolism. Professor A. D. Richie has noted that "the essential act of thought is symbolization" . . . , and art is as much symbolization as is speech. Art is a symbolic transformation of experience, and, as such, it invests and imbues experience—thus life—with beauty and aesthetic value and meaning.

Navajo culture is not just a food-gathering strategy; it is an artistic way of life. One is admonished to walk in beauty, speak in beauty, act in beauty, sing in beauty, and live in beauty. All things are to be made beautifully, and all activities are to be completed in beauty. The following daily prayer exemplifies the Navajo emphasis on beauty:

> With beauty before me, I walk
> With beauty behind me, I walk
> With beauty above me, I walk
> With beauty below me, I walk
> From the East beauty has been restored
> From the South beauty has been restored
> From the West beauty has been restored
> From the North beauty has been restored
> From the zenith in the sky beauty has been restored
> From the nadir of the earth beauty has been restored
> From all around me beauty has been restored.

The separation of mind and body—or, in the popular idiom, mind and heart—in Western metaphysics has led aesthetic analysis and interpretation into confusion as to what it is that the artist expresses in his work. Experience is divided into fragments which relate to the intellectual realm, the emotional realm, and the aesthetic realm. A major question, then, is whether a particular art work expresses an "idea," whether it expresses the emotions and feelings of the artist who created it, or whether it expresses nothing in the way of ideas or emotions and simply possesses significant and aesthetic form, a pure expression of beauty.

In the Navajo world, where mind and matter, thought and expression are inseparably connected, the aesthetic experience—the creation of beauty—is simultaneously intellectual, emotional, moral, aesthetic, and biological. Navajo life and culture are based on a unity of experience, and the goal of Navajo life—the creation, maintenance, and restoration of hózhǫ́—expresses that unity of experience. Hózhǫ́ expresses the intellectual concept of order, the emotional state of happiness, the moral notion of good, the biological condition of health and well-being, and the aesthetic dimensions of balance, harmony, and beauty. In Navajo art we find all these concepts, states, and conditions expressed.

As the essence of the Navajo conception of life is movement or motion, and the experience of beauty is dynamic and flowing, characteristic themes found in Navajo art express this emphasis on movement and activity. . . .

A Navajo often counts his wealth in the songs he knows and especially in the songs he has created. A poor Navajo is one who has no songs, for songs enrich one's experiences and beautify one's activities. Songs accompany and enrich both ceremonial and nonceremonial activities. There are riding songs, walking songs, grinding songs, planting songs, growing songs, and harvesting songs. There are songs to greet the sun in the morning and songs to bid it farewell in the evening. There are songs for horses, for sheep, and for various other animal species. There are songs for blessing a hogan and songs for taking a sweat bath. In the past there were even songs for bidding visitors farewell. And, of course, there are songs of love and romance. But the most powerful songs are those that are essential parts of ceremonial and ritual activities. The former type is a means by which Navajos maintain *hózhá* in their daily life experiences, while the latter type constitutes a means by which Navajos restore *hózhá* when it has been disrupted.

Professor David McAllester, who has spent over twenty-five years studying Navajo music, says Navajo music is characterized by its vigor, its power, and its acrobatic style. It is intense, at times almost "excessive," compared to Pueblo music which is low, controlled, and rehearsed. Navajo music seems to match the cultural emphasis on energy, activity, and motion. There is hardly ever a "held" note, except at the end of a song. . . .

In analyzing the First Snake Song, Professor McAllester finds that one of its chief characteristics is repetition. Repetition is a motif found all through Navajo life and culture. It is associated with the concepts of renewal, regeneration, rejuvenation, revolution, and restoration. Repetition enhances the compulsive power of the song. The repetitive nature of many Navajo songs is adorned with and enlivened by various modes of variation. . . .

In the First Snake Song there is a significant alternation in the *kind* of melodic activity. This is found between level sections based entirely or largely on the tonic, and active sections characterized by rapid and pulsing movement. McAllester considers this to be the quality in Navajo "chanting" that makes the term a misnomer. . . .

The verses of the First Snake Song also exhibit the principle of alternation. Here are found alternations in colors, in sex, in directions, and in jewel symbols. This is a way of presenting pairs of related objects. . . .

McAllester notes that although the First Snake Song is strophic and framed, it is progressive in that the pitch gradually rises from one song to the next. He relates this progression in pitch to a progression in textually expressed ideas where the movement is from mature male to immature female, from animate snake to inanimate hoop, from "holding," "dangling," "lugging" to "trundling." . . . As noted earlier . . . maturity is often thought of as a static and thus male-linked condition, whereas immaturity is associated with activity, process, and growth and is female-linked in the Navajo metaphor. Since the animate snake is obviously active and the inanimate hoop is static, the progression here seems to go from static to active and from active to static. This is contrasted by the progression of "holding," "dangling," "lugging," and "trundling," which starts from the static "holding" and gets progressively more active. . . .

Where Navajo music, singing, and poetry are artistic endeavors common to both men and women, the other two major domains of Navajo aesthetics, weaving and sandpainting, are sexually bifurcated. Weaving is primarily an activity of women, and sandpainting is primarily an activity of men. Some Navajo men weave, but this associates them with the category of *nádlééhí*, "transvestite." Such a person, however, is usually held in high esteem and is not normally the object of ridicule or unkind behavior. Reichard notes that Left-Handed Singer or Newcomb was a man who wove. She states that he was highly respected, and a person of superior intelligence combined with extreme gentleness and remarkable independence. As an accomplished singer or "medicine man," he wove primarily sandpainting tapestries. . . . Sandpainting is exclusively a male activity. Even female singers do not do sandpainting, although they may supervise the creation of a sandpainting.

It is relevant to note that the composition and design of Navajo sandpaintings are static; that is, the designs are rigidly established and must be created without significant change or alteration if they are to be an effective part of the particular ritual for which they are used. In contrast, a weaver seldom if ever repeats a design. Each rug woven is designed anew, so designs are always changing., flowing and moving. Thus the production of design in sandpainting and weaving seems to be appropriately associated with the generally static nature of male-linked endeavors and the dynamic nature of female-linked endeavors.

Before mass-produced retail goods became available to the Navajo, they had to produce their own blankets, garments, and moccasins. Although buckskin and other skins provided the raw materials to satisfy many of these needs, wool from sheep provided the major source of material for clothing and blankets. However, instead of just producing clothing and blankets to satisfy the pragmatic needs of warmth and protection from the elements, Navajo women turned the production of clothing and blankets into an artistic endeavor. Today, Navajo women weave rugs primarily for the use of non-Indians. Although they sell these rugs for cash, it has been estimated that the average weaver gets less than a quarter an hour for her work. Obviously, then, the motivation to weave is aesthetic as well as economic—probably even primarily aesthetic. Weaving is an effort in creative transformation. Navajo women transform the wool on the back of sheep into beautifully designed and delicately woven rugs. This is done through the processes of shearing, cleaning, dyeing, carding, spinning, and weaving. Additional color is added through vegetal dyes.

Navajo women develop and create designs in their minds, and then project them onto the world of external reality through the art of weaving. The intricate and often complex patterns created by Navajo weavers are generated in the mind and kept there through the whole process from dyeing through weaving. She must know exactly how much dye to use or exactly what amounts of black and white wool to mix in order to get the very exact color combinations and contrasts she has in her mind. . . .

. . . A woven rug is a product of the mind and the body. The inner form of the rug is in the mind; the outer form of the rug is projected onto the loom. . . .

In the patterns found on Navajo rugs, movement and activity are expressed by diagonal and zigzag lines (also associated with lightning), by the active colors of yellow (brown), blue (green), and red (pink), by appendages to various "static" centers, and by diamond shapes. In contrast, a static condition is expressed by straight lines and horizontal and vertical stripes, by squares and rectangles, and by the static colors of white, black, and grey. Motion goes in one of two directions: linear, continuative, incomplete motion, or circular, repetitious, complete, cyclical motion. In Navajo language the former is found in the important and extensively used imperfective and progressive modes and in the continuative aspect of Navajo verbs, while the latter is found in iterative and usitive modes and in the repetitive aspect of Navajo verbs. In addition linear and continuative motion is expressed by the verbal prefix *hi* which renders the idea of succession, while circular and repetitious actions and movements are expressed by the verbal prefixes *náá* and *ná* which express the ideas of repetition, revolution, and restoration.

In the language of Navajo weaving, linear, continuative, and incomplete motion is expressed by the successive alternation of static and active symbols—colors, lines, and designs. Linear movement thus follows the pattern or series of static-active-static-active. Circular and cyclical movement is expressed by the sequence already noted: static-active-active-static. This pattern is found in the sequence of color, direction, and growth, and in the daily and annual path of the sun. It is sunwise motion. There is also an opposite sequence, usually associated with witchcraft and its cure, but also associated with protection and with an emphasis on activity, that goes from active to static and static to active.

The former type of cyclical movement is mainly found in Navajo ritual where control and normality are emphasized, whereas the latter type of cyclical movement is often found in Navajo weaving and other art forms where creativity and activity are emphasized. . . .

Navajo sandpainting is a male-linked art form that accompanies most major Navajo ceremonials. The designs are established parts of the ritual and must not be significantly altered if the ritual is to be effective. These designs are made on the earthen floor of the hogan. The surface upon which the painting is made is cleaned and smoothed. The designs vary from a few inches to more than twenty feet in diameter, with most paintings averaging from three to six feet in diameter. The painting is done by letting dry pigments trickle through the thumb and flexed index finger. The dry pigments are made primarily from red, yellow, and white sandstone and various mixtures of these colors, but pigments made from colored corn meal, plant pollens, crushed flower petals, and charcoal are also used.

The sandpaintings are made by several men under the direction of the chanter or medicine man. Just as Reichard learned to weave, on many occasions I have enjoyed the opportunity to help create a sandpainting.

The sandpaintings depict the *Diyin Dine'é* and other sacred entities. They recall significant episodes of mythical drama. The mythical dramas revolve around a cultural hero's unfortunate plight and diseased condition, and his or her ultimate cure through identification with, and sometimes compulsive control of, a deity or deities. The disease is caused by some sort of disruption in the proper and normal order of things and is cured by a restoration of the proper order. The patient in his or her plight is identified with the cultural hero who contracted a similar disease or plight in the same way the patient did. In the curing ritual the patient follows in the footsteps of the hero of the myth, sings the songs he or she sang, prays the prayers he or she prayed, and ultimately acquires and exerts the power to restore health and order to his or her self and world that the hero acquired and exerted.

The myth, retold in the songs and prayers of the ritual, places the patient's illness in a cultural context where it can be understood and eventually cured. From the myth the patient learns that his or her plight and illness is not new, and that both its cause and treatment are known. To be cured, all the patient has to do is to repeat what has been done before. It has to be done sincerely, however, and this sincerity is expressed in concentration and dedication. The sandpainting depicts the desired order of things, and places the patient in this beautiful and ordered world. The patient thus becomes completely identified with the powerful and curing agents of the universe. The patient undresses to the extent modesty permits (men to a G-string and women to a skirt) and sits on the painting. Where appropriate and possible the patient's body parts—feet, knees, legs, etc.—are placed on the corresponding body parts of the deity with whom the patient is identified. In addition, the medicine man applies sand from the body parts of the depicted deity to corresponding body parts of the patient's body. Spectators and family members may also apply the sand to corresponding parts of their bodies as well. This is done for sanctification, blessing, and protection.

After the sandpainting has fulfilled its aesthetic and ritual purpose, the sand is carefully collected and deposited at some out-of-the-way place to the north. The symbolic representation of various sacred beings and things is considered to be effective in attracting them to the ceremonial hogan and thus enabling the patient to absorb their curative power.

Notwithstanding the important ritual functions of the sandpaintings, they also have great aesthetic appeal to Navajos. The painters take a special interest and pride in the quality of their work, and many men travel from ceremony to ceremony mainly to participate in the art forms—singing, poetry, drama, and painting—of the ritual. The ceremonies are really a symphony of the arts and they have great aesthetic appeal to Navajo participants and spectators. Where else can one go to and participate in a symphony of the arts while simultaneously being physically, morally, and intellectually sanctified and blessed?

The aesthetic appeal of the forms and designs of sandpaintings is also demonstrated in their extensive use in other Navajo art forms. This is particularly true in weaving where many designs and forms are taken from sandpaintings. These designs, however, also appear in Navajo silver work and in the oil paintings and drawings of contemporary Navajo artists. Such replications of these sacred designs and forms are potentially dangerous to their creators, and many purists among the Navajos deplore this secularization and profanation of sacred forms and symbols. Nevertheless, the aesthetic appeal of these designs and forms seems to have, in many cases, overridden the fear of the dangers inherent in the secular use of sacred forms. As elsewhere in Navajo culture, movement, repetition, balance and harmony, and controlled or restrained emotion and force are dominant themes in Navajo sandpaintings. . . .

Navajo art thus expresses Navajo experiences, and Navajo experiences are mediated by the concepts of and orientations to the world found in Navajo language and culture. All experiences are directed toward the ideals of *hózhǫ́*, and *hózhǫ́* is the intellectual, moral, biological, emotional, and aesthetic experience of beauty. A Navajo experiences beauty most poignantly in creating it and in expressing it, not in observing it or preserving it. The experience of beauty is dynamic; it flows to one and from one; it is found not in things, but in relationships among things. Beauty is not to be preserved but to be continually renewed in oneself and expressed in one's daily life and activities. To contribute to and be a part of this universal *hózhǫ́* is both man's special blessing and his ultimate destiny.

Currently a professor at San Francisco State University, Tim Drescher is also a mural artist and author. His book documenting murals of the Bay Area, San Francisco Murals: Community Creates Its Muse, 1914–1994, *was published in 1994 and has since been updated as* San Francisco Bay Area Murals: Communities Create Their Muses, 1904–1997.

Graffiti Language

An Interview with Jim Prigoff

Tim Drescher

All spray-can practitioners are known as "writers," regardless of whether they are putting up words or images or some combination of the two. This terminology obviously refers to the origins of the form, but it does not suggest recent extension far beyond mere words. Let's look at the categories and then at some of the issues spray-can/graffiti writing/art raises.

Henry Chalfant and Martha Cooper note the several types of graffiti in their important book, *Subway Art* (New York: Holt, Rinehart and Winston, 1984). The most common (and hated) examples are tags, which are initials or names or *noms d'aerosol* quickly written on any surface. They are ubiquitous throughout the inner cities of the United States and have spread throughout the world as well. They are written with any implement: magic markers, pencils, pens, paints, scratched into glass, plastic or wood surfaces. The motivation here is to "get up" as often as you can so that you gain prestige by having your mark (*placa* in Spanish) seen by as many people as possible. Tags are what most people have in mind when they refer to graffiti, but there are other types.

When letters are blown up and put up in outline form and then filled in with a different color; they are known as "throwups." These, too, are executed very quickly, but they have some suggestion of style to them.

With other types of graffiti, a debate begins. Jim Prigoff, co-author of *Spraycan Art* with Henry Chalfant (London and New York: Thames and Hudson, 1987), argues that all graffiti except for tags and throwups should be understood as **spray-can art** "to separate it from the street tags and graffiti." **Old school**, for example, originated in New York and refers to the block lettering and earlier types of writing done roughly before the 1980s. **New wave** refers to more current forms. **Wild style** denotes letters that are stylized to the point of being indecipherable—except by those in the know (and sometimes only to the writer). The issue is whether at this or any stage graffiti transforms into art, about which more in a moment.

The pinnacle of graffiti is the **piece**, short for masterpiece, which is a representational painting, a graffiti mural if you will, which often incorporates text along with the images.

Prigoff's categories are widely inclusive. Wild style, he says, "is a camouflage in essence, but it is simply a style of writing letters. When one writes with colors and better calligraphy, I include that in the whole category of pieces. Pieces can be just letters, they can be abstract, they can be letters with characters, they can be realist [sic] paintings of people done with spray cans."

Definition is a central issue here, Prigoff continues, because although graffiti has been around for a long time, "this is a new art form." He sees the word "graffiti" being used "to denigrate the art work of youth." To escape this prevalent association, Chalfant and Prigoff selected "Spraycan Art" as the title of their book. Prigoff continues, noting that "society has generally equated graffiti with gangs, violence and a youth culture gone mad. Plus, there was an almost total unwillingness to see the art work that had emerged from the scrawls. In some ways I saw myself giving dignity to their art work through the medium of the slides I was taking and through the exposure of these images in slide shows and lectures that I did."

While some attack these works, others study them with motives far beyond casual curiosity. *Spraycan Art* has sold more than 100,000 copies and continues to sell, Prigoff notes. "Advertising people, graphic designers, anthropologists, sociologists, to name just a few groups, have all been interested in this new form of communication." Of course, how one defines the work has a lot to do with whether one views it as a "new form of communication" or as property defacement. It is, of course, both.

Calling it either "graffiti" or "spraycan art" does not alter the fact of its presence virtually everywhere in our cities. Is this a political act? What are the politics of graffiti? Prigoff sees the politics embodied in the act more than in the contents. "Graffiti images are political because they use public space without permission, not always because there is a specific content to them. Spray painting is political just by the very nature of what it is. However, 90-odd percent of the youth who do it would deny that they have any concept of politics or social statement."

At the same time, he acknowledges that the form includes many macho and sexist images. Although there are a few especially powerful writers with a social/political conscience, the politics of the content derives primarily from the immediate experiences of the youths, from popular images (and attitudes) and from hip-hop culture.

For the most part, spray-can work is highly individual, a fact often suggested by the competitive nature of writing, in "crossing out" (writing your piece over someone else's) and in the pervasive tags. Even if you try to place the act in a (bogus) historical context by noting that "European fine artists traditionally signed their canvases, and now the signature has become the art form itself," the individualistic, even egotistical, nature of the practice is inescapable.

But this, too, is political, when seen as a response to a society increasingly "privatized," from which most youth are excluded. Prigoff notes "they are left out and therefore in many ways they are resentful of not having a share of the pie, and so private property for them represents, sometimes, the enemy. And, in a way, by utilizing the walls and the buildings and everything else, they are in some ways recapturing the property, or let's say they are aesthetically altering it, changing it, and making it more public."

Editor's note: All quotations are from an interview with Jim Prigoff in December, 1994. Prigoff, a retired business executive, is co-author of Spraycan Art *(1987) and one of the foremost documenters of murals and graffiti in its varied forms.*

Lorraine Ali and Devin Gordon are staff writers for Newsweek Magazine.

We Still Want Our MTV

Twenty Years On, the Music
Station Rocks Round the Clock

Lorraine Ali and Devin Gordon

A cacophony of teenage "wooohhhs!" fills the studio as MTV's most popular show, "Total Request Live" ("TRL"), begins rolling. Show host Carson Daly jumps to the task of entertaining like a boxer responds to the bell, while a producer eyes the studio audience for the next kid who will enthuse about his or her favorite track du jour. As each video plays back on the show, boxes called "mortises" periodically appear at the bottom of the screen and, inside, a screaming fan tells America why she loves the artist currently airing. It goes something like this: my name is Kendra, and I requested 'I Wanna Be Bad' by Willa Ford 'cause she's totally hot. Woooohh!!! During the next commercial break, the producer auditions a petite girl who looks younger than the show's required on-air age of 18. She starts off strong, but muffs the climactic howl. "OK, thanks," the producer says coolly, and moves on. After all, it's MTV's 20th anniversary year, and only the loudest wooohh will do.

On Aug. 1, MTV will kiss its teen years goodbye with a slew of promotional specials that track the station's rise from an obscure upstart to its current dominant role in music and popular culture. There is certainly plenty of ground to cover. MTV not only changed the way we listen to music, but the station turbocharged the careers of icons such as Madonna and Michael Jackson, inspired fashion trends (remember the Hammer flattop?) and even influenced the way movies and TV programs are made (its "Real World" series was a reality-TV pioneer). From the chortling idiocy of Beavis and Butt-head to the appeal of MTV's ever-morphing logo and eye-popping graphics, the Viacom-owned station's presence is now ubiquitous.

Its business track record is just as impressive. Last year revenues for MTV Networks, a business that now includes MTV2, VHl, Nickelodeon/Nick at Nite, TV Land, TNN and CMT, were $3.04 billion, almost triple the revenues in 1995. In the all-important ratings race, MTV is now the No. 1 cable network for the influential 12- to 24-year-old demographic, largely due to the success of the prime-time show "TRL." MTV is viewed in 342 million households worldwide, quite a leap from 1 million viewers in 1981.

But not everyone is feeling the love for MTV. Critics say the secret to its success is the result of a Faustian bargain, where the station sacrificed its initial credibility to cater to teens' most immediate and banal tastes. MTV's main-attraction artists are now bubblegum poppers like Britney Spears and 'N Sync, while its most popular shows consist of teens voting (and woohing) for their favorite videos, singing karaoke-style over hits and being made over into their favorite pop stars. Its prime-time hours (from 3:30 p.m. until dinner time) are filled with this fare, not to mention nonstop T&A in videos and beach-house specials, while more edgy artists are relegated to off-peak viewing hours or the smaller satellite station, MTV2. "It would be nice if MTV's music programming was as risk-taking as the people who run it," says former news anchor Tabitha Soren, who was at the station from 1991 to 1998. "It would be nice if their programming was more diverse. MTV now has enough power and has shown how irreverent and how creative it can be, so they should distinguish their programming from radio programming."

Even MTV's most famous in-house personality, master of ceremonies and latter-day Dick Clark, Daly, concedes that to stay on top of the heap, you must put your love for music aside and think about the all-mighty numbers. "Once you make music your business, there's no room for a polarized philosophy," says Daly. "I don't have time to be opinionated. I have a show to host and produce. It's like I'm a bartender: someone wants a Zima, and I might think it's kind of an iffy drink, but you know what? I'm gonna give it to him in a cold glass and hope he gives me a nice tip."

The very mind-set that frustrates hardcore music fans has made MTV one of the few music stations to stay consistently on top of fickle, teenage tastes. Since its inception in 1981, MTV's been able to jump from trend to trend— be it early-'80s new wave, late-'80s hair metal or early-'90s grunge and gangsta rap—and reinvent itself for each era. "Music television is a term that has to be redefined for each generation," says president of programming Brian Graden, who was instrumental in the station's recent shift toward teen pop. "You have to find new ways to package it, celebrate it, reinvent it, or somebody else would create tomorrow's music television."

MTV's last big moment of reinvention came with the advent of the Backstreet Boys. It was 1996, and the station was in a ratings slump because grunge had finally hit the skids, and hip-hop had yet to take over as a dominant ratings force. "I remember going to a meeting that year where they told us we were going after cutting-edge, freethinking, revolutionary minds," says Soren, who helped build MTV's credibility in the early '90s by producing smart, in-depth documentaries and covering the 1992 presidential elections. "But six months later we were told, 'Forget all that. Thirteen-year-olds are buying records. Britney Spears is gonna be the hottest thing since sliced bread. That's gonna be our base.' It was just this total flip." It's a turn of events that even the 19-year-old singer still finds hard to believe. "Oh, my goodness," says Spears. "I owe a lot of my success to MTV. I was really a nobody and they were playing my video like I was the most popular thing in the world. It was really, really sweet."

So sweet, in fact, that kids gobbled it up like candy. And movie and consumer-products marketers, desperate to tap the largest U.S. teen population on record (there are 31.6 million 12- to 19-year- olds in the United States, 65 percent of whom have TV sets in their own rooms), were willing to pay from $10,000 to $20,000 for a 30-second advertising slot. "If you're targeting young people, MTV has to be part of your strategy," says an ad buyer with one of MTV's top clients. "They know it too, and that tends to make them difficult to deal with. They have a very take-it-or-leave-it attitude."

Smaller advertisers and labels often complain that there is nowhere else to go since MTV purchased the Box three years ago and made it part of MTV2. "It's a monopoly, like Ticketmaster," says Jim DeRogatis, a former Rolling Stone editor and music critic for the Chicago Sun-Times. "If you want to rock on television, you can only go to MTV. You wanna buy a ticket to Madison Square Garden, you gotta go to Ticketmaster. It's the antithesis of everything that is rock and roll." But Kurt Loder, the station's news anchor for 13 years, does not see his mother ship as such an insidious entity. "MTV serves the purpose that 'American Bandstand' did," says Loder. "It reflects whatever's going on in pop culture at the moment. And if you like the moment, you're gonna like MTV. And if you don't, well, this too shall pass." Still, many industry insiders feel the rolling-with-the-tides philosophy is a cop-out for a station that was once daring enough to break revolutionary artists like Public Enemy and Nirvana. They say it's a bittersweet irony that many of the people behind what they view as today's most goofy programming are, at heart, risk-takers and highly creative thinkers. "Everybody there is really cool," says a source at one of the most successful independent labels in the business. "So you think that all the lame decisions must be happening above them. But you go up and up and up [in the company's leadership] and everyone's still really cool. So who is it? Who's gonna get mad at [president of the MTV Group] Judy McGrath if she tosses in a Badly Drawn Boy video after midnight?"

To its credit, the station does offer up some edgier side ventures. MTV2, the behemoth's baby-sister station, is a bone tossed to disgruntled music lovers. It offers 24-hour video programming of artists like Mos Def and Bjork and is what McGrath refers to as a "woo-free zone." The network also points with pride to its Internet sites, MTV.com and MTV2.com, where fans can listen to music by a wide array of artists. In the end, this is all part of an attempt to widen the network's appeal, and a pre-emptive strike of sorts: MTV knows better than anyone that current pop trends will change, and with these alterna-outlets, it can still maintain that it has one foot outside the world of mainstream pop. "It's good to keep all your windows and doors open," says McGrath.

The winds are already shifting. Record sales are down from last year, and the strong economy that's been driving the teen-music boom is sagging. "As soon as the public gets tired of this stuff, MTV will move on to something else," says Loder. "There is no loyalty in television." For people like DeRogatis, it's already too late. "The 'TRL' audience has been in a cocoon of creature comforts. But the economy is rapidly going in the toilet and the culture's taking a turn to the right. It's gonna be a bucket of ice water in the face, and to those kids, Eminem and Britney are not gonna be enough. I think they're gonna be biting the hand that's been feeding them all this crap." But for now, the kids are still hungry for the taste of sugar, and MTV is happily serving.

Novelist, poet, and children's fiction author, Alice Walker (b. 1944) received her B.A. from Sarah Lawrence College. She has earned critical and popular acclaim for her portrayals of African-American women and received the Pulitzer Prize for The Color Purple in 1983. Ms. Walker currently lives in San Francisco.

In Search of Our Mothers' Gardens

Alice Walker

I described her own nature and temperament. Told how they needed a larger life for their expression. . . . I pointed out that in lieu of proper channels, her emotions had overflowed into paths that dissipated them. I talked, beautifully I thought, about an art that would be born, an art that would open the way for women the likes of her. I asked her to hope, and build up an inner life against the coming of that day. . . . I sang, with a strange quiver in my voice, a promise song.

—Jean Toomer, "Avey,"
Cane

The poet speaking to a prostitute who falls asleep while he's talking—

When the poet Jean Toomer walked through the South in the early twenties, he discovered a curious thing: black women whose spirituality was so intense, so deep, so *unconscious*, that they were themselves unaware of the richness they held. They stumbled blindly through their lives: creatures so abused and mutilated in body, so dimmed and confused by pain, that they considered themselves unworthy even of hope. In the selfless abstractions their bodies became to the men who used them, they became more than "sexual objects," more even than mere women: they became "Saints." Instead of being perceived as whole persons, their bodies became shrines: what was thought to be their minds became temples suitable for worship. These crazy Saints stared out at the world, wildly, like lunatics—or quietly, like suicides; and the "God" that was in their gaze was as mute as a great stone.

Who were these Saints? These crazy, loony, pitiful women?

Some of them, without a doubt, were our mothers and grandmothers.

In the still heat of the post-Reconstruction South, this is how they seemed to Jean Toomer: exquisite butterflies trapped in an evil honey, toiling away their lives in an era, a century, that did not acknowledge them, except as "the *mule* of the world." They dreamed dreams that no one knew—not even themselves, in any coherent fashion—and saw visions no one could understand. They wandered or sat about the countryside crooning lullabies to ghosts, and drawing the mother of Christ in charcoal on courthouse walls.

They forced their minds to desert their bodies and their striving spirits sought to rise, like frail whirlwinds from the hard red clay. And when those frail whirlwinds fell, in scattered particles, upon the ground, no one mourned. Instead, men lit candles to celebrate the emptiness that remained, as people do who enter a beautiful but vacant space to resurrect a God.

Our mothers and grandmothers, some of them: moving to music not yet written. And they waited.

They waited for a day when the unknown thing that was in them would be made known; but guessed, somehow in their darkness, that on the day of their revelation they would be long dead. Therefore to Toomer they walked, and even ran, in slow motion. For they were going nowhere immediate, and the future was not yet within their grasp. And men took our mothers and grandmothers, "but got no pleasure from it." So complex was their passion and their calm.

To Toomer, they lay vacant and fallow as autumn fields, with harvest time never in sight: and he saw them enter loveless marriages, without joy; and become prostitutes, without resistance; and become mothers of children, without fulfillment.

For these grandmothers and mothers of ours were not Saints, but Artists; driven to a numb and bleeding madness by the springs of creativity in them for which there was no release. They were Creators, who lived lives of spiritual waste, because they were so rich in spirituality—which is the basis of Art—that the strain of enduring their unused and unwanted talent drove them insane. Throwing away this spirituality was their pathetic attempt to lighten the soul to a weight their work-worn, sexually abused bodies could bear.

What did it mean for a black woman to be an artist in our grandmothers' time? In our great-grandmothers' day? It is a question with an answer cruel enough to stop the blood.

Did you have a genius of a great-great-grandmother who died under some ignorant and depraved white overseer's lash? Or was she required to bake biscuits for a lazy backwater tramp, when she cried out in her soul to paint watercolors of sunsets, or the rain falling on the green and peaceful pasturelands? Or was her body broken and forced to bear children (who were more often than not sold away from her)—eight, ten, fifteen, twenty children—when her one joy was the thought of modeling heroic figures of rebellion, in stone or clay?

How was the creativity of the black woman kept alive, year after year and century after century, when for most of the years black people have been in America, it was a punishable crime for a black person to read or write? And the freedom to paint, to sculpt, to expand the mind with action did not exist. Consider, if you can bear to imagine it, what might have been the result if singing, too, had been forbidden by law. Listen to the voices of Bessie Smith, Billie Holiday, Nina Simone, Roberta Flack, and Aretha Franklin, among others, and imagine those voices muzzled for life. Then you may begin to comprehend the lives of our "crazy," "Sainted" mothers and grandmothers. The agony of the lives of women who might have been Poets, Novelists, Essayists, and Short-Story Writers (over a period of centuries), who died with their real gifts stifled within them.

And, if this were the end of the story, we would have cause to cry out in my paraphrase of Okot p'Bitek's great poem:

> O, my clanswomen
> Let us all cry together!
> Come,
> Let us mourn the death of our mother,
> The death of a Queen
> The ash that was produced
> By a great fire!
> O, this homestead is utterly dead
> Close the gates
> With *lacari* thorns,
> For our mother
> The creator of the Stool is lost!
> And all the young women
> Have perished in the wilderness!

But this is not the end of the story, for all the young women—our mothers and grandmothers, ourselves—have not perished in the wilderness. And if we ask ourselves why, and search for and find the answer, we will know beyond all efforts to erase it from our minds, just exactly who, and of what, we black American women are.

One example, perhaps the most pathetic, most misunderstood one, can provide a backdrop for our mothers' work: Phillis Wheatley, a slave in the 1700s.

Virginia Woolf, in her book *A Room of One's Own*, wrote that in order for a woman to write fiction she must have two things, certainly: a room of her own (with key and lock) and enough money to support herself.

What then are we to make of Phillis Wheatley, a slave, who owned not even herself? This sickly, frail black girl who required a servant of her own at times—her health was so precarious—and who, had she been white, would have been easily considered the intellectual superior of all the women and most of the men in the society of her day.

Virginia Woolf wrote further, speaking of course not of our Phillis, that "any woman born with a great gift in the sixteenth century [insert "eighteenth century," insert "black woman," insert "born or made a slave"] would certainly have gone crazed, shot herself, or ended her days in some lonely cottage outside the village, half witch, half wizard [insert "Saint"], feared and mocked at. For it needs little skill and psychology to be sure that a highly gifted girl who had tried to use her gift for poetry would have been so thwarted and hindered by contrary instincts [add "chains, guns, the lash, the ownership of one's body by someone else, submission to an alien religion"], that she must have lost her health and sanity to a certainty."

The key words, as they relate to Phillis, are "contrary instincts." For when we read the poetry of Phillis Wheatley—as when we read the novels of Nella Larsen or the oddly false-sounding autobiography of that freest of all black women writers, Zora Hurston—evidence of "contrary instincts" is everywhere. Her loyalties were completely divided, as was, without question, her mind.

But how could this be otherwise? Captured at seven, a slave of wealthy, doting whites who instilled in her the "savagery" of the Africa they "rescued" her from . . . one wonders if she was even able to remember her homeland as she had known it, or as it really was.

Yet, because she did try to use her gift for poetry in a world that made her a slave, she was "so thwarted and hindered by . . . contrary instincts, that she . . . lost her health. . . ." In the last years of her brief life, burdened not only with the need to express her gift but also with a penniless, friendless "freedom" and several small children for whom she was forced to do strenuous work to feed, she lost her health, certainly. Suffering from malnutrition and neglect and who knows what mental agonies, Phillis Wheatley died.

So torn by "contrary instincts" was black, kidnapped, enslaved Phillis that her description of "the Goddess"—as she poetically called the Liberty she did not have—is ironically, cruelly humorous. And, in fact, has held Phillis up to ridicule for more than a century. It is usually read prior to hanging Phillis's memory as that of a fool. She wrote:

> The Goddess comes, she moves divinely fair,
> Olive and laurel binds her *golden* hair.
> Wherever shines this native of the skies,
> Unnumber'd charms and recent graces rise. [My italics]

It is obvious that Phillis, the slave, combed the "Goddess's" hair every morning; prior, perhaps, to bringing in the milk, or fixing her mistress's lunch. She took her imagery from the one thing she saw elevated above all others.

With the benefit of hindsight we ask, "How could she?"

But at last, Phillis, we understand. No more snickering when your stiff, struggling, ambivalent lines are forced on us. We know now that you were not an idiot or a traitor; only a sickly little black girl, snatched from your home and country and made a slave; a woman who still struggled to sing the song that was your gift, although in a land of barbarians who praised you for your bewildered tongue. It is not so much what you sang, as that you kept alive, in so many of our ancestors, *the notion of song*.

B lack women are called, in the folklore that so aptly identifies one's status in society, "the *mule* of the world," because we have been handed the burdens that everyone else—*everyone else*—refused to carry. We have also been called "Matriarchs," "Superwomen," and "Mean and Evil Bitches." Not to mention "Castraters" and "Sapphire's Mama." When we have pleaded for understanding, our character has been distorted; when we have asked for simple caring, we have been handed empty inspirational appellations, then stuck in the farthest corner. When we have asked for love, we have been given children. In short, even our plainer gifts, our labors of fidelity and love, have been knocked down our throats. To be an artist and a black woman, even today, lowers our status in many respects, rather than raises it: and yet, artists we will be.

Therefore we must fearlessly pull out of ourselves and look at and identify with our lives the living creativity some of our great-grandmothers were not allowed to know. I stress *some* of them because it is well known that the majority of our great-grandmothers knew, even without "knowing" it, the reality of their spirituality, even if they didn't recognize it beyond what happened in the singing at church—and they never had any intention of giving it up.

H ow they did it—those millions of black women who were not Phillis Wheatley, or Lucy Terry or Frances Harper or Zora Hurston or Nella Larsen or Bessie Smith; or Elizabeth Catlett, or Katherine Dunham, either—brings me to the title of this essay, "In Search of Our Mothers' Gardens," which is a personal account that is yet shared, in its theme and its meaning, by all of us. I found, while thinking about the far-reaching world of the creative black woman, that often the truest answer to a question that really matters can be found very close.

In the late 1920s my mother ran away from home to marry my father. Marriage, if not running away, was expected of seventeen-year-old girls. By the time she was twenty, she had two children and was pregnant with a third. Five children later, I was born. And this is how I came to know my mother: she seemed a large, soft, loving-eyed woman who was rarely impatient in our home. Her quick, violent temper was on view only a few times a year, when she battled with the white landlord who had the misfortune to suggest to her that her children did not need to go to school.

She made all the clothes we wore, even my brothers' overalls. She made all the towels and sheets we used. She spent the summers canning vegetables and fruits. She spent the winter evenings making quilts enough to cover all our beds.

During the "working" day, she labored beside—not behind—my father in the fields. Her day began before sunup, and did not end until late at night. There was never a moment for her to sit down, undisturbed, to unravel her own private thoughts; never a time free from interruption—by work or the noisy inquiries of her many children. And yet, it is to my mother—and all our mothers who were not famous—that I went in search of the secret of what has fed that muzzled and often mutilated, but vibrant, creative spirit that the black woman has inherited, and that pops out in wild and unlikely places to this day.

But when, you will ask, did my overworked mother have time to know or care about feeding the creative spirit?

The answer is so simple that many of us have spent years discovering it. We have constantly looked high, when we should have looked high—and low.

For example: in the Smithsonian Institution in Washington, D.C., there hangs a quilt unlike any other in the world. In fanciful, inspired, and yet simple and identifiable figures, it portrays the story of the Crucifixion. It is considered rare, beyond price. Though it follows no known pattern of quilt-making, and though it is made of bits and pieces of worthless rags, it is obviously the work of a person of powerful imagination and deep spiritual feeling. Below this quilt I saw a note that says it was made by "an anonymous Black woman in Alabama, a hundred years ago."

If we could locate this "anonymous" black woman from Alabama, she would turn out to be one of our grandmothers—an artist who left her mark in the only materials she could afford, and in the only medium her position in society allowed her to use.

As Virginia Woolf wrote further, in *A Room of One's Own:*

> Yet genius of a sort must have existed among women as it must have existed among the working class. [Change this to "slaves" and "the wives and daughters of sharecroppers."] Now and again an Emily Brontë or a Robert Burns [change this to "a Zora Hurston or a Richard Wright"] blazes out and proves its presence. But certainly it never got itself on to paper. When, however, one reads of a witch being ducked, of a woman possessed by devils [or "Sainthood"], of a wise woman selling herbs [our root workers], or even a very remarkable man who had a mother, then I think we are on the track of a lost novelist, a suppressed poet, of some mute and inglorious Jane Austen. . . . Indeed, I would venture to guess that Anon, who wrote so many poems without signing them, was often a woman. . . .

And so our mothers and grandmothers have, more often than not anonymously, handed on the creative spark, the seed of the flower they themselves never hoped to see: or like a sealed letter they could not plainly read.

And so it is, certainly, with my own mother. Unlike "Ma" Rainey's songs, which retained their creator's name even while blasting forth from Bessie Smith's mouth, no song or poem will bear my mother's name. Yet so many of the stories that I write, that we all write, are my mother's stories. Only recently did I fully realize this: that through years of listening to my mother's stories of her life, I have absorbed not only the stories themselves, but something of the manner in which she spoke, something of the urgency that involves the knowledge that her stories—like her life—must be recorded. It is probably for this reason that so much of what I have written is about characters whose counterparts in real life are so much older than I am.

But the telling of these stories, which came from my mother's lips as naturally as breathing, was not the only way my mother showed herself as an artist. For stories, too, were subject to being distracted, to dying without conclusion. Dinners must be started, and cotton must be gathered before the big rains. The artist that was and is my mother showed itself to me only after many years. This is what I finally noticed:

Like Mem, a character in *The Third Life of Grange Copeland*, my mother adorned with flowers whatever shabby house we were forced to live in. And not just your typical straggly country stand of zinnias, either. She planted ambitious gardens—and still does—with over fifty different varieties of plants that bloom profusely from early March until late November. Before she left home for the fields, she watered her flowers, chopped up the grass, and laid out new beds. When she returned from the fields she might divide clumps of bulbs, dig a cold pit, uproot and replant roses, or prune branches from her taller bushes or trees—until night came and it was too dark to see.

Whatever she planted grew as if by magic, and her fame as a grower of flowers spread over three counties. Because of her creativity with her flowers, even my memories of poverty are seen through a screen of blooms—sunflowers, petunias, roses, dahlias, forsythia, spirea, delphiniums, verbena . . . and on and on.

And I remember people coming to my mother's yard to be given cuttings from her flowers; I hear again the praise showered on her because whatever rocky soil she landed on, she turned into a garden. A garden so brilliant with colors, so original in its design, so magnificent with life and creativity, that to this day people drive by our house in Georgia—perfect strangers and imperfect strangers—and ask to stand or walk among my mother's art.

I notice that it is only when my mother is working in her flowers that she is radiant, almost to the point of being invisible—except as Creator: hand and eye. She is involved in work her soul must have. Ordering the universe in the image of her personal conception of Beauty.

Her face, as she prepares the Art that is her gift, is a legacy of respect she leaves to me, for all that illuminates and cherishes life. She has handed down respect for the possibilities—and the will to grasp them.

For her, so hindered and intruded upon in so many ways, being an artist has still been a daily part of her life. This ability to hold on, even in very simple ways, is work black women have done for a very long time.

This poem is not enough, but it is something, for the woman who literally covered the holes in our walls with sunflowers:

> They were women then
> My mama's generation
> Husky of voice—Stout of
> Step
> With fists as well as
> Hands
> How they battered down
> Doors
> And ironed
> Starched white
> Shirts
> How they led
> Armies
> Headragged Generals
> Across mined

Fields
Booby-trapped
Kitchens
To discover books
Desks
A place for us
How they knew what we
Must know
Without knowing a page
Of it
Themselves.

Guided by my heritage of a love of beauty and a respect for strength—in search of my mother's garden, I found my own.

And perhaps in Africa over two hundred years ago, there was just such a mother; perhaps she painted vivid and daring decorations in oranges and yellows and greens on the walls of her hut; perhaps she sang—in a voice like Roberta Flack's—*sweetly* over the compounds of her village; perhaps she wove the most stunning mats or told the most ingenious stories of all the village storytellers. Perhaps she was herself a poet—though only her daughter's name is signed to the poems that we know.

Perhaps Phillis Wheatley's mother was also an artist.

Perhaps in more than Phillis Wheatley's biological life is her mother's signature made clear.

Virginia Woolf (1882–1941) was a British writer of the early 20ᵗʰ century and the author of novels, short stories, essays and criticisms, among them the early feminist classic, A Room of One's Own. *She was founder and president of London's Hogarth Press, a publishing house that paid special attention to women writers of the time. She is seen as a major feminist voice whose work still influences her readers.*

from A Room of One's Own

Virginia Woolf

Here am I asking why women did not write poetry in the Elizabethan age, and I am not sure how they were educated; whether they were taught to write; whether they had sitting-rooms to themselves; how many women had children before they were twenty-one; what, in short, they did from eight in the morning till eight at night. They had no money evidently; according to Professor Trevelyan they were married whether they liked it or not before they were out of the nursery, at fifteen or sixteen very likely. It would have been extremely odd, even upon this showing, had one of them suddenly written the plays of Shakespeare, I concluded, and I thought of that old gentleman, who is dead now, but was a bishop, I think, who declared that it was impossible for any woman, past, present, or to come, to have the genius of Shakespeare. He wrote to the papers about it. He also told a lady who applied to him for information that cats do not as a matter of fact go to heaven, though they have, he added, souls of a sort. How much thinking those old gentlemen used to save one! How the borders of ignorance shrank back at their approach! Cats do not go to heaven. Women cannot write the plays of Shakespeare.

Be that as it may, I could not help thinking, as I looked at the works of Shakespeare on the shelf, that the bishop was right at least in this; it would have been impossible, completely and entirely, for any woman to have written the plays of Shakespeare in the age of Shakespeare. Let me imagine, since facts are so hard to come by, what would have happened had Shakespeare had a wonderfully gifted sister, called Judith, let us say. Shakespeare himself went, very probably—his mother was an heiress—to the grammar school, where he may have learnt Latin—Ovid, Virgil and Horace—and the elements of grammar and logic. He was, it is well known, a wild boy who poached rabbits, perhaps shot a deer, and had, rather sooner than he should have done, to marry a woman in the neighbourhood, who bore him a child rather quicker than was right. That escapade sent him to seek his fortune in London. He had, it seemed, a taste for the theatre; he began by holding horses at the stage door. Very soon he got work in the theatre, became a successful actor, and lived at the hub of the universe, meeting everybody, knowing everybody, practising his art on the boards, exercising his wits in the streets, and even getting access to the palace of the queen. Meanwhile his extraordinarily gifted sister, let us suppose, remained at home. She was as adventurous, as imaginative, as agog to see the world as he was. But she was not sent to school. She had no chance of learning grammar and logic, let alone of reading Horace and Virgil. She picked up a book now and then, one of her brother's perhaps, and read a few pages. But then her parents came in and told her to mend the stockings or mind the stew and not moon about with books and papers. They would have spoken sharply but kindly, for they were substantial people who knew the conditions of life for a woman and loved their daughter—indeed, more likely than not she was the apple of her father's eye. Perhaps she scribbled some pages up in an apple loft on the sly, but was careful to hide them or set fire to them. Soon, however, before she was out of her teens, she was to be betrothed to the son of a neighbouring wool-stapler. She cried out that marriage was hateful to her, and for that she was severely beaten by her father. Then he ceased to scold her. He begged her instead not to hurt him, not to shame him in this matter of her marriage. He would give her a chain of beads or a fine petticoat, he said; and there were tears in his eyes. How could she disobey him? How could she break his heart? The force of her own gift alone drove her to it. She made up a small parcel of her belongings, let herself down by a rope one summer's night and took the road to London. She was not seventeen. The birds that sang in the hedge were not more musical than she was. She had the quickest fancy, a gift like her brother's, for the tune of words. Like him, she had a taste for the theatre. She stood at the stage door; she wanted to act, she said. Men laughed in her face. The manager—a fat, loose-lipped man—guffawed. He bellowed something about poodles dancing and women acting—no woman, he said, could possibly be an actress. He hinted—you can imagine what. She could get no training in her craft. Could she even seek her dinner in a tavern or roam the streets at midnight? Yet her genius was for fiction and lusted to feed abundantly upon the lives of men and women and the study of their ways. At last—for she was very young, oddly like Shakespeare the poet in her face, with the same grey eyes and rounded brows—at last Nick Greene the actor-manager took pity on her; she found herself with child by that gentleman and so—who shall measure the heat and violence of the poet's heart when caught and tangled in a woman's body?—killed herself one winter's night and lies buried at some cross-roads where the omnibuses now stop outside the Elephant and Castle.

That, more or less, is how the story would run, I think, if a woman in Shakespeare's day had had Shakespeare's genius. But for my part, I agree with the deceased bishop, if such he was—it is unthinkable that any woman in Shakespeare's day should have had Shakespeare's genius. For genius like Shakespeare's is not born among labouring, uneducated, servile people. It was not born in England among the Saxons and the Britons. It is not born today among the working classes. How, then, could it have been born among women whose work began, according to Professor Trevelyan, almost before they were out of the nursery, who were forced to it by their parents and held to it by all the power of law and custom? Yet genius of a sort must have existed among women as it must have existed among the working classes. Now and again an Emily Brontë or a Robert Burns blazes out and proves its presence. But certainly it never got itself on to paper. When, however, one reads of a witch being ducked, of a woman possessed by devils, of a wise woman selling herbs, or even of a very remarkable man who had a mother, then I think we are on the track of a lost novelist, a suppressed poet, of some mute and inglorious Jane Austen, some Emily Brontë who dashed her brains out on the moor or moped and mowed about the highways crazed with the torture that her gift had put her to. Indeed, I would venture to guess that Anon, who wrote so many poems without signing them, was often a woman. It was a woman Edward Fitzgerald, I think, suggested who made the ballads and the folk-songs, crooning them to her children, beguiling her spinning with them, or the length of the winter's night.

This may be true or it may be false—who can say?—but what is true in it, so it seemed to me, reviewing the story of Shakespeare's sister as I had made it, is that any woman born with a great gift in the sixteenth century would certainly have gone crazed, shot herself, or ended her days in some lonely cottage outside the village, half witch, half wizard, feared and mocked at. For it needs little skill in psychology to be sure that a highly gifted girl who had tried to use her gift for poetry would have been so thwarted and hindered by other people, so tortured and pulled asunder by her own contrary instincts, that she must have lost her health and sanity to a certainty.

Pulitzer prize nominee Ruth Forman is an award-winning African-American poet and the author of We Are the Young Magicians *(1993) and* Renaissance *(1998).*

Poetry Should Ride the Bus

Ruth Forman

poetry should hopscotch in a polka dot dress
wheel cartwheels
n hold your hand
when you walk past the yellow crackhouse

poetry should wear bright red lipstick
n practice kisses in the mirror
for all the fine young men with fades
shootin craps around the corner

poetry should dress in fine plum linen suits
n not be so educated that it don't stop in
every now n then to sit on the porch
and talk about the comins and goins of the world

poetry should ride the bus
in a fat woman's Safeway bag
between the greens n chicken wings
to be served with Tuesday's dinner

poetry should drop by a sweet potato pie
ask about the grandchildren
n sit through a whole photo album
on a orange plastic covered La-Z-Boy with no place to go

poetry should sing red revolution love songs
that massage your scalp
and bring hope to your blood
when you think you're too old to fight

yeah
poetry should whisper electric blue magic
all the years of your life
never forgettin to look you in the soul
every once in a while
n smile

Noted American poet and playright, Archibald MacLeish (1892–1982) earned several accolades for his work, including the Pulitzer prize (three-time recipient), the Presidential Medal of Freedom, a Tony Award, and an Academy Award. Although primarily known as a poet, his career included the roles of Librarian of Congress, Harvard professor, lawyer, television dramatist, and farmer. Some of his most awarded works include Conquistador *(1932),* Collected Poems: 1917–1952 *(1952), and* J.B.: A Play in Verse *(1958).*

Ars Poetica[1]

Archibald MacLeish

A poem should be palpable and mute
As a globed fruit,

Dumb
As old medallions to the thumb,

Silent as the sleeve-worn stone
Of casement ledges where the moss has grown—

A poem should be wordless
As the flight of birds.
             •
A poem should be motionless in time
As the moon climbs,

Leaving, as the moon releases
Twig by twig the night-entangled trees,

Leaving, as the moon behind the winter leaves,
Memory by memory the mind—

A poem should be motionless in time
As the moon climbs.
             •
A poem should be equal to:
Not true.

For all the history of grief
An empty doorway and a maple leaf.

For love
The leaning grasses and two lights above the sea—

A poem should not mean
But be.

Note

[1] "The Art of Poetry," title of a poetical treatise by the Roman poet Horace (65–8 B.C.).

Setting most of her work in her native Los Angeles, Chicana writer Helena Maria Viramontes addresses social issues, presenting a look at instances of oppression in the lives of ordinary women. She is co-founder of the Southern California Latina Writers and Filmmakers, and currently teaches on the faculty of the English department at Cornell University.

"Nopalitos": The Making of Fiction

Helena Maria Viramontes

Testimonio

Fiction is my jugular. For me it is a great consolation to know that whatever miserable things happen in my lifetime, goodness will inevitably result because I will write about it. There is strength in this when none is left in the soul.

I was born and raised in the U.S., East L.A., Califas, to be more exact on First Street not too far from Whittier Blvd., close enough to enable me to see the smoke from the Chicano Moratorium riots. I come from a family of eleven, six sisters and three brothers, but the family always extended its couch or floor to whomever stopped at our house with nowhere else to go. As a result, a variety of people came to live with us. Former boyfriends of my sisters who were thrown or pushed out of their own homes, friends who stayed the night but never left, relatives who crossed the border and stayed until enough was saved. Through all this I remember two things well: first, the late night kitchen meetings where everyone talked and laughed in low voices, played cards, talked of loneliness, plans for the future, of loves lost or won. I heard men cry drunken stories, women laughing. It was fascinating to listen in the dark, peek into the moments of their lives. For me, it seemed like a dream to wake up at midnight and hear the voices and listen to the soft music, see the light under the door. This was adulthood and I yearned to one day be the one on the other side of that door.

Little did I realize that this is the stuff good fiction is made of: the stories, the fascination of the subject matter, capturing the moments and fleeing with them like a thief or lover. I began my apprenticeship without even knowing it.

The other thing I remember is my mother. Her relentless energy. She must have been tired a good part of her life and yet she had to keep going and going and going. I also remember her total kindness, the way a sad story made her cry, the way she always found room somehow in an already-crowded household for those with the sad stories. The nights she would stay up, a small black and white TV blaring, waiting for the girls to come home. The mornings she would get up, KWKW Spanish radio on low, making the big stack of tortillas for the morning breakfast.

These two things, love of stories and love of my mother, or all that seemed female in our household, influenced me to such an extent that it became an unconscious part of me, so unconscious that I didn't realize it until just moments ago. In fact, the first story that I wrote, titled "Requiem for the Poor," opened with my mother awaking to make breakfast. To think: she was the first image in my mind, my heart, my hand. Naturally.

If my mother was the fiber that held a family together, it was my father who kept snapping it with his oppressive cruelty. With virtually no education, stressed with the responsibility of supporting such a large family, he worked as a hod carrier—a carrier of cement in construction. He drank, and was mean. Impatient, screaming a lot of the time, temper tantrums, we were often trembling in his presence. If my mother showed all that is good in being female, my father showed all that is bad in being male. I'm only now understanding the depth of this conclusion, and am making a serious effort to erase this black and white. See the good and bad in both sexes. That's the power of imagination, peeking beyond the fence of your personal reality and seeing the possibilities thereafter.

A basic problem for any writer is time. I lament the lack of time. As I pass my shelves of books, I think, these are books I will never read; or as my notebooks pile up, spilling over with plots, characters, great and moving sentences, I think, these are the words that will never find a story. Ideally, it would be bliss to manipulate the economic conditions of our lives and thus free our minds, our hands, to write. But there is no denying that this is a privilege limited to a certain sex, race and class. The only bad thing about privilege, Virginia Woolf wrote (I'm paraphrasing from Tillie Olsen), was that not everyone could have it.

How does one solve the problem of time? Fortunately, we *mujeres* are an inventive people. My mother, for example, faced the challenge of feeding eleven people every evening. Time and time again, I saw her cut four pork chops, add this and that and this, pour water, and miraculously feed all of us with a tasty *guiso*. Or the *nopales* she grew, cleaned, diced, scrambled with eggs, or meat, or chile, or really mixed with anything her budget could afford, and we had such a variety of tasty dishes!

I have never been able to match her *nopales*, but I have inherited her capacity for invention. I myself invent time by first conjuring up the voices and spirits of the women living under brutal repressive regimes. In the light of their reality, my struggles for a few hours of silence seem like such a petty problem. I am humbled, and no sooner do I think of their courage that I find my space on the kitchen table, my time long after midnight and before the start of the children's hectic morning. Because I want to do justice to their voices. To tell these women, in my own gentle way, that I will fight for them, that they provide me with my own source of humanity. That I love them, their children. Once seen in this perspective, the lack of sleep is more of an inconvenience than a sacrifice.

What little time we do invent we guard like our children. Interruption is a fact in our lives and is as common as pennies. Solely because we are women. A man who aspires to write is sanctioned by society. It is an acceptable and noble endeavor. As for us, writing is seen as a hobby we do after all our responsibilities are fulfilled. Nay, to write while the baby is crying is a crime punishable by guilt. Guilt is our Achilles' heel. Thus the work of the *mujer* suffers immensely, for the leisure of returning to her material, to rework it, polish it, is almost impossible. Because phones will ring, children will cry, or mothers will ask for favors. My mother, it seemed for a time, believed me to be half-baked for wanting desperately write. It was inconceivable to her that I spent mornings scratching a sharpened pencil against paper. She would stand and look over my shoulder, try to read a paragraph or two, and seeing that I was simply wasting my time staring into space, she'd ask me to go get some *tortillas*, or could you vacuum the living room, maybe water the plants outside? After turning her away with a harsh no, guilt would engulf me like a blob, and although I hated myself for doing it, there I was, once again, holding a garden hose, watering her roses.

We must come to understand that stifling a woman's imagination is too costly a price to pay for servitude. The world would be void of any depth or true comprehension if we were not allowed to exercise our imaginations. We must challenge those beliefs which oppress us within our family, our culture, in addition to those in the dominant culture.

Family ties are fierce. Especially for *mujeres*. We are raised to care for. We are raised to stick together, for the family unit is our only source of safety. Outside our home there lies a dominant culture that is foreign to us, isolates us, and labels us illegal alien. But what may be seen as a nurturing, close unit, may also become suffocating, manipulative, and sadly victimizing. As we slowly examine our own existence in and out of these cultures, we are breaking stereotypes, reinventing traditions for our own daughters and sons.

What a courageous task! In the past, we have been labeled as the weaker sex and it is logical to assume that we are of weaker minds as well. As women, we have learned to listen, rather than speak, causing us, historically to join with others who maintain we have nothing to say. Only now we are discovering that we do. And those who do not seem interested in knowing our voices are just plain foolish. To limit their knowledge of people, places, cultures, and sexes is to live in a narrow, colorless world. It is not only a tragedy, but just plain silly, for only foolish people would not be interested in embracing such knowledge.

We cannot, nor will we divorce ourselves from our families. But we need a change in their attitudes. If I am to succeed as a writer, I need my family to respect my time, my words, myself. This goes for my parents, brothers, sisters, my children, my husband. Respectability is a long and sometimes nasty struggle. But you'd be surprised at the progress one can make. Eventually, my mother proved to be very flexible. When I signed my first honorarium over to her, she discreetly placed it in her pocket. Later, as I spread my notebooks over the dining room table, she carried in a steaming cup of coffee, sweetened just the way I like it.

Now for some *nopalitos*.

Barbara Kingsolver (b. 1955) is a novelist, essayist, and human rights activist whose work includes The Bean Trees *(1988),* Animal Dreams *(1990),* The Poisonwood Bible *(1998), and* Small Wonder *(2002). In addition to writing, she has been a book reviewer for the* New York Times *since 1988 and the* Los Angeles Times *since 1989. She holds a M.S. from the University of Arizona, and makes her home in Tucson.*

Jabberwocky

Barbara Kingsolver

Once upon a time, a passing stranger sent me into exile. I was downtown in front of the Federal Building with a small crowd assembled to protest war in the Persian Gulf; he was in a black Ford pickup. As the truck roared by he leaned most of his upper body out the window to give me a better view of his finger, and he screamed, "Hey, bitch, love it or leave it!"

So I left.

He wasn't the first to give me that instruction; I've heard it since I was a nineteen-year-old in a scary barbershop haircut. Now I was thirty-four, mother of a child, with a decent reputation and pretty good hair. Why start listening *now*? I can only say he was finally one too many. I was on the verge of having a special kind of nervous breakdown, in which a person stalks through a Kmart parking lot ripping yellow ribbons off car antennas.

I realize that would have been abridging other people's right to free expression. What was driving me crazy was that very term "right to free expression," and how it was being applied in a nation at war. We were supposed to behave as though we had refrigerators for brains. Open, shove in a slab of baloney, close, stay cool. No questions. Our leaders told us this was a *surgical* war. *Very clean.* The language of the event was a perfect construct of nonmeaning. "Delivering the ordnance," they called it on the nightly news, which sounds nearly friendly. . . . "Why, here is your ordnance, friends, just sign on the line." "Deliver the ordnance" means "Drop the bomb."

But we bought the goods, or we kept our mouths shut. If we felt disturbed by the idea of pulverizing civilizations as the best way to settle our differences—or had trouble explaining that to our kids as adult behavior—we weren't talking about it. Typically, if I raised the debate, I was advised that if I liked Saddam so much I could go live in Iraq. As a matter of fact I *didn't* like Saddam, *or* the government of Kuwait. The two countries appeared practically indistinguishable; I doubt if many Americans could have guessed, a few years earlier (as we flooded Iraq with military aid), which one would turn out to be the Evil Empire, and which would require us to rush to its defense in the name of democracy. If *democracy* were really an issue we considered when going into that war, Iraq might have come out a nose ahead, Kuwait being a monarchy in which women held rights approximately equal to those of livestock. (*Since* the war, women's status in Kuwait has actually declined.) But the level of discourse allowed on this subject was "We're gonna kick butt." A shadow of doubt was viewed as treason.

I'm lucky enough to have a job that will follow me anywhere, so I left. I could contemplate from a distance these words on patriotism, written by the wise Garry Wills: "Love of one's country should be like love of one's spouse—a give-and-take criticism and affection. Although it is hoped one prefers one's spouse to other people . . . one does not prove that one loves one's wife by battering other women."

Give-and-take criticism and affection, out the window. And the battery was severe. Upon moving to Spain I read in the papers what was common knowledge, apparently, everywhere but in the U.S.: from the first night onward we bombed Iraqis relentlessly in their homes, killing thousands of civilians every day. Within months, more than 250,000 would be dead—most of them children—because of bombed-out water and sewer systems, hospitals with no antibiotics, hospitals with no roofs. To my horror I read that infections of hands and feet were rampant among Iraqi children, because of bombing debris, and the only available treatment was amputation. It had been an air war on civilians. The Commission of Inquiry for the International War Crimes Tribunal is still compiling the gruesome list of what the United States bombed in Iraq: all the country's major dams and most of its drinking water facilities; enough sewage treatment facilities to contaminate the Tigris River with waterborne killers; virtually all communications systems, leaving civilians unwarned of danger and unable to get help; civilian cars, buses, and taxis; 139 auto and railway bridges; food-processing, storage, and distribution systems; 100 percent of irrigation systems; wheat and grain fields (with incendiary bombs); 28 civilian hospitals and 52 community health centers; clothing factories; a cosmetics factory; an infant formula factory; 56 mosques; more than 600 schools. This was our surgical war.

Soon after the bombing ended, Ramsey Clark wrote a book called *The Fire This Time*, a meticulously researched account of the many ways the U.S.. violated the Geneva Convention and perpetrated crimes against civilians in the Persian Gulf War. Clark, as a former U.S. Attorney General, had once been appointed trustee of the nation's conscience. Now he asked us

I honestly never knew . . . →

to reckon with some awful responsibilities. But he encountered a truly American form of censorship: free enterprise in the hands of a monkey called See No Evil. His manuscript was rejected by eleven publishers— every major New York house. The editors did not turn it down for lack of merit, they said, but on grounds that it wouldn't be popular. (At length it was released by a small publisher called Thunder's Mouth; hurray for the alternative presses.)

No such hard luck for the memoirs of generals or celebrities, or O. J. Simpson's thoughts from jail while awaiting his verdict. The publisher of the latter (Little, Brown) claimed no moral qualms about providing a forum for Simpson at a time when he already commanded more media attention than has ever been held, probably, by any human being on the planet. The first printing was half a million copies.

This is a spooky proposition: an information industry that narrows down what we'll get to read and know about, mainly on the basis of how eagerly we'll lap it up. Producers and publishers who make these choices seem inclined, if confronted, to throw up their hands and exclaim, "I can't help it if that's what the people want!" A mother could say the same while feeding her baby nothing but jelly beans day after day; so could a physician who administers morphine for head colds. Both would be convicted of criminal neglect. Why is there no Hippocratic Oath for the professionals who service our intellects? Why is it that I knew, without wanting to, every possible thing about a figure skater who got whacked on the leg with a pipe—a melodrama that in the long run, let's face it, is utterly without consequence to anyone but the whackers and the whackee—but I had to go far out of my way to dig up the recent historical events that led to anarchy in Somalia and Haiti? (I learned, it's worth noting, that the U.S. did embarrassing things in both places.) News stations will move heaven and earth to get their own reporters into the likes of California vs. O. J. Simpson, or backstage with Tonya Harding, but not into hearings on the Clean Air Act. Producers will blame consumers, but blame is hardly the point if we are merrily dying of ignorance, and killing others with our apathy. Few U.S. citizens are aware, for example, that our government has routinely engineered assassinations of democratically elected heads of state in places like Chile and Guatemala, and replaced them with such monstrous confederates as Augusto Pinochet and Castillo Armas. Why do those dictators' names fail even to ring a bell in most red-blooded American heads? Possibly because our heads are too crowded with names like O. J. and Tonya. The guilt for that may not rest entirely with the producers or the consumers, but the crime has nevertheless occurred. To buy or to sell information as nothing more than a consumer product, like soda pop, is surely wrong. Marketed in that way, information's principal attribute must be universal palatability.

This is not to say we only get to tune in to *happy* news—there are wrecks and murders galore. But it's information that corroborates a certain narrow view of the world and our place in it. Exhaustive reports of rare, bizarre behaviors among the wealthy support the myth that violent crime is a random, unpreventable disaster, and obscure the blunt truth that most crime is caused by poverty. There's not much in the news to remind us, either, that poverty is a problem we could decently address, as all other industrialized countries have done. The safest marketing technique is to dispense with historical analysis, accountability, and even—apparently—critical thought.

When the Smithsonian deferred to what it called "public pressure" and canceled an exhibit on the historical use of the atomic bomb in Hiroshima and Nagasaki, Smithsonian Secretary I. Michael Heyman explained, "Veterans and their families were expecting, and rightly so, that the nation would honor and commemorate their valor and sacrifice. They were not looking for analysis, and, frankly, we did not give enough thought to the intense feeling that such analysis would evoke." *Analysis* in that case meant the most elementary connection between cause and effect: what happens when the Ordnance gets Delivered.

As a member of that all-important public, I'd like to state for the record that I'm offended. Give me the chance and I'll spend my consumer dollar on the story that relates to what kind of shape the world will be in fifty years from now. I'll choose analysis, every time, over placebo news and empty salve for my patriotic ego. I'm offended by the presumption that my honor as a citizen will crumple unless I'm protected from knowledge of my country's mistakes. I'm made of sturdier stuff than that, and I imagine, if he really thought about it, so is that guy who leaned out of a truck to give me the finger. What kind of love is patriotism, if it evaporates in the face of uncomfortable truths? What kind of honor sits quietly by while a nation's conscience flies south for a long, long winter?

Artists are as guilty as anyone in the conspiracy of self-censorship, if they succumb to the lure of producing only what's sure to sell. The good ones don't, and might still sell anyway, for humans have long accepted subconsciously that good art won't always, so to speak, match the sofa. "Poets are the unacknowledged legislators of the race," Percy Shelley said. They are also its margin of safety, like the canaries that used to be carried into mines because of their sensitivity to toxic gases; their silence can be taken as a sign of imminent danger.

The artist's maverick responsibility is sometimes to sugarcoat the bitter pill and slip it down our gullet, telling us what we didn't think we wanted to know. But in the U.S. we're establishing a modern tradition of tarpapering our messengers. The one who delivers the bitter pill, whether the vehicle is a war-crime documentary or a love story, is apt to be dismissed as a "political artist."

It's a Jabberwockish sort of label, both dreaded and perplexing. Technically the term "political" refers to campaigns, governments, and public institutions. But *Police Academy* was not called political. Barry Lopez is called political, and he writes about dying ecosystems and great blue herons and wolves, for heaven's sake. It took me years to work out what it is that earns this scalding label for an artist or an act.

Now I know, and this is how I know: during the Gulf War some young friends of mine wanted to set up a table in the shopping mall and hand out information about the less cheerful aspects of the war. The administrators of the mall refused permission. My friends contended, "But you let people hand out yellow ribbons and flags and 'We kick butt' bumper stickers!" The mall administrators explained their charter forbids anything political. "Handing out yellow ribbons is public service," they said, "but what *you* want to do is *political*."

Now you know. This subterfuge use of the word "political," which doesn't show up in my Random House Unabridged, means only that a thing runs counter to prevailing assumptions. If 60 percent of us support the war, then the expressions of the other 40 percent are political—and can be disallowed in some contexts for that reason alone. The really bad news is that the charter of the shopping mall seems to be standing in as a national artistic standard. Cultural workers in the U.S. are prone to be bound and gagged by a dread of being called political, for that word implies the art is not quite pure. Real art, the story goes, does not endorse a point of view. This is utter nonsense, of course (try to imagine a story or a painting with no point of view), and also the most thorough and invisible form of censorship I've ever encountered. When I'm interviewed about writing, I spend a good deal of time defending the possibility that such things as environmental ruin, child abuse, or the hypocrisy of U.S. immigration policy are appropriate subjects for a novel. I keep waiting for the interviewer to bring up *art* things, like voice and metaphor; usually I'm still waiting for that when the cows come home.

In rural Greece some people believe that if you drink very cold water on a very hot day, you will die; here, we have that kind of superstition about mixing art with conscience. It's a quaintly provincial belief that fades out fast at our borders. Most of the rest of the world considers social criticism to be, absolutely, the most legitimate domain of art. If you think I'm overstating this, look who's been winning Nobel Prizes in literature for the last ninety years:

Nadine Gordimer, who has spent her life writing against racism and apartheid in South Africa. Joseph Brodsky, who spent some years in Siberia because of his criticism of Soviet society. Wole Soyinka, who has also logged time in jail because of his criticisms of colonialism in Africa. Gabriel García Márquez, who is possibly the most gifted social critic in a whole continent of social-critic-writers. Czeslaw Milosz, who was active in the anti-Nazi underground and whose poetry is thoroughly ideological. Pablo Neruda, Aleksandr Solzhenitsyn, Miguel Asturias, Thomas Mann, George Bernard Shaw.

U.S. prizewinners do not dominate this list (as they do the Nobel categories of Physics, Chemistry, and Medicine), especially since the 1950s. It's not for lack of great writers, but perhaps because we've learned to limit our own access to serious content. The fear of being perceived as ideologues runs so deep in writers of my generation it undoubtedly steers us away from certain subjects without our knowing it. The fear is that if you fall short of perfect execution, you'll be called "preachy." But falling short of perfection when you've plunged in to say what needs to be said—is that so much worse, really, than falling short when you've plunged in to say what *didn't* need to be said?

And if you should by chance succeed—oh, then. Art has the power not only to soothe a savage breast, but to change a savage mind. A novel can make us weep over the same events that might hardly give us pause if we read them in a newspaper. Even though the tragedy in the newspaper happened to real people, while the one in the novel happened in an author's imagination.

A novel works its magic by putting a reader inside another person's life. The pace is as slow as life. It's as detailed as life. It requires you, the reader, to fill in an outline of words with vivid pictures drawn subconsciously from your own life, so that the story feels more personal than the sets designed by someone else and handed over via TV or movies. Literature duplicates the experience of living in a way that nothing else can, drawing you so fully into another life that you temporarily forget you have one of your own. That is why you read it, and might even sit up in bed till early dawn, throwing your whole tomorrow out of whack, simply to find out what happens to some people who, you know perfectly well, are made up. It's why you might find yourself crying, even if you aren't the crying kind.

The power of fiction is to create empathy. It lifts you away from your chair and stuffs you gently down inside someone else's point of view. It differs drastically from a newspaper, which imparts information while allowing you to remain rooted in your own perspective. A newspaper could tell you that one hundred people, say, in an airplane, or in Israel, or in Iraq, have died today. And you can think to yourself, "How very sad," then turn the page and see how the Wildcats fared. But a novel could take just one of those hundred lives and show you exactly how it felt to be that person rising from bed in the morning, watching the desert light on the tile of her doorway and on the curve of her daughter's cheek. You would taste that person's breakfast, and love her family, and sort through her worries as your own, and know that a death in that household will be the end of the only life that someone will ever have. As important as yours. As important as mine.

At the height of the Gulf War, I found in the *New York Times* this quote from Loren Thompson, director of the national security program at Georgetown University, explaining why the Pentagon wasn't releasing information about deaths in Iraq. When bomb damage is listed only in technical terms, he said, "you avoid talking about lives lost, and that serves both an esthetic and a practical purpose."

The esthetic and practical purpose, of course, is the loss of empathy. We seem to be living in the age of anesthesia and it's no wonder. Confronted with knowledge of dozens of apparently random disasters each day, what can a human heart do but slam its doors? No mortal can grieve that much. We didn't evolve to cope with tragedy on a global scale. Our defense is to pretend there's no thread of event that connects us, and that those lives are somehow not precious and real like our own. It's a practical strategy, to some ends, but the loss of empathy is also the loss of humanity, and that's no small tradeoff.

Art is the antidote that can call us back from the edge of numbness, restoring the ability to feel for another. By virtue of that power, it is political, regardless of content. If *Jane Eyre* is a great romance, it has also given thousands of men a female experience, and a chance to feel the constraints that weighed upon women of Jane's time. Through art, a woman can give a male reader the unparalleled athletic accomplishment of childbirth, or the annihilation of being raped; if every man knew both those things, I would expect the world to change tomorrow. We have all heard plenty about each other's troubles, but evidently it's not enough to be told, it has to be lived. And art is so very nearly the same as life.

I *know*, for example, that slavery was heinous, but the fate of sixty million slaves is too big a thing for a heart to understand. So it was not until I read Toni Morrison's *Beloved* that I honestly felt that truth. When Sethe killed her children rather than have them grow up in slavery, I was so far from my sheltered self I knew the horror that could make infanticide an act of love. Morrison carved the tragedy of those sixty million, to whom the book is dedicated, into something small and dense and real enough to fit through the door, get in my heart, and explode. This is how a novel can be more true than a newspaper.

One of my favorite writings about writing is this excerpt from Ursula K. Le Guin's introduction to her science-fiction novel *The Left Hand of Darkness*, in which she discusses fiction's role in what we call the truth:

Open your eyes; listen, listen. That is what the novelists say. But they don't tell you what you will see and hear. All they can tell you is what they have seen and heard, in their time in this world, a third of it spent in sleep and dreaming, another third of it spent in telling lies.

. . . Fiction writers, at least in their braver moments, do desire the truth: to know it, speak it, serve it. But they go about it in a peculiar and devious way, which consists in inventing persons, places, and events which never did and never will exist or occur, and telling about these fictions in detail and at length and with a great deal of emotion, and then when they are done writing down this pack of lies, they say, There! That's the truth!

. . . In reading a novel, any novel, we have to know perfectly well that the whole thing is nonsense, and then, while reading, believe every word of it. Finally, when we're done with it, we may find that we're a bit different from what we were before we read it, that we have been changed a little . . . crossed a street we never crossed before. But it's very hard to *say* just what we learned, how we were changed.

The artist deals with what cannot be said in words.

The artist whose medium is fiction does this *in words*. The novelist says in words what cannot be said in words.

This baffling manifesto is a command that rules my writing life. I believe it means there are truths we all know, but can't make ourselves feel: Slavery was horrible. Love thy neighbor as thyself, or we'll all go to hell in a handbasket. These are things that cannot be said in words because they're too familiar to move us, too big and bald and flat to penetrate our souls. The artist must craft missiles to deliver these truths so unerringly to the right place inside of us we are left panting, with no possibility of doubting they are true. The novelist must do this in story, image, and character. And make the reader believe.

To speak of this process as something that must fall either into the camp of "political" or "pure" is frankly absurd. Good art is political, whether it means to be or not, insofar as it provides the chance to understand points of view alien to our own. Its nature is the opposite of spiritual meanness, bigotry, and warfare. If it is disturbing at times, or unpalatable, it may be a good idea to buy it anyway.

In time, I came back from political exile. Not with my tail between my legs, having discovered the U.S.A. was after all the greatest place in the world. On the contrary, I loved the new experience of safety, the freedom to walk anywhere I pleased at any time of day, and the connected moral comfort of a society that cares for all its children, provides universal health care, and allows no one to be destitute. All these foreign things, and more, I loved: the sound of the ocean in my window, and the towering poinsettia trees that blossomed along the roadsides from Christmas till Easter. I missed a few things: Mexican food, certain familiar music on the radio, the blush of a Tucson sunset running hot and sweet up the face of the Santa Catalina Mountains. And I missed the sound of my mother tongue. By accident, it turns out, I've been apprenticed as a writer to my own language and culture. In the midst of a deeply American novel, high and dry in the Canary Isles, I had to beg friends back home for mundanities I couldn't recall—figures of speech, car makes, even commercial jingles.

More than anything, though, I missed people, the beloved relatives and friends I left behind. I had new friends, but it was finally on account of the old ones that I prepared to give up the expatriate's life.

As the time drew near, my feet balked. I dreaded leaving my kind new place to return to the land of the free (*free* to live behind locks at all times; *free* to walk in the evenings from library to parked car with sheer terror in my heart) and the home of the brave (well, yes, *brave*). The land where 7 percent of the world's souls guzzle the lion's share of the world's goods, pitch out a yearly average of sixteen hundred pounds of garbage apiece, and still can drive past homeless neighbors with little awareness of wrongdoing or alternatives. The place I was told to love or leave.

I found I could do neither. Not wholeheartedly. But like the boy who fought the Jabberwock in *Through the Looking Glass*, I took my vorpal sword in hand. For the sake of people who love me and the sight of mountains that move my soul, I would come galumphing back, to face the tyranny of words without meaning and monsters beyond my ken.

I came back because leaving was selfish. A country can be flawed as a marriage or a family or a person is flawed, but "Love it or leave it" is a coward's slogan. There's more honor in "Love it and get it right." Love it, love it. Love it and never shut up.

Searching for Truths

Nancy Rule Goldberger, Blythe McVicker Clinchy, Mary Field Belenky, and Jill Mattuck Tarule are feminist educators and researchers.

from Women's Ways of Knowing: On Gaining a Voice

Nancy Rule Goldberger, Blythe McVicker Clinchy, Mary Field Belenky, and Jill Mattuck Tarule

W e do not think of the average person as preoccupied with such difficult and profound questions as, "What is truth?" "What is authority?" "What counts for me as evidence?" "How do I know what I know?" Yet, to ask ourselves these questions and to reflect on our answers is more than an intellectual exercise, for our basic assumptions about the nature of truth and the origins of knowledge shape the way we see the world and ourselves as participants in it. In this chapter we describe five different perspectives from which women view reality and draw conclusions about truth, knowledge, and authority. Our description is based on extensive interviews with rural and urban American women of different ages, class and ethnic backgrounds, and educational histories. We examine how women's self-concepts and ways of knowing are intertwined. We describe how women struggle to gain a voice and claim the power of their own minds.

When the woman's voice is included in the study of human development, women's lives and qualities are revealed and the maps that chart the life cycle can be redrawn. Once these qualities are observed and acknowledged, we are more likely to observe their unfolding in the lives of men as well. The power of the women's voice in expanding our conceptions of epistemology and development is amply illustrated in Gilligan's (1982) work, which influenced our own thinking. By listening to girls and women resolve serious moral dilemmas in their lives, Gilligan has traced the development of a morality organized around notions of responsibility and care. This conception of morality contrasts sharply with the morality of rights described by Piaget (1965) and Kohlberg (1984), which is based on the study of the evolution of moral reasoning in boys and men. In recent work, Gilligan and Lyons (Lyons, 1983) have extended their study of gender-related differences in moral perspectives to the area of identity development. They have shown that a responsibility orientation tends to be more central to those whose conceptions of self are rooted in a sense of connection and a caring concern for others, whereas a rights orientation is more common to those who experience relationships in terms of objective fairness between separate individuals.

Lyons found that many more women than men define themselves in terms of their connected relationships to others, a point that has also been made by Chodorow (1978) and Miller (1976).

In addition to Gilligan's work, the work of Perry (1970, 1981) on developmental epistemology influenced our thinking. Based on interviews gathered each spring from male students as they moved through their undergraduate years at Harvard, Perry describes how students' conceptions of the nature and origins of knowledge evolve and how their understanding of themselves as knowers changes over time. Perry depicts a passage through a sequence of epistemological perspectives that he calls "positions." It is through these coherent interpretive frameworks that students give meaning to their educational experience. Perry traces a progression from an initial position, which he calls *basic dualism*—where the student views the world in polarities of right/wrong, black/white, we/they, and good/bad—through a position called *multiplicity*—in which the student perceives multiple perspectives on truth—to a position at which the *relativism* of all knowledge is recognized. Perry does not claim that his positions represent an invariant developmental sequence or stages; however, he does believe that each position "both includes and transcends the earlier ones" (1981, p. 78).

The Perry scheme stimulated our interest in modes of knowing and provided us with our first images of the paths women might take as they develop an understanding of their intellectual potential, as well as providing a description of the routes most often taken by men. Our work uncovers themes, epistemological perspectives, and catalysts for development that are prominent among women, but sketchy or missing in Perry's version of male development.

In summary, two major concerns led us to our current research on women's epistemology: 1) women appear to have difficulties in assuming authority and valuing their own minds, and 2) women's modes of thought and experience as knowers have been inadequately investigated. We believe that, until there is a better understanding of how women think and experience themselves as developing beings, families, educators, employers, and others who live and work with women will continue to be ill-informed about what women know and need to know.

The Analysis of the Women's Interviews

Our data consist of extensive interviews with 135 women of varied class and ethnic backgrounds drawn from three private liberal arts colleges, an inner-city community college, an urban public high school, a B.A. program for adults, and three rural human service agencies. The women ranged in age from sixteen to sixty-five; some were single or divorced, others married; many had borne and raised children.

Our open-ended interview was designed to investigate the respondent's structure of thought as well as her attitudes. The interview is similar in form to the Piagetian clinical interview that has been adopted in the research of many cognitive-developmentalists such as Perry (1970), Kohlberg (1984; Colby et al., 1983), and Gilligan (1977, 1982). Interviews were tape-recorded and transcribed; they ran from two to five hours in length. Because of our prior research at some of the sites, we had more than one interview with forty women in our sample, obtained anywhere from one to five years apart.

We told each participant that we were interested in her experience—and in women's experience—because it had been so often excluded as people sought to understand human development. We told her that we wanted to hear what was important about life and learning from her point of view. Each interview began with a question adapted from Perry's research—"Looking back, what stands out for you over the past few years?"—and proceeded gradually at the woman's own pace to questions concerning self-image, relationships of importance, education and learning, real-life decision making and moral dilemmas, accounts of personal change and growth, perceived catalysts for change and impediments to growth, and visions of the future. Embedded in the interview were also standard questions adapted from Kohlberg and Gilligan to elicit moral reasoning and concepts of self, and questions we developed for eliciting epistemological assumptions.

We used two approaches in analyzing the interviews. First, we separated out the section of the interview that was designed to yield information on epistemology. This section was scored by coders who were unaware of the woman's age, ethnicity, social class, institutional base, and other factors. We found that the women's thinking did not fit so neatly into Perry's positions. After much discussion about disagreements in scoring, and then about Perry's classification system itself, we decided to regroup and rename the epistemological perspectives to capture more adequately women's ways of knowing. We identified, in our group of women, five major epistemological perspectives or positions that are built upon Perry's, but also diverge from them. They are 1) Silence, 2) Received Knowledge, 3) Subjective Knowledge, 4) Procedural Knowledge, and 5) Constructed Knowledge. These will be described in the next section.

The question of why and when women shift from one mode of knowing to another, as many of our women evidently did at points in their life, is an important one, but is not answered conclusively with our data, which are, for the most part, limited to single interviews with individuals. Nevertheless, based on the repeated interviews available to us and the retrospective accounts of the women, it appears that, when context is held constant (for example, women of similar backgrounds studying at similar institutions), there is a developmental progression across the last four positions in the order we describe them. We believe, however, that it is premature to consider our five positions as stages, particularly as our data suggest that many women do not seem to follow this developmental sequence.

Our second approach to data analysis was what we called the *contextual analysis.* After coding the interviews for epistemological perspective, we reassembled the interviews and read and reread them in their entirety. Gradually we developed a number of additional coding categories (see Belenky et al., 1986, for a description), designed to capture the ways in which women construe their experience of themselves as developing beings and experience their learning environment. During this part of the interview analysis, we stayed alert to the socioeconomic realities of each woman's life. We tried to enter the woman's world so that we might get close to her experience. We asked ourselves, "What problems is this woman trying to solve? What is adaptive about the way she is trying to accommodate to the world as she sees it? What are the forces—psychological or social—that expand or limit her horizons? What are the growth metaphors that she uses to depict her experience of development?"

One growth metaphor in particular reverberated throughout the women's stories of their intellectual and ethical development. Again and again the women spoke of "gaining a voice," by which they meant gaining a sense of having something worthwhile to say and feeling the security within themselves to say it. As these women described their struggle to gain a voice, they also told us much about silence and listening, often using phrases such as "being silenced," "not being heard," "really listening," "words as weapons," "feeling deaf and dumb," "having no words," "saying what you mean," "listening to be heard," and so on in an endless variety of connotations all having to do with sense of authority and self-worth and feelings of isolation from or connection to others.

The tendency we observed for women to ground their epistemological premises in metaphors suggesting speaking and listening is at odds with the visual metaphors—such as equating knowledge with illumination, knowing with seeing, and truth with light—that scientists and philosophers must often use to express their sense of mind. Keller and Grontkowski (1983), tracing the metaphorical uses of vision in the history of Western intellectual thought, argue that such analogies have led to a favored cultural model for truth and the quest for mind. Visual metaphors, such as "the mind's eye," suggests a camera passively recording a static reality and promote the illusion that disengagement and objectification are central to the construction of knowledge. Visual metaphors encourage standing at a distance to get a proper view, removing, it is believed, subject and object from a sphere of possible intercourse.

By holding close to women's experience of voice, we have come to understand conceptions of the mind that are different from those held by individuals who find "the mind's eye" a more appropriate metaphor for expressing their experience with the intellect. For women, a sense of voice and a sense of mind appear to be intricately intertwined.

The Epistemological Positions: Women's Ways of Knowing

Silence

Only a few women fell into this category at the time of the interview. None of these women was currently in school; all were minimally educated. Although the designation "silence" is not parallel to the terms we have chosen for other epistemological positions, we selected it because the absence of voice in these women is so salient. This position, though rare, at least in our sample, is an important anchoring point for our epistemological scheme, representing an extreme in denial of self and dependence on external authority for direction.

Women at this position are utterly subject to the power and aggression of others. They are dwarfed by authority. Whereas they experience themselves in the world as passive, reactive, and dependent, they see all authorities as being powerful, if not omnipotent. Blind obedience to authorities is seen as being of utmost importance for "keeping out of trouble" and ensuring one's survival. One woman, who grew up in a family with a physically and sexually abusive father, said, "I spent my life, until recently, keeping quiet and looking for a safe place to hide."

Although these women view authorities, generally male, as omnipotent, the power that they see authorities as holding is not communicated through words imbued with shared meanings. Authorities seldom tell you what they want you to do. They apparently expect you to know in advance. If authorities do tell you what is right, they never tell you why it is right.

The references these women make to language suggests that words are not perceived as a means of communication, but as weapons. Authorities have used words to attack them, to denigrate, or to keep them in place. Using words to protest the actions of others—that is, "speaking out"—is to court danger and retaliation. Silence is the best policy. There is little evidence that these silent women actively listen to the content of authorities' voices. It is as if command and action are undifferentiated: to hear is to obey. One woman explained why her abusive husband ruled the roost: "You know, I used to hear his words, and his words kept coming out of my mouth. He had me thinking that I didn't know anything."

These women are not preverbal. Each has developed language. Yet their experience using language has been so limited they have not explored the power that words have for expressing or developing thought. To look for meaning in the words of others or to share one's experience with words seems impossible. Trying to talk to others typically leaves them feeling "deaf and dumb." They may sense that truth is passed from one person to another in the form of words, but they feel left out of the process and incapable of understanding what others know. Seeing themselves as incapable of receiving and retaining truths from others' words, or of having ideas of their own, they are dependent on the continual presence of authorities to guide their actions if they are not to be ruled by impulse. New situations evoke paralysis and the need to cling to others, too often to violent and deprecatory men. Some women speak of clinging to other women—mothers, aunts, friends—whom they feel have lived through similar experiences and share their plight.

Learning in traditional educational settings has been traumatic for them and only reinforced their image of themselves as stupid. They claim that only demonstration helps them to learn: "Someone has to show me—not tell me—or I can't get it." Their thought is utterly dependent on concrete everyday actions and experiences. Even their self-definition is embedded in concrete action. In response to our question, "How would you describe yourself to yourself?" they tended to describe themselves in terms of geographic space (if they could answer at all): "I am a person who likes to stay home. Before I got pregnant, I used to describe myself as not being home."

The world of the silent or silenced seems a static and unchangeable place to those within it. With language and thought so limited to the immediate and concrete, they have little ability to anticipate a different future. That anyone should emerge from their childhood years, into a modern society, with so little confidence in their meaning-making and meaning-sharing abilities signals the failure of the community to nurture all those entrusted to its care. To us, the situation of these women seemed to be in part the result of a cultural stereotype of femininity gone awry and at its most pernicious. These are women living in the worst imaginable social conditions as victims of physical abuse, incest, and neglect. Although the silent are by no means the only women in our sample who have experienced sexual and physical abuse, they are notable for their inability to speak out in protest.

Received Knowledge: Learning Through Listening to Others

At this position women are also oriented to authority outside themselves but believe that close attention to the words and wisdom of others is central to the knowing process. They conceive of themselves as capable of receiving, but not of creating, knowledge. The origins of knowledge lie outside the self. Because these women are subject to the standards, directions, and authority of others, they are conventional in the sense that they adhere to the prevailing cultural stereotypes and expectations of women. They rely on the words of others for self-knowledge; thus self-concept is organized around social expectations and roles. Approximately nine percent of our sample are in this category. This perspective was held by some of the youngest women in the sample; many of the older women, in particular those who had returned to school after spending years as homemakers, retrospectively describe themselves in these terms, even though their epistemological outlook may have recently shifted.

When striving to comprehend new ideas, the person at this position discounts the importance of her own experience and actions in the process of knowing. Truth is sought and found in the words of authorities. The woman does not really try to understand or evaluate new ideas. She has little notion of understanding as a process taking place over time. She collects facts, but does not develop opinions. Receiving, retaining, and returning the words of authorities are seen as synonymous with learning. Teachers are always right because ultimately "they can always look up the right answer in a book." Thus even authorities lack the capacity for constructing knowledge. Authorities must receive Truths from the words of even higher authorities.

These women (like Perry's dualists) divide the world into distinctive, polarized categories: true and false, good and evil, black and white, right and wrong. They assume that there is only one right answer to any question. All other answers and all contrary views are automatically wrong. There are no gradations of truth—no grey areas. When faced with controversy, there is for them a category of good authorities who have the right answers and bad ones who are either confused or misled (Perry, 1970, p. 68). Paradox is inconceivable as several contradictory ideas are never imagined to be simultaneously in accordance with fact. Ambiguity is intolerable. To impose oneself in the process of learning is improper: One reads the lines and follows the plot, but one should not read between the lines. People who see things between the lines are making them up. By dichotomizing the world, women at this position appear to value the objective over the subjective. Truth is thought to have a concrete, tangible existence independent of the mind.

• • •

The belief that there is a single right answer and that one can hear it in the words of others encourages women to become aware of and appreciative of their own listening skills. Wanting to do the right thing, but having no opinions of their own to give guidance, they listen to others and shape their behavior to fulfill the expectations and exhortations of others. They come to believe that a good woman listens and lets others do the talking. They listen closely and react to authorities and peers in their immediate community more readily than remote authority. We heard in the stories of our women a theme identified by Gilligan (1982) as characteristic of conventional female morality: that women should devote themselves to the care and empowerment of others while remaining selfless. Many of the women we interviewed had devoted a large part of their lives listening to others, stilling their voices so that others could be heard. Most felt a sense of pride in their response to the needs of others and indeed seemed quite attuned to the nuances and demands of human relationships.

Subjective Knowledge: The Inner Voice

At this position there is an emphasis on the authority within the self, on listening to the inner voice. The words, directives, and admonitions of external authorities fade and lose their power. Truth is defined as personal, private, and subjectively known or intuited.

Most women at this position have a difficult time identifying the source of their knowing, other than that it is within. It is like an inner conviction, a process that bypasses awareness. As one woman said, "I just know. I try not to think because if you trust yourself, you just know the answer." It is clear that these women do not see thought as central to the process of knowing. They do not experience themselves as constructors of truth, but as conduits through which truth emerges. . . .

Truth, then, is not universal. Women at this position claim that each person's experience makes her see a different reality from that of any other person. What is more, truth is necessarily a private matter, known only to oneself, and should not be imposed on others. Convergence of truths is possible; however, in the case of disagreement, one's own experience and inner voice are the final arbiters. Another person's opinion may be misguided or disagreeable but there is a tolerance for differences because others "must obviously believe in their opinion." These women recognize that others may disagree with them but seem less concerned than men in persuading others to their point of view, in part because they want to avoid battles that threaten to disrupt relationships. Whereas men claim they "have a right to their opinion" (Perry, 1970), women tend to state more cautiously, "It's just my opinion."

Many women at this position distrust logic, analysis, abstraction, and even language itself, perceiving these as alien territory belonging to men. They tend to argue against and stereotype those experts and remote authorities whom society promotes as holding the keys to truth—teachers, doctors, scientists, men in general. It is as if, after turning inward, they deny strategies for knowing that they perceive as belonging to the masculine world. Some seem never to have learned to use logic and theory as tools for knowing; others imply that they have and have rejected it. Generally they have vague and untested prejudices against a mode of thought that they believe is impersonal, inhuman, or unfeminine and possibly detrimental to their capacity for feeling. They prefer to rely on direct sensory experience and on real interactions and connections with real people—and ultimately on gut response—as a way of informing themselves about the world. Some of these women express a distrust of books and the written word, calling them instruments of oppression that are too often used against women. They prefer to express themselves nonverbally or artistically so as to bypass the categorizing and labeling that language implies.

In our sample, there were a large number of women who viewed reality from the position of subjectivism—46 percent of all we interviewed. They appeared in every educational and agency setting included in this study and cut across class, ethnic, age, and educational boundaries. What is most remarkable in the stories of our women is that the shift in perspective from adhering to external authority to knowing from the inside is not tied to any specific age or phase. We found that it was the predominant perspective on knowing in women as young as sixteen and as old as sixty, many of whom claimed that they had only come to this way of knowing very recently.

Women's discovery of the power of inner knowing is experienced as liberation, and greatly affects changing definitions of the self. Openness to change and novelty is the fulcrum around which their new identity revolves. Many women use the imagery of birth or rebirth to describe their experience of a nascent self.

We believe that a shift into subjectivism is a particularly significant reconceptualization of knowledge for women when and if it occurs. Women's emergent reliance on their intuitive processes is an important move in the service of self-protection, self-assertion, and self-definition. Over half of our large group of subjectivists had recently taken steps to end relationships with lovers or husbands, to reject further obligations to family members, and to move out and away on their own. For these women, subjectivism is a way of knowing that is safe from the dictates of others. It provides the space for a birth of the self without the constraints of social convention and it provides them with a reassuring sense of personal power and authority.

One women in her thirties described her recent liberation this way: "Now I only know with my gut. It helps me and protects me. It is perceptive and astute. My gut is my best friend—the one thing in the world that won't let me down or lie to me or back away from me."

Procedural Knowledge: The Voice of Reason

Most of the women in this category—24 percent of the sample—were attending or had recently graduated from prestigious colleges. Most were privileged, bright, white, and young, ranging in age from late teens to mid-twenties. One can hear in the stories of women in this category how they acquire the tools of reason and attitudes about knowledge that are valued in most of our esteemed institutions of higher education. These are women striving to join the academic elite and the professional public world of men.

All of the women at this position are absorbed in the business of acquiring and applying procedures for obtaining and communicating knowledge. Some seem passionately involved in the process, whereas others seem to treat it as a "game," but the emphasis on procedures, skills, and techniques is common to all. Developing procedures for knowing—such as critical thinking, textual analysis, and scientific method—becomes paramount, as does an emphasis on "learning the way they want you to think" (Perry, 1970, p. 100).

The woman at this position recognizes that some events are open to interpretation, and that some interpretations make better sense than others. Because one's ideas must "measure up to certain objective standards, one must speak in measured tones, or not speak at all." It is not sufficient to parrot the authorities' words or to blurt out the first thing that comes to mind. One should systematically muster support for one's opinions and be careful not to jump to conclusions.

For most of the women at this position, form predominates over content. It matters less what you think than that you have thought it through thoroughly. The women pride themselves on the skills they acquire. Asked what she valued most about her college education, one woman named her philosophy course. "I couldn't tell you right now the philosophies of most of the people we studied, but I can tell you how I would set about criticizing their arguments and what types of things you should look for."

Most women in this category retain or regain some trust in authority; authorities are perceived as relatively benign, neither dictatorial nor attacking. Authorities do not offer answers, only techniques for constructing answers. And, most important to the women, they judge, not opinions per se, but the procedures one uses to substantiate opinions. Authorities apparently do not seek to silence but to teach a new language.

However, some of these women, even as they go about developing their intellectual competence and authority, begin to express a deep ambivalence about the institutionalized pressure to conform to normative ideals about the right ways to learn and think. In the process of learning the new academic language, women do come to understand that we can know things that we have never seen or touched, that truth can be shared, and that expertise can be respected. They learn, too, that intuition can deceive and that gut reactions can be irresponsible. They are often told that first-hand experience has no place in the classroom. They are taught to look for general laws, for universal trends, and to avoid personalizing. They are taught that they isolate events and people from contexts in order to arrive at objective evaluations. They are taught to pay attention to objects in the external world, that is, for instance, to the painting itself rather than the feelings a painting arouses in oneself. Most of the women in our sample of procedural knowers have learned these lessons well and have demonstrated that they can excel in academic circles and adversarial debate. Some pride themselves, as the philosopher Sara Ruddick once did, on their "male minds" (Ruddick, 1984, p. 143).

But others speak of a sense of fraudulence about their proven academic abilities and success, feeling that, although they can perform adequately, they have lost a sense of their true selves. They talk about feeling like imposters who no longer aspire to having a male mind. Truth, for them, seems to lie somewhere outside the academy. The voice of reason that they have acquired, though it serves them well, is not necessarily their voice. Nor are the questions asked in academic circles necessarily their questions.

Some of these women have begun to experiment with more "feminine" procedures for knowing, procedures that are more personal and empathic. They speak of learning how to "open oneself up to ideas." The women in the next section have developed these procedures more fully.

Constructed Knowledge: Integrating the Voices

The women in this final category (18 percent of our sample) are all articulate and reflective people, some quite young, others among the oldest in our sample. All of them were attending or had graduated from college. At some time in their past, they said, they had felt deadened to their inner experience and inner selves; thinking and feeling were split asunder. They told us that their current way of knowing and viewing the world—the way of knowing we call *constructed knowledge*—began as an effort to reclaim the self by attempting to integrate knowledge that they felt intuitively was important with knowledge and methods of knowing that they had learned during their formal education. They had "moved outside the givens" of their social and intellectual world by removing themselves psychologically, and at times even geographically. Their stated intention was to take time out to get to know the self and to reflect on the contexts that confined and defined them. They described the development of a new way of thinking that emphasized not the extrication of the self in the process of knowing but a "letting the inside out and the outside in."

The central insight that distinguishes this position is that all knowledge is constructed and the knower is an intimate part of the known. The woman comes to see that the knowledge one acquires depends on the context or frame of reference of the knower who is seeking answers and on the context in which events to be understood have occurred. One woman put it this way: "We can assume that something exists out there—but "something" is thinking that something exists. Our consciousness is part of the world. We are creating the world at the time."

Recognizing that everything is relative, these women concern themselves with the basic assumptions that govern the kinds of questions being asked and the methods being used for getting answers. They are aware that even personal truths are a matter of history, circumstance, and timing, and are subject to change. Theories are seen not as truth but as models for approximating experience; theories are "educated guesswork."

Women at this position overcome the notion that there is One Right Answer or a Right Procedure in the search for truth. They see that there are various ways of knowing and methods of analysis. They feel responsibility for examining, choosing, questioning, and developing the systems that they will use for constructing knowledge. Question-posing and problem-posing become prominent methods of inquiry, strategies that some researchers have identified with the "fifth" stage of thought beyond formal-operational or logical thought (Arlin, 1975; Kitchener, 1983; Labouvie-Vief, 1980). The woman tends not to rely as readily or exclusively on hypothetico-deductive inquiry, which posits an answer (the hypothesis) prior to data collection. She prefers to examine the basic assumptions and the conditions in which a problem is cast. She can take, and often insists upon taking, a position outside a particular context or frame of reference and looks back on "who" is asking the question, "why" the question is asked at all, and "how" answers are arrived at.

The way of knowing prized by most constructivist women is anything but detached. For these women, intimate knowledge of the self not only precedes but always accompanies understanding. They are intensely aware of how perceptions are processed through the complex web of personal meaning and values; they resist excluding the self from the process of knowing for the sake of simplicity or "objectivity." They strive to find a way of weaving their passions and their intellectual life into some meaningful whole. All the old polarities—self and others, thought and feeling, subjective and objective, public and private, personal and impersonal, love and work—lose their saliency. The constructivist mode of thought, in women at least, stresses integration and balance and inclusion rather than exclusion and parsimony.

As we noted in the last section, "opening oneself up to ideas" (or people or poems) is stressed by some women as a procedure for knowing, but the relative lack of self-knowledge prevents the procedural knower from finding points of connection between that which she is trying to understand and her own experience. At the position of constructed knowledge, women often describe themselves in terms that denote passionate or "connected knowing"—a union of the knower with that which is to be known. Empathic seeing and feeling with the other is a central feature in the development of connected knowing. The empathic potential—the capacity for what Weil (1951) calls "attentive love" and Ruddick (1980) identifies with "maternal thinking"—is particularly characteristic of constructivist women. They use the language of intimacy and care to describe relationships with ideas as well as with people. Communion and communication are established with that which one is trying to understand. Women use such images as "conversing with nature," "getting closer to ideas," "having rapport with my reading matter," and "communicating with an author" in order to understand, rather than more masculine images such as "pinning an idea down," "getting on top of ideas," or "seeing through an argument."

Dialogue is at the center of this way of knowing. A balance is found between speaking and listening. The women here are able to listen to others without silencing their own voice, whereas at other positions they attend to only one or the other. They make a distinction between conversing and what they call "really talking" by which they mean a reciprocal drawing out of each other's ideas and meanings. "Really talking" requires careful listening; it implies a mutually shared agreement that together you are creating the optimum setting so that emergent ideas can grow. This mode of talk is something similar to what Habermas (1973) has called "the ideal speech situation." "Real talk" reaches deep into the experience of each; it also draws on the analytical abilities of each. It is as important in the public as the private sharing of knowledge. To this end, the women strive for an exploration of assumptions and intersubjective reality rather than a one-way didactic stating of views. Domination is absent; reciprocity and cooperation predominate.

These women strive to gain a public as well as a private voice. They want to communicate to others the complexities of the world as they experience it. However, even among women who have found a voice, problems of voice abound. In a society such as ours that values the words of male authority and often dismisses the woman's voice as soft or misguided, constructivist women are no more immune to the experience of feeling silenced than any other group of women.

Needless to say, the women at this position set themselves a difficult task. They want always to be sensitive to context, to include rather than exclude, to listen as often as to speak, to stay open to the ideas of others, to engage in "real talk," and to reevaluate continually their basic assumptions as they acquire knowledge. They do not claim that they always succeed at this task. Most of the women learn to live with compromise and to soften ideals that they find are unworkable. Nevertheless, they set an example of a refreshing mixture of idealism and realism. More than any other group of women, they are seriously preoccupied with the moral or spiritual dimensions in their lives. They actively reflect on how their judgments, attitudes, and behavior coalesce into some internal experience of moral consistency. For most of these women, the moral response is a caring response; an opinion is a commitment, something to live by. Further, they strive to translate their moral commitments into action, both out of a conviction that "one must act" and out of a feeling of responsibility to the larger community in which they live.

Implications for Human Development

The epistemological taxonomy that we describe is, at this point in our work, a beginning attempt to understand the variety of perspectives from which women know and view the world. Our descriptive scheme provides a framework for further research on gender similarities and differences in ways of knowing and on life experiences that shape thought. Our study, based on interviews with women, represents both an extension and modification of Perry's scheme of developmental epistemology, which was derived primarily from interviews with Harvard men. We recognize that the five ways of knowing we identify are not necessarily fixed or exhaustive categories; that they are abstract categories that will not always capture the complexities and uniqueness of an individual woman's thought and life; that other people might organize their observations differently; and that the scheme itself awaits further study and validation. The addition of new populations of women might extend the number of categories or lead to their modification. And it will only be with the study of men and women from equally mixed class, ethnic, and educational backgrounds that comparisons between the sexes can be made.

In spite of these cautions, we believe that our study does allow us to raise important questions about women's development and thought and to draw some conclusions. It also provides a firmer grounding than existed before for speculation about when and why women's concepts of self and ways of knowing change.

Because we approached this study with questions about women's sense of competence and authority, we paid particular attention to that part of their stories that dealt with their experience in two of the major social institutions that affect human development: families and schools. In their struggle to develop their voices and minds and hold onto their values in a society that tends to devalue women and their ideas, many women falter, deny their potential and values, accommodate to the views and expectations of others, and suffer from feelings of inauthenticity and/or powerlessness. Some women find their way out of the morass of accommodations, retreat, and self-denial largely on their own initiative, but sometimes with the help of perceptive, responsive families and schools or social agencies.

The women's interviews were, of course, quite diverse, but as we read and reread their accounts of what they had learned and failed to learn, of how they like to learn and were forced to learn, some common themes emerged, themes that may be distinctly, although surely not exclusively, feminine. We shall touch briefly on some of these themes here; we develop them more fully elsewhere (Belenky et al., 1986).

Confirmation of the Self as a Knower

Our interviews have convinced us that every woman, regardless of age, social class, ethnicity, and academic achievement, needs to know that she is capable of intelligent thought, and needs to know it sooner rather than later. Many women told us of personal incidents of being doubted, overlooked, and teased for their intellectual efforts even in well-intentioned families and schools. . . .

Women who attended the more prestigious colleges in the sample and who had a history of privilege and achievement were still uncertain of their abilities. Achievement did not protect them from self-doubt. The need for confirmation was even more prominent among the less privileged women, many of whom had grown up being told they were stupid. Their views of themselves began to change when they came across "maternal" social agencies that refused to treat them as dumb. What these women needed and what the agencies provided—perhaps more clearly, consistently, and sincerely than any other institutions we sampled—was confirmation that they could be trusted to know, to learn, and to share this knowledge with others. For these women to discover that they had opinions and experience of value to others was a lesson that they had missed during all their years of formal education. Most of the women we interviewed, rich and poor, educated or not, made it clear that they did not wish to be told merely that they had the "capacity" or the "potential" to become knowledgeable or wise. They needed to know that they already knew something (though by no means everything), that there was something good inside. They worried that there wasn't.

In the masculine myth, confirmation comes not at the beginning of education but at the end. Confirmation as a thinker and membership in a community of thinkers come as the climax of Perry's (1970) story of intellectual development in the college years. The student learns, according to Perry, that "we must all stand judgment" and must earn "the privilege of having [our] ideas respected" (p. 33). Having proved beyond reasonable doubt that he has learned to think in complex, contextual ways, the young man is admitted to the fraternity of powerful knowers. Certified as a thinker, he becomes one of Them (now dethroned to lower-case them). This scenario may capture the "natural" course of men's development in traditional, hierarchical institutions, but it does not work for women. For women, confirmation and community are prerequisites rather than consequences of development.

Collaboration, Community, and Trust

Most women say they learn best in groups and prefer collaborative work. When they are isolated from those who know by a wall of silence or status, their talents for learning through the drawing out of others are left untapped. Opportunities to match experiences, reveal insecurities and obtain reassurance, and try out ideas without fear of ridicule are possible where trust exists. And trust exists in classrooms and groups in which the "believing" rather than "doubting" game is played (Elbow, 1973). As Elbow says, the doubting game involves "putting something on trial to see whether it is wanting or not" (p. 173). The teacher or student playing the doubting game looks for something wrong—a loophole, a factual error, a logical contradiction, an omission of contrary evidence. Good teachers and good parents, according to women, are believers. They trust their students' or children's thinking and encourage them to expand it.

But in the psychological literature concerning the factors promoting cognitive development, doubt has played a more prominent role than belief. People are said to be precipitated into states of cognitive conflict when, for example, their ideas are challenged by some external event, and the effort to resolve conflict leads to cognitive growth. We do not deny that cognitive conflict can act as an impetus to growth; all of us can attest to such experiences in our own lives. But in our interviews, only a handful of women described a powerful and positive learning experience in which the teacher aggressively challenged their notions. Because so many women are already consumed with self-doubt, doubts imposed from outside seem at best redundant ("I'm always reprimanding myself") and at worst destructive, confirming women's own sense of themselves as inadequate knowers. This doubting model of teaching, then, may be particularly inappropriate for women, although we are not convinced that it is appropriate for men either.

Firsthand Experience

In considering how to design an education appropriate for women, suppose we were to begin by asking, simply: What does a woman know? Traditional courses do not begin there. They begin not with the student's knowledge but with the teacher's knowledge. Most of the women we interviewed, however, were drawn to the sort of knowledge that comes from firsthand observation, whereas most of the institutions they attended emphasized abstract out-of-context learning. The women spoke as often of the way students interacted in classes as of the course content; they were often more concerned about another's pride or shame than whether he or she supplied good answers; they were relieved when they could find some connection between the course material and their own experience.

For many women, the most powerful learning experiences took place out of school. The mothers usually name childbearing or child-rearing. The kind of knowledge that is gained in child-rearing is typical of the kind of knowledge that women value and schools do not. Ruddick (1980) has argued that "maternal thought" has rules of evidence and criteria for truth, just as do more esteemed modes of thought accepted with academic disciplines. The knowledge of mothers comes not from words but from action and observation, and much of it has never been translated into words, only into actions. As the philosopher Carol McMillan (1982) has noted, this kind of knowledge does not necessarily lead to general propositions. Good mothering, for instance, requires adaptive responding to changing phenomena; it is tuned to the concrete and particular. Mothers are understandably hesitant about "concocting theories about how other people should bring up their children" (McMillan, 1982). Most women are not opposed to abstractions per se. They find concepts useful as ways of making sense of their experiences, but they balk when the abstractions precede the experiences or push them out entirely. Even the women who were extraordinarily adept at abstract reasoning preferred to start with personal experience.

It should come as no surprise that the courses most often mentioned by women as powerful learning experiences were those that helped them translate private experience into a shared public language (for instance, courses on feminist theory or courses requiring the sharing of journals) and courses that provided experiential opportunities (for instance, collecting interviews from old-timers in the study of small-town life or co-managing a student theatrical group).

Models for Learning: Sharing and Listening

There is considerable evidence that parents who enter into a dialogue with their children, who draw out and respect their children's opinions, are more likely to have children whose intellectual and ethical development proceeds rapidly and surely (Baumrind, 1971; Haan, Smith and Block, 1968; Hauser et al., 1984; Lickona, 1983). Among our women, only the constructivists and a few procedural knowers described both parents as good listeners. Most women at the other positions came from families in which relationships among family members were hierarchical, with talking and listening unevenly divided between the members. Typically the husband spoke, the women and children listened. In these conventionally ordered families, fathers were depicted as being more like conventional teachers—bent on handing out truths; mothers were more like students—listening and trying to understand. The daughters from such families described themselves as students in much the same terms—obediently attentive students before all-wise lecturers. Constructivists, however, painted a different picture of their families and had a different vision of what makes a good teacher. They noticed and valued mothers who had gained a voice and fathers who had developed a listening ear. So, too, these women valued teachers who showed that they could both think and feel, that they could both speak and listen, that they could both teach and learn.

It can be argued, of course, that students need models of impeccable reasoning, that it is through imitating such models that students learn to reason. Perhaps. But none of the women we interviewed named this sort of learning as a powerful experience in their own lives. They did mention deflation of authority as a powerful learning experience. Women have been taught by generations of men that males have greater powers of rationality than females have. When a male professor presents only the impeccable products of his thinking, it is especially difficult for a woman student to believe that she could have produced such a thought. And it must be remembered that in spite of the women's movement, most of the teachers are still male, although more than half of the students are now female. Female students need opportunities to watch how female professors solve (and fail to solve) problems and male professors fail to solve (and succeed in solving) problems. They need role models of thinking as a human activity—as imperfect, yet attainable.

Growth and Change

Based on our research, it appears that women's intellectual growth and shifts in self-concept and worldview are often tied to events beyond classroom and parental teaching—events such as child-bearing and child-rearing, crises of self-doubt and feelings of inauthenticity, value conflicts in relationships, and the failure of male authority on whom the woman has depended. The fact that even well-intentioned families and teachers can hinder, as well as support, women's development has led us to question conventional assumptions about the education of women. In this chapter, we have touched on some correctives to educational practice that would benefit women, and perhaps men as well.

Significant developmental change, according to women's retrospective accounts, often occurs in middle adulthood. These transition points are accompanied by major shifts in the woman's assessment of her value, options, goals, and responsibilities. Most women experience a tremendous sense of growth as they begin to move away from silence and social stereotypes and rely on inner resources for knowing. For some, subjective knowing may be a stopping point and the predominant epistemology for much of their lives because reliance on inner authority provides a security that they need and hold on to. Other women, who have also come to value the power of rational and objective thought, gain a new sense of internal cohesion when they can find ways to balance subjective/intuitive and objective/rational knowledge. It is clear from our data that women's sense of self and voice flourish when they become what we call connected and passionate knowers. We argue that educators can help women develop their minds and authentic voices if they emphasize connection over separation, understanding and acceptance over assessment, collaboration over competition, and discussion over debate, and if they accord respect to and allow time for the knowledge that emerges from first-hand experience. We have learned these things by listening to the woman's voice.

References

Arlin, P. "Cognitive Development in Adulthood." *Developmental Psychology,* 11(1975): 602–606.

Baumrind, D. "Current Patterns and Parental Authority." *Developmental Psychology Monographs,* 4 (1, Pt. 2, 1971).

Belenky, M., B. Clinchy, N. Goldberger and J. Tarule. *Women's Ways of Knowing: The Development of Self, Voice, and Mind.* New York: Basic Books, 1986.

Belenky, M., J. Tarule and A. Landa, editors. *Education and Development.* Washington, DC: National Teachers Corp., 1979.

Chodorow, N. *The Reproduction of Mothering.* Berkeley: University of California Press, 1978.

Colby, A., L. Kohlberg, D. Candee, J. C. Gibbs, R. Hewer, K. Kaufman, C. Power and B. Speicher-Dubin. *Assessing Moral Judgments: A Manual.* New York: Cambridge University Press, 1983.

Elbow, P. *Writing Without Teachers.* London: Oxford University Press, 1973.

Gilligan, C. "In a Different Voice: Women's Conceptions of Self and of Morality." *Harvard Educational Review*, 47 (1977): 431–46.

Gilligan, C. "Woman's Place in Man's Life Cycle." *Harvard Educational Review*, 49 (1979): 431–46.

Gilligan, C. *In a Different Voice: Psychological Theory and Women's Development.* Cambridge, MA: Harvard University Press, 1982.

Haan, N., M. B. Smith and J. Block. "The Moral Reasoning of Young Adults: Political-Social Behavior, Family Background, and Personality Correlates." *Journal of Personality and Social Psychology*, 10 (1968): 183–201.

Habermas, J. *Legitimation Crisis*. Boston: Beacon Press, 1973.

Hauser, S., S. I. Powers, G. Noam, A. M. Jacobsen, B. Weiss, and D. J. Follansbee. "Familial Contexts of Adolescent Ego Development." *Child Development*, 55 (1984): 195–213.

Keller, E. and C. R. Grontkowski. "The Mind's Eye." In S. Harding and M. Hintikka, editors, *Discovering Reality*. Dordrecht, Holland: Reidel, 1983.

Kitchener, K. "Cognition, Metacognition, and Epistemic Cognition: A Three-Level Model of Cognitive Processing." *Human Development*, 26 (1983): 222–32.

Kohlberg, L. *The Psychology of Moral Development*. New York. Harper & Row, 1984.

Labouvie-Vief, G. "Beyond Formal Operations: Uses and Limits of Pure Logic in Life-Span Development." *Human Development*, 3 (1980): 141–61.

Lickona, T. *Raising Good Children: Helping Your Children Through the Stages of Moral Development*. New York: Bantam, 1983.

Lyons, N. "Two Perspectives on Self, Relationships and Morality." *Harvard Educational Review*, 53 (1983): 125–45.

McMillan, C. *Women, Reason, and Nature*. Princeton, NJ: Princeton University Press, 1982.

Miller, J. B. *Towards a New Psychology of Women*. Boston: Beacon Press, 1976.

Perry, W. G. *Forms of Intellectual and Ethical Development in the College Years*. New York: Holt, Rinehart & Winston, 1970.

Perry, W. G. "Cognitive and Ethical Growth: The Making of Meaning." In A. Chickering, editor, *The Modern American College*. San Francisco: Jossey-Bass, 1981.

Piaget, J. *The Moral Judgment of the Child*. New York: Free Press, 1965. Original work published in 1932.

Ruddick, S. "Maternal Thinking." *Feminist Studies*, 6 (1980): 70–96.

Ruddick, S. "New Combinations: Learning from Virginia Woolf." In C. Asher, L. DeSalvor and S. Ruddick, *Between Women*. Boston: Beacon Press, 1984.

Ruddick, S. and P. Daniels, editors. *Working it Out*. New York: Pantheon Books, 1977.

Weil, S. "Reflections on the Right Use of School Studies with a View to the Love of God." In S. Weil, *Waiting for God*. New York: Harper Colophon Books, 1951.

Larry Collins is Associate Professor of Spanish at the College of St. Catherine. He earned his Ph.D. from the University of Minnesota in 1968 (Medieval Spanish/Romance Linguistics). Before coming to CSC he taught at the UMN and UCO. He is interested in foreign study, international affairs, Spanish, and GSJ.

Critical Thinking

Larry Collins

Perhaps the single most frustrating aspect of dealing with justice is "Whom does one believe?" Which of the scholarly works do we accept, those of the liberal left, or those of the more conservative right?

Even more crucial than *what* we believe is *why* we believe it. One of the characteristics of an educated person should be the ability to explain why one believes in a certain point of view, rather than merely accepting uncritically what one is told. Obviously, no one is born with that ability. Some are born, as Ernest Hemingway has said, "with an ability to learn in a quicker ration to the passage of time," but it appears that, at one point or another, we must all *develop* the ability to think critically.

Within each academic discipline there exists a methodology, a set of procedures which, if followed, represent an attempt to arrive at objective, well-reasoned points of view. If we analyze these different methodologies (the historical method, the scientific approach, etc.) we will see that most of them share certain basic features:

- observation
- collection of data/facts
- evaluation of data/facts
- objectivity/suspending judgment
- working (tentative) hypothesis/analysis/synthesis
- statement of the problem (theory)
- causes of the problem
- goal/desired outcome
- possible solutions/courses of action
- assessment/evaluation of actions
- looking for bias in one's own thinking
- a willingness to change one's position, based on new evidence

In addition, there are certain "checks" which one can apply to one's own thinking. Although these checks are no guarantee of critical thought, they will, if applied *sincerely*, help to lead one along that path.

- *symptoms of the problem*: How are we aware that there is, in fact, a problem?

- *collection of data/facts*: What data / facts do we have to support our contention that there is a problem?

- *sources of information/authorities:* What are the sources of our information? Who are the authorities? How do we judge their reliability? How do the sources reveal biases by use of language (adjectives, emotion-filled terms, ideological "catch-phrases")?

- *objectivity/suspending judgment:* How well do we resist the temptation to prejudge? Do we stand back, removed from the issue? How involved are we from a personal, emotional point of view? Have we already made up our minds? Are we "bending" the facts to fit a conclusion we have already reached?

- *tentative (working) hypothesis/analysis/synthesis:* How willing am I to formulate a working hypothesis, analyze all the aspects of the problem within the context of that hypothesis, question the thesis (antithesis), and synthesize all aspects into a tentative statement of the problem? How willing am I to then question that tentative statement of the problem, and change it, if warranted?

- *statement of the problem (theory/thesis):*
  assumptions: What are the assumptions of my argument? Are those assumptions valid?

- *argumentation:*
  comprehensiveness: How complete is my argument? How well does it explain all the data? Does it account for (interpret) all events?

  consistency/contradiction: Does my argument "hold together"? Are there contradictions in what I say? Are my assumptions, my statements and my conclusions consistent?

  implications: What are the implications if this point of view is correct?

  logic: What is the particular method of explanation/understanding in my argument? What "laws" of thinking are implied? Where is the burden of proof? What is allowable as proof?

  evidence: How do I distinguish between fact and opinion? What evidence do I provide to support my argument? What kind of evidence is included/excluded? Should it be included/excluded?

  open-mindedness: Do I have biases in my thinking and reasoning? How do I guard against my biases? Am I *convinced* of a position?

How do I guard against the "danger of conviction," and attempt to introduce the "principle of uncertainty" into my deliberations?

intellectual honesty: Do I ignore (am I unwilling to consider) facts which are contrary to my point of view? Do I reject a valid argument because of the place of its origin (Marxism, for example)?

self-interest: Why do I think as I do? What is in it for me? Am I taking my position because of an objective analysis of the facts, out of ignorance, or because of my own self-interest? What are the self-interests of others' positions? What are their motivations?

- *conclusions:*
  Do my conclusions fit the facts, or am I attempting to find (bend) facts to fit a conclusion which I have already reached?

  conscious/unconscious thinking: How aware am I of the reasons for my position? Am I objectively analyzing the situation, or am I influenced by social and cultural traits and "myths" which I have absorbed by virtue of being born into a certain culture and being raised in a certain society?

  search for truth: Am I being completely honest with myself? Am I really searching for the truth of the matter? How will the truth affect me?

In considering justice, we would do well to ask ourselves how the sources of information are viewing the matter. Does the proposed explanation attempt to *ignore, eliminate* or *resolve* the problems? Does it consider the possibility that the problems, or similar problems, could be *avoided?*

Annette T. Rottenberg is a writer and philosopher whose books include Elements of Argument *(a text and reader), 1994, and* The Structure of Argument, *1994.*

from Elements of Argument

Annette T. Rottenberg

Chapter 1: Introduction to Argument

The Nature of Argument

A conversation overheard in the school cafeteria:

"Hey, how come you didn't order the meat loaf special? It's pretty good today."

"Well, I read this book about vegetarianism, and I've decided to give up meat. The book says meat's unhealthy and vegetarians live longer."

"Don't be silly. Americans eat lots of meat, and we're living longer and longer."

"Listen, this book tells how much healthier the Danes were during World War II because they couldn't get meat."

"I don't believe it. A lot of these health books are written by quacks. It's pretty dumb to change your diet after reading one book."

These people are having what most of us would call an argument, one that sounds dangerously close to a quarrel. There are, however, significant differences between the colloquial meaning of argument as a quarrel and its definition as a process of reasoning and advancing proof, although even the exchange reported above exhibits some of the characteristics of formal argument. The kinds of arguments we deal with in this text are not quarrels. They often resemble ordinary discourse about controversial issues. You may, for example, overhear a conversation like this one:

"This morning while I was trying to eat breakfast I heard an announcer describing the execution of that guy in Texas who raped and murdered a teen-aged couple. They gave him an injection, and it took him ten minutes to die. I almost lost my breakfast listening to it."

"Well, he deserved it. He didn't show much pity for his victims, did he?"

"Okay, but no matter what he did, capital punishment is really awful, barbaric. It's murder, even if the state does it."

"No, I'd call it justice. I don't know what else we can do to show how we feel about a cruel, pointless murder of innocent people. The punishment ought to be as terrible as we can make it."

167

Each speaker is defending a value judgment about an issue that tests ideas of good and evil, right and wrong, and that cannot be decided by facts.

In another kind of argument the speaker or writer proposes a solution for a specific problem. Two men, both aged twenty, are engaged in a conversation.

> *"I'm going to be broke this week after I pay my car insurance. I don't think it's fair for males under twenty to pay such high rates. I'm a good driver, much better than my older sister. Why not consider driving experience instead of age or sex?"*

> *"But I always thought that guys our age had the most accidents. How do you know that driving experience is the right standard to apply?"*

> *"Well, I read a report by the Highway Commission that said it's really driving experience that counts. So I think it's unfair for us to be discriminated against. The law's behind the times. They ought to change the insurance laws."*

In this case someone advocates a policy that appears to fulfill a desirable goal—making it impossible to discriminate against drivers just because they are young and male. Objections arise that the arguer must attempt to answer.

In these three dialogues, . . . human beings are engaged in explaining and defending their own actions and beliefs and opposing those of others. They do this for at least two reasons: to justify what they do and think both to themselves and to their opponents and, in the process, to solve problems and make decisions, especially those dependent on a consensus between conflicting views.

● ● ●

The Terms of Argument

One definition of argument, emphasizing audience, [is]: "Argumentation is the art of influencing others, through the medium of reasoned discourse, to believe or act as we wish them to believe or act." A distinction is sometimes made between argument and persuasion. Argument, according to most authorities, gives primary importance to logical appeals. Persuasion introduces the element of ethical and emotional appeals. The difference is one of emphasis. In real-life arguments about social policy, the distinction is hard to measure. In this book we use the term *argument* to represent forms of discourse that attempt to persuade readers or listeners to accept a claim, whether acceptance is based on logical or emotional appeals or, as is usually the case, on both. The following brief definition includes other elements: *An argument is a statement or statements offering support for a claim.*

An argument is composed of at least three parts: the claim, the support, and the warrant.[1]

The Claim

The claim (also called a *proposition*) answers the question "What are you trying to prove?" It may appear as the thesis statement of your essay, although in some arguments it may not be stated directly. There are three principal kinds of claim (discussed more fully in Chapter 2): claims of fact, of value, and of policy. (The three dialogues at the beginning of this chapter represent these three kinds of claim respectively.) *Claims of fact* assert that a condition has existed, exists, or will exist and are based on facts or data that the audience will accept as being objectively verifiable:

> The present cocaine epidemic is not unique. From 1885 to the 1920's, cocaine was as widely used as it is today.
>
> Horse racing is the most dangerous sport.
>
> California will experience colder, stormier weather for the next ten years.

All these claims must be supported by data. Although the last example is an inference or an educated guess about the future, a reader will probably find the prediction credible if the data seem authoritative.

Claims of value attempt to prove that some things are more or less desirable than others. They express approval or disapproval of standards of taste and morality. Advertisements and reviews of cultural events are one common source of value claims, but such claims emerge whenever people argue about what is good or bad, beautiful or ugly.

> One look and Crane [writing paper] says you have a tasteful writing style.
>
> *Tannhäuser* provides a splendid viewing as well as listening experience.
>
> Football is one of the most dehumanizing experiences a person can face. —Dave Meggyesy
>
> Ending a patient's life intentionally is absolutely forbidden on moral grounds.—Presidential Commission on Medical Ethics, 1983

Claims of policy assert that special policies should be instituted as solutions to problems. The expression *should, must,* or *ought to* usually appears in the statement.

> Prisons should be abolished because they are crime-manufacturing concerns.
>
> Our first step must be to immediately establish and advertise drastic policies designed to bring our own population under control.—Paul Ehrlich, biologist

The New York City Board of Education should make sure that qualified women appear on any new list [of candidates for Chancellor of Education].

Policy claims call for analysis of both fact and value.

The Support

Support consists of the materials used by the arguer to convince an audience that his or her claim is sound. These materials include *evidence* and *motivational appeals*. The evidence or data consists of facts, statistics, and testimony from experts. The motivational appeals are the ones that the arguer makes to the values and attitudes of the audience to win support for the claim. The word *motivational* points out that these appeals are the reasons that move an audience to accept a belief or adopt a course of action. For example, in his argument advocating population control, Ehrlich first offered statistical evidence to prove the magnitude of the population explosion. But he also made a strong appeal to the generosity of his audience to persuade them to sacrifice their own immediate interests to those of future generations.

The Warrant

The warrant is an inference or assumption, a belief or principle that is taken for granted. A warrant is a guarantee of reliability; in argument it guarantees the soundness of the relationship between the support and the claim. It allows the reader to make the connection between the support and the claim.

Warrants or assumptions underlie all the claims we make. They may be stated or unstated. If the arguer believes that the audience shares his assumption, he may feel it unnecessary to express it. But if he thinks that the audience is doubtful or hostile, he may decide to state the assumption in order to emphasize its importance or argue for its validity.

This is how the warrant works. In the dialogue beginning this chapter, one speaker made the claim that vegetarianism was more healthful than a diet containing meat. As support he offered the evidence that the authors of a book he had read recommended vegetarianism for greater health and longer life. He did not state his warrant—that the authors of the book were trustworthy guides to theories of healthful diet. In outline form the argument looks like this:

CLAIM: Adoption of a vegetarian diet leads to healthier and longer life.

SUPPORT: The authors of *Becoming a Vegetarian Family* say so.

WARRANT: The authors of *Becoming a Vegetarian Family* are reliable sources of information on diet.

A writer or speaker may also need to offer support for the warrant. In the case cited above, the second speaker is reluctant to accept the unstated warrant, suggesting that the authors may be quacks. The first speaker will need to provide support for the assumption that the authors are trustworthy, perhaps by introducing proof of their credentials in science and medicine. Notice that although the second speaker accepts the evidence, he cannot agree that the claim has been proved unless he also accepts the warrant. If he fails to accept the warrant—that is, if he refuses to believe that the authors are credible sources of information about diet—then the evidence cannot support the claim.

The following example demonstrates how a different kind of warrant, based on values, can also lead an audience to accept a claim.

CLAIM: Laws making marijuana illegal should be repealed.

SUPPORT: People should have the right to use any substance they wish.

WARRANT: No laws should prevent citizens from exercising their rights.

Support for repeal of the marijuana laws often consists of medical evidence that marijuana is harmless. Here, however, the arguer contends that an important ethical principle is at work: Nothing should prevent people from exercising their rights, including the right to use any substance, no matter how harmful. Let us suppose that the reader agrees with the supporting statement, that individuals should have the right to use any substance. But in order to accept the claim, the reader must also agree with the principle expressed in the warrant, that government should not interfere with the individual's right. He or she can then agree that laws making marijuana illegal should be repealed. Notice that this warrant, like all warrants, certifies that the relationship between the support and the claim is sound.

One more element of argument remains to be considered—*definition*. Definition, of course, is important in all forms of exposition, but it can be crucial in argument. For this reason we've devoted a whole chapter to it in this text. Many of the controversial questions you will encounter in your reading about public affairs are primarily arguments about the definition of terms. Such terms as *abortion, pornography, equality, poverty,* and *insanity* must be defined before useful public policies about them can be formulated.

The Audience

All arguments are composed with an audience in mind. We have already pointed out that an argument is an implicit dialogue or exchange. Often the writer of an argument about a public issue is responding to another writer or speaker who had made a claim that needs to be supported or opposed. In writing your own arguments, you should assume that there is a reader who may not agree with you. . . .

Speechmakers are usually better informed than writers about their audience. Some writers, however, are familiar with the specific persons or groups who will read their arguments; advertising copywriters are a conspicuous example. They discover their audiences through sophisticated polling and marketing techniques and direct their messages to a well targeted group of prospective buyers. Other professionals may be required to submit reports to persuade a specific and clearly defined audience of certain beliefs or courses of action: An engineer may be asked by an environmental interest group to defend his plans for the building of a sewage treatment plant; or a town planner may be called on to tell the town council why she believes that rent control may not work; or a sales manager may find it necessary to explain to his superior why a new product should be launched in the Midwest rather than the South.

In such cases the writer asks some or all of the following questions about the audience:

> Why has this audience requested this report? What do they want to get out of it?
>
> How much do they already know about the subject?
>
> Are they divided or agreed on the subject?
>
> What is their emotional involvement with the issues?

Assessing Credibility

Providing abundant evidence and making logical connections between the parts of an argument may not be enough to win agreement from an audience. In fact, success in convincing an audience is almost always inseparable from the writer's credibility, or the audience's belief in the writer's trustworthiness. Aristotle, the Greek philosopher who wrote a treatise on argument that has influenced its study and practice for more than two thousand years, considered credibility—what he called *ethos*—the most important element in the arguer's ability to persuade the audience to accept his or her claim.

Aristotle named "intelligence, character, and good will" as the attributes that produce credibility. Today we might describe these qualities somewhat differently, but the criteria for judging a writer's credibility remain essentially the same. First, the writer must convince the audience that he is knowledgeable, that he is as well informed as possible about the subject. Second, he must persuade his audience that he is not only truthful in the presentation of his evidence but also morally upright and dependable. Third, he must show that, as an arguer with good intentions, he has considered the interests and needs of others as well as his own.

As an example in which the credibility of the arguer is at stake, consider a wealthy Sierra Club member who lives on ten acres of a magnificent oceanside estate and who appears before a community planning board to argue against future development of the area. His claim is that more building will destroy the delicate ecological balance of the area. The board, acting in the interests of all the citizens of the community, will ask themselves: Has the arguer proved that his information about environmental impact is complete and accurate? Has he demonstrated that he sincerely desires to preserve the wilderness, not merely his own privacy and space? And has he also made clear that he has considered the needs and desires of those who might want to live in a housing development by the ocean? If the answers to all these questions are yes, then the board will hear the arguer with respect, and the arguer will have begun to establish his credibility.

A reputation for intelligence, character, and goodwill is not often won overnight. And it can be lost more quickly than it is won. Once a writer or speaker has betrayed an audience's belief in her character or judgment, she may find it difficult to persuade an audience to accept subsequent claims, no matter how sound her data and reasoning are. "We give no credit to a liar," said Cicero, "even when he speaks the truth."

Political life is full of examples of lost and squandered credibility. After it was discovered that President Lyndon Johnson had deceived the American public about U.S. conduct in the Vietnam War, he could not regain his popularity. After Senator Edward Kennedy failed to persuade the public that he had behaved honorably at Chappaquiddick, his influence and power in the Democratic party declined. After President Gerald Ford pardoned former President Richard Nixon for his complicity in the Watergate scandal, Ford was no longer a serious candidate for reelection.

We can see the practical consequences when an audience realizes that an arguer has been guilty of a deception—misusing facts and authority, suppressing evidence, distorting statistics, violating the rules of logic. But suppose the arguer is successful in concealing his or her manipulation of the data and can persuade an uninformed audience to take the action or adopt the idea that he or she recommends. Even supposing that the argument promotes a "good" cause, is the arguer justified in using evasive or misleading tactics?

The answer is no. To encourage another person to make a decision on the basis of incomplete or dishonestly used data is profoundly unethical. It indicates lack of respect for the rights of others—their right to know at least as much as you do about the subject, to be allowed to judge and compare, to disagree with you if they challenge your own interests. If the moral implications are still not clear, try to imagine yourself not as the perpetrator of the lie but as the victim.

There is also a danger in measuring success wholly by the degree to which audiences accept our arguments. Both as writers and readers, we must be able to respect the claim, or proposition, and what it tries to demonstrate. Toulmin has said: "To conclude that a proposition is true, it is not enough to know that this man or that finds it 'credible': the proposition itself must be *worthy* of credence."[2]

Acquiring Credibility

You may wonder how you can acquire credibility. You are not yet an expert in many of the subjects you will deal with in assignments, although you are knowledgeable about many other things, including your cultural and social activities. But there are several ways in which you can create confidence by your treatment of topics derived from academic disciplines, such as politics, psychology, economics, sociology, and art, on which most assignments will be based.

First, you can submit evidence of careful research, demonstrating that you have been conscientious in finding the best authorities, giving credit, and attempting to arrive at the truth. Second, you can adopt a thoughtful and judicious tone that reflects a desire to be fair in your conclusion. Tone expresses the attitude of the writer toward his or her subject. When the writer feels strongly about the subject and adopts a belligerent or complaining tone, for example, he or she forgets that readers who feel differently may find the tone disagreeable and unconvincing. In the following excerpt a student expresses his feelings about standard grading, that is, grading by letter or number on a scale that applies to a whole group.

> You go to school to learn, not to earn grades. To be educated, that's what they tell you. "He's educated, he graduated Magna Cum Laude." What makes a Magna Cum Laude man so much better than a man that graduates with a C? They are both still educated, aren't they? No one has a right to call someone less educated because they got a C instead of an A. Let's take both men and put them in front of a car. Each car has something wrong with it. Each man must fix his broken car. Our C man goes right to work while our Magna Cum Laude man hasn't got the slightest idea where to begin. Who's more educated now?

Probably a reader who disagreed with the claim—that standard grading should not be used—would find the tone, if not the evidence itself, unpersuasive. The writer sounds as if he is defending his own ability to do something that an honors graduate can't do, while ignoring the acknowledged purposes of standard grading in academic subjects. He sounds, moreover, as if he's angry because someone has done him an injury. Compare the preceding passage to the following one, written by a student on the same subject.

> Grades are the play money in a university Monopoly game. As long as the tokens are offered, the temptation will be largely irresistible to play for them. Students are so busy taking notes, doing tests, and getting tokens that they have forgotten to ask: Of what worth is all this? Or perhaps they ask and the grade is their answer.
>
> One certainly learns something in the passive lecture-note-read-note-test process: how to do it all more efficiently next time (in the hope of eventually owning Boardwalk and Park Place). As Marshall McLuhan has said, we learn what we do. In this process most students come to view learning as studying and remembering what other people have learned. They assume that knowledge is logically and for practical reasons divided up into discrete pieces called "disciplines" and that the highest knowledge is achieved by specializing in a discipline. By getting good grades in a lot of disciplines they conclude they have learned a lot. They have indeed, and it is too bad.[3]

Most readers would consider this writer more credible, in part because he has adopted a tone that seems moderate and impersonal. That is, he does not convey the impression that he is interested only in defending his own grades. Notice also that the language of this passage suggests a higher level of learning and research.

Sometimes, of course, an expression of anger or even outrage is appropriate and morally justified. But if readers do not share your sense of outrage, you must try to reach them through a more moderate approach. In his autobiography, Benjamin Franklin recounted his attempts to acquire the habit of temperate language in argument:

> Retaining . . . the habit of expressing myself in terms of modest diffidence; . . . never using, when I advanced anything that may possibly be disputed, the words "*certainly, undoubtedly,*" or any others that give the air of positiveness to an opinion; but rather say, I conceive or apprehend a thing to be so and so; it appears to me, *I should think it is so or so*, for such and such reasons; or *I imagine it to be so*; or *it is so, if I am not mistaken*. This habit, I believe, has been of great advantage to me when I have had occasion to inculcate my opinions, and persuade men into measures that I have been from time to time engaged in promoting.[4]

This is not to say that the writer must hedge his or her opinions or confess uncertainty at every point. Franklin suggests that the writer must recognize that other opinions may also have validity and that, although the writer may disagree, he or she respects the other opinions. Such an attitude will also dispose the reader to be more generous in evaluating the writer's argument.

A final method of establishing credibility is to produce a clean, literate, well-organized paper, with evidence of care in writing and proofreading. Such a paper will help persuade the reader to take your efforts seriously.

Chapter 2: Claims

Claims, or propositions, represent answers to the question: "'What are you trying to prove?" Although they are the conclusions of your arguments, they often appear as thesis statements. Claims can be classified as *claims of fact*, *claims of value*, and *claims of policy*.

Claims of Fact

Claims of fact assert that a condition has existed, exists, or will exist and their support consists of factual information—that is, information such as statistics, examples, and testimony that most responsible observers assume can be verified.

Many facts are not matters for argument. Our own senses can confirm them, and other observers will agree about them. We can argue that a certain number of students were in the classroom at a particular time, that lions make a louder sound than kittens, and that apples are sweeter than potatoes.

We can also agree about information that most of us can rarely confirm for ourselves—information in reference books, atlases, almanacs, and telephone directories; data from scientific resources about the physical world; and happenings reported in the media. We can agree on the reliability of such information because we trust the observers who report it.

However, the factual map is constantly being redrawn by new data in such fields as history and science that cause us to reevaluate our conclusions. For example, the discovery of the Dead Sea Scrolls in 1947 revealed that some books of the Bible—*Isaiah*, for one—were far older than we had thought. Researchers at New York Hospital-Cornell Medical Center say that many symptoms previously thought inevitable in the aging process are now believed to be treatable and reversible symptoms of depression.[5]

In your conversations with other students you probably generate claims of fact every day, some of which can be verified without much effort, others of which are more difficult to substantiate.

> CLAIM: Most of the students in this class come from towns within fifty miles of Boston.

To prove this the arguer would need only to ask the students in the class where they come from.

CLAIM: Students who take their courses Pass/Fail make lower grades than those who take them for specific grades.

In this case the arguer would need to have access to student records showing the specific grades given by instructors. (In most schools the instructor awards a letter grade, which is then recorded as a Pass or a Fail if the student has elected this option.)

CLAIM : The Red Sox will win the pennant this year.

This claim is different from the others because it is an opinion about what will happen in the future. But it can be verified (in the future) and is therefore classified as a claim of fact.

More complex factual claims about political and scientific matters remain controversial because proof on which all or most observers will agree is difficult or impossible to obtain.

CLAIM : The nuclear arsenal of the Soviet Union exceeds that of the United States.

CLAIM: The only life in the universe exists on this planet.

Not all claims are so neatly stated or make such unambiguous assertions. Because we recognize that there are exceptions to most generalizations, we often qualify our claims with words such as *generally, usually, probably, as a rule*. It would not be true to state flatly, for example, "College graduates earn more than high school graduates." This statement is generally true, but we know that some high school graduates who are electricians or city bus drivers or sanitation workers earn more than college graduates who are schoolteachers or nurses or social workers. In making such a claim, therefore, the writer should qualify it with a word that limits the claim.

To support a claim of fact, the writer needs to produce sufficient and appropriate data, that is, examples, statistics, and testimony from reliable sources. Provided this requirement is met, the task of establishing a factual claim would seem to be relatively straightforward. But as you have probably already discovered in ordinary conversation, finding convincing support for factual claims can pose a number of problems. Whenever you try to establish a claim of fact, you will need to ask at least three questions about the material you plan to use: What are sufficient and appropriate data? Who are the reliable authorities? and Have I made clear whether my statements are facts or inferences?

Sufficient and Appropriate Data

The amount and kind of data for a particular argument depend on the importance and complexity of the subject. The more controversial the subject, the more facts and testimony you will need to supply. Consider the claim "The nuclear arsenal of the Soviet Union is greater than that of the United States." If you want to prove the truth of this claim, obviously you will have to provide a larger quantity of data than for a claim that says "By following three steps, you can train your dog to sit and heel in fifteen minutes." In examining your facts and opinions, an alert reader will want to know if they are accurate, current, and typical of other facts and opinions that you have not mentioned.

The reader will also look for testimony from more than one authority, although there may be cases where only one or two experts, because they have achieved a unique breakthrough in their field, will be sufficient. These cases would probably occur most frequently in the physical sciences. The Nobel Prize winners James Watson and Francis Crick, who first discovered the structure of the DNA molecule, are an example of such experts. However, in the case of the so-called Hitler diaries that surfaced in 1983, at least a dozen experts—journalists, historians, bibliographers who could verify the age of the paper and the ink—were needed to establish that they were forgeries.

Reliable Authorities

Not all those who pronounce themselves experts are trustworthy. Your own experience has probably taught you cannot always believe the reports of an event by a single witness. The witness may be poorly trained to make accurate observations—about the size of a crowd, the speed of a vehicle, his distance from an object. Or his own physical conditions—illness, intoxication, disability—may prevent him from seeing or hearing or smelling accurately. The circumstances under which he observes the event—darkness, confusion, noise—may also impair his observation. In addition, the witness may be biased for or against the outcome of the event, as in a hotly contested baseball game, where the observer sees the play that he wants to see. You will find the problems associated with the biases of witnesses to be relevant to your work as a reader and writer of argumentative essays.

You will undoubtedly want to quote authors in some of your arguments. In most cases you will not be familiar with the authors. But there are guidelines for determining their reliability: the rank or title of the experts, the acceptance of their publications by other experts, their association with reputable universities, research centers, or think tanks. For example, for a paper on euthanasia, you might decide to quote from an article by Paul Ramsey, identified as the Harrington Spear Paine Professor of Religion at Princeton University. For a paper on prison reform you might want to use material supplied by Tom Murton, a professional penologist, formerly superintendent in the Arkansas prison system, now professor of criminology at the University of Minnesota. Most readers of your arguments would agree that these authors have impressive credentials in their fields.

What if several respectable sources are in conflict? What if the experts disagree? After a preliminary investigation of a controversial subject, you may decide that you have sufficient material to support your claim. But if you read further, you may discover that other material presented by equally qualified experts contradicts your original claim. In such circumstances you will find it impossible to make a definitive claim. [Later], in the treatment of support of a claim by evidence, you will find a more elaborate discussion of this vexing problem.

Facts or Inferences

We have defined a fact as a statement that can be verified. An inference is "a statement about the unknown on the basis of the known."[6] The difference between facts and inferences is important to you as the writer of an argument because an inference is an *interpretation,* or an opinion reached after informed evaluation of evidence. As you and your classmates wait in your classroom on the first day of the semester, a middle-aged woman wearing a tweed jacket and a corduroy skirt appears and stands in front of the room. You don't know who this woman is. However, based on what you do know about the appearance of many college teachers and the fact that teachers usually stand in front of the classroom, you may *infer* that this woman is your teacher. You will probably be right. But you cannot be certain until you have more information. Perhaps you will find out that this woman has come from the department office to tell you that your teacher is sick and cannot meet the class today.

You have probably come across a statement such as the following in a newspaper or magazine: "Excessive television viewing has caused the steady decline in the reading ability of children and teenagers." Presented this way, the statement is clearly intended to be read as a factual claim that has been or can be proved. But it is an inference. The facts, which can be, and have been, verified, are (1) the reading ability of children and teenagers has declined and (2) the average child views television for six or more hours a day. (Whether this amount of time is "excessive" is also an opinion.) The cause-effect relation between the two facts is an interpretation of the investigator who has examined both the reading scores and the amount of time spent in front of the television set and *inferred* that one is the cause of the other. The causes of the decline in reading scores are probably more complex than the original statement indicates. Since we can seldom or never create laboratory conditions for testing the influence of television separate from other influences in the family and the community, any statement about the connection between reading scores and television viewing can only be a guess.

By definition, no inference can ever do more than suggest probabilities. Of course, some inferences are much more reliable than others and afford a high degree of probability. Almost all claims in science are based on inferences, interpretations of data on which most scientists agree. Paleontologists find a few ancient bones from which they make inferences about an animal that might have been alive millions of years ago. We can never be absolutely certain that the reconstruction of the dinosaur in the museum is an exact copy of the animal it is supposed to represent, but the probability is fairly high because no other interpretation works so well to explain all the observable data—the existence of the bones in a particular place, their age, their relation to other fossils, and their resemblance to the bones of existing animals with which the paleontologist is familiar.

Inferences are profoundly important, and most arguments could not proceed very far without them. But an inference is not a fact. The writer of an argument must make it clear when he or she offers an inference, an interpretation, or an opinion that it is not a fact.

Defending a Claim of Fact

Here is a summary of the guidelines that should help you to defend a factual claim. (We'll say more about support of factual claims in Chapter 4.)

1. Be sure that the claim—what you are trying to prove—is clearly stated, preferably at the beginning of your paper.

2. Define terms that may be controversial or ambiguous. For example, in trying to prove that "radicals" had captured the student government, you would have to define "radicals," distinguishing them from "liberals" or members of other ideological groups, so that your readers would understand exactly what you meant.

3. As far as possible, make sure that your evidence—facts and opinions, or interpretations of the facts—fulfills the appropriate criteria. The data should be sufficient, accurate, recent, typical; the authorities should be reliable.

4. Make clear when conclusions about the data are inferences or interpretations, not facts. For example, you might write, "The series of lectures, 'Modern Architecture,' sponsored by our fraternity, was poorly attended because the students at this college aren't interested in discussions of art." What proof could you offer that this *was* the reason, that your statement was a *fact*? Perhaps there were other reasons that you hadn't considered.

5. Arrange your evidence in order to emphasize what is most important. Place it at the beginning or at the end, the most important positions in an essay, and devote more space to it.

• • •

Claims of Value

Unlike claims of fact, which attempt to prove that something is true and which can be validated by reference to the data, claims of value make a judgment. They express approval or disapproval. They attempt to prove that some action, belief, or condition is right or wrong, good or bad, beautiful or ugly, worthwhile or undesirable.

CLAIM: Democracy is superior to any other form of government.

CLAIM: Killing animals for sport is wrong.

CLAIM: The Sam Rayburn Building in Washington is an aesthetic failure.

Some claims of value are simply expressions of tastes, likes and dislikes, or preferences and prejudices. The Latin proverb "De gustibus non est disputandum" states that we cannot dispute about tastes. Suppose you express a preference for chocolate over vanilla. If your listener should ask why you prefer this flavor, you cannot refer to an outside authority or produce data or appeal to her moral sense to convince her that your preference is justified.

Many claims of value, however, can be defended or attacked on the basis of standards that measure the worth of an action, a belief, or an object. As far as possible, our personal likes and dislikes should be supported by reference to these standards. Value judgments occur in any area of human experience, but whatever the area, the analysis will be the same. We ask the arguer who is defending a claim of value: *What are the standards or criteria for deciding that this action, this belief or this object is good or bad, beautiful or ugly, desirable or undesirable? Does the thing you are defending fulfill these criteria?*

There are two general areas in which people often disagree about matters of value: aesthetics and morality. They are also the areas that offer the greatest challenge to the writer. What follows is a discussion of some of the elements of analysis that you should consider in defending a claim of value in these areas.

Aesthetics is the study of beauty and the fine arts. Controversies over works of art—the aesthetic value of books, paintings, sculpture, architecture, dance, drama, and movies—rage fiercely among experts and laypeople alike. They may disagree on the standards for judging or, even if they agree, may disagree about how successfully the art object under discussion has met these standards.

Consider a discussion about popular music. Hearing someone praise the singing of a well-known vocalist, Sheila Jordan, you might ask why she is so highly regarded. You expect Jordan's fan to say more than "I like her" or "Man, she's great." You expect the fan to give reasons to support this claim. "She's unique," he says. He shows you a short review from a widely read newspaper that says, "Her singing is filled with fascinating phrasings, twists, and turns, and she's been compared with Billie Holiday for her emotional intensity . . . She can be so heart-wrenching that conversations stop cold." Her fan agrees with the criteria for judging a singer given by the author of the review: uniqueness, fascinating phrasings, emotional intensity.

You may not agree that these are the only standards or even the significant ones for judging a singer. But the establishment of standards itself offers material for a discussion or an argument. You may argue about the relevance of the criteria, or, agreeing on the criteria, you may argue about the success of the singer in meeting them. Perhaps you prefer cool singers to intense ones. Or, even if you choose intensity over coolness, you may not think Sheila Jordan can be described as "expressive." Moreover, in any arguments about criteria, differences in experience and preparation acquire importance. You would probably take for granted that a writer with formal musical training who has listened carefully to dozens of singers over a period of years, who has read a good deal of musical criticism and discussed musical matters with other knowledgeable people would be a more reliable critic than someone who lacked these qualifications.

It is probably not surprising then, that, despite wide differences in taste, professional critics more often than not agree on criteria and whether an art object has met the criteria. For example, almost all movie critics agreed that *Back to the Future* and *Stand By Me* were superior films. They also agreed that *A Tomato Ate My Sister*, a horror film, was terrible.

Value claims about morality express judgments about the rightness or wrongness of conduct or belief. Here disagreements are as wide and deep as in the arts. The first two examples [above] reveal how controversial such claims can be. Although you and your reader may share many values, among them a belief in democracy, a respect for learning, and a desire for peace, you may also disagree, even profoundly, about other values. The subject of divorce, for example, despite its prevalence in our society, can produce a conflict between differing moral standards. Some people may insist on adherence to absolute standards, arguing that the values they hold are based on immutable religious precepts derived from God and Scripture. Since marriage is sacred, divorce is always wrong, they say, whether or not the conditions of society change. Other people may argue that their values are relative, based on the changing needs of societies in different places and at different times. Since marriage is an institution created by human beings at a particular time in history to serve particular social needs, they may say, it can also be dissolved when other social needs arise. The same conflicts between moral values might occur in discussions of abortion or suicide.

As a writer you cannot always know what system of values is held by your reader. Yet it might be possible to find a rule on which almost all readers agree. One such rule was expressed by the eighteenth-century German philosopher Immanuel Kant: "Man and, in general, every rational being exists as an end in itself and not merely as a means to be arbitrarily used by this or that will." Kant's prescription urges us not to subject any creature to a condition that it has not freely chosen. In other words, we cannot use other creatures, as in slavery, for our own purposes. (Some philosophers would extend this rule to the treatment of animals by human beings.) This standard of judgment has, in fact, been invoked in recent years against medical experimentation on human beings in prisons and hospitals without their consent and against the sterilization of poor or mentally defective women without their knowledge of the decision.

Nevertheless, even where there is agreement about standards for measuring behavior, you should be aware that a majority preference is not enough to confer moral value. If in a certain neighborhood most of the young men decide to harass a few homosexuals, that consensus does not make their action right. In formulating value claims, you should be prepared to ask and answer questions about the way in which your value claims and those of others have been arrived at. Lionel Ruby, an American philosopher, sums it up in these words: "The law of rationality tells us that we ought to justify our beliefs by evidence and reasons, instead of asserting them dogmatically."[7]

Of course, you will not always be able to persuade those with whom you argue that your values are superior to theirs and that they should therefore change their attitudes. Nor, on the other hand, would you want to compromise your values or pretend that they were different in order to win an argument. What you can and should do, however, as Lionel Ruby advises, is give *good reasons* why you think one thing is better than another. If as a child you asked why it was wrong to take your brother's toys, you might have been told by an exasperated parent, "Because I say so." Some adults still give such answers in defending their judgments, but such answers are not arguments and do nothing to win the agreement of others.

Defending a Claim of Value

The following suggestions are a preliminary guide to the defense of a value claim. (We discuss value claims further in Chapter 4.)

1. Try to make clear that the values or principles you are defending should have priority on any scale of values. Keep in mind that you and your readers may differ about their relative importance. For example, although your readers may agree with you that brilliant photography is important in a film, they may think that a well-written script is even more crucial to its success. And although they may agree that freedom of the press is a mainstay of democracy, they may regard the right to privacy as even more fundamental.

2. Suggest that adherence to the values you are defending will bring about good results in some specific situation or bad news if respect for the value is ignored. You might argue, for example, that a belief in freedom of the press will make citizens better informed and the country stronger while a failure to protect this freedom will strengthen the forces of authoritarianism.

3. Since value terms are abstract, use examples and illustrations to clarify meanings and make distinctions. Comparisons and contrasts are especially helpful. If you are using the term "heroism," can you provide examples to differentiate between "heroism" and "foolhardiness" or "exhibitionism"?

4. Use testimony of others to prove that knowledgeable or highly regarded people share your values.

Claims of Policy

Claims of policy argue that certain conditions should exist. As the name suggests, they advocate adoption of policies or courses of action because problems have arisen that call for solution. Almost always *should* or *ought to* or *must* is expressed or implied in the claim.

> CLAIM: Voluntary prayer should be permitted in public schools.

> CLAIM: A dress code should be introduced for all public high schools.

> CLAIM: A law should permit sixteen-year-olds and parents to "divorce" each other in cases of extreme incompatibility.

> CLAIM: Mandatory jail terms should be imposed for drunk driving violations.

In defending such claims of policy you may find that you must first convince your audience that a problem exists. This will require that, as part of your longer argument, you make a factual claim, offering data to prove that present conditions are unsatisfactory. You may also find it necessary to refer to the values that support your claim. Then you will be ready to introduce your policy, to persuade your audience that the solution you propose will solve the problem.

We will examine a policy claim in which all these parts are at work. The claim can be stated as follows: "The time required for an undergraduate degree should be extended to five years." Immediate agreement with this policy among student readers would certainly not be universal. Some students would not recognize a problem. They would say, "The college curriculum we have now is fine. There's no need for a change. Besides, we don't want to spend more time in school." First, then, the arguer would have to persuade a skeptical audience that there is a problem, that four years of college are no longer enough because the stock of knowledge in almost all fields of study continues to increase. The arguer would provide data to show how many more choices in history, literature, and science students have now compared to the choices in those fields a generation ago. She would also find it necessary to emphasize the value of greater knowledge and more schooling compared to the value of other goods the audience cherishes, such as earlier independence. Finally, the arguer would offer a plan for putting her policy into effect. Her plan would have to take into consideration initial psychological resistance, revision of the curriculum, the costs of more instruction, and the costs of lost production in the work force. Most important, she would point out the benefits for both individuals and society if this policy were adopted.

In this example, we assumed that the reader would disagree that a problem existed. In many cases, however, the reader may agree that there is a problem but disagree with the arguer about the way of solving it. Most of us, no doubt, will agree that we want to reduce or eliminate the following problems: misbehavior and vandalism in schools, drunk driving, crime on the streets, child abuse, pornography, pollution. But how shall we go about solving those problems? What public policy will give us well-behaved, diligent students who never destroy school property? Safe streets where no one is ever robbed or assaulted? Loving homes where no child is ever mistreated? Some members of society would choose to introduce rules or laws that punish infractions so severely that wrongdoers would be unwilling or unable to repeat their offenses. Other members of society would prefer policies that attempt to rehabilitate or reeducate offenders through training, therapy, counseling, and new opportunities.

Defending a Claim of Policy

The following steps will help you organize arguments for a claim of policy.

1. Make your proposal clear. The terms in the proposal should be precisely defined.

2. If necessary, establish that there is a need for change. If changes have been ignored or resisted, there may be good or at least understandable reasons why this is so. (It is often wrongly assumed that people cling to cultural practices long after their significance and necessity have eroded. But rational human beings do not continue to observe practices unless those practices serve a purpose. The fact that you and I may see no value or purpose in the activities of another is irrelevant.)

3. Consider the opposing arguments. You may want to state the opposing arguments in a brief paragraph in order to answer them in the body of your argument.

4. Devote the major part of your essay to proving that your proposal is an answer to the opposing arguments and that there are distinct benefits for your readers in adopting your proposal.

5. Support your proposal with solid data, but don't neglect the moral considerations and the common-sense reasons, which may be even more persuasive.

• • •

Chapter 4: Support

Types of Support: Evidence and Appeals to Needs and Values

All the claims you make—whether of fact, of value, or of policy—must be supported. Support for a claim represents the answer to the question, "What have you got to go on?"[8] There are two basic kinds of support in an argument: evidence and appeals to needs and values.

Evidence, as one dictionary defines it, is "something that tends to prove; ground for belief." When you provide evidence, you use facts, including statistics, and opinions, or interpretations of facts, both your own and those of experts. In the following conversation, the first speaker offers facts and the opinion of an expert to convince the second speaker that robots are exceptional machines.

> *"You know, robots do a lot more than work on assembly lines in factories."*
> *"Like what?"*
> *"They shear sheep, pick citrus fruit, and even assist in neurosurgery. And by the end of the century, every house will have a robot slave."*
> *"No kidding. Who says so?"*

"An engineer who's the head of the world's largest manufacturer of industrial robots."

A writer often appeals to readers' needs, that is, requirements for physical and psychological survival and well-being, and values, or standards for right and wrong, good and bad. In the following conversation, the first speaker makes an appeal to the universal need for self-esteem and to the principle of helping others, a value the second speaker probably shares.

"I think you ought to come help us at the nursing home. We need an extra hand."

"I'd like to, but I really don't have the time."

"You could give us an hour a week, couldn't you? Think how good you'd feel about helping out, and the old people would be so grateful. Some of them are very lonely."

Although they use the same kinds of support, conversations are less rigorous than arguments addressed to larger audiences in academic or public situations. In the debates on public policy that appear in the media and in the courts, the quality of support can be crucial in settling urgent matters. The following summary of a well-known court case demonstrates the critical use of both evidence and value appeals in the support of opposing claims.

On March, 30, 1981, President Ronald Reagan and three other men were shot by John W. Hinckley, Jr., a young drifter from a wealthy Colorado family. Hinckley was arrested at the scene of the shooting. In his trial the factual evidence was presented first: There were dozens of reliable witnesses who had seen the shooting at close range. Hinckley's diaries, letters, and poems revealed that he had planned the shooting to impress actress Jodie Foster. Opinions, consisting of testimony by experts, were introduced by both the defense and the prosecution. This evidence was contradictory. Defense attorneys produced several psychiatrists who defined Hinckley as insane. If this interpretation of his conduct convinced the jury, then Hinckley would be confined to a mental hospital rather than a prison. The prosecution introduced psychiatrists who interpreted Hinckley's motives and actions as those of a man who knew what he was doing and knew it was wrong. They claimed he was *not* insane by legal definition. The fact that experts can make differing conclusions about the meaning of the same information indicates that interpretations are less reliable than other kinds of support.

Finally, the defense made an appeal to the moral values of the jury. Under the law, criminals judged to be insane are not to be punished as harshly as criminals judged to be sane. The laws assume that criminals who cannot be held responsible for their actions are entitled to more compassionate treatment, confinement to a mental hospital rather than prison. The jury accepted the interpretive evidence supporting the claim of the defense, and Hinckley was pronounced not guilty by reason of insanity. Clearly the moral concern for the rights of the insane proved to be decisive.

In your arguments you will advance your claims, not unlike a lawyer, with these same kinds of support. But before you begin, you should ask two questions: Which kind of support should I use in convincing an audience to accept my claim? and How do I decide that each item of support is valid and worthy of acceptance? This chapter presents the different types of evidence and appeals you can use to support your claim and examines the criteria by which you can evaluate the soundness of that support.

Evidence

Factual Evidence

[Earlier] we defined facts as "statements possessing a high degree of public acceptance." In theory, facts can be verified by experience alone. Eating too much will make us sick; we can get from Hopkinton to Boston in a half hour by car; in the Northern Hemisphere it is colder in December than in July. The experience of any individual is limited in both time and space, so we must accept as fact thousands of assertions about the world that we ourselves can never verify. Thus we accept the report that human beings landed on the moon in 1969 because we trust those who can verify it. (Country people in Morocco, however, received the news with disbelief because they had no reason to trust the reporters of the event. They insisted on trusting their senses instead. One man said, "I can see the moon very clearly. If a man were walking around up there, wouldn't I be able to see him?")

Factual evidence appears most frequently as examples and statistics, which are a numerical form of examples.

Examples

Examples are the most familiar kind of factual evidence. In addition to providing support for the truth of a generalization, examples can enliven otherwise dense or monotonous prose.

In the following paragraph the writer supports the claim in the topic sentence by offering a series of specific examples. (The article claims that most airport security is useless.)

> Meanwhile, seven hijacking incidents occurred last year (twenty-one in 1980 and eleven the year before), despite the security system. Two involved the

use of flammable liquids. . . . In four other cases, hijackers claimed to have flammables or explosives but turned out to be bluffing. In the only incident involving a gun, a man brushed past the security system and brandished the weapon on the plane before being wrestled to the ground. One other hijacking was aborted on the ground, and the remaining five were concluded after some expense, fright, and delay—but no injuries or deaths.[9]

Hypothetical examples, which create imaginary situations for the audience and encourage them to visualize what might happen under certain circumstances, can also be effective. The following paragraph, taken from the same article as the preceding paragraph, illustrates the use of hypothetical examples.

> But weapons can get through nonetheless. Some are simply overlooked; imagine being one of those 10,000 "screeners" staring at X-rayed baggage, day in and day out. Besides, a gun can be broken down into unrecognizable parts and reassembled past the checkpoint. A hand grenade can be hidden in an aerosol shaving-cream can or a photographer's lens case. The ingredients of a Molotov cocktail can be carried on quite openly; any bottle of, say, duty-free liquor or perfume can be emptied and refilled with gasoline. And the possibilities for bluffing should not be forgotten; once on board, anyone could claim that a bottle of water was really a Molotov cocktail, or that a paper bag contained a bomb.[10]

All claims about vague or abstract terms would be boring or unintelligible without examples to illuminate them. For example, if you claim that a movie contains "unusual sound effects," you will certainly have to describe some of the effects to convince the reader that your generalization can be trusted.

Statistics

Statistics express information in numbers. In the following example statistics have been used to express raw data in numerical form.

> Surveys have shown that almost half of all male high school seniors—and nearly 20% of all 9th grade boys—can be called "problem drinkers.". . .
>
> Over 5000 teenagers are killed yearly in auto accidents due to drunken driving.[11]

These grim numbers probably have meaning for you, partly because you already know that alcoholism exists even among young teenagers and partly because your own experience enables you to evaluate the numbers. But if you are unfamiliar with the subject, such numbers may be difficult or impossible to understand. Statistics, therefore, are more effective in comparisons that indicate whether a quantity is relatively large or small and sometimes even whether a reader should interpret the result as gratifying or disappointing. For example, if a novice gambler were told that for every dollar wagered in a state lottery, 50 percent goes back to the players as prizes, would the gambler be able to conclude that the percentage is high or low? Would he be able to choose between playing the state lottery and playing a casino game? Unless he had more information, probably not. But if he were informed that in casino games, the return to the players is over 90 percent and in slot machines and racetracks the return is around 80 percent, the comparison would enable him to evaluate the meaning of the 50 percent return in the state lottery and even to make a decision about where to gamble his money.[12]

Comparative statistics are also useful for measurements over time.

> Tolerance of intermarriage has been gradually increasing in recent years. In a 1983 Gallup Poll on attitudes toward interracial marriage, 43 percent approved, 50 percent disapproved and 7 percent had no opinion. This contrasts with a 1978 Gallup Poll showing that 36 percent approved and 54 percent disapproved, and a 1968 Gallup Poll showing that only 20 percent approved while 72 percent disapproved.[13]

Diagrams, tables, charts, and graphs can make clear the relations among many sets of numbers. The following charts and diagrams allow readers to grasp the information more easily than if it were presented in paragraph form.

In a poll conducted by Louis Harris and Associates in 1985, voters were asked, "Do you think that the number of teen-age pregnancies in the United States is a serious problem, or a not-so-serious problem?" The results are shown in the pie chart[14] [below].

In a poll conducted by the Roper Organization in August 1986, voters in various age groups were asked to rank the most important issues facing the United States. Here the information from one group of respondents is summarized in the bar chart[15] [below].

Opinions: Interpretations of the Facts

We have seen how opinions of experts influenced the verdict in the trial of John Hinckley. Facts alone were not enough to substantiate the claim that Hinckley was guilty of attempted assassination. Both the defense and the prosecution relied on experts—psychiatrists—to interpret the facts. Opinions or interpretations about the facts are the inferences discussed in Chapter 2. They are an indispensable source of support for your claims.

Suppose a disco for teenagers—Studio 44: A Young Adult Dance Club—has opened in your town. That is a fact. What is the significance of it? Is the disco's existence good or bad? What consequences will it have for the community? Some parents oppose the idea of a disco, fearing that it may allow teenagers to escape from parental control and engage in dangerous

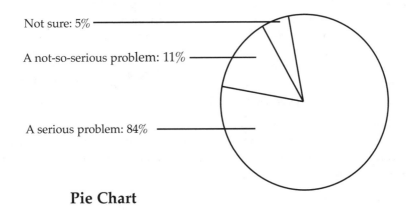

Not sure: 5%

A not-so-serious problem: 11%

A serious problem: 84%

Pie Chart

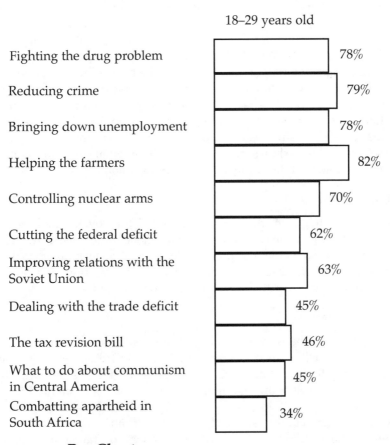

18–29 years old

Fighting the drug problem — 78%

Reducing crime — 79%

Bringing down unemployment — 78%

Helping the farmers — 82%

Controlling nuclear arms — 70%

Cutting the federal deficit — 62%

Improving relations with the Soviet Union — 63%

Dealing with the trade deficit — 45%

The tax revision bill — 46%

What to do about communism in Central America — 45%

Combatting apartheid in South Africa — 34%

Bar Chart

activities. Other parents approve of a disco, hoping that it will serve as a substitute for unsupervised congregation in the streets. The importance of these interpretations is that they, not the fact itself, help people decide what actions they should take. If the community accepts the interpretation that Studio 44 is a source of delinquency, they may decide to revoke the owner's license and close the disco. As one writer puts it, "The interpretation of data becomes a struggle over power."

Opinions or interpretations of facts generally take three forms: (1) They may suggest a causal connection between two sets of data or the cause for a condition; (2) they may offer predictions about the future; (3) they may suggest solutions to a problem.

Causal Connection

It is a fact that approximately two-thirds of all major crimes are committed by males between the ages of fifteen and twenty-four who are often poor and unemployed. What is the connection between the incidence of crime and the facts about the criminals? One interpretation was offered by former Vice President Hubert Humphrey, who inferred that poverty was the cause of crime. "Surely," he said, "the facts indicate that poverty, poor education, discrimination, lack of skills, and the ugliness of slums contribute to criminal behavior."[16] Other observers offer different interpretations of the same data, attributing crime by young adults to leniency by the courts: Certain research "not only debunks the myth that poverty causes crime, but it shows that the most fundamental contributing cause to rising crime is quite simply declining punishment."[17]

Predictions about the Future

The facts are that both the United States and the Soviet Union possess 50,000 nuclear weapons and plan to build 20,000 more nuclear warheads in the next decade. One interpretation predicts that such an arsenal will almost certainly lead to nuclear war. A contrary interpretation predicts that such an arsenal will act as a deterrent on both sides.

Solutions to Problems

In an article on the prevalence of graffiti on subway cars in New York City and the lack of success in deterring the graffitists, the author concludes, nevertheless, that a solution is possible. He has observed that trucks parked in lots and garages are seldom or never painted by the graffitists because, if they are caught by the truck drivers, they are severely beaten. He infers, therefore, that swift and unpleasant punishment for the graffitists would solve the problem of the painted subway cars.[18]

Expert Opinion

For many of the subjects you discuss and write about, you will find it necessary to accept and use the opinions of experts. Based on their reading of the facts, experts express opinions on a variety of controversial subjects: whether capital punishment is a deterrent to crime; whether legalization of marijuana will lead to an increase in its use; whether children, if left untaught, will grow up honest and cooperative; whether sex education courses will result in less sexual activity and fewer illegitimate births. The interpretations of the data are often profoundly important because they influence social policy and affect our lives directly and indirectly.

For the problems mentioned above, the opinions of people recognized as authorities are more reliable than those of people who have neither thought about nor done research on the subject. But opinions may also be offered by student writers in areas in which they are knowledgeable. If you were asked, for example, to defend or refute the statement that work has advantages for teenagers, you could call on your own experience and that of your friends to support your claim. You can also draw on your experience to write convincingly about your special interests.

One opinion, however, is not as good as another. The value of any opinion depends on the quality of the evidence and the trustworthiness of the person offering it.

Evaluation of Evidence

Before you begin to write, you must determine whether the facts and opinions you have chosen to support your claim are sound. Can they convince your readers? A distinction between the evaluation of facts and the evaluation of opinions is somewhat artificial because many facts are verified by expert opinion, but for our analysis we discuss them separately.

Evaluation of Factual Evidence

As you evaluate factual evidence, you should keep in mind the following questions:

1. Is the evidence up to date? The importance of up-to-date information depends on the subject. If you are defending the claim that suicide is immoral, you will not need to examine new data. For many of the subjects you write about, recent research and scholarship will be important, even decisive, in proving the soundness of your data. "New" does not always mean "best," but in fields where research is ongoing—education, psychology, technology, medicine, and all the natural and physical sciences—you should be sensitive to the dates of the research.

In writing a paper a few years ago warning about the health hazards of air pollution, you would have used data referring only to outdoor pollution produced by automobile and factory emissions. But writing about air pollution today, you would have to take into account new data about indoor pollution, which has become a serious problem as a result of attempts to conserve energy. Because research studies in indoor pollution are continually being updated, recent evidence will probably be more accurate than past research.

2. *Is the evidence sufficient?* The amount of evidence you need depends on the complexity of the subject and the length of your paper. Given the relative brevity of most of your assignments, you will need to be selective. For the claim that indoor pollution is a serious problem, one example would obviously not be enough. For a 750-to-1000-word paper, three or four examples should probably be sufficient. The choice of examples should reflect different aspects of the problem: in this case, different sources of indoor pollution—gas stoves, fireplaces, kerosene heaters, insulation—and the consequences for health.

Indoor pollution is a fairly limited subject for which the evidence is clear. But more complex problems require more evidence. A common fault in argument is generalization based on insufficient evidence. In a 1000-word paper you could not adequately treat the causes of unrest in the Middle East; you could not develop workable solutions for the health care crisis; you could not predict the development of education in the next century. In choosing a subject for a brief paper, determine whether you can produce sufficient evidence to convince a reader who may not agree with you. If not, the subject may be too large for a brief paper.

3. *Is the evidence relevant?* All the evidence should, of course, contribute to the development of your argument. Sometimes the arguer loses sight of the subject and introduces examples that are wide of the claim. In defending a national health care plan, one student offered examples of the success of health maintenance organizations, but such organizations, although subsidized by the federal government, are not the structure favored by sponsors of a national health care plan. The examples were interesting but irrelevant.

Also keep in mind that not all readers will agree on what is relevant. Is the unsavory private life of a politician relevant to his or her performance in office? If you want to prove that a politician is unfit to serve because of his or her private activities, you may first have to convince some members of the audience that private activities are relevant to public service.

4. *Are the examples representative?* This question emphasizes your responsibility to choose examples that are typical of all the examples you do not

use. Suppose you offered Vermont's experience to support your claim that passage of a bottle bill would reduce litter. Is the experience of Vermont typical of what is happening or may happen in other states? Or is Vermont, a small, mostly rural New England state, different enough from other states to make the example unrepresentative?

5. Are the examples consistent with the experience of the audience? The members of your audience use their own experiences to judge the soundness of your evidence. If your examples are unfamiliar or extreme, they will probably reject your conclusion. Consider the following excerpt from a flyer distributed on a university campus by the Revolutionary Communist Party.

> What is growing up female in a capitalist society? Growing up to Laverne and Shirley and the idea that female means scatter-brained broad? Being chained to the kitchen and let out on a leash to do cheap labor? Overburdened by the hardships of trying to raise children in this putrid, degenerate society—with or without husbands?

If most members of the audience find such a characterization of female experience inconsistent with their own, they will probably question the validity of the claim.

Evaluation of Statistics

The questions you must ask about examples also apply to statistics. Are they recent? Are they sufficient? Are they relevant? Are they typical? Are they consistent with the experience of the audience? But there are additional questions directed specifically to evaluation of statistics.

1. Do the statistics come from trustworthy sources? Perhaps you have read newspaper accounts of very old people, some reported to be as old as 135, living in the Caucasus or the Andes, nourished by yogurt and hard work. But these statistics are hearsay; no birth records or other official documents exist to verify them. Now two anthropologists have concluded that the numbers were part of a rural mythology and that the ages of the people were actually within the normal range for human populations elsewhere.[19]

Hearsay statistics should be treated with the same skepticism accorded to gossip or rumor. Sampling a population to gather statistical information is a sophisticated science; you should ask whether the reporter of the statistics is qualified and likely to be free of bias. Among the generally reliable sources are polling organizations such as Gallup, Roper, and Louis Harris and agencies of the U.S. government such as the Census Bureau and the Bureau of Labor Statistics. Other qualified sources are well-known research foundations, university centers, and insurance companies that prepare actuarial tables. Statistics from underdeveloped countries are less reliable for obvious reasons: lack of funds, lack of trained statisticians, lack of communication and transportation facilities to carry out accurate censuses.

2. *Are the terms clearly defined?* In an [earlier] example, the reference to "poverty" made clear that any statistics would be meaningless unless we knew exactly how "poverty" was defined by the user. "Unemployment" is another term for which statistics will be difficult to read if the definition varies from one user to another. For example, are seasonal workers "employed" or "unemployed" during the off-season? Are part-time workers "employed"? (In Russia they are "unemployed.") Are workers on government projects "employed"? (During the 1930s they were considered "employed" by the Germans and "unemployed" by the Americans.) The more abstract or controversial the term, the greater the necessity for clear definition.

3. *Are the comparisons between comparable things?* Folk wisdom warns us that we cannot compare apples and oranges. Population statistics for the world's largest city, for example, should indicate the units being compared. Greater London is defined in one way; greater New York in another; and greater Tokyo in still another. The population numbers will mean little unless you can be sure that the same geographical units are being compared.

4. *Has any significant information been omitted?* The Plain Truth, a magazine published by the World-Wide Church of God, advertises itself as follows:

> The Plain Truth has now topped 5,000,000 copies per issue. It is now the fastest growing magazine in the world and one of the widest circulated mass circulation magazines on earth. Our circulation is now greater than *Newsweek.* New subscribers are coming in at the rate of around 40,000 per week.

What the magazine neglects to mention is that it is *free.* There is no subscription fee, and the magazine is widely distributed free in drugstores, supermarkets, and airports. *Newsweek* is sold on newsstands and by subscription. The comparison therefore omits significant information.

Evaluation of Opinions

When you evaluate the reliability of opinions in subjects with which you are not familiar, you will be dealing almost exclusively with opinions of experts. Most of the following questions are directed to an evaluation of authoritative sources. But you can also ask these questions of students or of others with opinions based on their own experience and research.

1. *Is the source of the opinion qualified to give an opinion on the subject?* The discussion on credibility in Chapter 1 pointed out that certain achievements

by the interpreter of the data—publications, acceptance by colleagues—can tell us something about his or her competence. Although these standards are by no means foolproof—people of outstanding reputations have been known to falsify their data—nevertheless they offer assurance that the source is generally trustworthy. The answers to questions you must ask are not hard to find: Is the source qualified by education? Is the source associated with a reputable institution—a university or a research organization? Is the source credited with having made contributions to the field—books, articles, research studies? Suppose in writing a paper recommending relaxation of rules on prescription drugs you came across an article by Michael J. Halberstam. He is identified as follows:

> Michael J. Halberstam, MD, is a practicing cardiologist, associate clinical professor of medicine at George Washington University School of Medicine, and editor-in-chief of *Modern Medicine*. He is also a member of the advisory committee of the Center for Health Policy Research at the American Enterprise Institute.[20]

These credentials would suggest to almost any reader that Halberstam is a reliable source of information about prescription drugs.

If the source is not so clearly identified, you should treat the data with caution. Such advice is especially relevant when you are dealing with popular works about such subjects as miracle diets, formulas for instant wealth, and sightings of monsters and UFOs. Do not use such data until you can verify them from other, more authoritative sources.

In addition, you should question the identity of any source listed as "spokesperson" or "reliable source" or "an unidentified authority." The mass media are especially fond of this type of attribution. Sometimes the sources are people in public life who plant stories anonymously or off the record for purposes they prefer to keep hidden.

Even when the identification is clear and genuine, you should ask if the credentials are relevant to the field in which the authority claims expertise. So specialized are areas of scientific study today that scientists in one field may not be competent to make judgments in another. William Shockley is a distinguished engineer, a Nobel Prize winner for his contribution to the invention of the electronic transistor. But when he made the claim, based on his own research, that blacks are genetically inferior to whites, geneticists accused Shockley of venturing into a field where he was unqualified to make judgments. Similarly, advertisers invite stars from the entertainment world to express opinions about products with which they are probably less familiar than members of their audience. All citizens have the right to express their views, but this does not mean that all views are equally credible or worthy of attention.

2. Is the source biased for or against his or her interpretation? Even authorities who satisfy the criteria for expertise may be guilty of bias. Bias arises as a result of economic reward, religious affiliation, political loyalty, and other interests. The expert may not be aware of the bias; even an expert can fall into the trap of ignoring evidence that contradicts his or her own intellectual preferences. A British psychologist has said:

> The search for meaning in data is bound to involve all of us in distortion to greater or lesser degree. . . . Transgression consists not so much in a clear break with professional ethics, as in an unusually high-handed, extreme or self-deceptive attempt to promote one particular view of reality at the expense of all others.[21]

Before accepting the interpretation of an expert, you should ask: Is there some reason why I should suspect the motives of this particular source?

Consider, for example, an advertisement claiming that sweetened breakfast cereals are nutritious. The advertisement, placed by the manufacturer of the cereal, provides impeccable references from scientific sources to support its claims. But since you are aware of the economic interest of the company in promoting sales, you may wonder if they have reproduced only facts that favor their claims. Are there other facts that might prove the opposite? As a careful researcher you would certainly want to look further for data about the advantages and disadvantages of sugar in our diets.

It is harder to determine bias in the research done by scientists and university members even when the research is funded by companies interested in a favorable review of their products. If you discover that a respected biologist who advocates the use of sugar in baby food receives a consultant's fee from a sugar company, should you conclude that the research is slanted and that the scientist has ignored contrary evidence? Not necessarily. The truth may be that the scientist arrived at conclusions about the use of sugar legitimately through experiments that no other scientist would question. But it would probably occur to you that a critical reader might ask about the connection between the results of the research and the payment by a company that profits from the research. In this case you would be wise to read further to find confirmation or rejection of the claim by other scientists.

The most difficult evaluations concern ideological bias. Early in our lives we learn to discount the special interest that makes a small child brag, "My mother (or father) is the greatest!" Later we become aware that the claims of people who are avowed Democrats or Republicans or Marxists or Yankee fans or zealous San Franciscans or joggers must be examined somewhat more carefully than those of people who have no special commitment to a cause or a place or an activity. This is not to say that all partisan claims lack support. They may, in fact, be based on the best available support. But whenever special interest is apparent, there is always the danger that an argument will reflect this bias.

3. Has the source bolstered the claim with sufficient and appropriate evidence? In an article attacking pornography, one author wrote, "Statistics prove that the recent proliferation of porno is directly related to the increasing number of rapes and assaults upon women."[22] But the author gave no further information—neither statistics nor proof that a cause-effect relation exists between pornography and violence against women. The critical reader will ask, "What are the numbers? Who compiled them?"

Even those who are reputed to be experts in the subjects they discuss must do more than simply allege that a claim is valid or that the data exist. They must provide facts to support their interpretations.

When Experts Disagree

Authoritative sources can disagree. Such disagreement is probably most common in the social sciences. They are called the "soft" sciences precisely because a consensus about conclusions in these areas is more difficult to arrive at than in the natural and physical sciences. Consider the issue of merit pay for teachers. Should superior teachers be paid more? If so, how are superior teachers to be selected? This issue currently divides the educational profession. T. H. Bell, former U.S. secretary of education, believes that merit pay provides incentives for the best students to become teachers and for the best teachers to remain in the profession. But William McGuire, past president of the National Education Association, believes that decisions about raises under a merit pay system would depend on "personal relationships or subservient behavior rather than good teaching."[23] Resolving this issue is complicated by the difficulty of controlling all the factors that motivate human behavior.

But even in the natural and physical sciences, where the results of experiments are far more conclusive, you may encounter serious differences of opinion. A sharp debate has emerged in recent years about the origins of "yellow rain" in Southeast Asia. What is yellow rain? On one side is the view expressed by John Deutch, former dean of science at the Massachusetts Institute of Technology, with which other distinguished scientists agree: "In my judgment the weight of the evidence is remarkably on the side of the conclusion that mycotoxins have been used in Southeast Asia by man." On the other side is the view of Matthew S. Meselson, a Harvard biochemist, and other equally distinguished scientists, who have advanced the theory that "the yellow rain spots cited as evidence of chemical warfare in Southeast Asia may be little more than the excrement of bees."[24]

How can you choose between authorities who disagree? If you have applied the tests discussed so far and discovered that one source is less qualified by training and experience or makes claims with little support or appears to be biased in favor of one interpretation, you will have no difficulty in rejecting that person's opinion. If conflicting sources prove, as in the case above, to be equally reliable in all respects, then continue reading other authorities to determine whether a greater number of experts support one opinion rather than another. Although numbers alone, even of experts, don't guarantee the truth, nonexperts have little choice but to accept the authority of the greater number until evidence to the contrary is forthcoming. Finally, if you are unable to decide between competing sources of evidence, you may conclude that the argument must remain unsettled. Such an admission is not a failure; after all, such questions are considered controversial because even the experts cannot agree, and such questions are often the most interesting to consider and argue about. . . .

Appeals to Needs and Values

Good factual evidence is usually enough to convince an audience that your factual claim is sound. Using examples, statistics, and expert opinion, you can prove, for example, that women do not earn as much as men for the same work. But even good evidence may not be enough to convince your audience that unequal pay is wrong or that something should be done about it. In making value and policy claims, an appeal to the needs and values of your audience is absolutely essential to the success of your argument. If you want to persuade the audience to change their minds or adopt a course of action—in this case, to demand legalization of equal pay for equal work—you will have to show that assent to your claim will bring about what they want and care deeply about.

As a writer, you cannot always know who your audience is; it's impossible, for example, to predict exactly who will read a letter you write to a newspaper. Even in the classroom, you have only partial knowledge of your readers. You may not always know or be able to infer what the goals and principles of your audience are. You may not know how they feel about big government, the draft, private school education, feminism, environmental protection, homosexuality, religion, or any of the other subjects you might write about. If the audience concludes that the things you care about are very different from what they care about, if they cannot identify with your goals and principles, they may treat your argument with indifference, even hostility, and finally reject it. But you can hope that decent and reasonable people will share many of the needs and values that underlie your claims.

Appeals to Needs

Suppose that you are trying to persuade Joan Doakes, a friend who is still undecided, to attend college. In your reading you have come across a report about the benefits of a college education written by Howard Bowen, a former professor of economics at Claremont (California) Graduate School, former president of Grinnell College, and a specialist in the economics of higher education. Armed with this testimony, you write to Joan. As support for your claim that she should attend college, you offer evidence that (1) college graduates earn more throughout their lifetime than high school graduates; (2) college graduates are more active and exert greater influence in their communities than high school graduates; and (3) college graduates achieve greater success as partners in marriage and as thoughtful and caring parents.[25]

Joan writes back that she is impressed with the evidence you've provided—the statistics, the testimony of economists and psychologists—and announces that she will probably enroll in college instead of accepting a job offer.

How did you succeed with Joan Doakes? If you know your friend pretty well, the answer is not difficult. Joan has needs that can be satisfied by material success; more money will enable her to enjoy the comforts and luxuries that are important to her. She also needs the esteem of her peers and the sense of achievement that political activity and service to others will give her. Finally, she needs the rootedness to be found in close and lasting family connections.

Encouraged by your success with Joan Doakes, you write the same letter to another friend, Fred Fox, who has also declined to apply for admission to college. This time, however, your argument fails. Fred, too, is impressed with your research and evidence. But college is not for him, and he repeats that he has decided not to become a student.

Why such a different response? The reason, it turns out, is that you don't know what Fred really wants. Fred Fox dreams of going to Alaska to live alone in the wilderness. Money means little to him; influence in the community is irrelevant to his goals, and at present he feels no desire to become a member of a loving family.

Perhaps if you had known Fred better, you would have offered different evidence to show that you recognized what he needed and wanted. You could have told him that Bowen's study also points out that "college-educated persons are healthier than are others," that "they also have better ability to adjust to changing times and vocations," that "going to college enhances self-discovery" and enlarges mental resources, which encourage college graduates to go on learning for the rest of their lives. This information might have persuaded Fred that college would also satisfy some of his needs.

As this example demonstrates, you have a better chance of persuading your reader to accept your claim if you know what he or she wants and what importance he or she assigns to the needs that we all share. Your reader must, in other words, see some connection between your evidence and his or her needs.

The needs to which you appealed in your letters to Joan and Fred are the requirements for physiological or psychological well-being. The most familiar classification of needs was developed by the psychologist Abraham H. Maslow in 1954.[26] These needs, said Maslow, motivate human thought and action. In satisfying our needs, we attain both long- and short-term goals. Because Maslow believed that some needs are more important than others, he arranged them in hierarchical order from the most urgent biological needs to the psychological needs that are related to our roles as members of a society.

Physiological Needs. Basic bodily requirements: food and drink; health; sex

Safety Needs. Security; freedom from harm; order and stability

Belongingness and Love Needs. Love within a family and among friends; roots within a group or a community

Esteem Needs. Material success; achievement; power, status, and recognition by others

Self-actualization Needs. Fulfillment in realizing one's potential

For most of your arguments you won't have to address the audience's basic physiological needs for nourishment or shelter. The desire for health, however, now receives extraordinary attention. Appeals to buy health foods, vitamin supplements, drugs, exercise and diet courses, and health books are all around us. Many of the claims are supported by little or no evidence, but readers are so eager to satisfy the need for good health that they often overlook the lack of facts or authoritative opinion. The desire for physical well-being, however, is not so simple as it seems; it is strongly related to our need for self-esteem and love.

Appeals to our needs to feel safe from harm, to be assured of order and stability in our lives are also common. Insurance companies, politicians who promise to rid our streets of crime, and companies that offer security services all appeal to this profound and nearly universal need. (We say "nearly" because some people are apparently attracted to risk and danger.) At this writing the nuclear freeze movement has attempted both to arouse fears for our safety and to suggest ways of removing the dangers that make us fearful.

The last three needs in Maslow's hierarchy are the ones you will find most challenging to appeal to in your arguments. It is clear that these needs arise out of human relationships and participation in society. Advertisers make much use of appeals to these needs.

Belongingness and Love Needs.

"Gentlemen prefer Hanes."

"Whether you are young or old, the need for companionship is universal." (ad for dating service)

Esteem Needs.

"Enrich your home with the distinction of an Oxford library."

"Apply your expertise to more challenges and more opportunities. Here are outstanding opportunities for challenge, achievement and growth." (Perkin-Elmer Co.)

Self-actualization Needs.

"Be all that you can be." (U.S. Army)

"Are you demanding enough? Somewhere beyond the cortex is a small voice whose mere whisper can silence an army of arguments. It goes by many names: integrity, excellence, standards. And it stands alone in final judgment as to whether we have demanded enough of ourselves and, by that example, have inspired the best in those around us." (*New York Times*)

Of course, it is not only advertisers who use these appeals. We hear them from family and friends, from teachers, from employers, from editorials and letters to the editor, from people in public life.

Appeals to Values

Needs give rise to values. If we feel the need to belong to a group, we learn to value commitment, sacrifice, and sharing. And we then respond to arguments that promise to protect our values. It is hardly surprising that values, the principles by which we judge what is good or bad, beautiful or ugly, worthwhile or undesirable, should exercise a profound influence on our behavior. Virtually all claims, even those that seem to be purely factual, contain expressed or unexpressed judgments. The two scientists quoted in Chapter 2 who presented evidence that cocaine was "deadlier than we thought," did so not for academic reasons but because they hoped to persuade people that using the drug was bad.

For our study of argument, we will speak of groups or systems of values because any single value is usually related to others. People and institutions are often defined by such systems of values. We can distinguish, for example, between those who think of themselves as traditional and those who think of themselves as modern by listing their differing values. One writer contrasts such values in this way:

> Among the values of traditionalism are: merit, accomplishment, competition, and success; self-restraint, self-discipline, and the postponement of gratification; the stability of the family; and a belief in certain moral universals. The modernist ethos scorns the pursuit of success; is egalitarian and redistributionist in emphasis; tolerates or encourages sensual gratification; values self-expression as against self-restraint; accepts alternative or deviant forms of the family; and emphasizes ethical relativism.[27]

Systems of values are neither so rigid nor so distinct from one another as this list suggests. Some people who are traditional in their advocacy of competition and success may also accept the modernist values of self-expression and alternative family structures. One editorial writer explained the popularity of the governor of New York, Mario Cuomo:

> He embodies that rare combination of an old-fashioned liberal who has traditional, conservative family values—calling for compassion for the needy and afflicted while inveighing against a lack of discipline in American life.[28]

Values, like needs, are arranged in a hierarchy; that is, some are clearly more important than others to the people who hold them. Moreover, the arrangement may shift over time or as a result of new experiences. In 1962, for example, two speech teachers prepared a list of what they called "Relatively Unchanging Values Shared by Most Americans."[29] Included were "puritan and pioneer standards of morality" and "perennial optimism about the future." More than twenty years later, an appeal to these values might fall on a number of deaf ears.

You should also be aware of not only changes over time but also different or competing value systems that reflect a multitude of subcultures in our country. Differences in age, sex, race, ethnic background, social environment, religion, even in the personalities and characters of its members define the groups we belong to. Such terms as "honor," "loyalty," "justice," "patriotism," "duty," "responsibility," "equality," "freedom," and "courage" will be interpreted very differently by different groups.

All of us belong to more than one group, and the values of the several groups may be in conflict. If one group to which you belong, say, peers of your own age and class, is generally uninterested in and even scornful of religion, you may nevertheless hold to the values of your family and continue to place a high value on religious belief.

How can a knowledge of your readers' values enable you to make a more effective appeal? Suppose you want to argue in favor of a sex education program in the junior high school you attended. The program you support would not only give students information about contraception and venereal disease but also teach them about the pleasures of sex, the importance of small families, and alternatives to heterosexuality. If the readers of your argument are your classmates or your peers, you can be fairly sure that their agreement will be easier to obtain than that of their parents, especially if their parents think of themselves as conservative. Your peers are more likely to value experimentation, tolerance of alternative sexual practices, freedom, and novelty. Their parents are more likely to value restraint, conformity to conventional sexual practices, obedience to family rules, and foresight in planning for the future.

Knowing that your peers share your values and your goals will mean that you need not spell out the values supporting your claim; they are understood by your readers. Convincing their parents, however, who think that freedom, tolerance, and experimentation have been abused by their children, will be a far more challenging task. In one written piece you have little chance of changing their values, a result that might be achieved only over a longer period of time. So you might first attempt to reduce their hostility by suggesting that, even if a community-wide program were adopted, students would need parental permission to enroll. This might convince some parents that you share their values regarding parental authority and primacy of the family. Second, you might look for other values to which the parents subscribe and to which you can make an appeal. Do they prize maturity, self-reliance, responsibility in their children? If so, you could attempt to prove, with authoritative evidence, that the sex education program would promote these qualities in students who took the course.

But familiarity with the value systems of prospective readers may also lead you to conclude that winning assent to your argument will be impossible. It would probably be fruitless to attempt to persuade a group of lifelong pacifists to endorse the use of nuclear weapons. The beliefs, attitudes, and habits that support their value systems are too fundamental to yield to one or two attempts at persuasion.

Evaluation of Appeals to Needs and Values

If your argument is based on an appeal to the needs and values of your audience, the following questions will help you evaluate the soundness of your appeal.

1. Have the values been clearly defined? If you are appealing to the patriotism of your readers, can you be sure that they agree with your definition? Does patriotism mean "Our country, right or wrong!" or does it mean dissent, even violent dissent, if you think your country is wrong? Because value terms are abstractions, you must make their meaning explicit by placing them in context and providing examples.

2. Are the needs and values to which you appeal prominent in the reader's hierarchy at the time you are writing? An affluent community, fearful of further erosion of quiet and open countryside, might resist an appeal to allow establishment of a high-technology firm, even though the firm would bring increased prosperity to the area.

3. Is the evidence in your argument clearly related to the needs and values to which you appeal? Remember that the reader must see some connection between your evidence and his or her goals. Suppose you were writing an argument to persuade a group of people to vote in an upcoming election. You could provide evidence to prove that only 20 percent of the town voted in the last election. But this evidence would not motivate your audience to vote unless you could provide other evidence to show that their needs were not being served by such a low turnout.

Notes

[1] Some of the terms and analyses used in this text are adapted from Stephen Toulmin's *The Uses of Argument* (Cambridge: Cambridge University Press, 1958).

[2] *An Examination of the Place of Reason in Ethics* (Cambridge: Cambridge University Press, 1964), p. 71.

[3] Roy E. Terry in "Does Standard Grading Encourage Excessive Competitiveness?" *Change*, September 1974, p. 45.

[4] *The Autobiography of Benjamin Franklin* (New York: Pocket Library, 1954), pp. 22–23.

[5] *New York Times*, February 20, 1983, Sec. 22, p. 4.

[6] S. I. Hayakawa, *Language in Thought and Action* (New York: Harcourt, Brace, Jovanovich, 1978), p. 35.

[7] *The Art of Making Sense* (New York: Lippincott, 1968), p. 271.

[8] Stephen Toulmin, *The Uses of Argument* (Cambridge: Cambridge University Press, 1958), p. 98.

[9] Patrick Brogan, "The $310 Million Paranoia Subsidy," *Harper's*, September 1982, p. 18.

[10] Ibid.

[11] "The Kinds of Drugs Kids Are Getting Into" (Spring House, PA: McNeil Pharmaceutical, n.d.).

[12] Curt Suphee, "Lotto Baloney," *Harper's*, July 1983, p. 20.

[13] *New York Times*, June 20, 1984, Sec. C, p. 7.

[14] *Public Opinion*, September/October 1986, p. 37.

[15] *Public Opinion*, November/December 1986, p. 31.

[16] "Poverty Is a Major Cause of Crime," *The Causes of Crime*, edited by David L. Bender and Gary E. McCuen (Minneapolis: Greenhaven Press, 1977), p. 2.

[17] Warren T. Brooks, "The Myth That Poverty Causes Crime," in *The Causes of Crime*, p. 13.

[18] Nathan Glazer, "On Subway Graffiti in New York," *Public Interest*, Winter 1979, pp. 8–9.

[19] Richard B. Mazess and Sylvia H. Forman, "Longevity and Age Exaggeration in Vilcabamba, Ecuador," *Journal of Gerontology*, 1979, pp. 94–98.

[20] Michael Halberstam, "Too Many Drugs?" (Washington, DC: Center for Policy Health Research, 1979), inside cover.

[21] Liam Hudson, *The Cult of the Fact* (New York: Harper and Row, 1972), p. 125.

[22] Charlotte Allen, "Exploitation for Profit," *Daily Collegian* [University of Massachusetts], October 5, 1976, p. 2.

[23] *New York Times*, May 29, 1983, Sec. I, p. 1.

[24] *New York Times*, June 21, 1983, Sec. C, p. 1.

[25] "The Residue of Academic Learning," *Chronicle of Higher Education*, November 14, 1977, p. 13.

[26] *Motivation and Personality* (New York: Harper and Row, 1954), pp. 80–92.

[27] Joseph Adelson, "What Happened to the Schools," *Commentary*, March 1981, p. 37.

[28] *New York Times*, June 21, 1983, Sec. I, p. 29.

[29] Edward Steele and W. Charles Redding, "The American Value System: Premises for Persuasion," *Western Speech*, Vol. 26, Spring 1962, pp. 83–91.

Born in Hong Kong, Anita Ho (b. 1971) moved to Canada in 1990. She entered
Saint Mary's University in Halifax, Nova Scotia, and graduated in 1994 with a
B.A. in philosophy and a B. Comm. in marketing. In 1995, she received an M.A.
in philosophy from Dalhousie University in Halifax, Nova Scotia. She received
her M. Mus. in piano performance and Ph.D. in philosophy from the University
of Alberta in 2000. She has been teaching philosophy at the College of St. Catherine since the fall of 2000.

"It's So Judgmental!"

A Lesson on Subjectivity and Relativism

Anita Ho

"Iwouldn't do it, but how can I tell you that you can't do it either?" one
of my students comments on the issue of slavery. "I believe in equality,
and I think it is wrong for me to own slaves. But who am I to tell you that
you shouldn't own slaves? That's your decision to make, not mine!"
Other students from the class start to get into the discussion. One of them
says, "I agree. We should just mind our own business. How can we tell
others what to do and what not to do? It's so judgmental!"

Yes, we are talking about relativism and subjectivism. We are trying to
figure out if there are any absolute or universal moral standards that each
and every one of us should follow. We are wondering if there are certain
things that people should simply never do to another human being.
Almost all my students say that there is no such universal moral standard. Each culture has its own custom, and people outside of that culture
should not interfere. As a matter of fact, some students believe that each
person has his or her own moral beliefs, and people should not tell others that they are wrong.

Our discussion moves from slavery to the Holocaust. I ask, "What about
the Nazis? Can't we say that it was absolutely wrong for them to kill six
million Jews?"

Everyone looks at each other. A couple of them gently nod, but still say
that they cannot tell the Nazis what to do. One of them says that it was
horrible that the Nazis killed these people. She says she hopes that
nobody would ever do this again. However, she understands why they
did it. She says, "These people were taught to believe that the Jewish
people were subhuman. Obviously, I don't believe in that. But it is easy
for me to say that, because we don't have Hitler here. But if these people

were brought up in that environment, it is unfair for outsiders to judge them."

Other students make similar remarks. They say that the concentration camps were terrible, but they refuse to say that it was morally wrong for the Nazi Germans to kill all those people.

What's happening here? Really, can we not say that ethnic cleansing and slavery are absolutely wrong, no matter who you are, where you live, and when you live? Do these students really believe that we should not judge these actions, even though they also think that they themselves should not engage in these practices? Is it really so bad to be judgmental on some issues? I know some of these students are working in various volunteering projects to promote social justice, so why do they somehow deny that there is fundamental injustice in some practices? Are they simply confused about what they believe in?

Students often say that there is no such thing as a "universal moral standard." They insist that morality is simply a matter of one's own personal opinion. You have your opinion, and I have mine. You cannot tell me that I am wrong, and I also cannot tell you that you are wrong. They worry that believing in universal moral standards means that they are arrogant and are trying to impose their viewpoints on others. As Robert Simon says, students often think that any criticism of another culture's practices or ideologies is a kind of cultural imperialism.[1] There is the belief that if a practice is part of some people's cultural or moral belief, and if it has worked for them, then others should not pass judgment or interfere.

Worrying about being called judgmental and arrogant, many students say that they are *relativists*. They use the word in many different ways, but in general, they think that ethical beliefs or viewpoints are relative to societies and cultures. If your culture believes in footbinding, it is correct for your culture. If it does not, it is incorrect for your culture. Other cultures may have different ideas than your culture, and they can judge the rightness of this practice according to their own cultural beliefs. However, they cannot judge *your* culture's ideology, but can only determine for *themselves* what is right and wrong. If the Nazi Germans believe that ethnic cleansing was acceptable in their culture, contemporary Americans like my students simply cannot judge them, even if my students would not want that to happen here.

What is interesting in our discussion about relativism is that, students seem to believe that not only are cultures entitled to their traditions and beliefs, but so are individuals. When we start talking about whether it is absolutely wrong for an American today to own slaves, most students are still reluctant to say yes. I ask, "If you find out that your neighbor has a slave, you still don't think that is wrong?" One student says, "Well, I don't think I can tell anyone what to do. Of course I wouldn't own slaves, but what he does is not my business." In other words, it seems that my students believe that each and every individual is the only one who can decide what is right for himself or herself.

Surprised by the unanimous agreement among my students who almost never agree on anything, I proceed with the most awful and shocking example I can think of: "Suppose there is a group of people who believe that burning babies just for fun is acceptable." One student whispers, "Oh my god!" Another student quietly says, "Yuck!" Almost all of them give me a big, long, and disgusted stare. I realize that I am on dangerous ground, but I am hoping that a shocking and extreme example can get my students to rethink their position. I cautiously ask, "Can we tell them that it is absolutely wrong for them to do that? Can we say that it does not matter what their preference of entertainment may be, it is simply wrong for anyone to burn babies for fun?"

By the look of disbelief and shock on my students' faces, I start to think that they may be seriously questioning their position.

A few seconds lapse, and then I hear a quiet voice, "I guess it is awful for anyone to do that." A couple other nods follow.

I secretly think, *I am getting somewhere.*

Then, I hear a voice, "Yeah, but I still don't think we can make such a blank statement to say that it is wrong for anyone to do this. Sure, I think it is gross and everything, and like I said about slavery, I wouldn't do this myself. But again, I don't think I can tell these people what to do. I don't think we should be judgmental about what others do. I am not God. I can't tell others what is right and what is wrong."

Another voice follows, "I agree. I'm sitting here thinking, would I want others to tell me that what I do in my private life is wrong? No! I should be allowed to do whatever I believe in. I don't need to explain anything to other people. It's my life!"

Do students really believe that? Why do even the best students think that we can never say that there are things that are simply wrong?

When I probe the matter further, I realize that these students seem not only to be ethical relativists, but also subjectivists. They say that whether something is right or wrong depends solely on what you subjectively believe. For example, if I believe burning babies is a cruel and illegitimate way to derive pleasure, then it is wrong for me. If you believe it is the best form of entertainment, then it is right for you. People have different perspectives, and no one can say that one perspective is objectively better than another.

This is a worrying position. If everything is "free for all" and people can do whatever they want, wouldn't we have chaos? Why would our students believe in such a position?

Arguments for Ethical Relativism and Subjectivism

There are a few reasons why students are or at least think they are ethical relativists and subjectivists. "Evidence" of diversity is overwhelming. People of different times and places have vastly different or even conflicting ideologies and experiences. Anthropologists such as Ruth Benedict have given us numerous examples to show that it is not unusual for one society to approve of an act that is held to be abnormal or immoral by another.[2] When people around the world have vastly different customs and beliefs, it is unclear how we can evaluate them objectively. Some cultures avoid eating certain types of animals, while others use different kinds of animals for celebration. Some cultures avoid using certain numbers (e.g., "7" in the Chinese culture), while other societies think of the same number as lucky. Certain societies believe that female circumcision is an important element of cultural identity, while others believe that such practice is oppressive and barbaric. Some cultures require women to wear head-to-toe burkas, while other societies allow women to wear bikinis or even go to nude beaches.

On an individual level, there are also different ideas of the morality of practices such as abortion, capital punishment, and cloning. In the face of diversity, it is doubtful that we have any one custom or practice that is embraced by all. It is also unclear if anyone has a legitimate basis for interfering with customs and practices that are different from their own.

Ethical relativism and subjectivism also seem more plausible when we consider how there are various perspectives even among academics who are supposedly "experts" on ethics. They disagree on all the aforementioned ethical issues. If there is disagreement even among experts on the morality of various practices, it seems unlikely that there can be any absolute moral standard governing everyone. As one of my students says, "If these so-called experts can't straighten everything out for us, I doubt we can ever come to agreement anywhere else."

Another reason why many embrace ethical relativism and subjectivism is that they are uncertain if any culture or person should have the authority to determine for everyone else what is moral and immoral. As my students ask, who can be the judge, and how can we force others who have different ideologies to adopt our values? They claim that people of various societies should respect each other and not interfere with their culture and customs. They sometimes also say that whatever happens within a culture or society, it is a "domestic" or "private" matter of that society, and people outside of that society have no right to criticize its "domestic affairs." If certain societies require their women to wear a burka, we should simply respect their custom.

Foreign diplomats have said similar things. Chinese officials, for example, have repeatedly criticized the United States and other countries for trying to interfere with their domestic policies, such as how they deal with dissidents and criminal defendants. They argue that other countries have no right to impose their values on China. They insist that other countries that try to interfere with their internal affairs are claiming moral superiority and are therefore ethnocentric. In a speech regarding the China–U. S. relationship, President Jiang Zemin of The Republic of China argues that friendly relations and cooperation can only exist on the principles of "mutual non-aggression" and "non-interference in each other's internal affairs."[3] He insists that the United States cannot legitimately ask all countries to institute the same political system or to judge the various choices made by people of other countries according to their own values.

Many people also think that we can only have a harmonious society if we respect different ideologies. They worry that allowing some people to make decisions for everyone else will inevitably lead to an oppressive and totalitarian regime. This is especially an important concern for democratic societies like the United States, since we cannot consistently argue for democracy and at the same time impose certain beliefs on other cultures or even our own citizens. After all, democracy requires that all rational human beings be allowed to determine for themselves their way of life and personal values. It requires that others do not authoritatively impose their view as absolute and coerce everyone else to follow it. When there are different moral standards, we cannot simply ignore the perspectives of certain individuals. Imposing one's moral standard on others ignores people's ability to make decisions for themselves and violates their autonomy. As some of my students say, it seems to be pure arrogance for us to exalt our own morality as the only true one and dismiss all other ideas as false or inferior.

Responses to Ethical Relativists and Subjectivists

It is admirable that students want to respect different perspectives. But does respect require that we can never say that certain practices are illegitimate? Students are correct that there are many different beliefs in the world, and it is often difficult to find one right answer for any ethical dilemma. There are usually many complex issues involved in each case, and sometimes there is no simple way to reach an answer. In many instances, even after reflecting on various possible perspectives, we may still not know which perspective is the best one.

However, admitting the difficulty to determine which of the various perspectives is best is different from claiming that each perspective is equally valid, or that we cannot critically evaluate them. Just because there are numerous perspectives or ethical positions does not mean that everything reduces to cultural or personal opinions, or that there is no right or wrong answer to anything. While it is often difficult to find the right answer, we do not have to immediately reject the possibility that some perspectives have *more* validity than others. Although it is difficult to find *one* idea that will be agreeable for all, it is often possible for us to find out which viewpoints are at least more plausible than others. Sometimes even when we do not know what the best answer may be, we can still say that there are certain perspectives that are clearly objectionable. For example, although it is difficult to find a simple answer to the question of how we should treat other human beings, it is clear that there are good reasons to reject the idea that we can kill others whenever we want. Killing each other is a less plausible perspective *in any society* partly because life will become "nasty, brutish, and short," to use the philosopher Thomas Hobbes' phrase.[4]

It is admirable that students want to listen to and respect different perspectives. I agree that we need to refrain from assuming that there is always only one answer to each problem. There are times when there may be various plausible approaches to deal with an ethical issue. I also agree that we should not assume that we are always correct, and that dissenting viewpoints are automatically inferior or wrong. However, the argument that some perspectives are objectively better than others does not imply that one is presuming her moral superiority. Rather, the universal approach to morality only says that there are certain perspectives that are objectively more valid than others, and that these perspectives should apply to everyone. Our job is to *consider various perspectives carefully*, and then find out which ones are better than the rest, and why they are better. It is consistent for one to argue that some perspectives are better and deny that one actually is holding the better perspective. When we question the legitimacy of relativistic positions, we are not saying that we have to condemn *other* people's values. What we are saying is that we need to critically evaluate every perspective, *including our own*. Such a task acknowledges the possibility that we may be holding the wrong perspective.

In other words, it is a mistake to think that a universal approach to morality implies ethnocentrism. It is also a mistake to think that relativistic positions only ask us to withhold judgment of other people's cultural and personal beliefs. Relativism and subjectivism actually permits us to not even judge or evaluate our own beliefs. After all, under these relativistic positions, you do not need to question your beliefs. As one of my students says, she does not want anyone to tell her that she may be wrong, because she thinks she should be allowed to do whatever she believes in. Her idea is that, whatever you believe in is right for you. You do not have to explain or justify to others why you believe in certain things, and others have no right to impose their standard on you. In other words, there is no need for you to give reasons for your actions.

In this way, it is not the universal approach to morality that leads to ethnocentrism and unwillingness to question one's own beliefs. Rather, it is when we adopt a relativistic approach that we may fall into the idea that we are always correct in holding our own beliefs, so that we do not need to critically examine or correct one's own belief. After all, if we are all correct in our opinions, we never have to question whether our sense of morality is distorted. Ironically, it seems that by adopting the universal approach to morality that we can have a better chance of questioning our own beliefs.

It is admirable that students want to withhold judgment of other cultures and people. Certainly, people from different cultural and social backgrounds may not understand each other's viewpoint, and without such understanding it is arrogant to impose our views on others. Some societies have long-established traditions, and it may be difficult and traumatic to make them change their ways of life, since people may feel that they are losing their cultural identity. When we are non-judgmental, we can learn from each other and improve our understanding of others' viewpoints. Such tolerant attitude can help us to live harmoniously in a morally and culturally diverse society.

Moreover, it is only when we all respect others and remain tolerant that those of minority opinions have a fair chance to express their views. One of the reasons why democratic societies are appealing is that everyone has a legal right to express his or her ideas, even when his or her views are in the minority.[5] Maintaining such a tolerant attitude ensures that unpopular views are not being unfairly suppressed.

While these are all good reasons for us to keep an open mind, commitments to respect others and keep an open mind does not imply that ethical relativism and subjectivism are correct. While some customs and practices are relatively innocent and people should have a right to engage in them, not all practices fall into this category. Certainly, worshipping, burning incense, or not eating certain animals do not negatively affect the lives of human beings, and there is little reason to reject such practices even if we do not agree with them. However, it seems that there are limits on what people can do in the name of customs or personal beliefs. When one's action harms another person, as in the examples of ethnic cleansing and slavery, it is unclear if one can justify it simply by claiming that it is one's cultural or personal belief. It is also unclear if people can deny legitimacy of criticism or interference in the convenient name of "internal affairs" or "private matters."

John Stuart Mill's idea of liberty may be helpful here. As a moral philosopher who values liberty, Mill argues that the only justification for interfering with liberty is to prevent harm to others.[6] Mill acknowledges that people have different beliefs, and we need to have open dialogues to discuss such beliefs. He argues that freedom of expression should be allowed, since it is only when we have such freedom that we can fairly evaluate various perspectives and get closer to the truth. Mill also values diversity and originality. He argues that we should not try to shape people after one model, but should allow them to develop in their own ways. He argues that we should resist "forcing improvements on an unwilling people," since "the only unfailing and permanent source of improvement is liberty."[7] Mill argues that even when we disagree with each other's choices, *if such choices do not harm others*, we cannot interfere.

This last point is important. Mill treasures liberty and autonomy, and he thinks that we need to allow rational adults to express their own views and act on their own ideologies. However, he does not think that respect for others implies that we have to allow absolute freedom. There can still be limits to what people can do. As Mill says, "the fact of living in society renders it indispensable that each should be bound to observe a certain line of conduct towards the rest."[8] For example, people cannot injure the interests of another. After all, one cannot consistently argue for one's own freedom but harm another. In this way, respect for freedom does not imply that people should never be accountable for their actions. We can argue that people can engage in various activities in accordance with their cultural and personal ideology, *so long as their actions do not harm another human being's well being or violate another's freedom*. For example, ethnic cleansing and killing infants for entertainment purposes cannot be justified by cultural and personal ideologies, because they harm other people.

More Problems for Ethical Relativists and Subjectivists

Mill's "harm principle" brings out another inadequacy of ethical relativism and subjectivism. When pushed to the extreme, relativistic views run into trouble. Their view that morality is relative to one's cultural or individual beliefs makes it impossible for anyone to condemn or correct even the most atrocious practices. Ethical relativists and subjectivists do not distinguish between innocent customs and unethical practices. They seem to think that they are morally equivalent, i.e., they are all correct if you believe in them. Their failure to see the distinction may have led them to deny the legitimacy of condemning practices that are harmful to others. This is perhaps why many students refuse to say that the Nazi Germans were absolutely wrong in killing six million Jews. After all, we cannot condemn ethnic cleansing unless we accept the view that these practices are not "simply domestic affairs," and that they are wrong regardless of people's personal or cultural beliefs.

One may ask, does it matter whether one believes in relativism or subjectivism? What is the big deal? If we simply allow people to do what they believe in, can't we get along better?

No. I don't think we can get along better by being relativists. Yes. It is a big deal if people believe in relativism. It has enormous implication on social policies and justice issues. After all, we cannot do anything to "correct" injustice unless we can truly say that certain things that happened to people in the past were wrong. If we adopt a relativistic approach, we will be rejecting some of the most important ideas, such as the notion of human rights. Human rights are supposed to apply to all human beings regardless of who they are, where they live, and when they are born. No society or individual is allowed to violate these rights, regardless of their cultural or personal beliefs.

What will happen if we all become relativists? As shown in my class discussion, we will not be able to say that people were wrong in owning slaves, because they lived in a different time in which such practice was allowed. We also will not be able to talk intelligently about international tribunals prosecuting war crimes. If the Nazi Germans believed that it was morally legitimate to kill Jewish people, according to ethical relativism, it was right for them to do so. It makes no difference that other societies thought or continue to think that it was wrong for the Nazis to kill innocent people. We also cannot criticize the Taliban regime in Afghanistan, even though they publicly kill women who go outside without a male relative or a burka. If we accept relativism, we will have to say that all these actions are morally right for those who believe in them. If we disagree with such actions, all that means is that we will not condone it in our own society. However, acceptance of ethical relativism implies that we cannot interfere with or even intelligently criticize the Taliban's policies.

In the end, we will not act against injustice. If we cannot even say that certain things are morally wrong, of course we will not do anything to prevent or correct the wrong. We also do not need to strive for better societies. If the belief that we are entitled to our opinions implies that we are all correct in holding our opinions, then there is no point of questioning or improving ourselves. We will always be right! Ethical relativism and subjectivism seem to give us a convenient justification to never question our own viewpoints. It also provides justification for us to sit by and do nothing even when we have fundamental disagreement on moral matters.

It is no surprise that many proponents of ethical relativism, such as China and other regimes in the Middle East, have been the most flagrant violators of human rights. After all, if various cultures are entitled to their own moral standard and call their practices "domestic policies," other cultures cannot judge them or interfere with their policies. They are automatically immune from scrutiny. Feminists have criticized how many abuses of women are tolerated in the name of privacy and family autonomy. Women who suffer from abuse and other forms of inequality and violence often are not protected under relativistic positions, because what happens in a household or society is considered a private or domestic matter. Such matters cannot be interfered with, even if others may not agree with them. After all, under ethical relativism and subjectivism, whatever people believe is right for them.

What is most startling about ethical relativism and subjectivism is that, according to these doctrines, we can hold contradictory views and all be correct at the same time! According to relativism and subjectivism, part of the reason why we cannot criticize and interfere with each other's position is that we are each correct in holding our individual views! If I believe that physical assault is the right way to teach my spouse about his household duties, it is right for me to do so. If you are against such practice, your view is right for you. In the end, we are both right![9] This means that it is impossible for any culture to condone the wrong practice, or for any individual to believe in the wrong thing.

This is certainly a convenient but troubling position. If we accept the subjectivist idea and believe that we are each correct in believing contradicting positions, it is unclear if any society can legitimately have laws. It appears that under subjectivism, laws are inherently discriminatory, since they treat certain moral beliefs unfavorably. After all, laws that prohibit people from killing others or beating their spouse impose a standard on those who may have different beliefs. They prohibit these people to act on their beliefs.

Certainly, ethical relativists may argue that we need laws for practical reasons, since chaos will result if people can do anything that they "believe" in. However, the fact that we need laws to prevent chaos already shows that ethical relativists and subjectivists are mistaken. Contrary to what they believe, we simply cannot have a harmonious world or safe society if we take these relativistic positions seriously and allow people to do whatever they believe.

Putting aside the problem of chaos in accepting ethical relativism and subjectivism, it seems absurd that the correctness of a position depends on whether one believes in it. My students seem to think that whether slavery is wrong depends on whether people who own slaves believe in such a practice. (Of course, these students are not thinking about whether the slaves agree with such a practice!) But this makes all moral judgments arbitrary. If a culture or an individual happens to believe that owning slaves is wrong, it is wrong. However, if this culture or individual happens to hold the opposite belief, then owning slaves is moral. It does not ask *why* a certain culture or individual believes in various practices. It only asks *if* this culture or individual believes them.

However, it is unclear how my believing in certain things automatically makes it right. Relativistic positions do not require us to give independent reasons or logical arguments for holding such beliefs. They seem to believe that what we *think* is right is the same with what *is* right. The fact that some people believe in ethnic cleansing is sufficient to make it right for them. They do not need to provide any other supporting arguments to show *why* they believe such practice is right. If another group of people believe the opposite, they also do not need to explain why they hold such position.

If ethical relativism and subjectivism are true, moral dialogues or arguments will be meaningless. As I ask my students who are reluctant to say that anything is morally wrong, what is the point of studying ethics, if we are all correct in believing in whatever opinion we happen to hold? There is no point of evaluating different moral positions. And what is the point of trying to teach our children to become "moral citizens"? They can simply do whatever they want, and they will automatically be right! Moreover, what is the point of convincing others or even ourselves that our point of view may have merits? After all, others are also equally correct in holding their viewpoints.

When everyone is automatically right at all times, the whole notion of moral progress is also meaningless. Moral progress means an improvement from worse to better, and it implies an acknowledgement that certain ideologies are better than others. According to relativistic positions, however, we cannot say that the society we are living in right now is better than the one that allowed slavery. We cannot say that various anti-discriminatory practices enforced in the United States today are better than the discriminatory ones that resulted in the death of millions in Germany in 1940s.

It is difficult to balance tolerance and a critical perception of various cultural and individual ideologies. On the one hand, we need to be open-minded and allow other rational beings to reach moral judgements on their own. On the other hand, we also need to keep in mind that being open-minded does not mean that we cannot be critical of various ideas, or that every idea is equally valid. In other words, while we need to keep an open mind, we can still reject ethical relativism or subjectivism. Certainly, we need to be extremely careful in evaluating various views and imposing our views on others. We may be wrong, or there may be practical difficulties in imposing our views on others. However, a commitment to respect others and to keep an open mind does not imply that we can never make judgment about right and wrong. When we keep an open mind, we have a greater chance of understanding each other's viewpoints. At the same time, we will also be more equipped in critically evaluating various positions, including our own. Respect of others only requires that we carefully evaluate different perspectives, and give people of different ideologies an equal chance to explain and defend their respective positions. It requires that we do not assume authority on moral matters and automatically judge others' perspectives as inferior to ours. However, ethical relativism and subjectivism are not the best ways to keep us open-minded and respectful of others. In fact, they prevent us from understanding different viewpoints. The idea that there are universal moral standards may give us a better chance to critically evaluate various ideologies. The universal approach to morality does not argue that we are the ones who always have the right answer, and that others who have different ideologies are inferior. Rather, it requires that we all accept the possibility that everyone is susceptible to mistakes, and we all have to be patient and careful in investigating various moral positions.

I discuss all these issues with my students. Are they convinced? One of them says, "I guess I was wrong in thinking that I am a relativist. I am still not sure when we can impose our ideas on others, but I do think our laws prohibiting slavery and killing are right, and those who commit these acts should be punished." Another says, "I never thought that relativism might give people the perfect reason to sit by and watch injustice happening in the world, but I guess it inevitably leads to that." A few more students nod. As we are ready to leave the class, one student says, "Well, I guess that's your opinion. I still don't buy it." I respond, "And you can't tell me I am wrong."

Notes

[1] Robert Simon, "The Paralysis of Absolutophobia," *The Chronicle of Higher Education*, 27 June 1997, 85–86.

[2] Ruth Benedict, "Ethics Are Relative," in *Classical Philosophical Questions* 9th ed., ed. J. A. Gould (Upper Saddle River, NJ: Prentice Hall, 1998), 159–167.

[3] For the complete speech made by President Jiang, please see http://www.ncuscr.org/articles%20and%20speeches/jiang.speech.htmI

[4] Thomas Hobbes, *Leviathan* (1651; reprint, Harmondsworth, Middlesex: Penguin Books, 1975), 186.

[5] There are often other barriers to minorities actually voicing their opinions, even when they have the legal right to do so. For example, minorities may worry about the "tyranny of majority." They may worry that even when they have the "right" to voice their opinions, their unpopular views will still go unnoticed or are intentionally ignored. However, for the purpose of this essay, I will put aside this issue.

[6] John Stuart Mill, *On Liberty* (1859; reprint, London: Penguin Books, 1985).

[7] John Stuart Mill, 136.

[8] John Stuart Mill, 141.

[9] The ironic result of ethical relativism and subjectivism is that their proponents cannot prove that I am wrong. They cannot even try to convince me that they are correct. If I believe that there are universal moral standards, according to subjectivism, I am automatically correct! In the end, ethical relativism, subjectivism, and universal approach to morality are all correct!

David H. Freedman is the author of many articles and several books, including
Corps Business (2000), an examination of the organization and culture of the
United States Marine Corps as a management training program; Brainmaker
(1994), a study of new approaches to artificial intelligence, and of At Large
(1997), in which he writes about incidents of computer infiltration. A senior editor of Forbes ASAP, Freedman lives in Needham, MA.

The Aggressive Egg

David H. Freedman

Ah, fertilization—that miraculous process to which we all owe our
existence. Let's review: first, a wastefully huge swarm of sperm
weakly flops along, its members bumping into walls and flailing aim-
lessly through thick strands of mucus. Eventually, through sheer odds of
pinball-like bouncing more than anything else, a few sperm end up close
to an egg. As they mill around, the egg selects one and reels it in, pinning
it down in spite of its efforts to escape. It's no contest, really. The gigantic, hardy egg yanks this tiny sperm inside, distills out the chromosomes,
and sets out to become an embryo.

Or would you have put it differently? Until very recently, so would most
biologists. For decades they've been portraying sperm as intrepid warriors
battling their way to an aging, passive egg that can do little but await the
sturdy victor's final, bold plunge. But the first description is closer to the
truth, insists Emily Martin, a 47-year-old researcher at Johns Hopkins who
has spent the past seven years examining the metaphors used to describe
fertilization. Martin is not a biologist; she's a cultural anthropologist. But
her efforts to spotlight the male-skewed imagery that permeates our views
of reproduction have placed her at the center of a growing debate about
how cultural myths can turn into scientific myths, and vice versa.

Martin didn't set out to skewer biologists. Actually she was studying
biology, among other things, at the University of Michigan in 1965 when
a course on Japanese music hooked her on investigating other cultures.
After picking up a Ph.D. in cultural anthropology from Cornell in 1971,
she spent nine years traveling back and forth between the United States,
Taiwan, and China, where she was studying Chinese rituals and social
organization. Then, having done the study of a foreign culture that's traditionally expected of anthropologists, and being pregnant with her first
child, she started casting about for a new project closer to home. "Studying your own culture is harder," she says, "because everything seems so
normal to you."

Not until 1982, while attending a class for expectant parents before the birth of her second child, did Martin stumble on her topic. "It suddenly hit me that the way everyone was talking about their bodies was really weird," she recalls. "It was *the* body, *the* uterus, and *the* contraction—as if these things weren't a part of us. I realized that medical science was in need of some sort of interpretation, and my wedge would be reproductive issues." Martin started off by interviewing dozens of women on their feelings about every aspect of reproduction, from menstruation to menopause. Her book *The Woman in the Body*, published in 1987, explored the relation between images of the body and ideas about oneself. But by 1985 Martin realized that she had been looking at these issues from only one point of view. "I decided to do an ethnographic study in a scientific setting, to see how biologists thought about some of these questions," she says. "Also, I thought I should be including male reproductive processes as well." Fertilization research, she realized, would allow her to cover all the bases.

As she began her background studies, Martin was surprised to find that popular literature, textbooks, and even medical journals were crammed with descriptions of warrior sperm and damsel-in-distress eggs. Martin found that classic biology texts, for example, enthused about the human male's "amazing" productivity—some 200 million sperm every hour—while practically complaining over the "waste" of the 2 million immature eggs present in the human female at birth, only some 400 of which the ovaries ever "shed" for possible fertilization, with the rest destined to "degenerate" over the woman's lifetime. "The real mystery," says Martin, "is why the male's vast production of sperm is not seen as wasteful."

Less mysterious, in Martin's opinion, was the motivation for such biased language. "Men link potency to strong sperm," she says. "You'd like your sperm to be like you; no wonder everyone believed sperm were torpedoes." In all her searching, Martin came up with only a single depiction of less-than-mighty sperm: Woody Allen's portrayal of a neurotic sperm nervous about his imminent ejaculation in the movie *Everything You Always Wanted to Know About Sex But Were Afraid to Ask*.

Woody Allen aside, the durability of the masterful-sperm imagery astonished Martin. It continued to dominate the contemporary technical and popular literature despite a growing body of evidence that the egg plays anything but a passive role. From the early 1970s on, studies of the sperm and eggs of many species have revealed that molecules released by the egg are critical to guiding and "activating" the sperm—that is, triggering the sperm to release proteins that help it adhere to the egg. In fact, the egg might just as well be called eager as passive. Among many species of lizards, insects, some crustaceans, and even turkeys, the egg doesn't always wait for the sperm's arrival. It can begin dividing without fertilization, and females can reproduce without sperm at all.

Yet none of this had made a dent in biologists' language. "When I asked them about it, they told me I had a point," says Martin. "They claimed the imagery came up only when they needed to explain their research, and not in the lab. But I wanted to know what was really going on."

By 1986 Martin had begun hanging out with a team of researchers at Johns Hopkins who were observing sperm mobility in hopes of coming up with a strategy for a new contraceptive. They had started the year before with a simple experiment—measuring human sperm's ability to escape and swim away from a tiny suction pipet placed against the side of the sperm cell's head. To the team's great surprise, the sperm turned out to be feeble swimmers; their heads thrashed from side to side ten times more vigorously than their bodies pushed forward. "It makes sense," says Martin. "The last thing you'd want a sperm to be is a highly effective burrower, because it would end up burrowing into the first obstacle it encountered. You want a sperm that's good at getting away from things."

The team went on to determine that the sperm tries to pull its getaway act even on the egg itself, but is held down against its struggles by molecules on the surface of the egg that hook together with counterparts on the sperm's surface, fastening the sperm until the egg can absorb it. Yet even after having revealed the sperm to be an escape artist and the egg to be a chemically active sperm catcher, even after discussing the egg's role in "tethering" the sperm, the research team continued for another three years to describe the sperm's role as actively "penetrating" the egg.

Meanwhile, Martin was keeping an eye on two other fertilization groups. They too seemed at times to disregard their own observations when writing about fertilization. Researchers at the University of Wisconsin, for example, described the way sea urchin sperm first make contact with an egg by quickly stringing together protein molecules into a filament that extends out until it reaches the egg. But instead of describing this as an innocuous process of assembly and attachment, the group wrote—in a pioneering paper that otherwise points out the egg's ability to actively "clasp" and "entwine"—that the sperm's filament "shoots out and harpoons" the egg. Likewise, when a researcher at the Roche Institute of Molecular Biology in Nutley, New Jersey, wrote in 1987 of his discovery that mouse eggs carry a molecular structure on their coating that fits inside a complementary structure on the sperm, helping bind the two together, he described the two structures, naturally enough, as a lock and key—but he called the egg's protruding structure the lock and the sperm's engulfing structure the key.

Martin doesn't suggest that these researchers willfully distorted their imagery. In fact, she notes that one of the investigators at Johns Hopkins was her politically correct husband, Richard Cone. What's more, Martin concedes that she herself was slow to recognize the disparity between the discoveries at Johns Hopkins and the way the findings were written up. "It didn't strike me for a few years," she says. But innocent or not, she adds, the cultural conditioning these biologists had absorbed early in their careers influenced more than their writing: it skewed their research. "I believe, and my husband believes, and the lab believes, that they would have seen these results sooner if they hadn't had these male-oriented images of sperm. In fact, biologists could have figured out a hundred years ago that sperm are weak forward-propulsion units, but it's hard for men to accept the idea that sperm are best at escaping. The imagery you employ guides you to ask certain questions and to not ask certain others."

People preparing to dismiss Emily Martin as a humorless feminist have their work cut out for them. At once animated and easygoing in her cramped, cactus-strewn office, Martin chuckles as she goes through an inch-thick file of hapless-egg and macho-sperm imagery clipped from magazines. (In one Gary Larson cartoon, a housewife egg fends off a swarm of sperm trying to get past her by posing as phone repairmen, insurance salesmen, and UPS deliverymen.) "I just think this stuff is a riot," she says. In fact, it's the biologists who seem a little stuffy. Though she usually lectures to students, Martin recalls one lecture she gave to biologists at the Woods Hole Oceanographic Institution in 1990. "It was one of the most painful experiences of my life," she says. "I had gotten to the point where the audience is usually rolling in the aisles, and all I got was stony silence. I could see they were furious. On the other hand, I can understand their feelings; I get defensive when someone criticizes cultural anthropology."

One researcher who doesn't bristle at Martin's jabs is Scott Gilbert, a developmental biologist at Swarthmore College. Though he suggests Martin may go a little overboard in stressing the egg's aggressiveness—for example, he prefers to think of the egg as "engaging in a dialog" with the sperm rather than gluing it down—he does believe her views are a vast improvement over the conventional explanations. "Most studies clearly show that the sperm is attracted by the egg and activated by it," says Gilbert. "But if you don't have an interpretation of fertilization that allows you to look at the egg as active, you won't look for the molecules that can prove it. You simply won't find activities that you don't visualize."

Now that the discrepancy between experiment and interpretation is being brought out into the open, the professional literature seems to be coming around—although a recent issue of the biology journal *Cell Differentiation and Development* placed on its cover a Prince Charming sperm delivering a wake-up kiss to a long-eyelashed Sleeping Beauty egg. As for the popular press, Gilbert and Martin cite the same recent example as particularly egregious: an article titled "Sperm Wars" that appeared as a cover story in a national science magazine whose name you'd recognize in a minute, which referred to the sperm cell as "a formidable .00024-inch weapon, tipped with a chemical warhead" (see *Discover*, July 1991). On the other hand, *Developmental Biology*, the most popular college textbook in its subject area, takes great pains to point out the new, equal-opportunity view of fertilization. No wonder: Gilbert wrote it.

One reason the older interpretation is dying hard is that it tends to be self-reinforcing, not only in suggesting ready-made imagery that can skew observations but also in subtly determining who becomes a biologist in the first place. "This business has stopped certain people from entering the field," says Gilbert. "Why would a woman want to continue if people are telling her she's passive?"

Nevertheless, as Martin points out, a growing number of women *are* continuing in biology. But that won't guarantee more evenhanded interpretations. "Scientific training involves a rigorous socialization process that doesn't allow for different perspectives," she says. "It's hard to say that women biologists are any less guilty of these things than men."

Even if biologists do move away from the passive-egg myth, other images are waiting in the wings. These days, says Martin, researchers seem ready to confer a "spider woman" aspect on the egg. "Men have always turned to spider imagery when they are confronted with women who acquire power," she charges. Indeed, her file of magazine clippings contains several images in support of her claim. One striking example: the cartoonish silhouette employed as the emblem of the once-popular *Charlie's Angels* television series, which depicts the three starring female characters, guns and all, unmistakably merged into the eight-limbed shape of a spider.

Though Martin is the first to insist that much of the fertilization imagery is good for a laugh, she doesn't mean to let scientists dismiss it all as a big joke. "People say, 'Oh, what difference does it make?' as if this stuff doesn't affect anyone," she says. "But our culture *is* affected by these powerful visual images. We all put so much faith in science, and so much of the negative load lands on women."

She notes, as another example, that it's been known since the 1960s that women exposed to toxic chemicals bear children who run a higher risk of serious medical problems. Those findings reinforced the cultural notion that women should be sheltered, and some companies have rules to prevent women of reproductive age from working at jobs that might involve exposure to these chemicals. But only in the past few years have comparable studies shown that men exposed to high levels of lead, vinyl chloride, and about a dozen other chemicals also have children who are at higher risk. "It's the notion of invulnerable sperm," she claims, "that made it take so long for scientists and the public to accept the male role in birth defects and infertility."

Martin has recently shifted her focus to metaphors used in other areas of medical research. For example, she says, "when AIDS was seen as affecting only the 'dregs' of society, scientists described it as a monkey virus. Now that well-to-do white women are getting it, all of a sudden researchers are talking about AIDS being an autoimmune disease." There are, of course, other reasons that researchers' language might change, including a growing knowledge of how the AIDS virus in fact wreaks havoc on the host's immune system. Martin is still studying the literature and observing researchers in immunology labs. For now, she concedes, "all you can do is raise a question. It's often impossible to prove causality."

Although she is no longer studying fertilization imagery, Martin still lectures on the topic because, she contends, "the work shows that science can have social effects. When we anthropomorphize the egg and sperm, when we turn them into a miniature bride and groom complete with personalities, what effect does this have on abortion legislation? These effects aren't intended by scientists, but they happen. They blend moral and scientific issues together in a way that makes me want to stand up and say something."

There's further irony in the traditional metaphors. The notion of fiercely battling, competitive sperm suggests that they're battling each other in a "race" to the egg. In fact, says Cone, they have a hard time making their way through the mucus glop, and like a team of bicyclists they "take turns" up front parting strands of mucus. So in a sense sperm are cooperative. The egg, on the other hand, is the real competitive loner. Only one matures each month, and the one out in front suppresses the maturation of all the others. The macho image of sperm not only obscures this reality; it actually reverses what's been observed.

Can biased metaphors be eliminated from science? Martin doesn't think so. Even if they could be, she doesn't think that antiseptically neutral language would be desirable. Metaphor is, after all, a powerful vehicle for creative thinking. "The goal shouldn't be to clean the imagery out," she says, "but to be aware that it's there." It also helps, she adds, to be able to take a joke. "Humor takes away the sting," she says, "along with the potential for inculcating harmful ideas."

Lynn Payer (b. 1945) is author of several books and articles on science and medicine that have been published in Science, Medical Tribune, *the* New York Times, Vogue, Ms. *and others. She received her Masters degree at Columbia University's Graduate School of Journalism and has taught journalism at Columbia, New York University, and Indiana University. She maintains an online newsletter entitled* Lynn Payer's Medicine and Culture Update (http://www.healthcareland.com/medculture.htm).

Culture Bias in Medical Science

Lynn Payer

- An American opera singer in Vienna consulted an Austrian doctor, who prescribed suppositories for her headache. Not used to receiving headache medication in this form, she ate one.
- A British general practitioner took his wife to a North Carolina clinic where he was temporarily working to show her the position American women customarily assume for pelvic examination. Her judgment: "Why, that's barbaric!" Her husband performed the examination with women lying on their sides and, while he was ridiculed by the other North Carolina doctors, he soon found he had a queue of women outside his office who had heard he examined "the English way."
- A French professor on sabbatical in California suffered an attack of angina pectoris, for which his doctors recommended immediate bypass surgery. The professor consented, not realizing that at the time American rates of frequency for coronary bypass were twenty-eight times that of some European countries and that later studies were to show that bypasses rarely have to be done immediately, if at all.
- A young American working in Germany was told by her German gynecologist to take mud baths rather than antibiotics to treat her vaginal infection. "I don't want to sit in mud," wailed the woman later to a colleague. "All I want is a couple of pills!"
- World travelers who have had to see a doctor in a foreign country have usually discovered that medicine is not quite the international science that the medical profession would like us to believe. Not only do ways of delivering medical care differ from country to country; so does the medicine that is delivered. The differences are so great that one country's treatment of choice may be considered malpractice across the border.

Some of the most commonly prescribed drugs in France, drugs to dilate the cerebral blood vessels, are considered ineffective in England and America; an obligatory immunization against tuberculosis in France, BCG, is almost impossible to obtain in the United States. German doctors prescribe from six to seven times the amount of digitalis-like drugs as their colleagues in France and England, but they prescribe fewer antibiotics, with some German doctors maintaining antibiotics shouldn't be used unless the patient is sick enough to be in the hospital. Doses of the same drug may vary drastically, with some nationalities getting ten to twenty times what other nationals get. French people have seven times the chance of getting drugs in suppository form as do Americans. In the late 1960s American surgery rates were twice those of England; and the intervening years have seen this surgery gap widen, not close. Rates for individual operations vary even more. One study found three times as many mastectomies in New England as in England or Sweden, even though the rate of breast cancer was similar; another found that German-speaking countries had three times the rate of appendectomies of other countries; there are six times the number of coronary bypasses per capita in America when compared to England. Even if the operation has the same general name it may be done differently: West German doctors perform mostly vaginal hysterectomies; French doctors commonly perform subtotal hysterectomies; and English and U.S. doctors favor total abdominal hysterectomies.

The same clinical signs may even receive different diagnoses. Often, all one must do to acquire a disease is to enter a country where that disease is recognized—leaving the country will either cure the malady or turn it into something else. The American schizophrenic of a few years ago might well have found his disease called manic-depressive disease or even neurosis had he sought a second opinion in Britain; in France he likely would have been diagnosed as having a delusional psychosis. The Frenchman suffering from spasmophilia or the German from vasovegetative dystonia would be considered merely neurotic in Britain or perhaps a victim of panic disorder in the United States if he were considered sick at all.

Blood pressure considered treatably high in the United States might be considered normal in England; and the low blood pressure treated with eight-five drugs as well as hydrotherapy and spa treatments in Germany would entitle its sufferer to lower life insurance rates in the United States.

The differences are most marked for minor complaints but not at all limited to them. "Plenty of people," wrote Dr. M.N.G. Dukes in the *British Medical Journal*, "are still dying of diseases which other people do not believe in." One World Health Organization study found that doctors from different countries diagnosed different causes of death even when shown identical information from the same death certificates. There was a considerable amount of disagreement in coding infective and parasitic disease, "other heart" diseases, hypertension, pneumonia, nephritis and nephrosis, and diseases of the newborn. "There was fairly good agreement ... on whether a death was due to a malignant neoplasm [cancer] or not, but less agreement on the location of neoplasms ... ," a finding confirmed by another study sponsored by the American National Cancer Institute.

A psychiatric assessment of which patients are dangerous can result in their being locked up; yet when psychiatrists from six countries tried to agree on who was dangerous, the overall level of agreement was under 50 percent for three-quarters of the cases considered, and the psychiatrists did not agree any more among themselves than did nonpsychiatrists.

Even within a given country, of course, not all doctors diagnose and treat identically, and the differences among different specialists can often be particularly marked. But many comparisons have shown that while doctors within a given country differ somewhat, doctors from different countries differ even more.

How can medicine, which is commonly supposed to be a science, particularly in the United States, be so different in four countries whose peoples are so similar genetically? The answer is that while medicine benefits from a certain amount of scientific input, culture intervenes at every step of the way.

Take, for example, a very common situation in medicine. A patient is excessively tired, and makes an appointment with his doctor.

Already, a difference emerges. In England the patient would be obliged by the National Health Service to make an appointment with his general practitioner, whereas in the United States there are so few general practitioners that the patient would commonly choose some sort of specialist such as a gynecologist, pediatrician, or internist. Since even within a country different types of doctors treat the same illness differently, the different ratios of specialists will already have wide repercussions.

The physician faced with a tired patient will have several choices, since fatigue can be a sign of a number of diseases including viral illness, depression, cancer and heart disease. The doctor can examine the patient, and the frequency and thoroughness of examinations differ markedly from country to country. He can order tests, and here, too, enormous differences have been documented. He can delay, telling the patient to wait to see if his energy returns. Or he can come up with a diagnosis that will reassure the patient and hope that the placebo effect will then cure whatever it is. Often the physician feels this last approach is the best thing he can do for his patient.

The diagnosis he reaches in such a case will be strongly influenced by culture; what he learned in medical school, what he knows other doctors say, and what he knows will reassure the patient. A liver crisis will reassure a French patient while it would alarm an American one; the diagnosis of "a virus" would probably have opposite effects on each.

Many of the more scientifically minded physicians in all countries discount such "wastebasket diagnoses," claiming that they are really not scientific medicine at all. "In France, we would call vague digestive troubles a liver crisis; in the United States you would call it a food allergy. You prescribe anything at all, because it's not a scientific diagnosis, but rather a different use of placebos", said Henri Pequignot, a professor of medicine at Paris's Hôpital Cochin.

Most patients and most doctors, however, don't realize that they are using placebos, and as we shall see later, such wastebasket diagnoses influence so-called scientific medicine in a number of ways.

But for the time being let us accept Dr. Pequinot's comment that such diagnoses and treatments are unimportant, and look instead at what he would admit is "scientific medicine." Suppose, for example, that a doctor in one country decides to perform a scientific study. In planning his study, the doctor or other medical scientist must decide whether it will be randomized, controlled trial (RCT), in which patients are divided into at least two groups, the two groups treated differently, and the results eventually compared. The strength of such trials is that they are usually considered to provide the most scientific answer; the problem is that patients must be treated differently and the results then compared, and many doctors find this ethically distasteful. RCTs are also difficult to organize and carry out. While RCTs have to some extent been adopted in all the countries, they are done most often in England. One of their most vocal advocates, Dr. Archibald Cochrane, wrote in his book *Effectiveness and Efficiency*: "If some such index as the number of RCTs per 1,000 doctors per year for all countries were worked out and a map of the world shaded according to the level of the index (black being the highest), one would see the UK in black and scattered black patches in Scandinavia, the USA and a few other countries: The rest would be nearly white."

In the chapters that follow, the reason RCTs are considered so differently, as well as why it is easier to have a placebo-controlled trial in England than in America, will be considered. But for the moment, let us simply consider this point: *If a study is not performed as an RCT, it will probably not be accepted for publication in the English medical literature.* Which brings us to our next point: *Doctors in one country rarely read the medical literature of any country but their own.*

Dr. A.M.W. Porter, a general practitioner in Surrey, England, interviewed French and British doctors and found that the British doctors couldn't name a single French medical journal, and the French were only able to name an average of slightly over one British journal, mostly *The Lancet*. My own observations would suggest that the French are even more ignorant of the German medical literature, and vice versa. Communication may be somewhat better between the British and the Americans. But when a vice president of the American Cancer Society was informed in the mid-1970s of a study published in the *British Medical Journal* that showed women treated for early breast cancer by "tylectomy" (the British author's term for lumpectomy) survived just as long as those treated by radical mastectomy, his reply was: "We don't read much foreign literature here."

As a result of this mutual ignorance, the English and Americans are constantly rediscovering what the French and Germans have known for a long time, and vice versa. Dr. Marcel-Francis Kahn, a professor of rheumatology at Hôpital Bichat in Paris, pointed out that while a letter in the 1981 volume of the journal *Arthritis and Rheumatism* credited Churchill and his associates as the first to document disc-space infections in bacterial endocarditis, there had already been no fewer than ten articles in the French literature devoted to the subject, the first published in 1965.

Doctors claim that they stay on top of other countries'medical advances by attending international meetings, but presenting a paper at an international meeting is no guarantee that anyone is listening. To start with, there's the problem of language. Even the best simultaneous interpreter is going to have trouble dealing with the fact that *peptic ulcer* and *bronchitis* don't mean the same things in Britain as they do in the United States; that the U.S. *appendectomy* becomes the British *appendicectomy*; that the French tendency to exaggerate means there are never headaches in France, only migraines, and that the French often refer to real migraines as "liver crises"; that the German language has no word for chest pain, forcing the German patient to talk of heart pain, and that when a German doctor says "cardiac insufficiency" he may simply mean that the patient is tired.

A similar situation prevails in psychiatric language. "Even though bilingual dictionaries may give the impression that the English adjectives paranoid, paranoiac and delusional are the exact equivalents of French *paranoïde, paranoïaque* and *délirant*, French- and English-speaking psychiatrists use these terms quite differently and with vastly divergent frequencies," wrote Dr. Pierre Pichot, a French psychiatrist who is past president of the International Psychiatric Association.

Then, too, not all interpreters are top-notch, and the headphones may not work; at best they are irritating. At small meetings where scientists discuss a highly specialized topic in one language, communication is likely to be good; at large international congresses, doctors usually go to the sessions where their countrymen are speaking and spend the rest of the time sightseeing.

Dr. Sakari Härö, chief of the Department of Planning and Evaluation of the National Board of Health in Helsinki, Finland, put it this way: "At a meeting, the Finns tend to group with the English. The Germans stay together as a bloc, as do the Southern and Eastern Europeans. At a meeting I seldom discuss with the French—I'm half sleeping when French is being spoken."

If the language barrier is breached, and people understand the words, they will probably start to criticize the science. If a French or German doctor gives a paper, for example, a British doctor will often get up in the question-and-answer period and say scathingly, "I think it is scandalous that we are still hearing about uncontrolled trials."

Even if the science is understood and accepted, there may be no agreement as to what the study means for the practice of medicine. This is true even within a country: studies may show the consequence of a certain course of action, i.e., a treatment, but judging whether the consequence is good or bad can be highly subjective. Dr. E. M. Glaser, for example, writing in the *British Medical Journal*, pointed out the wide disparity of conclusions that had been drawn in the same issue of *BMJ*. One paper, reporting a near death from eating licorice, had no comment on future safety; another, on intestinal bypass operations for obesity, reported statistically significant liver damage in all patients studied and a 4 percent mortality but concluded that "further careful evaluation of the effects of intestinal bypass operations is required"; and a third that showed an adverse reaction in one of the 1,000 persons given an intravenous anesthetic induction agent concluded that this rate of side effects made the intravenous injection unacceptable.

If such very subjective conclusions concerning future courses of action can be drawn in a single issue of one medical journal, the possible range of subjectivity from country to country is, of course, even greater. Consider, for example, a study that shows that giving chemotherapy to elderly patients with cancer prolongs their lives by an average of a few months but also causes them severe, intractable, drug-induced vomiting. If one believes that length of life is the most important criterion, this study would indicate that such patients should be given chemotherapy; if one believes quality of life is more important it might indicate that chemotherapy should not be given.

In fact, the American authors of this particular paper felt the added months justified a recommendation for chemotherapy; Englishmen who commented on it in the *BMJ* felt this recommendation was off base. In neither commentary did the authors recommend that patients be asked how they felt about the matter.

If a study fits into the general scheme of medical thinking in a country, it is likely to be widely cited. This is particularly true if is shows that a drug is effective or an operation works, because the drug company and the surgeons concerned will see that the study gets written and talked about. If the study goes against medical thinking, medical professionals find it quite easy to ignore one study amid the thousands that are published each month. An RCT performed in 1922, for example, showed that women whose pubic hair was shaved before giving birth had more infections than those whose pubic hair wasn't shaved, and these results were shown again in 1965. Yet many hospital services in England and America (not in France) continued the practice, probably due to some puritanical feeling that pubic hair *should* be shaved. A 1986 paper in a prominent German medical journal proved that the horse-chestnut extracts already widely used in Germany to treat problems of circulation actually do work—and I'll wager that while the study will be widely cited in Germany, it will be completely ignored in the United States.

The Common Market countries theoretically allow free movement of goods and services among them. But the fact that one country allows a drug to be put on its market does not automatically put the drug on the market in other countries. In fact, in no case since the establishment of the Common Market have all the members accepted a drug just because it was accepted in one country. According to Dr. Gerald Jones of the Department of Health and Social Security in the United Kingdom, the differences were always related to risk-benefit ratios of the drugs: "We all use the same guidelines, yet different opinions are reached on the same pre-clinical or clinical data."

In general, doctors in all countries—except, as we shall see, England—favor studies that suggest new types of treatments rather than studies that show current treatments are unnecessary. For example, Dr. Umberto Veronesi, director of the Italian National Cancer Institute in Milan observed, "We did a trial showing that in malignant melanoma, after removal of the primary tumor, there is no need to remove the regional lymph nodes if they are not palpably involved. We followed up 600 patients for 12 years, and our results, published five years ago, are very clear. But the reaction of general surgeons has been strong and hostile—the majority of them still remove the regional lymph nodes."

In the United States, coronary artery bypass surgery was widely adopted before any studies had been shown it to be effective in preventing death or disability; yet, on the other hand, the practice of allowing women who have had a cesarean section to deliver vaginally a subsequent time will probably not be adopted—despite some twenty studies showing that under proper conditions such a practice is safe. The popularity of coronary bypass surgery concords with the American culture biases of aggressive treatment and with the American view of the body as a machine; while reducing the number of cesarean sections would contradict American values in favoring nonintervention and being mainly of psychological value to delivering women.

It is, of course, easier for doctors to reject a foreign study. Dr. Fritz Beller, a professor of gynecology at the University of Münster in West Germany, refers to the phenomenon as Beller's Rule Number One: A method developed on one continent has difficulty being accepted on another. One unnamed American researcher notes that, for many of his colleagues, "If we don't describe it first, our first reaction is always negative. We are very chauvinistic and have the attitude that if we haven't found something, it's probably wrong."

Rejection of study results may also be based on how doctors feel their patients would react. In response to evidence that cholera vaccination was of little value, the health authorities of one unnamed developed country explained: "The fear of cholera is strongly felt by a large part of the population which still trusts vaccination practice as a control measure against the disease. We feel that our population, as well as that of other countries, would not agree to drop a protective measure, even if it has been scientifically demonstrated to be of little value."

The way the doctor is paid, and the organization of medical care, will also influence acceptance. Dr. Henk Lamberts, a Dutch GP active in international organizations, said, "When you see a patient whose wound has been treated by a Spanish doctor, it will have two sutures, since in Spain doctors are paid by treating the wound. An Austrian doctor would have put in six sutures, and the Belgian doctor would have put in as many sutures as he could, as they are paid by the number of sutures."

Dr. Lamberts emphasized that he didn't mean to sound cynical. "Belgian culture values sutures, so they are put in. It's appreciated, so he gets paid for it."

The widespread ignorance that medicine in highly developed countries can be so different has a number of serious implications. First, all sorts of unjustified conclusions are currently being drawn from international statistics. A press handout concerning rates of coronary artery disease in various countries, for example, showed the rate to be low in West Germany. While the person who compiled the release had copied the figures correctly from international statistics, he was unaware that while West Germany reports relatively low rates of coronary artery disease, the country reports much higher rates of "other" heart disease than do England and the United States. If the rates of coronary artery disease and other heart disease are taken together, as it has been suggested they should, West Germany, England, and the United States have similar rates of heart disease.

Second, different ways that different countries treat the same disease constitute a sort of natural experiment; yet because most people are unaware of the experiment in the first place, they are unable to draw the conclusions that might result. For example, French doctors have widely prescribed calcium for a number of years, and a closer examination of osteoporosis rates there might help illuminate the role of calcium in this disease. As a corollary, a greater understanding of medical culture bias might predict the country in which side effects will first surface—or will be hidden. The neural side effects of bismuth were first discovered in France, where very high doses were prescribed for constipation; conversely, the very serious side effect that an antihypertensive drug, Selacryn, had on the liver were underestimated in France, because the French, who frequently attribute liver troubles to rich food and drink or a constitutionally "fragile" liver, would be less likely to see a drug as the culprit.

Finally, many of the medical mistakes made in each country can be best understood by cultural biases that blind both the medical profession and patients, causing them to accept some treatments too quickly and other treatments reluctantly or not at all. Understanding the cultural basis for these mistakes can perhaps prevent them—or at least lessen their impact.

Sandra Marie Schneiders, IHM (Immaculate Heart of Mary), is Professor of New Testament studies and Christian Spirituality at the Jesuit School of Theology at Berkeley. She is a lecturer on women and religious life and the author of several books, including Selling All: Commitment, Consecrated Celibacy, and Community in Catholic Religious Life *(2001), and* With Oil in Their Lamps: Faith, Feminism, and the Future *(2000).*

from Women and the Word
The Gender of God in the New Testament and the Spirituality of Women

Sandra Marie Schneiders

I. The Question about the Gender of God

A. The Modernity of the Question

. . . At the outset of this discussion it is important to be aware that the question of the gender of God is a thoroughly modern issue. No matter how entrenched in the imagination of the average Christian the image of a male God might be, theological tradition has never assigned sex to God.[1] St. Gregory of Nazianzus well represented the tradition when he affirmed that the terms "Father" and "Son" as applied to the persons of the Trinity were not names of natures or essences but of relations[2] and even in this case the terms are used metaphorically. In other words, God is neither a father nor a son but the first person of the Trinity is related to the second person as origin is related to that which is originated. Because the ancients believed that God was indeed personal, and because their defective biology ascribed all agency in procreation or personal originating activity to the male partner, their choice of "father" for the originating person of the Trinity was logical enough. And since they wished to affirm the absolute likeness and equality of the one originated to the divine principle they called the second person the "son." They were, however, quite aware of the metaphorical nature of their language and never intended to impute actual sexuality to the God whom Scripture affirms is pure Spirit (cf. Jn 4:24).

Second, theological tradition has virtually always maintained that the maleness of Jesus is theologically, christologically, soteriologically, and sacramentally irrelevant.[3] It has been suggested, not without reason, that the attempt of the Vatican's Congregation for the Doctrine of the Faith in its "Declaration on the Question of the Admission of Women to the Ministerial Priesthood" (*Inter Insignores*)[4] to assign theological significance to the sex of Jesus by maintaining that women Christians, because they are female, do not resemble Christ is not only non-traditional but also at least theologically confused if not strictly heretical.[5] As patristics scholar R. A. Norris states,

> The argument [against the ordination of women on the grounds that male sex is required for likeness to Christ] is virtually unprecedented. It does not in fact state any of the traditional grounds on which ordination to the presbyterate or episcopate has been denied to women. To accept this argument and its practical consequences, therefore, is not to maintain tradition but to alter it by altering its meaning.[6]

More important, however, than its non-traditionality is the threat it raises to a central theological affirmation about the incarnation, namely, that as Gregory of Nazianzus and numerous other Fathers of the Church have maintained, "*Tò gàr àpróslepton àtherápeuton*," i.e., "What is not assumed is not redeemed."[7] The Vatican argument attempts to make the maleness of Jesus a necessary precondition to his being who he is, God-with-us, and doing what he does, redeeming us by his paschal mystery. To do so, as Norris says, "is to qualify or deny the universality of his redemption."[8]

In short, the theological tradition of the Church never assigned sex to God and almost never (until the theologically faulty 1977 document) assigned any theological significance to the sex of Jesus. Why, then, is the gender of God such a troubling question for contemporary Christians, especially for women whose consciousness has been raised by the women's movement in our time?

B. The Dilemma for Women

As women have become aware of their inferior status and actual oppression in family, society, and Church, they have also become aware that the gender of God, God's presumed masculinity, has functioned as the ultimate religious legitimation of the unjust social structures which victimize women. First, the maleness of Jesus has been used in Christian cultures as a support from divine revelation for the age-old claim that maleness is normative for humanity and that men are superior to women. Most western languages themselves, in which the generic human is always masculine, testify incessantly to the misconception that humanity is originally and normatively male and that women are a derivative and subordinate, if not actually misbegotten, version of the essentially male species. Male privilege, based on this erroneous assumption of male superiority, is firmly entrenched in virtually every sector of human life.

Second the "fatherhood" of God has been used to justify patriarchy or father-rule, the social system which sacralizes male domination and legitimates virtually all forms of oppression of the weak by the strong. We will return to the topic of patriarchy shortly.

Third, the masculinity of God and of Jesus has been used, in the practical sphere, to deny the likeness of women to God and to Christ and to exclude them from full participation in the life of the Church. Whether this spiritual degradation takes the relatively mild form of excluding little girls from serving at the altar or the more serious forms of exclusion of women from decision-making positions in the Church and enforcement of their sacramental dependence on men, it has a destructive effect on women's spiritual self-image and perverts their relationships with male Christians and with God.

The masculinity of God, in other words, is not primarily an issue in speculative theology. It can easily be established that the God of Judaeo-Christian revelation and Christian theological tradition is not male and that Jesus' maleness is theologically irrelevant. This helps very little, however, because the real problem is not in the area of systematic theology but in the area of religious experience or spirituality.[9] How women experience themselves in relation to God, Christ, and Church is profoundly affected by the imputed masculinity of God which is operative in the imaginations of both male and female believers.

Once their consciousness is raised, women Christians can find themselves impaled on the horns of a dilemma. Either they can continue as Christians, accepting the spiritual consequences of their lack of resemblance to God and Christ and their consequent inferiority to and spiritual dependence on men in the Church (the position advocated by the Vatican Declaration despite its protestations to the contrary), or they can abandon Christianity as a hopelessly patriarchal religion and seek their spiritual home in a religious tradition in which women and women's experience are central and valued.[10] Unless educated and aware women can find a creative and liberating understanding of God and of Jesus, one which does not glorify masculinity at the expense of femininity and does not justify the oppression of women by men, they have no future in institutional Christianity.

II. Preliminary Clarifications

Before undertaking an exploration of the problem of God's "masculinity" and women's spirituality two clarifications are necessary. First, we must distinguish clearly between sex and gender because, as we will see, it is the *gender* of God and the *sex* of Jesus which are the real problems. Second, we have to distinguish between patriarchy (and paternalism) on the one hand and paternity or fatherhood on the other because it is only the former which is problematic. Fatherhood as such, provided that it is not used exclusively, is one appropriate metaphor for God.

A. Sex and Gender

Sex refers to biological identity, the possession of male or female sexual organs and the proportionate activity of male or female hormones which grounds the distinctive roles of men and women in the reproductive process. Gender, however, refers to the experience of self and others in terms of sexual identity. Although sex and gender normally coincide in humans, i.e., females experience themselves and are experienced by others as feminine and males as masculine, this is not always the case, nor is the experience always totally dichotomous. Thus, someone who is biologically a male might experience himself as feminine and might be experienced that way by others. And persons are sometimes experienced as both feminine and masculine, or androgynous. The point is that while sex is biologically determined by observation of empirically available data, gender refers to the way one experiences oneself or others.[11]

God, as we have said, is neither male nor female, i.e., God does not have a body and therefore does not have sex. But because all human persons have gender and we experience God as personal we tend to experience God anthropomorphically as either masculine or feminine or both, i.e., as male and female successively, or as androgynous. Our God-image, as we will explain below, is a function of the imagination, and the Christian religious imagination is deeply influenced by the belief in the personal nature of God, by the overwhelmingly male God-language in the Bible, and by the incarnation of God in the concrete humanity of a male human being, Jesus. Until very recently many if not most Christians, including those who were theologically convinced that God is Spirit, experienced God as almost exclusively masculine. Theologically well-informed people of both sexes have insisted vehemently on the maintenance of exclusively male language for God in public prayer.[12] To a large extent this insistence has more to do with maintaining male dominant power arrangements in family, society, and Church than with theological issues. But for many people the problem is genuinely religious. Their problem is a paralysis of the religious imagination. To imagine God or speak to God as feminine does not simply change the God image for these people; it destroys it.

If God is pure spirit, the same cannot be said about Jesus who was actually a male. However, although biologically male and masculine in gender, Jesus has also been experienced as distinctly feminine in many ways. Sentimental art provides a perverted testimony to this fact, but the motherhood of Jesus and of Christ is a consistent theme in medieval mystical literature. Bernard of Clairvaux, Julian of Norwich, Anselm of Canterbury, Gertrude of Helfta, Mechtild of Hackeborn, and Mechtild of Magdeburg are among the spiritual writers whose works are explored by medieval scholar Caroline Walker Bynum in her 1982 volume, *Jesus as Mother*.[13] The Gospel portrays Jesus as non-aggressive, non-competitive, meek and humble of heart, a nurturer of the weak, and a friend of the outcast. He manifested and preached a spirituality that was characterized by stereotypically feminine rather than masculine virtues. This femininity of Jesus has often enough proven difficult for men to assimilate, but it has always supported the spirituality of women. For women, the problem is not the gender of Jesus, his masculinity which is so inclusively feminine, but his sex. It is the biological fact that Jesus, by being a man rather than a woman, is irreducibly and irrevocably different from women that seems to exclude women from the fullness of identity with him. Furthermore, the maleness of Jesus cannot help but intensify the experience of God as masculine and of maleness as normative, i.e., as the best and fullest way to be human.

B. Patriarchy and Paternity

A second distinction important for our purposes is that between paternity on the one hand and patriarchy/paternalism on the other. Patriarchy is a social system based on the *patria potestas*, i.e., the absolute and unaccountable power over wives and concubines, children, servants, slaves, animals and real property enjoyed by the *paterfamilias*, i.e., the father who is head of the family, tribe, or clan. To the father of the family belonged, as property, all members of the extended household and all goods. In classical Greek and Roman societies this authority of ownership extended even to the power of life and death. Children, especially girls, were often deemed valueless to the father and left to die. Insubordinate wives or slaves could be sold or killed.[14] While sons, when they became adults, were emancipated and became patriarchs in their own right, daughters were passed, with or without their consent, from the control of the father to that of a husband,[15] i.e., from one patriarch to another.

In the patriarchal system authority and power were strictly coterminous and belonged totally and exclusively to the head of the household unless he delegated it to another. The authority and power of the *paterfamilias* were considered as divinely established, and thus the patriarchal system was unalterable and rebellion against the father was rebellion against God. Furthermore, even though in the absence of a man patriarchal power might sometimes be exercised by a woman, e.g., by a mother or a queen, and unemancipated males, e.g., minor sons and slaves, were as subject to the father's dominion as were females in the family, there is a vital connection in the patriarchal system among power, authority, property, and maleness. Conversely, powerlessness, exclusion from authority, dependence, and femaleness are closely linked. And the entire system is understood as the product and expression of the will of God.

For two reasons patriarchy is not just one social system among others. First, patriarchy is the basic principle of all major relational systems in the western world. As the former president of the World Council of Churches, Dr. W. A. Visser't Hooft, expressed it:

> . . . the patriarchal spirit and the doctrine upon which it is based have had an astonishingly wide influence, penetrating into many different spheres of life. Indeed, it has not been merely one of the many facets of society, but has rather formed its general pattern. . . . [Thus] emancipation [from patriarchy] concerns not only developments in family life, but also those in the state, the church and even in international relations.[16]

Visser't Hooft, like Rosemary Ruether, has pointed out that patriarchy is the basic principle underlying not only the subordination of women to men, but of one race to another, of colonies to master nations, of children to adults, of nations to divine right monarchs, of believers to clergy. In other words, patriarchy is the nerve of racism, ageism, classism, colonialism, and clericalism well as of sexism.[17] Patriarchy is fundamentally a masculine power in which all relationships are understood in terms of superiority and inferiority and social cohesion is assured by the exercise of dominative power.

The second reason why patriarchy is not just one system among others is that patriarchy is essentially hierarchy, i.e., the power and authority exercised over subordinates is believed to derive from the will of God and is exercised in the name of God. The patriarchal structure of the family was understood as divinely established for the good of all. When this structure was extended to other situations they were seen as quasi-families in which there is one adult and all others are minors. The feudal lord, the abbot in his monastery, the divine right monarch, the priest in his parish, the white European in the colonies, the husband in relation to his wife, the slave-holder with his "darkies," the Pope, were all father-figures caring for the "children" over which God had placed them. The difference, of course, between these extensions of patriarchy and its original locus, the family, is that these "children" are adults and, unlike real children, they are expected never to grow up. Thus, in a patriarchal system most people will remain subordinates all their lives and they cannot protest against this arrangement without challenging God "himself" who is the first patriarch and the legitimator of all others.

While not all men are patriarchs, women never are. Where patriarchy reigns women are subject to men. The man may be father, husband, slave-holder, priest, or Pope but the woman is always a minor. It is not surprising, then, that women, once they have analyzed the situation, repudiate patriarchy as the universal social structure and especially its claims to divine legitimacy. A patriarchal God, to feminist women, is at least a legitimator of women's victimization by men if not "himself" the very personification of the oppression of women.

However, it is important to distinguish sharply between patriarchy (including its more benign expression as paternalism) on the one hand, and paternity or fatherhood on the other. The association of fatherhood with patriarchy is so long-standing and widespread that the equation of the two is quite understandable and very often perfectly accurate. However, it is possible for a man to be a father to his minor children without assuming absolute power over them and to remain a father in relation to adult children whose autonomy and equality with himself he fully accepts. Likewise, it is possible for God to be experienced as paternal without being experienced as a patriarch. And a father-God who is not experienced as a patriarch can equally well be experienced as a mother-God without loss of status.

III. Imagination and Spirituality

In what has been said so far I have attempted to locate with some accuracy the problem of the gender of God. The problem is not the sex of God (which does not exist) but our experience of God as masculine; and it is not the masculinity of Jesus (who is anything but a glorification of machismo) but his male sex. However, the reason Jesus' male sex is a problem is because it is seen as a revelatory confirmation of the masculinity of God and therefore of the divinity of maleness. Jesus, the man, is the incarnation of the Son of the Father. Consequently, our primary concern must be with the experienced masculinity of God.

• • •

The tenacity of the patriarchal God-image is such that many feminists have decided that the only course open to women whose self-image has been healed of gender inferiority and whose world-image has been healed of hierarchy in general and patriarchy in particular is to abandon the Christian God altogether. I would like to suggest that just as the self and world images can be healed, so can the God-image. It cannot be healed, however, by rational intervention alone. Repeating the theological truth that God is Spirit may correct our ideas but a healthy spirituality requires a healing of the imagination which will allow us to think not only differently about God but to experience God differently. The imagination is accessible not primarily to abstract ideas but to language, images, interpersonal experience, symbolism, art—all the integrated approaches which appeal simultaneously to intellect, will, and feeling.

What must be undertaken is a therapy of the religious imagination, first in regard to God and then in regard to our relationship with Jesus Christ.

• • •

IV. The "Maleness" of God in the Old Testament

• • •

B. Old Testament Metaphors for God[18]

In the Old Testament there are numerous metaphors for God derived from human relationships. The vast majority, although not all, of the vehicles in these metaphors either are necessarily male, e.g., father or husband, or denote roles or activities which were virtually exclusively exercised by males in Israelite society. In the New Testament Jesus frequently used one of these metaphors, namely, father, at least in speaking to God and probably also in speaking about God. Fairly early in Christian history the father metaphor was literalized in religious imagination. The literalized metaphor, it must be remembered, no longer carries its "is not" but simply transfers to the referent all the characteristics of the vehicle. Thus, God the "father" came to be imagined as literally male. All the male metaphors for God in the Old Testament then tended to be drawn into this one metaphor. Since many of the Old Testament God-metaphors such as warlord and king were patriarchal the metaphorical fatherhood of God was not only literalized but patriarchalized. As both theologian Sallie McFague and biblical scholar Johanna Bos have pointed out, the literalized father metaphor for God has not only died but, in its ascription of maleness to God, it has become actually idolatrous.[19] We have created a false god and substituted "him" for the true God of Judaeo-Christian revelation.

It is highly enlightening, then, to examine the father metaphor as it actually occurs in the Old Testament. The most striking characteristic of this metaphor is how seldom it occurs. God is actually referred to as father only twelve times in the Hebrew Scriptures and never in direct address. Father is not a name for God but "a pointer to the free presence of God, which cannot be encapsulated in or manipulated by names."[20] Five of the references to God as father concern the special relation of God to the king. (2 Sam 7:14; 1 Chr 17:13; Ps 89:26; 1 Chr 22: 10; 28:6) and thus do not apply to the ordinary person. The other seven references (Ps 103:13; Dt 32:6, 18; Jer 3:4–5; 31:9; Is 63:16; Mal 1:6) all refer to God in the context of Israel's sin, repentance, and restoration and God's endless forgiveness.[21] The father metaphor in the Old Testament is nowhere used to present God as a patriarch dominating the people or exercising coercive power over them. On the contrary, the father metaphor is evoked precisely to describe the compassionate love of God who is like a parent spurned by ungrateful children but who is endless in patience and loving-kindness toward a rebellious people. The God who is presented as father in the Old Testament is like the father in the New Testament parable of the prodigal son, a paternal rather than patriarchal figure who is in no way a model for or a legitimation of patriarchy.

A second important point about the parental metaphor in the Old Testament is that it is not exclusively masculine. When Israel is referred to as a child the implied parent is sometimes masculine as in Deuteronomy 1:31 where Israel is reminded that "God bore you as a man bears his son." But at other times it is feminine as in Numbers 11:12 where the exasperated Moses demands of God, "Did I conceive all this people? Did I bring them forth, that thou should say to me, 'Carry them in thy bosom . . . ?'" clearly implying that God is the true mother of this people. At other times the metaphor is both masculine and feminine as in Hosea 11: 1–4:

> When Israel was a child, I loved him, and out of Egypt I called my son. The more I called them the more they went from me; they kept sacrificing to Baals, and burning incense to idols. Yet it was I who taught Ephraim to walk, I took them up in my arms; but they did not know that I healed them. I led them with cords of compassion, with the bands of love, and I became to them as one who eases the yoke on their jaws, and I bent down to them and fed them.

Thus, it is to be noted that, while they are not as frequent as even the infrequent paternal metaphors, there are clear maternal metaphors for God in the Old Testament as well as a pervasive maternal climate evoked by imagery based on the womb. In Deuteronomy 32:18 God clearly refers to herself, in feminine language, as "the God who gave you birth." In Isaiah 49:15 Israel is assured that God cherishes her people with a mother's love. In Isaiah 66:13 God says to Israel, "As one whom his mother comforts so will I comfort you." In Psalm 131:2 the psalmist says of reliance on God, "I have calmed and quieted my soul, like a child quieted at its mother's breast." As Phyllis Trible has pointed out[22] the typical Old Testament word for the compassion of God seems to be drawn from *rehem* the Hebrew word for womb, suggesting that God's tenderness is that of a mother for the child to whom she has given birth (cf. Is 63:15; Ex 34:6).[23] In Isaiah 42:14 God compares the divine anguish to that of a woman in the pangs of childbirth.[24]

In sum, an examination of the Old Testament father metaphor reveals that it was by no means a common, much less the preferred or only, metaphor for God, that it was never used to portray God as a patriarch in relation to the people, and that it is complemented by maternal imagery and metaphors which assure us that in no sense was the father metaphor meant to suggest that God is male[25] or that the divine parenthood is exclusively paternal.

Besides the father metaphor which, because of Jesus' use of it, exerted a powerful influence on the Christian imagination, there is one other Old Testament male metaphor for God which has had a major impact on the Christian God-image, namely, the spousal metaphor. Like the paternal metaphor which has been distorted into an exclusive and literalized support for male supremacy and patriarchy, the spousal metaphor has also exercised a perverse influence on the Christian imagination as a degradation of feminine sexuality and a justification of patriarchal marriage.

In some of the prophets, especially Jeremiah and Hosea, the relationship between God and Israel is depicted as marital union. God is the husband and Israel the wife in a marriage founded on love rather than on patriarchal authority and power. The extended metaphor is used, however, to describe the unfaithfulness of Israel to its faithful God. Israel, the wife, is a harlot. As feminist scholars have rightly pointed out, in this metaphor female sexuality is objectified and demonized. The male is assimilated to God and the female to sinful humanity.[26]

However, it must be realized that in the patriarchal culture of ancient Israel a husband could not really sin against his wife since he could do to her with impunity what he willed.[27] Marital fidelity was never absolutely required of men whereas a woman's infidelity was considered an offense against her husband's property rights. In such a culture, therefore, this metaphor could not have been structured in any other way. To make the point that God took the free initiative in choosing Israel, that God entered into a relationship of intimate love with Israel, and that Israel was unfaithful to that covenant, God had to be imaged as the husband who alone could act this way. However, in the husband role God acts not as a patriarch would have acted but as a wife would have acted. A husband who had been betrayed by his wife would at least have divorced her if he had not had her executed. A wife who had been betrayed would be expected, nevertheless, to be faithful and loving. God, in the marital metaphor, is a faithful lover who continually seeks reconciliation through the offer of forgiveness. In other words, the patriarchy of the metaphor is assumed because of the culture, but the message of the metaphor subverts patriarchy.

●   ●   ●

This brief exploration of the Old Testament language about God and the way this language has been used suggests several conclusions. God is not presented in the Old Testament in exclusively male terms. Even the two necessarily male metaphors, father and husband, are balanced by maternal imagery and the presentation of marital love as a relation of mutuality between equals. It is true that male imagery for God predominates, but this should serve to draw our attention to the unexpected feminine imagery which is perhaps more revelatory precisely because it cannot be adequately explained by the culture. In any case, any literalizing of God metaphors results not only in an impoverishment and distortion of the religious imagination but in a blasphemous assimilation of God to human categories and an idolatrous divinizing of human maleness.

Notes

[1] See Elizabeth A. Johnson, "The Incomprehensibility of God and the Image of God Male and Female," *Theological Studies* 45 (1984) 441–465.

[2] Gregory of Nazianzus, "The Third Theological Oration—on the Son," *Christology of the Later Fathers*, Vol. III, ed. E. R. Hardy (Philadelphia: Westminster, 1954), p. 171. Migne, *Patrologia Graeca* 36:93–96.

[3] The argument that priests had to be male to represent Christ is found in Bonaventure. See J. Rézette, "Le sacerdoce et la femme chez Saint Bonaventure," *Antonianum* 51 (1976) 520–527.

[4] *Acta Apostolicae Sedis* 69 (1977) 98–116; E. T. *Women Priests: A Catholic Commentary on the Vatican Declaration*, ed. L. and A. Swidler (New York: Paulist, 1977), pp. 37–49.

[5] See the excellent article by R. A. Norris, Jr., "The Ordination of Women and the 'Maleness' of Christ," *Supplementary Series of the Anglican Theological Review* 6 (June 1976) 69–80.

[6] Norris, "The Ordination of Women," p. 70.

[7] Gregory of Nazianzus, "Epistle 101," Hardy, *Christology*, p. 218. Migne, *P. G.* 37: 181.

[8] Norris, "The Ordination of Women," p. 74.

[9] See Gail R. Schmidt, "De Divinis Nominibus: The Gender of God," *Worship* 56 (1982) 117–131, for a discussion of how male God language affects liturgical experience.

[10] See, for example, the article by Carol P. Christ, "Why Women Need the Goddess: Phenomenological, Psychological, and Political Reflections," in *Womanspirit Rising: A Feminist Reader in Religion*, ed. C. P. Christ and J. Plaskow (San Francisco: Harper and Row, 1979), 273–287.

[11] Cf. Suzanne J. Kessler and Wendy McKenna, *Gender: An Ethnomethodological Approach* (Chicago: University of Chicago, 1985).

[12] On this subject, see Mary Collins, "Naming God in Public Prayer," *Worship* 59 (1985) 291–304.

[13] Caroline W. Bynum, *Jesus as Mother* (Berkeley: University of California, 1982).

[14] See R. Hamerton-Kelly, *God the Father: Theology and Patriarchy in the Teaching of Jesus* (Philadelphia: Fortress, 1979), pp. 55–60, for a good description of patriarchy in the Judaism of Jesus' time as well as in the Greco-Roman world of first century Christianity.

[15] See W. A. Visser't Hooft, *The Fatherhood of God in an Age of Emancipation* (Geneva: World Council of Churches, 1982), esp. chapters one to three, for a fuller description of this social system.

[16] Visser't Hooft, *Fatherhood*, p. 2.

[17] See Rosemary Ruether, "Feminists Seek Structural Change," *National Catholic Reporter* 20 (April 13, 1984) 4–6.

[18] I am indebted to my colleague, Dr. John Endres, and to Dr. Alice Laffey of Holy Cross College, Worcester, Massachusetts for their help on the Old Testament section of this paper.

[19] Cf. McFague, *Metaphorical Theology*, pp. 145–192; Bos, "When You Pray," p. 12.

[20] Bos, "When You Pray," p. 12.

[21] Cf. Diane Tennis, *Is God the Only Reliable Father?* (Philadelphia: Westminster, 1985), esp. pp. 82–83.

[22] See Phyllis Trible, *God and the Rhetoric of Sexuality* (Philadelphia: Fortress, 1978), pp. 34–56, and "Feminist Hermeneutics and Biblical Studies," *The Christian Century* 99 (Feb. 3–10, 1982)116–118.

[23] Mayer I. Gruber, in "The Motherhood of God in Second Isaiah," *Revue Biblique* 90 (1983) 351–359, challenges Trible's interpretation.

[24] It is interesting that John Paul II in his encyclical *Dives in Misericordia* (Nov. 13, 1980) has a long footnote (#52) in which he explores the feminine significance of *rahamīm*.

[25] Cf. Bos, "When You Pray," p. 12.

[26] Cf. T. Drorah Setel, "Prophets and Pornography: Female Sexual Imagery in Hosea," *Feminist Interpretation of the Bible*, ed. Letty M. Russell (Philadelphia: Westminster, 1985) 86–95.

[27] See Phyllis Trible, *Texts of Terror: Literary Feminist Readings of Biblical Narratives* (Philadelphia: Fortress, 1984) for evidences of the male attitude toward women and their rights.

Harold Kushner (b. 1935) is a Jewish rabbi and author of several inspirational books including the bestsellers When Bad Things Happen to Good People *(1981),* When All You've Ever Wanted Isn't Enough *(1986), and* Living a Life That Matters: Resolving the Conflict Between Conscience and Success *(2001). He lives in Natick, MA.*

from When Bad Things Happen to Good People

Harold Kushner

Why Do the Righteous Suffer?

There is only one question which really matters: why do bad things happen to good people? All other theological conversation is intellectually diverting; somewhat like doing the crossword puzzle in the Sunday paper and feeling very satisfied when you have made the words fit; but ultimately without the capacity to reach people where they really care. Virtually every meaningful conversation I have ever had with people on the subject of God and religion has either started with this question, or gotten there before long. Not only the troubled man or woman who has just come from a discouraging diagnosis at the doctor's office, but the college student who tells me that he has decided there is no God, or the total stranger who comes up to me at a party just when I am ready to ask the hostess for my coat, and says, "I hear you're a rabbi; how can you believe that . . ."—they all have one thing in common. They are all troubled by the unfair distribution of suffering in the world.

The misfortunes of good people are not only a problem to the people who suffer and to their families. They are a problem to everyone who wants to believe in a just and fair and livable world. They inevitably raise questions about the goodness, the kindness, even the existence of God . . .

One of the ways in which people have tried to make sense of the world's suffering in every generation has been by assumption that we deserve what we get, that somehow our misfortunes come as punishment for our sins:

> Tell the righteous it shall be well with them, for they shall eat the fruit of their deeds. Woe to the wicked, it shall be ill with him, for what his hands have done shall be done to him. (Isaiah 3:10–11)

> But Er, Judah's first born, was wicked in the sight of the Lord, and the Lord slew him. (Genesis 38:7)

No ills befall the righteous, but the wicked are filled with trouble. (Proverbs 12:21)

Consider, what innocent ever perished, or where have the righteous been destroyed? (Job 14:7)

This is an attitude we will meet later in the book when we discuss the whole question of guilt. It is tempting at one level to believe that bad things happen to people (especially other people) because God is a righteous judge who gives them exactly what they deserve. By believing that, we keep the world orderly and understandable. We give people the best possible reason for being good and for avoiding sin. And by believing that, we can maintain an image of God as all-loving, all-powerful and totally in control. Given the reality of human nature, given the fact that none of us is perfect and that each of us can, without too much difficulty, think of things he has done which he should not have done, we can always find grounds for justifying what happens to us. But how comforting, how religiously adequate, is such an answer?

The couple whom I tried to comfort, the parents who had lost their only child at age nineteen with no warning, were not profoundly religious people. They were not active in the synagogue; they had not even fasted on Yom Kippur, a tradition which even many otherwise nonobservant Jews maintain. But when they were stunned by tragedy, they reverted back to the basic belief that God punishes people for their sins. They sat there feeling that their daughter's death had been their faults; had they been less selfish and less lazy about Yom Kippur fast some six months earlier, she might still be alive. They sat there angry at God for having exacted His pound of flesh so strictly, but afraid to admit their anger for fear that He would punish them again. Life had hurt them, and religion could not comfort them. Religion was making them feel worse.

The idea that God gives people what they deserve, that our misdeeds cause our misfortune, is a neat and attractive solution to the problem of evil at several levels, but it has a number of serious limitations. As we have seen, it teaches people to blame themselves. It creates guilt even where there is no basis for guilt. It makes people hate God, even as it makes them hate themselves. And most disturbing of all, it does not even fit the facts.

Perhaps if we had lived before the era of mass communications, we could have believed this thesis, as many intelligent people of those centuries did. It was easier to believe then. You needed to ignore fewer cases of bad things happening to good people. Without newspapers and television, without history books, you could shrug off the occasional death of a child or saintly neighbor. We know too much about the world to do that today. How can anyone who recognizes the names Auschwitz and My Lai, or has walked the corridors of hospitals and nursing homes, dare to answer the question of the world's suffering by quoting Isaiah: "Tell the righteous it shall be well with them"? To believe that today, a person would either have to deny the facts that press upon him from every side, or else define what he means by "righteous" in order to fit the inescapable facts. We would have to say that a righteous person was anyone who lived long and well, whether or not he was honest and charitable, and a wicked person was anyone who suffered, even if that person's life was otherwise commendable. . . .

Sometimes we try to make sense of our life's trials by saying that people do in fact get what they deserve, but only over the course of time. At any given moment, life may seem unfair and innocent people may appear to be suffering. But if we wait long enough, we believe, we will see the righteousness of God's plan emerge.

So, for example, the Ninety-second Psalm praises God for the wonderful, flawlessly righteous world He has given us, and hints that foolish people find fault with it because they are impatient and don't give God the time it takes for His justice to emerge.

> How great are Your deeds, O Lord,
> Your thoughts are very deep.
> The ignorant man does not comprehend them,
> Nor does the fool understand them.
> When the wicked spring up like grass,
> And the workers of inequity flourish,
> It is that they may be destroyed forever...
> The righteous shall flourish like the palm tree,
> And grow mighty like a cedar of Lebanon...
> To declare that the Lord is upright,
> My Rock in Whom there is no unrighteousness. (Psalm 92:6–8,13,16)

The psalmist wants to explain the world's apparent evil as in no way compromising God's justice and righteousness. He does it by comparing the wicked to grass, and the righteous to a palm tree or cedar. If you plant grass seed and a palm tree seed on the same day, the grass will start to sprout much sooner. At that point, a person who knew nothing about nature might predict that the grass would grow to be higher and stronger that the palm tree, since it was growing faster. But the experienced observer would know that the head start of the grass was only temporary, that it would wither and die in a few months, while the tree would grow slowly, but would grow to be tall and straight and would last for more than a generation.

So too, the psalmist suggests, foolish impatient people see the prosperity of the wicked and the suffering of the upright, and jump to the conclusion that it pays to be wicked. Let them observe the situation over the long run, he notes, and they will see the wicked wither like the grass, and the righteous prosper slowly but surely, like the palm tree or cedar.

If I could meet the author of the Ninety-second Psalm, I would first congratulate him on having composed a masterpiece of devotional literature. I would acknowledge that he has said something perceptive and important about the world we live in, that being dishonest and unscrupulous often gives people a head start, but that justice catches up to them. As Rabbi Milton Steinberg has written, "Consider the pattern of human affairs: how falsehood, having no legs, cannot stand; how evil tends to destroy itself; how every tyranny has eventually invoked its own doom. Now set against this the staying power of truth and righteousness. Could the contrast be so sharp unless something in the scheme of things discouraged evil and favored the good?"

But having said that, I would be obliged to point out that there is a lot of wishful thinking in his theology. Even if I were to grant that wicked people don't get away with their wickedness, that they pay for it in one way or another, I cannot say Amen to his claim that "the righteous flourish like the palm tree." The psalmist would have us believe that, given enough time, the righteous will catch up and surpass the wicked in attaining the good things of life. How does he explain the fact that God, who is presumably behind this arrangement, does not always give the righteous man time to catch up? Some good people die unfulfilled; others find length of days to be more of a punishment than a privilege. The world, alas, is not so neat a place as the psalmist would have us believe. . . .

Often, victims of misfortune try to console themselves with the idea that God has His reasons for making this happen to them, reasons that they are in no position to judge. I think of a woman I know named Helen.

The trouble started when Helen noticed herself getting tired after walking several blocks or standing in line. She chalked it up to getting older and having put on some weight. But one night, coming home after dinner with friends, Helen stumbled over the threshold of the front door, sent a lamp crashing to the floor, and fell to the floor herself. Her husband tried to joke about her getting drunk on two sips of wine, but Helen suspected that it was no joking matter. The following morning, she made an appointment to see a doctor.

The diagnosis was multiple sclerosis. The doctor explained that it was a degenerative nerve disease, and that it would gradually get worse, maybe quickly, maybe gradually over many years. At some point Helen would find it harder to walk without support. Eventually she would be confined to a wheelchair, lose bowel and bladder control, and become more and more of an invalid until she died.

The worst of Helen's fears had come true. She broke down and cried when she heard that. "Why should this happen to me? I've tried to be a good person. I have a husband and young children who need me. I don't deserve this. Why should God make me suffer like this?" Her husband took her hand and tried to console her: "You can't talk like that. God must have His reasons for doing this, and it's not for us to question him. You have to believe that if He wants you to get better, you will get better, and if He doesn't, there has to be some purpose to it."

Helen tried to find peace and strength in those words. She wanted to be comforted by the knowledge that there was some purpose to her suffering, beyond her capacity to understand. She wanted to believe that it made sense at some level. All her life, she had been taught—at religious school and in science classes alike—that the world made sense, that everything happened for a reason. She wanted so desperately to go on believing that, to hold on to her belief that God was in charge of things, because if He wasn't, who was? It was hard to live with multiple sclerosis, but it was even harder to live with the idea that things happened to people for no reason, that God had lost touch with the world and nobody was in the driver's seat.

Helen didn't want to question God or be angry at Him. But her husband's words only made her feel more abandoned and more bewildered. What kind of higher purpose could possibly justify what she would have to face? How could this in any way be good? Much as she tried not to be angry at God, she felt angry, hurt, and betrayed. She had been a good person; not perfect, perhaps, but honest, hard-working, helpful, as good as most people and better than many who were walking around healthy. What reasons could God possibly have for doing this to her? And on top of it all, she felt guilty for being angry at God. She felt alone in her fear and suffering. If God had sent her this affliction, if He, for some reason, wanted her to suffer, how could she ask Him to cure her of it?

• • •

Let us consider another question: Can suffering be educational? Can it cure us of our faults and make us better people? Sometimes religious people who would like to believe that God has good reasons for making us suffer, try to imagine what those reasons might be. In the words of one of the great Orthodox Jewish teachers of our time, Rabbi Joseph B. Soloveitchik, "Suffering comes to ennoble man, to purge his thoughts of pride and superficiality, to expand his horizons. In sum, the purpose of suffering is to repair that which is faulty in a man's personality."

Just as a parent sometimes has to punish a child whom he loves, for the child's sake, so God has to punish us. A parent who pulls his child out of a busy roadway, or refuses to give him a candy bar before supper, is not being mean or punitive or unfair. He or she is just being a concerned, responsible parent. Sometimes a parent even has to punish a child, with a spanking or a deprivation, in order to drive home a lesson. The child may feel that he is being arbitrarily deprived of something all the other children have, and he may wonder why an ostensibly loving parent should treat him that way, but that is because he is still a child. When he grows up, he will come to understand the wisdom and necessity of it.

Similarly, we are told, God treats us the way a wise and caring parent treats a naive child, keeping us from hurting ourselves, withholding something we may think we want, punishing us occasionally to make sure we understand that we have done something seriously wrong, and patiently enduring our temper tantrums at His "unfairness" in the confidence that we will one day mature and understand that it was all for our own good. "For whom the Lord loves, He chastises, even as a father does to the son he loves." (Proverbs 3:12). . . .

Consider the case of Ron, a young pharmacist who ran a drugstore with an older partner. When Ron bought into the business, his older colleague told him that the store had recently been the target of a series of holdups by young drug addicts looking for drugs and cash. One day, when Ron was almost ready to close up, a teenage junkie pulled a small-caliber handgun on him and asked for drugs and money. Ron was willing to lose a day's receipts rather than be a hero. He went to open the cash register, his hands trembling as he did so. As he turned , he stumbled and reached for the counter to brace himself. The robber thought he was going for a gun, and fired. The bullet went through Ron's abdomen and lodged in his spinal cord. Doctors removed it, but the damage had been done. Ron could never walk again.

Friends tried to console him. Some held his hand and commiserated with him. Some told him of experimental drugs doctors were using on paraplegics, or of miraculous spontaneous recoveries they had read about. Others tried to help him understand what had happened to him, and to answer his question, "Why me?"

"I have to believe," one friend said, "that everything that happens in life, happens for a purpose. Somehow or other, everything that happens to us is meant for our good. Look at it this way. You were always a pretty cocky guy, popular with girls, flashy cars, confident you were going to make a lot of money. You never really took time to worry about the people who couldn't keep up with you. Maybe this is God's way of teaching you a lesson, making you more thoughtful, more sensitive to others. Maybe this is God's way of purging you of pride and arrogance, and thinking about how you were going to be such a success. It's His way of making you a better, more sensitive person."

The friend wanted to be comforting, to make sense of this senseless accident. But if you were Ron, what would your reaction have been? Ron remembers thinking that if he hadn't been confined to a hospital bed, he would have punched the other man. What right did a normal, healthy person—a person who would soon be driving home, walking upstairs, looking forward to playing tennis—have to tell him that what had happened to him was good and was in his best interest?

The problem with a line of reasoning like this one is that it isn't really meant to help the sufferer or to explain his suffering. It is meant primarily to defend God, to use words and ideas to transform bad into good and pain into privilege. Such answers are thought up by people who believe very strongly that God is a loving parent who controls what happens to us, and on the basis of that belief adjust and interpret the facts to fit their assumption. It may be true that sometimes we have to do painful things to people we love for their benefit, but not every painful thing that happens to us is beneficial.

I would find it easier to believe that I experience tragedy and suffering in order to "repair" that which is faulty in my personality if there were some clear connection between the fault and the punishment. A parent who disciplines a child for doing something wrong, but never tells him what he is being punished for, is hardly a model of responsible parenthood. Yet, those who explain suffering as God's way of teaching us to change are at a loss to specify just what it is about us we are supposed to change.

Equally unhelpful would be the explanation that Ron's accident happened not to make *him* a more sensitive person, but to make his friends and family more sensitive to the handicapped than they would otherwise have been. Perhaps women give birth to dwarfed or retarded children as part of God's plan to deepen and enlarge their souls, to teach them compassion and a different kind of love. . . .

If we cannot satisfactorily explain suffering by saying we deserve what we get, or by viewing it as a "cure" for our faults, can we accept the interpretation of tragedy as a test? Many parents of dying children are urged to read the twenty-second chapter of the Book of Genesis to help them understand and accept their burden. In that chapter, God orders Abraham to take his son Isaac, whom he loves, and offer him to God as a human sacrifice. The chapter begins with the words "It came to pass after all these matters that the Lord tested Abraham." God had Abraham go through that ordeal to test his loyalty and the strength of his faith. When he passed the test, God promised to reward him liberally for the strength he had shown.

For those who have difficulty with the notion of a God who plays such sadistic games with His most faithful follower, proponents of this view explain that God knows how the story will end. He knows that we will pass the test, as Abraham did, with our faith intact (though, in Abraham's case the child did not die). He puts us to the test so that we will discover how strong and faithful we are.

The Talmud, the compilation of the teachings of the rabbis between the years 200 B.C. and A.D. 500, explains Abraham's test this way: If you go to the marketplace, you will see the potter hitting his clay pots with a stick to show you how strong and solid they are. But the wise potter hits only the strongest pots, never the flawed ones. So too, God sends such tests and afflictions only to people He knows are capable of handling them, so that they and others can learn the extent of their spiritual strength.

I was the parent of a handicapped child for fourteen years, until his death. I was not comforted by this notion that God had singled me out because He recognized some special spiritual strength within me and knew that I would be able to handle it better. It didn't make me feel "privileged" nor did it help me understand why God has to send handicapped children into the lives of a hundred thousand unsuspecting families every year.

Writer Harriet Sarnoff Schiff has distilled her pain and tragedy into an excellent book, *The Bereaved Parent*. She remembers that when her young son died during an operation to correct a congenital heart malfunction, her clergyman took her aside and said, "I know that this is a painful time for you. But I know that you will get through it all right, because God never sends us more of a burden than we can bear. God only let this happen to you because He knows that you are strong enough to handle it." Harriet Schiff remembers her reaction to those words: "If only I was a weaker person, Robbie would still be alive."

Does God "temper the wind to the shorn lamb"? Does He never ask more of us that we can endure? My experience, alas, has been otherwise. I have seen people crack under the strain of unbearable tragedy. I have seen marriages break up after the death of a child, because parents blamed each other for not taking proper care or for carrying the defective gene, or simply because the memories they shared were unendurably painful. I have seen some people made noble and sensitive through suffering, but I have seen many more people grow cynical and bitter. I have seen people become jealous of those around them, unable to take part in the routines of normal living. I have seen cancers and automobile accidents take the life of one member of a family, and functionally end the lives of five others, who could never again be the normal, cheerful people they were before disaster struck. If God is testing us, He must know by now that many of us fail the test. If He is only giving us burdens we can bear, I have seen Him miscalculate far too often.

When all else fails, some people try to explain suffering by believing that it comes to liberate us from a world of pain and lead us to a better place. I received a phone call one day informing me that a five-year-old boy in our neighborhood had run out into the street after a ball, had been hit by a car and killed. I didn't know the boy; his family was not part of the congregation. But several children from the congregation had known him and played with him. Their mothers attended the funeral, and some of them told me about it afterwards.

In the eulogy, the family's clergyman had said "This is not a time of sadness or tears. This is a time for rejoicing, because Micheal has been taken out of this world of sin and pain with his innocent soul unstained by sin. He is in a happier land now where there is no pain and no grief; let us thank God for that."

I heard that, and I felt so bad for Micheal's parents. Not only had they lost a child without warning, they were being told by the representative of their religion that they should rejoice in the fact that he had died so young and innocent, and I couldn't believe that they felt much like rejoicing at that moment. They felt hurt, they felt angry, they felt that God had been unfair to them, and here was God's spokesman telling them to be grateful to God for what had happened.

Sometimes in our reluctance to admit that there is unfairness in the world, we try to persuade ourselves that what has happened is not really bad. We only think that it is. It is only our selfishness that makes us cry because five-year-old Micheal is with God instead of living with us. Sometimes, in our cleverness, we try to persuade ourselves that what we call evil is not real, does not really exist, but is only a condition of not enough goodness, even as "cold" means "not enough heat," or darkness is a name we give to the absence of light. We may thus "prove" that there is really no such thing as darkness or cold, but people do stumble and hurt themselves because of the dark, and people die of exposure to cold. Their deaths and injuries are no less real because of our verbal cleverness.

Sometimes, because our souls yearn for justice, because we so desperately want to believe that God will be fair to us, we fasten our hopes on the idea that life in this world is not the only reality. Sometimes beyond this life is another world where "the last shall be first" and those whose lives were cut short here on earth will be reunited with those they loved, and will spend eternity with them.

Neither I nor any other living person can know anything about the reality of that hope. We know that our physical bodies decay after we die. I for one believe that the part of us which is not physical, the part we call the soul or personality, does not and cannot die. But I am not capable of imagining what a soul without a body looks like. Will we be able to recognize disembodied souls as being the people we had known and loved? Will a man who lost his father at a young age, and then lived a full life, be older, younger, or the same age as his father in the world-to-come? Will the souls of the retarded or the short-tempered be somehow made whole in Heaven?

People who have been close to death and recovered tell of seeing a bright light and being greeted by someone they had loved, now deceased. After our son's death, our daughter dreamed that she had died and was welcomed into Heaven by her brother, now grown normal, and by her grandmother (who had died the year before). Needless to say, we have no way of knowing whether these visions are intimations of reality or products of our own wishful thinking.

Belief in a world to come where the innocent are compensated for their suffering can help people endure the unfairness of life in this world without losing faith. But it can also be an excuse for not being troubled or outraged by injustice around us, and not using our God-given intelligence to try to do something about it. The dictate of practical wisdom for people in our situation might be to remain mindful of the possibility that our lives continue in some form after death, perhaps in a form our earthly imaginations cannot conceive of. But at the same time, since we cannot know for sure, we would be well advised to take this world as seriously as we can, in case it turns out to be the only one we will ever have, and to look for meaning and justice here.

All the responses to tragedy which we have considered have at least one thing in common. They all assume that God is the cause of suffering, and they try to understand why God would want us to suffer. Is it for our own good, or is it a punishment we deserve, or could it be that God does not care what happens to us? Many of the answers were sensitive and imaginative, but none was totally satisfying. Some led us to blame ourselves in order to spare God's reputation. Others asked us to deny reality or to repress our true feelings. We were left either hating ourselves for deserving such a fate, or hating God for sending it to us when we did not deserve it.

There may be another approach. Maybe God does not cause our suffering. Maybe it happens for some reason other than the will of God. The psalmist writes, "I lift mine eyes to the hills; from where does my help come? My help comes from the Lord, maker of Heaven and earth." (Psalm 121:1–2) He does not say, "My pain comes from the Lord," or "my tragedy comes from the Lord." He says "my *help* comes from the Lord."

Could it be that God does not cause the bad things that happen to us? Could it be that He doesn't decide which families shall give birth to a handicapped child, that He did not single out Ron to be crippled by a bullet or Helen by a degenerative disease, but rather that He stands ready to help them and us cope with our tragedies if we could only get beyond the feelings of guilt and anger that separate us from Him? Could it be that "How could God do this to me?" is really the wrong question for us to ask?

* * *

No Exceptions for Nice People

The story is told of the youngster who came home from Sunday School, having been taught the biblical story of the crossing of the Red Sea. His mother asked him what he had learned in class, and he told her: "The Israelites got out of Egypt, but Pharaoh and his army chased after them. They got to the Red Sea and they couldn't cross it. The Egyptian army was getting closer. So Moses got on his walkie-talkie, the Israeli air force bombed the Egyptians, and the Israeli navy built a pontoon bridge so the people could cross." The mother was shocked. "Is that the way they taught you the story?" "Well no," the boy admitted, "but if I told it to you the way they taught it to us, you'd never believe it."

Centuries ago, people found reassuring proof of God in stories of miracles. They would tell of how God divided the sea to let the Israelites cross on dry land. They would recount stories about God sending rain in answer to a righteous person's prayer, or about rivers reversing their courses and the sun moving backward in its flight. They would remember tales of Daniel emerging unhurt from the den of lions, and Shadrach, Meshach, and Abednego surviving the fiery furnace. The point of all these stories was to prove that God cared about us so much that He was willing to suspend the laws of nature to support and protect those whom He favored.

But we today are like the little boy in the Sunday School story. We are told those stories and we are skeptical. If anything, we find proof of God precisely in the fact that laws of nature do not change. God has given us a wonderful, precise, orderly world. One of the things that makes the world livable is the fact that the laws of nature are precise and reliable, and always work the same way. There is gravity: heavy objects always fall toward the earth, so a builder can build a house without having his materials float away. There is chemistry: mixing certain elements in certain proportions always yields the same result, so a doctor can prescribe medication and know what will happen. We can even predict when the sun will rise and set on any given day. We can even predict when the moon will block the sun for certain areas, causing an eclipse. To the ancients, an eclipse was an unnatural event which they interpreted as God's way of warning them. To us, it is a perfectly natural event, a reminder of how precise a universe God has given us.

Our human bodies are miracles, not because they defy laws of nature, but precisely because they obey them. Our digestive systems extract nutrients from food. Our skins help to regulate body temperature by perspiring. The pupils of our eyes expand and contract in response to light. Even when we get sick, our bodies have built-in defense mechanisms to fight the illness. All these wonderful things happen, usually without our being aware of them, in accordance with the most precise laws of nature. That, not the legendary splitting of the Red Sea, is the real miracle.

But the unchanging character of these laws, which makes medicine and astronomy possible, also causes problems. Gravity makes objects fall. Sometimes they fall on people and hurt them. Sometimes gravity makes people fall off mountains and out of windows. Sometimes gravity makes people slip on ice or sink under water. We could not live without gravity, but that means we have to live with the dangers it causes.

Laws of nature treat everyone alike. They do not make exceptions for good people or for useful people. If a man enters a house where someone has a contagious disease, he runs the risk of catching the disease. It makes no difference why he is in the house. He may be a doctor or a burglar; disease germs cannot tell the difference. If Lee Harvey Oswald fires a bullet at President John Kennedy, laws of nature take over from the moment that bullet is fired. Neither the course of the bullet nor the seriousness of the wound will be affected by questions of whether or not President Kennedy was a good person, or whether the world would be better off with him alive or dead.

Laws of nature do not make exceptions for nice people. A bullet has no conscience; neither does a malignant tumor or an automobile gone out of control. That is why good people get sick and get hurt as much as anyone. No matter what stories we were taught about Daniel or Jonah in Sunday School, God does not reach down to interrupt the workings of laws of nature to protect the righteous from harm. This is a second area of our world which causes bad things to happen to good people, and God does not cause it and cannot stop it.

And really, how could we live in this world if He did? Let us suppose, for purposes of argument, that God was determined not to let anything happen to a good and pious person. If an Oswald shoots at the president, no matter how carefully he aims, God will make the bullet miss. If a wing falls off Air Force One, God will make it land safely. Would this be a better world, if certain people were immune to laws of nature because God favored them, while the rest of us had to fend for ourselves?

Let us suppose, again for purposes of argument, that I was one of those righteous people to whom God would not let anything bad happen, because I was an observant, charitable person with a young family, spending my life helping people. What would that mean? Would I be able to go out in my shirtsleeves in cold weather and not get sick, because God would prevent the workings of nature from doing me harm? Could I cross streets against lights in the face of heavy traffic, and not be injured? Could I jump out of high windows when I was in too much of a hurry to wait for an elevator, and not hurt myself? A world in which good people suffer from the same natural dangers that others do causes problems. But a world in which good people were immune to those laws would cause even more problems.

Insurance companies refer to earthquakes, hurricanes and other natural disasters as "acts of God." I consider that a case of using God's name in vain. I don't believe that an earthquake that kills thousands of innocent victims without reason is an act of God. It is an act of nature. Nature is morally blind, without values. It churns along, following its own laws, not caring who or what gets in the way. But God is not morally blind. I could not worship Him if I thought He was. God stands for justice, for fairness, for compassion. For me, the earthquake is not an "act of God." The act of God is the courage of people to rebuild their lives after the earthquake, and the rush of others to help them in whatever way they can.

If a bridge collapses, if a dam breaks, if a wing falls off an airplane and people die, I cannot see that as God's doing. I cannot believe that He wanted all those people to die and had no choice but to condemn the others along with them. I believe that these calamities are all acts of nature, and that there is no moral reason for those particular victims to be singled out for punishment. Perhaps, as human beings apply their God-given intelligence to the area of natural disasters, we will one day be able to understand the physical processes behind earthquakes, hurricanes, and metal fatigue, and learn how to anticipate them or even prevent them. When that happens, fewer innocent people will fall victim to these so-called "acts of God."

I don't know why one person gets sick, and another does not, but I can only assume that some natural laws which we don't understand are at work. I cannot believe that God "sends" illness to a specific person for a specific reason. I don't believe in a God who has a weekly quota of malignant tumors to distribute, and consults His computer to find out who deserves one most or who could handle it best. "What did I do to deserve this?" is an understandable outcry from a sick and suffering person, but it is not a matter of what God decides that we deserve. The better question is "if this has happened to me, what do I do now, and who is there to help me do it?" As we saw in the previous chapter, it becomes much easier to take God seriously as the source of moral values if we don't hold Him responsible for all the unfair things that happen in the world.

• • •

I believe in God. But I do not believe the same things about Him that I did years ago, when I was growing up or when I was a theological student. I recognize His limitations. He is limited in what He can do by laws of nature and by the evolution of human nature and human moral freedom. I no longer hold God responsible for illness, accident, and natural disasters, because I realize that I gain little and lose so much when I blame God for those things. I can worship a God who hates suffering but cannot eliminate it, more easily than I can worship a God who chooses to make children suffer and die, for whatever exalted reason. Some years ago, when the "death of God" theology was a fad, I remember seeing a bumper sticker that read "My God is not dead; sorry about yours." I guess my bumper sticker reads "My God is not cruel; sorry about yours."

God does not cause our misfortunes. Some are caused by bad luck, some are caused by bad people, and some are simply an inevitable consequence of our being human and being mortal, living in a world of inflexible natural laws. The painful things that happen to us aren't punishments for our misbehavior, nor are they in any way part of some grand design on God's part. Because the tragedy is not God's will, we need not feel hurt or betrayed by God when tragedy strikes. We can turn to Him for help in overcoming it, precisely because we can tell ourselves that God is as outraged by it as we are.

• • •

And finally, to the person who asks "What good is God? Who needs religion, if these things happen to good people and bad people alike?" I would say that God may not prevent the calamity, but He gives us the strength and the perseverance to overcome it. Where else do we get these qualities which we did not have before? The heart attack which slows down a forty-six-year-old businessman does not come from God, but the determination to change his life-style, to stop smoking, to care less about expanding his business and care more about spending time with his family, because his eyes have been opened to what is truly important to him—those things come from God. God does not stand for heart attacks; those are nature's responses to the body's being overstressed. But God does stand for self-discipline and for being part of a family.

The flood that devastates a town is not an "act of God," even if the insurance companies find it useful to call it that. But the efforts people make to save lives, risking their own lives for a person who might be a total stranger to them, and the determination to rebuild their community after the flood waters have receded, do qualify as acts of God.

When a person is dying of cancer, I do not hold God responsible for the cancer or for the pain he feels. They have other causes. But I have seen God give such people the strength to take each day as it comes, to be grateful for a day full of sunshine or one in which they are relatively free of pain.

When people who were never particularly strong become strong in the face of adversity, when people who tended to think only of themselves become unselfish and heroic in an emergency, I have to ask myself where they got these qualities which they would freely admit they did not have before. My answer is that this is one of the ways in which God helps us when we suffer beyond the limits of our own strength.

Life is not fair. The wrong people get sick and the wrong people get robbed and the wrong people get killed in wars and in accidents. Some people see life's unfairness and decide, "There is no God; the world is nothing but chaos." Others sees the same unfairness and ask themselves, "Where do I get my sense of what is fair and what is unfair? Where do I get my sense of outrage and indignation, my instinctive response of sympathy when I read in the paper about a total stranger who has been hurt by life? Don't I get these things from God? Doesn't He plant in me a little bit of His own divine outrage at injustice and oppression, just as He did for the prophets of the Bible? Isn't my feeling of compassion for the afflicted just a reflection of the compassion He feels when He sees the suffering of His creatures?" Our responding to life's unfairness with sympathy and with righteous indignation, God's compassion and God's anger working through us, may be the surest proof of all of God's reality.

Religion alone can affirm the afflicted person's sense of self-worth. Science can describe what has happened to a person; only religion can call it a tragedy. Only the voice of religion, when it frees itself from the need to defend and justify God for all that happens, can say to the afflicted person, "You are a good person, you deserve better. Let me come and sit with you so that you will know that you are not alone."

Voltaire is the pen name of French author and philosopher Francois Marie Arouet (1694–1778). Although generally considered one of France's greatest writers, Voltaire spent much of his life in exile from his homeland, due to his out-spoken writings criticizing the government and church alike. He wrote prolifi-cally, using his intelligence and humor as a backdrop for his condemnation of slavery, religious intolerance, and persecution. To this day, his books, plays, pam-phlets, and letters are considered vital reading in the study of philosophy.

The Story of a Good Brahmin

Voltaire

On my travels I met an old Brahmin, a very wise man, of marked intel-lect and great learning. Furthermore, he was rich and, consequently, all the wiser, because, lacking nothing, he needed to deceive nobody. His household was very well managed by three women who set themselves out to please him. He passed the time in philosophizing. Near his house, which was beautifully decorated and had charming gardens attached, there lived a narrow-minded old Indian woman: she was simple of mind and rather poor.

Said the Brahmin to me one day: 'I wish I had never been born!' On my ask-ing why, he answered: 'I have been studying forty years, and that is forty years wasted. I teach others and myself am ignorant of everything. Such a state of affairs fills my soul with so much humiliation and disgust that my life is intolerable. I was born in Time, I live in Time, and yet I do not know what Time is. I am at a point between two eternities, as our wise men say, and I have no conception of eternity. I am composed of matter: I think, but I have never been able to learn what produces my thought. I do not know whether or no my understanding is a simple faculty inside me, such as those of walking and digesting, and whether or no I think with my head as I grip with my hands. Not only is the cause of my thought unknown to me; the cause of my actions is equally a mystery. I do not know why I exist, and yet every day people ask me questions on all these points. I have to reply, and as I have nothing really worth saying I talk a great deal, and am ashamed of myself afterward for having talked.

'It is worse still when I am asked if Brahma was born of Vishnu or if they are both eternal. God is my witness that I have not the remotest idea, and my ignorance shows itself in my replies. "Ah, Holy One," people say to me, "tell us why evil pervades the earth." I am in as great a difficulty as those who ask me this question. Sometimes I tell them that everything is as well as can be, but those who have been ruined and broken in the wars do not believe a word of it—and no more do I. I retire to my home stricken at my own curiosity and ignorance. I read our ancient books, and they double my darkness. I talk to my companions: some answer me that we must enjoy life and make game of mankind; others think they know a lot and lose themselves in a maze of wild ideas. Everything increases my anguish. I am ready sometimes to despair when I think that after all my seeking I do not know whence I came, whither I go, what I am nor what I shall become.'

The good man's condition really worried me. Nobody was more rational or more sincere than he. I perceived that his unhappiness increased in proportion as his understanding developed and his insight grew. The same day I saw the old woman who lived near him. I asked her if she had ever been troubled by the thought that she was ignorant of the nature of her soul. She did not even understand my question. Never in all her life had she reflected for one single moment on one single point of all those which tormented the Brahmin. She believed with all her heart in the metamorphoses of Vishnu and, provided she could obtain a little Ganges water wherewith to wash herself, thought herself the happiest of women.

Struck with this poor creature's happiness, I returned to my wretched philosopher. 'Are you not ashamed,' said I, 'to be unhappy when at your very door there lives an old automaton who thinks about nothing, and yet lives contentedly?'

'You are right,' he replied. 'I have told myself a hundred times that I should be happy if I thought as little as my neighbor, and yet I do not desire such happiness.'

My Brahmin's answer impressed me more than all the rest. I set to examining myself, and I saw that in truth I would not care to be happy at the price of being a simpleton.

I put the matter before some philosophers, and they were of my opinion. 'Nevertheless,' said I, 'there is a tremendous contradiction in this mode of thought, for, after all, the problem in this life is how to be happy. What does it matter whether one has brains or not? Further, those who are contented with their lot are certain of their contentment, whereas those who reason are not certain that they reason correctly. It is quite clear, therefore,' I continued, 'that we must choose not to have common sense, however little common sense may contribute to our discomfort.' Everyone agreed with me, but I found nobody, notwithstanding, who was willing to accept the bargain of becoming a simpleton in order to become contented. From which I conclude that if we consider the question of happiness we must consider still more the question of reason.

But on reflection it seems that to prefer reason to happiness is to be very senseless. How can this contradiction be explained? Like all the other contradictions. It is matter for much talk.

Parker J. Palmer (b. 1939) is a Quaker writer, teacher, and activist for education, spirituality, and social change. He received a B.A. in sociology and philosophy from Carleton College and an M.A. and Ph.D. from the University of California at Berkeley. Palmer is the author of many books and articles, including The Courage to Teach: Exploring the Inner Landscape of a Teacher's Life *(1997) and* Let Your Life Speak *(1999).*

Now I Become Myself

Parker J. Palmer

A Vision of Vocation

With twenty-one words, carefully chosen and artfully woven, May Sarton evokes the quest for vocation—at least, my quest for vocation—with candor and precision:

> Now I become myself.
>
> It's taken time, many years and places.
>
> I have been dissolved and shaken,
>
> Worn other people's faces. . . .[1]

What a long time it can take to become the person one has always been! How often in the process we mask ourselves in faces that are not our own. How much dissolving and shaking of ego we must endure before we discover our deep identity—the true self within every human being that is the seed of authentic vocation.

I first learned about vocation growing up in the church. I value much about the religious tradition in which I was raised: its humility about its own convictions, its respect for the world's diversity, its concern for justice. But the idea of "vocation" I picked up in those circles created distortion until I grew strong enough to discard it. I mean the idea that vocation, or calling, comes from a voice external to ourselves, a voice of moral demand that asks us to become someone we are not yet—someone different, someone better, someone just beyond our reach.

That concept of vocation is rooted in a deep distrust of selfhood, in the belief that the sinful self will always be "selfish" unless corrected by external forces of virtue. It is a notion that made me feel inadequate to the task of living my own life, creating guilt about the distance between who I was and who I was supposed to be, leaving me exhausted as I labored to close the gap.

Today I understand vocation quite differently—not as a goal to be achieved but as a gift to be received. Discovering vocation does not mean scrambling toward some prize just beyond my reach but accepting the treasure of true self I already possess. Vocation does not come from a voice "out there" calling me to become something I am not. It comes from a voice "in here" calling me to be the person I was born to be, to fulfill the original selfhood given me at birth by God.

It is a strange gift, this birthright gift of self. Accepting it turns out to be even more demanding than attempting to become someone else! I have sometimes responded to that demand by ignoring the gift, or hiding it, or fleeing from it, or squandering it—and I think I am not alone. There is a Hasidic tale that reveals, with amazing brevity, both the universal tendency to want to be someone else and the ultimate importance of becoming one's self: Rabbi Zusya, when he was an old man, said, "In the coming world, they will not ask me: 'Why were you not Moses?' They will ask me: 'Why were you not Zusya?'"[2]

If you doubt that we all arrive in this world with gifts and as a gift, pay attention to an infant or a very young child. A few years ago, my daughter and her newborn baby came to live with me for a while. Watching my granddaughter from her earliest days on earth, I was able, in my early fifties, to see something that had eluded me as a twenty-something parent: my granddaughter arrived in the world as *this* kind of person rather than *that*, or *that*, or *that*.

She did not show up as raw material to be shaped into whatever image the world might want her to take. She arrived with her own gifted form, with the shape of her own sacred soul. Biblical faith calls it the image of God in which we are all created. Thomas Merton calls it true self. Quakers call it the inner light, or "that of God" in every person. The humanist tradition calls it identity and integrity. No matter what you call it, it is a pearl of great price.

In those early days of my granddaughter's life, I began observing the inclinations and proclivities that were planted in her at birth. I noticed, and I still notice, what she likes and dislikes, what she is drawn toward and repelled by, how she moves, what she does, what she says.

I am gathering my observations in a letter. When my granddaughter reaches her late teens or early twenties, I will make sure that my letter finds its way to her, with a preface something like this: "Here is a sketch of who you were from your earliest days in this world. It is not a definitive picture—only you can draw that. But it was sketched by a person who loves you very much. Perhaps these notes will help you do sooner something your grandfather did only later: remember who you were when you first arrived and reclaim the gift of true self."

We arrive in this world with birthright gifts—then we spend the first half of our lives abandoning them or letting others disabuse us of them. As young people, we are surrounded by expectations that may have little to do with who we really are, expectations held by people who are not trying to discern our selfhood but to fit us into slots. In families, schools, workplaces, and religious communities, we are trained away from true self toward images of acceptability; under social pressures like racism and sexism our original shape is deformed beyond recognition; and we ourselves, driven by fear, too often betray true self to gain the approval of others.

We are disabused of original giftedness in the first half of our lives. Then—if we are awake, aware, and able to admit our loss—we spend the second half trying to recover and reclaim the gift we once possessed.

When we lose track of true self, how can we pick up the trail? One way is to seek clues in stories from our younger years, years when we lived closer to our birthright gifts. A few years ago, I found some clues to myself in a time machine of sorts. A friend sent me a tattered copy of my high school newspaper from May 1957 in which I had been interviewed about what I intended to do with my life. With the certainty to be expected of a high school senior, I told the interviewer that I would become a naval aviator and then take up a career in advertising.

I was indeed "wearing other people's faces," and I can tell you exactly whose they were. My father worked with a man who had once been a navy pilot. He was Irish, charismatic, romantic, full of the wild blue yonder and a fair share of the blarney, and I wanted to be like him. The father of one of my boyhood friends was in advertising, and though I did not yearn to take on his persona, which was too buttoned-down for my taste, I did yearn for the fast car and other large toys that seemed to be the accessories of his selfhood!

These self-prophecies, now over forty years old, seem wildly misguided for a person who eventually became a Quaker, a would-be pacifist, a writer, and an activist. Taken literally, they illustrate how early in life we can lose track of who we are. But inspected through the lens of paradox, my desire to become an aviator and an advertiser contain clues to the core of true self that would take many years to emerge: clues, by definition, are coded and must be deciphered.

Hidden in my desire to become an "ad man" was a lifelong fascination with language and its power to persuade, the same fascination that has kept me writing incessantly for decades. Hidden in my desire to become a naval aviator was something more complex: a personal engagement with the problem of violence that expressed itself at first in military fantasies and then, over a period of many years, resolved itself in the pacifism I aspire to today. When I flip the coin of identity I held to so tightly in high school, I find the paradoxical "opposite" that emerged as the years went by.

If I go farther back, to an earlier stage of my life, the clues need less deciphering to yield insight into my birthright gifts and callings. In grade school, I became fascinated with the mysteries of flight. As many boys did in those days, I spent endless hours, after school and on weekends, designing, crafting, flying, and (usually) crashing model airplanes made of fragile balsa wood.

Unlike most boys, however, I also spent long hours creating eight- and twelve-page books about aviation. I would turn a sheet of paper sideways; draw a vertical line down the middle; make diagrams of, say, the cross-section of a wing; roll the sheet into a typewriter; and peck out a caption explaining how air moving across an airfoil creates a vacuum that lifts the plane. Then I would fold that sheet in half along with several others I had made, staple the collection together down the spine, and painstakingly illustrate the cover.

I had always thought that the meaning of this paperwork was obvious: fascinated with flight, I wanted to be a pilot, or at least an aeronautical engineer. But recently, when I found a couple of these literary artifacts in an old cardboard box, I suddenly saw the truth, and it was more obvious than I had imagined. I didn't want to be a pilot or an aeronautical engineer or anything else related to aviation. I wanted to be an author, to make books—a task I have been attempting from the third grade to this very moment!

From the beginning, our lives lay down clues to selfhood and vocation, though the clues may be hard to decode. But trying to interpret them is profoundly worthwhile—especially when we are in our twenties or thirties or forties, feeling profoundly lost, having wandered, or been dragged, far away from our birthright gifts.

Those clues are helpful in counteracting the conventional concept of vocation, which insists that our lives must be driven by "oughts." As noble as that may sound, we do not find our callings by conforming ourselves to some abstract moral code. We find our callings by claiming authentic selfhood, by being who we are, by dwelling in the world as Zusya rather than straining to be Moses. The deepest vocational question is not "What ought I to do with my life?" It is the more elemental and demanding "Who am I? What is my nature?"

Everything in the universe has a nature, which means limits as well as potentials, a truth well known by people who work daily with the things of the world. Making pottery, for example, involves more than telling the clay what to become. The clay presses back on the potter's hands, telling her what it can and cannot do —and if she fails to listen, the outcome will be both frail and ungainly. Engineering involves more than telling materials what they must do. If the engineer does not honor the nature of the steel or the wood or the stone, his failure will go well beyond aesthetics: the bridge or the building will collapse and put human life in peril. .

The human self also has a nature, limits as well as potentials. If you seek vocation without understanding the material you are working with, what you build with your life will be ungainly and may well put lives in peril, your own and some of those around you. "Faking it" in the service of high values is no virtue and has nothing to do with vocation. It is an ignorant, sometimes arrogant, attempt to override one's nature, and it will always fail.

Our deepest calling is to grow into our own authentic selfhood, whether or not it conforms to some image of who we *ought* to be. As we do so, we will not only find the joy that every human being seeks—we will also find our path of authentic service in the world. True vocation joins self and service, as Frederick Buechner asserts when he defines vocation as "the place where your deep gladness meets the world's deep need."[3]

Buechner's definition starts with the self and moves toward the needs of the world: it begins, wisely, where vocation begins—not in what the world needs (which is everything), but in the nature of the human self, in what brings the self joy, the deep joy of now knowing that at we are here on earth to be the gifts that God created.

Contrary to the conventions of our thinly moralistic culture, this emphasis on gladness and selfhood is not selfish. The Quaker teacher Douglas Steere was fond of saying that the ancient human question "Who am I?" leads inevitably to the equally important question "Whose am I?"—for there is no selfhood outside of relationship. We must ask the question of selfhood and answer it as honestly as we can, no matter where it takes us. Only as we do so can we discover the community of our lives.

As I learn more about the seed of true self that was planted when I was born, I also learn more about the ecosystem in which I was planted—the network of communal relations in which I am called to live responsively, accountably, and joyfully with beings of every sort. Only when I know both seed and system, self and community, can I embody the great commandment to love both my neighbor and myself.

•   •   •

Selfhood, Society, and Service

By surviving passages of doubt and depression on the vocational journey, I have become clear about at least one thing: self-care is never a selfish act—it is simply good stewardship of the only gift I have, the gift I was put on earth to offer to others. Anytime we can listen to true self and give it the care it requires, we do so not only for ourselves but for the many others whose lives we touch.

There are at least two ways to understand the link between selfhood and service. One is offered by the poet Rumi in his piercing observation: "If you are here unfaithfully with us, you're causing terrible damage."[7] If we are unfaithful to true self, we will extract a price from others. We will make promises we cannot keep, build houses from flimsy stuff, conjure dreams that devolve into nightmares, and other people will suffer—if we are unfaithful to true self.

I will examine that sort of unfaithfulness, and its consequences, later in this book. But a more inspiring way of understanding the link between selfhood and service is to study the lives of people who have been here *faithfully* with us. Look, for example, at the great liberation movements that have served humanity so well—in eastern Europe, Latin America, and South Africa, among women, African Americans, and our gay and lesbian brothers and sisters. What we see is simple but often ignored: the movements that transform us, our relations, and our world emerge from the lives of people who decide to care for their authentic selfhood.

The social systems in which these people must survive often try to force them to live in a way untrue to who they are. If you are poor, you are supposed to accept, with gratitude, half a loaf or less; if you are black, you are supposed to suffer racism without protest; if you are gay, you are supposed to pretend that you are not. You and I may not know, but we can at least imagine, how tempting it would be to mask one's truth in situations of this sort—because the system threatens punishment if one does not.

But in spite of that threat, or because of it, the people who plant the seeds of movements make a critical decision: they decide to live "divided no more." *They decide no longer to act on the outside in a way that contradicts some truth about themselves that they hold deeply on the inside.* They decide to claim authentic selfhood and act it out—and their decisions ripple out to transform the society in which they live, serving the selfhood of millions of others.

I call this the "Rosa Parks decision" because that remarkable woman is so emblematic of what the undivided life can mean. Most of us know her story, the story of an African American woman who, at the time she made her decision, was a seamstress in her early forties. On December 1, 1955, in Montgomery, Alabama, Rosa Parks did something she was not supposed to do: she sat down at the front of a bus in one of the seats reserved for whites—a dangerous, daring, and provocative act in a racist society.

Legend has it that years later a graduate student came to Rosa Parks and asked, "Why did you sit down at the front of the bus that day?" Rosa Parks did not say that she sat down to launch a movement, because her motives were more elemental than that. She said, "I sat down because I was tired." But she did not mean that her feet were tired. She meant that her soul was tired, her heart was tired, her whole being was tired of playing by racist rules, of denying her soul's claim to selfhood.[8]

Of course, there were many forces aiding and abetting Rosa Parks's decision to live divided no more. She had studied the theory and tactics of nonviolence at the Highlander Folk School, where Martin Luther King Jr. was also a student. She was secretary of the Montgomery chapter of the National Association for the Advancement of Colored People, whose members had been discussing civil disobedience.

But in the moment she sat down at the front of the bus on that December day, she had no guarantee that the theory of nonviolence would work or that her community would back her up. It was a moment of existential truth, of claiming authentic selfhood, of reclaiming birthright giftedness—and in that moment she set in motion a process that changed both the lay and the law of the land.

Rosa Parks sat down because she had reached a point where it was essential to embrace her true vocation—not as someone who would reshape our society but as someone who would live out her full self in the world. She decided, "I will no longer act on the outside in a way that contradicts the truth that I hold deeply on the inside. I will no longer act as if I were less than the whole person I know myself inwardly to be."

Where does one get the courage to "sit down at the front of the bus" in a society that punishes anyone who decides to live divided no more? After all, conventional wisdom recommends the divided life as the safe and sane way to go: "Don't wear your heart on your sleeve." "Don't make a federal case out of it." "Don't show them the whites of your eyes." These are all the clichéd ways we tell each other to keep personal truth apart from public life, lest we make ourselves vulnerable in that rough-and-tumble realm.

Where do people find the courage to live divided no more when they know they will be punished for it? The answer I have seen in the lives of people like Rosa Parks is simple: these people have transformed the notion of punishment itself. They have come to understand that *no pun-*

ishment anyone might inflict on them could possibly be worse than the punishment they inflict on themselves by conspiring in their own diminishment.

In the Rosa Parks story, that insight emerges in a wonderful way. After she had sat at the front of the bus for a while, the police came aboard and said, "You know, if you continue to sit there, we're going to have to throw you in jail."

Rosa Parks replied, "You may do that...," which is a very polite way of saying, "What could your jail of stone and steel possibly mean to me, compared to the self-imposed imprisonment I've suffered for forty years—the prison I've just walked out of by refusing to conspire any longer with this racist system?"

The punishment imposed on us for claiming true self can never be worse than the punishment we impose on ourselves by failing to make that claim. And the converse is true as well: no reward anyone might give us could possibly be greater than the reward that comes from living by our own best lights.

You and I may not have Rosa Parks's particular battle to fight, the battle with institutional racism. The universal element in her story is not the substance of her fight but the selfhood in which she stood while she fought it—for each of us holds the challenge and the promise of naming and claiming true self.

But if the Rosa Parks story is to help us discern our own vocations, we must see her as the ordinary person she is. That will be difficult to do because we have made her into superwoman—and we have done it to protect ourselves. If we can keep Rosa Parks in a museum as an untouchable icon of truth, we will remain untouchable as well: we can put her up on a pedestal and praise her, world without end, never finding ourselves challenged by her life.

Since my own life runs no risk of being displayed in a museum case, I want to return briefly to the story I know best—my own. Unlike Rosa Parks, I never took a singular, dramatic action that might create the energy of transformation around the institutions I care about. Instead, I tried to abandon those institutions through an evasive, crablike movement that I did not want to acknowledge, even to myself.

But a funny thing happened on the way to my vocation. Today, twenty-five years after I left education in anger and fear, my work is deeply related to the renewal of educational institutions. I believe that this is possible only because my true self dragged me, kicking and screaming, toward honoring its nature and needs, forcing me to find my rightful place in the ecosystem of life, to find a right relation to institutions with which I have a lifelong lover's quarrel. Had I denied my true self, remaining "at my post" simply because I was paralyzed with fear, I would almost certainly be lost in bitterness today instead of serving a cause I care about.

Rosa Parks took her stand with clarity and courage. I took mine by diversion and default. Some journies are direct, and some are circuitous; some are heroic, and some are fearful and muddled. But every journey, honestly undertaken, stands a chance of taking us toward the place where our deep gladness meets the world's deep need.

As May Sarton reminds us, the pilgrimage toward true self will take "time, many years and places." The world needs people with the patience and the passion to make that pilgrimage not only for their own sake but also as a social and political act. The world still waits for the truth that will set us free—my truth, your truth, our truth—the truth that was seeded in the earth when each of us arrived here formed in the image of God. Cultivating that truth, I believe, is the authentic vocation of every human being.

Notes

[1] May Sarton, "Now I Become Myself," in *Collected Poems, 1930–1973* (New York: Norton, 1974), 156.

[2] Martin Buber, *Tales of the Hasidim: The Early Masters* (New York: Schocken Books, 1975), 251.

[3] Frederick Buechner, *Wishful Thinking: A Seeker's ABC* (San Francisco: Harper San Francisco, 1993), 119.

[4] Phil Cosineau, *The Art of Pilgrimage* (Berkeley: Conari Press 1998), xxiii.

[5] Parker J. Palmer, *The Company of Strangers: Christians and the Renewal of America's Public Life* (New York: Crossroads, 1981).

[6] See Howard H. Brinton, *The Pendle Hill Idea: A Quaker Experiment in Work, Worship, Study* (Wallingford, PA: Pendle Hill, 1950), and Eleanor Price Mather, *Pendle Hill: A Quaker Experiment in Education and Community* (Wallingford, PA: Pendle Hill, 1980).

[7] Rumi, "Forget Your Life," in *The Enlightened Heart*, ed. Stephen Mitchell (New York: HarperCollins, 1989), 56.

[8] Rosa Parks, *Rosa Parks: My Story* (New York: Dial Books, 1992), 116.

Working Toward Community and Justice

Mohandas K. Gandhi (1869–1948) was called the Mahatma (Great Soul); he is known as a great national and spiritual leader of India, who helped free India from British rule through nonviolent resistance. He was assassinated in 1948.

from Principles of Nonviolence

Mohandas K. Gandhi

53

I see so much misapprehension about *satyagraha* amongst us, as well as amongst Englishmen that, though I have said and written much about it, I think it proper to say something even at the risk of repetition.

Satyagraha was a word coined in South Africa to name a certain movement. First, even the Gujarati word for the great movement that our countrymen in South Africa were carrying on was "passive resistance." Once I happened to address a meeting of Europeans in connection with the movement, and on that occasion the European president of the meeting said there was nothing active in the power of the Indians—who were voteless and unarmed—to offer passive resistance, which could only be a weapon of the weak. He was my friend. He expressed these views without meaning any insult to us, but I felt humiliated. I was conscious that the nature of the fight that the Indians were offering in South Africa was not the result of their weakness. They had purposely decided on that sort of agitation. I took the earliest opportunity to correct my friend's views and demonstrate to him that it was beyond the power of weak men to put up a fight of the nature the Indians in South Africa were doing. They were exhibiting greater courage than that required of a soldier.

Whilst I was in England, in connection with the same movement, I saw that the suffragist women were burning buildings and whipping officers and calling their agitation "passive resistance," and the people also called it so. In the agitation of the Indians in South Africa there was no room for these violent acts. I thus saw that to let our movement be known by the name of "passive resistance" was fraught with dangers. I could not find an English word that could correctly express our movement. In the meeting of Europeans above referred to I called our movement one of "soul force." But I did not dare to make the word current as expressive of our movement. Some capable Englishmen could see the imperfectness of the words "passive resistance," but they could not suggest a better phrase. I now see that "Civil Resistance" is the phrase which can correctly express our movement. Some time ago I somehow hit upon this phrase, and so I have now been using it in English. "Civil Resistance" expresses much more than is conveyed by the phrase "Civil Disobedience," though it expresses much less than *satyagraha*.

I also saw that in South Africa, truth and justice were our only weapons, that the force we were putting forth was not brute force but soul force, be it ever so little. This force is not found to be within the power of brutes, and as truth ever contains soul force, the South African agitation began to be known in our vernacular by the name of *satyagraha*.

That *satyagraha* is thus based on purity is no exaggeration. We can now understand that *satyagraha* is not merely Civil Disobedience. At times, it may be *satyagraha* not to offer Civil Disobedience. When it appears to us to be our duty to offer Civil Disobedience—when not to offer it seems to us derogatory to our manliness and to our soul—then only Civil Disobedience can be *satyagraha*.

This *satyagraha* can be offered not only against Government but against family and society. In short, *satyagraha* may be used as between husband and wife, [between] father and son, and between friends. We may use this weapon in any sphere of life and to get redress of any grievance. The weapon purifies the one who uses it as well as the one against whom it is used. A good use of the weapon can never be undesirable and it is ever infallible. If *satyagraha* is converted into *duragraha* and thus becomes fruitful of evil results, *satyagraha* cannot be blamed.

This sort of *satyagraha* consciously or unconsciously appears to be used mostly in families. That is to say, if a son finds that his father is unjust to him, he does not put up with the injustice, and he pays the penalty with pleasure. In the end he succeeds in winning over his callous father and in having justice from him. But a deadening inertia prevents us from carrying *satyagraha* beyond the family sphere. And I have therefore thought the use of *satyagraha* in the political and social sphere to be a new experiment. Tolstoy in one of his letters drew attention to the fact that this was a new experiment.

There are some who believe that *satyagraha* may be used only in the religious sphere. My wide experience points to a contrary conclusion. We may use it in other spheres and spiritualize them, and by so doing we hasten the victory and are saved many a false thing. I am firmly of the opinion that *satyagraha* contains the observance of the manifest laws of economics, and therefore I believe *satyagraha* to be a practical affair. *Satyagraha* being, as I have shown above, a new weapon, it may take time to be understood and accepted by the people—and things pregnant with results great and good do take time—but when it pervades the land, then political and social reforms, which today take very long to be achieved, will be obtained in comparatively less time, the gulf that separates rulers and the ruled will be bridged over, and trust and love will take the place of distrust and estrangement.

There is only one thing needful for a wide propagation of *satyagraha*. If the leaders understand it correctly and put it before the people, I am sure the people are ready to welcome it. To understand its true beauty one should have unflinching faith in Truth and nonviolence. Truth does not require to be explained. I do not mean to enter here into a minute explanation of non-violence. It means, in brief, that we should not be actuated by spite against him from whom we seek to obtain justice, that we should never think of obtaining anything from him by any violence to his person, but by pure civility. If we can trust ourselves to be equal to only this much nonviolence, the required reforms can be easily achieved.

When the whole nation adopts *satyagraha* as an eternal weapon, all our movements will take a new form. We shall be spared much of the hubbub and stump oratory, much of the petition making and passing of resolutions, and much of our mean selfishness. I see nothing in which lies social, eco-nomic, and political advancement of the nation so much as in *satyagraha*.

Satyagraha differs from Passive Resistance as the North Pole from the South. The latter has been conceived as a weapon of the weak and does not exclude the use of physical force or violence for the purpose of gaining one's end. Whereas, the former has been conceived as a weapon of the strongest and excludes the use of violence in any shape or form. . . .

Satyagraha is utter self-effacement, greatest humiliation, greatest patience, and brightest faith. It is its own reward. . . .

54

Its [*satyagraha's*] root meaning is holding on to Truth, hence Truth force. I have called it Love force or Soul force. I discovered in the earliest stages that pursuit of Truth did not admit of violence being inflicted on one's opponent, but that he must be weaned from error by patience and sympa-thy. For, what appears to be Truth to the one may appear to be error to the other. And patience means self-suffering. So the doctrine came to mean vindication of Truth, not by infliction of suffering on the opponent, but on oneself.

When I refuse to do a thing that is repugnant to my conscience, I use soul force. For instance, the government of the day has passed a law which is applicable to me. I do not like it. If, by using violence, I force the govern-ment to repeal the law, I am employing what may be termed body force. If I do not obey the law, and accept the penalty for its breach, I use soul force. It involves sacrifice of self.

Soul force begins when man recognizes that body force, be it ever so great, is nothing compared to the force of the soul within, which pervades not only him but all creation.

55

The fact that there are so many men still alive in the world shows that it is based not on the force of arms but on the force of truth or love. Therefore, the greatest and most unimpeachable evidence of the success of this force is to be found in the fact that, in spite of the wars of the world, it still lives on.

Thousands, indeed tens of thousands, depend for their existence on a very active working of this force. Little quarrels of millions of families in their daily lives disappear before the exercise of this force. Hundreds of nations live in peace. History does not and cannot take note of this fact.

56

History is really a record of every interruption of the even working of the force of love or of the soul. Two brothers quarrel, one of them repents and reawakens the love that was lying dormant in him, the two again begin to live in peace; nobody takes note of this. But if the two brothers, through the intervention of solicitors or for some other reason, take up arms or go to law—which is another form of the exhibition of brute force—their doings would be immediately noticed in the press, they would be the talk of their neighbors and would probably go down in history.

And what is true of families and communities is true of nations. There is no reason to believe that there is one law for families and another for nations. History, then, is a record of interruptions in the course of nature. Soul force, being natural, is not noted in history.

57

I have more than once dilated in my writings on the limits of *satyagraha*. *Satyagraha* presupposes self-discipline, self-control, self-purification, and a recognized social status in the person offering it. A *satyagrahi* must never forget the distinction between evil and the evil-doer. He must not harbor ill will or bitterness against the latter. He may not even employ needlessly offensive language against the evil person, however unrelieved his evil might be. For it should be an article of faith with every *satyagrahi* that there is no one so fallen in this world but can be converted by love. A *satyagrahi* will always try to overcome evil by good, anger by love, untruth by truth, *himsa* by *ahimsa*. *There is no other way of purging the world of evil.* Therefore, a person who claims to be a *satyagrahi* always tries by close and prayerful self-introspection and self-analysis to find out whether he is himself completely free from the taint of anger, ill will and such other human infirmities, whether he is not himself capable of those very evils against which he is out to lead a crusade. In self-purification and penance lies half the victory of a *satyagrahi*. A *satyagrahi* has faith that the silent and undemonstrative action of truth and love produces far more permanent and abiding results than speeches or such other showy performances. . . .

60

It is a fundamental principle of *satyagraha* that the tyrant whom the *satyagrahi* seeks to resist has power over his body and material possessions, but he can have no power over the soul. The soul can remain unconquered and unconquerable even when the body is imprisoned. The whole science of *satyagraha* was born from a knowledge of this fundamental truth.

61

Defeat has no place in the dictionary of nonviolence.

The path of a *satyagrahi* is beset with insurmountable difficulties. But in true *satyagraha* there is neither disappointment nor defeat. As truth is all-powerful, *satyagraha* can never be defeated.

There is no time limit for a *satyagrahi*, nor is there a limit to his capacity for suffering. Hence, there is no such thing as defeat in *satyagraha*. The so-called defeat may be the dawn of victory. It may be the agony of birth. . . .

64

The triumph of *satyagraha* consists in meeting death in the insistence on Truth.

65

From the standpoint of pure Truth, the body too is a possession. It has been truly said that desire for enjoyment creates bodies for the soul. When this desire vanishes, there remains no further need for the body, and man is free from the vicious cycle of births and deaths. The soul is omnipresent; why should she care to be confined within the cagelike body or do evil and even kill for the sake of that cage? We thus arrive at the ideal of total renunciation and learn to use the body for the purposes of service so long as it exists, so much so that service, and not bread, becomes with us the staff of life. We eat and drink, sleep and wake, for service alone. Such an attitude of mind brings us real happiness and the beatific vision in the fullness of time. . . .

70

The man who is saturated with the spirit of nonviolence has never any quarrel with a single individual. His opposition is directed to a system, to the evil in man, not against the man himself.

Dr. Martin Luther King, Jr., leader of the U.S. Civil Rights movement in the 1960s, was an orator and minister in Atlanta, GA. A proponent of Gandhi's non-violent resistance, he was assassinated in 1968.

Letter from Birmingham Jail

Martin Luther King, Jr.

Birmingham City Jail
April 16, 1963

Bishop C. C. J. Carpenter
Bishop Joseph A. Durick
Rabbi Milton L. Grafman
Bishop Paul Hardin
Bishop Nolan B. Harmon
The Reverend George M. Murray
The Reverend Edward V. Ramage
The Reverend Earl Stallings

Very eloquent

My dear Fellow Clergymen,

While confined here in Birmingham City jail, I came across your recent statement calling our present activities "unwise and untimely." Seldom, if ever, do I pause to answer criticism of my work and ideas. If I sought to answer all of the criticisms that cross my desk, my secretaries would be engaged in little else in the course of the day and I would have no time for constructive work. But since I feel that you are men of genuine good will and your criticisms are sincerely set forth, I would like to answer your statement in what I hope will be patient and reasonable terms.

I think I should give the reason for my being in Birmingham, since you have been influenced by the argument of "outsiders coming in." I have the honor of serving as president of the Southern Christian Leadership Conference, an organization operating in every Southern state with head-quarters in Atlanta, Georgia. We have some eighty-five affiliate organiza-tions all across the South—one being the Alabama Christian Movement for Human Rights. Whenever necessary and possible we share staff, edu-cational, and financial resources with our affiliates. Several months ago our local affiliate here in Birmingham invited us to be on call to engage in a nonviolent direct action program if such were deemed necessary. We readily consented and when the hour came we lived up to our promises. So I am here, along with several members of my staff, because we were invited here. I am here because I have basic organizational ties here.

Beyond this, I am in Birmingham because injustice is here. Just as the eighth century prophets left their little villages and carried their "thus saith the Lord" far beyond the boundaries of their home town, and just as the Apostle Paul left his little village of Tarsus and carried the gospel of Jesus Christ to practically every hamlet and city of the Graeco-Roman world, I too am compelled to carry the gospel of freedom beyond my particular home town. Like Paul, I must constantly respond to the Macedonian call for aid.

Moreover, I am cognizant of the interrelatedness of all communities and states. I cannot sit idly by in Atlanta and not be concerned about what happens in Birmingham. Injustice anywhere is a threat to justice everywhere. We are caught in an inescapable network of mutuality tied in a single garment of destiny. Whatever affects one directly affects all indirectly. Never again can we afford to live with the narrow, provincial "outside agitator" idea. Anyone who lives inside the United States can never be considered an outsider anywhere in this country.

You deplore the demonstrations that are presently taking place in Birmingham. But I am sorry that your statement did not express a similar concern for the conditions that brought the demonstrations into being. I am sure that each of you would want to go beyond the superficial social analyst who looks merely at effects, and does not grapple with underlying causes. I would not hesitate to say that it is unfortunate that so-called demonstrations are taking place in Birmingham at this time, but I would say in more emphatic terms that it is even more unfortunate that the white power structure of this city left the Negro community with no other alternative.

In any nonviolent campaign there are four basic steps: (1) collection of the facts to determine whether injustices are alive; (2) negotiation; (3) self-purification; and (4) direct action. We have gone through all of these steps in Birmingham. There can be no gainsaying of the fact that racial injustice engulfs this community. Birmingham is probably the most thoroughly segregated city in the United States. Its ugly record of police brutality is known in every section of this country. Its unjust treatment of Negroes in the courts is a notorious reality. There have been more unsolved bombings of Negro homes and churches in Birmingham than any city in this nation. These are the hard, brutal, and unbelievable facts. On the basis of these conditions Negro leaders sought to negotiate with the city fathers. But the political leaders consistently refused to engage in good faith negotiation.

Then came the opportunity last September to talk with some of the leaders of the economic community. In these negotiating sessions certain promises were made by the merchants—such as the promise to remove the humiliating racial signs from the stores. On the basis of these promises Rev. Shuttlesworth and the leaders of the Alabama Christian Movement for Human Rights agreed to call a moratorium on any type of demonstrations. As the weeks and months unfolded we realized that we were the victims of a broken promise. The signs remained. As in so many experiences of the past we were confronted with blasted hopes, and the dark shadow of a deep disappointment settled upon us. So we had no alternative except that of preparing for direct action, whereby we would present our very bodies as a means of laying our case before the conscience of the local and national community. We were not unmindful of the difficulties involved. So we decided to go through a process of self-purification. We started having workshops on nonviolence and repeatedly asked ourselves the questions, "Are you able to accept blows without retaliating?" "Are you able to endure the ordeals of jail?"

We decided to set our direct action program around the Easter season, realizing that with the exception of Christmas, this was the largest shopping period of the year. Knowing that a strong economic withdrawal program would be the by-product of direct action, we felt that this was the best time to bring pressure on the merchants for the needed changes. Then it occurred to us that the March election was ahead, and so we speedily decided to postpone action until after election day. When we discovered that Mr. Connor was in the runoff, we decided again to postpone action so that the demonstrations could not be used to cloud the issues. At this time we agreed to begin our nonviolent witness the day after the runoff.

This reveals that we did not move irresponsibly into direct action. We too wanted to see Mr. Connor defeated; so we went through postponement after postponement to aid in this community need. After this we felt that direct action could be delayed no longer.

You may well ask, "Why direct action? Why sit-ins, marches, etc.? Isn't negotiation a better path?" You are exactly right in your call for negotiation. Indeed, this is the purpose of direct action. Nonviolent direct action seeks to create such a crisis and establish such creative tension that a community that has constantly refused to negotiate is forced to confront the issue. It seeks so to dramatize the issue that it can no longer be ignored. I just referred to the creation of tension as a part of the work of the nonviolent resister. This may sound rather shocking. But I must confess that I am not afraid of the word tension. I have earnestly worked and preached against violent tension, but there is a type of constructive nonviolent tension that is necessary for growth. Just as Socrates felt that it was necessary to create a tension in the mind so that individuals could rise from the bondage of myths and half-truths to the unfettered realm of creative analysis and objective appraisal, we must see the need of having nonviolent gadflies to create the kind of tension in society that will help men rise from the dark depths of prejudice and racism to the majestic heights of understanding and brotherhood. So the purpose of the direct action is to create a situation so crisis-packed that it will inevitably open the door to negotiation. We, therefore, concur with you in your call for negotiation. Too long has our beloved Southland been bogged down in the tragic attempt to live in monologue rather than dialogue.

One of the basic points in your statement is that our acts are untimely. Some have asked, "Why didn't you give the new administration time to act?" The only answer that I can give to this inquiry is that the new administration must be prodded about as much as the outgoing one before it acts. We will be sadly mistaken if we feel that the election of Mr. Boutwell will bring the millennium to Birmingham. While Mr. Boutwell is much more articulate and gentle than Mr. Connor, they are both segregationists dedicated to the task of maintaining the status quo. The hope I see in Mr. Boutwell is that he will be reasonable enough to see the futility of massive resistance to desegregation. But he will not see this without pressure from the devotees of civil rights. My friends, I must say to you that we have not made a single gain in civil rights without determined legal and nonviolent pressure. History is the long and tragic story of the fact that privileged groups seldom give up their privileges voluntarily. Individuals may see the moral light and voluntarily give up their unjust posture; but as Reinhold Niebuhr has reminded us, groups are more immoral than individuals.

We know through painful experience that freedom is never voluntarily given by the oppressor; it must be demanded by the oppressed. Frankly I have never yet engaged in a direct action movement that was "well timed," according to the timetable of those who have not suffered unduly from the disease of segregation. For years now I have heard the word "Wait!" It rings in the ear of every Negro with a piercing familiarity. This "wait" has almost always meant "never." It has been a tranquilizing thalidomide, relieving the emotional stress for a moment, only to give birth to an ill-formed infant of frustration. We must come to see with the distinguished jurist of yesterday that "justice too long delayed is justice denied." We have waited for more than three hundred and forty years for our constitutional and God-given rights. The nations of Asia and Africa are moving with jet-like speed toward the goal of political independence, and we still creep at horse and buggy pace toward the gaining of a cup of coffee at a lunch counter.

I guess it is easy for those who have never felt the stinging darts of segregation to say wait. But when you have seen vicious mobs lynch your mothers and fathers at will and drown your sisters and brothers at whim; when you have seen hate-filled policemen curse, kick, brutalize, and even kill your black brothers and sisters with impunity; when you see the vast majority of your twenty million Negro brothers smothering in an airtight cage of poverty in the midst of an affluent society; when you suddenly find your tongue twisted and your speech stammering as you seek to explain to your six-year-old daughter why she can't go to the public amusement park that has just been advertised on television, and see tears welling up in her little eyes when she is told that Funtown is closed to colored children, and see the depressing clouds of inferiority begin to form in her little mental sky, and see her begin to distort her little personality by unconsciously developing a bitterness toward white people; when you have to concoct an answer for a five-year-old son asking in agonizing pathos: "Daddy, why do white people treat colored people so mean?"; when you take a cross-country drive and find it necessary to sleep night after night in the uncomfortable corners of your automobile because no motel will accept you; when you are humiliated day in and day out by nagging signs reading "white" men and "colored"; when your first name becomes "nigger" and your middle name becomes "boy" (however old you are) and your last name becomes "John," and when your wife and mother are never given the respected title "Mrs."; when you are harried by day and haunted by night by the fact that you are a Negro, living constantly at tip-toe stance never quite knowing what to expect next, and plagued with inner fears and outer resentments; when you are forever fighting a degenerating sense of "nobodiness";—then you will understand why we find it very difficult to wait. There comes a time when the cup of our endurance runs over, and men are no longer willing to be plunged into an abyss of injustice where they experience the bleakness of a corroding despair. I hope, sirs, you can understand our legitimate and unavoidable impatience.

You express a great deal of anxiety over our willingness to break laws. This is certainly a legitimate concern. Since we so diligently urge people to obey the Supreme Court's decision of 1954 outlawing segregation in the public schools, it is rather strange and paradoxical to find us consciously breaking laws. One may well ask, "How can you advocate breaking some laws and obeying others?" The answer is found in the fact that there are two types of laws. There are *just* laws and there are *unjust* laws. I would be the first to advocate obeying just laws. One has not only a legal but moral responsibility to obey just laws. Conversely, one has a moral responsibility to disobey unjust laws. I would agree with Saint Augustine that "An unjust law is no law at all."

Now what is the difference between the two? How does one determine when a law is just or unjust? A just law is a man-made code that squares with the moral law or the law of God. An unjust law is a code that is out of harmony with the moral law. To put it in the terms of Saint Thomas Aquinas, an unjust law is a human law that is not rooted in eternal and natural law. Any law that uplifts human personality is just. Any law that degrades human personality is unjust. All segregation statutes are unjust because segregation distorts the soul and damages the personality. It gives the segregator a false sense of superiority and the segregated a false sense of inferiority. To use the words of Martin Buber, the great Jewish philosopher, segregation substitutes an "I-it" relationship for the "I-thou" relationship, and ends up relegating persons to the status of things. So segregation is not only politically, economically, and sociologically unsound, but it is morally wrong and sinful. Paul Tillich has said that sin is separation. Isn't segregation an existential expression of man's tragic separation, an expression of his awful estrangement, his terrible sinfulness? So I can urge men to obey the 1954 decision of the Supreme Court because it is morally right, and I can urge them to disobey segregation ordinances because they are morally wrong.

Let us turn to a more concrete example of just and unjust laws. An unjust law is a code that a majority inflicts on a minority that is not binding on itself. This is *difference* made legal. On the other hand a just law is a code that a majority compels a minority to follow that it is willing to follow itself. This is *sameness* made legal.

Let me give another explanation. An unjust law is a code inflicted upon a minority which that minority had no part in enacting or creating because they did not have the unhampered right to vote. Who can say the legislature of Alabama which set up the segregation laws was democratically elected? Throughout the State of Alabama all types of conniving methods are used to prevent Negroes from becoming registered voters and there are some counties without a single Negro registered to vote despite the fact that the Negro constitutes a majority of the population. Can any law set up in such a state be considered democratically structured?

These are just a few examples of unjust and just laws. There are some instances when a law is just on its face but unjust in its application. For instance, I was arrested Friday on a charge of parading without a permit. Now there is nothing wrong with an ordinance which requires a permit for a parade, but when the ordinance is used to preserve segregation and to deny citizens the First Amendment privilege of peaceful assembly and peaceful protest, then it becomes unjust.

I hope you can see the distinction I am trying to point out. In no sense do I advocate evading or defying the law as the rabid segregationist would do. This would lead to anarchy. One who breaks an unjust law must do it *openly, lovingly* (not hatefully as the white mothers did in New Orleans when they were seen on television screaming "nigger, nigger, nigger") and with a willingness to accept the penalty. I submit that an individual who breaks a law that conscience tells him is unjust, and willingly accepts the penalty by staying in jail to arouse the conscience of the community over its injustice, is in reality expressing the very highest respect for law.

Of course there is nothing new about this kind of civil disobedience. It was seen sublimely in the refusal of Shadrach, Meshach, and Abednego to obey the unjust laws of Nebuchadnezzar because a higher moral law was involved. It was practiced superbly by the early Christians who were willing to face hungry lions and the excruciating pain of chopping blocks, before submitting to certain very unjust laws of the Roman Empire. To a degree our academic freedom is a reality today because Socrates practiced civil disobedience.

We can never forget that everything Hitler did in Germany was "legal" and everything the Hungarian freedom fighters did in Hungary was "illegal." It was "illegal" to aid and comfort a Jew in Hitler's Germany. But I am sure that, if I had lived in Germany during that time, I would have aided and comforted my Jewish brothers even though it was illegal. If I lived in a communist country today where certain principles dear to the Christian faith are suppressed, I believe I would openly advocate disobeying these antireligious laws.

I must make two honest confessions to you, my Christian and Jewish brothers. First I must confess that over the last few years I have been gravely disappointed with the white moderate. I have almost reached the regrettable conclusion that the Negroes' great stumbling block in the stride toward freedom is not the White Citizens' "Councilor" or the Ku Klux Klanner, but the white moderate who is more devoted to "order" than to justice; who prefers a negative peace which is the absence of tension to a positive peace which is the presence of justice; who constantly says "I agree with you in the goal you seek, but I can't agree with your methods of direct action"; who paternalistically feels that he can set the timetable for another man's freedom; who lives by the myth of time and who constantly advises the Negro to wait until a "more convenient season." Shallow understanding from people of good will is more frustrating than absolute misunderstanding from people of ill will. Lukewarm acceptance is much more bewildering than outright rejection.

I had hoped that the white moderate would understand that law and order exist for the purpose of establishing justice, and that when they fail to do this they become the dangerously structured dams that block the flow of social progress. I had hoped that the white moderate would understand that the present tension in the South is merely a necessary phase of the transition from an obnoxious negative peace, where the Negro passively accepted his unjust plight, to a substance-filled positive peace, where all men will respect the dignity and worth of human personality. Actually, we who engage in nonviolent direct action are not the creators of tension. We merely bring to the surface the hidden tension that is already alive. We bring it out in the open where it can be seen and dealt with. Like a boil that can never be cured as long as it is covered up but must be opened with all its pus-flowing ugliness to the natural medicines of air and light, injustice must likewise be exposed, with all of the tension its exposing creates, to the light of human conscience and the air of national opinion before it can be cured.

In your statement you asserted that our actions, even though peaceful, must be condemned because they precipitate violence. But can this assertion be logically made? Isn't this like condemning the robbed man because his possession of money precipitated the evil act of robbery? Isn't this like condemning Socrates because his unswerving commitment to truth and his philosophical delvings precipitated the misguided popular mind to make him drink the hemlock? Isn't this like condemning Jesus because His unique God consciousness and never-ceasing devotion to His will precipitated the evil act of crucifixion? We must come to see, as federal courts have consistently affirmed, that it is immoral to urge an individual to withdraw his efforts to gain his basic constitutional rights because the quest precipitates violence. Society must protect the robbed and punish the robber.

I had also hoped that the white moderate would reject the myth of time. I received a letter this morning from a white brother in Texas which said: "All Christians know that the colored people will receive equal rights eventually, but is it possible that you are in too great of a religious hurry? It has taken Christianity almost 2000 years to accomplish what it has. The teachings of Christ take time to come to earth." All that is said here grows out of a tragic misconception of time. It is the strangely irrational notion that there is something in the very flow of time that will inevitably cure all ills. Actually time is neutral. It can be used either destructively or constructively. I am coming to feel that the people of ill will have used time much more effectively than the people of good will. We will have to repent in this generation not merely for the vitriolic words and actions of the bad people, but for the appalling silence of the good people. We must come to see that human progress never rolls in on wheels of inevitability. It comes through the tireless efforts and persistent work of men willing to be co-workers with God, and without this hard work time itself becomes an ally of the forces of social stagnation.

We must use time creatively, and forever realize that the time is always ripe to do right. Now is the time to make real the promise of democracy, and transform our pending national elegy into a creative psalm of brotherhood. Now is the time to lift our national policy from the quicksand of racial injustice to the solid rock of human dignity.

You spoke of our activity in Birmingham as extreme. At first I was rather disappointed that fellow clergymen would see my nonviolent efforts as those of the extremist. I started thinking about the fact that I stand in the middle of two opposing forces in the Negro community. One is a force of complacency made up of Negroes who, as a result of long years of oppression, have been so completely drained of self-respect and a sense of "somebodiness" that they have adjusted to segregation, and of a few Negroes in the middle class who, because of a degree of academic and economic security, and because at points they profit by segregation, have unconsciously become insensitive to the problems of the masses. The other force is one of bitterness and hatred and comes perilously close to advocating violence. It is expressed in the various black nationalist groups that are springing up over the nation, the largest and best known being Elijah Muhammad's Muslim movement. This movement is nourished by the contemporary frustration over the continued existence of racial discrimination. It is made up of people who have lost faith in America, who have absolutely repudiated Christianity, and who have concluded that the white man is an incurable "devil." I have tried to stand between these two forces saying that we need not follow the "do-nothingism" of the complacent or the hatred and despair of the black nationalist. There is the more excellent way of love and nonviolent protest. I'm grateful to God that, through the Negro church, the dimension of nonviolence entered our struggle. If this philosophy had not emerged I am convinced that by now many streets of the South would be flowing with floods of blood. And I am further convinced that if our white brothers dismiss us as "rabble rousers" and "outside agitators"—those of us who are working through the channels of nonviolent direct action—and refuse to support our nonviolent efforts, millions of Negroes, out of frustration and despair, will seek solace and security in black nationalist ideologies, a development that will lead inevitably to a frightening racial nightmare.

Oppressed people cannot remain oppressed forever. The urge for freedom will eventually come. This is what has happened to the American Negro. Something within has reminded him of his birthright of freedom; something without has reminded him that he can gain it. Consciously and unconsciously, he has been swept in by what the Germans call the *Zeitgeist*, and with his black brothers of Africa, and his brown and yellow brothers of Asia, South America, and the Caribbean, he is moving with a sense of cosmic urgency toward the promised land of racial justice. Recognizing this vital urge that has engulfed the Negro community, one should readily understand public demonstrations. The Negro has many pent-up resentments and latent frustrations. He has to get them out. So let him march sometime; let him have his prayer pilgrimages to the city hall; understand why he must have sit-ins and freedom rides. If his repressed emotions do not come out in these nonviolent ways, they will come out in ominous expressions of violence. This is not a threat; it is a fact of history. So I have not said to my people, "Get rid of your discontent." But I have tried to say that this normal and healthy discontent can be channeled through the creative outlet of nonviolent direct action. Now this approach is being dismissed as extremist. I must admit that I was initially disappointed in being so categorized.

But as I continued to think about the matter I gradually gained a bit of satisfaction from being considered an extremist. Was not Jesus an extremist in love? "Love your enemies, bless them that curse you, pray for them that despitefully use you." Was not Amos an extremist for justice—"Let justice roll down like waters and righteousness like a mighty stream." Was not Paul an extremist for the gospel of Jesus Christ—"I bear in my body the marks of the Lord Jesus." Was not Martin Luther an extremist—"Here I stand; I can do none other so help me God." Was not John Bunyan an extremist—"I will stay in jail to the end of my days before I make a butchery of my conscience." Was not Abraham Lincoln an extremist—"This nation cannot survive half slave and half free." Was not Thomas Jefferson an extremist—"We hold these truths to be self-evident that all men are created equal." So the question is not whether we will be extremist but what kind of extremist will we be. Will we be extremists for hate or will we be extremists for love? Will we be extremists for the preservation of injustice—or will we be extremists for the cause of justice? In that dramatic scene on Calvary's hill three men were crucified. We must never forget that all three were crucified for the same crime—the crime of extremism. Two were extremists for immorality, and thus fell below their environment. The other, Jesus Christ, was an extremist for love, truth, and goodness, and thereby rose above His environment. So, after all, maybe the South, the nation, and the world are in dire need of creative extremists.

I had hoped that the white moderate would see this. Maybe I was too optimistic. Maybe I expected too much. I guess I should have realized that few members of a race that has oppressed another race can understand or appreciate the deep groans and passionate yearnings of those that have been oppressed, and still fewer have the vision to see that injustice must be rooted out by strong, persistent, and determined action. I am thankful, however, that some of our white brothers have grasped the meaning of this social revolution and committed themselves to it. They are still all too small in quantity, but they are big in quality. Some like Ralph McGill, Lillian Smith, Harry Golden, and James Dabbs have written about our struggle in eloquent, prophetic, and understanding terms. Others have marched with us down nameless streets of the South. They have languished in filthy, roach-infested jails, suffering the abuse and brutality of angry policemen who look on them as "dirty nigger lovers." They, unlike so many of their moderate brothers and sisters, have recognized the urgency of the moment and sensed the need for powerful "action" antidotes to combat the disease of segregation.

Let me rush on to mention my other disappointment. I have been so greatly disappointed with the white Church and its leadership. Of course there are some notable exceptions. I am not unmindful of the fact that each of you has taken some significant stands on this issue. I commend you, Rev. Stallings, for your Christian stand on this past Sunday, in welcoming Negroes to your service on a non-segregated basis. I commend the Catholic leaders of this state for integrating Springhill College several years ago.

But despite these notable exceptions I must honestly reiterate that I have been disappointed with the Church. I do not say that as one of those negative critics who can always find something wrong with the Church. I say it as a minister of the gospel, who loves the Church; who was nurtured in its bosom; who has been sustained by its spiritual blessings and who will remain true to it as long as the cord of life shall lengthen.

I had the strange feeling when I was suddenly catapulted into the leadership of the bus protest in Montgomery several years ago that we would have the support of the white Church. I felt that the white ministers, priests, and rabbis of the South would be some of our strongest allies. Instead, some have been outright opponents, refusing to understand the freedom movement and misrepresenting its leaders; all too many others have been more cautious than courageous and have remained silent behind the anesthetizing security of stained glass windows.

In spite of my shattered dreams of the past, I came to Birmingham with the hope that the white religious leadership of this community would see the justice of our cause and, with deep moral concern, serve as the channel through which our just grievances could get to the power structure. I had hoped that each of you would understand. But again I have been disappointed.

I have heard numerous religious leaders of the South call upon their worshippers to comply with a desegregation decision because it is the law, but I have longed to hear white ministers say: "Follow this decree because integration is morally right and the Negro is your brother." In the midst of blatant injustices inflicted upon the Negro, I have watched white churches stand on the sideline and merely mouth pious irrelevancies and sanctimonious trivialities. In the midst of a mighty struggle to rid our nation of racial and economic injustice, I have heard so many ministers say, "Those are social issues with which the Gospel has no real concern." and I have watched so many churches commit themselves to a completely otherworldly religion which made a strange distinction between body and soul, the sacred and the secular.

So here we are moving toward the exit of the twentieth century with a religious community largely adjusted to the status quo, standing as a taillight behind other community agencies rather than a headlight leading men to higher levels of justice.

I have travelled the length and breadth of Alabama, Mississippi, and all the other Southern states. On sweltering summer days and crisp autumn mornings I have looked at her beautiful churches with their spires pointing heavenward. I have beheld the impressive outlay of her massive religious education buildings. Over and over again I have found myself asking: "Who worships here? Who is their God? Where were their voices when the lips of Governor Barnett dripped with words of interposition and nullification? Where were they when Governor Wallace gave the clarion call for defiance and hatred? Where were their voices of support when tired, bruised, and weary Negro men and women decided to rise from the dark dungeons of complacency to the bright hills of creative protest?"

Yes, these questions are still in my mind. In deep disappointment, I have wept over the laxity of the Church. But be assured that my tears have been tears of love. There can be no deep disappointment where there is not deep love. Yes, I love the Church; I love her sacred walls. How could I do otherwise? I am in the rather unique position of being the son, the grandson, and the great-grandson of preachers. Yes, I see the Church as the body of Christ. But, oh! How we have blemished and scarred that body through social neglect and fear of being nonconformist.

There was a time when the Church was very powerful. It was during that period when the early Christians rejoiced when they were deemed worthy to suffer for what they believed. In those days the Church was not merely a thermometer that recorded the ideas and principles of popular opinion; it was a thermostat that transformed the mores of society. Wherever the early Christians entered a town the power structure got disturbed and immediately sought to convict them for being "disturbers of the peace" and "outside agitators." But they went on with the conviction that they were a "colony of heaven" and had to obey God rather than man. They were small in number but big in commitment. They were too

God-intoxicated to be "astronomically intimidated." They brought an end to such ancient evils as infanticide and gladiatorial contest.

Things are different now. The contemporary Church is so often a weak, ineffectual voice with an uncertain sound. It is so often the arch-supporter of the status quo. Far from being disturbed by the presence of the Church, the power structure of the average community is consoled by the Church's silent and often vocal sanction of things as they are.

But the judgment of God is upon the Church as never before. If the Church of today does not recapture the sacrificial spirit of the early Church, it will lose its authentic ring, forfeit the loyalty of millions, and be dismissed as an irrelevant social club with no meaning for the twentieth century. I am meeting young people every day whose disappointment with the Church has risen to outright disgust.

Maybe again I have been too optimistic. Is organized religion too inextricably bound to the status quo to save our nation and the world? Maybe I must turn my faith to the inner spiritual Church, the church within the Church, as the true *eccelesia* and the hope of the world. But again I am thankful to God that some noble souls from the ranks of organized religion have broken loose from the paralyzing chains of conformity and joined us as active partners in the struggle for freedom. They have left their secure congregations and walked the streets of Albany, Georgia, with us. They have gone through the highways of the South on torturous rides for freedom. Yes, they have gone to jail with us. Some have been kicked out of their churches and lost the support of their bishops and fellow ministers. But they have gone with the faith that right defeated is stronger than evil triumphant. These men have been the leaven in the lump of the race. Their witness has been the spiritual salt that has preserved the true meaning of the Gospel in these troubled times. They have carved a tunnel of hope through the dark mountain of disappointment.

I hope the Church as a whole will meet the challenge of this decisive hour. But even if the Church does not come to the aid of justice, I have no despair about the future. I have no fear about the outcome of our struggle in Birmingham, even if our motives are presently misunderstood. We will reach the goal of freedom in Birmingham and all over the nation, because the goal of America is freedom. Abused and scorned though we may be, our destiny is tied up with the destiny of America. Before the pilgrims landed at Plymouth, we were here. Before the pen of Jefferson etched across the pages of history the majestic words of the Declaration of Independence, we were here. For more than two centuries our foreparents labored in this country without wages; they made cotton "king"; and they built the homes of their masters in the midst of brutal injustice and shameful humiliation—and yet out of a bottomless vitality they con-

inspiring!

tinued to thrive and develop. If the inexpressible cruelties of slavery could not stop us, the opposition we now face will surely fail. We will win our freedom because the sacred heritage of our nation and the eternal will of God are surely embodied in our echoing demands.

I must close now. But before closing I am impelled to mention one other point in your statement that troubled me profoundly. You warmly commended the Birmingham police force for keeping "order" and "preventing violence." I don't believe you would have so warmly commended the police force if you had seen its angry violent dogs literally biting six unarmed, nonviolent Negroes. I don't believe you would so quickly commend the policemen if you would observe their ugly and inhuman treatment of Negroes here in the city jail; if you would watch them push and curse old Negro women and young Negro girls; if you would see them slap and kick old Negro men and young Negro boys; if you will observe them, as they have done on two occasions, refuse to give us food because we wanted to sing our grace together. I'm sorry that I can't join you in your praise for the police department.

It is true·that they have been rather disciplined in their public handling of the demonstrators. In this sense they have been rather publicly "nonviolent." But for what purpose? To preserve the evil system of segregation. Over the last few years I have consistently preached that nonviolence demands that the means we use must be as pure as the ends we seek. So I have tried to make it clear that it is wrong to use immoral means to attain moral ends. But now I must affirm that it is just as wrong, or even more so, to use moral means to preserve immoral ends. Maybe Mr. Connor and his policemen have been publicly nonviolent, as Chief Prichett was in Albany, Georgia, but they have used the moral means of nonviolence to maintain the immoral end of flagrant racial injustice. T. S. Eliot has said that there is no greater treason than to do the right deed for the wrong reason.

I wish you had commended the Negro sit-inners and demonstrators of Birmingham for their sublime courage, their willingness to suffer, and their amazing discipline in the midst of the most inhuman provocation. One day the South will recognize its real heroes. They will be the James Merediths, courageously and with a majestic sense of purpose, facing jeering and hostile mobs and the agonizing loneliness that characterizes the life of the pioneer. They will be old, oppressed, battered Negro women, symbolized in a seventy-two year old woman of Montgomery, Alabama, who rose up with a sense of dignity and with her people decided not to ride the segregated buses, and responded to one who inquired about her tiredness with ungrammatical profundity: "My feets is tired, but my soul is rested." They will be young high school and college students, young ministers of the gospel and a host of the elders, courageously and nonviolently sitting in at lunch counters and willingly going to jail for conscience sake. One day the South will know that when these disinherited children of God sat down at lunch counters they were in reality standing up for the best in the American dream and the most sacred values in our Judeo-Christian heritage, and thus carrying our whole nation back to great wells of democracy which were dug deep by the founding fathers in the formulation of the Constitution and the Declaration of Independence.

Never before have I written a letter this long (or should I say a book?). I'm afraid that it is much too long to take your precious time. I can assure you that it would have been much shorter if I had been writing from a comfortable desk, but what else is there to do when you are alone for days in the dull monotony of a narrow jail cell other than write long letters, think strange thoughts, and pray long prayers?

If I have said anything in this letter that is an overstatement of the truth and is indicative of an unreasonable impatience, I beg you to forgive me. If I have said anything in this letter that is an understatement of the truth and is indicative of my having a patience that makes me patient with anything less than brotherhood, I beg God to forgive me.

I hope this letter finds you strong in the faith. I also hope that circumstances will soon make it possible for me to meet each of you, not as an integrationist or a civil rights leader, but as a fellow clergyman and a Christian brother. Let us all hope that the dark clouds of racial prejudice will soon pass away and the deep fog of misunderstanding will be lifted from our fear-drenched communities and in some not too distant tomorrow the radiant stars of love and brotherhood will shine over our great nation with all of their scintillating beauty.

Yours for the cause of Peace and Brotherhood

Martin Luther King, Jr.

Professor of psychology and education at Mount Holyoke College and practicing clinical psychologist, Beverly Daniel Tatum gained national attention in 1997 when her book Why Are All the Black Kids Sitting Together in the Cafeteria?: And Other Conventions about Race *was published; she was one of three authors on the panel for President Clinton's national town meeting on race in December of that year. Her writing focuses on the psychology of racism, including issues such as blacks in predominantly white settings, multiracial families, and self-segregation. She and her husband Travis make their home in Northampton, MA.*

Defining Racism

"Can We Talk?"

Beverly Daniel Tatum

Early in my teaching career, a White student I knew asked me what I would be teaching the following semester. I mentioned that I would be teaching a course on racism. She replied, with some surprise in her voice, "Oh, is there still racism?" I assured her that indeed there was and suggested that she sign up for my course. Fifteen years later, after exhaustive media coverage of events such as the Rodney King beating, the Charles Stuart and Susan Smith cases, the O. J. Simpson trial, the appeal to racial prejudices in electoral politics, and the bitter debates about affirmative action and welfare reform, it seems hard to imagine that anyone would still be unaware of the reality of racism in our society. But in fact, in almost every audience I address, there is someone who will suggest that racism is a thing of the past. There is always someone who hasn't noticed the stereotypical images of people of color in the media, who hasn't observed the housing discrimination in their community, who hasn't read the newspaper articles about documented racial bias in lending practices among well-known banks, who isn't aware of the racial tracking pattern at the local school, who hasn't seen the reports of rising incidents of racially motivated hate crimes in America—in short, someone who hasn't been paying attention to issues of race. But if you are paying attention, the legacy of racism is not hard to see, and we are all affected by it.

The impact of racism begins early. Even in our preschool years, we are exposed to misinformation about people different from ourselves. Many of us grew up in neighborhoods where we had limited opportunities to interact with people different from our own families. When I ask my college students, "How many of you grew up in neighborhoods where most of the people were from the same racial group as your own?" almost every hand goes up. There is still a great deal of social segregation in our communities. Consequently, most of the early information we receive about "others"—people racially, religiously, or socioeconomically differ- ent from ourselves—does not come as the result of firsthand experience. The secondhand information we do receive has often been distorted, shaped by cultural stereotypes, and left incomplete.

Some examples will highlight this process. Several years ago one of my students conducted a research project investigating preschoolers' con- ceptions of Native Americans.[1] Using children at a local day care center as her participants, she asked these three- and four-year-olds to draw a picture of a Native American. Most children were stumped by her request. They didn't know what a Native American was. But when she rephrased the question and asked them to draw a picture of an Indian, they readily complied. Almost every picture included one central feature: feathers. In fact, many of them also included a weapon—a knife or tom- ahawk—and depicted the person in violent or aggressive terms. Though this group of children, almost all of whom were White, did not live near a large Native American population and probably had had little if any personal interaction with American Indians, they all had internalized an image of what Indians were like. How did they know? Cartoon images, in particular the Disney movie *Peter Pan*, were cited by the children as their number-one source of information. At the age of three, these chil- dren already had a set of stereotypes in place. Though I would not describe three-year-olds as prejudiced, the stereotypes to which they have been exposed become the foundation for the adult prejudices so many of us have.

Sometimes the assumptions we make about others come not from what we have been told or what we have seen on television or in books, but rather from what we have *not* been told. The distortion of historical infor- mation about people of color leads young people (and older people, too) to make assumptions that may go unchallenged for a long time. Consider this conversation between two White students following a discussion about the cultural transmission of racism:

"Yeah, I just found out that Cleopatra was actually a Black woman."

"What?"

The first student went on to explain her newly learned information. The second student exclaimed in disbelief, "That can't be true. Cleopatra was beautiful!"

What had this young woman learned about who in our society is consid- ered beautiful and who is not? Had she conjured up images of Elizabeth Taylor when she thought of Cleopatra? The new information her class- mate had shared and her own deeply ingrained assumptions about who is beautiful and who is not were too incongruous to allow her to assimilate the information at that moment.

Omitted information can have similar effects. For example, another young woman, preparing to be a high school English teacher, expressed her dismay that she had never learned about any Black authors in any of her English courses. How was she to teach about them to her future students when she hadn't learned about them herself? A White male student in the class responded to this discussion with frustration in his response journal, writing "It's not my fault that Blacks don't write books." Had one of his elementary, high school, or college teachers ever told him that there were no Black writers? Probably not. Yet because he had never been exposed to Black authors, he had drawn his own conclusion that there were none.

Stereotypes, omissions, and distortions all contribute to the development of prejudice. *Prejudice* is a preconceived judgment or opinion, usually based on limited information. I assume that we all have prejudices, not because we want them, but simply because we are so continually exposed to misinformation about others. Though I have often heard students or workshop participants describe someone as not having "a prejudiced bone in his body," I usually suggest that they look again. Prejudice is one of the inescapable consequences of living in a racist society. Cultural racism—the cultural images and messages that affirm the assumed superiority of Whites and the assumed inferiority of people of color—is like smog in the air. Sometimes it is so thick it is visible, other times it is less apparent, but always, day in and day out, we are breathing it in. None of us would introduce ourselves as "smog-breathers" (and most of us don't want to be described as prejudiced), but if we live in a smoggy place, how can we avoid breathing the air? If we live in an environment in which we are bombarded with stereotypical images in the media, are frequently exposed to the ethnic jokes of friends and family members, and are rarely informed of the accomplishments of oppressed groups, we will develop the negative categorizations of those groups that form the basis of prejudice.

People of color as well as Whites develop these categorizations. Even a member of the stereotyped group may internalize the stereotypical categories about his or her own group to some degree. In fact, this process happens so frequently that it has a name, *internalized oppression*. Some of the consequences of believing the distorted messages about one's own group will be discussed in subsequent chapters.

Certainly some people are more prejudiced than others, actively embracing and perpetuating negative and hateful images of those who are different from themselves. When we claim to be free of prejudice, perhaps what we are really saying is that we are not hatemongers. But none of us is completely innocent. Prejudice is an integral part of our socialization, and it is not our fault. Just as the preschoolers my student interviewed are not to blame for the negative messages they internalized, we are not at fault for the stereotypes, distortions, and omissions that shaped our thinking as we grew up.

To say that it is not our fault does not relieve us of responsibility, however. We may not have polluted the air, but we need to take responsibility, along with others, for cleaning it up. Each of us needs to look at our own behavior. Am I perpetuating and reinforcing the negative messages so pervasive in our culture, or am I seeking to challenge them? If I have not been exposed to positive images of marginalized groups, am I seeking them out, expanding my own knowledge base for myself and my children? Am I acknowledging and examining my own prejudices, my own rigid categorizations of others, thereby minimizing the adverse impact they might have on my interactions with those I have categorized? Unless we engage in these and other conscious acts of reflection and reeducation, we easily repeat the process with our children. We teach what we were taught. The unexamined prejudices of the parents are passed on to the children. It is not our fault, but it is our responsibility to interrupt this cycle.

Racism: A System of Advantage Based on Race

Many people use the terms *prejudice* and *racism* interchangeably. I do not, and I think it is important to make a distinction. In his book *Portraits of White Racism*, David Wellman argues convincingly that limiting our understanding of racism to prejudice does not offer a sufficient explanation for the persistence of racism. He defines racism as a "system of advantage based on race."[2] In illustrating this definition, he provides example after example of how Whites defend their racial advantage—access to better schools, housing, jobs—even when they do not embrace overtly prejudicial thinking. Racism cannot be fully explained as an expression of prejudice alone.

This definition of racism is useful because it allows us to see that racism, like other forms of oppression, is not only a personal ideology based on racial prejudice, but a *system* involving cultural messages and institutional policies and practices as well as the beliefs and actions of individuals. In the context of the United States, this system clearly operates to the advantage of Whites and to the disadvantage of people of color. Another related definition of racism, commonly used by antiracist educators and consultants, is "prejudice plus power." Racial prejudice when combined with social power—access to social, cultural, and economic resources and decision-making—leads to the institutionalization of racist policies and practices. While I think this definition also captures the idea that racism is more than individual beliefs and attitudes, I prefer Wellman's definition because the idea of systematic advantage and disadvantage is critical to an understanding of how racism operates in American society.

In addition, I find that many of my White students and workshop participants do not feel powerful. Defining racism as prejudice plus power has little personal relevance. For some, their response to this definition is the following: "I'm not really prejudiced, and I have no power, so racism has nothing to do with me." However, most White people, if they are really being honest with themselves, can see that there are advantages to being White in the United States. Despite the current rhetoric about affirmative action and "reverse racism," every social indicator, from salary to life expectancy, reveals the advantages of being White.[3]

The systematic advantages of being White are often referred to as White privilege. In a now well-known article, "White Privilege: Unpacking the Invisible Knapsack," Peggy McIntosh, a White feminist scholar, identified a long list of societal privileges that she received simply because she was White.[4] She did not ask for them, and it is important to note that she hadn't always noticed that she was receiving them. They included major and minor advantages. Of course she enjoyed greater access to jobs and housing. But she also was able to shop in department stores without being followed by suspicious salespeople and could always find appropriate hair care products and makeup in any drugstore. She could send her child to school confident that the teacher would not discriminate against him on the basis of race. She could also be late for meetings, and talk with her mouth full, fairly confident that these behaviors would not be attributed to the fact that she was White. She could express an opinion in a meeting or in print and not have it labeled the "White" viewpoint. In other words, she was more often than not viewed as an individual, rather than as a member of a racial group.

This article rings true for most White readers, many of whom may have never considered the benefits of being White. It's one thing to have enough awareness of racism to describe the ways that people of color are disadvantaged by it. But this new understanding of racism is more elusive. In very concrete terms, it means that if a person of color is the victim of housing discrimination, the apartment that would otherwise have been rented to that person of color is still available for a White person. The White tenant is, knowingly or unknowingly, the beneficiary of racism, a system of advantage based on race. The unsuspecting tenant is not to blame for the prior discrimination, but she benefits from it anyway.

For many Whites, this new awareness of the benefits of a racist system elicits considerable pain, often accompanied by feelings of anger and guilt. These uncomfortable emotions can hinder further discussion. We all like to think that we deserve the good things we have received, and that others, too, get what they deserve. Social psychologists call this tendency a "belief in a just world."[5] Racism directly contradicts such notions of justice.

Understanding racism as a system of advantage based on race is antithetical to traditional notions of an American meritocracy. For those who have internalized this myth, this definition generates considerable discomfort. It is more comfortable simply to think of racism as a particular form of prejudice. Notions of power or privilege do not have to be addressed when our understanding of racism is constructed in that way.

The discomfort generated when a systemic definition of racism is introduced is usually quite visible in the workshops I lead. Someone in the group is usually quick to point out that this is not the definition you will find in most dictionaries. I reply, "Who wrote the dictionary?" I am not being facetious with this response. Whose interests are served by a "prejudice only" definition of racism? It is important to understand that the system of advantage is perpetuated when we do not acknowledge its existence.

Racism: For Whites Only?

Frequently someone will say, "You keep talking about White people. People of color can be racist, too." I once asked a White teacher what it would mean to her if a student or parent of color accused her of being racist. She said she would feel as though she had been punched in the stomach or called a "low-life scum." She is not alone in this feeling. The word *racist* holds a lot of emotional power. For many White people, to be called racist is the ultimate insult. The idea that this term might only be applied to Whites becomes highly problematic for after all, can't people of color be "low-life scum" too?

Of course, people of any racial group can hold hateful attitudes and behave in racially discriminatory and bigoted ways. We can all cite examples of horrible hate crimes which have been perpetrated by people of color as well as Whites. Hateful behavior is hateful behavior no matter who does it. But when I am asked, "Can people of color be racist?" I reply, "The answer depends on your definition of racism." If one defines racism as racial prejudice, the answer is yes. People of color can and do have racial prejudices. However, if one defines racism as a system of advantage based on race, the answer is no. People of color are not racist because they do not systematically benefit from racism. And equally important, there is no systematic cultural and institutional support or sanction for the racial bigotry of people of color. In my view, reserving the term *racist* only for behaviors committed by Whites in the context of a White-dominated society is a way of acknowledging the ever-present power differential afforded Whites by the culture and institutions that make up the system of advantage and continue to reinforce notions of White superiority. (Using the same logic, I reserve the word *sexist* for men. Though women can and do have gender-based prejudices, only men systematically benefit from sexism.)

Despite my best efforts to explain my thinking on this point, there are some who will be troubled, perhaps even incensed, by my response. To call the racially motivated acts of a person of color acts of racial bigotry and to describe similar acts committed by Whites as racist will make no sense to some people, including some people of color. To those, I will respectfully say, "We can agree to disagree." At moments like these, it is not agreement that is essential, but clarity. Even if you don't like the definition of racism I am using, hopefully you are now clear about what it is. If I also understand how you are using the term, our conversation can continue—despite our disagreement.

Another provocative question I'm often asked is "Are you saying all Whites are racist?" When asked this question, I again remember that White teacher's response, and I am conscious that perhaps the question I am really being asked is, "Are you saying all Whites are bad people?" The answer to that question is of course not. However, all White people, intentionally or unintentionally, do benefit from racism. A more relevant question is what are White people as individuals doing to interrupt racism? For many White people, the image of a racist is a hood-wearing Klan member or a name-calling Archie Bunker figure. These images represent what might be called *active racism*, blatant, intentional acts of racial bigotry and discrimination. *Passive racism* is more subtle and can be seen in the collusion of laughing when a racist joke is told, of letting exclusionary hiring practices go unchallenged, of accepting as appropriate the omissions of people of color from the curriculum, and of avoiding difficult race-related issues. Because racism is so ingrained in the fabric of American institutions, it is easily self-perpetuating.[6] All that is required to maintain it is business as usual.

I sometimes visualize the ongoing cycle of racism as a moving walkway at the airport. Active racist behavior is equivalent to walking fast on the conveyor belt. The person engaged in active racist behavior has identified with the ideology of White supremacy and is moving with it. Passive racist behavior is equivalent to standing still on the walkway. No overt effort is being made, but the conveyor belt moves the bystanders along to the same destination as those who are actively walking. Some of the bystanders may feel the motion of the conveyor belt, see the active racists ahead of them, and choose to turn around, unwilling to go to the same destination as the White supremacists. But unless they are walking actively in the opposite direction at a speed faster than the conveyor belt—unless they are actively antiracist—they will find themselves carried along with the others.

So, not all Whites are actively racist. Many are passively racist. Some, though not enough, are actively antiracist. The relevant question is not whether all Whites are racist, but how we can move more White people from a position of active or passive racism to one of active antiracism? The task of interrupting racism is obviously not the task of Whites alone. But the fact of White privilege means that Whites have greater access to the societal institutions in need of transformation. To whom much is given, much is required.

It is important to acknowledge that while all Whites benefit from racism, they do not all benefit equally. Other factors, such as socioeconomic status, gender, age, religious affiliation, sexual orientation, mental and physical ability, also play a role in our access to social influence and power. A White woman on welfare is not privileged to the same extent as a wealthy White heterosexual man. In her case, the systematic disadvantages of sexism and classism intersect with her White privilege, but the privilege is still there. This point was brought home to me in a 1994 study conducted by a Mount Holyoke graduate student, Phyllis Wentworth.[7] Wentworth interviewed a group of female college students, who were both older than their peers and were the first members of their families to attend college, about the pathways that lead them to college. All of the women interviewed were White, from working-class backgrounds, from families where women were expected to graduate from high school and get married or get a job. Several had experienced abusive relationships and other personal difficulties prior to coming to college. Yet their experiences were punctuated by "good luck" stories of apartments obtained without a deposit, good jobs offered without experience or extensive reference checks, and encouragement provided by willing mentors. While the women acknowledged their good fortune, none of them discussed their Whiteness. They had not considered the possibility that being White had worked in their favor and helped give them the benefit of the doubt at critical junctures. This study clearly showed that even under difficult circumstances, White privilege was still operating.

It is also true that not all people of color are equally targeted by racism. We all have multiple identities that shape our experience. I can describe myself as a light-skinned, well-educated, heterosexual, able-bodied,

Christian African American woman raised in a middle-class suburb. As an African American woman, I am systematically disadvantaged by race and by gender, but I systematically receive benefits in the other categories, which then mediate my experience of racism and sexism. When one is targeted by multiple isms—racism, sexism, classism, heterosexism, ableism, anti-Semitism, ageism—in whatever combination, the effect is intensified. The particular combination of racism and classism in many communities of color is life-threatening. Nonetheless, when I, the middle-class Black mother of two sons, read another story about a Black man's unlucky encounter with a White police officer's deadly force, I am reminded that racism by itself can kill.

The Cost of Racism

Several years ago, a White male student in my psychology of racism course wrote in his journal at the end of the semester that he had learned a lot about racism and now understood in a way he never had before just how advantaged he was. He also commented that he didn't think he would do anything to try to change the situation. After all, the system was working in his favor. Fortunately, his response was not typical. Most of my students leave my course with the desire (and an action plan) to interrupt the cycle of racism. However, this young man's response does raise an important question. Why should Whites who are advantaged by racism *want* to end that system of advantage? What are the *costs* of that system to them?

A *Money* magazine article called "Race and Money" chronicled the many ways the American economy was hindered by institutional racism.[8] Whether one looks at productivity lowered by racial tensions in the workplace, or real estate equity lost through housing discrimination, or the tax revenue lost in underemployed communities of color, or the high cost of warehousing human talent in prison, the economic costs of racism are real and measurable.

As a psychologist, I often hear about the less easily measured costs. When I ask White men and women how racism hurts them, they frequently talk about their fears of people of color, the social incompetence they feel in racially mixed situations, the alienation they have experienced between parents and children when a child marries into a family of color, and the interracial friendships they had as children that were lost in adolescence or young adulthood without their ever understanding why. White people are paying a significant price for the system of advantage. The cost is not as high for Whites as it is for people of color, but a price is being paid.[9] Wendell Berry, a White writer raised in Kentucky, captures this psychic pain in the opening pages of his book, *The Hidden Wound:*

If white people have suffered less obviously from racism than black people, they have nevertheless suffered greatly; the cost has been greater perhaps than we can yet know. If the white man has inflicted the wound of racism upon black men, the cost has been that he would receive the mirror image of that wound into himself. As the master, or as a member of the dominant race, he has felt little compulsion to acknowledge it or speak of it; the more painful it has grown the more deeply he has hidden it within himself. But the wound is there, and it is a profound disorder, as great a damage in his mind as it is in his society.[10]

The dismantling of racism is in the best interests of everyone.

A Word about Language

Throughout this chapter I have used the term *White* to refer to Americans of European descent. In another era, I might have used the term *Caucasian*. I have used the term *people of color* to refer to those groups in America that are and have been historically targeted by racism. This includes people of African descent, people of Asian descent, people of Latin American descent, and indigenous peoples (sometimes referred to as Native Americans or American Indians).[11] Many people refer to these groups collectively as non-Whites. This term is particularly offensive because it defines groups of people in terms of what they are not. (Do we call women "non-men?") I also avoid using the term *minorities* because it represents another kind of distortion of information which we need to correct. So-called minorities represent the majority of the world's population. While the term *people of color* is inclusive, it is not perfect. As a workshop participant once said, White people have color, too. Perhaps it would be more accurate to say "people of more color," though I am not ready to make that change. Perhaps fellow psychologist Linda James Myers is on the right track. She refers to two groups of people, those of acknowledged African descent and those of unacknowledged African descent, reminding us that we can all trace the roots of our common humanity to Africa.

I refer to people of acknowledged African descent as Black. I know that *African American* is also a commonly used term, and I often refer to myself and other Black people born and raised in America in that way. Perhaps because I am a child of the 1960s "Black and beautiful" era, I still prefer *Black*. The term is more inclusive than *African American*, because there are Black people in the United States who are not African American—Afro-Caribbeans, for example—yet are targeted by racism, and are identified as Black.

When referring to other groups of color, I try to use the terms that the people themselves want to be called. In some cases, there is no clear consensus. For example, some people of Latin American ancestry prefer

Latino, while others prefer *Hispanic* or, if of Mexican descent, *Chicano*.[12] The terms *Latino* and *Hispanic* are used interchangeably here. Similarly, there are regional variations in the use of the terms *Native American, American Indian,* and *Indian*. *American Indian* and *Native people* are now more widely used than *Native American,* and the language used here reflects that. People of Asian descent include Pacific Islanders, and that is reflected in the terms *Asian/Pacific Islanders* and *Asian Pacific Americans*. However, when quoting others I use whichever terms they use.

My dilemma about the language to use reflects the fact that race is a social construction.[13] Despite myths to the contrary, biologists tell us that the only meaningful racial categorization is that of human. Van den Berghe defines race as "a group that is socially defined but on the basis of *physical* criteria," including skin color and facial features.[14]

Racial identity development, a central focus of this book, usually refers to the process of defining for oneself the personal significance and social meaning of belonging to a particular racial group. The terms *racial identity* and *ethnic identity* are often used synonymously, though a distinction can be made between the two. An ethnic group is a socially defined group based on *cultural* criteria, such as language, customs, and shared history. An individual might identify as a member of an ethnic group (Irish or Italian, for example) but might not think of himself in racial terms (as White). On the other hand, one may recognize the personal significance of racial group membership (identifying as Black, for instance) but may not consider ethnic identity (such as West Indian) as particularly meaningful.

Both racial and ethnic categories are socially constructed, and social definitions of these categories have changed over time. For example, in his book *Ethnic Identity: The Transformation of White America*, Richard Alba points out that the high rates of intermarriage and the dissolution of other social boundaries among European ethnic groups in the United States have reduced the significance of ethnic identity for these groups. In their place, he argues, a new ethnic identity is emerging, that of European American.[15]

Throughout this book, I refer primarily to racial identity. It is important, however, to acknowledge that ethnic identity and racial identity sometimes intersect. For example, dark-skinned Puerto Ricans may identify culturally as Puerto Rican and yet be categorized racially by others as Black on the basis of physical appearance. In the case of either racial or ethnic identity, these identities remain most salient to individuals of racial or ethnic groups that have been historically disadvantaged or marginalized.

The language we use to categorize one another racially is imperfect. These categories are still evolving as the current debate over Census classifications indicates.[16] The original creation of racial categories was in the service of oppression. Some may argue that to continue to use them is to continue that oppression. I respect that argument. Yet it is difficult to talk about what is essentially a flawed and problematic social construct without using language that is itself problematic. We have to be able to talk about it in order to change it. So this is the language I choose.

Notes

1. C. O'Toole, "The effect of the media and multicultural education on children's perceptions of Native Americans" (senior thesis, Department of Psychology and Education, Mount Holyoke College, South Hadley, MA, May 1990).

2. For an extended discussion of this point, see David Wellman, *Portraits of White Racism* (Cambridge: Cambridge University Press, 1977), ch. 1.

3. For specific statistical information, see R. Farley, "The common destiny of Blacks and Whites: Observations about the social and economic status of the races," pp. 197–233 in H. Hill and J. E. Jones, Jr. (Eds.), *Race in America: The Struggle for Equality* (Madison: University of Wisconsin Press, 1993).

4. P. McIntosh, "White Priveledge: Unpacking the Invisible Knapsack," *Peace and Freedom* (July/August 1989): 10–12.

5. For further discussion of the concept of "belief in a just world," see M. J. Lerner, "Social Psychology of Justice and Interpersonal Attraction," in T. Huston (Ed.), *Foundations of Interpersonal Attraction* (New York: Academic Press, 1974).

6. For a brief historical overview of the institutionalization of racism and sexism in our legal system, see "Part V: How It Happened: Race and Gender Issues in U.S. law," in P. S. Rothenberg (Ed.), *Race, Class, and Gender in the United States: An Integrated Study*, 3rd. ed. (New York: St. Martin's Press, 1995).

7. P. A. Wentworth, "The identity development of non-traditionally aged first-generation women college students: An exploratory study" (master's thesis, Department of Psychology and Education, Mount Holyoke College, South Hadley, MA, 1994).

8. W. I. Updegrave, "Race and Money," *Money* (December 1989): 152–72.

9. For further discussion of the impact of racism on Whites, see B. Bowser and R. G. Hunt (Eds.), *Impacts of Racism on White Americans* (Thousand Oaks, CA: Sage, 1981); P. Kivel, *Uprooting Racism: How White People Can Work for Racial Justice* (Philadelphia: New Society Publishers, 1996); and J. Barndt, *Dismantling Racism: The Continuing Challenge to White America* (Minneapolis: Augsburg Press, 1991).

10. W. Berry, *The Hidden Wound* (San Francisco: North Point Press, 1989), pp. 3–4.

11. It is important to note here that these groups are not necessarily mutually exclusive. For example, people of Latin America descent may have European, African, and Native American ancestors. The politics of racial categorization has served to create artificial boundaries between groups with shared ancestry.

¹² It is difficult to know which is the preferred term to use because different sub-groups have different preferences. According to Amado Padilla, younger U.S.-born university-educated individuals of Mexican ancestry prefer *Chicano(a)* to *Mexican American* or *Hispanic*. On the other hand, *Latino* is preferred by others of Mexican ancestry or other Latin American origin. Those of Cuban ancestry may prefer *Cuban American* to *Latino,* wheras recent immigrants from Central America would rather be identified by their nationality (e.g., *Guatematecos* or *Salvadorenos*). A. Padilla (Ed.), *Hispanic Psychology* (Thousand Oaks, CA: Sage 1995).

¹³ For an expanded discussion of the social construction of race, see M. Omi and H. Winant, *Racial Formation in the United States,* 2nd ed. (New York: Routledge, 1994).

¹⁴ P. L. Van den Berghe, *Race and Racism* (New York: Wiley, 1967).

¹⁵ See R. Alba, *Ethnic Identity: The Transformation of White America* (New Haven: Yale University Press, 1990).

¹⁶ For a discussion of the census classification debate and the history of racial classification in the United States, see L. Wright, "One Drop of Blood," *The New Yorker* (July 25, 1994): 46–55.

Peggy McIntosh, Ph.D., is the Associate Director of the Wellesley College Center for Research on Women, and is founder and co-director of the national S.E.E.D. (Seeking Educational Equity and Diversity) Project on Inclusive Curriculum. She has lectured worldwide and is considered an authority on multicultural and gender-fair curricula in higher education. Her many articles have examined aspects of race and the integration of feminist theories into traditional curricula.

White Privilege: Unpacking the Invisible Knapsack

Peggy McIntosh

Through work to bring materials from Women's Studies into the rest of the curriculum, I have often noticed men's unwillingness to grant that they are over-privileged, even though they may grant that women are disadvantaged. They may say they will work to improve women's status, in the society, the university, or the curriculum, but they can't or won't support the idea of lessening men's. Denials which amount to taboos surround the subject of advantages which men gain from women's disadvantages. These denials protect male privilege from being fully acknowledged, lessened or ended.

Thinking through unacknowledged male privilege as a phenomenon, I realized that since hierarchies in our society are interlocking, there was most likely a phenomenon of white privilege which was similarly denied and protected. As a white person, I realized I had been taught about racism as something which puts others at a disadvantage, but had been taught not to see one of its corollary aspects, white privilege, which puts me at an advantage.

I think whites are carefully taught not to recognize white privilege, as males are taught not to recognize male privilege. So I have begun in an untutored way to ask what it is like to have white privilege. I have come to see white privilege as an invisible package of unearned assets which I can count on cashing in each day, but about which I was 'meant' to remain oblivious. White privilege is like an invisible weightless knapsack of special provisions, maps, passports, codebooks, visas, clothes, tools and blank checks.

Describing white privilege makes one newly accountable. As we in Women's Studies work to reveal male privilege and ask men to give up some of their power, so one who writes about having white privilege must ask, "Having described it, what will I do to lessen or end it?"

After I realized the extent to which men work from a base of unacknowledged privilege, I understood that much of their oppressiveness was unconscious. Then I remembered the frequent charges from women of color that white women whom they encounter are oppressive. I began to understand why we are justly seen as oppressive, even when we don't see ourselves that way. I began to count the ways in which I enjoy unearned skin privilege and have been conditioned into oblivion about its existence.

My schooling gave me no training in seeing myself as an oppressor, as an unfairly advantaged person, or as a participant in a damaged culture. I was taught to see myself as an individual whose moral state depended on her individual moral will. My schooling followed the pattern my colleague Elizabeth Minnich has pointed out: whites are taught to think of their lives as morally neutral, normative, and average, and also ideal, so that when we work to benefit others, this is seen as work which will allow "them" to be more like "us."

I decided to try to work on myself at least by identifying some of the daily effects of white privilege in my life. I have chosen those conditions which I think in my case *attach somewhat more to skin-color privilege* than to class, religion, ethnic status, or geographical location, though of course all these other factors are intricately intertwined. As far as I can see, my African American co-workers, friends and acquaintances with whom I come into daily or frequent contact in this particular time, place, and line of work cannot count on most of these conditions.

1. I can if I wish arrange to be in the company of people of my race most of the time.
2. If I should need to move, I can be pretty sure of renting or purchasing housing in an area which I can afford and in which I would want to live.
3. I can be pretty sure that my neighbors in such a location will be neutral or pleasant to me.
4. I can go shopping alone most of the time, pretty well assured that I will not be followed or harassed.
5. I can turn on the television or open to the front page of the paper and see people of my race widely represented.
6. When I am told about our national heritage or about "civilization," I am shown that people of my color made it what it is.
7. I can be sure that my children will be given curricular materials that testify to the existence of their race.
8. If I want to, I can be pretty sure of finding a publisher for this piece on white privilege.

9. I can go into a music shop and count on finding the music of my race represented, into a supermarket and find the staple foods which fit with my cultural traditions, into a hairdresser's shop and find someone who can cut my hair.

10. Whether I use checks, credit cards, or cash, I can count on my skin color not to work against the appearance of financial reliability.

11. I can arrange to protect my children most of the time from people who might not like them.

12. I can swear, or dress in second hand clothes, or not answer letters, without having people attribute these choices to the bad morals, the poverty, or the illiteracy of my race.

13. I can speak in public to a powerful male group without putting my race on trial.

14. I can do well in a challenging situation without being called a credit to my race.

15. I am never asked to speak for all the people of my racial group.

16. I can remain oblivious of the language and customs of persons of color who constitute the world's majority without feeling in my culture any penalty for such oblivion.

17. I can criticize our government and talk about how much I fear its policies and behavior without being seen as a cultural outsider.

18. I can be pretty sure that if I ask to talk to "the person in charge," I will be facing a person of my race.

19. If a traffic cop pulls me over or if the IRS audits my tax return, I can be sure I haven't been singled out because of my race.

20. I can easily buy posters. postcards, picture books, greeting cards, dolls, toys, and children's magazines featuring people of my race.

21. I can go home from most meetings of organizations I belong to feeling somewhat tied in, rather than isolated, out-of-place, outnumbered, unheard, held at a distance, or feared.

22. I can take a job with an affirmative action employer without having co-workers on the job suspect that I got it because of race.

23. I can choose public accommodation without fearing that people of my race cannot get in or will be mistreated in the places I have chosen.

24. I can be sure that if I need legal or medical help, my race will not work against me.

25. If my day, week, or year is going badly, I need not ask of each negative episode or situation whether it has racial overtones.

26. I can choose blemish cover or bandages in "flesh" color and have them more or less match my skin.

I repeatedly forgot each of the realizations on this list until I wrote it down. For me white privilege has turned out to be an elusive and fugitive subject. The pressure to avoid it is great, for in facing it I must give up the myth of meritocracy. If these things are true, this is not such a free country; one's life is not what one makes it; many doors open for certain people through no virtues of their own.

In unpacking this invisible knapsack of white privilege, I have listed conditions of daily experience which I once took for granted. Nor did I think of any of these perquisites as bad for the holder. I now think that we need a more finely differentiated taxonomy of privilege, for some of these varieties are only what one would want for everyone in a just society, and others give license to be ignorant, oblivious, arrogant and destructive.

I see a pattern running through the matrix of white privilege, a pattern of assumptions which were passed on to me as a white person. There was one main piece of cultural turf; it was my own turf, and I was among those who could control the turf. *My skin color was an asset for any move I was educated to want to make.* I could think of myself as belonging in major ways, and of making social systems work for me. I could freely disparage, fear, neglect, or be oblivious to anything outside of the dominant cultural forms. Being of the main culture, I could also criticize it fairly freely.

In proportion as my racial group was being made confident, comfortable, and oblivious, other groups were likely being made inconfident, uncomfortable, and alienated. Whiteness protected me from many kinds of hostility, distress, and violence, which I was being subtly trained to visit in turn upon people of color.

For this reason, the word "privilege" now seems to me misleading. We usually think of privilege as being a favored state, whether earned or conferred by birth or luck. Yet some of the conditions I have described here work to systematically overempower certain groups. Such privilege simply *confers dominance* because of one's race or sex.

I want, then, to distinguish between earned strength and unearned power conferred systemically. Power from unearned privilege can look like strength when it is in fact permission to escape or to dominate. But not all of the privileges on my list are inevitably damaging. Some, like the expectation that neighbors will be decent to you, or that your race will not count against you in court, should be the norm in a just society. Others, like the privilege to ignore less powerful people, distort the humanity of the holders as well as the ignored groups.

We might at least start by distinguishing between positive advantages which we can work to spread, and negative types of advantages which unless rejected will always reinforce our present hierarchies. For example, the feeling that one belongs within the human circle, as Native Americans say, should not be seen as privilege for a few. Ideally it is an *unearned entitlement*. At present, since only a few have it, it is an *unearned advantage* for them. This paper results from a process of coming to see that some of the power which I originally saw as attendant on being a human being in the U.S. consisted in *unearned advantage* and *conferred dominance*.

I have met very few men who are truly distressed about systemic, unearned male advantage and conferred dominance. And so one question for me and others like me is whether we will be like them, or whether we will get truly distressed, even outraged, about unearned race advantage and conferred dominance and if so, what we will do to lessen them. In any case, we need to do more work in identifying how they actually affect our daily lives. Many, perhaps most, of our white students in the U.S. think that racism doesn't affect them because they are not people of color; they do not see "whiteness" as a racial identity. In addition, since race and sex are not the only advantaging systems at work, we need similarly to examine the daily experience of having age advantage, or ethnic advantage, or physical ability, or advantage related to nationality, religion, or sexual orientation.

Difficulties and dangers surrounding the task of finding parallels are many. Since racism, sexism, and heterosexism are not the same, the advantaging associated with them should not be seen as the same. In addition, it is hard to disentangle aspects of unearned advantage which rest more on social class, economic class, race, religion, sex and ethnic identity than on other factors. Still, all of the oppressions are interlocking, as the Combahee River Collective Statement of 1977 continues to remind us eloquently.

One factor seems clear about all of the interlocking oppressions. They take both active forms which we can see and embedded forms which as a member of the dominant group one is taught not to see. In my class and place, I did not see myself as a racist because I was taught to recognize racism only in individual acts of meanness by members of my group, never in invisible systems conferring unsought racial dominance on my group from birth.

Disapproving of the systems won't be enough to change them. I was taught to think that racism could end if white individuals changed their attitudes. [But] a "white" skin in the United States opens many doors for whites whether or not we approve of the way dominance has been conferred on us. Individual acts can palliate, but cannot end, these problems.

To redesign social systems we need first to acknowledge their colossal unseen dimensions. The silences and denials surrounding privilege are the key political tool here. They keep the thinking about equality or equity incomplete, protecting unearned advantage and conferred dominance by making these taboo subjects. Most talk by whites about equal opportunity seems to me now to be about equal opportunity to try to get into a position of dominance while denying that systems of dominance exist.

It seems to me that obliviousness about white advantage, like obliviousness about male advantage, is kept strongly inculturated in the United States so as to maintain the myth of meritocracy, the myth that democratic choice is equally available to all. Keeping most people unaware that freedom of confident action is there for just a small number of people props up those in power, and serves to keep power in the hands of the same groups that have most of it already.

Though systemic change takes many decades, there are pressing questions for me and I imagine for some others like me if we raise our daily consciousness on the perquisites of being light-skinned. What will we do with such knowledge? As we know from watching men, it is an open question whether we will choose to use unearned advantage to weaken hidden systems of advantage, and whether we will use any of our arbitrarily-awarded power to try to reconstruct power systems on a broader base.

Ursula K. Le Guin (b. 1929), a feminist science fiction writer, is author of numerous poems, plays, short stories and novels for adults and children. She has been the recipient of numerous Nebula and Hugo Awards for her work, including her popular Earthsea *trilogy.* The Birthday of the World: And Other Stories *(2002) is her latest book.*

The Ones Who Walk Away from Omelas

Ursula K. Le Guin

With a clamor of bells that set the swallows soaring, the Festival of Summer came to the City of Omelas, bright-towered by the sea. The rigging of the boats in harbor sparkled with flags. In the streets between houses and red roofs and painted walls, between old moss-grown gardens and under avenues of trees, past great parks and public buildings, processions moved. Some were decrous: old people in long stiff robes of mauve and grey, grave master workmen, quiet, merry women carrying their babies and chatting as they walked. In other streets the music beat faster, a shimmering of gong and tambourine, and the people went dancing, the procession was a dance. Children dodged in and out, their high calls rising like the swallows' crossing flights over the music and the singing. All the processions wound towards the north side of the city, where on the great water-meadow called the Green Fields boys and girls, naked in the bright air, with mud-stained feet and ankles and long, lithe arms, exercised their restive horses before the race. The horses wore no gear at all but a halter without bit. Their manes were braided with streamers of silver, gold, and green. They flared their nostrils and pranced and boasted to one another; they were vastly excited, the horse being the only animal who has adopted our ceremonies as his own. Far off to the north and west the mountains stood up half encircling Omelas on her bay. The air of morning was so clear that the snow still crowning the Eighteen Peaks burned with white-gold fire across the miles of sunlit air, under the dark blue of the sky. There was just enough wind to make the banners that marked the racecourse snap and flutter now and then. In the silence of the broad green meadows one could hear the music winding through the city streets, farther and nearer and ever approaching, a cheerful faint sweetness of the air that from time to time trembled and gathered together and broke out into the great joyous clanging of the bells.

Joyous! How is one to tell about joy? How describe the citizens of Omelas?

They were not simple folk, you see, though they were happy. But we do not say the words of cheer much any more. All smiles have become archaic. Given a description such as this one tends to make certain assumptions. Given a description such as this one tends to look next for the King, mounted on a splendid stallion and surrounded by his noble knights, or perhaps in a golden litter borne by great-muscled slaves. But there was no king. They did not use swords, or keep slaves. They were not barbarians. I do not know the rules and laws of their society, but I suspect that they were singularly few. As they did without monarchy and slavery, so they also got on without the stock exchange, the advertisement, the secret police, and the bomb. Yet I repeat that these were not simple folk, not dulcet shepherds, noble savages, bland utopians. They were not less complex than us. The trouble is that we have a bad habit, encouraged by pedants and sophisticates, of considering happiness as something rather stupid. Only pain is intellectual, only evil interesting. This is the treason of the artist: a refusal to admit the banality of evil and the terrible boredom of pain. If you can't lick 'em, join 'em. If it hurts, repeat it. But to praise despair is to condemn delight, to embrace violence is to lose hold of everything else. We have almost lost hold; we can no longer describe a happy man, nor make any celebration of joy. How can I tell you about the people of Omelas? They were not naïve and happy children—though their children were, in fact, happy. They were mature, intelligent, passionate adults whose lives were not wretched. O miracle! but I wish I could describe it better. I wish I could convince you. Omelas sounds in my words like a city in a fairy tale, long ago and far away, once upon a time. Perhaps it would be best if you imagined it as your own fancy bids, assuming it will rise to the occasion, for certainly I cannot suit you all. For instance, how about technology? I think that there would be no cars or helicopters in and above the streets; this follows from the fact that the people of Omelas are happy people. Happiness is based on a just discrimination of what is necessary, what is neither necessary nor destructive, and what is destructive. In the middle category, however— that of the unnecessary but undestructive, that of comfort, luxury, exuberance, etc.—they could perfectly well have central heating, subway trains, washing machines, and all kinds of marvelous devices not yet invented here, floating light-sources, fuelless power, a cure for the common cold. Or they could have none of that; it doesn't matter. As you like it. I incline to think that people from towns up and down the coast have been coming to Omelas during the last days before the Festival on very fast little trains and double-decked trams, and that the train station of Omelas is actually the handsomest building in town, though plainer than the magnificent Farmers' Market. But even granted trains, I fear that Omelas so far strikes some of you as goody-goody. Smiles, bells, parades, horses, bleh. If so,please add an orgy. If an orgy would help, don't hesitate. Let us not, however, have temples from which issue beautiful nude priests and priestesses already half in ecstasy and ready to copulate with any man or woman, lover or stranger, who desires union with the deep godhead of the blood, although that was my first idea. But really it would be better not to have any temples in Omelas—at least, not manned temples. Religion yes, clergy no. Surely the beautiful nudes can just wander about, offering themselves like divine soufflés to the hunger of the needy and the rapture of the flesh. Let them join the processions. Let tambourines be struck above the copulations, and the glory of desire be proclaimed upon the gongs, and (a not unimportant point) let the offspring of these delightful rituals be beloved and looked after by all. One thing I know there is none of in Omelas is guilt. But what else should there be? I thought at first there were no drugs, but that is puritanical. For those who like it, the faint insistent sweetness of *drooz* may perfume the ways of the city, *drooz* which first brings a great lightness and brilliance to the mind and limbs, and then after some hours a dreamy languor, and wonderful visions at last of the very arcana and inmost secrets of the Universe, as well as exciting the pleasure of sex beyond belief; and it is not habit-forming. For more modest tastes I think there ought to be beer. What else, what else belongs in the joyous city? The sense of victory, surely, the celebration of courage. But as we did without clergy, let us do without soldiers. The joy built upon successful slaughter is not the right kind of joy; it will not do; it is fearful and it is trivial. A boundless and generous contentment, a magnanimous triumph felt not against some outer enemy but in communion with the finest and fairest in the souls of all men everywhere and the splendor of the world's summer: this is what swells the hearts of the people of Omelas, and the victory they celebrate is that of life. I really don't think many of them need to take *drooz*.

Most of the processions have reached the Green Fields by now. A marvelous smell of cooking goes forth from the red and blue tents of the provisioners. The faces of small children are amiably sticky; in the benign gray beard of a man a couple of crumbs of rich pastry are entangled. The youths and girls have mounted their horses and are beginning to group around the starting line of the course. An old woman, small, fat, and laughing, is passing out flowers from a basket, and tall young men wear her flowers in their shining hair. A child of nine or ten sits at the edge of the crowd, alone, playing on a wooden flute. People pause to listen, and they smile, but they do not speak to him, for he never ceases playing and never sees them, his dark eyes wholly rapt in the sweet, thin magic of the tune.

He finishes, and slowly lowers his hands holding the wooden flute.

As if that little private silence were the signal, all at once a trumpet sounds from the pavilion near the starting line: imperious, melancholy, piercing. The horses rear on their slender legs, and some of them neigh in answer. Sober-faced, the young riders stroke the horses' necks and soothe them, whispering, "Quiet, quiet, there my beauty, my hope . . . ." They begin to form in rank along the starting line. The crowds along the race-course are like a field of grass and flowers in the wind. The Festival of Summer has begun.

Do you believe? Do you accept the festival, the city, the joy? No? Then let me describe one more thing.

In a basement under one of the beautiful public buildings of Omelas, or perhaps in the cellar of one of its spacious private homes, there is a room. It has one locked door, and no window. A little light seeps in dustily between cracks in the boards, secondhand from a cobwebbed window somewhere across the cellar. In one corner of the little room a couple of mops, with stiff, clotted, foul-smelling heads, stand near a rusty bucket. The floor is dirt, a little damp to the touch, as cellar dirt usually is. The room is about three paces long and two wide: a mere broom closet or dis-used tool room. In the room a child is sitting. It could be a boy or a girl. It looks about six, but actually is nearly ten. It is feeble-minded. Perhaps it was born defective, or perhaps it has become imbecile through fear, malnutrition, and neglect. It picks its nose and occasionally fumbles vaguely with its toes or genitals, as it sits hunched in the corner farthest from the bucket and the two mops. It is afraid of the mops. It find them horrible. It shuts its eyes, but it knows the mops are still standing there; and the door is locked; and nobody will come. The door is always locked; and nobody ever comes, except that sometimes—the child has no under-standing of time or interval—sometimes the door rattles terribly and opens, and a person, or several people, are there. One of them may come in and kick the child to make it stand up. The others never come close, but peer in at it with frightened, disgusted eyes. The food bowl and the water jug are hastily filled, the door is locked, the eyes disappear. The people at the door never say anything, but the child, who has not always lived in the tool room, and can remember sunlight and its mother's voice, sometimes speaks. "I will be good," it says. "Please let me out. I will be good!" They never answer. The child used to scream for help at night, and cry a good deal, but now it only makes a kind of whining "eh-haa, eh-haa" and it speaks less and less often. It is so thin there are no calves to its legs; its belly protrudes; it lives on a half-bowl of corn meal and grease a day. It is naked. Its buttocks and thighs are a mass of festered sores, as it sits in its own excrement continually.

They all know it is there, all the people of Omelas. Some of them have come to see it, others are content merely to know it is there. They all know that it has to be there. Some of them understand why, and some do not, but they all understand that their happiness, the beauty of their city, the tenderness of their friendships, the health of their children, the wisdom of their scholars, the skill of their makers, even the abundance of their harvest and the kindly weathers of their skies, depend wholly on this child's abominable misery.

This is usually explained to children when they are between eight and twelve, whenever they seem capable of understanding; and most of those who come to see the child are young people, though often enough an adult comes, or comes back, to see the child. No matter how well the matter has been explained to them, these young spectators are always shocked and sickened at the sight. They feel disgust, which they had thought themselves superior to. They feel anger, outrage, impotence, despite all the explanations. They would like to do something for the child. But there is nothing they can do. If the child were brought up into the sunlight out of that vile place, if it were cleaned and fed and comforted, that would be a good thing, indeed; but if it were done, in that day and hour all the prosperity and beauty and delight of Omelas would wither and be destroyed. Those are the terms. To exchange all the goodness and grace of every life in Omelas for that single, small improvement: to throw away the happiness of thousands for the chance of the happiness of one: that would be to let guilt within the walls indeed.

The terms are strict and absolute; there may not even be a kind word spoken to the child.

Often the young people go home in tears, or in a tearless rage, when they have seen the child and faced this terrible paradox. They may brood over it for weeks or years. But as time goes on they begin to realize that even if the child could be released, it would not get much good of its freedom: a little vague pleasure of warmth and food, no doubt, but little more. It is too degraded and imbecile to know any real joy. It has been afraid too long ever to be free of fear. Its habits are too uncouth for it to respond to humane treatment. Indeed, after so long it would probably be wretched without walls about it to protect it, and darkness for its eyes, and its own excrement to sit in. Their tears at the bitter injustice dry when they begin to perceive the terrible justice of reality, and to accept it. Yet it is their tears and anger, the trying of their generosity and the acceptance of their helplessness, which are perhaps the true source of the splendor of their lives. Theirs is no vapid, irresponsible happiness. They know that they, like the child, are not free. They know compassion. It is the existence of the child, and their knowledge of its existence, that makes possible the nobility of their architecture, the poignancy of their music, the profundity of their science. It is because of the child that they are so gentle with children. They know that if the wretched one were not there snivelling in the dark, the other one, the flute-player, could make no joyful music as the young riders line up in their beauty for the race in the sunlight of the first morning of summer.

Now do you believe in them? Are they not more credible? But there is one more thing to tell, and this is quite incredible.

At times one of the adolescent girls or boys who go to see the child does not go home to weep or rage, does not, in fact, go home at all. Sometimes also a man or woman much older falls silent for a day or two, and then leaves home. These people go out into the street, and walk down the street alone. They keep walking, and walk straight out of the city of Omelas, through the beautiful gates. They keep walking across the farmlands of Omelas. Each one goes alone, youth or girl, man or woman. Night falls; the traveler must pass down village streets, between the houses with yellow-lit windows, and on out into the darkness of the fields. Each alone, they go west or north, towards the mountains. They go on. They leave Omelas, they walk ahead into the darkness, and they do not come back. The place they go towards is a place even less imaginable to most of us than the city of happiness. I cannot describe it at all. It is possible that it does not exist. But they seem to know where they are going, the ones who walk away from Omelas.

Audre Lorde (1934–1992), born in New York of West Indian parents, was a self-described "black feminist lesbian poet, mother of two and member of an interracial couple." A writer and activist, her poetry and essays have made a significant contribution to the contemporary feminist movement.

The Transformation of Silence into Language and Action

Audre Lorde

I have come to believe over and over again that what is most important to me must be spoken, made verbal and shared, even at the risk of having it bruised or misunderstood. That the speaking profits me, beyond any other effect. I am standing here as a Black lesbian poet, and the meaning of all that waits upon the fact that I am still alive, and might not have been. Less than two months ago I was told by two doctors, one female and one male, that I would have to have breast surgery, and that there was a 60 to 80 percent chance that the tumor was malignant. Between that telling and the actual surgery, there was a three-week period of the agony of an involuntary reorganization of my entire life. The surgery was completed, and the growth was benign.

But within those three weeks, I was forced to look upon myself and my living with a harsh and urgent clarity that has left me still shaken but much stronger. This is a situation faced by many women, by some of you here today. Some of what I experienced during that time has helped elucidate for me much of what I feel concerning the transformation of silence into language and action.

In becoming forcibly and essentially aware of my mortality and of what I wished and wanted for my life, however short it might be, priorities and omissions became strongly etched in a merciless light, and what I most regretted were my silences. Of what had I *ever* been afraid? To question or to speak as I believed could have meant pain, or death. But we all hurt in so many different ways, all the time, and pain will either change or end. Death, on the other hand, is the final silence. And that might be coming quickly, now, without regard for whether I had ever spoken what needed to be said, or had only betrayed myself into small silences, while I planned someday to speak, or waited for someone else's words. And I began to recognize a source of power within myself that comes from the knowledge that while it is most desirable not to be afraid, learning to put fear into a perspective gave me great strength.

I was going to die, if not sooner then later, whether or not I had ever spoken myself. My silences had not protected me. Your silence will not protect you. But for every real word spoken, for every attempt I had ever made to speak those truths for which I am still seeking, I had made contact with other women while we examined the words to fit a world in which we all believed, bridging our differences. And it was the concern and caring of all those women which gave me strength and enabled me to scrutinize the essentials of my living.

The women who sustained me through that period were Black and white, old and young, lesbian, bisexual, and heterosexual, and we all shared a war against the tyrannies of silence. They all gave me a strength and concern without which I could not have survived intact. Within those weeks of acute fear came the knowledge—within the war we are all waging with the forces of death, subtle and otherwise, conscious or not—I am not only a casualty, I am also a warrior.

What are the words you do not yet have? What do you need to say? What are the tyrannies you swallow day by day and attempt to make your own, until you will sicken and die of them, still in silence? Perhaps for some of you here today, I am the face of one of your fears. Because I am woman, because I am Black, because I am lesbian, because I am myself— a Black woman warrior poet doing my work—come to ask you, are you doing yours?

And of course I am afraid, because the transformation of silence into language and action is an act of self-revelation, and that always seems fraught with danger. But my daughter, when I told her of our topic and my difficulty with it, said, "Tell them about how you're never really a whole person if you remain silent, because there's always that one little piece inside you that wants to be spoken out, and if you keep ignoring it, it gets madder and madder and hotter and hotter, and if you don't speak it out one day it will just up and punch you in the mouth from the inside."

In the cause of silence, each of us draws the face of her own fear—fear of contempt, of censure, or some judgment, or recognition, of challenge, of annihilation. But most of all, I think, we fear the visibility without which we cannot truly live. Within this country where racial difference creates a constant, if unspoken, distortion of vision, Black women have on one hand always been highly visible, and so, on the other hand, have been rendered invisible through the depersonalization of racism. Even within the women's movement, we have had to fight, and still do, for that very visibility which also renders us most vulnerable, our Blackness. For to survive in the mouth of this dragon we call America, we have had to learn this first and most vital lesson—that we were never meant to survive. Not as human beings. And neither were most of you here today, Black or not. And that visibility which makes us most vulnerable is that which also is the source of our greatest strength. Because the machine will try to grind you into dust anyway, whether or not we speak. We can sit in our corners mute forever while our sisters and our selves are wasted, while our children are distorted and destroyed, while our earth is poisoned; we can sit in our safe corners mute as bottles, and we will still be no less afraid.

In my house this year we are celebrating the feast of Kwanza, the African-American festival of harvest which begins the day after Christmas and lasts for seven days. There are seven principles of Kwanza, one for each day. The first principle is Umoja, which means unity, the decision to strive for and maintain unity in self and community. The principle for yesterday, the second day, was Kujichagulia—self-determination—the decision to define ourselves, name ourselves, and speak for ourselves, instead of being defined and spoken for by others. Today is the third day of Kwanza, and the principle for today is Ujima—collective work and responsibility—the decision to build and maintain ourselves and our communities together and to recognize and solve our problems together.

Each of us is here now because in one way or another we share a commitment to language and to the power of language, and to the reclaiming of that language which has been made to work against us. In the transformation of silence into language and action, it is vitally necessary for each one of us to establish or examine her function in that transformation and to recognize her role as vital within that transformation.

For those of us who write, it is necessary to scrutinize not only the truth of what we speak, but the truth of that language by which we speak it. For others, it is to share and spread also those words that are meaningful to us. But primarily for us all, it is necessary to teach by living and speaking those truths which we believe and know beyond understanding. Because in this way alone we can survive, by taking part in a process of life that is creative and continuing, that is growth.

And it is never without fear—of visibility, of the harsh light of scrutiny and perhaps judgment, of pain, of death. But we have lived through all of those already, in silence, except death. And I remind myself all the time now that if I were to have been born mute, or had maintained an oath of silence my whole life long for safety, I would still have suffered, and I would still die. It is very good for establishing perspective.

And where the words of women are crying to be heard, we must each of us recognize our responsibility to seek those words out, to read them and share them and examine them in their pertinence to our lives. That we not hide behind the mockeries of separations that have been imposed upon us and which so often we accept as our own. For instance, "I can't possibly teach Black women's writing—their experience is so different from mine." Yet how many years have you spent teaching Plato and Shakespeare and Proust? Or another, "She's a white woman and what could she possibly have to say to me?" Or, "She's a lesbian, what would my husband say, or my chairman?" Or again, "This woman writes of her sons and I have no children." And all the other endless ways in which we rob ourselves of ourselves and each other.

We can learn to work and speak when we are afraid in the same way we have learned to work and speak when we are tired. For we have been socialized to respect fear more than our own needs for language and definition, and while we wait in silence for that final luxury of fearlessness, the weight of that silence will choke us.

The fact that we are here and that I speak these words is an attempt to break that silence and bridge some of those differences between us, for it is not difference which immobilizes us, but silence. And there are so many silences to be broken.

Rumi (Mevlana Jalaluddin Rumi) (1207–1273) was a Sufi mystic poet and author of the Mathnawi, *a six-volume work of spiritual teaching on metaphysics, religion, ethics, and mysticism. He was also the founder of the Mevlevi, the Sufi order known as the "Whirling Dervishes" for their love of music and dancing as an expression of their spiritual realization.*

A Community of the Spirit

Rumi

There is a community of the spirit.
Join it, and feel the delight
of walking in the noisy street,
and *being* the noise.

Drink *all* your passion,
and be a disgrace.

Close both eyes
to see with the other eye.

Open your hands,
if you want to be held.

Sit down in this circle.

Quit acting like a wolf, and feel
the shepherd's love filling you.

At night, your beloved wanders.
Don't accept consolations.

Close your mouth against food.
Taste the lover's mouth in yours.

You moan, "She left me." "He left me."
Twenty more will come.

Be empty of worrying.
Think of who created thought!

Why do you stay in prison
when the door is so wide open?

Move outside the tangle of fear-thinking.
Live in silence.

Flow down and down in always
widening rings of being.

There's a strange frenzy in my head,
of birds flying,
each particle circulating on its own.
Is the one I love *everywhere?*

Drunks fear the police,
but the police are drunk too.

People in this town love them both
like different chess pieces.

from The New Revised Standard Version of the Bible

The Good Samaritan

(Luke 10: 29–37)

But wanting to justify himself, he asked Jesus, "And who is my neighbor?" Jesus replied, "A man was going down from Jerusalem to Jericho and fell into the hands of robbers, who stripped him, beat him, and went away, leaving him half dead. Now by chance a priest was going down that road; and when he saw him, he passed by on the other side. So likewise a Levite, when he came to the place and saw him, passed by on the other side. But a Samaritan while traveling came near him; and when he saw him, he was moved to pity. He went to him and bandaged his wounds, having poured oil and wine on them. Then he put him on his own animal, brought him to an inn, and took care of him. The next day he took out two denarii, gave them to the innkeeper, and said, 'Take care of him; and when I come back, I will repay whatever you spend.' " "Which of these three, do you think, was a neighbor to the man who fell into the hands of robbers?" He said, "The one who showed him mercy." Jesus said to him, "Go and do likewise."

Paul's Teaching on Love

(I Cor. 13: 1–13)

If I speak in tongues of mortals and of angels, but do not have love, I am a noisy gong or a clanging cymbal. And if I have prophetic powers, and understand all mysteries and all knowledge, and if I have all faith, so as to remove mountains, but do not have love, I am nothing. If I give away all my possessions, and hand over my body so that I may boast, but do not have love, I gain nothing.

Love is patient; love is kind; love is not envious or boastful or arrogant or rude. It does not insist on its own way; it is not irritable or resentful; it does not rejoice in wrongdoing, but rejoices in truth. It bears all things, believes all things, hopes all things, endures all things.

Love never ends. But as for the prophecies, they will come to an end; as for tongues, they will cease; as for knowledge, it will come to an end. For we know only in part; and we prophesy only in part; but when the complete comes, the partial will come to an end. When I was a child, I spoke like a child, I thought like a child, I reasoned like a child; when I became an adult, I put an end to the childish ways. For now we see in a mirror, dimly, but then we will see face to face. Now I know only in part; then I will know fully, even as I have been fully known. And now faith, hope, and love abide, these three; and the greatest of these is love.

Sermon on the Mount

(Matthew 5: 1–16)

When Jesus saw the crowds he went up the mountain; and after he sat down, his disciples came to him. Then he began to speak, and taught them saying:

"Blessed are the poor in spirit, for theirs is the kingdom of heaven."

"Blessed are those who mourn, for they will be comforted."

"Blessed are the meek, for they will inherit the earth."

"Blessed are those who hunger and thirst for righteousness, for they will be filled."

"Blessed are the merciful, for they will receive mercy."

"Blessed are the pure in heart, for they will see God."

"Blessed are the peacemakers, for they will be called children of God."

"Blessed are you when people revile you and persecute you and utter all kinds of evil against you falsely on my account. Rejoice and be glad, for your reward is great in heaven, for in the same way they persecuted the prophets who were before you."

"You are the salt of the earth; but if salt has lost its taste, how can its saltiness be restored? It is no longer good for anything, but is thrown out and trampled under foot."

"You are the light of the world. A city built on a hill cannot be hid. No one after lighting a lamp puts it under a bushel basket, but on the lampstand, and it gives light to all in the house. In the same way, let your light shine before others, so that they may see your good works and give glory to your father in heaven."

Thomas H. West (b. 1942 in Minneapolis) entered the University of Minnesota in 1960 on an Evans Scholarship. He graduated in 1964 with a B.A. in Humanities, then completed a M.A. in Theology at Marquette University. After studying philosophy and theology in Germany from 1967–69, he began work on a Ph.D. in the Philosophy of Religion, a program offered jointly by the University of California, Berkeley, and the Graduate Theological Union. He received his Ph.D. in 1975, and, after teaching at Santa Clara University and the University of St. Thomas, took a position at the College of St. Catherine in 1979 where he is currently professor of Theology. Dr. West is author of Ultimate Hope without God: The Atheistic Eschatology of Ernst Bloch *(Peter Lang, 1991) and* Jesus and the Quest for Meaning: Entering Theology *(Fortress, 2001).*

Love into Justice: The Good Samaritan Revisited

Thomas H. West

Most Christians would say that the foundation of social justice is love, especially love of neighbor, *agape.* But how do we get from agape to an active commitment to social justice? We do not answer this question well if we say simply that agapic love and social justice are the same thing. They are not. Yet I want to argue that work for social justice is a necessary expression of agapic love.

In the New Testament, the epitome of agapic love is the Good Samaritan. We do not ordinarily think of the Good Samaritan as practicing social justice. We see him as practicing compassion, performing an act of charity, carrying out a mission of mercy, not, surely, working for social justice. What the Good Samaritan did and what a social reformer like Martin Luther King Jr. did are clearly very different things.

But is social justice so sharply different from agapic love? In this chapter I shall argue that there is indeed a distinction between agapic love and social justice, but it is a distinction within a unity.

Luke's Parable of the Good Samaritan

Here is the parable of the Good Samaritan as told in Luke's gospel:

> Just then a lawyer stood up to test Jesus. "Teacher," he said, "what must I do to inherit eternal life?" He said to him, "What is written in the law? What do you read there?" He answered, "You shall love the Lord your God with all your heart, and with all your soul, and with all your strength, and with all your mind; and your neighbor as yourself." And he said to him, "You have given the right answer; do this, and you will live."

But wanting to justify himself, he asked Jesus, "And who is my neighbor?" Jesus replied, "A man was going down from Jerusalem to Jericho, and fell into the hands of robbers, who stripped him, beat him, and went away, leaving him half dead." Now by chance a priest was going down the road; and when he saw him, he passed by on the other side. So likewise a Levite, when he came to the place and saw him, passed by on the other side. But a Samaritan while traveling came near him; and when he saw him, he was moved with compassion. He went to him and bandaged his wounds, having poured oil and wine on them. Then he put him on his own animal, brought him to an inn, and took care of him. The next day he took out two denarii, gave them to the innkeeper, and said, "Take care of him; and when I come back, I will repay you whatever more you spend" (Luke 10:25–35).

Luke situates the parable of the Good Samaritan within the "travel narrative" (Luke 9: 51–19: 27) that follows Jesus' journey from Galilee to Jerusalem.[1]

During the journey Jesus frequently pauses to instruct his followers in the way of discipleship. One day he instructed them by telling the parable of the Good Samaritan.

The Good Samaritan parable is classified by Joachim Jeremias as a "parable of realized discipleship,"[2] though it is not a parable in the narrow or typical sense. Rather, it is an *example story*, not an extended metaphor or simile where the figures and events symbolize something else, as when the mustard seed symbolizes the reign of God (see Mt. 13: 31–32) or the generous vineyard owner (see Mt. 20: 1–16), God's unconditional love.[3] The Good Samaritan parable does not refer beyond itself in this way. Jesus is not saying that "God acts like the Good Samaritan," but rather, "You should act like the Good Samaritan."

The Good Samaritan story does, however, display other elements typical of a parable, most obviously the element of surprise. The surprise is not that the priest and the Levite (a Temple official subordinate to the priests) pass by an injured man. Out in the countryside, "anti-clericalism" was widespread among Jews. That Jesus would portray Temple officials as morally callous would evoke a knowing murmur from his Jewish audience. His audience would then expect Jesus to finish off his story by having an Israelite layperson like themselves stop and do the right thing.[4] Instead, the *Samaritan* stops, and, "moved with compassion," does the right thing. This is a major surprise to Jesus' Jewish audience. John Donahue reminds us: "Centuries of pious reflection have dulled our sensibilities to the hatred that existed between Jews and Samaritans." Jews regarded Samaritans not only as a mongrel people who had intermarried with pagan invaders, but as deserters of the Jewish religion.[5] That a Jew could love the Samaritan as a neighbor, and a Samaritan could love the Jew as a neighbor, well, it's a scandal, it's out of the question. When the lawyer asked Jesus, "Who is my neighbor?" he was being serious. There was genuine debate among Jews at this time about who was included under "neighbor." According to Jeremias, "It was generally agreed that the term connoted fellow countrymen, including full proselytes."[6] It did not include Samaritans. Jesus defines *neighbor* to include the hated Samaritan, depicting the Samaritan as one who is a neighbor precisely by treating the injured Jew as a neighbor. This is a surprise. This is a shock.

In the parable of the Good Samaritan, Jesus offers an example of agapic love in action. Such love imitates the love shown by Jesus, and Jesus' love is in turn an imitation of God's love. Such is the nature of Jesus' radical moral demand on those called to the mission of bringing people into the reign of God. In the parable, agapic love shows the following qualities:

- It is unconditional. The Samaritan does not demand that the person injured fulfill any conditions before the Samaritan is willing to give help.
- This love is universal. The Samaritan does not care to which gender, race, class, religion, or ethnic group the injured person belongs. A human being is hurt. This Samaritan would have reached out to any human being who was suffering.
- This love is unconcerned with merit or just deserts. The Samaritan does not say to himself, "This person in the ditch half dead does not deserve my help because he had it coming. He didn't take sufficient care to avoid the threat of robbery." The Samaritan does not say to himself, "There is probably some past sin in the victim's life. God through this violent assault and robbery is punishing him."
- It is love moved by compassion. The Samaritan is moved by feeling. Indeed, one can imagine him seized by feeling and impelled to the ditch beside the road.
- It is a love that is spontaneous and uncalculating. The Samaritan is moved to act, quickly. He is not shown pondering the pros and cons. He is not shown engaging in subtle calculations about precisely what he should do. He spends no time in rational analysis.
- It is a love that goes beyond the minimum one would expect of even the most decent person. That is, it is supererogatory; it goes beyond what is asked. He doesn't just bandage the injured man's wounds and get him to the next town, but stays with him, takes care of him, pays his lodging, and then—and here is the special touch—says to the innkeeper: "If it comes to more than this, I'll pay the difference on my way back." Here the Samaritan shows himself to be a virtuoso of the supererogatory.[7]

These qualities constitute agapic, that is, Christian, love in action, in the public sphere, among strangers, who through love become neighbors and friends.

Now if the Christian moral life were simply a matter of letting oneself be moved to uncalculating love towards any human being in special need, we would have no need for lengthy books on Christian morality and justice. But the Christian moral life often requires us to go beyond spontaneous acts of agapic love. Morality then becomes more complex, and when it does, it begins to move from agapic love pure and simple to agapic love that expresses itself in the work of justice.

2. Love into Interpersonal Justice

The great American theologian Reinhold Niebuhr said that Christian love becomes justice when there are three or more people in the room.[8] Expanding on the story of the Good Samaritan, let us imagine that the Samaritan, instead of discovering one robbery victim in the ditch, discovers three. The Samaritan is moved by compassion to go over to the three victims, but as soon as he arrives, he finds himself having to step back from the situation and from his feeling in order to engage in some rational analysis and calculation. He finds himself engaged in what we today call *triage*. Triage is a system of principles and rules by which one judges how one can best treat victims like these, given one's resources. Whenever my family calls our Health Maintenance Organization after hours, we talk first to the triage nurse; using a complex system of principles and rules she decides what the HMO can and should do for us given our ailments and given their resources.

Coming upon the three victims, the Good Samaritan must also practice triage. The principles and rules of triage he uses will be undoubtedly less explicit and formalized than those of the HMO triage nurse; nevertheless, if he is to do *justice* to these three victims he will have to turn his thoughtful attention to *some* principles and rules, however rudimentary they might be.

In practicing triage, the Samaritan does not completely turn from feeling to thought, but he does distance himself enough to allow a rational analysis of the situation. If he lets himself be ruled only by feeling, he might spontaneously attend first to the victim who is screaming and moaning the loudest, but to do so would be unjust. One of the first principles of triage is that one should attend first to the victim who is most seriously injured and then make a judgment about whether one has the resources to help him or her. The Samaritan coolheadedly turns his attention very self-consciously towards this principle and sets about putting it into practice. He first gathers empirical data about the condition of the victims. He discovers that the victim screaming the loudest is a teenage boy holding his ankle. A second victim is very quiet, is not bleeding, but he has a weak pulse. A third victim is bleeding profusely from the neck. He decides to help her first, and bandages her wounds, and stops the bleeding. On her he decides to concentrate his maximum effort. He has acted justly.

Yet it would be unfair, it would be unjust, if he were to cease thinking about the other two. They, after all, are human beings, with their inherent dignity and worth. He can*not* give them his *maximum* effort in this situation, but he feels bound to give them at least a minimum of attention. But what precisely is the minimum he owes them in this situation? The answer requires another calculation on his part. To the boy holding his ankle, he decides that the injury is not that serious, and he limits himself to wrapping the ankle and uttering words of comfort. And he double-checks the person with the weak pulse to make sure that he still is alive.

At this point the Samaritan is now expressing his love in the form of justice, and specifically, *interpersonal* justice. Interpersonal justice refers to the justice that is practiced by one individual to another in a situation where the person practicing the justice has to distance himself somewhat from his feelings, consult a set of principles and rules, gather data about this situation, and make a rational decision about what should be done. Interpersonal justice requires attention to the questions of what is equal treatment, what is fair treatment, what is the minimum one owes each individual who is present, and what is the maximum one can offer, given one's resources. This kind of analysis tells the Samaritan that it would be wrong, it would violate the principles of interpersonal justice, if he were to spend himself totally in selfless and supererogatory love on only one of the victims that now confront him. He must therefore carefully and rationally distribute his efforts in an equal yet fair manner, giving the most he can give to one without at the same time totally neglecting the others.

Interpersonal justice is not only practiced in the kind of extraordinary situation in which the Samaritan finds himself. It is in fact the stuff of ordinary daily life, in a way that heedless agapic love can never be. Every day we have many encounters with our fellow human beings. Not every encounter is, or should be, an occasion for agapic love in the pure form. Rather, we should treat those individuals we encounter every day with a simple, interpersonal justice, with a basic respect for their worth, dignity, and autonomy.[9] There is a minimum that we owe everyone. Some might require more than the minimum from us. We must weigh matters and decide what we can give. Knowing how this is done takes much training and learning. Some people take to this very well and show an acute ethical intelligence.

Let us return to our story. The Samaritan has bound the wounds of the woman bleeding, attended to the man with the weak pulse, and calmed the boy with the injured ankle. Somehow, after making a whole series of further decisions, all accompanied by considerable rational analysis, he gets them to the nearest town and arranges for their care, though this time a check of his financial resources precludes an offer to pay the innkeeper and the local physician. He has done justice to these people.

But the whole experience has left him angry. For the fourth time this month he has encountered victims of brutal robberies left to die in the ditch. What would have happened to these poor people had he not happened along? The Samaritan thinks on the many others who were passed by and left to suffer and die. This tragic situation is more than he as an individual can manage. He is moved to conclude that one-to-one agapic love and interpersonal justice are not enough. He decides to move into social justice.

3. Love into Social Justice

The Good Samaritan decides to involve the larger community and attempt a more systematic solution to this terrible problem of assault and robbery.[10] He decides thereby to make the move from *interpersonal* justice to the work of *social* justice. Social justice is justice practiced by a group or community towards individuals or other groups or communities. Social justice is a social endeavor, which involves the creation of *social structures*.

Social structures have two elements: the mental and the institutional. The *first* element is concerned with the consciousness, the mind, the attitude, the ethos, of the community. It is obvious to the Samaritan that many people are passing by these victims in the ditch and not doing anything to help. "There is a deeply faulty ethos in these parts," he says to himself. "People around here are indifferent to this kind of human misery."

The Good Samaritan resolves to change the ethos, to raise consciousness, to change the mentality. On his next trip down this road, he stops at each village and gives a little talk to the villagers, alerting them to the suffering of the victims of these robberies and urging them not to pass by the victims. He talks about the basic dignity and equality of all human beings. All human beings, he insists, have a claim on our love and justice, especially those who are suffering. He even includes in his talk a rudimentary introduction to triage. In his efforts to create a new social mentality, the Samaritan enjoys some success. People become more sensitized. More people than before are reaching out with agapic love and interpersonal justice.

In one village this new consciousness becomes so pervasive that helping robbery victims becomes what sociologists call an *institution*, that is, an *established pattern of behavior*, which is the *second* element of a social structure.[11] Helping victims is something that villagers practice without hesitation. The institution in this case is a *custom*, a pattern of behavior that establishes itself quite spontaneously and lacks formal organization.

Nevertheless, this proves to be not enough. There are still many victims and many people are passing them by. The ethos of reaching out to help is indeed deeper and more widespread, but it is far from pervasive. Human beings, after all, are free to defy ethos and custom and are especially prone to do so when they are asked to go outside themselves for someone else's sake. And so the Samaritan decides to move beyond custom and create a more formal institution.

He decides to create an institution in which groups of volunteers will patrol the road in shifts in search of victims.[12] To insure that these volunteers will be skilled in applying triage, he arranges for training sessions. He rents several buildings in the villages in which to hold these sessions. Since those who conduct the sessions will be engaged in virtually full-time work, he decides to pay them. Realizing that he does not have enough money for rent and salaries, he sets out to raise money, trusting that the ethos he created earlier is wide and deep enough to produce people willing to contribute. He organizes a fund drive, to occur on a regular basis. His institution comes thereby to depend on both the willingness of people to volunteer their time to work on the patrols and their willingness to contribute money on a regular basis. And since the contributions of time and money depend on the continued vitality of the ethos, the Samaritan must continue to give talks to raise ethical consciousness; that is, he must continue to be concerned with the element of mentality.

The Samaritan has thus created not only a new mentality, but also new institutions. And many robbery victims are helped.

Yet, many victims continue to die in the ditch, unhelped. The crime rate is up. Also, there are difficulties with the Samaritan's institutional structure. The patrols are staffed largely by unpaid volunteers, who are free to cease volunteering, and quite regularly one or more will suddenly and unpredictably pull out. On nights before holidays, the most dangerous nights, whole patrols have to be canceled for lack of volunteers.

Funding is a continuing problem. The regional economy fluctuates wildly and along with that, financial contributions fluctuate wildly. Sometimes the Samaritan has the funds to do the training, sometimes not. A fickleness and unpredictability pervade the institution making for a fickle and unpredictable service to the victims along the road. One of the principles of justice is universality of coverage: all persons will receive the minimum due them. This institution is failing to provide that coverage, which causes acute pangs of conscience in the Samaritan. The compassion that moved him to that first act of agapic love has now moved him towards the work of justice that aims to reach all those suffering, but he is *not* reaching them all in any consistent way.

For a while the Samaritan considers going to what we now call the free-market approach. In order to guarantee more predictable and reliable staff he could staff the patrols with paid professionals. To pay for them, he could market their services by charging the victims—with some provision for their ability to pay—or by selling their services to villages along the road or to groups of travelers. To raise the initial capital outlay for this service, he could sell shares to the enterprise and then pay the shareholders out of the profits.

But he decides against going into the market. He is not opposed to the market as such, for he is a businessperson and believes firmly that some goods and services are best delivered to people through the market. But he has come to believe that a robbery victim in the ditch has not just a *need* for help, but also a *right* to help. A right means that the victim has an absolute claim on the community for a consistent, predictable, and skilled response to his or her suffering. The free market approach introduces the profit motive and with that the inevitable tendency to provide the best service to those who have the most money to pay for it. But this is the kind of service that every human being has a right to, irrespective of wealth or social position.

So the Samaritan chooses another step, namely, he decides to go to the state, that is, to the institutions of government. This road is in a province under the jurisdiction of Rome. He decides to go to the Roman governor and ask that a new social structure be created. While talking with the governor and his aides, he learns that the problems occurring along this road are occurring on roads throughout the province. The governor is responsive. He petitions Rome for the permission to create a new structure and collect a tax to pay for it. The Roman senate passes a law, the emperor approves it, and the governor's bureaucrats work out detailed policies, that is, principles and rules, to guide the new institution in its service. Paid governmental patrols are put in place along the roads. They deliver medical help more quickly and predictably and thus provide coverage that approaches universal. Because the government owns the means of legalized violence, it equips the patrols with the physical means to pursue, subdue, and arrest the violent robbers who are causing so much human suffering.[13] And since the taxes are set and levied by law, funding is more predictable year-to-year.

The Good Samaritan is quite satisfied with his work. He has moved from agapic love to interpersonal justice, and finally, to social justice. To be sure, he has not ceased practicing agapic love—indeed, just the other night an opportunity again presented itself and he reached out to help a victim—but he has spent most of his time these past several years on the long march through social structures.

Despite his general satisfaction, the Samaritan has frequently found the work of social justice tedious and boring. Giving ethical pep talks, finding buildings to rent, training volunteers, writing up detailed policy suggestions for the governor—more than once during all this he has felt a slackening in his original agapic motivation. Indeed there have been moments when he becomes wistful for the spontaneous purity of that original act of agapic love. He recalls the deep joy and peace he felt after he had paid the innkeeper, knowing that he had done the right thing.

In addition, he is no naïve reformer. He has seen the negative side of this movement from agapic love to social justice. He worries, for example, about the impersonality of the new government structure. He has talked with some members of the patrols and found that quite a few are not motivated by the desire to help their neighbors but by the desire to advance their careers. Some government administrators appear less interested in providing a good service than in protecting their turf and increasing their budgets. He worries that with the movement to a government structure, the community ethos will decline. There is already much grumbling about the new taxes. Taxes, after all, are coercive. They are extracted by law and backed by the organized violence of the state. The other day he heard someone say, "They're confiscating my hard-earned money to pay for these patrols—I never even take those roads. It's not fair!" He fears that giving this work of social justice over to the state will diminish the motivating energy of agapic love to the point where individuals will pass by victims in the ditch with the excuse, "I don't need to stop, a patrol will be by soon." He has even heard rumors that some patrols are abusing their power and using their instruments of violence not to protect the victims but to blackmail them. Social justice, when it is carried out by the structures of government, has its dark side.

But all in all, despite these concerns, the Samaritan remains cautiously proud of his work. He is convinced that this new social structure has reduced the total amount of human suffering. Social justice has accomplished more than his individual acts of agapic love ever could.

As we watch the Samaritan move from agapic love to social justice from our perspective in the twentieth century, we notice something missing from his vision and practice. At no time does the Samaritan engage in an in-depth social, political, and economic analysis of his society. He does not ask himself why there are so many robberies. He does not link the rise in the crime rate with the high concentration of wealth in the hands of a few large absentee landowners. He fails to bring into view the many tenant farmers who live in virtual slavery.[14] Many are so poor that they are drawn to lives of crime. As he journeys to see the governor, he does not wonder if perhaps his work of social justice wouldn't be more effective if this region were not under imperial rule and if Jews and Samaritans were independent peoples with grassroots, egalitarian political structures more immediately responsive to crime and its victims. This kind of analysis might very well have led the Samaritan to a vision of radical and sweeping change in the social, economic, and political structures of his day. But this kind of analysis, and the radical vision that often goes with it, is a relatively recent development in the history of ethical intelligence. Jesus did not undertake this kind of analysis.[15] Nor did the early Church. And the Catholic Church was indifferent, sometimes even hostile, to this kind of analysis until late in the nineteenth century. In our day, however, virtually all Christians engaged in the work of social justice are aware of the need for complex social analysis.

I hope that my revisit of the Good Samaritan story has shown that the distinctions among agapic love, interpersonal justice, and social justice are real, but not hard and fast. Agapic love, Christian love, is not *replaced* by interpersonal and social justice, but continues to accompany both as their motivational fount, energizing both,[16] preventing each from becoming impersonal and bloodless. Justice has been described as the *public* expression of love, a definition that strikes me as particularly apt. The movement from agapic love to social justice is continuous and necessary. Any theology that draws too sharp a separation between love and justice, or which sees them as belonging to utterly different spheres, or which sees them in opposition, is a deeply flawed theology.

Just as there is a natural movement from agapic love to social justice, so too is there a natural move from social justice to agapic love. Even the most intense, one-to-one expression of agapic love does not occur in a social vacuum. Social structures—mentality, ethos, custom, laws, institutions—all pre-shape even the most private actions. The Good Samaritan, after all, is a member of a schismatic Jewish sect whose members followed the Torah, the Jewish law found in the first five books of the Hebrew Bible. The heart of this law is the two-fold commandment to love God and love your neighbor as yourself. This two-fold law was part of the Samaritan ethos and passed on to the Good Samaritan through the institutions of religious learning and instruction. The religious and ethical logic of the two-fold law led him to oppose a mentality that would forbid him to help an injured Jew. And therefore his spontaneous act of agapic love as told in Jesus' story did not arise solely out of his own spontaneity, it was not utterly his own, *sui generis*, but in part was the consequence of a social structure. Indeed the very spontaneity of his action is partly a sign of how thoroughly he was socialized by the redemptive elements of this structure.[17] And we must not forget, the parable of the Good Samaritan was told by Jesus, who was raised a Jew and was taught the same two-fold law of love.

We must, therefore, be wary of drawing overprecise distinctions among Christian love, interpersonal justice, and social justice. The distinctions are real, but within an unfolding unity. In his story of the Good Samaritan, Jesus beautifully captured the first and decisive moment of agapic love. Yet we can well imagine that the logic of love carried the Good Samaritan, as it should carry us, into the work of justice.

But with all this talk of social justice we dare not forget that the direction of agapic love is not only out into the public sphere of social structures.[18] There is the other direction, towards the intimacy of full mutuality, towards friendship, romantic love, and family. What is the final purpose of just social structures if not a world where mutuality can flourish? Mutuality with God and mutuality with others. The full terror of a corrupt social structure is the way its destructive power makes even the intimacy of mutuality impossible. Agapic love achieves public expression in justice, but its fulfillment in mutual self-giving.[19]

Notes

[1] See John Donahue, *The Gospel in Parable: Metaphor, Narrative, and Theology in the Synoptic Gospels* (Philadelphia: Fortress Press, 1988), 126ff.

[2] Joachim Jeremias, *The Parables of Jesus* (New York: Charles Scribner's Sons, 2nd rev. ed., 1972), 198ff.

[3] Donahue, *The Gospel in Parable*, 12f.

[4] Jeremias, *The Parables of Jesus*, 204.

[5] Donahue, *The Gospel in Parable*, 130f., supplies a short history of the relations between Jews and Samaritans to show why they were such enemies.

[6] Jeremias, *The Parables of Jesus*, 202.

[7] Donahue, *The Gospel in Parable*, tells us that the Samaritan's extra help at the inn is more than just a sign of the supererogatory: "As a paradigm for compassionate entry into the world of an injured brother or sister, this final action is indispensable. According to the law at the time, a person with an unpaid debt could be enslaved until the debt was paid (see Matt. 18:23–35). Since the injured man was robbed and stripped—deprived of all resources—he could have been at the mercy of the innkeeper, a profession that had a bad reputation for dishonesty and violence. The parable assures the injured man's freedom and independence" (133).

[8] Actually, Niebuhr said it more abstractly than that: "An immediately felt obligation towards obvious need may be prompted by the emotion of pity. But a continued sense of obligation rests upon and expresses itself in rational calculations of the needs of others as compared with our own interests. A relation between the self and one other may be partly ecstatic; and in any case the cal-

culation of relative interests may be reduced to a minimum. But as soon as a third person is introduced into the relation even the most perfect love requires a rational estimate of conflicting needs and interests." Reinhold Niebuhr, *The Nature and Destiny of Man: A Christian Interpretation. Volume II: Human Destiny*, (New York: Charles Scribner's Sons, 1943), 248.

9 Following the rules of common courtesy can fulfill more than a small part of interpersonal justice on a day-to-day level. It is amazing how much of the advice that Ms. Manners gives in her syndicated newspaper column can be seen as the application of interpersonal justice. She shows an acute sense for the intersection of morality and manners. Though insofar as her rulings on courtesy precipitate a widespread pattern of behavior in society, she is creating a social structure; that is, she is doing the work of social justice.

10 Another re-telling of the Good Samaritan story, which makes much the same move to social justice as I make here, is that of Stephen Mott. See his *Biblical Ethics and Social Change* (New York: Oxford University Press, 1982), 58f. I am not indebted to Mott's re-telling, but the parallel is striking. For the Mott reference I am indebted to Garth L. Hallet, *Christian Neighbor Love: An Assessment of Six Rival Positions* (Washington, D.C.: Georgetown University Press, 1989), 118.

11 On institutionalization, see Peter L. Berger and Thomas Luckmann, *The Social Construction of Reality: A Treatise on the Sociology of Knowledge* (New York: Doubleday Anchor Books, 1967), 54–61.

12 A volunteer patrol is a good example of what Catholic social teaching calls a "mediating structure" or an "intermediate structure." Such structures carry out the "principle of subsidiarity," which could be summed up this way: before creating larger, governmental structures, first create smaller, local, nongovernmental structures. See Fred Kammer, *Doing Faithjustice: An Introduction to Catholic Social Thought* (New York: Paulist Press, 1991), 184.

13 Here we have an example of the twin functions of government. On the one hand, it has the more positive function of extending medical help to all who need it. On the other hand, it has the more negative function of countering violence with violence, of enforcing order against the forces of anarchy and destruction. There are two traditions in Western political theory that tend to focus on one function at the expense of the other. Martin Luther (and before him Augustine and after him Hobbes) tends to reduce government to the "negative" function, that is, "to bear the secular sword and punish the wicked" (see "Secular Authority: To What Extent it Should be Obeyed," in John Dillenberger, ed., *Martin Luther Selections from his Writings* [New York: Doubleday Anchor Books, first published in 1523, this edition, 1961] 363–402, here 374). Government indeed is willed by God, but by God's "left hand." Its work is God's work, yet an "alien work" (377). If there had been no sin there would be no government. The scriptural source for this tradition can be found in Rom. 13:4 and 1 Pet. 1: 13. Another tradition, going back to Plato and Aristotle, stresses that government is a good, and natural to human life. Christian socialists and welfare state liberals add to this the agapic motivation and welcome government structures in their "positive" function of meeting a broad range of human needs. Reinhold Niebuhr keeps these two traditions in good balance: "All structures of justice do indeed presuppose the sinfulness of man, and are all

partly systems of restraint which prevent the conflict of wills and interests from resulting in a consistent anarchy. But they are also all mechanisms by which men fulfill their obligations to their fellow men, beyond the possibilities offered in direct and personal relationships. The Kingdom of God and the demands of perfect love are therefore relevant to every political system and impinge upon every social situation in which the self seeks to come to terms with the claims of other life." See *The Nature and Destiny of Man: A Christian Interpretation. Volume II: Human Destiny*, 192.

[14] One of the effects of the widespread indebtedness among the peasants in Palestine was virtual slavery for those who could not pay their debts. Many took to banditry. See Richard A. Horsley, *Sociology and the Jesus Movement* (New York: Crossroad, 1989), 88–90.

[15] I am not denying that people in Jesus' time could not have visions of a new world where life would be radically different. Jesus had that vision, as did the many other "millenarian prophets" of his time. What I don't see is the combination of radical vision and social analysis, as epitomized, for example, in the work of Karl Marx.

[16] In the words of Fred Kammer: "Instead of a tension between love and justice, love as the soul of justice gives the Christian passion for building a more just order." See *Doing Faithjustice: An Introduction to Catholic Social Thought* (New York: Paulist Press, 1991), 181.

[17] An extraordinary example of agapic love practiced spontaneously more because of communal ethos than individual heroic virtue is the story of the French mountain village of Le Chambon, whose 5000 inhabitants sheltered 5000 Jews during World War II. The documentary, produced by Pierre Sauvage, that tells the story has many interviews with individuals who participated in this good work. What is remarkable is how self-effacing they are. Indeed, they appear somewhat baffled by the attention. What emerges out of the interviews is that these people performed individual acts of love because that is what one does if one is a member of that community. There appears to have been very little agonizing over the risks. It was the triumph of an ethos and thus of the work of social justice. See also Philip P. Hallie, *Lest Innocent Blood Be Shed: The Story of the Village of Le Chambon and How Goodness Happened There* (New York: Harper and Row, 1979). And yet reading Hallie's book reveals how mysteriously complex all this is. For the ethos of Le Chambon would not have attained its spontaneous strength without the inspired work of two individuals, the pastor and his wife, André and Magda Trocmé. For a very interesting philosophical examination of both the village ethos and the moral achievement of the Trocmés, see Lawrence A. Blum, *Moral Perception and Particularity* (New York: Cambridge University Press, 1994), 73–4, 85–9, 91–2, 151–2, 175–80.

[18] Within the public sphere of social justice there are several sub-spheres that correspond to different kinds of social justice. These sub-spheres are: 1) basic human rights and freedoms: freedom of speech, of worship, of movement, and so on; 2) economic justice: the duty of society to ensure that goods and services are fairly and equally distributed and the duty of individuals to contribute to the production of goods and services; 3) political justice: the duty of society to ensure that political power is fairly and equally distributed and the duty of

individuals to contribute to political decision-making; 4) criminal justice: the duty of the society to fairly and equally enforce the law and the duty of individuals to obey the law; 5) environmental justice: the duty to protect the inor- . ganic and organic world so that all being will flourish, not just human being; 6) intergenerational justice: duty of the present generation to pass on just social structures to the next generation and not overburden the next generation with debt and environmental degradation; 7) international justice: the duty of nations to live in comity with other nations and to create international social structures to solve social problems that are global in their effects. To all these duties are corresponding rights; indeed, one of the tasks of social justice is to find the proper balance of duties (responsibilities) and rights (entitlements), or to put it another way, the proper mix of what the larger society should distribute to sub-societies and individuals, and what individuals and sub-societies should contribute to the larger society.

[19] The works of two contemporary theorists of agapic love show these two tendencies. Gene Outka in his *Agape: an Ethical Analysis* (New Haven: Yale University Press, 1972), defines agapic love as "universal equal regard." Although he does accept mutuality as a proper fulfillment of agape, his understanding of agape leads his analysis more naturally towards justice. Stephen Post, in his *A Theory of Agape: On the Meaning of Christian Love* (Lewisburg, PA: Bucknell University Press, 1990) shows agapic love as seeking out mutual response in "special relations." My own view is that both tendencies must be kept together in dialectical unity. I like the words of Gilbert Meilander: "We ought not give up the desire for mutual love and try to be stoics. Neither ought we permit our love to be limited to the small circle of those who return it." See *Friendship: A Study in Theological Ethics* (South Bend: University of Notre Dame Press, 1981), 50.

Nancy A. Heitzeg, Ph.D. is an Associate Professor of Sociology and Program Director for Critical Studies of Race/Ethnicity. Nancy has taught several sections of GSJ, in the topic areas of Environmental Justice, Voices of Dissent, and Dismantling Racism. As a sociologist, Nancy has long been interested in issues of inequality and their intersection. The role of race, class, gender, sexual orientation, ability and age are central and consistent themes in every course she teaches, all her writings and professional presentations, and all her interdisciplinary work in Global Search for Justice, Women's Studies, Critical Studies of Race/Ethnicity, and the Honors Program. In addition, these issues, and, most importantly, their eventual resolution are her personal passion.

Justice (not just us): The Personal Is Political

Nancy A. Heitzeg

"First they came for the socialists, and I did not speak out because I was not a socialist.

Then they came for the trade unionists, and I did not speak out because I was not a trade unionist.

Then they came for the Jews, and I did not speak out because I was not a Jew.

Then they came for me and there was no one left to speak . . ." Pastor Martin Niemöller

Introductory Remarks

Consider the following points:

- The wealthiest 1 percent of Americans controls over 20 percent of all annual income, and 60 percent of all wealth. The richest 10 Americans have a combined net worth of over $300 billion. They are overwhelmingly white, male, and over 50 years of age. Over 60 percent of the richest 1 percent has directly inherited their wealth.

- The richest 400 Americans of a net worth of $1.2 trillion which is 1,000 times greater than the net worth of the 40 million poorest Americans.

- Only 31 women are listed among the 400 richest Americans. Of those, 25 directly inherited their wealth. Oprah Winfrey is one of two African Americans on the list and the only "rags to riches" story of the Forbes 400.

- Over 32 million Americans live in official poverty (i.e., annual income of approximately $8,000 for a single person, $11,000 for a two-person household, and $17,000 for a family of four). A more accurate indication (i.e., relative poverty) would count 50 million Americans as poor.

- The poorest Americans control 3 percent of annual income, and less than 1 percent of wealth in the U.S.

- Forty percent of the poor are children; another 10 percent are 18 to 24 years of age. Ten percent of the poor are elderly, most of them are women and/or racial/ethnic minorities. Among the adults (18 to 64 years of age) poor, 40 percent are working.

- Racial/ethnic minorities, women, and children are disproportionately in poverty. Female-headed single-parent households represent 60% of the poor, and one-third of all female-headed households, one-third of racial/ethnic minorities, two-thirds of minority children, and one-fifth of all children in the U.S. live in official poverty.

- The U.S. has the highest rate of child poverty, and the greatest income/wealth inequality, of any First World country.

- The U.S. government annually disperses $200 billion in corporate welfare (i.e., subsidies, tax write-offs/breaks, overseas marketing grants, etc.), and a mere $60 billion in individual welfare, including $16 billion for AFDC/TANF.

- One to two million Americans are homeless at some point during the course of a year. Over 50% percent are families with children; 10 percent are over 65 years of age.

- Need-based welfare expenditures represent a fraction of the $1.7 trillion Federal budget ($60 billion). The top expenditures include age-graded entitlement programs (i.e. Social Security/$407 billion, Defense/$300 billion, Medicare/$203 billion), and interest on the more than $2 trillion debt/$220 billion).

- In average, the maximum state welfare payment represents only 15% of the annual estimated living wage.

- Women still earn only 70 cents for every dollar men make.

- Women and people of color remain under represented in the professions and over represented in blue- and "pink-"collar occupations.

- The typical woman with a Ph.D. degree earns less than the typical male with a B.A. degree.

- Globally, women do over 65% of the world's unpaid labor.

- Two of every three illiterate people worldwide are women.

- Nearly one half of the world's 6 billion people live on the equivalent of $2 per day.

(Gans; Kozol; McChesney; Seager; Walker, Spohn and DeLone; Wilson; www.arc.org; www.census.gov; www.gpo.gov)

A re these justice issues? It is likely that most of us would answer yes. When pressed, however, to elaborate as to why, and how, and for what reasons, we may have more difficulty responding. Justice, it seems, is easy to intuitively acknowledge, more difficult to articulate.

One of the goals of TRW (and, a primary purpose of GSJ) is to clarify our place in the community, be it local, national and global. This requires, in part, an interdisciplinary understanding of justice—what it means for us as well as others. Justice is difficult to define, perhaps uncomfortable to act upon. For our purposes, there are several dimensions of justice that we should consider.

First of all, justice is ultimately a collective, rather than individual concern. Justice issues have a broad impact, and even seemingly isolated incidents often have global connections. Many grassroots actions for justice emerge at the local level only to uncover links with global goals. Consider Lois Gibbs and Love Canal. In 1978, Lois Gibbs was a lower-middle-class housewife in Niagara Falls, who, with other women in her neighborhood, "became politicized by the life and death issues directly affecting their children and their homes" (Merchant, pp. 192–3). Gibbs and other members of the Love Canal Homeowners Association conducted studies documenting the health problems associated with the Hooker Chemical and Plastic waste site and succeeded in obtaining redress from the state of New York. As the involvement of these women deepened, they came to realize that the hazardous waste was not an isolated local problem. Similar action by women globally linked them together as cultural ecofeminists. As Carolyn Merchant writes, "From initial Not In My Back Yard (NIMBY) concerns, the movement has changed to Not In Anybody's Back Yard (NIABY) to Not On Planet Earth (NOPE) (p. 193).

Secondly, justice issues are often systemic issues, i.e. they reflect larger structural patterns of inequality and disparity. All of the aforementioned statistics reveal structured inequality both globally and nationally. Consideration of justice issues as systemic requires distinguishing between what sociologist C. Wright Mills calls "personal troubles and social issues" (p.45). If, for example, someone becomes poor due to laziness, bad habits, and inertia, that is a personal trouble. When, however, 40 million people (most of them women, children and senior citizens) live in absolute poverty in the richest nation in the world, that can no longer be attributed to personal failing. That is an issue of structured inequality, an issue of justice.

Thirdly, justice issues imply, indeed, impel action. Justice and action are inextricably linked. Justice claims are more often than not, accompanied by calls to action. Conversely, spontaneous action is later linked to broader justice issues. The Stonewall riots provide an example. On the fringes of what was called the homophile movement, the gay men, lesbians and street queens who frequented the Stonewall Inn (a Greenwich Village bar) wanted to dance and socialize. But a night in late June 1969 changed all that. Fed up with perpetual police harassment and arrests, the patrons fought back as yet another police raid unfolded. The officers were outnumbered, and three days of street fights and skirmishes ensued. The event, now referred to as the Stonewall riots, is widely regarded as the symbolic beginning of the gay liberation movement. Action led to activism (out of the closets and into the streets . . .) and many disenfranchised Stonewall patrons became part of the general movement for GLBT rights (Duberman). What was initially a very specific response to perceived injustice became linked with general justice issues and broader goals. (The links between justice and action are extensive, and cannot be addressed in their totality here. That is the subject of GSJ and a more detailed treatment of the connections will occur in the context of that course.)

Finally, justice, despite its complexities and often, emotional overtones, can be critically analyzed. That is our primary objective here, to ferret out the general themes and commons that characterize the wide range of perspectives on justice. What follows is an overview of the existing literature on justice, an acknowledgment of its limitations for interdisciplinary analysis, and the suggestion of a schema for analyzing justice frameworks by examining sources, standards, and scope.

Prevailing Approaches to Justice

Justice. A seemingly simple word—a word we have spoken countless times, a word we intuitively claim to comprehend. Justice, we might say, is fairness, equality, freedom, and rights for all. It appears to be as easy as that.

On closer examination, however, the seemingly simple becomes increasingly complex, and we are left with a series of questions. Justice for whom? By what standards? According to which perspectives—social, economic, political, legal, divine, ecological? To what end? What exactly do fairness, equality and freedom mean? What rights do we have, should we have?

What is justice? How might we achieve it? I, too, asked these questions. My own struggle with the issues of justice and action began as I prepared to teach this course. While my position was clear, I searched, in vain it seems, for course material that would capture the range of interdisciplinary perspectives and positions relative to justice and action. Discipline specific material seemed too limiting—the philosophers had a lot to say about certain views of justice, but little that spoke of action. The political theorists, on the other hand, discussed justice and action in the context of governments and official documents, but often ignored the grassroots activists. And, the activists, well, they were activists who often engaged the issues of justice without much analysis or theorizing. None of the existing writings on justice and action seemed to provide a larger framework for comparison and critical analysis. The interdisciplinary literature I sought was not there.

The possibility of creating such an analytic scheme to critically compare justice perspectives and action options occurred to me as I was examining factions of the Civil Rights Movement in detail. The Southern Christian Leadership Conference (SCLC), the Student Non-violent Coordinating Committee (SNCC), the Nation of Islam (NOI), Malcolm X and the Black Panther Party (BPP) all emerged from the same struggle, but they had diverse goals and tactics. The ways in which these groups varied, however, could be systematically analyzed and discussed. Their justice arguments emanated from different sources; they applied varying standards, and also diverged regarding the scope of these justice standards. In addition, the proposed course of action for all these groups varied markedly. SCLC, SNCC, NOI and the BPP differed with respect to goals, positions on the appropriateness of nonviolence vs. militant action, leadership styles and strategies. If, then, we could identify variables that provided a framework for comparing and contrasting elements of the Civil Rights Movement, couldn't we also utilize that framework to compare justice and action across disciplines and movements? This was where I began; what follows is the result. I trust it will be of assistance for an interdisciplinary understanding of justice.

Debates over justice are timeless and as varied as historical experience. Often these discussions are explicit, expressly directed towards defining justice and delineating the conditions and contingencies of action. Such is the case with many religious tracts, political treatises, and philosophical essays. Similarly, analyses of justice are also found in the writings of sociologists, social workers, historians and political scientists, among others. Issues of justice also form the foundation for many areas of interdisciplinary studies, which emphasize the vantage point of disenfranchised groups. Women's Studies, GLBT Studies, Multicultural and Post-Colonial Studies are all cases in point. In all the aforementioned areas, issues of justice are at the fore; indeed, a primary goal of the discussion/discipline is to advance discourse on issues of justice and related options for action.

On other occasions, perspectives on justice are emergent, less overtly articulated, but present nonetheless. Some of these are implicit in the theoretical paradigms and applications of various disciplines including the natural and social sciences, the humanities, and certain areas of professional study. Here, notions of equity, of balance, of resource allocation, provide a seminal justice/action framework. Other emergent views of justice and action emanate from the grassroots, from every day understandings of the cosmos, from patterns of interaction with others, nature and the unseen. These are worldviews, ways of life which are based on a taken-for-granted notion of what constitutes justice and right action. Grassroots perspectives on justice and action also arise under duress, from spontaneous collective responses (e.g. demonstrations, riots, and revolt) to perceived injustice. Latent definitions of justice may become manifest in the face of oppression and what was unclear becomes certain as the people respond. In other words, notions of justice may be embedded in ways of thinking and being; these are implied rather than explicitly stated, but become apparent under closer examination.

Both implicit and explicit approaches are essential to a comprehensive interdisciplinary understanding of justice. Indeed, they provide the foundation for the ensuing discussion. For our purposes, however, detailed analysis of the specific points of each approach is limiting. For example, the explicit theoretical discourse on justice is often discipline-specific, fettered by academic jargon and abstraction. And, with some noted exceptions, it has been dominated by Western, often Eurocentric, male points of view, particularly those of philosophers, political theorists and theologians. Implicit claims, on the other hand, are just that. Awareness of the justice/action issues requires extrapolation, interpretation, case-by-case analysis and post-hoc speculation. In the many cases, we are unguided by first hand accounts and documentation.

Further, even in combination, these perspectives per se constrain our discussion by failing to consistently draw the connection between justice and action. In many cases, one is emphasized at the expense of the other, with very few acknowledgements of the conceptual and practical linkages between the two. And, finally, any systematic examination of the range of viewpoints represents an insurmountable task. It is impossible to quantify perspectives on justice/action—there may be 6 or 600 or 6 billion. Such an endeavor is fruitless and loses sight of the common threads that run through these discussions. Over-attention to the specifics here leads to the proverbial dilemma of losing sight of the forest for the trees. What is needed, and what is lacking is an overview of the common themes that provide a basis for comparing perspectives on justice.

A New View of Justice

How then, are we to proceed in untangling an endless web of justice? Perhaps a broader view, a meta-analysis of justice frameworks will offer a starting point. Interdisciplinary analysis of justice may require a search for themes and patterns among the vast array of perspectives and experiences.

As noted earlier, there is a dearth of literature that provides an overarching look at the similarities, differences, common questions, points of contention and convergence. All the explicit and implicit approaches to justice grapple with comparable concerns. They emerge from identifiable sources and also name certain contingencies of justice that translate into concrete goals and strategies. Those proverbial trees, in short, do constitute a forest, and it is that forest that will be explored here. The goal of the ensuing discussion is to provide an overview of the conceptual variations in justice frameworks. There are certainly other ways of organizing these ideas and, while what is presented is representative, it may not exhaust all the complexities of justice and action. Consider this a beginning, rather than a definitive end point for this discussion.

Further, the goal is to provide a descriptive, general outline of justice frameworks. Hopefully, this might illuminate more specific discussions of justice. The aim here is not to advocate for any particular perspective on justice, nor to evaluate the relative efficacy of various actions. Those indeed are valid discussions, which this outline may ideally inform and inspire. Figure 1 outlines the issues so central to justice frameworks, and will serve as a point of reference for the discussion that follows.

Justice Frameworks

SOURCES

- Theological/spiritual
  (e.g. Catholic, Protestant, Judaic, Islamic, Eastern, Native American spirituality, feminist theology, revitalization)
- Politial
  (e.g. Nationalist, Democratic/Pluralist, Socialist/Communist, Anarchist, international accords)
- Philosophical/Cosmological
  (e.g. idealism, materialism, utilitarianism, libertarian, communitarian, existentialism, feminist philosophy, post-modernism, Eastern philosophies, Afrocentric cosmology)
- Natural/Social Scientific
  (e.g. ecological, biological, psychological, anthropological, sociological, economic, demographic)

STANDARDS

- universalism/absolutism
  particularism/relativism
- distributive/commutative
  retributive/restorative
- merit
- need
- liberty/freedom
- equality/equal rights/equal access

SCOPE

- human-centered
  (e.g. exclusion/inclusion based on class, race/ethnicity, gender, sexual orientation, age, ability, religion, and nationality)
- eco-centered
  (e.g. earth-based religious/political movements, animal rights, Gaia hypothesis)

Figure 1. Justice Frameworks: An Overview

Justice Frameworks

In general, discourses on justice share common features: all emerge from specific sources that frame the nature of the discussion; all identify standards by which justice/injustice is measured and meted out, and all, in varying degree, address the scope of justice—the range of Beings to which the standards apply. And finally, all, directly or indirectly suggest actions appropriate for achieving justice. Each will be considered in turn.

Sources

Justice frameworks may be most immediately analyzed with reference to their inspirational sources. Perspectives on justice or conversely, injustice began with a particular worldview, a vantage point from which to gauge and assess. Historically and currently, justice has been defined from several vantage points: religious/spiritual, philosophical, political, and scientific. Historically and currently, these sources continue to frame most discussions of justice.

The world's religions provide some of the oldest and most diverse perspectives on justice. Here justice is divinely revealed absolute. All of the major world religions as well as nature-based perspectives of indigenous peoples include notions of duties, rights and standards of conduct. These outline just relationships between humans, the divine, and nature. Often, religious perspectives on justice have both sacred and secular implications. Divinely inspired justice should pervade this world as well as the next. (Catholic social teaching provides an excellent example of this and is discussed in detail in Dr. Connors' article in this text). Indeed, for much of human history, sacred justice was synonymous with secular justice; it was "on Earth as it is in Heaven" (Klass; Lehman and Meyers; Gudorf).

Philosophy is an equally significant source regarding justice. From the early Greeks to the present day, explicit discussions of justice remain a central topic of philosophical debate. Indeed philosophical views of the common good, universal rights and ethics, and just distribution, and retribution have shaped both political and scientific views of justice (Isnay; Shute and Hurley). More recent philosophical treatments of justice have rejected the notion of absolute justice that is the trademark of the modern era. Justice here is situated, relative and subject to change (Kaufman).

Political theorists, governmental legal systems and international bodies offer secular views of justice in treaties, constitutions, documents and accords. The common sense understandings that many hold regarding justice and the relationship between citizens and the state, civil rights and liberties, access to resources and just law and punishment. Originally, political notions of justice were most often discussed relative to the nation state. Many current political discussions of justice, however, are global; these emerge from international bodies such as the United Nations or transnational nongovernmental organizations (NGO's) (United Nations, Amnesty International).

The sciences, both natural and social, are less explicit sources on the topic of justice. Like political sources, earlier philosophical perspectives often inform these views. Although the term per se is rarely used, rudimentary perspectives on justice are embedded in their analyses of the social institutions and arrangements, the psyche and the natural world. The conflict paradigm in sociology for example, presents a clear commentary on structured inequality and its correlation with classism, racism, sexism, heterosexism, and ageism (Collins, 1975, 1994). Similarly, ecology incorporates mechanistic models of science into a holistic view that emphasizes balance, biodiversity and sustainability (Naess; Miller). All the previous justice questions regarding distribution, rights, responsibilities and equity are implicit in these approaches.

It is crucial to note that these sources do not provide unified perspectives on justice. These sources of justice, in fact, are neither internally consistent nor mutually exclusive. There are vast disagreements within categories as well as points of congruence between them. Philosophers, for example, have debated for centuries over the nature of justice—is it an absolute ideal or constructed relative to material circumstances. Is justice best represented by "the greatest good for the greatest number" or "from each according to his/her ability to each according to his/her need"? Is liberty, equal treatment, or equal opportunity the standard (Ishay; Lebacqz)? Such is also the case with religious, political, and scientific sources; they share a certain starting point for framing justice, but diverge on its precise meaning.

There are, on the other hand, many similarities that exist between the different sources. Although emanating from religious and scientific sources respectively, Native American spirituality and deep ecology arrive at strikingly similar views of environmental justice and a balanced relationship between humans and nature. Whether other species are perceived to be our spiritual kin or other species within ecosystem, the resultant definition of justice is the same. Perhaps one of the most striking examples of this congruency can be found in the life and work of Dr. Martin Luther King Jr. As a minister, president of the Southern Christian Leadership Conference, and a leader in the struggle for civil rights, he moved with ease from framing justice religiously and politically. Full civil rights for African Americans, he argued, must be granted for moral reasons and constitutional reasons. The Bible and the Bill of Rights both spoke to the issue, and, for King, were completely compatible sources on justice (Carson, et al.; Washington).

Sister Helen Prejean, CSJ, provides another excellent example of drawing upon the congruencies among justice frameworks. The author of *Dead Man Walking* and presenter at a CSC Core convocation in the fall of 1999, Sister Helen opposes the death penalty on several grounds: moral/theological, philosophical and political. As honorary chair of Moratorium 2000, a global grassroots campaign that aims towards the ultimate abolition of capital punishment, Sister Helen Prejean eloquently opposes the death penalty, first on the basis of Catholic social teaching on life. She also notes high financial and political costs as well as race and class disparities. All suggest U.S. constitutional violations of due process and equal protection as well as violations of standards set by the U.N. Commission on Human Rights. Still other views draw upon common themes from disparate sources to create hybrid perspectives on justice.

Liberation theology is a prime example here. Grounding Catholic social teachings' preference for the poor in a Marxist critique of capitalism, liberation theology imbues faith with political implications. The liberation is spiritual, economic, and political (Hennelly). Similar fusion is found in the revitalization movements of other oppressed peoples past and present: the Handsome Lake Revival of the Iroquois Nations, Ghost Dance movements among North American Plains Tribes, and the Rastafarians of Jamaica. Rastafarians, for example, fuse Biblical prophecy with Pan-African political ideology to create a critique of Western culture, a vision of African Liberation and an entire lifestyle (Brown; Lewis; Campbell). In all these cases, mergers of native religions, Christianity, and political ideologies shape the view of justice.

This sort of cross-sectional accord is closely related to questions of justice standards and scope. What constitutes justice? Who is justice for? Thinkers from all the sources have grappled with the many dimensions of this issue and their tentative answers are explored in the ensuing sections.

Standards

As the foregoing discussion implies, the sources for framing justice arguments are only a starting point. The issue of how justice might be measured—what are the standards for justice—is at the heart of all discussions. Again, there are many questions and no definitive answers.

Two general dimensions will be considered here. First of all, justice standards may be construed as universalist or particularist. Proponents of the universalist position argue that justice standards are universally applicable, transcending time, culture, and social context—and often absolute. Until recently, the universalist approach has characterized most theological, philosophical, political and scientific views of justice. Discussions of divine and natural law, "the inalienable rights of citizens," and universal human rights as set forth by the United Nations all suggest universalist standards (Declaration of Independence, United Nations). The majority of explicit theological, philosophical, and political justice tracts are grounded in universal standards. So, too, are many of the more implicit justice perspectives that emerge from the sciences and the humanitarians as well as indigenous religions, and grassroots social movements.

Others argue that justice standards emanate from particular historical circumstances, perspectives or situations of oppression. This perspective is frequently associated with the post-modern, post-colonial critique of what bell hooks calls "the white supremacist capitalist patriarchy" (hooks, 1992 p. 22). This perspective is often rooted in a critique of supposedly universalistic standards as non-inclusive, and proceeds from the perspective of excluded groups. Particularistic standards of justice are explicitly expressed in strands of existential and feminist philosophy, in the identity politics of racial/ethnic minorities, women, GLBT persons, and Third World nationalists; and in the religious/political agendas of revitalization movements (Brown, Collier, Cruikschank; Fanon; Hennelly; Kaufman; Lewis). Perhaps, the anthropological debate over "cultural relativism" represents one of the clearest expositions of particularistic views of justice in the social sciences. In addition, particularist perspectives of justice are implicit in the standpoint critiques of theory in the social sciences, the interdisciplinary approaches of women's, multicultural, and GLBT studies and some local-level grassroots movements whose initial impetus is often very specific situations of injustice (Collins, Patricia, 1990; Fisher, 1994; hooks, 1984; Kendall; Merchant; Rothenberg).

One of the most heated debates over universal/particular justice standards is centered on the practice of female genital mutilation (FGM), which involves the removal of all or part of the external female genitalia without anesthetic. While FGM is practiced in other regions of the world, it is most widely practiced in Northern Africa, where over 100 million women have undergone the procedure. First brought to Western attention in the work of Alice Walker (i.e. *Possessing the Secret of Joy* and *Warrior Marks*), FGM clearly illustrates the tension between universal and relativist views of justice. Proponents contend that it is a cultural tradition that can only be understood and addressed from within (El Saadawi). Opponents cite a long list of physical complications (e.g. infection, pain-induced shock, urine and menstrual retention, damage to the urethra, painful intercourse, greater risk of STD infection, and obstructed labor) and maintain that FGM is a human rights violation and, perhaps, grounds for asylum (Noble, Covetz and Janagishita; Seager pp. 52–53).

As Alice Walker so succinctly puts it, "Torture is not culture" (Walker and Parmar, p. 95).

Discussions of the general or specific applicability of justice standards are closely intertwined with the universalistic/particularistic debate. Here, the debate centers on the extent to which justice standards apply to all areas of social life or are limited to certain select concerns. Philosophers and political theorists have provided most of the explicit discourse, here often dividing justice into four areas: distributive (i.e. distribution of rewards and resources), commutative (i.e. justice in exchange), retributive (i.e. justice in punishment), and restorative (i.e. justice in compensation) (LeBacqz, pp. 9–10). Perspectives on justice may encompass some or all of these. Many theological and political perspectives often encompass all four, as part of divinely sacred and secular justice (Thompson; Ishtay). Certain political perspectives and grassroots movements, on the other hand, narrow the focus. Libertarians, for example, emphasize commutative justice in exchange, arguing that the only just government intervention involves minimal regulation of the economy to insure equitable exchange (Nozick). In contrast, civil rights movements of disenfranchised groups often argue for distributive justice. Globally, for example, women perform over 65% of the world's unpaid labor, are more likely than men to live in poverty, and earn 70% less of what men make for comparable work. Women are over-represented in the lower wage sectors of economies, and are disproportionately employed in the unprotected enterprise zones of the global economy (Seager). These are clearly issues of distributive justice. Retributive and restorative justice are concerns for groups who focus on issues related to the criminal, civil, and administrative law, such as racial profiling, incarceration, capital punishment, political prisoners, calls for compensation and reparations (Amnesty International, Feagin). The post-apartheid hearings on Truth and Reconciliation in South Africa as well as calls for reparations for the descendants of slaves in the U.S. are both examples of restorative justice.

The final dimension relative to justice standards is the hallmark, the ultimate measure of justice. This is the subject of much debate within and between all the perspectives on justice and is at the heart of much theological, philosophical, and political literature on justice. In general, discussions of justice often make reference to central concepts: merit and/or need, liberty/freedom, equality and rights. Again, these are illusive concepts, which are defined in disparate ways in religious documents, philosophical tracts and the constitutions of nation states (Ishtay; Shute and Hurley).

Most national constitutions for example, enumerate the rights and freedoms available to all or particular groups of citizens. The United Nations

Universal Declaration of Human Rights, however, lists rights that seem applicable to everyone regardless of nationality; ". . . recognition of the inherent dignity and of the equal and inalienable rights of all members of the human family is the foundation of freedom, justice and peace in the world" (United Nations, p. 21) (See Appendix A).

More importantly, however, is the prioritizing of these standards. Liberals, particularly those in Western democracies, tend to hold freedom and liberty central to justice. The rights of individuals, then, especially those safeguarding freedoms, take precedent over equality. The rights of free speech, to keep and bear arms, to own/accumulate private property, to pursue happiness, are supposedly universal standards of justice. In the U.S. however, their primacy in law and public opinion leads to constricted definitions of equality. Equal access to all social resources, in most liberal analyses of justice, is a lesser hallmark of justice that is limited by individual merit, rights, and liberties (LeBacqz, pp. 10–11; Howard and Donnelly). Equality, then, is frequently defined in the most minimal of terms, as equal protection under the law. It has rarely meant equal access to rewards and resources, a point that is painfully clear to the poor, people of color and women.

Marxists/socialists, on the other hand, regard economic equality and freedom from economic oppression as the preconditions for justice. Need, not merit, is the measure; a longstanding Marxian dictum speaks directly to this point—"from each according to their ability to each according to their need" (Marx). Further, individual freedoms, especially those related to material accumulation, are defined as lesser considerations subject to restraint in pursuit of the higher standard and the communal good (Marx and Engels, 1948; Feuer; Kautsky; Trotsky; Shiva). Indeed, much historical conflict over the ideologies of capitalism and socialism/communism revolve around the standards of justice and the value of freedom vs. equality, merit vs. need, the right to accumulate wealth vs. the right to basic necessities of survival.

Finally, the definitions of justice standards such as freedom, equality, and rights are shaped by considerations of the scope of justice, i.e. justice for whom and why?

Scope

The scope of justice is one of the most significant elements that shape justice perspectives. Scope, here, refers to the range of persons and/or beings to which justice standards apply. It includes considerations of inclusivity and discrimination, as well as human-centered and eco-centered claims.

The majority of explicit and implicit justice frameworks focus on justice as a concept that is applicable and available to humans. On closer examination, however, it is clear that historical and contemporary perspectives have frequently narrowed the concept of justice, which permits the exclusion of certain categories of persons.

Prior to the twentieth century, the classical philosophical, theological, and political perspectives of the West have limited justice to those who were deserving by nature of either nationality or morality. Almost invariably, this led to the dehumanization and subsequent oppression of persons who failed to meet the standards of "reason" or "morality." As Richard Rorty notes, "For most white people, until very recently, black people did not so count. For most Christians, up until the seventeenth century or so, most heathens did not so count. For the Nazis, Jews did not so count. For most males, in countries where the average annual income is under $4000, most females still do not so count. Whenever tribal and national rivalries become important, members of rival tribes and nations will not so count" (p. 263).

Philosophically and theologically, such a narrow scope of justice allowed seemingly "righteous" and "reasonable" men to endorse slavery, conduct inquisitions, colonize, and exterminate indigenous peoples globally, brutalize women and children in the name of discipline and property rights, and execute anyone who deviated from proscribed norms of sexual conduct (Golden, et al.).

Politically, this constricted view of personhood allowed even the "enlightened" Western democracies to limit those so-called universal and "inalienable" rights to white men who owned property. At the time of its writing, the rights and freedoms enumerated in the U.S. Constitution were only available to white, adult, property-owning males. Native Americans—the only indigenous Americans—are mentioned in the Declaration of Independence as the "merciless Indian savages, whose known rule of warfare, is an undistinguished destruction of all ages, sexes, and conditions" (Declaration of Independence, p. 7). African Americans, then enslaved, were counted as three-fifths of a person for purposes of determining state population size and subsequent representation. They remained property (a point reinforced by several Supreme Court decisions) until the ratification of the Thirteenth Amendment in 1865 (The Constitution of the United States, pp. 14, 42). Women, of course, were not citizens either and were, for all intents and purposes, the property of their parents or husbands. Full Constitutional rights were finally extended to women with the passage of the Nineteenth Amendment in 1920 (Ibid, p. 48).

Constricted views of personhood and consequently the scope of justice are not limited to the past. In the U.S., federal law did not prohibit discrimination against racial/ethnic minorities, women, the differently abled, and senior citizens until the mid-1960s. GLBT persons and those under eighteen still do not have the full rights of citizenship here, and GLBT persons, in particular, are denied federal civil rights protections against discrimination in several areas including employment, housing, family relationships, the military, security clearances, and matters of the criminal law (Hunter, Michaelson and Stoddard). In addition, many contend that the theoretical inclusion of formerly disenfranchised groups in constitutional claims of justice does not necessarily translate into justice in practice. As noted before, equal protection under the law does not translate into equal access to social resources. The persistence of institutionalized classism, racism, sexism, heterosexism and ageism is well documented and continues to be regarded as just by certain groups of religious and political conservatives (Doob, Kendall, Rothenberg).

Globally, the scope of justice also continues to be narrowly construed. Despite the broadly based universal human rights outlined in a series of international accords, a variety of explicit theological and political views, and implicit socio-political perspectives exclude certain persons from the purview of justice. Race/ethnicity, gender, sexual orientation, age, and religion remain the source of devalued status in many regions of the world. The system of apartheid in South Africa remained legal until 1992, and the ill effects are still felt by the black majority (Bratton). Similarly, post-colonial religious and ethnic conflict rages from Bosnia to Indonesia. Women are still denied social and legal rights in many areas of the world. They remain the property of men, are denied access to education, restricted in their movements, are bought, sold, beaten, mutilated, forced to labor, raped and killed at will. In many of the Middle Eastern Islamic theocracies, the movement and dress of women is also restricted (Seager). Prior to its collapse in 2002, the Taliban in Afghanistan "banned employment for women, halted formal female education pending the development of an 'appropriate' curriculum, imposed strict dress codes, and introduced strict controls on the movement of women outside the home" (Marsden, pp. 88–89). Similarly draconian policies persist in many other countries in the Middle East.

So, too, in most of the world, GLBT persons and children are often excluded from the scope of justice. Same-sex activity is still illegal in most nations of the world, and GLBT persons continue to be religiously and politically persecuted. Children are parental property and, in spite of international standards to the contrary, over 75 million children under fifteen labor, often in sweatshop conditions. Female children, particularly in areas of Central and East Asia, are viewed as economic and social liabilities and are disproportionately subject to abortion, infanticide, and abandonment (Seager; Noble, Cover, and Janagishita).

The scope of justice is not always so narrow. More inclusive perspectives flourish as well. Historically, these can be found in some strands of early Greek philosophy, and the nature-based religions of many indigenous peoples, the universal tenets of Buddhism which extend to all sentient beings; and the informal, non-stratified political arrangements of foraging bands (Barnes; Ishtay; LaDuke; Ward). Some of these perspectives are supported by extensive writings, others are reported in the anthropological and historical literature. All, however, limit social differentiation and inequality and extend the scope of justice at minimum, to all humans.

Several Western-based theological, philosophical, and political perspectives also broaden the scope. Progressive interpretations of Christianity include all people and often advocate for secular justice for all, as well. Many Catholic and Protestant theologians have been involved in the struggle for civil rights, economic justice, and women's rights on religious as well as political grounds. Catholic social teaching holds up the dignity of every person and the preference for the poor as key tenets (Thompson). Feminist theology has also expanded traditional interpretations of Christianity to be more inclusive of the role(s) of women, both spiritually, and in institutional roles on the church (Plaskow and Christ; Johnson, Sallie).

In the past 150 years, the identity politics of disenfranchised groups have expressed both explicit and implicit claims for inclusion within justice frameworks. The poor, racial/ethnic minorities, women, religious sects, senior citizens, the differently abled, and GLBT persons through social action and interdisciplinary writings have continued to push the margins of justice debates. Much of this work is rooted in a critique of the narrow Eurocentric patriarchal view of justice held by many Western political and philosophical frameworks. A vast array of work is included here: socialist critique of capitalism ranging from Marx to the present; feminist and post-colonial philosophy, political theory; critical conflict, and standpoint theory in sociology; multicultural and feminist perspectives in a variety of disciplines, and political demands for inclusion that range from abolition and Seneca Falls, to the Civil Rights Act and era and beyond (Carson, et al.; Collins, Patricia; Feuer; Marx and Engels; Kendall; Rothenberg; Wallace; Weitz; Wallace and Wolf). The common feature of all is a broad-based scope of justice that seeks to include all persons within existing socio-political parameters of justice or abandon them in favor of non-discriminatory alternatives.

At the heart of all these claims are several key points. Oppressions intersect; class, race, gender, sexual orientation and age are sources of interrelated disadvantages and subsequent injustice. Further, justice is not a commodity that can be parceled out to some and not all. It is an all or nothing proposition. As Martin Luther King Jr. so aptly noted in "Letter from Birmingham Jail": "Injustice anywhere is a threat to justice everywhere. We are caught in an inescapable network of mutuality tied in a single garment of destiny" (p. 85). Whatever affects one directly affects all indirectly.

Finally, the scope of justice may be extended to non-human species and, in fact, the entire planet. Eco-centered perspectives in justice contend that classical configurations limit the scope of justice to human centered concerns, thus overlooking a range of beings who may also be entitled to rights, freedoms and equality. While some of these justice arguments are centuries old, many have emerged in the late 20th century in conjunction with the ecology and animal rights movements (Merchant; Finsen and Finsen).

Historically, eco-centric views of justice are found in non-Western religions such as Native American spirituality. In fact, according to anthropological evidence indigenous animistic religions are the oldest in the world. Many still persist and, in the U.S., Native American spirituality continues to inform both the religious and ecological positions of many Native Americans. In *All Our Relations*, Winona LaDuke quotes Anishinabe elder Eddie Benton, "There are two separate roads to choose from—the road to technology and the other road to spiritualism. The elders feel that the road of technology represents a continuation of headlong rush to technological development. This is the road that has led to modern society, to a damaged and scorched earth. . . . The other road represents the slower path that traditional native people have traveled and are now seeking again. The earth is not scorched on this trail. The grass is still growing there" (p. 198). Buddhism also extends the scope of justice to non-humans. Buddhism has long held that the utmost earthly goal is to "Bear the burden of all beings. . . . Make the vow to save all beings, to set free all beings. . . . As long as the world remains, as long as sentient beings remain, then so too shall I remain to ease the suffering of the world" (Ishtay, p. 6). Similar notions are also found in the teachings of several other religions including Taoism and Hinduism.

More recently, eco-centered conceptions of justice have begun to be included in Western theological thought. Feminist theology in particular, is a key contributor here. Elisabeth Johnson CSJ, in *Women, Earth, and Creator Spirit* argues for an ecofeminist reconsideration of "hierarchical dualism" which has relationships between God/Man, Man/Woman, and Man/Nature. Johnson writes, "Hierarchical dualism . . . places the privileged, so-called rational man apart from and above other persons such as the poor and people of color . . . . Feminist analysis insists that the devastating ecological consequences of this two-tiered vision cannot be fully addressed until we face it as a whole. . . . We need to realize that the natural environment is oppressed, manipulated and abused in ways analogous to the patriarchal use of women" (pp. 11–12).

Eco-inclusive perspectives on justice extend beyond theology. Philosophy has made significant contributions including further development of eco-feminist ideas. Perhaps, most importantly, philosophy paved the way for continued challenges to human-centered views of justice on several fronts. Norwegian philosopher Arne Naess coined the term deep ecology in 1972 (Naess). As Carolyn Merchant notes, deep ecology "has now become the legitimating framework for an array of ecological movements from spiritual greens to radical EarthFirst!ers" (p. 86). Philosophers were also among the first to critique speciesism and make the case for animal rights. Peter Singer and Tom Regan in particular, inspired the contemporary animal rights movement with their respective works, *Animal Liberation* and *The Case for Animal Liberation* (Finsen and Finsen).

Several perspectives found in the natural and social sciences comparably widen the scope of justice. Physicists, biologists, and chemists have begun to question the predominance of the Western mechanistic view of science (Naess; Sheldrake, 1981, 1985). Holistic approaches, which view the earth as an ecosystem or a complex organism, itself, imply that balance, equality, and in fact, justice, require a consideration of non-human nature. In fact, one scientific approach—the Gaia hypothesis—contends that the entire earth itself is a complex organism that should receive consideration as such (Miller).

The social sciences and interdisciplinary areas of study have also begun to expand their scope of inquiry to the environment and other species. Increasingly, sociology, psychology, women's studies, and multicultural studies have considered the relationship between social and environmental inequality. Eco-psychology and the study of environmental racism, sexism, and classism are all cases in point (Bullard; Roszak; Roszak, Gomes and Kanner). Similarly, the sociological interest in social movements has provided analyses of the green and animal rights movements as well as exposés of animal abuse in a variety of settings (Kunkel; Catton and Dunlap).

Finally, more inclusive, eco-centered views of justice have emerged from political thought and practice. Rudimentary notions of eco-justice can be found in the socialist writings of Marx and Engels, as well as the early anarchists (Merchant, pp. 134–4; Runkle). Both critique economic and political relations as oppressive and exploitive to humans as well as the environment. These ideas find contemporary manifestation in the writings and activism of the socialist ecologists, socialist eco-feminists, and anarchist social ecologists (Chase; Shiva). These perspectives have informed much of the green movement in the U.S. as well as indigenous efforts globally to maintain ecologically sound practices.

National legislation and international treaties have also begun to reflect more expansive views of justice. Animals and the environment have limited legal protection here, and there is continued lobbying and political pressure to expand our legal notions of animal and environmental rights. Political proponents are for a variety of changes in our legal system including enhanced penalties for animal cruelty, the abolition of animal experimentation and factory farming, and moratoria on nuclear energy, urban sprawl, and the use of fossil fuels (Bullard; Merchant; Newkirk; Saign; Wise).

In addition, international bodies and agencies are increasingly called upon to consider the environment and other species in political treaties and agreements. Pressures from indigenous peoples and environmental groups globally have led to agreements on sustainable development, pollution reduction, and endangered species protection. Examples include the inaugural Earth Summit held in Rio de Janeiro in 1992, and the United Nations Declaration of Indigenous People's Rights (Saign; Ewen). While many such documents are motivated by human-based concerns, they do nonetheless extend the concept of justice, rights, and protections to non-humans as well.

Justice frameworks, then, provide an analytical basis from which to identify and evaluate justice arguments. Justice frameworks may be characterized by their implicit or explicit definitions of justice—its source, standards and scope. As the foregoing suggests, even this rudimentary classification schema quickly becomes complicated with comparisons and caveats, and, at best, serves as a rough guide to the intricacies of justice.

Concluding Remarks

Justice. We end as we began, albeit a bit closer to capturing the complexities of this concept. As the discussion and examples indicate, this word does indeed have many different dimensions, many different meanings. The foregoing descriptive overview is an initial attempt to locate the common threads among various perspectives; to synthesize the insights provided by a multiplicity of disciplines and experiences.

And yet, this is only half the story. Once justice has been conceptualized, its realization inevitably comes into question. Justice without action is mere intellectual exercise; the circumstances of everyday life and engaged citizenship demand much more. Once we have identified a justice issue analyzed its parameters and our own position, we are called to act. May the epitaph of Karl Marx be our guide—"The philosophers have merely described the world—the goal, however, is to change it."

Questions for Discussion

(#1) Identify your own perspective on justice. What are the sources, standards, and scope of your definition of justice? What actions would you recommend in pursuit of justice? Address the goals, conditions, and strategies of action. What factors have influenced your view of justice and action?

(#2) Review the United Nation's Universal Declaration of Human Rights. Does this list adequately capture the rights that should be available to all people? Is anything or anyone missing? Is it even possible to claim or identify universal standards of justice? Why/why not?

(#3) Why should women be particularly concerned about justice? What justice issues do women face globally? Nationally? Locally? What actions can you take to address the issues cited here?

Appendix A

Universal Declaration of Human Rights

Adopted and proclaimed by General Assembly

Resolution 217 A (III) of 10 December 1948

On December 10, 1948 the General Assembly of the United Nations adopted and proclaimed the Universal Declaration of Human Rights the full text of which appears in the following pages. Following this historic act the Assembly called upon all Member countries to publicize the text of the Declaration and "to cause it to be disseminated, displayed, read and expounded principally in schools and other educational institutions, without distinction based on the political status of countries or territories."

Article 1.

All human beings are born free and equal in dignity and rights. They are endowed with reason and conscience and should act towards one another in a spirit of brotherhood.

Article 2.

Everyone is entitled to all the rights and freedoms set forth in this Declaration, without distinction of any kind, such as race, colour, sex, language, religion, political or other opinion, national or social origin, property, birth or other status. Furthermore, no distinction shall be made on the basis of the political, jurisdictional or international status of the country or territory to which a person belongs, whether it be independent, trust, non-self-governing or under any other limitation of sovereignty.

Article 3.

Everyone has the right to life, liberty and security of person.

Article 4.

No one shall be held in slavery or servitude; slavery and the slave trade shall be prohibited in all their forms.

Article 5.

No one shall be subjected to torture or to cruel, inhuman or degrading treatment or punishment.

Article 6.

Everyone has the right to recognition everywhere as a person before the law.

Article 7.

All are equal before the law and are entitled without any discrimination to equal protection of the law. All are entitled to equal protection against any discrimination in violation of this Declaration and against any incitement to such discrimination.

Article 8.

Everyone has the right to an effective remedy by the competent national tribunals for acts violating the fundamental rights granted him by the constitution or by law.

Article 9.

No one shall be subjected to arbitrary arrest, detention or exile.

Article 10.

Everyone is entitled in full equality to a fair and public hearing by an independent and impartial tribunal, in the determination of his rights and obligations and of any criminal charge against him.

Article 11.

(1) Everyone charged with a penal offence has the right to be presumed innocent until proved guilty according to law in a public trial at which he has had all the guarantees necessary for his defence.

(2) No one shall be held guilty of any penal offence on account of any act or omission which did not constitute a penal offence, under national or international law, at the time when it was committed. Nor shall a heavier penalty be imposed than the one that was applicable at the time the penal offence was committed.

Article 12.

No one shall be subjected to arbitrary interference with his privacy, family, home or correspondence, nor to attacks upon his honour and reputation. Everyone has the right to the protection of the law against such interference or attacks.

Article 13.

(1) Everyone has the right to freedom of movement and residence within the borders of each state.

(2) Everyone has the right to leave any country, including his own, and to return to his country.

Article 14.

(1) Everyone has the right to seek and to enjoy in other countries asylum from persecution.

(2) This right may not be invoked in the case of prosecutions genuinely arising from non-political crimes or from acts contrary to the purposes and principles of the United Nations.

Article 15.

(1) Everyone has the right to a nationality.

(2) No one shall be arbitrarily deprived of his nationality nor denied the right to change his nationality.

Article 16.

(1) Men and women of full age, without any limitation due to race, nationality or religion, have the right to marry and to found a family. They are entitled to equal rights as to marriage, during marriage and at its dissolution.

(2) Marriage shall be entered into only with the free and full consent of the intending spouses.

(3) The family is the natural and fundamental group unit of society and is entitled to protection by society and the State.

Article 17.

(1) Everyone has the right to own property alone as well as in association with others.

(2) No one shall be arbitrarily deprived of his property.

Article 18.

Everyone has the right to freedom of thought, conscience and religion; this right includes freedom to change his religion or belief, and freedom, either alone or in community with others and in public or private, to manifest his religion or belief in teaching, practice, worship and observance.

Article 19.

Everyone has the right to freedom of opinion and expression; this right includes freedom to hold opinions without interference and to seek, receive and impart information and ideas through any media and regardless of frontiers.

Article 20.

(1) Everyone has the right to freedom of peaceful assembly and association.

(2) No one may be compelled to belong to an association.

Article 21.

(1) Everyone has the right to take part in the government of his country, directly or through freely chosen representatives.

(2) Everyone has the right of equal access to public service in his country.

(3) The will of the people shall be the basis of the authority of government; this will shall be expressed in periodic and genuine elections which shall be by universal and equal suffrage and shall be held by secret vote or by equivalent free voting procedures.

Article 22.

Everyone, as a member of society, has the right to social security and is entitled to realization, through national effort and international co-operation and in accordance with the organization and resources of each State, of the economic, social and cultural rights indispensable for his dignity and the free development of his personality.

Article 23.

(1) Everyone has the right to work, to free choice of employment, to just and favourable conditions of work and to protection against unemployment.

(2) Everyone, without any discrimination, has the right to equal pay for equal work.

(3) Everyone who works has the right to just and favourable remuneration ensuring for himself and his family an existence worthy of human dignity, and supplemented, if necessary, by other means of social protection.

(4) Everyone has the right to form and to join trade unions for the protection of his interests.

Article 24.

Everyone has the right to rest and leisure, including reasonable limitation of working hours and periodic holidays with pay.

Article 25.

(1) Everyone has the right to a standard of living adequate for the health and well-being of himself and of his family, including food, clothing, housing and medical care and necessary social services, and the right to security in the event of unemployment, sickness, disability, widowhood, old age or other lack of livelihood in circumstances beyond his control.

(2) Motherhood and childhood are entitled to special care and assistance. All children, whether born in or out of wedlock, shall enjoy the same social protection.

Article 26.

(1) Everyone has the right to education. Education shall be free, at least in the elementary and fundamental stages. Elementary education shall be compulsory. Technical and professional education shall be made generally available and higher education shall be equally accessible to all on the basis of merit.

(2) Education shall be directed to the full development of the human personality and to the strengthening of respect for human rights and fundamental freedoms. It shall promote understanding, tolerance and friendship among all nations, racial or religious groups, and shall further the activities of the United Nations for the maintenance of peace.

(3) Parents have a prior right to choose the kind of education that shall be given to their children.

Article 27.

(1) Everyone has the right freely to participate in the cultural life of the community, to enjoy the arts and to share in scientific advancement and its benefits.

(2) Everyone has the right to the protection of the moral and material interests resulting from any scientific, literary or artistic production of which he is the author.

Article 28.

Everyone is entitled to a social and international order in which the rights and freedoms set forth in this Declaration can be fully realized.

Article 29.

(1) Everyone has duties to the community in which alone the free and full development of his personality is possible.

(2) In the exercise of his rights and freedoms, everyone shall be subject only to such limitations as are determined by law solely for the purpose of securing due recognition and respect for the rights and freedoms of others and of meeting the just requirements of morality, public order and the general welfare in a democratic society.

(3) These rights and freedoms may in no case be exercised contrary to the purposes and principles of the United Nations.

Article 30.

Nothing in this Declaration may be interpreted as implying for any State, group or person any right to engage in any activity or to perform any act aimed at the destruction of any of the rights and freedoms set forth herein.

References

Abu-Jamal, Mumia. *Live from Death Row*. Reading, MA: Addison-Wesley, 1995.

———. *Death Blossoms: Reflections from a Prisoner of Conscience*. Farmington, MA: The Plough Publishing House, 1996.

Adam, Barry. *The Rise of a Gay and Lesbian Movement*. Rev. ed. New York, NY: Twayne, 1995.

Alexander, A. *The Farrakhan Factor*. New York, NY: Grove Press, 1998.

Alexander, Ewan, ed. *Voice of Indigenous Peoples*. Santa Fe, NM: Clear Light Publishers, 1994.

Amnesty International. *United States of America: Rights for All*. New York, NY: Amnesty International, 1998.

————. *Amnesty Report 2001*. New York, NY: Amnesty International, 2001.

————. *Broken Bodies, Shattered Minds: Torture and Ill-treatment of Women*. New York, NY: Amnesty International, 2001.

————. *Refugees*. New York, NY: Amnesty International, 1997.

————. *Torture Worldwide*. New York, NY: Amnesty International, 2000.

Anderson, M. and Patricia Hill Collins, ed. *Race, Class, and Gender: An Anthology*. Belmont, CA: Wadsworth, 1998.

Arden, Harvey, ed. *Prison Writings: My Life Is a Sundance: Leonard Peltier United States Prisoner # 89637–132*. New York: St. Martin's Press, 1999.

Bell, Derrick. *Faces at the Bottom of the Well: The Permanence of Racism*. New York, NY: Basic Books, 1992.

Bloods and Crips. "Bloods/Crips Proposal for L.A.'s Face-Lift." *Why L.A. Happened*. Ed. H. Madhubuti. Los Angeles, CA: Third World Press, 1993.

Bové, Jose and Francois Dufour. *The World Is Not for Sale: Farmers against Junk Food*. NY: Verso, 2001.

Boyte, Harry. *Commonwealth: A Return to Citizen Politics*. New York, NY: Free Press, 1989.

Branch, Taylor. *Parting the Waters: America in the King Years, 1954–63*. New York, NY: Simon and Schuster, 1988.

————. *Pillar of Fire: America in the King Years, 1963–65*. New York, NY: Simon and Schuster, 1998.

Bratton, M. "After Mandela's Miracle in South Africa." *Current History* 97 (1998): 214–219.

Breitman, G., ed. *Malcolm X Speaks: Selected Speeches and Statements*. New York, NY: Grove Press, 1965.

Broude, Norma and Mary D. Garrard, ed. *The Power of Feminist Art*. New York, NY: Harry Abrams, Inc., 1994.

Brown, Dee. *Bury My Heart at Wounded Knee*. New York, NY: Holt, Rinehart and Winston, 1971.

Bullard, Robert. *Confronting Environmental Racism: Voices from the Grassroots*. Boston, MA: South End Press, 1993.

Burgos-Debray, E., ed. *I, Rigoberta Menchú: An Indian Woman in Guatemala*. London: Verso, 1984.

Burns, Stewart. *Social Movements of the 1960s: Searching for Democracy*. New York, NY: Twayne, 1990.

Campbell, H. *Rasta and Resistance: From Marcus Garvey to Walter Rodney*. Trenton, NJ: Africa World Press, 1987.

Carmichael, Stokley and Charles Hamilton. *Black Power: The Politics of Liberation in America*. New York, NY: Random House, 1967.

Carson, Claybonne, David J. Janow, Gerald Gill, Vincent Hardy, and Darlene Clark Hines, ed. *The Eyes on the Prize Civil Rights Reader: Documents, Speeches and Firsthand Accounts from the Black Freedom Struggle*. New York, NY: Penguin Books, 1991.

Chinosole, ed. *Schooling the Generations in the Politics of Prison*. Berkeley, CA: New Earth Publications, 1996.

Chomsky, Noam. *Secrets, Lies and Democracy*. Tucson, AZ: Odonian Press, 1994.

———. *The Prosperous Few and the Restless Many*. Tucson, AZ: Odonian Press, 1994.

———. *9–11*, New York, NY: Seven Stories Press, 2001.

Chuck D. with Y. Yah. *Fight the Power: Rap, Race and Reality*. New York, NY: Delacorte Press, 1997.

Clark, Steve, ed. *Nelson Mandela Speaks: Foraging a Democratic Nonracial South Africa*. New York: Pathfinder, 1993.

Cleaver, Eldridge. *Soul on Ice*. New York, NY: Random House, 1968.

Cockcraft, Eva, John Weber and James Cockcraft. *Toward a People's Art: The Contemporary Mural Movement*. New York, NY: E. P. Dutton, 1977.

Collins, Patricia Hill. *Black Feminist Thought: Knowledge, Consciousness and the Politics of Empowerment*. Boston, MA: Unwin Hyman, 1990.

Cone, James. *Martin and Malcolm: A Dream or a Nightmare*. Maryknoll, NY: Orbis, 1991.

———. *Black Theology and Black Power*. Maryknoll, NY: Orbis Books, 1997.

Cooper, Martha and Henry Chalfant. *Subway Art*. New York: Henry Holt and Company, 1984.

Cornell, T., R. Ellsberg and J. Forest, ed. *A Penny a Copy: Readings from the Catholic Worker*. Mary Knoll, NY: Orbis, 1995.

Cose, Ellis. *Color-Blind: Seeing Beyond Race in a Race-Obsessed World*. New York, NY: Harper Perennial, 1997.

Cruikshank, M. *The Gay and Lesbian Liberation Movement*. New York, NY: Routledge, Chapman and Hall, 1992.

Dalton, H. *Racial Healing: Confronting the Fear between Blacks and Whites*. New York, NY: Anchor, 1995.

Davis, Angela. *Women, Race and Class*. New York, NY: Random House, 1981.

Declaration of Independence and the Constitution of the United States. New York, NY: Penguin, 1995.

Deloria, Vine, Jr. *Custer Died for Your Sins*. New York, NY: Macmillan, 1969.

————. *Behind the Trail of Broken Treaties*. New York, NY: Delacorte, 1974.

Denisoff, R. Serge. *Sing a Song of Social Significance*. Bowling Green: KY Bowling Green University Press, 1972.

Doob, C. B. *Racism: An American Caldron*. New York, NY: Longman, 1999.

Draher, Patricia and John P. Pierce, ed. *Compassion and Protest*. New York: Cross River Press, 1991.

Duberman, Martin. *Stonewall*. New York, NY: Plume, 1993.

Due, L. *Joining the Tribe: Growing Up Gay and Lesbian in the '90s*. New York, NY: Anchor, 1995.

Elliott, M. "The New Radicals." *Newsweek* 13 (1999) Dec. 21–25.

Faludi, Susan. *Backlash: The Undeclared War against American Women*. New York, NY: Crown, 1991.

Fanon, Franz. *The Wretched of the Earth*. New York, NY: Grove Press, 1963.

Feinberg, Leslie. *Transgender Warriors*. Boston: Beacon Press, 1996.

Felshin, Nina, ed. *But Is It Art? The Spirit of Art as Activism*. Seattle, WA: Bay Press, 1995.

Feree, M. and B. Hess. *Controversy and Coalition: The New Feminist Movement across Three Decades of Change*. Rev. ed. New York, NY: Twayne, 1995.

Fletcher, J., T. Jones and S. Latringer. *Still Black, Still Strong: Survivors of the War against Black Revolutionaries*. New York, NY: Semiotext(e), 1993.

Foner, P., ed. *The Black Panthers Speak*. Philadelphia: J. B. Lippincott, 1970.

Friedan, Betty. *The Feminine Mystique*. New York, NY: Dell, 1963.

Golden, R., M. McConnell, P. Mueller, C. Popper, and M. Turkovic. *Dangerous Memories: Invasion and Resistance Since 1492*. Chicago, IL: Chicago Religions Task Force on Central America, 1991.

Gomez-Quinones, J. *Mexican Students Por la Razda: The Chicano Student Movement in Southern California, 1969–1977*. Santa Barbara, CA: Editorial la Causa, 1978.

Hacker, Andrew. *Two Nations: Black and White, Separate, Hostile, Unequal*. New York, NY: Ballantine Books, 1992.

Hampton, H. and S. Fayer, ed. *Voices of Freedom: An Oral History of the Civil Rights Movement from the 1950s Through the 1980s*. New York, NY: Bantam, 1991.

Harris, B. "The Scoop on the WTO." *Mother Jones*, Nov 30, 1991: 21–25.

Harris, D. "WTO Watch: Explaining the Mess." *Mother Jones*, Dec. 7, 1999: 14–17.

Harwood, R. *Mandela*. New York, NY: Plume, 1987.

Hennelly, A., ed. *Liberation Theology: A Documentary History*. Maryknoll, NY: Orbis, 1990.

hooks, bell. *Black Looks: Race and Representation*. Boston, MA: South End Press, 1992.

———. *Feminist Theory from Margin to Center*. Boston, MA: South End Press, 1984.

———. *Killing Rage: Ending Racism*. New York, NY: Henry Holt, 1995.

———. *Where We Stand: Class Matters*. New York, NY: Routledge, 2000.

Hunter, N., Michaelson, S., & Stoddard, T. *ACLU Handbook: The Rights of Lesbians and Gay Men*. 3rd ed. Carbondale, IL: Southern Illinois University Press, 1992.

Ishay, M., ed. *The Human Rights Reader: Major Political Essays, Speeches and Documents from the Bible to the Present*. New York, NY: Routledge, 1997.

Jacobs, Karrie and Steven Heller. *Angry Graphics: Protest Posters of the Reagan/Bush Era*. Layton, UT: Gibbs-Smith, 1992.

Jacobson, D., ed. *The Immigration Reader: America in Multidisciplinary Perspective*. Malden, MA: Blackwell, 1998.

James, J., ed. *The Angela Y. Davis Reader*. Malden, MA: Blackwell, 1998.

Jencks, Christopher. *Rethinking Social Policy: Race, Poverty and the Underclass*. New York, NY: Harper Perennial, 1992.

Jones, Charles, ed. *The Black Panthers Reconsidered*. Baltimore, MD: Black Classics, 1998.

Joseph, A., Jr., T. Thomas and J. Eden. *Wounded Knee: Lest We Forget*. 2nd ed. Cody, WY: Buffalo Bill Historical Center, 1993.

Kendall, D. *Race, Class and Gender in a Diverse Society*. Needham Heights, MA: Allyn and Bacon, 1997.

Klass, M. *Ordered Universes: Approaches to the Anthropology of Religion*. Boulder, CO: Westview, 1995.

Kotlowitz, Alex. *There Are No Children Here*. New York, NY: Anchor, 1991.

Kozol, Jonathan. *Amazing Grace: The Lives of Children and the Conscience of the Nation*. New York, NY: Harper Perennial. 1995.

—————. *Savage Inequalities: Children in America's Schools*. New York, NY: Harper Perennial, 1992.

LaDuke, Winona. *All Our Relations: Native Struggles for Land and Life*. Boston, MA: South End Press, 1999.

Levy, J. *Cesar Chavez: Autobiography of a La Causa*. New York, NY: W.W. Norton, 1975.

Lewis, W. *Soul Rebels: The Rastafari*. Prospect Heights, IL: Waveland Press, 1993.

Lorde, Audre. *Sister Outsider: Essays and Speeches*. Freedom, CA: Crossing Press, 1984.

Lubiano, W., ed. *The House That Race Built*. New York, NY: Vintage Books, 1988.

Madhubuti, H., ed. *Why L.A. Happened*. New York, NY: World Press, 1993.

Malcolm X. *Malcolm X Speaks*. New York, NY: Grove Press, 1965.

—————. *Two Speeches by Malcolm X*. New York, NY: Pathfinder, 1965.

Mandela, Nelson. *Nelson Mandela Speaks: Forging a Democratic Nonracial South Africa*. New York, NY: Pathfinder, 1993.

Marcus, E. *Making History: The Struggle for Gay and Lesbian Equal Rights, 1945–1990*. New York, NY: HarperCollins, 1992.

Martin, P., and E. Midgey. "Immigration to the United States." *Population Bulletin*. 54 Jun. 1999: 12.

Matthiessen, Peter. *Sal Si Puedes: Cesar Chavez and the New American Revolution*. New York, NY: Dell, 1969.

————. *In the Spirit of Crazy Horse: The Story of Leonard Peltier and the FBI's War on AIM*. New York, NY:Vintage,1991.

McChesney, Robert W. *Rich Media, Poor Democracy*. New York, NY: New Press, 1999.

McCloud, B. *African American Islam*. New York, NY: Routledge, 1995.

McKissack, Patricia and Frederick L. McKissack. *American Slave Revolts: Rebels against Slavery*. New York, NY: Scholastic, 1999.

Millman, M., and R. Moss Kanter, ed. *Another Voice: Feminist Perspectives on Social Life and Social Science*. New York, NY: Octagon, 1976.

Mills, C. Wright. *The Sociological Imagination*. New York, NY: Oxford University Press, 1959.

Mooney, Patrick H. and Theo J. Majka. *Farmers' and Farm Workers' Movement: Social Protest in American Agriculture*. New York, NY: Twayne, 1995.

Moraga, C. and G. Anzaldua, ed. *This Bridge Called My Back: Writings by Radical Women of Color*. Watertown, MA: Persephone Press, 1981.

Morrison, Toni. *Beloved*. New York, NY: Plume, 1987.

————. "Home" *The House That Race Built*. Ed. W. Lubiano. New York, NY: Vintage, 1997.

————. *The Bluest Eye*. New York, NY: Holt, Rhinehart & Winston, 1970.

Munoz, C. *Youth, Identity and Power: The Chicano Movement*. New York, NY: Verso, 1989.

Murton, Thomas. *Gandhi on Non-Violence*. New York, NY: New Directions, 1965.

Nelson-Pallmeyer, Jack. *School of the Assassins:Guns, Greed, and Globalization*. Maryknoll, NY: Orbis Books, 2001.

Noble, J., J. Cover and M. Janagashita. *The World's Youth*. Washington, DC: Population Reference Bureau, 1996.

Novick, G. *Genocide against the Indians*. New York, NY: Pathfinder, 1970.

Patterson, Orlando. *The Ordeal of Integration: Progress and Resentment in America's Racial Crisis*. New York, NY: Civitas/Counterpoint, 1997.

————. *Rituals of Blood: Consequences of Slavery in Two American Centuries*. New York, NY: Basic Civitas, 1998.

Patton, Susan. *African-American Art*. New York, NY: Oxford University Press, 1998.

Payne, Charles. "Ella Baker and Models of Social Change." *Signs* 14:4 (1989): 885–899.

Plaskow, J. and Carol P. Christ, ed. *Weaving the Visions: New Patterns in Feminist Spirituality*. San Francisco, CA: Harper and Row, 1989.

Powell, Richard J. *Black Art and Culture in the 20th Century*. London: Thames and Hudson, 1997.

Reagan Johnson, Bearnice. "Coalition Politics: Turning the Century." *Homegirls: A Black Feminist Anthology*. ed. B. Smith. New York, NY: Kitchen Table Press, 1983.

Roediger, D., ed. *Black on White: Black Writers on What It Means to Be White*. New York, NY: Schocken, 1998.

Rose, Tricia. *Black Noise: Rap Music and Black Culture in Contemporary America*. Hanover, NH: Wesleyan University Press, 1994.

Rothenberg, P., ed. *Race, Class and Gender in the U. S.: An Integrated Study*. 4th ed. New York, NY: St. Martin's Press, 1998.

Rowbotham, S. *Women in Movement: Feminism and Social Action*. NY: Routledge, Chapman and Hall, 1992.

Sakorsky, R. and F. Wei-Han Ho., ed. *Sounding Off! Music as Subversion/Resistance/Revolution*. Brooklyn, NY: Autonomedia, 1995.

Schlosser, Eric, *Fast Food Nation*, Boston: Houghton Mifflin, 2001.

Seager, Joan. *The State of Women in the World Atlas*. New York, NY: Penguin, 1997.

Shakur, Sanyika. *Monster: The Autobiography of an LA Gang Member*. New York, NY: Penguin, 1993.

Shaw, Randy. *The Activists Handbook: A Primer for the 1990s and Beyond*. Berkeley: University of California Press, 1996.

Shilts, Randy. *And the Band Played On: People, Politics and the AIDS Epidemic*. New York, NY: Penguin, 1988.

Shiva, Vandana. "Staying Alive: Development, Ecology and Women." *The Human Rights Reader: Major Political Essays, Speeches and Documents from the Bible to the Present*. ed. M. Ishay. New York, NY: Routledge, 1997: 253–263.

———. *Biopiracy*. Boston, MA: South End Press, 1997.

———. *Stolen Harvest*. Boston, MA: South End Press, 2000.

———. *Water Wars*. Boston, MA: South End Press, 2002.

Shute, S. and S. Hurley, ed. *On Human Rights: Oxford Amnesty Lectures.* New York, NY: Basic Books, 1993.

Signorile, M. *Queer in America: Sex, Media and the Closets of Power.* New York, NY: Anchor, 1993.

Smith, Anna Deavere. *Fires in the Mirror.* New York, NY: Anchor, 1993.

———. *Twilight: Los Angeles,* 1992. New York, NY: Anchor, 1994.

Smith, Dorothy. (1987). *The Everyday World as Problematic: A Feminist Sociology.* Boston, MA: Northeastern University Press, 1987.

Stan, Adele. *Debating Sexual Correctness.* New York, NY: Anchor, 1994.

Sturgeon, Noel. *Ecofeminist Natures: Race, Gender, Feminist Theory and Practical Action.* New York, NY: Routledge, 1997.

Sturken, Marita. *Tangled Memories: Vietnam War, The AIDS Epidemic and the Politics of Remembering.* Berkely, CA: University of California Press, 1997.

Taylor, R. *Sweatshops in the Sun: Child Labor on the Farm.* Boston, MA: Beacon Press, 1973.

———. *Chavez and the Farmworkers: A Study in the Acquisition of Power.* Boston, MA: Beacon Press, 1975.

Thompson, B. and S. Tyagi, ed. *Names We Call Home: Autobiography of Racial Identity.* New York, NY: Routledge, 1996.

Thomas, Janet, *The Battle in Seattle,* Golden, CO: Fulcrum, 2000.

United Nations. *Human Rights: A Compilation of International Instruments.* Vol. 1. New York, NY: United Nations Publications, 1999.

Upchurch, C. *Convicted in the Womb: One Man's Journey from Prisoner to Peacemaker.* New York, NY: Bantam, 1997.

Walker, Alice. *In Search of Our Mother's Gardens.* New York, NY: Harcourt Brace Jovanovich, 1983.

———. *Possessing the Secret of Joy.* New York, NY: Harcourt Brace Jovanovich, 1992.

———. *The Color Purple.* New York, NY: Harcourt Brace, 1982.

Walker, Alice and P. Parmar. *Warrior Marks: Female Genital Mutilation and the Sexual Blinding of Women.* New York, NY: Harcourt Brace Jovanovich, 1993.

Walker, S., C. Spohn and M. Delone. *The Color of Justice: Race, Ethnicity and Crime in America.* 3rd ed. Belmont, CA: Wadsworth, 2000.

Wallace, R., ed. *Feminism and Sociological Theory*. Newbury Park, CA: Sage, 1989.

Ward, Martha C. *A World Full of Women*. 2nd ed. Boston, MA: Allyn and Bacon, 1999.

Washington, J., ed. *I Have a Dream: Writing and Speeches That Changed the World/Martin Luther King Jr*. New York, NY: HarperCollins, 1992.

Weitz, R., ed. *The Politics of Women's Bodies: Sexuality, Appearance and Behavior*. New York, NY: Oxford, 1998.

Welton, Neva and Linda Wolf. *Global Uprising*, Gabriola Island, BC: New Society, 2001.

West, Cornell. *Race Matters*. New York, NY: Vintage, 1993.

Whelehan, I. *Modern Feminist Thought*. New York, NY: University Press, 1995.

Wilson, William Julius. *The Truly Disadvantaged: The Inner City, the Underclass and Public Policy*. Chicago: University of Chicago Press, 1987.

———. *When Work Disappears: The New World of the Urban Poor*. New York, NY: Alfred A. Knopf, 1996.

Wilson, S. K., ed. *The Crisis Reader: Stories, Poetry and Essays from the NAACP's Crisis Magazine*. New York, NY: Random House, 1999.

———. *The Opportunity Reader: Stories, Poems and Essays from the Urban League's Opportunity Reader*. New York, NY: Random House, 1999.

Wolf, Naomi. *The Beauty Myth*. New York, NY: Anchor, 1991.

www.arc.org

www.census.gov

www.forbes.com

www.gpo.gov

www.acf.dhhs.gov

Yanker, Gary. *Prop Art: Over 1000 Contemporary Political Posters*. New York, NY: Darien House, Inc. 1972.

Supplemental Readings

American poet Walt Whitman (1819–1892) is remembered for his unconventional and revolutionary literary style that exalted both the individual and American democracy. His collection of poems, Leaves of Grass (1855), is considered one of the great works of American literature.

Song of Myself

Walt Whitman

[1]

I CELEBRATE MYSELF,
And what I assume you shall assume,
For every atom belonging to me as good belongs to you.

I loafe and invite my soul,
I lean and loafe at my ease . . . . observing a spear of summer grass.

[2]

Houses and rooms are full of perfumes . . . . the shelves are crowded
   with perfumes,
I breathe the fragrance myself, and know it and like it,
The distillation would intoxicate me also, but I shall not let it.

The atmosphere is not a perfume . . . . it has no taste of the distillation
   . . . . it is odorless,
It is for my mouth forever . . . . I am in love with it,
I will go to the bank by the wood and become undisguised and naked,
I am mad for it to be in contact with me.

The smoke of my own breath,
Echoes, ripples, and buzzed whispers . . . . loveroot, silkthread, crotch and
   vine,
My respiration and inspiration . . . . the beating of my heart . . . . the passing of blood and air through my lungs,
The sniff of green leaves and dry leaves, and of the shore and darkcolored
   sea-rocks, and of hay in the barn,
The sound of the belched words of my voice . . . . words loosed to the
   eddies of the wind,

A few light kisses . . . . a few embraces . . . . a reaching around of arms,
The play of shine and shade on the trees as the supple boughs wag,

The delight alone or in the rush of the streets, or along the fields and hill-
    sides,
The feeling of health . . . . the full-noon trill . . . . the song of me rising from
    bed and meeting the sun.

Have you reckoned a thousand acres much? Have you reckoned the earth
    much?
Have you practiced so long to learn to read?
Have you felt so proud to get at the meaning of poems?

Stop this day and night with me and you shall possess the origin of all
    poems,
You shall possess the good of the earth and sun . . . . there are millions of
    suns left,
You shall no longer take things at second or third hand . . . . nor look through
    the eyes of the dead . . . . nor feed on the spectres in books,
You shall not look through my eyes either, nor take things from me,
You shall listen to all sides and filter them from yourself.

[3]
I have heard what the talkers were talking . . . . the talk of the beginning
    and the end,
But I do not talk of the beginning or the end.

There was never any more inception than there is now,
Nor any more youth or age than there is now;
And will never be any more perfection than there is now,
Nor any more heaven or hell than there is now.

Urge and urge and urge,
Always the procreant urge of the world.

Out of the dimness opposite equals advance . . . . Always substance and
    increase,
Always a knit of identity . . . . always distinction . . . . always a breed of life.
To elaborate is no avail . . . . Learned and unlearned feel that it is so.

Sure as the most certain sure . . . . plumb in the uprights, well entretied,
    braced in the beams,
Stout as a horse, affectionate, haughty, electrical,
I and this mystery here we stand.

Clear and sweet is my soul . . . . and clear and sweet is all that is not my
    soul.

Lack one lacks both . . . . and the unseen is proved by the seen,
Till that becomes unseen and receives proof in its turn.

Showing the best and dividing it from the worst, age vexes age,
Knowing the perfect fitness and equanimity of things, while they discuss
    I am silent, and go bathe and admire myself.

Welcome is every organ and attribute of me, and of any man hearty and
    clean,
Not an inch nor a particle of an inch is vile, and none shall be less famil-
    iar than the rest.

I am satisfied . . . . I see, dance, laugh, sing;
As God comes a loving bedfellow and sleeps at my side all night and
    close on the peep of the day,
And leaves for me baskets covered with white towels bulging the house
    with their plenty,
Shall I postpone my acceptation and realization and scream at my eyes,
That they turn from gazing after and down the road,
And forthwith cipher and show me to a cent,
Exactly the contents of one, and exactly the contents of two, and which is
    ahead?

[4]

Trippers and askers surround me,
People I meet . . . . the effect upon me of my early life. . . . of the ward and
    city I live in . . . . of the nation,
The latest news . . . . discoveries, inventions, societies . . . . authors old and
    new,
My dinner, dress, associates, looks, business, compliments, dues,
The real or fancied indifference of some man or woman I love,
The sickness of one of my folks—or of myself . . . . or ill-doing . . . .or loss or
    lack of money . . . . or depressions or exaltations,
They come to me days and nights and go from me again,
But they are not the Me myself.

Apart from the pulling and hauling stands what I am,
Stands amused, complacent, compassionating, idle, unitary,
Looks down, is erect, bends an arm on an impalpable certain rest,
Looks with its sidecurved head curious what will come next,
Both in and out of the game, and watching and wondering at it.

Backward I see in my own days where I sweated through fog with lin
    guists and contenders,
I have no mockings or arguments . . . . I witness and wait.

[5]

I believe in you my soul . . . . the other I am must not abase itself to you,
And you must not be abased to the other.

Loafe with me on the grass . . . . loose the stop from your throat,
Not words, not music or rhyme I want . . . . not custom or lecture, not
    even the best,
Only the lull I like, the hum of your valved voice.

I mind how we lay in June, such a transparent summer morning;
You settled your head athwart my hips and gently turned over upon me,
And parted the shirt from my bosom-bone, and plunged your tongue to
    my barestript heart,
And reached till you felt my beard, and reached till you held my feet.

Swiftly arose and spread around me the peace and joy and knowledge
    that pass all the art and argument of the earth;
And I know that the hand of God is the elderhand of my own,
And I know that the spirit of God is the eldest brother of my own,
And that all the men ever born are also my brothers . . . . and the women
    my sisters and lovers,
And that a kelson of the creation is love;
And limitless are leaves stiff or drooping in the fields,
And brown ants in the little wells beneath them,
And mossy scabs of the wormfence, and heaped stones, and elder and
    mullen and pokeweed.

Barbara Kingsolver (b. 1955) is a novelist, essayist, and human rights activist whose work includes The Bean Trees *(1988),* Animal Dreams *(1990),* The Poisonwood Bible *(1998), and* Small Wonder *(2002). In addition to writing, she has been a book reviewer for the* New York Times *since 1988 and the* Los Angeles Times *since 1989. She holds a M.S. from the University of Arizona, and makes her home in Tucson.*

Civil Disobedience at Breakfast

Barbara Kingsolver

I have a child who was born with the gift of focus, inclined to excel at whatever she earnestly pursues. Soon after her second birthday she turned to the earnest pursuit of languor, and shot straight through the ranks to world-class dawdler. I thought it might be my death.

Like any working stiff of a mother keeping the family presentable and solvent, I lived in a flat-out rush. My daughter lived on Zen time. These doctrines cannot find peace under one roof. I tried everything I could think of to bring her onto my schedule: five-minute countdowns, patient explanations of our itinerary, frantic appeals, authoritarianism, the threat of taking her to preschool *exactly* however she was dressed when the clock hit seven. (She went in PJs, oh delight! Smug as Brer Rabbit in the briars.) The more I tried to hurry us along, the more meticulously unhurried her movements became.

My brother pointed out that this is how members of the Japanese Parliament carry out a filibuster—by shuffling up to the voting box so extremely slowly it can take one person an hour to get across the room, and a month or two to get the whole vote in. It's called "cow walking," he reported. Perfect, I said. At my house we are having a Cow Life.

And that's how it was, as I sat at breakfast one morning watching my darling idle dangerously with her breakfast. I took a spectacularly deep breath and said, in a voice I imagined was calm, "We need to be going very soon. Please be careful not to spill your orange juice."

She looked me in the eye and coolly knocked over her glass.

Bang, my command was dead. Socks, shirt, and overalls would have to be changed, setting back the start of my workday another thirty minutes. Thirty-five, if I wanted to show her who was boss by enforcing a five-minute time-out. She knew exactly what she was doing. A filibuster.

I'd been warned the day would dawn when my sweet, tractable daughter would become a Terrible Two. And still this entirely predictable thing broadsided me, because in the beginning she was *mine*—as much a part of my body, literally, as my own arms and legs. The milk I drank knit her bones in place, and her hiccups jarred me awake at night. Children come to us as a dramatic coup of the body's fine inner will, and the process of sorting out "self" from "other" is so gradual as to be invisible to a mother's naked soul. In our hearts, we can't expect one of our own limbs to stand up one day and announce its own agenda. It's too much like a Stephen King novel.

Later in the day I called a friend to tell my breakfast war story. She had a six-year-old, so I expected commiseration. The point of my call, really, was to hear that one could live through this and that it ended. Instead, my friend was quiet. "You know," she said finally, "Amanda never went through that. I worry about her. She works so hard to please everybody. I'm afraid she'll never know how to please herself."

A land mine exploded in the back of my conscience. My child was becoming all I'd ever wanted.

The way of a parent's love is a fool's progress, for sure. We lean and we lean on the cherished occupation of making ourselves obsolete. I applauded my child's first smile, and decoded her doubtful early noises to declare them "language." I touched the ground in awe of her first solo steps, as if she alone among primates had devised bipedal locomotion. Each of these events in its turn—more than triumph and less than miracle—was a lightening, feather by feather, of the cargo of anxious hope that was delivered to me with my baby at the slip of our beginning.

"We teach our children one thing only, as we were taught: to wake up," claims Annie Dillard. That's just about the whole truth, a parent's incantation. Wake up, keep breathing, look alive. It's only by forming separateness and volition that our children relieve us of the deepest parental dread: that they might somehow *not* wake up, after all, but fail to thrive and grow, remaining like Sleeping Beauty in the locked glass case of a wordless infancy. More times than I could count, in those early days, I was stopped, in the grocery by some kindly matron who exclaimed over my burbling pastel lump of baby: "Don't you wish you could keep them like that forever?" Exactly that many times, I bit the urge to shout back, "Are you out of your mind?"

From the day she emerged open-mouthed in the world, I've answered my child's cries with my own gaping wonder, scrambling to part the curtains and show the way to wakefulness. I can think or feel no more irresistible impulse. In magnificent pantomime, I demonstrate to my small shadow the thousand and one ways to be a person, endowed with opinions. How could it be a surprise that after two years the lessons started to take? The shadow began to move of its own accord, exhibiting the skill of opinion by any means necessary. Barreling pell-mell through life was not my daughter's style; a mother ought to arrange mornings to allow time for communing with the oatmeal—that was her first opinion. How could I fail to celebrate this new red-letter day? There had been a time when I'd reduced my own personal code to a button on my blue-jeans jacket that advised: *question authority*. A few decades later, the motto of my youth blazed resplendent on my breakfast table, the color of Florida sunshine. I could mop up, now, with maternal pride, or eat crow.

Oh, how slight the difference between "independent" and "ornery." A man who creates spectacular sculptures out of old car bodies might be a wonderful character, until he moves in next door. Children who lip off to their parents are cute in movies because they're in movies, and not in our life. Another of my brother's wise nuggets, offered over the phone one Saturday while I tried to manage family chaos and pour a cement porch foundation, was: "Remember, kids are better in the abstract than in the concrete." Of all kid abstractions, independence may be the hardest one to accept in the concrete, because we're told how we'll feel about it long before it arrives. It's the mother of all childhood stereotypes, the Terrible Twos.

Now there are stereotypes that encircle a problem like a darn good corral, and there are stereotypes that deliver a problem roaring to our doorstep, and I'm suspicious of this one, the Terrible Twos. If we'd all heard half so much about, say, the "Fat Fours," I'd bet dollars to donuts most four-year-olds would gain lots of weight, and those who didn't would be watched for the first sign of puffiness. Children are adept at becoming what we expect them to be. "Terrible" does not seem, by any stretch, to be a wise expectation. My Spanish-speaking friends—who, incidentally, have the most reliably child-friendly households in my acquaintance—tell me there's no translation for "Terrible Twos" in their language.

The global truth, I think, is that the twos are time-consuming and tidiness-impaired, but not, intrinsically, terrible. A cow in parliament is not a terrible cow. It's just a question of how it fits in with the plan.

The plan in our culture, born under the sign of freedom with mixed-message ascendant, is anyone's guess. The two developmental stages we parents are most instructed to dread—the twos and teens—both involve a child's formation of a sovereign identity. This, a plumb horror of assertive children, in the land of assertiveness training and weekend seminars on getting what you want through creative visualization. Expert advice on the subject of children's freedom is a pawnshop of clashing platitudes:

We are to cultivate carefully the fragile stem of self-esteem. We are to consider a thing called "tough love," which combines militarist affection with house arrest, as remedy for adolescent misbehavior. We are to remember our children are only passing through us like precious arrows launched from heaven, but in most states we're criminally liable for whatever target they whack. The only subject more loaded with contradictions is the related matter of sex, which—in the world we've packaged for adolescents—is everywhere, visibly, the goal, and nowhere allowed. Let them eat it, drink it, wear it on their jeans, but don't for heaven's sakes pass out condoms, they might be inspired to *do* it. This is our inheritance, the mixed pedigree of the Puritans and Free Enterprise. We're to dream of our children growing up to be decision makers and trend setters, and we're to dream it through our teeth, muttering that a trend-setting toddler is a pain, and a teenager's decisions are a tour down the River Styx. How, then, to see it through?

The traditional camp says to hold the reins hard until the day we finally drop them, wish our big babies Godspeed, and send them out to run the world. I say, Good luck, it sounds like we'll have men and women with the mental experience of toddlers running domestic and foreign policy. (And, in fact, it sometimes appears that we do.) This is the parenting faction that also favors spanking. Studies of corporal punishment show, reliably, that kids who are spanked are more likely to be aggressive with their peers. For all the world, you'd think they were just little people, learning what they were taught.

I hold with those who favor allowing kids some freedom to work out problems their own way, and even make some messes, before we set them on Capitol Hill. I do not hold that this is easy. The most assiduous task of parenting is to divine the difference between boundaries and bondage. In every case, bondage is quicker. Boundaries, however carefully explained, can be reinterpreted creatively time and again. Yes, it's okay to pet the dog, and yes again on taking a bath, but *not* the dog *in* the tub. No to painting on the wall, no again to painting on the dog. I spent many years sounding to myself like Dr. Seuss: Not in a box! Not with a fox! Not on a train! Not in the rain!

The hardest boundaries to uphold are those that I know, in my heart, I have drawn for no higher purpose than my own convenience. I swore when I was pregnant I would never say to my child those stupid words "Because I said so!" Lord, have mercy. No contract I've ever signed has cost me so much. "Because I said so!" is not a real reason. But how about "Because if you do that again Mommy will scream, run into the bushes, pluck out the ovaries that made you, and cast them at the wild dogs." What price mental health? When your kid knocks over the orange juice, or ditches school, do you really have to listen to her inner wishes or can you just read the riot act?

Maybe both. Maybe there's not time for both right this minute—there never is, because life with children always bursts to fullness in the narrowest passages, like a life raft inflating in the emergency exit. If that's the case, then maybe the riot act now, and the other, listening to inner wishes, as soon as possible after you've worked free of the burning wreck.

During my short tenure as a parent I've relived my own childhood in a thousand ways while trying to find my path. Many of the things my parents did for me—most, I would say—are the things I want to do for my own child. Praise incessantly. Hold high expectations. Laugh, sing out loud, celebrate without cease the good luck of getting set down here on a lively earth.

But the world has changed since *Howdy Doody Time*, and some things nearly all parents did back then have been reconsidered. Spanking is one. Another, a little harder to define, has to do with structuring the family's time. My mother's job was me. But now I'm a mother with other work too, and fewer hours each day to devote to my main preoccupation of motherhood. I represent the norm for my generation, the throng of maternal employed, going about the honest work of the planet with gusto and generally no real alternative. The popular wisdom is that families used to be more kid-centered than they are now. I'm not so sure that's true. It's just different. My mother had kids to contend with from dawn till doom. She was (is) educated, creative, and much of the time the only people around for her to talk with had snakes in their pockets. My father worked very hard, as good fathers verily did. I had the guarantee of three squares daily, the run of several hundred acres of farms and wild Kentucky hills, the right to make a pet of anything nonvenomous, and a captive audience for theatrical projects. When my mother is canonized, I will testify that she really did sit through a hundred virtually identical productions, staged by my siblings and me, of the play titled approximately "The Dutch Boy Who Saved His Town by Putting His Finger in the Hole in the Dike." I have no idea why we did this. It seems truly obsessive. I can only offer as defense that we had a soft gray blanket with a hole in it, an irresistible prop. We took rave reviews for granted.

We also understood clearly that, during major family outings and vacations, our parents needed desperately to enjoy themselves. They bundled us into the back of the station wagon and begged us to go into hibernation for two thousand miles, so they could finish a conversation they'd started the previous autumn. I'm sure there were still plenty of times they sacrificed their vacation goals on the altar of my selfishness; I have forgotten these entirely. What I particularly remember instead is one nonstop auto trip to Key West, during which my sibs and I became bored beyond human limits. "Try counting to a million," my father suggested. And this is the point I am getting to: we actually did.

This seems amazing to me now. I could claim to be a victim, but that would be fatuous; my childhood was blessed. In the spectrum of the completely normal fifties family, nuclear units kept pretty much to themselves, and in the interest of everyone's survival, kids had to learn a decent show of obedience.

I'm amazed by the memory of counting to one million in a station wagon, not because I resent having done it myself, but because I can't imagine asking my daughter to do that, or, more to the point, *needing* for her to do it. When she and I head out on a car trip, we fall right into a fierce contest of White Horse Zit or license-plate alphabet. Childish enterprises, since they aren't my job, are in a sense my time off, my vacation. In spite of the well-publicized difficulties of balancing career and family, when I compare my life to my mother's I sometimes feel like Princess Grace. Each day I spend hours in luxurious silence, doing the work I most love; I have friends and colleagues who talk to me about interesting things, and never carry concealed reptiles. At the end of the day, when Camille and I are reunited after our daily cares, I'm ready for joyful mayhem.

For this reason I was also prepared to search through the pockets of my own soul on the day she and I arrived at our orange-juice impasse. I kept up a good authoritarian front at the time, but understood my daughter's implicit request. What was called for here was some Cow Time, stress free, no holds barred. I decided that after work we would go somewhere, out of the house, away from the call of things that require or provoke an orderly process. Together my two-year-old and I would waste the long last hours of an afternoon.

We went to the zoo. Not very far *into* the zoo, actually; we made it through the front gate and about twenty steps past, to the giant anteater den. There Camille became enraptured with a sturdy metal railing that was meant, I gather, to hold the public back from intimate contact with the giant anteaters. There was no danger, so I let her play on the metal bar.

And play.

After ten minutes I longed to pull her on toward the elephants, because frankly there's only so much looking a right-minded person can do at a giant anteater. But our agenda here was to have no agenda. I did my part.

Looked again at those long anteating noses and those skinky anteating tongues.

Other children materialized on the bar. They clung and they dropped, they skinned the cat and impersonated tree sloths, until their parents eventually pulled them off toward the elephants. My eyes trailed wistfully after those departing families, but I knew I was being tested, and this time I knew I could win. I could refrain from asking my toddler to hurry up even longer than she could persist in sloth. After something less than an hour, she got down from the bar and asked to go home.

Five years have passed since then. Now it sometimes happens that Camille gets up, dresses herself in entirely color-coordinated clothes, and feeds the dog, all before the first peep of the alarm clock. I never cease to be amazed at this miracle, developmental biology. For any parent who needs to hear it today, I offer this: whatever it is, you can live through it, and it ends.

Plenty of psychologists have studied the effects of parents' behavior on the mental health of their children, but few have done the reverse. So Laurence Steinberg's study of 204 families with adolescents broke some new ground. All the families lived in Wisconsin but were otherwise diverse: rural, urban, white, black, brown, single-parented, remarried, nuclear. Steinberg uncovered a truth that crosses all lines: teenagers can make you crazy. Forty percent of the study parents showed a decline in psychological well-being during their children's adolescence. Steinberg even suggests that the so-called "midlife crisis" may be a response to living with teenagers, rather than to the onset of wrinkles and gray hair *per se*. The forty-four-year-old parent with a thirteen-year-old, it turns out, is far more disposed to crisis than the forty-four-year-old parent with an eight-year-old. Marital happiness tends to decline in households with teens, and single parents are more likely to experience difficulty with remarriage. But the study produced one hopeful note for the modern parent: in all family configurations, work is a buffer. Parents with satisfying careers had the best chance of sailing through the storms of their children's adolescence.

Here at last is a rallying cry for the throng of maternal employed. The best defense against a teenager's independence, and probably a toddler's as well, may simply be a matter of quitting before we're fired. Or not *quitting*, exactly, but backing off from eminent domain, happily and with dignity, by expressing ourselves in the serious pursuits and pleasures that we hold apart from parenting. Individuation goes both ways: we may feel less driven to shape a child in our own image if instead we can shape policy or sheet metal, or teach school, or boss around an employee or two. Luckiest of all is the novelist: I get to invent people who will live or die on the page, do exactly as I wish, *because I said so!*

I'm told it is terribly hard to balance career and family and, particularly, creativity. And it is, in fact. Good mothering can't be done by the clock. There are days I ache to throw deadlines to the wind and go hunt snipes. I wish for time to explain the sensible reason for every "no." To wallow in "yes," give over to a cow's timetable, stop the clock, stop watching the pot so it might splendidly boil.

I also long for more time of my own, and silence. My jaw drops when I hear of the rituals some authors use to put themselves in the so-called mood to write: William Gass confesses to spending a couple of hours every morning photographing dilapidated corners of his city. Diane Ackerman begins each summer day "by choosing and arranging flowers for a Zenlike hour or so." She listens to music obsessively, then speed-walks for an hour, every single day. "I don't know whether this helps or not," she allows, in *A Natural History of the Senses*. "My muse is male, has the radiant, silvery complexion of the moon, and never speaks to me directly."

My muse wears a baseball cap, backward. The minute my daughter is on the school bus, he saunters up behind me with a bat slung over his shoulder and says oh so directly, "Okay, author lady, you've got six hours till that bus rolls back up the drive. You can sit down and write, *now*, or you can think about looking for a day job."

As a mother and a writer, I'd be sunk if either enterprise depended on corsages or magic. I start a good day by brushing my teeth; I don't know whether it helps or not, but it does fight plaque. I can relate at least to the utilitarian ritual of Colette, who began her day's writing after methodically picking fleas from her cat. The remarkable poet Lucille Clifton was asked, at a reading I attended, "Why are your poems always short?" Ms. Clifton replied, "I have six children, and a memory that can hold about twenty lines until the end of the day."

I would probably trade in my whole Great Books set for an epic-length poem from the pen of Lucille Clifton. But I couldn't wish away those six distracting children, even as a selfish reader, because I cherish Clifton's work precisely for its maternal passions and trenchant understanding of family. This is the fence we get to walk. I might envy the horses that prance unbridled across the pastures on either side of me, but I know if I stepped away from my fence into the field of "Only Work" or "Only Family," I would sink to my neck. I can hardly remember how I wrote before my child made a grown-up of me, nor can I think what sort of mother I would be if I didn't write. I hold with Dr. Steinberg: by working at something else I cherish, I can give my child room to be a chip off any old block she wants. She knows she isn't the whole of my world, and also that when I'm with her she's the designated center of my universe. On the day she walks away from my house for good, I'll cry and wave a hanky from my lonely balcony; then I'll walk to my study, jump for joy, and maybe do the best work of my life.

It's never easy to take the long view of things, especially in a society that conveys itself to us in four-second camera shots. But in a process as slow and complex as parenting, an eye to the future is an anchor. Raising children is a patient alchemy, which can turn applesauce into an athlete, ten thousand kissed bruises into one solid confidence, and maybe orneriness to independence. It all adds up. From the get-go I've been telling my child she is not just taking up space here, but truly valuable. If she's to believe it, I have to act as if I do. That means obedience is not an absolute value. Hurting people is out of the question, but an obsession with the anteater bar can and will be accommodated. I hope to hold this course as her obsessions grow more complex. For now, whenever the older, wiser parents warn, "Just wait till she's a teenager," I smile and say, "I'm looking forward to that." They think I am insane, impudent, or incredibly naïve. Probably I am. Call it creative visualization.

My time here is up today, for I'm being called to watch a theatrical production entitled approximately "The Princess Fairy Mermaids Who Save the Castle by Murderizing the Monsters and Then Making Them Come Back Alive with Fairy Dust and Be Nice." I've seen this show before. Some days I like it, especially when they tie up the monster with Day-Glo shoelaces and pantyhose. Other days my mind drifts off to that spare, uncluttered studio where I will arrange flowers, Zenlike, when I'm sixty. I'll write great things, and I'll know once and for all the difference between boundaries and bondage.

Writer, poet, and instructor, Patricia Hampl (b. 1946) is Regents' Professor of English at the University of Minnesota, Twin Cities. She is the editor of Burning Bright, *an anthology of sacred poetry (Judaism, Christianity, Islam), and has offered readings, lectures, and workshops both nationally and internationally.*

Look at a Teacup

Patricia Hampl

She bought the teacup in 1939, of all years. It was on sale downtown, because it was a discontinued pattern. Even on sale, it was an extravagance as far as her new in-laws were concerned; it set her apart. She used to say how she just put the money down on that counter and let Aunt Gert sigh as loud as she pleased.

1939. My mother was buying dishes that had come from Czechoslovakia, because they made the best china and she was marrying an American Czech. Most of the teacups are still unbroken. They're mine now, because I'm her daughter and she cleaned out her china cabinet last week. Each piece has a tiny "Czechoslovakia" stamped on the bottom. The cup is thin—you can almost see through its paleness when it's empty; right now, there's tea in it, and its level can be gauged from the shadow outside. The cup is the palest water-green imaginable. Sometimes, in certain lights, it is so pale it doesn't seem green at all, just something not white. It is shiny, and there are thin bands of gold around the edges of the saucer and cup, and again midway down the bowl of the cup and at its base, which is subtly formed into a semi-pedestal. There is also a band of gold on the inner circle of the saucer, but it has been worn away, after so many years, except for a dulled, blurred line. There is no other decoration on the outside of the cup—a bland precision of lines and curved light.

But inside the cup there are flowers, as if someone had scattered a bouquet and it had tumbled into separate blossoms, falling in a full circle around the inside. Some have fallen faster to the bottom of the cup, while some are still floating. The blossoms don't seem to be pasted on the surface like decals, they really appear to be caught in motion. And now, for the first time, alone in my own house (I've never been alone with one of these cups before; they were her company dishes), I see that no two flowers on the cup or the saucer are the same. Each a different flower—different colors, different altitudes of falling, nothing to create a pattern. Yet the cup and saucer together are pure light, something extremely delicate but definite. As refined as a face.

My mother's face, which has fallen into sadness. Nothing tragic ever happened to her—"nothing big," she'll say. I am the one who has wanted something big.

"I know the most important thing in the world," I told her when I was ten.

"Well, what is it?" she asked.

"Work. Work is the most important thing."

Her face showed fear. "Oh, no," she said quickly, trying to sweep away the thought. "No. Family is the important thing. Family, darling." Even then, her voice was sounding a farewell, the first of all those goodbyes mothers say to their daughters.

Or maybe our parting began one day when Dad came up behind her in the kitchen. He kissed her on the back of the neck. She thought they were alone, but my brother and I had followed him into the kitchen. He kissed her neck just where the hair stops. She turned from the sink like a swaying stem, with her hands all full of soapsuds, and put her stem arms around his neck. Her eyes were closed, her arms heavy and soapy. Pure and passionate soap arms of my mother. He drew her down suddenly in a swooping joke of an embrace—a Valentino bend, an antic pose for us giggling kids. He swept her in his arms and gave her lips a clownish kiss. We giggled, and our father laughed and turned to grin at his audience. "My dahling, I *luff* you!" he said to her soulfully. Her body struggled awkwardly, her eyes flew open, and she tried to rise from his clownish embrace.

"No, no," she said. No, no to any joke. She stood at the edge of her red-petalled life. There are buds that never open. "Just let me up," she said. "I've got these dishes to do. Let me *up*." And she plunged her hands back into the dishwater. Every night, she swam with her thoughts in that small sea.

In the cup, amid the bundle of pastel falling flowers at the bottom of the bowl there is another firm, thin gold circlet. It shines up just below the most deeply submerged flower, like a shoreline submerged by a momentary tide of morning tea. The engulfed flowers become oranges and violets—those colors. Above the tea-line there are green leaves and several jots of blue flowers, not deep and bright like cornflowers but a powdery, toneless blue, a monochrome without shadow or cloud. Also, there is the shape of the flowers. Some are plump, all curve and weight. There is a pale lavender rose on the saucer, with a rounded, balled-up cabbage head of petals; and on the opposite side a spiky, orange dahlia-like flower. None of the flowers looks real. They are suggestions, pale, almost unfinished, with occasional sparks of brightness, like a replica of memory itself. There is a slur of recollection about them, something imprecise, seductive, and foggy but held together with a bright bolt of accuracy— perhaps a piercing glance from a long-dead uncle, whose face, all the features, has otherwise faded and gone.

In 1939, in Chicago, my mother was a bride. That was the first year of the war, when Europe began to eat itself raw. In the newspaper picture announcing the marriage, her head had a halo. A golden light was around her head.

"I wasn't one for buying a lot of stuff," she tells me. "You only need so much. I bought what I needed when I got married." In the past few years, she's been giving me many of those things, piece by piece. Every time I go over to visit, she says, "Well, you might as well take the yellow tablecloth." Or there will be a pile of silverware she'll want me to have. These teacups. I'm always walking off with something.

I try to get her to talk about her life, but she won't do that. It's not that she thinks I'm prying. "Well, honey, what do you want to know?" she says. "I mean, what's there to say?" And she pushes her hair, which is still more blond than anything else, away from her face, and she looks really beautiful. I start talking fast, saying how everybody *knows* the world has changed a lot since the Second World War ended, and she was alive when Hitler was in power, for God's sake, and she's lived through something, and it's part of history.

"It wasn't *that* long ago," she says, and flips her honey hair again and lights a cigarette. "Besides, you'd have to talk to somebody from Europe about all that. They lived through it." Once she told me that in high school she'd had an assignment to write an essay about why Hitler was good for Germany. "Personally, I never liked him," she said. "We were always Democrats. But we had that assignment."

So I go over to visit, and we talk and I ask all these questions and she says, "You sound like one of those oral-history projects," and I say, "No, really, I'm interested." I'm always telling her, anything you can remember, any detail—it's really important. Everybody's life is important, I say. I'm interested. I can't even explain why.

Sometimes she says things like "You know, I bet you won't believe this, but we girls, way back—and this wasn't in the country, either—we used to use cotton strips all bundled up, instead of Kotex. And we'd wash them out and use them over again." Or, "The first pair of nylon stockings I bought, they lasted two years. Then stockings started not lasting." Once, she looked across the kitchen table at me and said, almost experimentally, as if she wanted to hear how it would sound aloud, "You know, one time your father came home, just an ordinary day, and I looked up and I wasn't even thinking, it just darted into my head: Someday he'll walk in and I just won't be here, I'll just leave. But it never happened."

None of it amounts to anything, though. Her details don't add up to a life story. Maybe that's why she's been giving me all these things the past few years—her possessions, everything she bought in 1939, the year of her marriage. This teacup, which I look at closely, for a long time, sitting at my own white-and-yellow kitchen table, alone, across the city from her.

The teacup was made in a country far away, of which other countries knew little. An English politician (but you can't go just blaming *him*, my mother says) shook a nation away as he tightly furled his black umbrella. A country lost its absorption in peaceful work, lost its pure science of flinging flowers onto the sides of teacups.

I tell her I believe that something could have been different. What would have happened if someone with an important black umbrella had considered the future of teacups, if powerful men bowed their heads at the difficulties of implanting the waxy tulip on porcelain? Old questions— certain people have tried to answer them, there are books. But many of us still live with the details; the souvenirs of some places are never broken. This cup is a detail, a small uncharred finger from the mid-century bonfire.

I visit my mother. We sit in her blue-and-white kitchen. My mother stands up for the future. "Life goes on, you can't keep going over things," she says. "It's the *flow* of life that counts." She wants me to ride forward into the golden light that she says is the future and all its possibility. "Look ahead," she tells me.

I try, but everything drives me into the past that she insists is safely gone. How can I ride forward on her errand when all the world, even the smallest object, sends me back, sets me wondering over and over about our own strange life and country, always trying to understand history and sexuality. Details, however small, get sorted into their appropriate stories, all right, but I am always holding out for the past and thinking how it keeps coming back at us. No details are disparate, I tell her. Mother, the cups were discontinued because a country was discontinued.

"Oh, but now you're talking politics," she says, and clears off the kitchen table. "Over my head, over my head," she says.

But it's not. That's what makes me mad. She *knows*. They all do, those brides who chose their china in 1939. Many things fell that year, for those brides—not only flowers into teacups. Their bodies fell, paired with other bodies, on beds together for the first time. "But that was no tragedy," she says, smiling, with her hands on the back of a chair. Smiling because she knows after all our talks that I think something was wasted when she first fell. Because I have refused to fall. "Some people just don't want to get married—I know that," she says broadmindedly. But she knows I'm saying marriage isn't *there* anymore; the flowered flannel nightgown isn't being hung on a peg in a closet next to a pair of striped drawstring pajamas anymore. We don't get married anymore, Mother. Don't blame me; I didn't think it up.

"Don't talk like a sausage," she'll say. "Some people—there are always some people who do not *want* to get married. I understand this. I understand you. You don't want to get married. Fine. That's just fine. It's fine. Many people live . . . that way."

Her own marriage, I agree, was no tragedy. It was the old bow pulled across the cello, making its first sexual sound again. Another generation joining the long, low moan. The falling of flowers down the sides of teacups, the plunging bodies on white sheets—I know people could take any amount of this pain. But the falling of the other bodies, the rain of bodies in Europe, that happened that year too, Mother.

Marriage, that's one thing; we agree that for her it was no tragedy, wasn't the end, really. But Europe was already broken, broken for good; there was no replacing a nation of glassblowers. Bodies fell that year in Madrid, too. In the cities of Spain, women looked up at the sky in terror. In Barcelona, almost for the first time in history, a woman carrying home a branch of forsythia wrapped in waxed paper ran for cover, hiding from the air. In that war, bombs fell on women from the air, and it was planned.

My mother says she can't get over how I'm always connecting things.

"Everybody I know talks this way," I say. "Does it embarrass you?"

"No. Just—well, tell the truth."

"I will. I'll try to."

The only real difference between us, between my mother and me, is all the talking I do. Her cello voice was drowned somewhere in the sound of falling flowers, in marriage, in the new thought of bombs falling on women with flowers, with teacups. But this particular teacup and its golden shoreline escaped, and she and I have both sat with it in our kitchens. She gave it to me.

Mothers know their daughters go to their bedrooms and try on the strange clothes women wear and look at themselves in the full-length mirror, trying to understand the future, the lipstick, the bras. Is there a mother who gives a daughter a teacup and thinks it is not also inspected?

"Mother," I said last week when I was over to visit and she was putting red tulips in a vase, talking about how everybody she knew smoked and how she was glad I'd never taken it up. "Mother, everybody I know, they're always talking about their parents, trying to figure out their mothers. Did you do that? My friends, we all do that."

"No," she said. "We didn't, I guess. We didn't talk the way you do. We didn't, you know, have *relationships*." Then she remembered about the teacups, and we changed the conversation.

If she were alone having a cup of tea, as I am now, she would be smoking a cigarette, staring dreamily out the kitchen window, absently rubbing her index finger over the nail of her thumb (she still uses nail polish) in circle after circle. The smoke would be circling around her head of honey-and-smoke hair. Just sitting. I can see her.

This afternoon, though, it is my finger looped in the ear of this European cup. She is not the only submerged figure I see—she and this buoyant cabbage-head rose. There is so much sinking, no hand can hold all that has happened.

We sit around a kitchen table, my friends and I, and try to describe even one thing, but it flies apart in words. Whole afternoons go. Women often waste time this way. But history has to get written somehow. There are all these souvenirs in our houses. We have to wash and dust them. They get handed down when there's no way of explaining things. It's as if my mother has always been saying, Darling, look at the teacup. It has more to say.

Melvin Rader (1903–1981) was Professor Emeritus of Philosophy at the University of Washington, Seattle. His work covered poetry, literature, art, history, and politics, all within the scope of philosophy. In 1948, Rader was blacklisted as a Communist, and spent the next several years proving his innocence. In his 1969 book, False Witness, *he related the struggle to clear his name during the anti-communism hysteria of the 1950s. Writer, philosopher, and teacher, Bertram Jessup (1899–?) studied value theory, aesthetics, and the philosophy of art. He was Professor Emeritus of Philosophy at the University of Oregon. He co-authored* Art and Human Values *(1976) with Rader.*

Aesthetic Object

Melvin Rader and Bertram Jessup

The Aesthetic Object and Its Qualities

We can begin our discussion [of aesthetic objects] by pointing out typical examples of aesthetic objects, thus indicating in a rough way what we are talking about. Such pointing is illustrated by Stephen Pepper in the following passage:

> In the aesthetic field, for example, it is generally acknowledged that the poems, pictures, statues, musical compositions of the great artists are aesthetic materials, and also many buildings such as medieval cathedrals, and fondly made tools like paddles and baskets and pottery of primitive peoples, and dance and ritual, and also certain perceptions of nature like the sea and starry nights and sunsets and pleasant pastures and groves and sometimes fear-inspiring scenes like storms and mountains, and waterfalls.[1]

As Pepper remarks, to deny that these are works of art or objects of beauty or sublimity is contrary to common sense, and any plausible definition of the aesthetic field must fit such examples.

But pointing out aesthetic objects does not take us very far. We can conclude from Pepper's examples and other similar listings that both human artifacts and natural objects may be aesthetic, and we can note the great variety of things that are so classified. We can remark that things such as waterfalls and sunsets, or the pictures and statues and musical compositions of great artists, are all vivid objects and fascinating to see or hear. We may be a little hesitant about including paddles and baskets and pottery, asking ourselves just how "fondly" they must be fashioned before they become aesthetic and cease to be merely utilitarian. Or we may note that rituals, among the things listed by Pepper, may be humdrum and not truly felt as aesthetic. We can question why certain things are not included, such as very sentimental pictures, or awkward mechanical contraptions, or landscapes so flat and monotonous that we hardly give them a second glance, wondering whether these objects are incorrigibly nonaesthetic, or whether in certain moods or from certain perspectives they take on aesthetic quality. As soon as we ask these questions, we are doing more than pointing—we are interpreting and theorizing. We do not even know what to point at until we have some idea of the difference between aesthetic and nonaesthetic objects.

It is not so difficult to tell the difference in pointing to objects in nature. Any natural thing or quality can be considered "aesthetic" if it delights the beholder by the bare fact of its being apprehended. "Let that be called *beauty*," said Saint Thomas Aquinas, "the very perception of which pleases."[2] No more simple and satisfactory definition of beauty has ever been suggested. It contains two ideas. First, beautiful things give pleasure. Second, not everything that gives pleasure is beautiful, but only that which gives pleasure in immediate perception. We do not call a thing beautiful if it gives us pleasure for some other reason, for example, because it is useful or edifying. The sublime in nature is also considered aesthetic. Sublimity is contrasted with "beauty" in the narrow sense, but it is a subdivision of "beauty" in the very wide sense. So considered, it is a quality in objects "the very perception of which pleases" by awakening awe, reverence, lofty emotion, a sense of immense power or magnitude. In the narrow sense of beauty, a daisy is beautiful but the starry heavens are not; but in the wide, robust sense of beauty, few natural objects are as beautiful as the stars in all their splendor. There are other qualities in nature (such as gracefulness) that are aesthetic, but most of these can be considered subdivisions of beauty.

It is much more difficult to identify human artifacts as aesthetic or nonaesthetic. One reason is that there are many different kinds of things that are called works of art. There are things made by artists and placed on public display, such as statues and paintings in art museums, or similar works displayed in the privacy of a home or office. Then there are prints and copies of paintings and copies or casts of sculpture as distinguished from the originals. There are also etchings or lithographs rendered in multiple copies, each one of which is equally "original." There are novels, poems, and texts of plays extant in few or many copies; and there are literary works transmitted only by oral tradition, such as the Indian *Vedas* before the invention of written language, and folk songs preserved only in memory and occasional performance. There are scores and scripts that are no more than instructions for performers, and performances of plays, television scripts, musical compositions, and ballets that follow more or less faithfully the instructions. There are clowns, acrobats, dance improvisers, and persons engaged in "happenings" following no instructions at all. There are many buildings, machines and tools designed for some useful purpose that may nevertheless evoke aesthetic appreciation. Similarly, there are performances, such as sports, military parades, and religious rituals, that are carried on for some end other than aesthetic. All of these, including those not so intended, may be the objects of aesthetic contemplation.

We shall not undertake to answer the extremely difficult epistemological question, that of the mode of existence of these innumerable objects and artifacts. But it is clear that they exist in various stages and modes, some in the mind, some in preliminary sketch, and some in physical actualization. Also, some are duplicates, others are not; some are originals, others are copies. Some works of art, like nonprogrammatic music and nonfigurative painting, refer to nothing beyond themselves, others symbolize or represent things in "real life," and these representations and symbolizations likewise evoke aesthetic interest.

When the objective component in aesthetic value is so varied, it may seem impossible to pin it down or sum it up in a definition. But it seems to us possible, if not to define, at least to reach valid conclusions. We can say that an outstanding characteristic of incontestably aesthetic objects, whether they be works of art or things in nature, is their qualitative force and vivacity. Take any arresting objects, such as migrant birds passing from darkness into darkness across the moon, and they become aesthetic the moment they are appreciated as sheer spectacle. Unless there is some quality to arrest attention, unless the object has character and distinction, unless it stands out as vivid and memorable, unless it has a peculiar lustre of its own that we can snatch from the common dust, there is likely to be little aesthetic value or none at all. The object of aesthetic value, we can conclude, is a thing or quality that is fascinating in direct apprehension. We are using the word "quality," let us not forget, in a very inclusive sense to denote any aspect, characteristic, or attribute of a thing, including its intrinsic and relational properties, its form and its constituents. It might be objected that we are slipping back into the purely objective or nonrelational view that aesthetic value is in the object alone and that the subjective part is simply one of recognition. Our intention, however, is not to contradict the relational theory. In the first place, the object may be purely imaginary, the fine arts being the very homeland of creative imagination. And in the second place, few objects, if any, are incorrigibly nonaesthetic. Even a handful of grass, said Walt Whitman, can excite marvelling contemplation. Some of the devices of avant-garde artists, such as John Cage's evocation of strange, hitherto unnoticed sounds and silences, or the "minimal" artist's gouging out an interesting shape in mud, are intended to broaden people's ideas of what is "quality to arrest attention." We must recognize, nevertheless, that some objects are much more fit to be aesthetically appreciated than others. A very simple object, such as a single isolated dot, could scarcely attract or long hold aesthetic interest. Unless we are to discount the objective factor altogether, we must recognize that some objects, because of their inherent limitations, are aesthetically worthless or nearly so. Here, as elsewhere, we are simply insisting on the relational nature of aesthetic value—two sets of factors are always involved: those in the object and those in the percipient.

What is worthy of aesthetic appreciation may pass unnoticed until there is someone who looks with fresh eyes. So enslaved are most people to the stereotypes of expectation that they are unable to see what is plainly before them. Custom lies upon them, "with a weight, heavy as frost, and deep almost as life." As Victor Sklovskij, a Russian literary critic, writes:

> People living at the seashore grow so accustomed to the murmur of waves that they never hear it. By the same token, we scarcely ever hear the words which we utter. . . . We look at each other, but we do not see each other any more. Our perception of the world has withered away: what has remained is mere recognition.[3]

The function of the artist, according to Sklovskij, is to excite a sense of the strangeness and beauty of even the most common thing. This he does by seeing it afresh and lifting it to the "sphere of new perception." Similarly Wordsworth, in his famous *Preface to the Lyrical Ballads*, speaks of "a certain coloring of the imagination, whereby ordinary things should be presented to the mind in an unusual way." Coleridge noted Wordsworth's "gift of spreading the tone, the atmosphere, and with it the depth and height of the ideal world around forms, incidents, and situations, of which, for the common view, custom had bedimmed all the lustre, had dried up the sparkle and the dew drops."[4] Charles Peirce cites the example of our ordinary perceptions of color as contrasted with the perceptions of the gifted painter:

> When the ground is covered by snow on which the sun shines brightly except where shadows fall, if you ask any ordinary man what its color appears to be, he will tell you white, pure white, whiter in the sunlight, a little greyish in the shadow. But that is not what is before his eyes that he is describing: it is his theory of what ought to be seen. The artist will tell him that the shadows are not grey but a dull blue and the snow in the sunshine is a rich yellow.[5]

The impressionist movement, as represented by such painters as Monet, Pissarro, Sisley, and Bonnard, was an attempt to see and capture the splendors of color, the subtleties of light and shade, and the shimmering atmospheric veil that enwraps a scene under certain optical conditions.

The impressionist movement provoked such derisory comments as the retort, "I never saw a purple cow." But given the necessary optical conditions, there are purple cows and the man who is blind to such fugitive impressions is the poorer for his blindness. If the spectator is to see objects as they really appear, he has to trust his eyes and ignore his expectations.

The painter, of course, may choose to stress quite other features of objects than these evanescent effects. Paul Cezanne began as an impressionist but developed an idiom and vision of his own. He noticed, as had the impressionists, that light both reveals and destroys form, sometimes robbing the object of its own color and solidity and bathing it in an iridescent atmosphere. To record these transient appearances did not interest him. In his most characteristic painting, he emphasized solid and massive forms, building up sturdy three-dimensional shapes by the structural use of color, and relating conceptualized objects to one another in both pattern and deep space. His favorite subject was the massive shape of Mont Sainte-Victoire, the creation of innumerable centuries of geological formation and attrition. He preferred to paint still objects, whether a mountain or an arrangement of fruit, impatiently bidding his posing wife, "Be an apple!" Characteristically, he remarked that nature can be resolved into the cylinder, the sphere, and the cone. His paintings are exercises in a kind of Platonic geometry which clarifies the enduring essences and structural harmonies of nature.

Both Monet and Cezanne make us see afresh, make us see what otherwise we would not see at all. The contrast between these two painters is instructive because they call attention to opposite qualities, but actually they do not contradict each other. Whatever they as artists or others as critics may say about their respective art practices, they do not gainsay each other. Art works of differing kinds do not say or imply, this is the way things really are, but rather, things are also this way. The artist, in effect does not ask what is something truly, but asks rather, what else is it? Given honest perception, art collectively contains no contradictions, no denials, no corrections. It rounds and fills out the world of appreciations, and does not subtract from that world. The works of both Monet and Cezanne, and indeed of every artist, can be cited as evidence that art leads to a heightened and extended awareness. "To follow the arts is to walk the earth with heightened awareness," as Brooks Atkinson has said.[6]

•   •   •

We have scarcely more than hinted at the range of even a single art such as painting. If, in addition, we include all the qualities embodied in dance, music, sculpture, and architecture and in all the literary and dramatic arts, the variations are inexhaustible. This whole gamut of aesthetic qualities—natural and artificial, introspective and extrospective, representational and presentational, real and visionary, intellectual and emotional—is infinite in scope and variety.

• • •

The Principles of Form

A work of art is indivisible; it cannot be broken up into units with independent meanings. Yet critics and aestheticians talk about distinguishable principles of form, such as rhythm and thematic variation, and any keen observer notices such formal aspects. There is no harm in distinguishing them as long as we bear in mind the involvement of every element and aspect in the total fabric of the work.

The principles of form are referred to by such terms as thematic repetition and variation, balance, rhythm, progress or evolution, emphasis and subordination, and conformity to type. In addition, there is the all-embracing principle of unity in variety—a principle metaphorically designated as "living form" or "organic unity."

Thematic repetition and variation. The same pattern may be repeated in a wallpaper design; the same color may appear in separated areas of a painting; a tonic chord may be repeated in a musical composition; identical columns may appear in a building; or the same refrain may appear in a poem or song. Although exact repetition is sometimes very effective, its danger is monotony. Hence the need for variation, as in the repetition of a musical motif by some other voice or instrument, for example, when the melody inaugurated by the cello in Schubert's *Symphony in B minor* is repeated by all the strings, or when the theme of the second movement of Rimsky-Korsakov's *Scheherezade* is rendered successively by bassoon, oboe, strings, and flute. To repeat with a difference is one of the common devices in all the arts. In combining familiarity with strangeness, it avoids the monotony of mere repetition and the chaos of mere difference. In music, there may be repetition on different instruments, at different tempos, with different keys, with different intervals, with different harmonies, or with variations in melodic pattern. In the visual and plastic arts, there may be variation in size, hue, intensity, lightness or darkness, line, shape, mass, texture, perspective, symbolism, or representational detail. It is possible to illustrate repetition and variation with examples drawn from literature, music, dance, sculpture, painting, moving pictures, architecture, and the industrial arts, but a single illustration from Shakespeare's *Hamlet* must suffice. The following sketchy analysis of parts of the first and second scenes is suggestive of the continuity in other parts of the play.

The opening scene is that of a change of guard on the ramparts of the castle of Elsinore. It is deep night and very cold. A misdirected challenge on the part of the oncoming guard suggests a state of extreme tension. One of the guards on post says to his replacement:

For this relief much thanks. 'Tis bitter cold And I am sick at heart.

He is never seen or heard of again in the play, and he might be passed over at first reading as merely a fill-in or bit character in the background. But his words "I am sick at heart," emotional material already supported by the night, the bitter coldness, and the loneliness of the watch, soon turn out to be the first striking of a major theme of the drama. In the next scene, the theme is taken up, varied, and enlarged. It is treated first in sheer spectacle through contrast, visual and auditory. The stage is dominated by the royal procession, the king and queen, councilors and attendants. There is color, pomp, gaiety, laughter and lively conversation, fanfare of trumpets. And against all this, at a distance behind, the lone, silent, somber figure of Hamlet in "inky cloak"—visual, "heartsickness" the theme. The dialogue, when he is soon drawn in by the king and queen, repeats it and varies it, and finally when the court goes off and leaves him alone, the heartsickness is uttered directly in the soliloquy, "O that this too too solid flesh would melt."

The theme, of course, continues through the play. But this is enough to show its substance and direction. A bit of action compounded of night, cold, military routine, royal pomp, dejection, and conflict of emotion and will, all strung on a thread of "heartsickness," yields a marvelously intricate yet closely composed experience, in which there is both thematic continuity and progression toward the tragic denouement.

Balance. The meaning of balance may be illustrated by a playground see-saw. If the seesaw is to work, there must be balance either symmetrical or asymmetrical. Children of the same weight may balance each other by sitting in the same relative position; or the weight of an adult may be balanced by the weight of two children; or a child who is heavier may balance a child who is lighter by moving closer to the center. Thus, there may be a balance of similarity or contrast, but in either case there must be some equality of weight.

In a work of art, balance likewise involves some kind of equality—of scale, emphasis, proportion, or interest. Lack of balance produces lopsidedness—for example, when one side of a painting lacks interest in comparison with the other. As in the example of the seesaw, the balance may be of likes or unlikes, and of any degree of likeness or unlikeness. The balance of similars is called symmetry, and of dissimilars, asymmetrical balance or contrast. Often the two are combined. For example, in a painting the lines and masses might balance symmetrically while the colors might balance asymmetrically (a cold blue, for example, balancing a warm orange). The balance may be on a horizontal, vertical or diagonal axis.

Symmetry is more applicable to the spatial arts, such as painting, sculpture, and architecture, than to the more dynamic temporal arts, such as music, dancing, moving pictures, and drama. But even in the spatial arts, perfect symmetry is likely to prove uninteresting, because it involves less variety than does contrast. Hence many architects, sculptors, and painters prefer asymmetrical balance. In music, there is frequently a symmetrical balance between the earlier and later parts of a composition—for example, in the length of the movements; and symmetry is employed, to some extent, in all the other temporal arts.

Contrast may be illustrated by innumerable examples—between light and dark, warm and cold, and bright and dull colors; straight and curved and horizontal and vertical lines; heavy and light, and big and little masses; near and distant objects; blank and patterned surfaces; rough and smooth textures; high and low, and loud and soft notes, sound and silence; slow and fast movements; calm and excited moods, and gay emotions; good and bad, comic and tragic, male and female, and young and old characters; victorious and defeated forces in a novel or play. When each of the contrasting factors is given approximately equal emphasis, there is a balance of contrasts, and this is often more satisfying than a disproportionate emphasis upon one factor as opposed to another. But it is necessary to take account of the need for emphasis and subordination—a principle that may run counter to balance, to some extent, in all the other temporal arts.

Rhythm. This is not a separate principle but a combination of balance and repetition. In the rhythm of waves, for example, the crests are balanced by the dips, and both crests and dips are repeated. But rhythm is so important that it deserves separate consideration. It may be achieved in numerous ways, for example, by size: large-small; by length in duration: long-short; by tempo: swift-fast; by accent: loud-soft; by pitch: high-low, by color: warm-cold, bright-dull, light-dark. Whenever there is measured alternation, there is one kind of rhythm.

Rhythm is very important in the temporal arts, especially poetry, dancing, and music. Eduard Hanslick, the famous musical aesthetician, called it the "main artery of the musical organism."[7] But the exploration of recurrent similarities and differences in spatial objects may have a rhythmical character. The up and down thrust of a zigzag line, for example, appears rhythmical to an observer who takes the time to run his eye along it. Similarly, rhythm can be felt whenever one surveys the measured alternation of light and dark, of contrasting hues, of contrasting shapes, of large and small units, of filled and empty spaces, of near and far objects, of horizontals and verticals, or of other effects.

Rhythms may be varied in innumerable ways. Instead of contrasting pairs, there may be an alternating of more complex clusters. The compound and complex rhythms of poetry, music, dancing, and even the visual arts, may be highly involved. The rhythms may be regular—when similar measures occur in sequence—or irregular—when dissimilar measures occur. Rhythms may cross, conflict, or commingle.

To be interesting, rhythm must be somewhat complex and varied, as in musical syncopation. No one can sustain interest in rhythms that are as simple and monotonous as the ticking of a clock. The variations in rhythm are frequently expressive of a changing mood or meaning. A faster rhythm may express joy; a slower rhythm, sorrow. In Shelley's "Stanzas Written in Dejection Near Naples," the poem begins with a lilting rhythm:

> The sun is warm, the sky is clear,
> The waves are dancing fast and bright.

But the rhythm gradually changes, as the mood of dejection deepens, to a slower pace, until the lines that envisage the poet's death by drowning take on a solemn and majestic tempo:

> Till death like sleep might steal on me,
> And I might feel in the warm air
> My cheek grow cold, and hear the sea
> Breathe o'er my dying brain its last monotony.

Expressive variation in rhythm is one of the main sources of aesthetic effect.

Progress or evolution. In rhythm, there is no necessary development but only an alternation. Different is the way a novel, a play, a moving picture, or a musical composition as a whole unfolds, with a progress from beginning to end. Here there is no mere alternation but a growth and accumulation—a real evolution. The earlier parts contribute to the later; the later parts depend upon the earlier; so that there is a definite and irreversible movement from beginning to end. A story cannot be told backwards or a musical composition played backwards without ludicrous results.

Evolution obviously applies to the temporal arts, but there may also be movement and a felt sense of direction in the visual arts. In surveying a Gothic cathedral, the eye naturally starts at the bottom and sweeps upward until it reaches the topmost spire, rather than vice versa. In many of the paintings of El Greco, there is a similar upward lift; and in mural paintings, there may be a natural movement from one side to the other and from one picture to another, as the contemplator progresses through a related series of paintings.

Progress often takes the form of following a sequence of graduated qualities. As Stephen Pepper, in his *Principles of Art Appreciation*, points out, "a
gradation consists in following a sequence of nearly related qualities. . . .
Thus a sequence of grays from black to white would be a gradation, or a
sequence of hues from red through orange to yellow." A similar progression "is possible with lengths and widths and degrees of curvature of
lines, with sizes and volumes, with shapes such as gradations from circles into narrower and narrower ellipses, or from squares into narrower
and narrower rectangles. In sound there is a gradation of pitches low to
high, and of intensities from soft to loud. And so with all sense qualities."[8] Even identical objects can appear as gradations. For example, identical columns when seen in perspective diminish in apparent size. Or,
again, identical circles look more and more elliptical when spaced farther
and farther away; or identical sounds appear softer and softer as we
move away, or louder and louder as we approach. Whether the gradation
is real or apparent, its contemplation involves a kind of progression. For
example, when we run up the notes of a musical scale, we feel that we are
"getting somewhere," and when we run through a gradation of colors,
we have a similar sense of movement.

Emphasis and subordination. Certain qualities tend to be more emphatic
than others: the loud rather than the soft, the bright rather than the dull,
the big rather than the small, the swift rather than the slow, the discordant rather than the concordant, the tense rather than the relaxed. When
the qualities in a graduated series are so arranged that there is a progression toward a high point of emphasis and interest, we can speak of
movement toward a climax. We are all familiar with climaxes in plays,
novels, musical compositions, and moving pictures, but to a lesser extent
we find climax in the visual arts when our attention passes through a
graduated series to a peak of interest and intensity. Such a peak is usually
in the center of a painting, and the gradations lead from the periphery
into the center. For example, there may be color gradation from darker to
lighter, beginning at the sides and reaching a climax in light, brilliant
color at the central focus, as in Fra Angelico's "Madonna of Humility." In
the temporal arts, the climax often comes before the end, and the earlier
upward movement is balanced by a swift downward movement, the resolution or denouement. Sometimes, as in Shakespeare's *Macbeth*, there
are a number of climaxes, a succession of rises and falls—for example, in
many symphonies, plays, novels, and dances. Emphasis may be achieved
in other ways—by repetition, contrast, discord, focal position, size, color,
tone, suspense, fullness of elaboration—without necessarily mounting to
a climax.

Whenever there is emphasis there is subordination. To emphasize everything is to emphasize nothing; for example, no emphasis would be gained

by italicizing every word in a book. Hence an artist must learn to modulate this emphasis—to practice restraint. He must work out a hierarchy of details, giving to each the relative degree of emphasis or subordination that is suitable. With the judicious use of subordination and emphasis, a work of art can contain a great wealth of detail without being cluttered. It is one of the principal means of reconciling unity with variety.

Type. One of the commonest ways of achieving organization is conformity to type. A type is any set of characteristics that serve to mark off a class of objects. When we look at the painting of a nude woman, for example, we have in mind the characteristics of the female human form. We recognize the type and see the details as fitting into a preconceived whole. The eyes, ears, nose, mouth, and hair fit together to constitute the head; and the head, arms, legs, stomach, breasts, and other features combine to form the larger pattern of the body. The nude figure, as a recognizable type, thus provides a compositional scheme to bring together and unify many details. In providing such schemes, representational subject matter has an important unifying function. But many artists prefer to deviate greatly from naturalistic appearance for the sake of a more beautiful, or a more original and expressive, composition.

We have concepts of innumerable natural objects—animals, plants, mountains, streams, clouds, and so forth. To these we can add the man-made things—tables, chairs, articles of clothing, automobiles and airplanes or any other human artifact. Each of these has a recognizable structure which can serve as a unifying factor in representational art. Usually a number of natural objects or artifacts are represented in a single work of art, and there is an overall subject that unites the various recognizable parts. Arrangement in terms of perspective, which is a type of spatial organization, is a scheme often used to order and unite the objects. In literature the overall scheme may be an incident or story. The Greek dramatists, for example, used the myths of gods and heroes to provide a familiar narrative structure. Types of character can also serve as schemata, as in Moliere's depiction of hypocrisy, avarice, jealousy, hypochondria, religious bigotry, and other obsessions.

Not only are there human and natural types but such recurrent abstract forms as circles, squares, rectangles, triangles, cubes, spheres, and pyramids. These are quite as recognizable as the types of natural objects or human artifacts—and they may have a similar organizing function. One of the characteristics of the cubist movement in painting was stress upon such abstract forms. In much "nonfigurative" painting and sculpture and in a great deal of architecture, the forms of circles, triangles, spheres, arches, and so forth are the essential patterns. Many of these forms are elements in a larger comprehensive pattern, but this larger pattern, in turn, may be circular, triangular, pyramidal, or of some similar abstract type.

Finally, there are artistic types—such as the sonnet, the waltz, the sonata, the fugue, the minuet, the Corinthian column. Artistic types are especially frequent in poetry, music, and dancing. Styles in architecture, such as the Romanesque or the Dutch Colonial, are artistic types; and in the other arts, too, there are formal conventions that characterize the works of the various "schools" of artists. Such types are helpful in providing a ready-made compositional scheme. To the artist with sufficient genius, the type is not a rigid mold but a plastic receptable which he can fill with new content. An example is the use of the sonnet by Shakespeare, Milton, Wordsworth, and Keats. Each of these poets achieved superb and highly individual effects with a relatively strict traditional type. In music, Bach provides illustrations:

> Bach was one of the most conventional composers who ever existed. He accepted forms and formulas ready-made from his predecessors, chiefly German and Italian, but French and English also, and he was none the worse for it, because he succeeded, in spite of the self-imposed blinkers to his fancy, in making something greater out of precedent than it had ever been before.[9]

But a mediocre artist may employ type patterns to conceal the poverty of his imagination or as a short-cut in obtaining a slick effect. To conform to a traditional type when new materials, techniques, functions, and intentions require a different treatment is a mark of mediocrity. One of the banes of architecture is the tendency to be traditional when tradition is out of place.

To the contemplator of a work of art, recognition of type characteristics gives the pleasure of recognition, but this pleasure tends to be transient and superficial. In the last analysis, every work of art is individual and concrete, and unless the beholder goes beyond schemata to grasp the vivid original essence of the work, he has missed the boat. But the knowledge of types may be an invaluable preparation for and aid to enjoyment.

Organic unity. This is the all-inclusive principle of form to which all the other principles contribute. The term "organize unity," used to emphasize the similarity between an organism and a work of art, is a metaphor derived from Aristotle and other classical aestheticians. An organism is a unitary being composed of interdependent parts constituted for subserving vital processes. Thus there is a total functional integration, the life of the whole, which is the end of the parts. Now a work of art is not, in this sense, alive, but it resembles a living organism with respect to adequacy, economy, and internal coherence.

There should be nothing lacking that is required to give wholeness and integrity to the work. The test of adequacy is whether the beholder is satisfied, not whether the work of art resembles a natural organism in its completeness. "If it pleases a futurist to paint a lady with only one eye, or a quarter of an eye," Jacques Maritain remarked, "nobody denies him such a right: all one is entitled to require—and here is the whole problem—that the quarter eye is all the lady needs *in the given case*."[10] The only valid test of adequacy is the test of imagination: Does the work seem to be completely executed—is it a satisfying whole rather than a mere fragment?

Another mark of organic unity is economy. The work should not be cluttered with distracting and unnecessary details. This means, not that details should be few, but that none should be superfluous. Many of Rembrandt's paintings are rich in details, but by the masterly use of unifying principles—especially emphasis and subordination—they achieve a remarkable integration. The ideal is to be more unified without being less inclusive. If we combine adequacy with economy, we have enough for unity but not too much.

An organic unity is not a mere arithmetical sum of separate and distinct parts but a configuration of interdependent parts. Consider this line from Wordsworth's poem "Michael":

> And never lifted up a single stone.

Although strikingly prosaic when detached from the poem, it is beautiful and expressive in its context. One mark of organic unity is that the parts do thus function in context, lending their value to the whole and deriving value from that whole. The total effect determines whether any detail should be added, omitted, or altered. Every inconsistent detail cries out for change and alterations; or if it is included, the whole must be reorganized so as to achieve a unified effect. This sort of unity in variety, with nothing lacking, nothing superfluous, and all the parts cohering, is organic unity.

It can be violated in innumerable ways: by subject matter inconsistent with the nature of the medium (such as the representation of a light and transient movement in heavy inflexible stone); by static paintings that try to tell stories; by machines with incongruous decorations; by moving pictures in which songs are artificially introduced; by novels in which the propagandistic element is "dragged in"; by operas in which the acting, music, and scenery are imperfectly integrated; by architecture in which the traditional style ill fits the modern materials and functions of the building; or by any work of art in which there are unrelated, inconsistent, insufficient, or redundant details.

Lest "organic unity" be interpreted too narrowly, we should consider two characteristics of organisms pointed out by Aristotle. First, he distinguished between the essential and the accidental. In the human organism, the functioning of the heart is essential, the length of the hair is accidental. The clipping of hair or fingernails is not serious, the loss of an arm of leg is serious, total damage to the brain is catastrophic. The analogy with a work of art is obvious, because some parts of the work are much more essential than others. The "Venus de Milo," for example, is beautiful in its broken state, but it would be more seriously damaged if its head in addition to its arms were missing. As Ruth Saw has remarked, "Part of the beauty of the statue is the way the head is held on the shoulders, and if neck and head were missing, this might be completely lost."[11] Because a well-wrought work of art is a gestalt, in which the character of the whole permeates every part, even a torso may be extremely beautiful. But the impairment cannot go beyond a certain point without a fundamental loss.

In a small work, such as a sonnet, the requirement of organic wholeness is much more stringent than in a big work, such as a novel or an epic. *War and Peace* is a masterpiece, although much could be eliminated without mutilation. But there is danger in huge size, as the fate of the dinosaurs indicates. In the fossil record of the rocks, it is "always the gigantic individuals who appear at the end of each chapter."[12] Comparing a too-lengthy play with an imaginary animal a mile long, Aristotle implied that both real animal and good play must have organic limits.[13]

Second, Aristotle insisted that each organism has a "soul"—a word that he used in a special sense to designate its functional unity. Among the terms he employed to characterize the soul are "the determining principle of life," "the essential and enduring character of a living body," and "the form of a natural body endowed with the capacity of life." Although only a living being can have a soul, we can speak of a functional object as if it had.

> Suppose, for example, that an instrument such as an axe were a natural body. Its character of being an axe would be its "whatness, or essential thinghood," and therefore its "soul"; if this were taken away it would no longer be an axe except in name.[14]

The soul is its nature, which makes it possible for the axe to function as an axe. We can speak similarly of the parts of a living body. "If the eye were an independent organism," Aristotle remarks, "sight would be its soul, for it is in terms of sight that the essential whatness of the eye must be defined."[15] What is true of a bodily organ must be no less true of the whole organism—its soul must be defined in functional terms. The soul of a cat, for example, is the principle of life, or animating force, that enables it to function as a feline organism.

If, by analogy, this notion of soul is applied to a work of art, it would follow that its "soul" is its capacity to fulfill its function. We maintain that the function of a work of art is to express values. Hence the "soul" of the work of art is its value-expressiveness. This leads us to the next division of our chapter.

What Is Good Taste?

The concept of aesthetic value as a relational complex . . . helps us to resolve the conflict between objectivism and subjectivism. Some writers have put all the emphasis on the subject pole of the relation and others on the objective pole. Both extremes are mistaken. Because the value is relational, it is to be found not solely in the interest or solely in the object, but in the worthiness of each to contribute to the aesthetic experience. The object is fit to excite an appreciative attitude in the beholder, and the beholder is fit to appreciate the object. The aesthetic goodness is the result of a felt harmony between the appreciator and the thing appreciated, each being fit or worthy for the other. An excellent work of art is more worthy of being appreciated than trash, and a gifted art-lover is better fitted to appreciate it than an insensitive spectator. When the experience is poor, the fault may be either in the work or the beholder or both. The work may be insipid, chaotic, trite, sentimental, or otherwise defective. The beholder may be inattentive, biased, uncultivated, insensitive, or fatigued. When a person does not like a work of art, he should consider whether the deficiency is in the object or in himself. If the latter is the case, he should not condemn the work of art, but, if possible, improve his taste. This he may do solely through the use of his own critical faculties or with the help and guidance of a critic.

This brings us to the question, What is good taste? The answer we shall propose is not original. It is intended to set forth what is commonly meant by "good taste."

It has often been said that good taste is rooted in but not guaranteed by native sensory equipment—good eyes, good ears, an alert mind, etc. Good taste is not innate or ready-made. For good taste, besides being a keen taste, is an educated taste, it is informed, experienced, and cultivated. In its operations it is discriminating, broad, tolerant, and unconfused. In its articulations it is sincere. It is a taste that is refined but at the same time robust, not so overrefined that it loses its gusto and becomes finicky. Its interest in the orchid must not dull it to the primrose and the dandelion.

Conversely, "bad taste" in common usage means, besides a taste that is insensitive because of impaired sense faculties or dullness of mind or emotions, a taste that is ignorant, uninformed, inexperienced, narrow, intolerant, confused, or oversophisticated. But one deficiency does not entail all the others. A person of narrow taste may, for example, be informed, experienced and sensitive to whatever he reacts to within the range of his interests. But still, to call a taste "narrow" is to subtract something from it qualitatively.

A few illustrations will serve to enforce these characterizations. Good taste is discriminating. A person of good taste will not react, for example, in a single lump of indiscriminate feeling to John Bunyan's *Grace Abounding* because he meets there an uncongenial theological doctrine; he will rather note that fact as an unpalatable ingredient and then go on to feel pleasantly the charm of innumerable little incidents told by the way and enjoy the admirable honesty and excellence of the simple English prose style.

A person of good taste is tolerant in his responses. He is not quick to feel displeasure in the presence of a kind of art with which he is unfamiliar, of which he does not have experience and about which he does not have understanding. He will not feel antipathy out of hand to an avant-garde design because it answers to nothing in his previous experience. He will not break into derisive guffaws at a native south African dance because it is not European ballet. Nothing is more stifling than continually insisting that all works of art should conform to an already established norm. Art can never to reduced to a recipe, and genius refuses to be fenced in. The greatest figures in the history of art have almost invariably been rebels against established taste, and it is only after their works have lost their virtue as catalytic agents that they become "classics." Something new and unprecedented, such as the "barbaric yawp" of Walt Whitman, strikes most people initially as outrageous. To cite a more contemporary example, the combination of loud "rock music," psychedelic "light show" including "strobe" effects, and free, inner-directed dancing, might seem the epitome of "bad taste," but Robert Joffrey, the ballet director, recognized the vitality of these "hippy" art forms and incorporated them into one of the finest ballets. In view of such examples, we should be leary of condemning works of art that do not fit into the standards of *conventional* "good taste."

Good taste is broad. It is a various taste. Many kinds of objects engage its interest and command its approval. It will warm not only to modern art but to classical too. It will like not only classical music but swing and jazz also. It will enjoy the novel as good reading but not to the exclusion of poetry. It is not provincial. Artistic merits being equal, it will find pleasure in a Japanese landscape as much as in a typical homeland scene. It is not one-sided. It will not exalt purely formal beauties above those of content, nor those of thought above those of sensuous surface.

But every person has his limitations; no one can like everything that is worthy of being enjoyed. Human temperaments are bound to vary, and different works will appeal to different temperaments. To the bored opera-goer, who has been told that opera is excellent but is incapable of feeling it, the "knowledge" that he is listening to fine opera is cold comfort. For him the opera as art does not exist. If he can truly appreciate a simple folk story, it is aesthetically better for him than the grand opera. He may eventually learn to enjoy opera and other difficult musical forms, but in the meantime, there is no justification for trying to fool himself and others into thinking that he enjoys what he does not enjoy. As Henry James declared:

> Nothing, of course, will ever take the place of the good old fashion of "liking" a work of art or not liking it: the most improved criticism will not abolish that primitive, that ultimate test.[16]

It is a test of honesty both for the critic and the public. The well-known fact that taste can be cultivated implies that it can be broadened and improved. But the last thing we should seek to cultivate is a *cult* of good taste.

Aesthetic taste, to be honest and good, must be really aesthetic. A taste is not good aesthetic taste if it is not aesthetic taste at all. If an object of art is valued for its snob appeal, the taste is not aesthetic. If a poem is liked because it is scientifically true or morally uplifting, it is not valued poetically. If a building impresses because of its cost, it is not valued architecturally. If a painting is favorably received because of its religious or irreligious content, it is not valued as art. And if a work is found interesting because it throws light on a page of history, it is a cognitive and not an aesthetic interest that is satisfied. And so on.

The nonaesthetic interest may, of course, be perfectly worthy, and by itself does not result in bad aesthetic taste. But when aesthetic worth is imputed to the total object on the basis of a separately considered, nonaesthetic ingredient in it, then confusion of value and in that sense "bad taste" does occur. When for example, a thing of great cost is deemed *ipso facto* a thing of high aesthetic value, the corruption of taste which in one of its meanings is called "vulgar taste" sets in.

Aesthetic taste to be good must be adequately perceptive. This means simply that what is responded to must be really there in the work and that what is really there must be responded to. To be adequately perceptive is to be fully and relevantly perceptive. The work of art must be seen or heard in whole and not merely in part. Correct response is total response. Inadequate response may also be described as failure to respond to the work as object and to use it rather as a trigger to set off memories, feelings, and sentiments which are related to the object only by psychological privacies or eccentricities of the beholder. In that case the taste is directed not upon the object but upon the recalled and outside incidents and interests of the beholder's life. If, for example, in reading Shakespeare's

   All the world's a stage And all the men and women merely players,

the reader feels confirmed in his conviction that life is showy and superficial, and if he stops there in the satisfied feeling of being confirmed by Shakespeare, then he has not arrived at an adequate perception of Shakespeare's play, nor even of the lines themselves. He is responding to the thought rather than through the thought to the character who is made to utter it and is thereby perceptually defined. He has failed to see that Shakespeare does not make the assertion, but uses it—that is, makes something of it. The reader's perception has failed and his taste has been misdirected. A misdirected taste is a bad taste.

"Good taste," to be a meaningful concept, must mean more than my taste and your taste and any taste. It must represent a normality of response based on normality of capacity to respond. A good taste is one that is able to see what sharp eyes can see, to hear what good ears can hear, to take in what a good mind can encompass, and to feel what an emotionally sensitive person can feel. Good taste is the actual full possession and exercising of these capacities. Thus, for example, Dr. Samuel Johnson's hardness of hearing is correctly inferred to account in part at least not only for his lack of enjoyment of music, but also for his critically unfavorable appraisals of certain poems in which tonal excellence is fundamental.

What Is a Good Work of Art?

If we turn from a consideration of good taste to the consideration of good works of art, we again offer a sample of common-sense criteria without entering into the intricacies of advanced critical theory.

1. Beauty. "Beauty" is frequently used in casual conversation, as in remarking "What a beautiful day!" When applied to works of art, it may indicate nothing more specific than an attitude of approval or enjoyment. To say that a work is beautiful tells us very little about it or the motives for its creation. Even if beauty is characteristic of the work, it is a unique beauty, as we can see if we compare the beauty of works by El Greco and Rembrandt, or of Chaucer and Shelley, or of Mozart and Stravinsky. Hence the concept is too vague to function effectively as a tool for explaining artistic phenomena or directing aesthetic choice. It is mainly useful in indicating that the aesthetic object pleases, for as St. Thomas said, "The beautiful is something pleasant to apprehend."[17]

The judgment that a work of art is beautiful may be, in a particular instance, irrelevant or misapplied. The spectator may ask of the work, "How beautiful is this?" when the artist was not interested in beauty. It is true that an artist may create beauty when he is intent upon something else, and that the spectator may be interested only in this incidental effect. All expressive art may require some foundation of formal beauty if it is not to fall faulty, but its value is not reducible to beauty alone, and the person who looks always and only for beauty will miss much of the distinctive value. The expressive content of many words is bitter, gloomy, heart-rending, even horrible and ugly. Art has explored the depths of life as thoroughly as it has explored the heights.

2. Originality. Uniqueness or originality is an important characteristic of a genuine or good work of art. The language of appreciation and criticism is replete with terms which recognize the quality. An excellent work of art is "inimitable." To ascribe to an artist "originality" in conception or style is basic praise. Conversely, to be derivative is in a work of art to be less than great. It is always better to be the Shakespeare than to be Shakespearean; better to be the Tolstoy than to be, like Sholokov, "the most Tolstoyan of Soviet novelists."[18]

Uniqueness, originality, is a prime character or art. But the uniqueness that is possible to a work of art and in terms of which we praise it is a relative, not an absolute or total, uniqueness. This is seen in the fact that once we have established the uniqueness of an artist we do not hesitate to compare others with him. We say that there is something in the sonnets of Keats at his best which is Shakespearean, or that there is something of Michelangelo in Rubens. And if we read or look with attentive and trained discrimination, we will not be at a total loss to say what the something or the somewhat is.

The assertion has been made of many great composers, whether classic (Ockheghen, Bach, Handel, Mozart) or modern (Ives, Stravinsky, Bartok) that they have "stolen" or "borrowed" themes from other composers. Shakespeare derived his plots from Seneca, Plutarch, Holinshed, or the Gesta Romanorum, and much of his dramatic technique from Kyd and Marlowe. Turner is said to have lifted many of his compositions from Claude Lorrain. Picasso, Braque, and Gris in their cubist period, or Henry Moore and Barbara Hepworth in much of their sculpture, closely resemble each other. The idea that each artist stands alone, or that every work of art is entirely unique, is not borne out by the history of art. We are not questioning the value of originality, but we are saying that it has its taproots, its vital connections with what has already been created.

Uniqueness, if pursued too far, produces novelty—a quality of negative aesthetic weight. The book of the month, or the play of the season, or the stunt painting has it, but not the work of the centuries. The work that takes its place enduringly has something more than uniqueness, something equally primary. It has the character that makes it a particular embodiment, no matter how new and strange, of art as a continuing and shared reality.

3. Formal integration. The qualities in works of art are elements in relation or relations among the elements; they are never properly grasped in disconnection. When the integration is complete, the duality of form and content disappears. The parts attain their keenest lyrical beauty by reason of their relation to the whole; and the whole attains its vivid expressiveness because it is articulated in and through the parts. Such "organic unity"—with nothing essential lacking, nothing redundant, and all the parts contributing to, and being governed by, the total configuration—is the supreme mark of good art viewed from the standpoint of form.

It is possible that the vividness of the individual qualities may detract from the formal excellence of the work. One might think that the more arresting each detail, the better will be the work of art in the total ensemble in its qualities. But as Plato remarked:

> Suppose that we were painting a statue, and some one came up to us and said, Why do you not put the most beautiful colors on the most beautiful parts of the body—the eyes ought to be purple, but you have made them black—to him we might fairly answer, Sir, you would not surely have us beautify the eyes to such a degree that they are no longer eyes; consider rather whether, by giving this and the other features their due proportion, we make the whole beautiful.[19]

In judging how the details should be treated, we must bear in mind the intent of the work. Let us suppose a painter is aiming at beauty of design, in the sense of a beautiful organization of colors, lines, shapes, and volumes. Attention to striking subject matter would distract from attention to design. Hence the subject matter, in this instance, should be made relatively inconspicuous, and figurative detail either subordinated or cut out altogether.

If there is enough skill, impressive representational subject matter can be perfectly harmonized with the form. In the works of great masters such as Giotto and Rembrandt—to mention only painters—there is a superb harmonization of all aspects of the work: the sensuous materials, the subject matter, and the design enhance one another rather than compete. Provided that the unity and expressiveness of the whole are served, deeply expressive subject matter is aesthetically all to the good. Art can thus combine significant content, including representational matter movingly portrayed, with significant form. Indeed, in the wide sense of "form," the subject matter is a constituent within the form. In this broad meaning— and it is the meaning that we here intend—form is the integration of all the elements and aspects that comprise the work of art.

Form has often been characterized as unity in variety. If there is too little unity in comparison with the variety, or too little variety in comparison with the unity, the form is comparatively unimpressive. Superb art is more unified without being less inclusive, and more inclusive without being less unified. Plenty is synthesized into harmony. Hence, Aristotle recognized, a certain magnitude, bringing with it amplitude and variety, as long as the whole is coherent and perspicuous throughout, is necessary for the greatest art.

More inwardly conceived, form is a kind of dynamic psychological equilibrium. It has been characterized by Coleridge in a well-known passage:

> [The imagination] reveals itself in the balance or reconciliation of opposite or discordant qualities; of sameness, with difference; of the general, with the concrete; the idea, with the image; the individual, with the representative; the sense of novelty and freshness, with old and familiar objects; a more than usual state of emotion, with more than usual order. . . .[20]

Similar is the contention of Schiller and Kant that the unity and manifoldness of the aesthetic object is inwardly reflected in the unimpeded exercise and mutual facilitation of our basic human faculties. This free play, balance, and harmonization of diverse, or even discordant, impulses and faculties has been called "synaesthesis," and I. A. Richards has proposed to make it the main criterion of aesthetic excellence.[21] But his theory is stated too exclusively in response language rather than object language. As we have so often said, object and response are indissolubly united in aesthetic value.

4. Memorable experience. We need, in addition to formal standards, a wider and freer criterion of good art. John Dewey has suggested such a wider standard in "an experience that is an experience"—that is to say, an experience that is rich, satisfying, creative, memorable. Stephen Pepper, in characterizing this standard, has said:

> The stress is on the experience, the unique quality of the experience, and it is this that is quantified to give the contextualistic aesthetic standard. *The more vivid the experience and the more intense and rich its quality, the greater its aesthetic value* . . . Dewey frequently chooses the word "seizure" to designate the highest aesthetic experience. It is an experience in which a total situation is absorbed in a vivid fused satisfying quality.[22]

Among the ways suggested to attain the optimum vividness of quality are the freshness and sharpness of details to avoid dullness and banality, the discreet use of conflict to stimulate alertness, and the interrelating and convergence of qualities to achieve a total vivid seizure.

It might be objected that the standard of memorable experience applies only to the beholder's response, and not to the work of art. This objection overlooks the relational character of aesthetic values. As Dewey and Pepper recognize, the vivid values that evoke a memorable experience in the perceiver are qualities in the object. The standard can be stated in terms of either object language or response language. Really there are not two separate standards, one objective and grounded in the work and the other subjective and grounded in the response, but rather one single standard, that of the vivid fused satisfying quality which characterizes the object as much as it characterizes the subject, because it is a product of the conjunction of the two.

The criterion of memorable experience is akin to the standard of "greatness" enunciated by Longinus, who defended elevation and intensity of content as against correctness of form.[23] Similarly, Walter Pater, at the end of his "Essay on Style," declared that the distinction between "good art" and "bad art" depends not on form but on subject matter.[24] Rejecting this dichotomy of form and content, Lascelles Abercrombie has said that "the greatness of poetry is . . . greatness of the scope of its unifying harmony." For example, "the art of interpretation," such as the poetry of Chaucer, is greater than "the art of refuge," such as the poetry of Spenser, "for the harmony it effects cannot but be a fuller and richer version of life."[25] The great artist contrives a rich texture of intensities and complexities which combine into a total form of impressive range and power. It is exemplified by a great symphony, a majestic architectural structure, or a monumental painting or statue; and is the result of the teamwork of all the qualities, representational and presentational, which contextually interpenetrate and give the impression of mystery, complexity, and depth.

Difficult Art

All these marks of excellence may be present in works of art, and yet the works, because of their complexity, intensity, breadth, or strangeness, may not be appreciated. The spectator or listener may have to return to the work again and again and analyze it in great detail before he can grasp its intricate structure. Even after prolonged effort, the complexity of the form may elude him. Also, some works of art are so intense that they put heavy demands upon the observer. The high tension of great tragedy, for example, calls for an intense response-strong emotion and extreme concentration. The sublime, in many of its aspects, requires an exalted mood and abundant spiritual energy; when a person is fatigued, or in a light, playful frame of mind, he may be unmoved by sublimity. Some works of art demand a freedom from prejudice and a tolerant outlook; the comedy of Ben Jonson or the satire of Rabelais, for example, may offend the prudish. Conservatives may be repelled by left-wing art, such as that of Aumier or Orozco; orthodox people may not be able to enjoy heterodox religious art. Some works are so strange, so different from the usual, that they require a great readjustment before they can be appreciated. We tend to like what we already know—the familiar is easy to like; the unfamiliar requires much more effort to enjoy. A person may need special training or experience, such as familiarity with the musical idiom of Arnold Schoenberg or Miltron Babbitt, in order to enjoy the work of art. The factors that we have been mentioning—complexity, intensity, breadth, and strangeness—are not the only sources of difficulty in appreciating art, but they are among the most important.[26]

Difficult art may repel at first, but if the object is worthy and the beholder can cultivate a taste for it, it will likely be a richer source of aesthetic satisfaction than an object that is easy to appreciate. Many excellent works of art do not immediately make themselves felt—they require familiarity and cultivation. This fact is well to bear in mind when we judge works of art, because it will keep us from making hasty and superficial judgments.

The distinction between easy and difficult works of art points up the main idea of this chapter, that aesthetic value is neither in the object alone nor in the subject alone but in the relation between the two. Aesthetic value in full measure can be actualized only when the object is worthy to be appreciated and the beholder is worthy to appreciate it. The depth of appreciation must meet and match the depth of expressiveness in the object. As long as interest and object do not interlock, there is aesthetic value only in potentiality. The actualized value exists if and only if (1) the necessary conditions for its existence are present in the object, and (2) the requisite capabilities to appreciate the object are present and operative in the beholder. Until both of these conditions are fulfilled, the natural object or artifact remains a bare skeleton, neutral and dumb. Relativism, which puts exclusive emphasis upon the subjective factors, and absolutism, which puts exclusive emphasis on the object factors, are equally misleading and one-sided. The valid alternative is a subject-object relationship that accords due weight to both subjective and objective components.

Summary and Conclusion

We have characterized aesthetic value as a gestalt consisting of three components—the object, the interest, and their interrelation. Having devoted most of Chapters 1 through 4 to an elucidation of this concept, we shall now gather together the threads of our discussion.

The aesthetic object is any thing or quality, whether imaginary or real, that has enough vividness and poignancy to make us appreciate it simply as given. Nothing is excluded that can excite aesthetic interest, even though it be a blade of grass; but some objects are much better fitted to arouse and sustain aesthetic interest than others. The distinction between content and form is a relative one, the content being the elements in relation and the form being the relationship among the elements. The elements comprise all kinds of qualities—natural and artifactual, introspective and extrospective, representational and presentational, primary, secondary, and tertiary—all qualities whatsoever that are fascinating to sense, imagine, or apprehend for their own sake. The formal principles that bind together these qualities include thematic repetition and variation, balance, rhythm, evolution, and emphasis and subordination. All serve the master principle of organic unity—the adequacy, integrity, and internal coherence that make a work of art resemble a living organism.

Values as they occur in art and aesthetic experience are concrete and individuated, but in addition, we can speak of aesthetic value in a wider and more generic sense. We can think of art and aesthetic experience as a way of life, and we can ask what good is that way. Just as we can ask what is the good of science, or what is the good of religion, so we can ask what is the good of the aesthetic way. To bring the question to a focus, we can consider what would be lost if art and aesthetic experience should entirely disappear from human life. The loss, we believe, would be catastrophic, for aesthetic value is very pervasive and primordial. Only when we gain some sense of that loss can be understand the "good" of art and aesthetic experience.

We can speak not only of the value of art, in the sense of the generic good of this way of life, but also of values in art—namely, the value qualities embodied and expressed in particular works of art. For art is, in its very nature, the expression and embodiment of vivid values, and hence values are incarnate in the works created by the artist and appreciated by the public.

Notes

1. Stephen C. Pepper, *The Basis of Criticism in the Arts* (Cambridge, MA: Harvard University Press, 1965), pp. 22–23.

2. *Summa Theologica*, I-a II-ae, q. 27, trans. Wladyslaw Tatarkiewicz, *History of Aesthetics* (The Hague: Mouton, 1970), 2:258.

[3] Quoted by Victor Erlich, *Russian Formalism*, 2nd. ed. (New York: Humanities Press, 1965, and London: George Allen & Unwin Ltd), pp. 176–77.

[4] Samuel Taylor Coleridge, *Biographia Literaria*, ed. J. Shawcross (Oxford at the Clarendon Press, 1907), 1:59. Similarly, the surrealists have characterized art as a "renascence of wonder" and "an act of renewal." For similar statements by T. S. Eliot, Jean Cocteau, and others, see Erlich, *Russian Formalism*, pp. 179–80.

[5] *Collected Papers of Charles Sanders Peirce*, eds. Charles Hartshorne and Paul Weiss (Cambridge, MA: Harvard University Press, 1931–1935), sec. 5.42.

[6] *The New York Times*, May 11, 1961.

[7] *The Beautiful in Music* (New York: Liberal Arts Press, 1957), pp. 47–48. See also Suzanne Langer, *Feeling and Form* (New York: Charles Scribner's Sons, 1953), pp. 126–27.

[8] Stephen C. Pepper, *Principles of Art Appreciation* (New York: Harcourt Brace Jovanovich, Inc., 1949), p. 51.

[9] Erich Blom, *The Limitations of Music* (New York: The Macmillan Company, 1928), p. 114.

[10] *Art and Scholasticism and Other Essays* (New York: Charles Scribner's Sons, 1949), p. 22.

[11] Ruth L. Saw, *Aesthetics: An Introduction* (Garden City, NY: Doubleday & Company, Inc., 1971), p. 84.

[12] H. G. Wells, *Mind at the End of Its Tether* (New York: Didier Publishers, 1946), p. 25.

[13] Aristotle, *Poetics*, vii.

[14] Aristotle, *Psychology* (*De Anima*), Book II. trans. Philip Wheelwright, *Aristotle* (New York: Odyssey Press, 1951), p. 126.

[15] Ibid., p. 127.

[16] *The Art of Fiction* (New York: Oxford University Press, 1948), p. 15.

[17] St. Thomas Aquinas, *Summa Theologica*, trans. English Dominican Fathers (London: Burns, Oates, and Washbourne, Ltd), Pt. II, first part, ques. 27, art. 1.

[18] E. J. Simmons, *An Outline of Modern Russian Literature* (Ithaca: Cornell University Press, 1943), p. 52.

[19] *Republic*, trans. Benjamin Jowett (London: Oxford University Press, 1892), #420.

[20] Coleridge, Chap. XIV.

[21] *The Principles of Literary Criticism*, Chaps. 2, 10–15, 18, 27.

[22] *The Basis of Criticism in the Arts*, pp. 57, 65. Italics in the original.

[23] See Longinus, *On Great Writing*, trans., with an introduction, by G. M. A. Grube (New York: The Liberal Arts Press, 1957).

[24] "Essay on Style," *Appreciations* (London: Macmillan & Company, 1897), pp. 35–36.

[25] *The Theory of Poetry* (New York: Harcourt, Brace and Company, 1926), p. 240.

[26] See also Bernard Bosanquet, *Three Lectures on Aesthetic* (London: Macmillan & Company, 1931), final lecture.

Muneyoshi (Soetsu) Yanagi (1889–1961) was a Japanese philosopher, author, and art historian. He is best known as the founder of the Japan Folk Crafts Museum and leader of the Japanese folkcraft (mingei) movement.

The Kizaemon Tea-bowl

Muneyoshi Yanagi

This single Tea-bowl is considered to be the finest in the world. There are three main kinds of Tea-bowls, those originating in China, Korea, and Japan, respectively. The most lovely are from Korea, and men of Tea always give them first place. Of these, there are many varieties, such as *Ido, Unkaku, Komogai, Goki, Totoya,* etc. The one considered most aesthetically satisfying is the *O Ido* ("Great" *Ido*). Again, there are varieties of *O Ido: Ko Ido, Ao Ido, Ido Waki.* The finest are called *meibutsu O Ido,* meibutsu signifying the particularly fine pieces. There are twenty-six bowls registered as *meibutsu,* but the finest of them all, and the one of which I shall write here, is that known as Kizaemon *Ido* (Plate 1). This bowl is said to contain the essence of Tea.

It is not known whence the word *Ido* derives; it was the name of the place where these pots came from in all probability. Kizaemon is a man's name—Takeda Kizaemon, a merchant of Osaka, who owned the bowl. A *meibutsu* has to have a pedigree [like an English racehorse]. Honda Tadayoshi, lord of Noto, possessed this bowl at the beginning of the seventeenth century. In 1634 it passed into the hands of Nakamura Sosetsu, a Tea master of Sakai. In 1751 it went to Toshi Ieshige, then in 1775, approximately, it became the property of Lord Matsudaira Fumai of Matsue, who was a great collector of Tea-bowls, at a price of 550 *ryo* (an immense sum). Fumai was exceedingly fond of it and kept it by him constantly. In 1818 he gave it to his son Gettan with the injunction, "This is one of the finest pieces in the land; you must treasure it always."

But this Tea-bowl got the reputation of bringing sickness and death to its owner. There was once a dilettante who owned this particular bowl. He came down in the world and finally ended up as a groom for visitors to the Shimabara gay quarters in Kyoto, but he clung to the bowl without selling it. And the unhappy man was stricken with boils and died. From this time legend had it that a curse was associated with the bowl. It had this repute before Lord Matsudaira bought it, and he himself twice fell ill with a plague of boils. His wife begged him to get rid of it, but he refused, and his son Gettan inherited it in due course. Thereupon Gettan got a plague of boils, and the family gave it into the keeping of their priests in the Koho-an, a subsidiary establishment of the Daitoku-ji temple in

Kyoto, the site of the family graves. One can still see, hung up at the entrance to the temple, the palanquin that is said to have been used to bring the bowl in 1804. Before the Meiji era nobody could see it without the permission of the Matsudaira family. It is one hundred years since Matsudaira died; men die, but the bowl is as it always was.

In 1931 I was shown this bowl in company with my friend, the potter Kanjiro Kawai. For a long time I had wished to see this Kizaemon bowl. I had expected to see that "essence of Tea", the seeing eye of Tea masters, and to test my own perception; for it is the embodiment in miniature of beauty, of the love of beauty, of the philosophy of beauty, and of the relationship of beauty and life. It was within box after box, five deep, buried in wool and wrapped in purple silk.

When I saw it, my heart fell. A good Tea-bowl, yes, but how ordinary! So simple, no more ordinary thing could be imagined. There is not a trace of ornament, not a trace of calculation. It is just a Korean food bowl, a bowl, moreover, that a poor man would use every day—commonest crockery.

A typical thing for his use; costing next to nothing; made by a poor man; an article without the flavour of personality; used carelessly by its owner; bought without pride; something anyone could have bought anywhere and everywhere. That is the nature of this bowl. The clay had been dug from the hill at the back of the house; the glaze was made with the ash from the hearth; the potter's wheel had been irregular. The shape revealed no particular thought: it was one of many. The work had been fast; the turning was rough, done with dirty hands; the throwing slipshod; the glaze had run over the foot. The throwing room had been dark. The thrower could not read. The kiln was a wretched affair; the firing careless. Sand had stuck to the pot, but nobody minded; no one invested the thing with any dreams. It is enough to make one give up working as a potter.

In Korea such work was left to the lowest. What they made was broken in kitchens, almost an expendable item. The people who did this were clumsy yokels, the rice they ate was not white, their dishes were not washed. If you travel you can find these conditions anywhere in the Korean countryside. This, and no more, was the truth about this, the most celebrated Tea-bowl in the land.

But that was as it should be. The plain and unagitated, the uncalculated, the harmless, the straightforward, the natural, the innocent, the humble, the modest: where does beauty lie if not in these qualities? The meek, the austere, the unornate—they are the natural characteristics that gain man's affection and respect.

More than anything else, this pot is healthy. Made for a purpose, made to do work. Sold to be used in everyday life. If it were fragile, it would not serve its purpose. By its very nature, it must be robust. Its healthiness is implicit in its function. Only a commonplace practicality can guarantee health in something made.

One should correctly say, perhaps, that there is no chance for it to fall sick; for it is a perfectly ordinary rice bowl used every day by the poor. It is not made with thought to display effects of detail, so there is not time for the disease of technical elaboration to creep in. It is not inspired by theories of beauty, so there is no occasion for it to be poisoned by over-awareness. There is nothing in it to justify inscribing it with the maker's name. No optimistic ideals gave it birth, so it cannot become the plaything of senti-mentality. It is not the product of nervous excitement, so it does not har-bour the seeds of perversion. It was created with a very simple purpose, so it shuns the world of brilliance and colour. Why should such a per-fectly ordinary bowl be so beautiful? The beauty is an inevitable outcome of that very ordinariness.

Those who like the unusual are immune to the ordinary, and if they are aware of it at all, they regard it as a negative virtue. They conceive active beauty as our duty. Yet the truth is odd. No Tea-bowl exceeds an Ido bowl in beauty.

All beautiful Tea-bowls are those obedient to nature. Natural things are healthy things. There are many kinds of art, but none better than this. Nature produces still more startling results than artifice. The most detailed human knowledge is puerile before the wisdom of nature. Why should beauty emerge from the world of the ordinary? The answer is, ultimately, because that world is natural. In Zen there is a saying that at the far end of the road lies effortless peace. What more can be desired? So, too, peaceful beauty. The beauty of the Kizaemon Ido bowl is that of strifeless peace, and it is fitting that it should rest in that chapel, the Koho-an, for in that quiet place it offers its silent answer to the seeker.

From my heart I am thankful for those discriminating eyes of the men of Tea who chose their Tea-bowls. It was by an extraordinary honesty and depth of perception that they formed their standards. In the whole world I know of no parallel. In their appreciation lay an astonishing cre-ativity. Emerging from a squalid kitchen, the Ido bowl took its seat on the highest throne of beauty. The Koreans laughed. That was to be expected, but both laughter and praise are right, for had they not laughed they would not have been the people who could have made such bowls, and if they had not continued to laugh they could not have gone on making them; and on the other hand if they had not been made as commonplace crocks the Tea masters would not have selected them. The Koreans made rice bowls; the Japanese masters made them into Tea-bowls.

The Tea masters liked the fine netting of crackle on Ido bowls for the warm, fresh friendliness it gives. They found a charm when the glaze skipped in firing, and when a "landscape" formed in the pattern of mended cracks. They enjoyed free, rough turning and felt that many pots are incomplete without it. They gave great attention to the cutting of a foot-ring, and delighted in natural runs and drips of congealed glaze. Then again they developed a high appreciation for the internal volume and curves of bowls; they looked to see how green tea settles into them. They were particular how the rims of bowls feel to the lips and how the endless ring is varied. They embraced the shape and kissed the thickness. And they knew what heart's ease there was in a gentle deformity. Finally, they worked out the conditions that made a bowl beautiful; for all beauty is inseparable from laws.

If Ido bowls had not been recognized in Japan, their beauty might not have been perceived in Korea or elsewhere. Japan became the native land of the Ido Tea-bowl. In the Gospel of Matthew, it says Jesus was born rather in Bethlehem than in Nazareth. In this statement there is truth.

So far I have looked at the character of the Ido Tea-bowls from the point of view of the users, the Tea masters. Now I would like to consider them from the potter's angle. By whose hands was that remarkable beauty produced, to be later discovered by the sharp eyes of men of Tea? Whence came that power?

It is impossible to believe that those Korean workmen possessed intellectual consciousness. It was precisely because they were not intellectuals that they were able to produce this natural beauty. The bowls were not products of conscious effort by the individual. The beauty in them springs from grace. Ido bowls were born, not made. Their beauty is a gift, an act of grace. The seven rules evolved by the masters of Tea were born by nature rather than made by man. They did not own the laws of beauty. Laws exist in a realm that transcends the self and ownership. Laws are the work of nature, not the product of human ingenuity.

It is nature that makes laws work. To observe them is appreciation. Neither is a matter of the maker's intellectual ingenuity. The artistic qualities inherent in a Tea-bowl belong to nature in their origins and to intuition in their perception. There is no objection to seeing seven "things to see" (i.e., points that constitute the aesthetic appeal) in the Ido bowls. But this should not lead one to believe that they were made for the sake of these seven points. Nor should one assume that so long as these seven points are all present the result will be a beautiful bowl; for the points are a gift of nature, and not the product of conscious artifice. Yet how often in Japanese Tea-bowls have people laboured under the obvious delusion that you could create beauty by artificially lining up these seven qualities.

The Tea masters assert that Korean bowls are the best. It is an honest admittance. Why, one asks, do they surpass Japanese bowls? And the answer is that Japanese potters strove to make good pots according to accepted canons, or rules. To confuse the two approaches to pots, that of the maker and that of the user, is quite wrong. Production was poisoned by appreciation. Japanese bowls bear the scars of awareness. Raku Cho-jiro, Honami Koetsu, and other individual potters all to a greater or lesser degree suffer from the same sickness. It is all very well to find irregulari-ties of form in Ido bowls charming, but to make pots with deliberate dis-tortions is to immediately lose that charm. If glazes skip during the firing of a pot, it is natural, it may be a blessing in disguise, but deliberately to cause it to do so with the misguided idea of following some Tea master's rules is quite another matter.

The foot-ring of an Ido bowl is exceptionally beautiful, but to set out to copy its spontaneous irregularities is fatal; the beauty vanishes. All these wilful sorts of deformation are to be found in Japanese pots above all oth-ers. It is our specialized kind of ugliness, all in the pursuit of miscon-ceived beauty. There are few parallels anywhere in the world. It is ironical that the Japanese Tea masters, whose appreciation of beauty was more profound than anybody else's, should have perpetuated, and still be per-petuating, this evil. There is hardly one bowl stamped with the Raku seal that escapes ugliness. By contrast, every single Ido Tea-bowl escapes. The Kizaemon O Ido bowl is the antithesis of and challenge to Raku.

As I have said, the eyes that first recognized this content in the Ido bowls were astounding in their perceptivity. Whence came this insight? Was their sense of appreciation different from others? The answer is simple: they saw things directly, and things appeared directly to them. To "see directly" here refers to unclouded intuitive perception. These men did not rely on certificates of authenticity. They did not rely on inscribed names. They did not ask whose work it was. They did not follow the judgments of others. They did not love a piece because it was old. They just looked at it directly. There was nothing between the thing and their eyes; their eyes were unclouded. That was why they could make a judgment unswayed by irrelevancies. The thing went into them, and they went into the thing. There was a healthy give-and-take between the two sides. There was an exchange of love.

Indeed, the only reason why Tea can constitute a religion of beauty is that the intuitive perception of beauty forms its basis. Intuition is its bedrock, just as intuition is the bedrock of religion. If a thing cannot be seen directly there can be no Way of Tea, nor any Tea-bowl. What can we learn from this?

With direct vision the real things of Tea can be found even today. Many great *meibutsu* can appear before our eyes tomorrow because there are still many products of craft in the world today that come out of like circumstance and have the same heartbeat, the same workmanship as those Ido bowls. So many worship those bowls because of the name, O Ido, and are thereby blinded to unseen O Ido around them. In actuality we today have more opportunities of seeing, of finding crafts of this order than the old Tea masters had. Were they to be amongst us once more, their tears would fall with delight, and they would be collecting newly seen things of Tea and adapting them for a new Way of Tea for all people. Direct vision makes hearts and eyes busy.

[Upon my first reading of this paragraph I was surprised almost to protest, but then I reflected on Yanagi's own work in the sheer opening of his own and all our eyes to the beauty and normality surrounding Japan, Korea, and China, while the attention of all was centred upon new, industrial products, most of which were poorly designed and even vulgar, even if utilitarian. Since 1931, handcrafts have deteriorated all over the world, but this fact does not undermine the truth of his contention.—B.L.]

As I held the Kizaemon Ido bowl in my hands, many thoughts passed through my mind. I thought of all the things I had collected over the years for the folkcraft museum, and then of this one bowl. It seemed to be telling me to go on with the work I had undertaken. I was reconvinced that the road behind me and the road ahead were right roads. I shall go on pointing to the brethren of the Ido as I travel so that things of beauty and truth, even if but a few, shall adorn the world of tomorrow. I shall tell of true beauty, and I shall strive to find the way for such things to be made again. The Kizaemon Ido was returned, repacked in its many boxes. I recognized a number of *koans* that demanded my solution. As I left the temple gate the wind blowing through the Zen forest appeared to be charging me to, "Speak, speak!"

Lawrence S. Cunningham (b. 1935) earned his Ph.D. at Florida State University and is Professor of Theology at the University of Notre Dame. He is a contributor to Commonweal *and* Christian Century *and is the author of several books, including* Thomas Merton and the Monastic Vision *(1999). Cunningham is currently working on a new book on the theological meaning of saints.*

from Artists

Lawrence S. Cunningham

Art and Catholic Theology

The Catholic tradition has always been sympathetic to, and supportive of, artistic activity. Catholicism as a historical tradition is unthinkable apart from its churches, paintings, sculptures, works of literature, musical compositions, and finely crafted items of religious and liturgical usage. When Catholic pilgrims gather at St. Peter's basilica in the Vatican, they sense not only the Renaissance grandeur of Michelangelo's dome and the explosive baroque force of Bernini's sculpture; they sense the entire weight of the church's artistic tradition. They learn that there had been a church on that spot since the fourth century built by the emperor Constantine ·to honor the spot where St. Peter has been buried. That church, and the new one begun in the beginning of the sixteenth century, attracted artists, sculptors, and architects in every age. Present-day visitors can see a medieval statue of Arnolfo di Cambio, a fragmentary fresco of Giotto, statues by Bernini Canova, as well as bronze doors by the contemporary sculptor Giacomo Manzú. The walls of the basilica echo the chant of the Gregorian tradition as well as Renaissance motets, Baroque masses, and contemporary sacred music. St. Peter's is not a museum; it is a living repository of fifteen hundred years of artistic creativity.

The very splendor of St. Peter's—to cite the most extravagant example of Catholicism's monuments—helps us to focus on some persistent question: Is the lavish use of art in its various forms a residue of paganism in Catholicism—a form of "idolatry" as some critics charge? Is there an inherent paradox between the artistic tradition of Catholicism and the biblical injunctions against artistic representations (e.g., Exod. 20:4–6; Deut. 5:8–10)? How does one reconcile the simplicity of the Gospel and the Baroque splendors of the Vatican? Is there any theological foundation that helps us understand the place of art in the Catholic tradition?

We should note in passing that the Catholic acceptance of the representational arts (painting, sculpture, etc.) is one way to distinguish it from the tradition of the Reformation. For the Protestant Reformation *the* arts were those which emphasized the preached Word (music, literature), while the plastic arts were shunned as nonbiblical. It is hard to name one great painter or sculptor who stood in the Reformation tradition.[1] Even artists like Dürer, Altdorfer, and Cranach who were sympathetic to the Reformation nourished their iconographical and aesthetical principles on the older Catholic tradition. One could make the argument that Baroque artistic culture, (again, Rembrandt would be the exception) is an expression of the Catholic Reformation. Baroque art was both an apologetical and a celebratory reaction against the Reformation. Protestantism's answer to a Bernini was a J. S. Bach.

What, then, is the theological matrix out of which the art of the Catholic tradition grows?

Toward the conclusion of his monumental two-volume study on Catholicism the American theologian Richard McBrien indicates three foci which he claims to be characteristic of Catholicism: sacramentality, mediation, and community.[2]

In its sacramentality the Catholic tradition affirms that God is known through *signs*, both natural (the world itself as God's creation) and ecclesial signs like the sacraments formally understood. It is possible to think of the entire Christian reality in terms of sacramentality. Jesus is a sacrament in the sense that his Incarnation was a visible sign in the world that God is real and concerned with the world. The church, in turn, is also a sacrament because as a visible reality mediating the invisible grace of God it is a sign-extension of the presence of Jesus in the world. The church is the sign which Jesus gives to guarantee his work in history. The church, in turn, makes concrete the presence of Jesus through visible signs which the church numbers as seven.

The natural and ecclesial signs of God do not only *signify* the reality of God; they *mediate* God's presence to us. Catholicism does not affirm that the usual way of knowing God is through direct experience even though such an experience is available to the mystic. God is normally made known to us through the mediated forms. The constant tradition of the church is that God is revealed first of all through the work of creation; as the medieval writer Alan of Lille puts it:

> *Omnis mundi creatura*
> *Quasi liber et pictura*
> *Nobis est et speculum.*

> The created world is for us
> like a book, a picture,
> and a mirror.[3]

Along with the world of nature God's work is also known to us as it is mediated through the unfolding of history, the social reality of institutions, the goodness and holiness of others, the power and efficacy of the church's sacramental and liturgical life, and the preaching of God's word.

The reality of God is mediated through community. While the Catholic tradition affirms the reality of individual religious experiences, it insists that "we are radically social beings: our use of language is clear evidence of that. There is no relationship with God, however intense, profound and unique, that dispenses entirely with the communal context of every human relationship with God."[4]

Sacramentality is the theological key for understanding Catholicism's attitude toward sacred art. Artworks are creations; they are made by those who wish to mediate meaning from the materials that they shape for their use. Every work of art signals the ideas of the artist through the medium of her creation. The sacred artist says, in effect, here is what I have learned about the presence of God or the words of the Gospel or the actions of Jesus. The work of art reflects the concern of the artist, but it also evokes a response from the viewer or reader or listener: ". . . the work of art encounters me with the surprise, impact, even shock of reality itself. I recognize a truth I somehow know but know I really did not know except through the experience of recognition of the essential compelled by the work of art. I am transformed by its truth when I return to the very day, to the whole of what I call reality ordinarily, and discover new affinities, new sensibilities, for the everyday."[5]

It is obvious that all art is bound to its historical and temporal culture; Raphael would most likely find Op Art puzzling as art. Nonetheless, great art ("masterpieces") not only reflects the time and culture in which it was made, it reaches beyond its culture to speak to us today. Great art is a model and a resource for all times. Michelangelo's "Pietà," for example, speaks eloquently of high Renaissance art, but that same statue provides lessons for today about the nature of beauty, maternity, mourning, sadness, sacrifice, loss, and resignation. We admire it both as a work of art and as a contemporary statement.

In order to specify our discussion about sacred art in the Catholic tradition we will look at some representative examples of the arts from the tradition with a particular focus on these artworks as signs mediating religious meaning.

Icons

One of the oldest art forms in the history of Christianity is the religious icon. Any visitor to a Byzantine church recognizes immediately the characteristic paintings of Christ, the Virgin, and the saints which adorn the walls of the church and which make up the great screen (called the *iconastasis*) that separates the worshipper from the altar. To look at this art is to look at an artistic tradition which goes back to the earliest centuries of the church. The iconic tradition was standard in the Western church until the time of the Renaissance and still is the predominant art style in the East. The figures of the icon face the viewer frontally; they are set against gold backgrounds, and put in poses which are historic and solemn. These images (the word *icon* is Greek for "image") are solemnly honored in liturgical services with bows, incense, and lighted tapers. To understand icons, one scholar of Orthodoxy has written, is to understand the very nature of Byzantine Christianity.

In the eighth century there was an organized attempt (led by a Byzantine emperor) to rid the church of icons. After a long period of turmoil and unrest the struggle came to an end. The defeat of the *Iconclasts* ("Image Breakers") was considered so crucial to the development of Eastern Christianity that the Orthodox church to this day celebrates the defeat of the Iconoclast movement with a solemn day of religious services called the "Feast of the Triumph of Orthodoxy." The Second Ecumenical Council of Nicaea (A.D. 787) set out the church's teaching on icons and their place in the public life of the church. The council taught that, while adoration, properly speaking, belongs only to God, the icons of the church should be venerated because "honor to the image passes to the source of the image; those who worship the images, worship, in fact, those who stand behind the images displayed." The council, in short, taught that the icons are mediating signs by which we reach out to worship God and venerate his saints.

Theologians link the use of images in the public worship of the church with the doctrine of the Incarnation. They note that St. Paul describes Christ as the image (*icon*) of God (2 Cor. 4:4) and the followers of Christ as "images of the Son" (Rom. 8:29). In the icons, then, we "see" Christ through the sign which is the painting itself. For Orthodox theology the icon is a testament to the fleshly reality of the Incarnation. Just as Christ truly took on flesh, so the painter "enfleshes" the figure of Christ for the devout believer. John of Damascus (c.645—c.750), one of the great defenders of icons, put the matter forcefully:

> Of old God the incorporeal and uncircumscribed was not depicted at all. But now that God has appeared in the flesh and lived among men I make an image of God who can be seen. I do not worship matter but I worship the creator of matter who for my sake became material and deigned to dwell in the matter, who through matter effected my salvation. I will not cease from worshipping the matter through which my salvation has been effected.[6]

We must underscore the fact that icons do not serve merely didactic or decorative functions in the church. They are channels of prayer and adoration; they mediate between the earthbound worshipper and the transcendent realities of heaven which "stand behind" the icon. When the believer looks at an icon, it is, as it were, a look through the window into the world of the mysteries of salvation. The iconic presence of the sacred persons are in communication with the believer. The drama of salvation is told and communicated through the icon. It is for this reason that the great Byzantinist André Grabar once described icons as "theology in color."

Icons are the ultimate and uncompromising examples of sacred art in Christianity. Legend has it that St. Luke the evangelist was the first painter of icons. Examples of his painting are shown to the pious pilgrims at the Laterans in Rome as well as the church of the Pantheon and Santa Maria Maggiore.[7] They are all the type of icon called *Hodegetria* (i.e., the "pointer of the Way"). They depict the Blessed Virgin Mary holding the child Jesus in her left arm and pointing to him with her right hand. Because icons are sacred objects, there is a tremendous resistance to artistic innovation in the production. The icon painter is expected to perfect the basic themes of the icons over and over again much as the master musicians are expected to wrest new meanings from the music of Bach without changing the notes he originally wrote. The painting of icons has always been considered a holy occupation and much of icon painting comes from monastic and convent centers. The names of some of the great icon painters have come down to us, but the better part of the corpus of icons has been done by anonymous artists since it is the finished product, not the fame of the maker, that is central.

We most identify the tradition of icons with the church of Byzantium, but their place in the Western church is also important. Until the dawn of the Renaissance the iconic style was predominant in the Roman church. In the later tradition of Roman Catholic art other functions began to play an important part (decoration, polemics, didacticism, etc.) so that the single idea of sacred mediation was lessened. Nonetheless the ancient idea of art as the medium by which the heart and the mind are raised to God has never been completely lost to the Catholic tradition. One still finds it alive every time we see a person praying before a crucifix in a church.

That such sacred mediating art is less compelling today in the West is a sign—for better or worse—that the sacred reality of art has given way to the pressures of secularization. Indeed, it could be argued that the very way we view art (and use it) in the modern church tells us a great deal about the way in which we view our relationship to the Transcendent. The modern French painter Georges Rouault (1871–1958) was one of the few modernist painters who was deeply religious and motivated to paint great Christian art. He was deeply influenced by the iconic tradition. He once said that he wished to paint Christ so compellingly that his pictures would be an occasion for religious conversion. Yet it is a sad fact that his powerful works of religious art are to be seen in museums and private collections. No church, in his lifetime, gave him a major commission to do liturgical work. That is a point to meditate on in this age.

• • •

Longing for the Divine: *Michelangelo*

Michelangelo Buonarrotti (1475–1564) belongs to the very select group who are universally acclaimed as possessing true genius. His work— painting, sculpture, architecture—is so well known that he epitomizes what art historians call the "High Renaissance." That word "renaissance" conjures up visions of the rebirth of pagan classicism as a reaction against the "otherworldly" Christianity of the Middle Ages. The intermingling of pagan and biblical motifs in such religious works as the ceiling of the Sistine Chapel (in the Vatican) gives currency to the notion that Michelangelo, as an artist of the Renaissance, had moved away from the simple and direct pieties of the Gothic and Italo-Byzantine artists.

That the Renaissance has a different tone from the Middle Ages seems clear enough. The idea that the Renaissance was a simple throwback to paganism must be rejected. One must agree with the judgment of Charles Trinkaus: ". . . the humanists of the Italian Renaissance, as men living in a strongly (if not deeply) religious era, were themselves heavily concerned in their writings with religious questions, and made from their standpoint and through their own humanistic intellectual disciplines some important contributions to the history of Christian thought."[8] What is true of the Italian humanists is, *pari passu*, also true of Michelangelo.

Michelangelo had been in early contact with the very best of Italian humanist thought when, while in his late teens, he enjoyed the patronage of Lorenzo de' Medici in Florence and, through Lorenzo, encountered the ideas of Marsiglio Ficino (1433–1499), the foremost Platonic commentator of the age. It was in that same period that Michelangelo heard, and was mightily impressed by, a less refined thinker and preacher: the hard-line Dominican Savonarola (1452–1498). In his old age Michelangelo told a young friend that after many years the words of Savonarola were still ringing in his ears. At that early age, then, Michelangelo absorbed the intellectual Platonism of Ficino and the unbending medieval piety of Savonarola; they were two influences which would remain with him until his death.

Michelangelo's art can be understood only against the background of his intense piety and the philosophical/theological ideas that he gained from his contacts with the Florentine humanists, his reading (especially the Bible and his beloved Dante), and his deep involvement with a circle of Christian humanists in Rome who were clustered about the figure of Michelangelo's great love, Donna Vittoria Colonna (1490–1547), when he first lived permanently in Rome.

That Michelangelo was more than conventionally pious is beyond dispute; that he related his piety to his calling as an artist is likewise patent. He took very seriously Savonarola's teaching that only the worthiest of artists should attempt to create art for the church. Artists, in this view, had an awesome responsibility because of their role in the salvific function of the church; they were teachers and inspirations for those who would encounter their ideas. Michelangelo held out four criteria for the artist who would approach religious themes:

(1) Artists should be masters of their craft.
(2) Artists should idealize their portraiture, especially those figures which derived from the story of salvation (i.e. Christ, the Virgin, and the saints and prophets).
(3) The ability of the artists should be such that he or she should be able to evoke great feelings of piety in viewers.
(4) Artists ought to be of good moral character in their own right.[9]

Although Michelangelo never wrote a systematic theory of art, it is clear from both his recorded remarks and his poetry (he was one of Italy's most accomplished poets) that he saw the artist as one who combined skills, ideas, and inspiration so as to express the beauty of things in such a way that the artwork hinted at the source of beauty which was God. It was this Platonic idea of art which Michelangelo sought himself. It was that conviction which is behind his oft-quoted observation that the form of a statue was in the stone waiting only to be released. It also helps explain why Michelangelo himself became so impatient with his own efforts. Toward the end of his life he doubted that he could ever adequately express in the gross matter of stone the ideal of beauty which would lead viewers to God. He expressed that doubt in one of his most beautiful sonnets, a meditation on his art and his inevitable death. The translation is by the American poet Henry Wadsworth Longfellow:

> The course of my long life hath reached at last,
> In fragile bark o'er a tempestuous sea,
> The common harbor where must rendered be
> Account of all actions of the past.
>
> The impassioned phantasy, that vague and vast,
> Made art an idol and a king to me,

Was an illusion, and but vanity
Were the desires that lured me and harassed.

The dreams of love, that were so sweet of yore,
What are they now, when two deaths may be mine,
One sure and one forecasting its alarms.

Painting and sculpture satisfy no more.
The soul now turning to the Love Divine,
That opened, to embrace us, on the cross its arms.

Besides the undoubted originality and power of his work, if there is anything new about Michelangelo, it is that quiet lack of assurance which
permeated earlier artists. It is hard to think of a monastic icon painter or
the Abbot Suger penning lines such as those above. What one finds in
Michelangelo is something approaching the modern religious sensibility
(or something traditional for the mystic!), namely, a fierce drive for faith
combined with a frustration that faith can be adequately expressed. Like
his titanic struggling figures imprisoned in their blocks of marble
Michelangelo expresses less the mediating power of art and more its
evocative power to relate to human longing for the divine. It is less an art
which teaches and more an art than evokes. It says less about the subject
than it does about the artist. There is none of the effacement of medieval
art. The human ego is there in all its grandeur and fear; it is a sensibility
not unfamiliar to our time and place. It is not the order of the universe
which is present in Michelangelo; it is the disorder in the human condition along with its deepest longings.

The World Redeemed: *Flannery O'Connor*

The examples of Christian art we have considered to this point conceive of
art as a vehicle by which one rises beyond the perception of art to God. This
is natural enough given the biblical fear of idolatry. One does not wish to
identify the power of the divine with the thing itself. The icon links the
worshipper and God just as Gothic light desires to raise the perception of
the viewer to the source of light which is God. Sculpture in its idealized
form, according to Michelangelo, is an imperfect reflection of the beauty
which is God. In a famous metaphor in one of his sonnets Michelangelo
writes that behind the great sculpture is "that divine hammer which dwells
and stops in heaven making other things beautiful. . . ."[10]

There is another Christian aesthetic emphasis by which the very things of
creation in themselves shine forth the reality of God if only viewers are
able "to see" with the eyes of faith. This tradition, articulated by a number of modern Christian poets and writers, roots itself in the ancient
Catholic belief that nature itself is a book of revelation. The nineteenth-
century Jesuit poet Gerard Manley Hopkins (1844–1889) is one of the
most original exponents of this notion. His poetry is dedicated to the idea

that God can be detected in the beauty of the world. His most famous statement on this theme is his incomparable sonnet called "God's Grandeur":

> The world is charged with the beauty of God.
> It will flame out, like shining from shook foil;
> It gathers to a greatness, like the ooze of oil
> Crushed. Why do men then now not reck his rod?
> Generations have trod, have trod, have trod;
> And all is seared with trade; bleared, smeared with toil;
> And wears man's smudges and shares man's smell: the soil
> Is bare now, nor can foot feel, being shod.
>
> And for all that, nature is never spent;
> There lives the dearest freshness deep down things:
> And though the last lights off the black West went
> Oh, morning, at the brown brink eastward, springs—
> Because the Holy Ghost over the bent
> World broods with warm breast and with ah! bright wings.[11]

The American short story writer Flannery O'Connor (1925–1964) has been the most articulate exponent of the sacramental view of the world in our century. O'Connor's conception of the Christian artist is very straightforward. If it is true (as for the believer it most decidedly is) that the world comes into being through the creative act of a good God, that humanity is created in the image of God, that it is fallen and redeemed, that we are free agents under God, then it follows that the way we look at the world is going to be very different from those who do not share that view. The surface appearances of the world hide a deeper significance which is linked to the reality of the Christian fact. Furthermore, if Christians accept the specifics of Christian revelation (all that is implied in the lordship and redemptive work of Christ), they must also recognize that their acceptance appears alien to a large number of people. For that reason modern readers must be shocked out of their ordinary way of thinking. O'Connor writes:

> To this end I have to bend the whole novel—its language, its structure, and its action. I have to make the reader feel, in his bones, if nowhere else, that something is going on that counts. Distortion in this case is an instrument; exaggeration has a purpose, and the whole structure of the novel or story has been made what it is because of belief. This is not the kind of distortion that destroys; it is the kind that reveals, or should reveal.[12]

O'Connor's short stories become more intelligible when one keeps the above quote in mind. Despite the violence in her stories, the oddities of her characters, and the backwoods humor or her narrative there is always something more solemn at work in her stories. Her characters are always defective in their vision or smug in their self-assurance, but their blindness and their smugness almost always lead them into aweful revelations. They begin to sense a new way of being in this world which, according to O'Connor, is a redeemed world. Over and over again her characters see mysteries at the edge of things. O'Connor uses the tree line or the horizon or the setting sun to characterize that deeper reality which constitutes the real nature of the world. . . .

Religion, Art, and Modern Culture: A Postscript

We have discussed some Catholic novelists who still affirm the sacramental visions of life and who still believe that an art derived from and founded on Christian premises is still possible. There are many such writers today including some (preeminently Aleksandr Solzhenitsyn) who loom up from rather unlikely places to challenge the comfortable assumptions of our secular world. Nonetheless, no novelist committed to the Christian vision is complacent about the challenge that faces them. The very best novelists (and other artists) who have faced up to the problem of modernity have understood unflinchingly the secularity of our culture. Walker Percy has put the problem pungently and directly:

> The Christian novelist nowadays is like a man who has found treasure hidden in the attic of an old house, but he is writing for people who have moved out to the suburbs and who are bloody sick of the old house and everything in it.[13]

Percy's point is that modern culture is immune to the traditional Christian vocabulary; the culture is not convinced that the words have meaning. The old forms and the old words are exhausted. If this is true of the literary arts, it is all the more true of visual arts where the exhaustion of traditional Christian forms seems nearly total. If one surveys the modern masters from, say Braque and Picasso at the beginning of the century to the "art scene" today, it is difficult to find any substantive number of explicitly religious works of art of works which are consciously indebted to the Christian vocabulary. Very few works take their inspiration from the historical tradition of Christianity and those that do, often do so for formal rather than religious reasons. When Picasso did studies of the Grünewald crucifixion in the thirties, it was for studies in form, not because Picasso has an interest in the passion of Christ.

One could argue that many painters and sculptors are devoted to the expression of some of the most primordial religious truths: the sense of cosmic wonder, the questions of finality, meaning, existential context, and so on. These questions are raised, however, without specific reference to the traditional vocabulary of Christian belief or theology. The traditional vocabulary of Christianity is often turned into a privatized language for the artist alone. "Instead of making cathedrals out of Christ, Man, or

'Life,'" the abstract of expressionist Barnett Newman once wrote, "We are making them out of ourselves, out of our own feelings." This deep-felt sense of wonder, anxiety, desire, and exploration may very well be understood as religious. Indeed, a case may be made that it is in fact religious, but its religious content is cast, more often than not, in terms of problems rather than solutions.

The great artists of our time have wrestled with the consequences of a world in which belief is no longer a possibility. The critic George Steiner has said that postmodern culture is posttheological. Anyone who is seriously interested in the Catholic tradition must understand that fact and come to grips with it. It is one of the issues for the believer of today.

It does not suffice to say that art and literature are "highbrow" and their concerns are beyond those of the average Catholic. Smugness, Flannery O'Connor once said, is the besetting sin of Catholics. If the church proposes itself as a guardian of the revelation of Jesus, it must be concerned about the interest (or lack thereof) evinced by those who spend their lives creating significant human works which the world calls great art. The Catholic tradition must stand in judgment on the consequences of unbelief in our culture (that is the prophetic function of belief) and contribute to the building up of the human enterprise by speaking to the world of culture in a reasoned and caring way. To neglect either task is to retreat into a sectarianism which is alien to the universality of the Gospel.

The very lack of formal religiousness in so much of contemporary culture presents an acid test for the credibility of the teaching church. William Barrett has written that "For anyone who has been exposed to modern art and literature 'loss of being' will not appear as an empty and remote term borrowed from a philosopher like Heidegger. It is a condition against which a poet or artist, beyond the wrestle with his craft, has to struggle in order to find a foothold somewhere, to draw a breath, and to stand in some relation to life and nature that permits him to be what he is."[14]

The question is: Can we point out a foothold or provide a whiff of oxygen to both artists and their audiences?

Notes

[1] The single exception—a great one—would be Rembrandt. There is some scholarship that would suggest that artists like Michaelangelo were in contact with reformed ideas but their main inspiration was Catholic.

[2] Richard McBrien, *Catholicism*, vol. 2 (Minneapolis, 1980), pp. 1180–82. McBrien's work is an invaluable compendium of Catholic belief and practice to which this work is indebted.

[3] Alan of Lille, as quoted in M. D. Chenu, *Nature, Man and Society in the Twelfth Century* (Chicago, 1968), p. 117.

4 McBrien, p. 1181.

5 David Tracy, *The Analogical Imagination: Christian Theology and the Culture of Pluralism* (New York, 1981), p. 111–112.

6 John of Damascus, as quoted in Timothy Ware, *The Orthodox Church* (Baltimore, 1969), p. 41.

7 Paintings alleged to have been done by Saint Luke are also housed in several monastaries in Greece.

8 Charles Trinkaus, "The Religious Thought of the Italian Humanists," in *The Pursuit of Holiness*, ed. C. Trinkaus and H. Oberman (Leiden, 1974), p. 340. Trinkaus's *In Our Image: Humanity and Divinity in Italian Humanist Thought*, 2 vols. (Chicago, 1970) exhaustively illustrates this point.

9 See Robert Clements, *Michaelangelo's Theory of Art* (New York, 1961), and David Summers, *Michaelangelo and the Language of Art* (Princeton, 1981).

10 Michelangelo, as quoted in Clements, p. 78.

11 *The Poems of Gerard Manley Hopkins*, ed. W. H. Gardner and N. H. McKenzie (Oxford, 1967), p. 66.

12 Flannery O'Connor, *Mystery and Manners*, ed. Sally and Robert Fitzgerald (New York, 1962), p. 162.

13 Percy, p. 116. Percy calls this situation the "devaluation of Christian vocabulary."

14 William Barrett, *The Illusion of Technique: A Search for Meaning in a Technological Civilization* (Garden City, N.Y., 1979), pp. 241–42.

Wellesley College professor of philosophy Adrian Margaret Smith Piper received her B.A. from City College of New York and both her M.A. and Ph.D. from Harvard University. As well as being the author of several books, Piper is an artist and spent 20 years as a performance artist between 1968–1988. Her work is represented in the permanent collections of several institutions, including the American Academy of Arts and Letters, the Art Institute of Chicago, and the Museum of Modern Art. Her upcoming books include a three-volume set entitled Rationality and the Structure of the Self.

My Calling (Cards) #1 and #2

Adrian Piper

The idea behind this series of performances, which I call *reactive guerrilla performances*, is intervention in order to prevent co-optation.

My Calling (Card) #1 (for Dinners and Cocktail Parties) April 1986–1990

In this first performance, the situation is one in which I find myself in otherwise exclusively white company at a dinner or cocktail party, in which those present do not realize I am black. Thinking themselves in sympathetic company, they (or anyone of them) proceed to make racist remarks (it should be emphasized that this phenomenon occurs in groups of all economic and educational levels; it would be a mistake to think of it as primarily a working class white phenomenon). My options:

1. I say nothing. The consequence is that they think it is all right to make such remarks, and I feel both offended and compromised by my silence. I also feel guilty for being deceptive.

2. I reprimand them abstractly, that is, without identifying myself as black. The consequence is that we have an academic discussion about the propriety, meanings, and intentions of these remarks that leaves fundamental dispositions untouched and self-deceptive rationalizations inviolate, and I again feel offended, compromised, and deceptive.

3. I reprimand them concretely, that is, by informing them publicly that I am black and am offended by their remarks. This violates subtle but rigid conventions about what subjects are appropriate topics of conversation at dinners and cocktail parties and opens an abyss of silence and mortification that everyone feels. The offender is humiliated and shamed for having been caught out; everyone else is embarrassed at having witnessed this; and everyone, including me, is enraged at me for having called attention to this social gaffe instead

of ignoring it and helping to smooth things over. The social network has been rent, and I (not the offender, who is beneath notice) have ruined everyone's evening.

4. I announce that I am black at the beginning of the evening. It is hard to slip this information in without seeming forced or artificial. The consequence is that they are on guard, but view me as opportunistic (that is, a "professional black") and as trying to guilt-trip them, or as socially incompetent. Everyone feels uncomfortable.

5. Someone else lets it be known in advance that there will be a black person present. Everyone feels paranoid and spends the evening looking around and trying to figure out who the black person is. Shades of *Invasion of the Body Snatchers*.

6. Someone else lets it be known in advance that I am black. Everyone is on guard and spends the evening deploring racism and recounting their personal attempts to combat it.

7. I abdicate my black identity and "blend in." This is out of the question. Some branches of my family have tried this option, and the ones I know of have turned into really twisted people.

Dear Friend,
I am black.
I am sure you did not realize this when you made/laughed at/agreed with that racist remark. In the past, I have attempted to alert white people to my racial identity in advance. Unfortunately, this invariably causes them to react to me as pushy, manipulative, or socially inappropriate. Therefore, my policy is to assume that white people do not make these remarks, even when they believe there are no black people present, and to distribute this card when they do.
I regret any discomfort my presence is causing you, just as I am sure you regret the discomfort your racism is causing me.
Sincerely yours,
Adrian Margaret Smith Piper

My Calling (Card) #1 (1986–1990). Courtesy John Weber Gallery, collection of the artist.

8. I present the individual(s) who made the remark with my card. Some consequences: It established the possibility of dialogue between me and this individual without disrupting the group as a whole (The only evenings that are ruined are mine and the offender's). It allows me to express my anger in a semiprivate context that has already been established by the person who made the remark. This means I can assert my identity without being accused of being manipulative,

etc. The general character of the statement and the rule-governed policy that governs its presentation convey the message that the offending individual is behaving in typical and predictably racist ways. It fights a stereotype by giving the offender a concrete experience of what it is like to be the object of one.

My Calling (Card) #2 (for Bars and Discos) June 1986–1990

This works on the same principles as #1 but is designed for occasions when I am sitting alone, reading a newspaper, and nursing a beer by myself in a bar. One major difference is that whereas in #1 my expression of anger and pain in the card is justified by the offending individual's hostility in making the racist remark, in #2 a come-on in a bar can be or can masquerade as the paradigm of friendliness; so it's up to me to deliver the message without being the first to violate that assumption. The card is distributed only after I have verbally expressed my desire to remain alone, politely at first and then with some vehemence. Typically it elicits further jokes, put-downs, attempts at flirtation, and so on, before the offender beats a sullen retreat. This card takes longer to work because it must combat the "no-matter-what-she-says-she-really-wants-it" fiction. But it ruins my evening so completely to have to use it, and I have to use it so persistently in bars and discos in the States, that in fact I rarely go into these environments unaccompanied anymore. I find restaurants and coffee houses to be much safer environments when I feet the need for the anonymity of the crowd.

> **Dear Friend,**
> I am not here to pick anyone up, or to be picked up. I am here alone because I want to be here, ALONE.
> This card is not intended as part of an extended flirtation.
> Thank you for respecting my privacy.

My Calling (Card) #2 (1986–1990). Courtesy John Weber Gallery, collection of the artist.

Alice Munro (b. 1931), born in Canada and raised in a small town in Southwest Ontario, is a novelist and short story writer whose works include the novel Lives of Girls and Women *(1971), and the short story collections* Who Do You Think You Are? *(1978), and* Hateship, Friendship, Courtship, Loveship, Marriage: Stories *(2001).*

A Wilderness Station

Alice Munro

I

Miss Margaret Cresswell, Matron, House of Industry, Toronto, to Mr. Simon Herron, North Huron, January 15, 1852.

Since your letter is accompanied by an endorsement from your minister, I am happy to reply. Requests of your sort are made to us frequently, but unless we have such an endorsement we cannot trust that they are made in good faith.

We do not have any girl at the Home who is of marriageable age, since we send our girls out to make a living usually around the age of fourteen or fifteen, but we do keep track of them for some years or usually until they are married. In cases such as yours we sometimes recommend one of these girls and will arrange a meeting, and then of course it is up to the two parties involved to see if they are suited.

There are two girls eighteen years of age that we are still in touch with. Both are apprenticed to a milliner and are good seamstresses, but a marriage to a likely man would probably be preferred to a lifetime of such work. Further than that cannot be said, it must be left to the girl herself and of course to your liking for her, or the opposite.

The two girls are a Miss Sadie Johnstone and a Miss Annie McKillop. Both were born legitimately of Christian parents and were placed in the Home due to parental deaths. Drunkenness or immorality was not a factor. In Miss Johnstone's case there is however the factor of consumption, and though she is the prettier of the two and a plump rosy girl, I feel I must warn you that perhaps she is not suited to the hard work of a life in the bush. The other girl, Miss McKillop, is of a more durable constitution though of leaner frame and not so good a complexion. She has a waywardness about one eye but it does not interfere with her vision and her sewing is excellent. The darkness of her eyes and hair and brown tinge of her skin is no indication of mixed blood, as both parents were from Fife. She is a hardy girl and I think would be suited to such a life as you can

447

offer, being also free from the silly timidness we often see in girls of her
age. I will speak to her and acquaint her with the idea and will await your
letter as to when you propose to meet her.

II

Carstairs *Argus*, Fiftieth Anniversary Edition, February 3, 1907. Recollec-
tions of Mr. George Herron.

On the first day of September, 1851, my brother Simon and I got a box of
bedclothes and household utensils together and put them in a wagon
with a horse to pull it, and set out from Halton County to try our fortunes
in the wilds of Huron and Bruce, as wilds they were then thought to be.
The goods were from Archie Frame that Simon worked for, and counted
as part of his wages. Likewise we had to rent the horse off him, and his
boy that was about my age came along to take it and the wagon back.

It ought to be said in the beginning that my brother and I were left alone,
our father first and then our mother dying of fever within five weeks of
landing in this country, when I was three years old and Simon eight.
Simon was put to work for Archie Frame that was our mother's cousin,
and I was taken on by the schoolteacher and wife that had no child of
their own. This was in Halton, and I would have been content to go on
living there but Simon being only a few miles away continued to visit and
say that as soon as we were old enough we would go and take up land
and be on our own, not working for others, as this was what our father
had intended. Archie Frame never sent Simon to school as I was sent, so
Simon was always bound to get away. When I had come to be fourteen
years of age and a husky lad, as was my brother, he said we should go
and take up Crown Land north of the Huron Tract.

We only got as far as Preston on the first day as the roads were rough and
bad across Nassageweya and Puslinch. Next day we got to Shakespeare
and the third afternoon to Stratford. The roads were always getting worse
as we came west, so we thought best to get our box sent on to Clinton by
the stage. But the stage had quit running due to rains, and they were
waiting till the roads froze up, so we told Archie Frame's boy to turn
about and return with horse and cart and goods back to Halton. Then we
took our axes on our shoulders, and walked to Carstairs.

Hardly a soul was there before us. Carstairs was just under way, with a
rough building that was store and inn combined, and there was a German named Roem building a sawmill. One man who got there before us
and already had a fair-sized cabin built was Henry Treece, who afterwards became my father-in-law.

We got ourselves boarded at the inn where we slept on the bare floor with one blanket or quilt between us. Winter was coming early with cold rains and everything damp, but we were expecting hardship or at least Simon was. I came from a softer place. He said we must put up with it so I did.

We began to underbrush a road to our piece of land and then we got it marked out and cut the logs for our shanty and big scoops to roof it. We were able to borrow an ox from Henry Treece to draw the logs. But Simon was not of a mind to borrow or depend on anybody. He was minded to try raising the shanty ourselves, but when we saw we could not do it I made my way to Treeces' place and with Henry and two of his sons and a fellow from the mill it was accomplished. We started next day to fill up the cracks between the logs with mud and we got some hemlock branches so we would not be out money anymore for staying at the inn but could sleep in our own place. We had a big slab of elm for the door. My brother had heard from some French-Canadian fellows that were at Archie Frame's that in the lumber camps the fire was always in the middle of the shanty. So he said that was the way we should have ours, and we got four posts and were building the chimney on them, house-fashion, intending to plaster it with mud inside and out. We went to our hemlock bed with a good fire going, but waking in the middle of the night we saw our lumber was all ablaze and the scoops burning away briskly also. We tore down the chimney and the scoops being green basswood were not hard to put out. As soon as it came day, we started to build the chimney in the ordinary way in the end of the house and I thought it best not to make any remark.

After the small trees and brush was cleared out a bit, we set to chopping down the big trees. We cut down a big ash and split it into slabs for our floor. Still our box had not come which was to be shipped from Halton so Henry Treece sent us a very large and comfortable bearskin for our cover in bed but my brother would not take the favour and sent it back saying no need. Then after several weeks we got our box and had to ask for the ox to bring it on from Clinton, but my brother said that is the last we will need to ask of any person's help.

We walked to Walley and brought back flour and salt fish on our back. A man rowed us across the river at Manchester for a steep price. There were no bridges then and all that winter not a good enough freeze to make it easy going over the rivers.

Around Christmastime my brother said to me that he thought we had the place in good enough shape now for him to be bringing in a wife, so we should have somebody to cook and do for us and milk a cow when we could afford one. This was the first I had heard of any wife and I said that I did not know he was acquainted with anybody. He said he was not but he had heard that you could write to the Orphanage Home and ask if they hid a girl there that was willing to think about the prospect and that they would recommend, and if so he would go and see her. He wanted one between eighteen and twenty-two years of age, healthy and not afraid of work and raised in the Orphanage, not taken in lately, so that she would not be expecting any luxuries or to be waited on and would not be recalling about when things were easier for her. I do not doubt that to those hearing about this nowadays it seems a strange way to go about things. It was not that my brother could not have gone courting and got a wife on his own, because he was a good-looking fellow, but he did not have the time or the money or inclination, his mind was all occupied with establishing our holding. And if a girl had parents they would probably not want her to go far away where there was little in comforts and so much work.

That it was a respectable way of doing things is shown by the fact that the minister Mr. McBain, who was lately come into the district, helped Simon to write the letter and sent word on his own to vouch for him.

So a letter came back that there was a girl that might fit the bill and Simon went off to Toronto and got her. Her name was Annie but her maiden name I have forgotten. They had to ford the streams in Huller and trudge through deep soft snow after leaving the stage in Clinton, and when they got back she was worn out and very surprised at what she saw, since she said she had never imagined so much bush. She had in her box some sheets and pots and dishes that ladies had given her and that made the place more comfortable.

Early in April my brother and I went out to chop down some trees in the bush at the farthest corner of our property. While Simon was away to get married, I had done some chopping in the other direction towards Treeces', but Simon wanted to get all our boundaries cut clear around and not to go on chopping where I had been. The day started out mild and there was still a lot of soft snow in the bush. We were chopping down a tree where Simon wanted, and in some way, I cannot say how, a branch of it came crashing down where we didn't expect. We just heard the little branches cracking where it fell and looked up to see it and it hit Simon on the head and killed him instantly.

I had to drag his body back then to the shanty through the snow. He was a tall fellow though not fleshy, and it was an awkward task and greatly wearying. It had got colder by this time and when I got to the clearing I saw snow on the wind like the start of a storm. Our footsteps were filled in that we had made earlier. Simon was all covered with snow that did not melt on him by this time, and his wife coming to the door was greatly puzzled, thinking that I was dragging along a log.

In the shanty Annie washed him off and we sat still a while not knowing what we should do. The preacher was at the inn as there was no church or house for him yet and the inn was only about four miles away, but the storm had come up very fierce so you could not even see the trees at the edge of the clearing. It had the look of a storm that would last two or three days, the wind being from the north-west. We knew we could not keep the body in the shanty and we could not set it out in the snow fearing the bobcats would get at it, so we had to set to work and bury him. The ground was not frozen under the snow, so I dug out a grave near the shanty and Annie sewed him in a sheet and we laid him in his grave, not staying long in the wind but saying the Lord's Prayer and reading one psalm out of the Bible. I am not sure which one but I remember it was near the end of the Book of Psalms and it was very short.

This was the third day of April, 1852.

That was our last snow of the year, and later the minister came and said the service and I put up a wooden marker. Later on we got our plot in the cemetery and put his stone there, but he is not under it as it is a foolish useless thing in my opinion to cart a man's bones from one place to another when it is only bones and his soul has gone on to judgement.

I was left to chop and clear by myself and soon I began to work side by side with the Treeces, who treated me with the greatest kindness. We worked all together on my land or their land, not minding if it was the one or the other. I started to take my meals and even to sleep at their place and got to know their daughter Jenny who was about of my age, and we made our plans to marry, which we did in due course. Our life together was a long one with many hardships but we were fortunate in the end and raised eight children. I have seen my sons take over my wife's father's land as well as my own since my two brothers-in-law went away and did well for themselves in the West.

My brother's wife did not continue in this place but went her own way to Walley.

Now there are gravel roads running north, south, east, and west and a railway not a half mile from my farm. Except for woodlots, the bush is a thing of the past and I often think of the trees I have cut down and if I had them to cut down today I would be a wealthy man.

The Reverend Walter McBain, Minister of the Free Presbyterian Church of North Huron, to Mr. James Mullen, Clerk of the Peace, Walley, United Counties of Huron and Bruce, September 10, 1852.

I write to inform you, sir, of the probable arrival in your town of a young woman of this district, by the name of Annie Herron, a widow and one of my congregation. This young person has left her home here in the vicinity of Carstairs in Holloway Township, I believe she intends to walk to Walley. She may appear at the Gaol there seeking to be admitted, so I think it my duty to tell you who and what she is and her history here since I have known her.

I came to this area in November of last year, being the first minister of any kind to venture. My parish is as yet mostly bush, and there is nowhere for me to lodge but at the Carstairs Inn. I was born in the west of Scotland and came to this country under the auspices of the Glasgow Mission. After applying to know God's will, I was directed by Him to go to preach wherever was most need of a minister. I tell you this so you may know what sort I am that bring you my account and my view of the affairs of this woman.

She came into the country late last winter as the bride of the young man Simon Herron. He had written on my advice to the House of Industry in Toronto that they might recommend to him a Christian, preferably Presbyterian, female suitable to his needs, and she was the one recommended. He married her straight away and brought her here to the shanty he had built with his brother. These two young lads had come into the country to clear themselves a piece of land and get possession of it, being themselves orphans and without expectations. They were about this work one day at the end of winter when an accident befell. A branch was loosed while chopping down a tree and fell upon the elder brother so as to cause instant death. The younger lad succeeded in getting the body back to the shanty and since they were held prisoner by a heavy snowstorm they conducted their own funeral and burial.

The Lord is strict in his mercies and we are bound to receive his blows as signs of his care and goodness for so they will prove to be.

Deprived of his brother's help, the lad found a place in a neighboring family, also members in good standing of my congregation, who have accepted him as a son, though he still works for title to his own land. This family would have taken in the young widow as well, but she would have nothing to do with their offer and seemed to develop an aversion to everyone who would help her. Particularly she seemed so towards her brother-in-law, who said that he had never had the least quarrel with her, and towards myself. When I talked to her, she would not give any answer or sign that her soul was coming into submission. It is a fault of mine that I am not well-equipped to talk to women. I have not the ease to win their trust. Their stubbornness is of another kind than a man's.

I meant only to say that I did not have any good effect on her. She stopped appearing at services, and the deterioration of her property showed the state of her mind and spirit. She would not plant peas and potatoes though they were given to her to grow among the stumps. She did not chop down the wild vines around her door. Most often she did not light a fire so she could have oat-cake or porridge. Her brother-in-law being removed, there was no order imposed on her days. When I visited her the door was open and it was evident that animals came and went in her house. If she was there she hid herself, to mock me. Those who caught sight of her said that her clothing was filthy and torn from scrambling about in the bushes, and she was scratched by thorns and bitten by the mosquito insects and let her hair go uncombed or plaited. I believe she lived on salt fish and bannock that the neighbors or her brother-in-law left for her.

Then while I was still puzzling how I might find a way to protect her body through the winter and deal with the more important danger to her soul, there comes word she is gone. She left the door open and went away without cloak or bonnet and wrote on the shanty floor with a burnt stick the two words: 'Walley, Gaol'. I take this to mean she intends to go there and turn herself in. Her brother-in-law thinks it would be no use for him to go after her because of her unfriendly attitude to himself, and I cannot set out because of a deathbed I am attending. I ask you therefore to let me know if she has arrived and in what state and how you will deal with her. I consider her still as a soul in my charge, and I will try to visit her before winter if you keep her there. She is a child of the Free Church and the Covenant and as such she is entitled to a minister of her own faith and you must not think it sufficient that some priest of the Church of England or Baptist or Methodist be sent to her.

In case she should not come to the Gaol but wander in the streets, I ought to tell you that she is dark-haired and tall, meagre in body, not comely but not ill-favoured except having one eye that goes to the side.

Mr. James Mullen, Clerk of the Peace, Walley, to the Reverend Walter McBain, Carstairs, North Huron, September 30, 1852.

Your letter to me arrived most timely and appreciated, concerning the young woman Annie Herron. She completed her journey to Walley unharmed and with no serious damage though she was weak and hungry when she presented herself at the Gaol. On its being inquired what she did there, she said that she came to confess to a murder, and to be locked up. There was consultation round and about, I was sent for, and it being near to midnight, I agreed that she should spend the night in a cell. The next day I visited her and got all particulars I could.

Her story of being brought up in the Orphanage, her apprenticeship to a milliner, her marriage, and her coming to North Huron, all accords pretty well with what you have told me. Events in her account begin to differ only with her husband's death. In that matter what she says is this:

On the day in early April when her husband and his brother went out to chop trees, she was told to provide them with food for their midday meal, and since she had not got it ready when they wanted to leave, she agreed to take it to them in the woods. Consequently she baked up some oat-cakes and took some salt fish and followed their tracks and found them at work some distance away. But when her husband unwrapped his food he was very offended, because she had wrapped it in a way that the salty oil from the fish had soaked into the cakes, and they were all crumbled and unpleasant to eat. In his disappointment he became enraged and promised her a beating when he was more at leisure to do it. He then turned his back on her, being seated on a log and she picked up a rock and threw it at him, hitting him on the head so that he fell down uncon-scious and in fact dead. She and his brother then carried and dragged the body back to the house. By that time a blizzard had come up and they were imprisoned within. The brother said that they should not reveal the truth as she had not intended murder, and she agreed. They then buried him—her story agreeing again with yours—and that might have been the end of it, but she became more and more troubled, convinced that she had surely been intending to kill him. If she had not killed him, she says, it would only have meant a worse beating, and why should she have risked that? So she decided at last upon confession and as if to prove something handed me a lock of hair stiffened with blood.

This is her tale, and I do not believe it for a minute. No rock that this girl could pick up, combined with the force that she could summon to throw it, would serve to kill a man. I questioned her about this, and she changed her story, saying that it was a large rock that she had picked up in both hands and that she had not thrown it but smashed it down on his head from behind. I said why did not the brother prevent you, and she said, he was looking the other way. Then I said there must indeed be a bloodied rock lying somewhere in the wood, and she said she had washed it off with the snow. (In fact it is not likely a rock would come to hand so eas-ily, with all such depth of snow about.) I asked her to roll up her sleeve that I might judge of the muscles in her arms, to do such a job, and she said that she had been a huskier woman some months since.

I conclude that she is lying, or self-deluded. But I see nothing for it at the moment but to admit her to the Gaol. I asked her what she thought would happen to her now, and she said, well, you will try me and then you will hang me. But you do not hang people in the winter, she said, so I can stay here till spring. And if you let me work here, maybe you will want me to go on working and you will not want me hanged. I do not know where she got this idea about people not being hanged in the winter. I am in perplexity about her. As you may know, we have a very fine new Gaol here where the inmates are kept warm and dry and are decently fed and treated with all humanity, and there has been a complaint that some are not sorry—and at this time of year, even happy—to get into it. But it is obvious that she cannot wander about much longer, and from your account she is unwilling to stay with friends and unable to make a tolerable home for herself. The Gaol at present serves as a place of detention for the Insane as well as criminals, and if she is charged with Insanity, I could keep her here for the winter perhaps with removal to Toronto in the spring. I have engaged for a doctor to visit her. I spoke to her of your letter and your hope of coming tos ee her, but I found her not at all agreeable to that. She asks that nobody be allowed to see her excepting a Miss Sadie Johnstone, who is not in this part of the country.

I am enclosing a letter I have written to her brother-in-law for you to pass on to him, so that he may know what she has said and tell me what he thinks about it. I thank you in advance for conveying the letter to him, also for the trouble you have been to, in informing me as fully as you have done. I am a member of the Church of England, but have a high regard for the work of other Protestant denominations in bringing an orderly life to this part of the world we find ourselves in. You may believe that I will do what is in my power to do, to put you in a position to deal with the soul of this young woman, but it might be better to wait until she is in favour of it.

The Reverend Walter McBain to Mr. James Mullen, November 18, 1852.

I carried your letter at once to Mr. George Herron and believe that he has replied and given you his recollection of events. He was amazed at his sister-in-law's claim, since she never said anything of this to him or to anybody else. He says that it is all her invention or fancy, since she was never in the woods when it happened and there was no need for her to be, as they had carried their food with them when they left the house. He says that there had been at another time some reproof from his brother to her, over the spoiling of some cakes by their proximity to fish, but it did not happen at this time. Nor were there any rocks about to do such a deed on impulse if she had been there and wished to do it.

My delay in answering your letter, for which I beg pardon, is due to a bout of ill health. I had an attack of the gravel and a rheumatism of the stomach worse than any misery that ever fell upon me before. I am somewhat improved at present and will be able to go about as usual by next week if all continues to mend.

As to the question of the young woman's sanity, I do not know what your Doctor will say but I have thought on this and questioned the Divinity and my belief is this. It may well be that so early in the marriage her submission to her husband was not complete and there would be carelessness about his comfort, and naughty words, and quarrelsome behaviour, as well as the hurtful sulks and silences her sex is prone to. His death occurring before any of this was put right, she would feel a natural and harrowing remorse, and this must have taken hold of her mind so strongly that she made herself out to be actually responsible for his death. In this way, I think many fold are driven mad. Madness is at first taken on by some as a kind of play, for which shallowness and audacity they are punished later on, by finding out that it is play no longer, and the Devil has blocked off every escape.

It is still my hope to speak to her and make her understand this. I am under difficulties at present not only of my wretched corpus but being lodged in a foul and noisy place obliged to hear day and night such uproars as destroy sleep and study and intrude even on my prayers. The wind blows bitterly through the logs, but if I go down to the fire there is swilling of spirts and foulest insolence. And outside nothing but trees to choke off every exit and icy bog to swallow man and horse. There was a promise to build a church and lodging but those who made such a promise have grown busy with their own affairs and it seems to have been put off. I have not however left off preaching even in my illness and in such barns and houses as are provided. I take heart remembering a great man, the great preacher and interpreter of God's will, Thomas Boston, who in the latter days of his infirmity preached the grandeur of God from his chamber window to a crowd of two thousand or so assembled in the yard below. So I mean to preach to the end though my congregation will be smaller.

Whatsoever crook there is in one's lot, it is of God's making. Thomas Boston.

This world is a wilderness, in which we may indeed get our station changed, but the move will be out of one wilderness station unto another. Ibid.

Mr. James Mullen to the Reverend Walter McBain, January 17, 1853.

I write to you that our young woman's health seems sturdy, and she no longer looks such a scarecrow, eating well and keeping herself clean and tidy. Also she seems quieter in her spirits. She has taken to mending the linen in the prison which she does well. But I must tell you that she is firm as ever against a visit, and I cannot advise you to come here as I think your trouble might be for nothing. The journey is very hard in winter and it would do no good to your state of health.

Her brother-in-law has written me a very decent letter affirming that there is no truth to her story, so I am satisfied on that.

You may be interested in hearing what the doctor who visited her had to say about her case. His belief is that she is subject to a sort of delusion peculiar to females, for which the motive is a desire for self-importance, also a wish to escape the monotony of life or the drudgery they may have been born to. They may imagine themselves possessed by the forces of evil, to have committed various and hideous crimes, and so forth. Sometimes they may report that they have taken numerous lovers but these lovers will be all imaginary and the woman who thinks herself a prodigy of vice will in fact be quite chaste and untouched. For all this he—the doctor—lays the blame on the sort of reading that is available to these females, whether it is of ghosts or demons or of love escapades with Lords and Dukes and suchlike. For many, these tales are a passing taste given up when life's real duties intervene. For others they are indulged in now and then, as if they were sweets or sherry wine, but for some there is complete surrender and living within them just as in an opium-dream. He could not get an account of her reading from the young woman, but he believes she may by now have forgotten what she has read, or conceals the matter out of slyness.

With his questioning there did come to light something further that we did not know. On his saying to her, did she not fear hanging? she replied, no, for there is a reason you will not hang me. You mean that they will judge that you are mad? said he, and she said, oh, perhaps that, but is it not true also that they will never hang a woman that is with child? The doctor then examined her to find out if this were true, and she agreed to the examination, so she must have made the claim in good faith. He discovered however that she had deceived herself. The signs she took were simply the results of her going so long underfed and in such a reduced state, and later probably of her hysteria. He told her of his findings, but it is hard to say whether she believes him.

It must be acknowledged that this is truly a hard country for women. Another insane female has been admitted here recently, and her case is more pitiful for she has been driven insane by a rape. Her two attackers have been taken in and are in fact just over the wall from her in the men's section. The screams of the victim resound sometimes for hours at a stretch, and as a result the prison has become a much less pleasant shelter. But whether that will persuade our self-styled murderess to recant and take herself off, I have no idea. She is a good needlewoman and could get employment if she chose.

I am sorry to hear of your bad health and miserable lodgings. The town has grown so civilized that we forget the hardship of the hinterlands. Those like yourself who choose to endure it deserve our admiration. But you must allow me to say that it seems pretty certain that a man not in robust health will be unable to bear up for long in your situation. Surely your Church would not consider it a defection were you to choose to serve it longer by removing to a more comfortable place.

I enclose a letter written by the young woman and sent to a Miss Sadie Johnstone, on King Street, Toronto. It was intercepted by us that we might know more of the state of her mind, but resealed and sent on. But it has come back marked 'Unknown'. We have not told the writer of this in hopes that she will write again and more fully, revealing to us something to help us decide whether or not she is a conscious liar.

Mrs. Annie Herron, Walley Gaol, United Counties of Huron and Bruce, to Miss Sadie Johnstone, 49 King Street, Toronto, December 20, 1852.

Sadie, I am in here pretty well and safe and nothing to complain of either in food or blankets. It is a good stone building and something like the Home. If you could come and see me I would be very glad. I often talk to you a whole lot in my head, which I don't want to write because what if they are spies. I do the sewing here, the things was not in good repare when I came but now they are pretty good. And I am making curtains for the Opera House, a job that was sent in. I hope to see you. You could come on the stage right to this place. Maybe you would not like to come in the winter but in the springtime you would like to come.

Mr. James Mullen to the Reverend Walter McBain, April 7,1853.

Not having had any reply to my last letter, I trust you are well and might still be interested in the case of Annie Herron. She is still here and busies herself at sewing jobs which I have undertaken to get her from outside. No more is said of being with child, or of hanging, or of her story. She has written once again to Sadie Johnstone but quite briefly and I enclose her letter here. Do you have an idea who this person Sadie Johnstone might be?

I don't get any answer from you, Sadie, I don't think they sent on my letter. Today is the First of April, 1853. But not April Fool like we used to fool each other. Please come and see me if you can. I am in Walley Gaol but safe and well.

Mr. James Mullen from Edward Hoy, Landlord, Carstairs Inn, April 19, 1853.

Your letter to Mr. McBain sent back to you, he died here at the inn February 25. There is some books here, nobody wants them.

III

Annie Herron, Walley Gaol, to Sadie Johnstone, Toronto. Finder Please Post.

George came dragging him across the snow. I thought it was a log he dragged. I didn't know it was him. George said, it's him. A branch fell out of a tree and hit him, he said. He didn't say he was dead. I looked for him to speak. His mouth was part way open with snow in it. Also his eyes part way open. We had to get inside because it was starting to storm like anything. We dragged him in by the one leg each. I pretended to myself when I took hold of his leg that it was still the log. Inside where I had the fire going it was warm and the snow started melting off him. His blood thawed and ran a little around his ear. I didn't know what to do and I was afraid to go near him. I thought his eyes were watching me.

George sat by the fire with his big heavy coat on and his boots on. He was turned away. I sat at the table, which was of half-cut logs. I said, how do you know if he is dead? George said, touch him if you want to know. But I would not. Outside there was terrible storming, the wind in the trees and over top of our roof, I said, Our Father who art in Heaven, and that was how I got my courage. I kept saying it every time I moved. I have to wash him off, I said. Help me. I got the bucket where I kept the snow melting. I started on his feet and had to pull his boots off, a heavy job. George never turned around or paid attention or helped me when I asked. I didn't take the trousers or coat off of him, I couldn't manage. But I washed his hands and wrists. I always kept the rag between my hand and his skin. The blood and wet where the snow had melted off him was on the floor under his head and shoulders so I wanted to turn him over and clean it up. But I couldn't do it. So I went and pulled George by his arm. Help me, I said. What? he said. I said we had to turn him. So he came and helped me and we got him turned over, he was laying face down. And then I saw, I saw where the axe had cut.

Neither one of us said anything. I washed it out, blood and what else. I said to George, go and get me the sheet from my box. There was the good sheet I wouldn't put on the bed. I didn't see the use of trying to take off his clothes though they were good cloth. We would have had to cut them away where the blood was stuck and then what would we have but the rags. I cut off the one little piece of his hair because I remembered when Lila died in the Home they did that. Then I got George to help me roll him on to the sheet and I started to sew him up in the sheet. While I was sewing I said to George, go out in the lee of the house where the wood is piled and maybe you can get in enough shelter there to dig him a grave. Take the wood away and the ground is likely softer underneath.

I had to crouch down at the sewing so I was nearly laying on the floor beside him. I sewed his head in first folding the sheet over it because I had to look in his eyes and mouth. George went out and I could hear through the storm that he was doing what I said and pieces of wood were thrown up sometimes hitting the wall of the house. I sewed on, and every bit of him I lost sight of I would say even out loud, there goes, there goes. I had got the fold neat over his head but down at the feet I didn't have material enough to cover him, so I sewed on my eyelet petticoat I made at the Home to learn the stitch and that way I got him all sewed in.

I went out to help George. He had got all the wood out of the way and was at the digging. The ground was soft enough, like I had thought. He had the spade so I got the broad shovel and we worked away, him digging and loosening and me shovelling.

Then we moved him out. We could not do it now one leg each so George got him at the head and me at the ankles where the petticoat was and we rolled him into the earth and set to work again to cover him up. George had the shovel and it seemed I could not get enough dirt on to the spade so I pushed it in with my hands and kicked it in with my feet any way at all. When it was all back in, George beat it down flat with the shovel as much as he could. Then we moved all the wood back searching where it was in the snow and we piled it up in the right way so it did not look as if anybody had been at it. I think we had no hats on or scarves but the work kept us warm.

We took in more wood for the fire and put the bar across the door. I wiped up the floor and I said to George, take off your boots. Then, take off your coat. George did what I told him. He sat by the fire. I made the kind of tea from catnip leaves that Mrs. Treece showed me how to make and I put a piece of sugar in it. George did not want it. Is it too hot, I said. I let it cool off but then he didn't want it either. So I began, and talked to him.

You didn't mean to do it.

It was in anger, you didn't mean what you were doing.

I saw him other times what he would do to you. I saw he would knock you down for a little thing and you just get up and never say a word. The same way he did to me.

If you had not have done it, some day he would have done it to you.

Listen, George. Listen to me.

If you own up what do you think will happen? They will hang you. You will be dead, you will be no good to anybody What will become of your land? Likely it will all go back to the Crown and somebody else win get it and all the work you have done will be for them.

What will become of me here if you are took away?

I got some oat-cakes that were cold and I warmed them up. I set one on his knee. He took it and bit it and chewed it but he could not get it down and he spit it on to the fire.

I said, listen. I know things. I am older than you are. I am religious too, I pray to God every night and my prayers are answered. I know what God wants as well as any preacher knows and I know that he does not want a good lad like you to be hanged. All you have to do is say you are sorry Say you are sorry and mean it well and God will forgive you. I will say the same thing, I am sorry too because when I saw he was dead I did not wish, not one minute, for him to be alive. I will say, God forgive me, and you do the same. Kneel down.

But he would not. He would not move out of his chair. And I said, all right. I have an idea. I am going to get the Bible. I asked him, do you believe in the Bible? Say you do. Nod your head.

I did not see whether he nodded or not but I said, there. There you did. Now. I am going to do what we all used to do in the Home when we wanted to know what would happen to us or what we should do in our life. We would open the Bible any place and poke our finger at a page and then open our eyes and read the verse where our finger was and that would tell you what you needed to know. To make double sure of it just say when you close your eyes, God guide my finger.

He would not raise a hand from his knee, so I said, all right. Ail right, I'll do it for you. I did it, and I read where my finger stopped. I held the Bible close in to the fire so I could see.

It was something about being old and gray-headed, *oh God forsake me not*, and I said, what that means is that you are supposed to live till you are old and gray-headed and nothing is supposed to happen to you before that. It says so, in the Bible.

Then the next verse was so-and-so went and took so-and-so and conceived and bore him a son.

It says you will have a son, I said. You have to live and get older and get married and have a son.

But the next verse I remember so well I can put down all of it. *Neither can they prove the things of which they now accuse me.*

George, I said, do you hear that? *Neither can they prove the things of which they now accuse me.* That means that you are safe.

You are safe. Get up now. Get up and go and lay on the bed and go to sleep.

He could not do that by himself but I did it. I pulled on him and pulled on him until he was standing up and then I got him across the room to the bed which was not his bed in the comer but the bigger bed, and got him to sit on it then lay down. I rolled him over and back and got his clothes off down to his shirt. His teeth were chattering and I was afraid of a chill or the fever. I heated up the flat-irons and wrapped them in cloth and laid them down one on each side of him close to his skin. There was not whisky or brandy in the house to use, only the catnip tea. I put more sugar in it and got him to take it from a spoon. I rubbed his feet with my hands, then his arms and his legs, and I wrung out cloths in hot water which I laid over his stomach and his heart. I talked to him then in a different way quite soft and told him to go to sleep and when he woke up his mind would be clear and all his horrors would be wiped away.

A tree branch fell on him. It was just what you told me. I can see it falling. I can see it coming down so fast like a streak and little branches and crackling all along the way, it hardly takes longer than a gun going off and you say, what is that? and it has hit him and he is dead.

When I got him to sleep I laid down on the bed beside him. I took off my smock and I could see the black and blue marks on my arms. I pulled up my skirt to see if they were still there high on my legs, and they were. The back of my hand was dark too and sore still where I had bit it.

Nothing bad happened after I laid down and I did not sleep all night but listened to him breathing and kept touching him to see if he was warmed up. I got up in the earliest light and fixed the fire. When he heard me, he waked up and was better.

He did not forget what had happened but talked as if he thought it was all right. He said, we ought to have had a prayer and read something out of the Bible. He got the door opened and there was a big drift of snow but the sky was clearing. It was the last snow of the winter.

We went out and said the Lord's Prayer. Then he said, where is the Bible? Why is it not on the shelf? When I got it from beside the fire he said, what is it doing there? I did not remind him of anything. He did not know what to read so I picked the 131st Psalm that we had to learn at the Home. *Lord my heart is not haughty nor mine eyes lofty. Surely I have behaved and quieted myself as a child that is weaned of his mother, my soul is even as a weaned child.* He read it. Then he said he would shovel out a path and go and tell the Treeces. I said I would cook him some food. He went out and shovelled and didn't get tired and come in to eat like I was waiting for him to do. He shovelled and shovelled a long path out of sight and then he was gone and didn't come back. He didn't come back until near dark and then he said he had eaten. I said, did you tell them about the tree? Then he looked at me for the first time in a bad way. It was the same bad way his brother used to look. I never said anything more to him about what had happened or hinted at it in any way. And he never said anything to me, except he would come and say things in my dreams. But I knew the difference always between my dreams and when I was awake, and when I was awake it was never anything but the bad look.

Mrs. Treece came and tried to get me to go and live with them the way George was living. She said I could eat and sleep there, they had enough beds. I would not go. They thought I would not go because of my grief but I wouldn't go because somebody might see my black and blue, also they would be watching for me to cry. I said I was not frightened to stay alone.

I dreamed nearly every night that one or other of them came and chased me with the axe. It was him or it was George, one or the other. Or sometimes not the axe, it was a big rock lifted in both hands and one of them waiting with it behind the door. Dreams are sent to warn us.

I didn't stay in the house where he could find me and when I gave up sleeping inside and slept outside I didn't have the dream so often. It got warm in a hurry and the flies and mosquitoes came but they hardly bothered me. I would see their bites but not feel them, which was another sign that in the outside I was protected. I got down when I heard anybody coming. I ate berries both red and black and God protected me from any badness in them.

I had another kind of dream after a while. I dreamed George came and talked to me and he still had the bad look but was trying to cover it up and pretend that he was kind. He kept coming into my dreams and he kept lying to me. It was starting to get colder out and I did not want to go back in the shanty and the dew was heavy so I would be soaking when I slept in the grass. I went and opened the Bible to find out what I should do.

And now I got my punishment for cheating because the Bible did not tell me anything that I could understand, what to do. The cheating was when I was looking to find something for George, and I did not read exactly where my finger landed but looked around quick and found something else that was more what I wanted. I used to do that too when we would be looking up our verses in the Home and I always got good things and nobody ever caught me or suspected me at it. You never did either, Sadie.

So now I had my punishment when I couldn't find anything to help me however I looked. But something put it into my head to come here and I did. I had heard them talking about how warm it was and tramps would be wanting to come and get locked up, so I thought, I will too, and it was put into my head to tell them what I did. I told them the very same lie that George told me so often in my dreams, trying to get me to believe it was me and not him. I am safe from George here is the main thing. If they think I am crazy and I know the difference I am safe. Only I would like for you to come and see me.

And I would like for that yelling to stop.

When I am finished writing this, I will put it in with the curtains that I am making for the Opera House. And I will put on it, Finder Please Post. I trust that better than giving it to them like the two letters I give them already that they never have sent.

IV

Miss Christena Mullen, Walley, to Mr. Leopold Henry, Department of History, Queen's University, Kingston July 8, 1959.

Yes I am the Miss Mullen that Treece Herron's sister remembers coming to the farm and it is very kind of her to say I was a pretty young lady in a hat and veil. That was my motoring-veil. The old lady she mentions was Mr. Herron's grandfather's sister-in-law, if I have got it straight. As you are doing the biography, you will have got the relationships worked out. I never voted for Treece Herron myself since I am a Conservative, but he was a colorful politician and as you say a biography of him will bring some attention to this part of the country—too often thought of as 'deadly dull.'

I am rather surprised the sister does not mention the car in particular. It was a Stanley Steamer. I bought it myself on my twenty-fifth birthday in 1907. It cost twelve hundred dollars, that being part of my inheritance from my grandfather James Mullen who was an early Clerk of the Peace in Walley. He made money buying and selling farms.

My father having died young, my mother moved into my grandfather's house with all us five girls. It was a big cut—stone house called Traquair, now a Home for Young Offenders. I sometimes say in joke that it always was!

When I was young, we employed a gardener, a cook, and a sewing woman. All of them were 'characters,' all prone to feuding with each other, and all owing their jobs to the fact that my grandfather had taken an interest in them when they were inmates at the County Gaol (as it used to be spelled) and eventually had brought them home.

By the time I bought the Steamer, I was the only one of my sisters living at home, and the sewing-woman was the only one of these old servants who remained. The sewing-woman was called Old Annie and never objected to that name. She used it herself and would write notes to the cook that said, 'Tea was not hot, did you warm the pot? Old Annie.' The whole third floor was Old Annie's domain and one of my sisters— Dolly—said that whenever she dreamed of home, that is, of Traquair, she dreamed of Old Annie up at the top of the third-floor stairs brandishing her measuring stick and wearing a black dress with long fuzzy black arms like a spider.

She had one eye that slid off to the side and gave her the air of taking in more information than the ordinary person.

We were not supposed to pester the servants with questions about their personal lives, particularly those who had been in the Gaol, but of course we did. Sometimes Old Annie called the Gaol the Home. She said that a girl in the next bed screamed and screamed, and that was why she— Annie—ran away and lived in the woods. She said the girl had been beaten for letting the fire go out. Why were you in jail, we asked her, and she would say, 'I told a fib!' So for quite a while we had the impression that you went to jail for telling lies!

Some days she was in a good mood and would play hide-the-thimble with us. Sometimes she was in a bad mood and would stick us with pins when she was evening our hems if we turned too quickly or stopped too soon. She knew a place, she said, where you could get bricks to put on children's heads to stop them growing. She hated making wedding dresses (she never had to make one for me) and didn't think much of any of the men that my sisters married. She hated Dolly's beau so much that she made some kind of deliberate mistake with the sleeves which had to be ripped out, and Dolly cried. But she made us all beautiful ball gowns to wear when the Governor-General and Lady Minto came to Walley.

About being married herself, she sometimes said she had been and sometimes not. She said a man had come to the Home and had all the girls
paraded in front of him and said, 'I'll take the one with the coal-black
hair.' That being Old Annie, but she refused to go with him, even though
he was rich and came in a carriage. Rather like Cinderella but with a different ending. Then she said a bear killed her husband, in the woods, and
my grandfather had killed the bear, and wrapped her in its skin and
taken her home from the Gaol.

My mother used to say, 'Now, girls. Don't get Old Annie going. And
don't believe a word she says.'

I am going on at great length filling in the background but you did say
you were interested in details of the period. I am like most people my age
and forget to buy milk but could tell you the color of the coat I had when
I was eight.

So when I got the Stanley Steamer, Old Annie asked to be taken for a ride.
It turned out that what she had in mind was more of a trip. This was a
surprise since she had never wanted to go on trips before and refused to
go to Niagara Falls and would not even go down to the Harbor to see the
fireworks on the First of July. Also she was leery of automobiles and of
me as a driver. But the big surprise was that she had somebody she
wanted to go and see. She wanted to drive to Carstairs to see the Herron
family, who she said were her relatives. She had never received any visits or letters from these people, and when I asked if she had written to ask
if we might visit she said, 'I can't write.' This was ridiculous—she wrote
those notes to the cooks and long lists for me of things she wanted me to
pick up down on the Square or in the city. Braid, buckram, taffeta—she
could spell all of that.

'And they don't need to know beforehand,' she said. 'In the country it's
different.'

Well, I loved taking jaunts in the Steamer. I had been driving since I was
fifteen but this was the first car of my own and possibly the only Steam
car in Huron County. Everybody would run to see it go by. It did not
make a beastly loud noise coughing and clanking like other cars but
rolled along silently more or less like a ship with high sails over the lake
waters and it did not foul the air but left behind a plume of steam. Stanley Steamers were banned in Boston, because of steam fogging the air. I
always loved to tell people, I used to drive a car that was banned in
Boston!

We started out fairly early on a Sunday in June. It took about twenty-five
minutes to get the steam up and all that time Old Annie sat up straight in
the front seat as if the show were already on the road. We both had our

motoring-veils on, and long dusters, but the dress Old Annie was wearing underneath was of plum-colored silk. In fact it was made over from the one she had made for my grandmother to meet the Prince of Wales in.

The Steamer covered the miles like an angel. It would do fifty miles an hour—great then—but I did not push it. I was trying to consider Old Annie's nerves. People were still in church when we started, but later on the roads were full of horses and buggies making the journey home. I was polite as all get-out, edging by them. But it turned out Old Annie did not want to be so sedate and she kept saying, 'Give it a squeeze,' meaning the horn, which was worked by a bulb under a mudguard down at my side.

She must not have been out of Walley for more years than I had been alive. When we crossed the bridge at Saltford (that old iron bridge where there used to be so many accidents because of the turn at both ends), she said that there didn't used to be a bridge there, you had to pay a man to row you.

'I couldn't pay but I crossed on the stones and just hiked up my skirts and waded,' she said. 'It was that dry a summer.'

Naturally I did not know what summer she was talking about.

Then it was, Look at the big fields, where are the stumps gone, where is the bush? And look how straight the road goes, and they're building their houses out of brick! And what are those buildings as big as churches?

Barris, I said.

I knew my way to Carstairs all right but expected help from Old Annie once we got there. None was forthcoming. I drove up and down the main street waiting for her to spot something familiar. 'If I could just see the inn,' she said, 'I'd know where the track goes off behind it.'

It was a factory town, not very pretty in my opinion. The Steamer of course got attention, and I was able to call out for directions to the Herron farm without stopping the engine. Shouts and gestures and finally I was able to get us on the right road. I told Old Annie to watch the mailboxes but she was concerned with finding the creek. I spotted the name myself, and turned us in at a long lane with a red brick house at the end of it and a couple of these barns that had amazed Old Annie. Red-brick houses with verandas and key windows were all the style then, they were going up everywhere.

'Look there!' Old Annie said, and I thought she meant where a herd of cows was tearing away from us in the pasture-field alongside the lane. But she was pointing at a mound pretty well covered with wild grape, a few logs sticking out of it. She said that was the shanty. I said, "Well, good—now let's hope you recognize one or two of the people.'

There were enough people around. A couple of visiting buggies were pulled up in the shade, horses tethered and cropping grass. By the time the Steamer stopped at the side veranda, a number were lined up to look at it. They didn't come forward—not even the children ran out to look close up the way town children would have done. They all just stood in a row looking at it in a tight-lipped sort of way.

Old Annie was staring off in the other direction.

She told me to get down. Get down, she said, and ask them if there is a Mr. George Herron that lives here and is he alive yet, or dead?

I did what I was told. And one of the men said, that's right. He is. My father.

Well, I have brought somebody, I told them. I have brought Mrs. Annie Herron.

The man said, that so?

(A pause here due to a couple of fainting-fits and a trip to the hospital. Lots of tests to use up the taxpayers' money. Now I'm back and have read this over, astounded at the rambling but too lazy to start again. I have not even got to Treece Herron, which is the part you are interested in, but hold on, I'm nearly there.)

These people were all dumbfounded about Old Annie, or so I gathered. They had not known where she was or what she was doing or if she was alive. But you mustn't think they surged out and greeted her in any excited way. Just the one young man came out, very mannerly, and helped first her then me down from the car. He said to me that Old Annie was his grandfather's sister-in-law. It was too bad we hadn't come even a few months sooner, he said, because his grandfather had been quite well and his mind quite clear—he had even written a piece for the paper about his early days here—but then he had got sick. He had recovered but would never be himself again. He could not talk, except now and then a few words.

This mannerly young man was Treece Herron.

We must have arrived just after they finished their dinner. The woman of the house came out and asked him—Treece Herron—to ask us if we had eaten. You would think she or we did not speak English. They were all very shy—the women with their skinned-back hair, and men in dark-blue Sunday suits, and tongue-tied children. I hope you do not think I am making fun of them—it is just that I cannot understand for the life of me why it is necessary to be so shy.

We were taken to the dining-room which had an unused smell—they must have had their dinner elsewhere—and were served a great deal of food of which I remember salted radishes and leaf lettuce and roast chicken and strawberries and cream. Dishes from the china cabinet, not their usual. Good old Indian Tree. They had sets of everything. Plushy living-room suite, walnut dining-room suite. It was going to take them a while, I thought, to get used to being prosperous.

Old Annie enjoyed the fuss of being waited on and ate a lot, picking up the chicken bones to work the last shred of meat off them. Children lurked around the doorways and the women talked in subdued, rather scandalized voices out in the kitchen. The young man, Treece Herron, had the grace to sit down with us and drink a cup of tea while we ate. He chatted readily enough about himself and told me he was a divinity student at Knox College. He said he liked living in Toronto. I got the feeling he wanted me to understand that divinity students were not all such sticks as I supposed or led such a stringent existence. He had been tobogganing in High Park, he had been picnicking at Hanlan's Point, he had seen the giraffe in the Riverdale Zoo. As he talked, the children got a little bolder and started trickling into the room. I asked the usual idiocies . . . How old are you, what book are you in at school, do you like your teacher? He urged them to answer or answered for them and told me which were his brothers and sisters and which his cousins.

Old Annie said, 'Are you all fond of each other, then?' which brought on funny looks.

The woman of the house came back and spoke to me again through the divinity student. She told him that Grandpa was up now and sitting on the front porch. She looked at the children and said, 'What did you let all them in here for?'

Out we trooped to the front porch, where two straight-backed chairs were set up and an old man settled on one of them. He had a beautiful full white beard reaching down to the bottom of his waistcoat. He did not seem interested in us. He had a long, pale, obedient old face.

Old Annie said, 'Well, George,' as if this was about what she had expected. She sat on the other chair and said to one of the little girls, 'Now bring me a cushion. Bring me a thin kind of cushion and put it at my back.'

I spent the afternoon giving rides in the Stanley Steamer. I knew enough about them now not to start in asking who wanted a ride, or bombarding them with questions, such as, were they interested in automobiles? I just went out and patted it here and there as if it was a horse, and I looked in the boiler. The divinity student came behind and read the name of the

Steamer written on the side. 'The Gentleman's Speedster' He asked was it my father's.

Mine, I said. I explained how the water in the boiler was heated and how much steam-pressure the boiler could withstand. People always wondered about that—about explosions. The children were closer by that time and I suddenly remarked that the boiler was nearly empty. I asked if there was any way I could get some water.

Great scurry to get pails and man the pump! I went and asked the men on the veranda if that was all right, and thanked them when they told me, help yourself. Once the boiler was filled, it was natural for me to ask if they would like me to get the steam up, and a spokesman said, it wouldn't hurt. Nobody was impatient during the wait. The men stared at the boiler, concentrating. This was certainly not the first car they had seen but probably the first steam car.

I offered the men a ride first, as it was proper to. They watched skeptically while I fiddled with all the knobs and levers to get my lady going. Thirteen different things to push or pull! We bumped down the lane at five, then ten miles an hour. I knew they suffered somewhat, being driven by a woman, but the novelty of the experience held them. Next I got a load of children, hoisted in by the divinity student telling them to sit still and hold on and not be scared and not fall out. I put up the speed a little, knowing now the ruts and puddle-holes, and their hoots of fear and triumph could not be held back.

I have left out something about how I was feeling but will leave it out no longer, due to the effects of a martini I am drinking now, my late-afternoon pleasure. I had troubles then I have not yet admitted to you because they were love-troubles. But when I had set out that day with Old Annie, I had determined to enjoy myself as much as I could. It seemed it would be an insult to the Stanley Steamer not to. All my life I found this a good rule to follow—to get as much pleasure as you could out of things even when you weren't likely to be happy.

I told one of the boys to run around to the front veranda and ask if his grandfather would care for a ride. He came back and said, 'They've both gone to sleep!'

I had to get the boiler filled up before we started back, and while this was being done, Treece Herron came and stood close to me.

'You have given us all a day to remember,' he said.

I wasn't above flirting with him. I actually had a long career as a flirt ahead of me. It's quite a natural behavior, once the loss of love makes you give up your ideas of marriage.

I said he would forget all about it, once he got back to his friends in Toronto. He said no indeed, he would never forget, and he asked if he could write to me. I said nobody could stop him.

On the way home I thought about this exchange and how ridiculous it would be if he should get a serious crush on me. A divinity student. I had no idea then of course that he would be getting out of Divinity and into Politics.

'Too bad old Mr. Herron wasn't able to talk to you,' I said to Old Annie.

She said, 'Well, I could talk to him.'

Actually, Treece Herron did write to me, but he must have had a few misgivings as well because he enclosed some pamphlets about Mission Schools. Something about raising money for Mission Schools. That put me off and I didn't write back. (Years later I would joke that I could have married him if I'd played my cards right.)

I asked Old Annie if Mr. Herron could understand her when she talked to him, and she said, 'Enough.' I asked if she was glad about seeing him again and she said yes. 'And glad for him to get to see me,' she said, not without some gloating that probably referred to her dress and the vehicle.

So we just puffed along in the Steamer under the high arching trees that lined the roads in those days. From miles away the lake could be seen just glimpses of it, shots of light, held wide apart in the trees and hills so that Old Annie asked me if it could possibly be the same lake, all the same one that Walley was on?

There were lots of old people going around then with ideas in their heads that didn't add up—though I suppose Old Annie had more than most. I recall her telling me another time that a girl in the Home had a baby out of a big boil that burst on her stomach, and it was the size of a rat and had no life in it, but they put it in the oven and it puffed up to the right size and baked to a good color and started to kick its legs. (Ask an old woman to reminisce and you get the whole ragbag, is what you must be thinking by now.)

I told her that wasn't possible, it must have been a dream.

'Maybe so,' she said, agreeing with me for once. 'I did used to have the terriblest dreams.'

Philip E. Simmons is associate professor of English at Lake Forest College in Illinois. Although he is now disabled with ALS (Lou Gehrig's disease), Simmons continues to write and is a contributing editor of UU World, *the journal of the Unitarian Universalist Association, and the author of* Deep Surfaces *(1997) and* Learning to Fall: The Blessings of an Imperfect Life *(2002). He and his family live in New Hampshire.*

Unfinished Houses

Philip Simmons

Even as a child I shared my mother's fascination with houses. Driving around town on errands or taking me and my brothers to the beach, she would comment on old houses we drove past. Sometimes she and I would go out just to look at some house that had recently been put up for sale. I remember once turning up a dirt drive into a yard gone to foot-high grass and weeds. It was summer, with the smell of summer dust and heat, katydids fluttering up at each step, and behind the house, crickets chorusing in a neglected field that was filling with juniper and birch. We worked our way around the old white clapboard farmhouse, peering through windows, our shoes crunching the stubbled remains of flower beds. Hands cupped against my forehead, nose to the glass, I gazed through the glare into a succession of empty rooms, sensing in those worn floorboards, skewed doorframes, and faded floral wallpapers the possibilities for another life from the one I knew.

My mother had no intention of buying. We were already settled into an old white clapboard farmhouse of our own. I say we were settled, but perhaps this was not entirely so. Our house, like most in these parts, was a work in progress. Already my parents had reshingled the back wall, installed a large kitchen window to give us a view of the Ossipee mountains, reclaimed an ancient fireplace hidden behind wallboard, torn down the two-hole privy leaning off the back of the ell and replaced it with a set of steps, and made enough plans for future changes to keep them busy for years. Ralph Waldo Emerson once wrote that "people wish to be settled; only so far as they are unsettled is there any hope for them." I suppose that with her restless interest in other houses, her continued improvement of our own, her ceaseless imagining of other possibilities for herself and her family, there was, and still is, hope for my mother. And I want to consider what hope there might be for all of us who in some way or other remain unsettled.

I am writing this in January, and if ever there was a time of year to be settled, this is it. Here in New Hampshire preparing for winter is a year-

472

round occupation, and by now we've long ago gotten the wood in, staked the driveway for the plow, and watched the first snows bury our summer's work in garden, yard, and field. Here in winter's deep, dark time, a season that finds us denned, burrowed, and hunkered through long nights and brief days, it may seem foolish to search for some virtue in being unsettled in our houses. But let me do my best, in the spirit of Emerson when he wrote, "I unsettle all things."

• • •

My mother's interest in houses is part of a larger history. When my parents came up from Massachusetts looking for a country house, they were part of a wave of such people that lasted through the 1950s and 1960s. Our town's population had reached a low of around 600 people, lower than it had been since soon after the town's founding in the late 1700s. My parents' cohort bought and renovated old houses all over town, employing a growing number of younger tradesmen and craftsmen who in turn bought and built houses of their own, and now with their families have doubled the town's year-round population and made Sandwich the happy small place it is today. So it's no wonder that we're interested in houses, and that everyone I know is happy to talk at length about them. Ours is not the bland talk of real estate prices and interest rates that you hear in suburban communities. In my town you're expected to know your girts from your beams, your headers from your ledgers, your rafters from your collar ties. At church suppers, at our children's birthday parties, on the sidelines at soccer practice, or during intermission at the Christmas concert, we talk stud walls and stress-skin panels and Typar and hurricane bracing; we talk vapor barriers and blueboard and poly-isocyanurate insulation; we talk shallow wells and drilled wells, septic tanks and leaching fields. You have never witnessed passion until you've heard your neighbors discourse on the virtues of full-dimension lumber or "low-e glass." The words themselves are charged, erotic, tasted in the mouth like delicacies: *shiplap, splined boards, tongue and groove.*

Maybe it's because we so enjoy talking about our houses that we never finish them. After all, if we finished them, what would we have to talk about? So we leave drywall unpainted, closets without doors, windows without trim. We live for years with plywood subfloors over which someday we fully intend to install the wide-board oak of our dreams. Fact is, almost no one I know here lives in an entirely finished house, and those few who do are embarrassed to admit it. And whether our houses are finished or not, most of us have a drawer somewhere with sketches of various rooms and outbuildings yet to be constructed. I know that in some places people live differently. I know there are places, lying south of Concord, I suppose, where people move into finished houses, where everything is spic and span, the windows washed and the hinges oiled and even the clock on the stove set to the right time. But this is the country, and we live differently.

This essay was inspired by a friend of mine, recently returned to town after a year away, who planned on renting a house for the winter. The house was unfinished, with exposed insulation in the walls. No matter: My friend, the single mother of a ten-year-old boy, whose family has been in this town for 150 years, said that she would "just throw up some Sheetrock." What struck me was not only her resilience and good spirit in the face of challenge, but that she could assume, correctly, that I would think "throwing up some Sheetrock" to make a house livable for the winter not at all an unusual thing to do. This is a place where respectable people staple plastic over their windows and stack hay bales against their foundations. If our town were a country, its national flag would be the blue tarp. Thrown over leaky roofs, old cars, and unfinished outbuildings, its a fitting symbol of a nation dedicated to the provisional and the temporary. Its cheerful presence outside our houses proclaims the frugality an craftiness with which we cheat time and our own limits.

• • •

What else keeps us from finishing our houses? Reasons are not hard to find: We lack the money, or choose to spend it otherwise; those of us who insist on doing the work ourselves are too busy with other chores, including the eternal chore of making a living. In most cases we simply get used to things as they are, and the pain of unfinished tasks diminishes to a dull and manageable ache. Still, a certain shame remains, and we show visitors the unfinished features of our houses with a look of hangdog guilt at our own inefficiency and sloth. This guilt, however, barely conceals a deeper pride. Those of us who are non-natives have come here, we know, for therapy, as part of a lifelong project of getting in touch with our inner Yankee. A degree of make-do shabbiness is required to show we are making progress. Yankees, whether by birth or adoption, have always found ways to let their neighbors know the extent of their thrift and stoicism, and native and newcomer alike find a too-finished house as out of place as a mink coat worn to the post office.

But when we push even deeper we discover yet another level of feeling: not guilt, not pride, but despair. For on our bad days, in our dark moments, we see in our unfinished houses the surest sign of calamity. That unpainted dry-wall, that missing piece of trim remind us that the world is too much with us, that we have lost our grip, that life hurls more at us than we can handle. At such times we find ourselves aboard time's driverless train, rushing toward doom. For we know, don't we, that we will never get it all done, that we are never good enough, and that surely it will all get away from us, that our fields will fill with brush, our stone walls topple, our houses collapse and sink into the earth to become more of the cellar holes scattered through these woods and hills like so many monuments to failure.

Such dark days have their flip side, of course, when in manic rebound we indulge our fantasies: For we also know, don't we, that someday when our kids are grown, when our ex-husbands finally pony up with child support, when we sell that screenplay, when we get that new job selling condo time-shares, when we have *really* figured out the World Wide Web, when we finally learn to balance our checkbooks, when all our ships come sailing in, all our cows are cashed, when maple trees grow money, when at last our lives take that stunning upswing and we ascend into the glittering hoo-hah of a destiny we knew all along was ours, then, *then* we'll put cedar shingles on that wall that has been wraped in Typar since our children were born, *then* we will drill a deep well so that our teenage daughters can take end-less hot showers and we can water our tomatoes until they grow fat, *then* we will install a radiant floor heating system so that we can walk cozily barefoot in February, *then* we will add on that master bedroom suite with the indoor Jacuzzi and the outdoor hot tub, *then* we'll build that cupola with the hammock hanging in it from which we can gaze at stars. And then will all the scattered pieces of ourselves be gathered up, all that has been lost returned to us, all our wounds healed, all our griefs assuaged, and all our days will pass in happiness, our nights in bliss.

But that hasn't happened yet, has it? Fact is, most of us make do with our duct tape and blue tarps, our patched and cobbled houses giving physi-cal form to all that remains unfinished and imperfect in our own cramped and needful selves. Don't get me wrong: I love my house. Sitting with a cup of coffee at the table, basking in the low January sun that fills our house with light while outside spindrift whips over the fields, I am the luckiest man on God's frozen earth. Still, most of us most of the time, and all of us some of the time, live in houses that remind us of the many ways in which life has turned out to be *not quite what we had in mind*.

My unsettling suggestion is that perhaps this is a good thing.

Our houses, like our lives, will never be finished, never be settled. The only thing that will settle the affairs of this life is death itself. To be too settled in this life is, in Emerson's sense, to die while still living, to live a sort of death-in-life. Only so far as we are unsettled is there any hope for us. Let us remain unsettled, therefore, in order that we may truly live.

But to follow this line of inquiry further, I need to tell you now about Orrin Tilton, and how he lived and died. That old clapboard farmhouse we lived in when I was a child was on Tilton Hill Road, and when we moved there the last Tiltons still living on the road were our next door neighbors. When I first knew him, Orrin Tilton was a man in his 50s, living with his disabled father in a house that hadn't seen paint in decades and was heated by the monstrous Glenwood cookstove in a kitchen lit by a single bare bulb. Orrin's father, I remember, used to sit in a chair in the kitchen, or in the yard when it was warm, and try to sell us wood scraps from a bucket he kept at his feet.

Orrin, like many New Hampshire folk who had seen an entire agricultural world vanish around them, made his living as a carpenter and handyman, occasionally firing up his old tractor to hay the field he still owned across from our house. He was not given to idle talk; about the most flamboyant thing he ever did was on one Fourth of July, when he fired off his antique brass cannon using the supply of black powder that he stored under his bed. But in those first years he helped us flatlanders get settled in, steering my father patiently over the shoals of cranky plumbing, shallow wells, and rotting sills. He refinished our pine floors and put a new roof on our barn, and sometimes my mother had him over for a spaghetti supper. I remember him most clearly as he sat at our table, a wiry man with strongly muscled arms, thin, close-cropped gray hair, ears that stood well out from his head, gray eyes that swam behind thick lenses, and a drop of spaghetti sauce on his chin.

Years later, when as a teenager I lay in bed late at night memorizing Robert Frost's poem "An Old Man's Winter Night," it was Orrin Tilton I imagined clomping through his empty house, going about the humble and ordinary business of putting himself and all the countryside he cared for to bed, while outside, ominously, "all out of doors looked darkly in at him." So many nights in that drafty old farmhouse next door to Orrin's on Tilton Hill Road, nestled into my pocket of warmth beneath several hundred pounds of blankets, I listened to the same "roar of trees and crack of branches" the poem describes and puzzled over its final lines:

> One aged man—one man—can't keep a house,
> A farm, a countryside, or if he can,
> It's thus he does it of a winter night.

Some time after his father died, Orrin sold his house and most of his lands to a neighbor who, like us, had come up from Massachusetts. He kept one small field and a few acres of woods for himself but moved to a trailer park in Laconia. We didn't hear any more from him until several years later, when he began to return to our road—to his road—to build himself a new house. He worked alone, on weekends and at odd hours, by now a man well into his 70s with a heart condition, building with his own hands the house in which he planned to live out his retirement. I saw him finish the house. I was home for Thanksgiving from college in Massachusetts, and Orrin Tilton was there every day that week, getting the roofing on before the first snow. By Sunday, he had got the roof on, and that afternoon in the early dusk, as I was driving away from our house, back to school, he had just finished splitting the winter's firewood. Actually, Orrin was leaving, too, headed back down to Laconia. His car stood in the road, blocking my way. As I waited for him to move, a neighbor came out of the nearby house (the daughter of the man who had bought Orrin's old house and land) and told me she had already called the police. By the time I got out and looked into his car, he was already gone: head sunk forward against the steering wheel, his face the color of parchment.

He had finished his house.

We stood with the blue lights of the police car flashing into the woods, a cold night coming on. I listened to branches crack and trunks creak, and the ground seemed to harden beneath my feet. I don't know what Orrin was feeling at the end, sitting in his car as the light failed. I suspect he had learned long before then what the poem tells us: that one man can't keep a house, a farm, a countryside, for as the psalm reminds us, "all things are transient, as insubstantial as dreams." And I suspect he also knew that if we can keep a house, it is through humble and ordinary acts such as hammering shingles and hauling wood, work performed not in a vain bid for immortality but out of plain reverence for the fact of being alive. His work was his worship, for such chores pay homage to the very impermanence of all we build. As Emerson wrote, "in nature every moment is new; the past is always swallowed up and forgotten; the coming only is sacred. Nothing is secure but life, transition, the energizing spirit."

• • •

The old houses in our town were built to last, but the cellar holes in our woods remind us that houses, like bodies, don't endure forever. I don't know whether Orrin was religious or whether he would have been comforted by the apostle Paul's words: "We know that if the earthly house we live in is destroyed, we have a building from God, a house not made with hands, eternal in the heavens." Even those who don't believe in the afterlife described by Paul can share the feeling behind his words. On some level all religious feeling begins with the sense that our true home lies elsewhere, however we may choose to define elsewhere: as psychic wholeness; as life in the beloved community; as a place of justice; as a harmonious relation to the natural world; as union of our spirits with the divine. In the journey to the elsewhere of our fond imagining we wish ourselves far from here, far from the suffering of our lives, far from our unfinished houses and our unfinished selves.

The unsettling news is that we'll never reach that elsewhere of our long-ing as long as we remain in this life, as long as we remain human. Heaven has its place, and our desire for it may guide us, ethically and spiritually, to work for the good. But in our desire always to be elsewhere than here, we can lose what measure of heaven may be ours on earth. When our fan-tasies of a better life consume us, when our memories of past hurts bind us and fears of pending calamity drive us, we are robbed of the only gift—the greatest gift—we can be sure of possessing: the present moment. We cannot summon the future, we cannot remake the past. The present moment is the unfinished house in which we dwell.

I don't know what awaits me after death: reincarnation as a houseplant or, if I've really racked up the bad karma, as a plastic surgeon in San Diego. Maybe the afterlife really is wings and harps and Mahalia Jackson, the Queen of Gospel, singing "In the Upper Room." Maybe it's nothing, absolutely nothing. I try not to make too much of those moments when I've had what Wordsworth called "intimations of immortality," when I have sensed the presence of another order of existence flickering like orange flames at the edges of the one I now know. Maybe these percep-tions, and all religious feelings, are just delusional constructs that give the human species some evolutionary adaptive advantage by keeping us from annihilating one another even more efficiently than we do now. But I do know that whatever communion with the divine I may have when this life is done will surely be prepared for by my seeking always to dwell in the divine as I find it here, in this life, in this very moment. In each unfinished and imperfect day I struggle to find myself at home in this body, however flawed and failing, in this breath, however labored, in this speech, however halting. Each day, I work to make my home among the people I find about me. I write these words to make a sort of house in which you and I may dwell together for a time. Only in such work, in building a house of peace in the present moment, a house of peace not only for ourselves but for all who may be in our presence or our hearts—only in such work can we be made whole. We are here, in the unfinished house of the now, for the duration. The joy is in the building.

My mother eventually looked through the windows of enough farm-houses to want to sell our old one on Tilton Hill Road and move into a bigger, even older farmhouse on the other side of town. And a few years ago, my parents gave my wife and me the several acres of land on which we have built a house near theirs and in which we have the pleasure of hunkering through these long winter nights. Back when we were just starting to think about building, I was standing at a window in their house, looking out across the field to the section of dense woods where I was planning to build. It was a subzero December night, and the wind was up, lashing pines and blowing snow, the whole forest howling. I said to my mother then, "I can't imagine that we're really going to live out there." I suppose I was asking for her reassurance, and she gave it, saying simply, "You'll be fine." And we built the house, and we are fine, and I keep a file full of sketches for the addition, with its master bedroom and outdoor hot tub, its Count Rumford fireplace and radiant floor heat, its oak floors and cherry trim. And on some cold winter nights with the woodstove stoked, I lie awake beside my wife and listen to "the roar of trees and crack of branches" that Frost described, and I'm thankful for the chance to be at home for this one night, for this one moment, in this unfinished house.

Alex Kotlowitz (b. 1955) has written several books exploring race problems in the U.S., including There Are No Children Here: The Story of Two Boys Growing Up in the Other America *(1991) and* The Other Side of the River: A Story of Two Towns, a Death and America's Dilemma *(1998). He has written for the* Wall Street Journal, *the* New York Times Sunday Magazine, *the* MacNeil-Lehrer NewsHour, *National Public Radio and various magazines. Mr. Kotlowitz grew up in New York City and is a graduate of Wesleyan University in Middletown, CT. He and his family currently live near Chicago.*

Colorblind

Alex Kotlowitz

One Christmas day seven years ago, I'd gone over to the Henry Horner Homes in Chicago to visit with Lafeyette and Pharoah, the subjects of my book "There Are No Children Here." I had brought presents for the boys, as well as a gift for their friend Rickey, who lived on the other side of the housing complex, an area controlled by a rival gang. Lafeyette and Pharoah insisted on walking over with me. It was eerily quiet, since most everyone was inside, and so, bundled from the cold, we strolled toward the other end in silence. As we neared Damen Avenue, a kind of demilitarized zone, a uniformed police officer, a white woman, approached us. She looked first at the two boys, neither of whom reached my shoulder, and then at me. "Are you O.K.?" she asked.

About a year later, I was with Pharoah on the city's North Side, shopping for high-tops. We were walking down the busy street, my hand on Pharoah's shoulder, when a middle-aged black man approached. He looked at me, and then at Pharoah. "Son," he asked, "are you O.K.?"

Both this white police officer and middle-aged black man seemed certain of what they witnessed. The white woman saw a white man possibly in trouble; the black man saw a black boy possibly in trouble. It's all about perspective—which has everything to do with our personal and collective experiences, which are consistently informed by race. From those experiences, from our histories, we build myths, legends that both guide us and constrain us, legends that include both fact and fiction. This is not to say the truth doesn't matter. It does, in a big way. It's just that getting there may not be easy, in part because everyone is so quick to choose sides, to refute the other's myths and to pass on their own.

We'd do well to keep this in mind as we enter the yearlong dialogue on race convened by President Clinton. Yes, conversation is critical, but not without self-reflection, both individually and communally. While myths help us make sense of the incomprehensible, they can also confine us, confuse us and leave us prey to historical laziness. Moreover, truth is not always easily discernible—and even when it is, the prism, depending on which side of the river you reside on, may create a wholly different illusion. Many whites were quick to believe Susan Smith, the South Carolina mother who claimed that a black man had killed her children. And with the reawakening of the Tawana Brawley case, we learn that, although a grand jury has determined otherwise, many blacks still believe she was brutally raped by a group of white men. We—blacks and whites—need to examine and question our own perspectives. Only then can we grasp each other's myths and grapple with the truths.

In 1992, I came across the story of a 16-year-old black boy, Eric McGinnis, whose body had been found a year earlier floating in the St. Joseph River in southwestern Michigan. The river flows between Benton Harbor and St. Joseph, two small towns whose only connections are two bridges and a powerful undertow of contrast.

St. Joseph is a town of 9,000, and, with its quaint downtown and brick-paved streets, resembles a New England tourist haunt. But for those in Benton Harbor, St. Joseph's most defining characteristic is its racial makeup: it is 95 percent white. Benton Harbor, a town of 12,000 on the other side of the river, is 92 percent black and dirt poor. For years, the municipality so hurt for money that it could not afford to raze abandoned buildings.

Eric, a high-school sophomore whose passion was dancing, was last seen at the Club, a teen-age nightspot in St. Joseph, where weeks earlier he had met and started dating a white girl. The night Eric disappeared, a white man said he caught the boy trying to break into his car and chased him away from the river, past an off-duty white deputy sheriff. That was the last known moment he was seen alive, and it was then that the myths began.

I became obsessed with Eric's death, and so for five years moved in and out of these two communities, searching for answers to both Eric's disappearance and to matters of race. People would often ask which side of the river I was staying on, waiting to gauge my allegiance. And they would often ask about the secrets of those across the way or, looking for affirmation, repeat myths passed on from one generation to the next.

Once, during an unusually bitter effort by white school-board members to fire Benton Harbor's black superintendent, one black woman asked me: "How do you know how to do this? Do you take lessons? How do you all stick together the way you do?" Of course, we don't. Neither community is as unified or monolithic as the other believes. Indeed, contrary to the impression of those in St. Joseph, the black community itself was deeply divided in its support for the superintendent, who was eventually fired.

On occasion, whites in St. Joseph would regale me with tales of families migrating to Benton Harbor from nearby states for the high welfare benefits. It is, they would tell me, the reason for the town's economic decline. While some single mothers indeed moved to Benton Harbor and other Michigan cities in the early 80s to receive public assistance, the truth is that in the 30s and 40s, factories recruited blacks from the South, and when those factories shut down, unemployment, particularly among blacks, skyrocketed.

But the question most often asked was: "Why us? Why write about St. Joseph and Benton Harbor?" I would tell them that while the contrasts between the towns seem unusually stark, they are, I believe, typical of how most of us live: physically and spiritually isolated from one another.

It's not that I didn't find individuals who crossed the river to spend time with their neighbors. One St. Joseph woman, Amy Johnson, devotes her waking hours to a Benton Harbor community center. And Eric McGinnis himself was among a handful of black teen-agers who spent weekend nights at the Club in St. Joseph. Nor is it that I didn't find racial animosity. One St. Joseph resident informed me that Eric got what he deserved: "That nigger came on the wrong side of the bridge," he said. And Benton Harbor's former schools superintendent, Sherwin Allen, made no effort to hide his contempt for the white power structure.

What I found in the main, though, were people who would like to do right but don't know where to begin. As was said of the South's politicians during Jim Crow, race diminishes us. It incites us to act as we wouldn't in other arenas: clumsily, cowardly and sometimes cruelly. We circle the wagons, watching out for our own.

That's what happened in the response to Eric's death. Most everyone in St. Joseph came to believe that Eric, knowing the police were looking for him, tried to swim the river to get home and drowned. Most everyone in Benton Harbor, with equal certitude, believes that Eric was killed—most likely by whites, most likely because he dated a white girl. I was struck by the disparity in perspective, the competing realities, but I was equally taken aback by the distance between the two towns—which, of course, accounts for the myths. Jim Reeves, the police lieutenant who headed the investigation into Eric's death, once confided that this teen-ager he'd never met had more impact on him than any other black person.

I'm often asked by whites, with some wonderment, how it is that I'm able to spend so much time in black communities without feeling misunderstood or unwelcomed or threatened. I find it much easier to talk with blacks about race than with fellow whites. While blacks often brave slights silently for fear that if they complain they won't be believed, when asked, they welcome the chance to relate their experiences. Among whites, there's a reluctance—or a lack of opportunity—to engage. Race for them poses no urgency; it does not impose on their daily routines. I once asked Ben Butzbaugh, a St. Joseph commissioner, how he felt the two towns got along. "I think we're pretty fair in this community," he said. "I don't know that I can say I know of any out-and-out racial-type things that occur. I just think people like their own better than others. I think that's pretty universal. Don't you? . . . We're not a bunch of racists. We're not anything America isn't." Butzbaugh proudly pointed to his friendship with Renée Williams, Benton Harbor's new school superintendent. "Renée was in our home three, four, five days a week," he noted. "Nice gal. Put herself through school. We'd talk all the time." Williams used to clean for Butzbaugh's family.

As I learned during the years in and out of these towns, the room for day-to-day dialogue doesn't present itself. We become buried in our myths, certain of our truths—and refuse to acknowledge what the historian Allan Nevins calls "the grains of stony reality" embedded in most legends. A quarter-century ago, race was part of everyday public discourse; today it haunts us quietly, though on occasion—the Rodney King beating or the Simpson trial or Eric McGinnis's death—it erupts with jarring urgency. At these moments of crisis, during these squalls, we flail about, trying to find moral ballast. By then it is usually too late. The lines are drawn. Accusations are hurled across the river like cannon fire. And the cease-fires, when they occur, are just that, cease-fires, temporary and fragile. Even the best of people have already chosen sides.

Born in Texas in 1944, Olivia Castellano has used her childhood frustrations of feeling unsupported by both the Mexican and Anglo-American cultures to build a unique voice as a poet. She uses symbolism from both these backgrounds in her poetry, frequently employing the colors blue and yellow to represent the large sky and parched soil of Texas, and blends language styles of English and her native Spanish. Currently Ms. Castellano is a professor of English at California State University, Sacramento.

Canto, locura y poesía

Olivia Castellano

In Comstock, the Tex-Mex border town about 15 miles from the Rio Grande where I spent the first 12 years of my life, I saw the despair that poverty and hopelessness had etched in the faces of young Chicano men who, like my father, walked back and forth on the dusty path between Comstock and the Southern Pacific Railroad station. They would set out every day on rail carts to repair the railroad. The women of Comstock fared no better. Most married early, I had seen them in their kitchens toiling at the stove, with one baby propped on one hip and two toddlers tugging at their skirts. Or, they followed their working mothers' route, cleaning house and doing laundry for rich Texan ranchers who paid them a pittance. I decided very early that this was not the future I wanted.

In 1958 my father, tired of seeing days fade into each other without promise, moved us to California, where we became farmworkers in the San Jose area (then a major agricultural center). I saw the same futile look in the faces of young Chicanos and Chicanas working beside my family. Those faces already lined so young with sadness made me deadly serious about my books and my education.

At a young age—between 11 and 14—I began my intellectual and spiritual rebellion against my parents and society. I fell in love with books and created space of my own where I could dare to dream. Yet, in school I remained shy and introverted, terrified of my white, male professors. In my adolescence, I rebelled against my mother's insistence that Mexican girls should marry young, as she did at 18. But, I didn't care if my cousins Alicia and Anita were getting married and having babies early "I was put on this earth to make books, not babies!" I announced and ran into my room.

Books became my obsession. I wanted to read everything that I was not supposed to. By 14 I was already getting to know the Marquis de Sade, Rimbaud, Lautréamont, Whitman, Dostoyevsky, Marx. I came by these writers serendipitously. To get from home to Sacramento High School, I had to walk through one of the toughest neighborhoods in the city, Oak Park. There were men hanging out with liquor in brown paper bags, playing dice, shooting craps and calling from cars: "Hey, baby, get in here with me!" I'd run into the small Oak Park Library which turned out to have a little bit of everything. I would walk around staring at the shelves, killing time till the shifty-eyed men would go away.

The librarians knew and tolerated me with skepticism: "Are you sure you're going to read the Marquis de Sade? Do your parents know you're checking out this material? What are you doing with the Communist Manifesto?" One librarian even forbade me to check the books out, so I'd sit in the library reading for hours on end. Later, at 16 or 17, 1 was allowed to check out anything I wanted.

The librarians gave me *carte blanche* circulation, so it was that I came to grapple with tough language and ideas. These books were hot! Yet I also was obsessed with wanting to be pretty, mysterious, silent and sexy. I wanted to have long curly hair, red lips and long red nails; to wear black tight dresses and high heels. I wanted desperately to look like the sensuous femmes fatales of the Mexican cinema—María Félix, one of the most beautiful and famous of Mexico's screen goddesses, and Libertad Lamarque, the smoky-voiced, green-eyed Argentinian singer. These were the women I admired when my mother and I went to the movies. But these were my "outward" models. My "inward" models, the voices of the intellect that spoke to me when I shut the door to my room, were, as you have gathered, a writer of erotica, two mad surrealists, a crazy Romantic, an epileptic literary genius, and a radical socialist.

I needed to sabotage society in a major, intellectually radical way. I needed to be a warrior who would catch everyone off guard. But to be a warrior, you must never let your opponent figure you out. When the bullets of racism and sexism are flying at you, you must be very clever in deciding how you want to live. I knew that everything around me— school, teachers, television, friends, men, even my own parents, who in their own internalized racism and self-hatred didn't really believe I'd amount to much though they hoped like hell life would prove them wrong—everything was against me and this I understood fully.

To protect myself, I fell in love with Language—all of it, poems, stories, novels, plays, songs, biographies, "cuentos" or little vignettes, movies— all manifestations of spoken and written language. I fell in love with ideas, with essays by writers like Bacon and Montaigne. I began my serious reading crusade around age 11, when I was already convinced that books alone would save my life. Only through them and through songs, I felt, would I be free to shape some kind of future for myself.

I wanted to prove to anyone who cared to ask (though by now I was convinced no one gave a damn) that I, the daughter of a laborer-farmworker, could dare to be somebody. Try to imagine what it is like to be full of rage—rage at everything: at white teachers who could never pronounce my name (I was called anything from "Odilia" to "Otilia" to "Estela"); rage at those teachers who asked me point blank, "But how did you get to be so smart? You are Mexican, aren't you?"; rage at my 11th-grade English teacher who said to me in front of the whole class, "You stick to essay writing; never try to write a poem again because a poet you are not!" (This after I had worked for two diligent weeks on an imitation of "La Belle Dame Sans Merci"! Now I can laugh. Then it was pitiful).

From age 13, I was also angry at boys who hounded me for dates. When I'd reject them they'd yell, "So what do you plan to do for the rest of your life, fuck a book?" Angry at my Chicana classmates in high school who, perhaps jealous of my high grades, would acuse, "What are you trying to do, be like the whites?" And regrettably, I was angry at my parents, exasperated by their docility, their limited expectations of life. I knew they were proud; but sometimes, in their own misdirected rage (maybe afraid of my little successes), they would make painful comments. "Te vas a volver loca con esos jodidos libros" ("You'll go nuts with those damned books") was my mother's frequent warning. Or the even more sickening, "Esta nunca se va a casar." ("Give up on this one; she'll never get married.") This was the tenor of my adolescent years. When nothing on either side of the two cultures, Mexican or Anglo-American, affirms your existence, that is how rage is shaped.

While I managed to escape at least from the obvious entrapments—a teen pregnancy, a destructive early marriage—I did not escape years of being told I wasn't quite right, that because of my ethnicity and gender I was somehow defective, incomplete. Those years left wounds on my self-esteem, wounds so deep that even armed with my books and stolen knowledge I could not entirely escape deep feelings of unworthiness.

By the time I graduated from high school and managed to get a little scholarship to California State University, Sacramento, where I now teach (in 1962 it was called Sacramento State College), I had become very unassertive, immensely shy. I was afraid to look unfeminine if I raised my hand in class, afraid to seem ridiculous if I asked a "bad" question and all eyes turned on me. A deeper part of me was afraid that my rage might rear its ugly head and I would be considered "one more angry Mexican accusing everybody of racism." I was painfully concerned with my physical appearance: wasn't I supposed to look beautiful like Félix and Lamarque? Yet while I wanted to look pretty for the boys, the thought of having sex terrified me. What if I got pregnant, had to quit college and couldn't read my books any more? The more I feared boys, the more I made myself attractive for them, the more they made advances, the more I rejected them.

This constant tension sapped my energy and distracted me from my creative journeys into language. Oh, I would write little things (poems, sketches for stories, journal entries), but I was afraid to show them to anyone. Besides, no one knew I was writing them. I was so frightened by my white, male professors, especially in the English department—they looked so arrogant and were so ungiving of their knowledge—that I didn't have the nerve to major in English, though it was the subject I loved.

Instead, I chose to major in French. The "Parisiens" and "Québecois" in the French department faculty admired my French accent: "Mademoiselle, êtes-vous certaine que vous n'êtes pas Parisienne?" they would ask. In short, they cared. They engaged me in dialogue, asked why I preferred to study French instead of Spanish ("I already know Spanish," I'd say.) So French became my adopted language. I could play with it, sing songs in it and sound exotic. It complemented my Spanish; besides, I didn't have to worry about speaking English with my heavy Spanish accent and risk being ridiculed. At one point, my spoken French was better than my oral Spanish and my written French has remained better than my written Spanish.

Thus, at 23, armed with a secondary school teaching credential and a B.A. in French with an English minor, I became a high school teacher of French and English. Soon after that, I began to work for a school district where the majority of the students were Chicanos and Blacks from families on welfare and/or from households run by women.

After two years of high school teaching, I returned to Cal State at Sacramento for the Master's degree. Professionally and artistically, it was the best decision I have ever made. The Master's program in which I was accepted was a pilot program in its second year at CSU Sacramento. Called the "Mexican American Experienced Teachers Fellowship," it was run by a team of anthropology professors, central among whom was Professor Steven Arvizu. The program was designed to turn us graduates into "agents of social change." It was 1969 and this was one of the first federally funded (Title V) programs to address Mexican-American students' needs by re-educating their teachers.

My interests were literary, but all 20 of us "fellows" had to get an M.A. in social anthropology, since this experiment took the "anthropolgizing education" approach. We studied social dynamics, psycholinguistics, history of Mexico, history of the American Southwest, community activism, confrontational strategies and the nature of the Chicano Movement. The courses were eye-openers. I had never heard the terms Chicano, bicul-

turalism, marginality, assimilation, Chicanismo, protest art. I had never
heard of César Chávez and the farmworkers nor of Luis Valdéz and his
Teatro Campesino. I had never studied the nature of racism and identity.
The philosophy of the program was that culture is a powerful tool for
learning, self-expression, solidarity and positive change. Exploring it can
help Chicano students understand their bicultural circumstances.

The program brought me face to face with nineteen other Chicano men
and women, all experienced public school teachers like myself, with
backgrounds like mine. The program challenged every aspect of my life.
Through group counseling, group encounter, classroom interaction,
course content and community involvement I was allowed to express my
rage and to examine it in the company of peers who had a similar anger.
Most of our instructors, moreover, were Chicano or white professors sensitive to Chicanos. For the first time, at 25, I had found my role models. I
vowed to do for other students what these people had done for me.

Eighteen years of teaching, primarily white women students, Chicanos,
and Blacks at California State University, Sacramento have led me to see
myself less as a teacher and more as a cultural worker, struggling against
society to undo the damage of years of abuse. I continue to see myself as
a warrior empowered by my rage. Racism and sexism leave two clear-cut
scars on my students: internalized self-hatred and fear of their own creative passion, in my view the two most serious obstacles in the classroom.
Confronting this two-headed monster made me razor-sharp. Given their
tragic personal stories, the hope in my students' eyes reconfirms daily the
incredible beauty, the tenacity of the human spirit.

Teaching white women students (ages 30–45) is no different from working with Chicano and Black students (both men and women): you have
to bring about changes in the way they view themselves, their abilities,
their right to get educated, and their relation to a world that has systematically oppressed them simply for being who they are. You have to help
them channel and understand the seething rage they carry deep inside, a
rage which, left unexpressed, can turn them against each other and, more
sadly, against themselves.

I teach four courses per semester: English 109G, Writing for Proficiency
for Bilingual Bidialectal Students (a course taken mainly by Chicano and
Black students, ages 19–24); English 115A, Pedagogy/Language Arts for
Prospective Elementary School Teachers (course taken mainly by women
aged 25–45, 50 percent white, 50 percent Chicano); English 180G, Chicano
Literature, an advanced studies General Education course for non-Eng-
lish majors (taken by excellent students, aged 24–45, about 40 percent
white, 40 percent Chicano, 20 percent Black/Vietnamese/Filipino/South
American). The fourth course is English 1, Basic Language Skills, a pre-

freshman composition course taken primarily by Black and Chicano freshmen, male and female, aged 18–22, who score too low on the English Placement Test to be placed in "regular" Freshman Composition.

Mine is a teaching load that, in my early teaching years, used to drive me close to insanity from physical, mental and spiritual exhaustion—spiritual from having internalized my students' pain. Perhaps not fully empowered myself, not fully emplumed in the feather of my own creativity (to borrow the "emplumada" metaphor coined by Lorna Dee Cervantes, the brilliant Chicana poet), I allowed their rage to become part of mine. This kind of rage can kill you. And so through years of working with these kinds of students I have learned to make my spirit strong with "canto, locura y poesía" (song, madness and poetry).

Truly, it takes a conjurer, a magus with all the teaching cards up her sleeve, to deal with the fragmented souls that show up in my classes. Among the Chicanos and Blacks, I get ex-offenders (mostly men but occasionally a woman who has done time)', orphans, single women heads of household, high school dropouts who took years to complete their Graduation Equivalency Diploma.

I get women who have been raped or have been sexually abused either by a father figure or by male relatives—Sylvia Tracey, for example, a 30-year-old Chicana feminist, mother of two, whose parents pressured her to marry her rapist and who is going through divorce after ten years of marriage. I get battered women who are still in a violent marriage or finally got the courage to say enough. And, of course, I get the young Chicano and Black young yuppies who don't believe the world existed before 1970, who know nothing about the sixties' history of struggle and student protest, who—in the case of the Chicanos—feel ashamed that their parents speak English with an accent or were once farmworkers. Most of my students are ashamed of their writing skills and have never once been told that they could succeed in school.

Annetta Jones is typical. A 45-year-old Black woman who single-handedly raised three children, all college-educated and successful, she is still married to a man who served ten years in prison for being a "hit man." She visited him faithfully in prison and underwent all kinds of humiliation at the hands of correctional officers—even granting them sexual favors for conjugal visits with her husband. When her husband completed his time, he fell in love with a young woman from Chicago, where he now lives.

Among my white women students (ranging in age from 25 to 40, though occasionally I get a 45- or 50-year-old "re-entry" woman who wants to be an elementary or high school teacher and "help out young kids so they won't have to go through what I went through"—their exact words) I get women who are either divorced or divorcing; rarely do I get a "happily" married woman. This is especially true of the white women who take my Chicano literature and my credential-pedagogy classes. Take Lynne Trebeck, for instance, a white woman about 40 years old who runs a farm. When she entered the university, her husband objected, so she divorced him! They continue to live in the same house (he refused to leave), "but now he has no control over me," as she told me triumphantly midway through the semester. She has two sons, 15 and 18-years-old; as a young woman, she did jail time as the accomplice of a convicted drug dealer.

Every semester I get two or three white lesbian feminists. This semester there was Vivianne Rose, about 40, in my Chicano literature class. On the first day of class she wore Levi pants, a baggy sweat shirt, white tennis shoes and a beige baseball cap. But, apparently sensing too much conservatism in the students, and knowing that she wanted to be an elementary school teacher, she chose to conceal her sexual orientation By the end of the first week she had switched to ultrafeminine dresses and flowery skirts, brightly colored blouses, nylons and medium-heeled black shoes, along with lipstick and eye makeup. When she spoke in class she occasionally made references to "my husband who is Native-American." She and Sylvia Tracey became very close friends. Halfway through the course, they informed me that "Shit, it's about time we tell her." (This from Sylvia.) "Oh, hell, why not," Vivianne said; "my husband is a woman." Vivianne Rose lived on a reservation for years and taught Native-American children to read and write. She speaks "Res" (reservation speech) and has adopted her "husband's" last name.

Among my white women students there are also divorced women who are raising two to four children, usually between the ages of eight and seventeen. The most confident are the older, widowed white women who are taking classes for their own enjoyment, not for a degree. They also tell stories of torment: rapes, beatings, verbal and emotional harassment from their men. On occasion, as I said, I get women who have done jail time, usually for taking the rap for drug-connected boyfriends. Among the older married women, the litany echoes again and again: "My husband doesn't really want me in school." "My husband doesn't really care what I do in college as long as I take care of his needs and the kids' needs." "My husband doesn't really know what I'm studying—he has never asked and I've never told him."

Most of the white women as well as the minority students come to the university through special programs. There is the "Educational Opportunity Program" for students who do not meet all university entrance requirements or whose high school grade point average is simply too low for regular admission. The "Student Affirmative Action Program" is for students who need special counseling and tutoring to bring their academic skills up to par or deal with emotional trauma. And the "College Assistance Migrant Program" assists students whose parents are migrant farmworkers in the agricultural areas surrounding the city of Sacramento. There is a wonderful program called PASAR for older women students entering the university for the first time or returning after a multiple-year absence. The Women's Resource Center also provides small grants and scholarships for these re-entry women. A large number of my students (both white and minority women) come severely handicapped in their basic language, math and science skills; a large number have never used a computer. It is not uncommon (especially among Chicanos and Blacks) to get an incoming student who scores at the fifth- and sixth-grade reading levels. Imagine the damage I must help repair!

The task is Herculean, the rewards spiritually fulfilling. I would not have it any other way. Every day is a lesson in humility and audacity. That my students have endured nothing but obstacles and put-downs yet have the courage and strength to seek a college education, humbles me. They are, like me, walking paradoxes. They have won against all the odds, (their very presence on campus attests to that). Yet, they haven't won: their deeply ingrained sense of inferiority convinces them that they are not worthy of success.

This is my challenge, I embrace it wholeheartedly. There is no other place I'd rather be, no profession more noble. Sure, I sometimes have doubts; every day something new, sad, even tragic comes up. Just as I was typing this article, for instance, Vicky, one of the white students in my Chicano literature class, called in tears, barely able to talk. "Professor, I can't possibly turn in my paper to your mailbox by four o'clock," she cried. "Everything in my house is falling apart! My husband just fought with my oldest daughter [from a previous marriage], has thrown her out of the house. He's running up and down the street, yelling and threatening to leave us. And I'm sitting here trying to write your paper! I'm going crazy. I feel like walking away from it all!" I took an hour from writing this article to help her contain herself. By the end of our conversation, I had her laughing. I also put her in touch with a counselor friend of mine and gave her a two-day extension for her final paper. And naturally I was one more hour late with my own writing!

I teach in a totally non-traditional way. I use every trick in the book: much positive reinforcement, both oral and written; many one-on-one conferences. I help women develop a network with each other, refer them to professor friends who can help them; connect them with graduate students and/or former students who are already pursuing careers. In the classroom, I force students to stand in front of their classmates, to explain concepts or read and evaluate their essays aloud. I create panels representing opposing viewpoints and hold debates—much oral participation, role-playing, reading their own texts. Their own writing and opinions become part of the course. On exams I ask them questions about their classmates' presentations. I meet with individual students in local coffee houses or taverns; it's much easier to talk about personal pain over coffee or a beer or a glass of wine than in my office. My students, for the most part, do not have a network of support outside of the university. There are no supportive husbands, lovers (except on rare occasions, as with my lesbian students), no relatives saying, "Yes, you can do it."

Is it any wonder that when these students enter the university they have a deep sense of personal shame about everything—poor skills, being older students. They are angry at the schools for having prepared them poorly; at their parents for not having had high enough expectations of them or (in the case of the women) for having allowed them to marry so young. Sylvia, my Chicana feminist student, put it best when I was pointing out incomplete sentences in her essay: "Where the hell was I when all this was being taught in high school? And why didn't anybody give a damn that I wasn't learning it?"

I never teach content for the first two weeks of the semester. I talk about anger, sexism, racism and the sixties—a time when people believed in something larger than themselves. I allow them space to talk—about prisons and why so many Chicano and Black young men are behind bars in California; why people fear differences; why our society is gripped by homophobia. I give my students a chance to talk about their anger ("coraje" in Spanish). I often read them a poem by my friend and colleague José Montoya, called "Eslipping and Esliding," in which he talks about "locura" (craziness) and says that with a little locura, a little eslipping and esliding, we can survive the madness that surrounds us. We laugh at ourselves, sharing our tragic, tattered pasts, undoing everything and letting the anger out. "I know why so many of you are afraid of doing well," I say. "You've been told you can't do it, and you're so angry about it, you can't concentrate." Courage takes pure concentration. By the end of these initial two or three weeks we have become friends and defined our mutual respect. Only then do we enter the course content.

I am not good at endings; I prefer to celebrate beginnings. The struggle continues, and the success stories abound. Students come back, year after year, to say "Thank you." Usually, I pull these visitors into the classroom: "Tell my class that they can do it. Tell them how you did it!" The visitors start talking and can't stop. "Look, Olivia, when I first came into your class," said Sylvia, "I couldn't even put a fucking sentence together. And now look at me, three years later I'm even writing poetry!"

Inés Maria Talamantez is Associate Professor of Religion Studies at the University of California, Santa Barbara, and managing editor of New Scholar: An Americanist Review. *She founded and directs the first (and only) doctoral program in the U.S. on Native American Religious Traditions. She has written several books on Native American oral tradition, and numerous articles on women, religion and the environment.*

Seeing Red: American Indian Women Speaking about Their Religious and Political Perspectives

Inés Maria Talamantez

With the dawn breaking in the east over the Sacramento Mountains of New Mexico, the barrenness of the white gypsum sand dunes glimmers to the west. The early desert sun of the Tularosa Valley is already hot. I was born less than one hundred miles south from where I am now standing, and I am remembering what the women of this place have taught me. It is their stories that have helped me explore who I am today. They have given me the sense of self and place. Learning our stories as we move through our lives, collecting and gathering until we fill our baskets to the brim (or our files to overflowing, and we move on to entering our ideas on computer disks), we are reminded of the minds and imaginations of our ancestors and how they acquired the knowledge necessary to survive the struggle throughout the centuries.

Central to these teachings from Native American traditions are the elaborate explanations about the beginning of the cosmos and the role of female deities who were present at the time of creation. The role of many Native American women today is still influenced by the teachings passed on to us by those that went before us and their concern for the generations to follow. Acknowledging the perseverance of indigenous women for social justice and religious freedom is as necessary for Native American women as for American feminists. In a world where distorted images of native women's spirituality abound, spiritually impoverished American women often appropriate those aspects of our lives that fill their needs. Our struggle continues.

Those who write without knowing the truth provide glib, shallow accounts of what they consider to be "other," and the perspective they take places them beyond accountability to those on whose lives they draw for spiritual nourishment. Neither are they native women, nor do they want to be connected to their own female ancestors. They are

494

detached from knowledge of their own past and seek meaning in the lives of others who are in no position to object. This is offensive and con-stitutes a form of intellectual imperialism. The belief that the traditions of others may be appropriated to serve the needs of self is a peculiarly West-ern notion that relies on a belief that knowledge is disembodied rather than embedded in relationships, intimately tied to place, and entails responsibilities to others and a commitment and discipline in learning.

Feminist explorations of the distinctive knowledge that women's distinc-tive experiences generate provide a helpful perspective on the struggle of native women to be heard and to see their traditions respected and their truths acknowledged. Diane Bell, Australian feminist, has argued that women's experience of subordination predisposes them to a reflexive stance on their lives and those of others.[1] Within this schema, Native American women may speak in a specially true and insightful voice. Of course, men as well may write of their experiences, which reflect their truths and their lives, but their narratives do not always represent the clearest expositions of what it means to be a gendered, colonized subject.

This work is not just a research project; it is part of my life. I am connected to these women and their truths. We are taught in our cultures that as young girls we are moving through the world with others, that we are moving in relationships with others, including the lives of the flora and the fauna. We are told to respect the lives and movements of others. The invis-ible forces at work in the natural world are revealed through the wondrous world created in the sacred narratives, the stories that provide the frame of reference through which we are instructed about our heritage as women of Native America. It is this aesthetic, created in the minds of our ancestors, that has given us a different way of looking at and thinking about time and place. The cycles of growth in the natural world or the movement of the sun, for example, explicate time as cyclical rather than linear, as repre-sented on my digital wristwatch, on which of course I also depend.

The natural cycles of growth are closely watched, as is decay. Complex rituals embedded in our ceremonial structures provide a perspective into the world of the supernatural. The sacred is reflected in everyone and in everything, in our minds and worlds, in the moving bodies of dancers and in the voices of singers. However, we face profound political and sociocultural challenges in keeping our cultures alive through creative and religious introspection and work and not letting the devastating forces of change overwhelm us. Yet we know through understanding our ceremonies that transformation brings change. It is, however, the knowl-edge gained through ritual transformation that then gives us the respon-sibility to apply the lessons learned to our lives and the lives of those around us. It is here that we understand both the values and the social systems under which all individuals in diverse cultural locations must operate in order to maintain balance within their societies.

The indigenous framework within which many of us work reveals the systems of relatedness, obligation, and respect that govern the lives of many native women. There is a driving purpose behind our work; we know what we are expected to do. There are political commitments to social justice, concerns for what constitutes activism in our present day, complex issues of identity and naming ourselves. The political survival issues of the day—land claims, freedom of religion, environmental racism, lack of appropriate health, education, and employment, for example—engage us as persons who labor under the twin oppressions of being woman and native. This narrative of inquiry requires deep reflection. It is an exploration in both humility and authority. Insight is gained through analysis, interpretation, and critique.

In practice today our lives are shaped by the complex intertwining of several controlling regimes that discriminate against us in a variety of ways. Native American women living on reservations are subject to the will of tribal governments, which are under the control of the Bureau of Indian Affairs, an arm of the Department of the Interior. The concerns of women are not a priority for the bureaucrats or the elected officials, any more than they are in the dominant society. For urban Indian women, who are not registered in federal government records—that is, have no number indicating that they are enrolled and are therefore "legitimate Indians" according to the government—social services and benefits are difficult or almost impossible to obtain. For example, those who do make it through the school system and plan to attend a junior college or university are denied access to scholarships unless they can prove that they are Indian. No one else in this country has to prove their ethnicity; why do we?

Health care issues are also viewed in this way. If you are enrolled, you qualify for federal Indian Health programs, but if you are not enrolled, you are just another minority woman seeking health care. In reforming the health care system, the particular needs of those of us who are women and native need to be addressed. We are American women. We are indigenous women. We share many of the health concerns of other American women, but we have been disproportionately exposed to some additional health risks. In seeking to heal our bodies, we look to religion, land, and medicine in ways that the present health care system finds difficult to accommodate. As Meredith Begay [an Apache medicine woman] tells us, medicine, health, ceremony are all intertwined, and her work as a cross-cultural communicator shows one path forward.

Churches are also guilty. Many Christian churches, especially in areas largely populated by Indians, still require that their parishioners give up participating in their own religious traditions if they wish to be Christians. This discrimination has been met in a variety of ways. Some native women continue to resist completely all forms of Christianity and practice their own native ways, which beautifully blend culture and spirituality in one complete worldview. Other women continue to follow their cultural ways and have found a method that allows them to be Indians from a specific culture but yet accept and embrace Christian dogma. And of course some Indian women have accepted Christianity completely and have opted for assimilation into the dominant American culture.

The struggle for religious freedom and a land-based pedagogy require that we reconfigure the roles of native women and their distinctive features. We are looking at tangled historical processes and systems that integrate cultural, political, and ecological dimensions. We need a new schemata, one that frees us from the constraints of a Western patriarchal paradigm of control, one that takes us beyond victim status and blame. We need a framework that enables us to understand our own cultures as well as allows us to teach about them. We must not forget, however, that we are working within institutions that have continued to exert control over the very substance of our research, the publication of our work—institutions that have the power to determine what counts as scholarship. It will take reflection and a willingness to scrutinize the power of church and state before native and non-native, men and women can share in a meaningful way. It will be a long time before we can be equal partners in a dialogue. We women are at a historical juncture where as workers, mothers, scholars, healers, poets, we have the necessary tools to move forward. Our fight for religious freedom is a fight for life and for land. If you are fighting for social justice, you are fighting for our freedom. If you are raising children, you are fighting for our freedom. If you are writing as a woman, you are fighting for our freedom.

Voices of Wisdom

Having articulated the underlying philosophy, albeit in the abstract, and alluded to the complexity of the context within which we give expression to our beliefs, let me now ground this discussion in the specific writings of Native American scholars. Indian societies, long before the coming of Europeans to America, were in the process of significant and dynamic development in the areas of religious practice, economic production, and artistic and material achievements. These were hardly simple, savage, or "primitive" peoples. Alfonso Ortiz from San Juan Pueblo and professor of anthropology at the University of Albuquerque, remembers that in New Mexico

long ago, when first informing their worlds with meaning, the San Juan people took their three-tiered social order and projected it outwards and
upwards to encompass the whole of their physical world as well by imbuing
that world with a three-tiered spiritual meaning, one both reflecting and
reinforcing their social order. The fit among their ideas of order in society, in
the physical world, and in the spiritual realm is ingenious, for these three
orders interlock and render order into everything within the Tewa world.[2]

In Keres Pueblo, in New Mexico, Paula Gunn Allen (Laguna/Sioux, and
professor of English at UCLA), tells us that Sun Woman, who was present
at and participated in the creation of the universe, left to go to the east
and it is said that she will return in times to come. At Laguna, Gunn tells
us, people believe that she has already returned in the form of the
atomic/hydrogen "suns," which were put together in her original lands.
These are the lands that provided the uranium that was mined to create
the atomic devastations.[3]

Vickie Downey, writing of her home pueblo, Tesuque, tells us about keeping alive the religious traditions of the Southwest Pueblos in spite of
Spanish priests and soldiers:

> About our religion, yes, we've kept that alive even with exploitation that
> came in and tried to wipe out our religion. We've maintained that. Among
> the pueblos there's a church in each pueblo. With the Spanish they brought
> the priests along with the soldiers. Together they tried to exterminate our
> communities, our villages, our spirit. But we've maintained our way to this
> time. It's been a struggle, but we've maintained it. A lot of other Indian reser-
> vations, they've also maintained it.[4]

The settlers who came even later to this land felt the need to exploit it even
further for its natural resources in the name of what they believed to be
civilization. Their attitudes were very different from those of the diverse
tribal societies they encountered. The sharp contrast in ideals and values
that affected the way the newcomers viewed the religious practices of
these societies is still felt today. The settlers feared nature and wilderness;
they were, after all, from another land and ecosystem. Perhaps the settlers
were haunted by memories of former times and the fear of going back to
the earlier uncivilized states that had existed in Europe if they were not
successful in mastering this new, strange land and its peoples.

The way these colonists acted toward this land had less to do with the
natural world than with their ideals of individualism and independence
and their desperate need for a new beginning in a new world. In shaping
their own adjustment to this new environment, they inherited much from
the Native American societies they encountered but were more concerned with conquering than understanding. Their belief that God had
given them this natural world to exploit allowed them to rationalize their
behaviors in the name of European manifest destiny, civilization, and

Christianity. Everywhere, in every direction, the consequence was the laying waste of souls and natural resources.

Many Dene (Navajo) women today are dealing with these issues in an ongoing struggle for religious freedoms and social justice. To be a Dene woman requires living in and practicing the Dene way of life. The power manifested by Changing Woman, a female deity in the myth of the Blessingway ceremonial complex, is a power that Dene women call upon in their struggles today, especially their struggle for a land base, for they continue to be forced to relocate from what they consider to be their spiritual homeland. According to a Dene woman traditionalist and friend involved in this political, religious struggle, to be moved away from her place means to be living out of balance and harmony. The ideas set forth in the concepts of Blessingway provide the sanctions for Dene peoples' roles in human life and require participation in ceremonial life in a specific land base.[5]

In the *Kináálá*, the girls' initiation ceremony, Dene girls are instructed to live their lives modeled after Changing Woman. Women's beliefs about the attributes of Changing Woman and the nature of her interconnectedness to all living entities is of great significance and clarifies for the initiates what their roles and responsibilities will be as Dene women. Female sponsors for the initiates derive their power from a codified body of ceremonial knowledge and personal experience. The ceremony itself requires of the women sponsors that they be responsible for ritually guiding the initiates from childhood through the doors of adolescence into womanhood. This is a tremendous task that requires rigorous, dedicated religious commitment if the ceremony is to be effective. Initiated women will sometimes gain prestige in the community by learning from their own sponsors how to carry on the *Kináálá* ceremony. This of course takes years of apprenticeship if it is to be done correctly. The important fact here is that initiated women often become the carriers of the Dene female tradition. Dene women, who are also known to perform the ceremonial roles of Hand Tremblers, praying over a patient's body with trembling hands as they search for answers, or of Diagnosticians, locating the source of an illness and then referring the patient to the appropriate ceremonies, are usually not free to pursue these demanding roles until after menopause.[6]

The struggle to pursue one's religion has many faces. For example, Flora Jones, a Wintu religious leader, like Pilulaw Khus, a Chumash elder, is concerned with desecration by the federal government and commercial interests of lands considered sacred and central to the continuity of their ceremonial life and practices. Flora has complained she has not been able to collect essential medicines in the forests of north-

ern California.[7] Pilulaw has fought oil companies whose development
would desecrate Chumash ceremonial areas. When there are oil spills,
she is the first out there to clean up the beaches and to assist the endangered animals. Knowledge of a sustainable environment, revealed in the
languages in which the myths are told and in the concept of Mother Earth
and the interconnectedness of all living things, is central to what it means
to be indigenous to a place.

The tensions between the spiritual forces at work in Native America and
the ideas of forced religious conversion, along with new introduced technologies, have had a tremendous impact on the lives of native women. In
the sphere of religion, men were moved into positions of power over religious women leaders. Too often missionization meant the disempower-
ment of women. This is made explicit in *Jesuit Relations*, the journals of
the Jesuit missionaries of the seventeenth century, which advocates placing men in religious leadership roles and counsels against dealing with
women in positions of religious or political power.[8] Despite the pervasive
power of these agents of change, the resistance of native women persists.
Though often graciously stepping aside from former leadership roles,
they continue in many places to be respected for their religious knowledge and women's wisdom.

The women of the Iroquois Longhouse, for example, have not permitted
patriarchal distortion of the natural world or newly introduced technologies and commodities, such as fast food, disposable diapers, and television, to diffuse their powerful cultural positions as clan mothers and
keepers of the Longhouse ceremonial complex. They are responsible for
choosing the chiefs of the clan, who can govern only if they are in agreement with the rest of the clan members. The final decisions are made by
the careful consideration of the clan mothers, who are concerned for the
well-being of all the people, especially the young children.[9] This, of
course, is a very different perspective on Indian women from one that
blends many traditions into the stereotype of the Indian woman as subservient. It is important that we remember that women had many and
varied tasks, ceremonies, and social roles, in different places, at different
times, and in different nations. Yet when we look to the historic record
and ethnographic accounts, women are often invisible.

One notable exception is Ella Cara Deloria's (Yankton Sioux) novel
Waterlily. Writing of the dramatic changes taking place in her society in
the late nineteenth century, she paints a moving portrait of the elaborate
rite *hunka*, or "child beloved," a ceremony for children who are selected
for a place of honor in Teton society. Through this rite the girl Waterlily is
taught the knowledge necessary for understanding the principles of daily
life and why ritual practices are important for both men and women.[10]

In the American Southwest, interreligious dialogue in churches and at conferences has ignored the religious life of Native American women and our relationships with other indigenous women of the borderlands. Historically Chicana and Mexican women south of the border have been denied access to knowledge of their indigenous heritage in a manner similar to that of their sisters in the north. Church and state have combined in powerful ways to divide and conquer, yet the religious and medical practices of these women today demonstrate a rich complex blend of ideas, commitments, and identities. Coatlicue (an Aztec female deity), Guadalupe (a melding of an Aztec deity and sixteenth-century Spanish Catholicism), Curanderas (Mexican folk healers), Parteras (midwives), and more recently Mexican and Chicana Espiritualistas stand as testimony to the strength and creativeness of women of the borderlands. Today, Chicana and indigenous women, in dialogue with our elders, are finding a place for ourselves as we redefine the history of our religious experience. *Mujeres Activas en Letras y Cambio Social* is an important forum for exploring these matters.[11] Rigoberta Menchu, Quiche woman of Guatemala, has so brilliantly named our struggle as the spirituality of the Western hemisphere.[12]

My own identity incorporates the richness of my Apache, Mexican Indian, and Chicana heritage. It was that background and my female kin that guided me along a path of even deeper reflection and understanding of the diverse roles of women. When I draw on the tradition of the Sun Clan at the Mescalero Apache Reservation in New Mexico, I make the linkages among myself, my research, and my political activism as a woman. In elaborate detail the Sun Clan creation myth, when told in Apache, relates that from the very beginning of time, the earth existed and was in a process of continual change, which was seen and continues to be seen as the manifestation of the cyclical powers of nature.

In the ceremony *'Isánáklésh Gotal*, which marks the transition from girlhood to womanhood, the symbols used to influence the young girls vary in their function, but their overall purpose is to convince the adolescent that she will undergo good and positive changes if she participates fully in the ceremony. However, it is up to the girl herself to decide if she wishes to undertake this responsibility. At this young age girls are thought of as soft and moldable, suggesting that they are still capable of being conditioned and influenced by female kin. It is easier to convince some girls to participate than others. Some need to be awakened to their female identity, while others need to be calmed down and taught to be more feminine. Within the ritual design of the ceremony two concepts are at work: one is awakening the initiate to the world around her and to her abilities, and the other is to carefully calm down the unrestrained nature of adolescence. Both concepts are nurtured and encouraged in the young girl's everyday activities.

Preparation for the ceremony begins early in the life of a young girl. She is slowly and carefully made ready, then suddenly uprooted from her special privileged childhood in a family where female kin watch over her from the time of her birth. Menarche signals a physiological marker that the young girl immediately recognizes. Suddenly her life changes. Her first menstruation is usually celebrated by family and kin. At this time she is sung over to emphasize the importance of this intimate celebration, the gift of 'Isánáklésh to a young changing woman. Nearly all girls had this ritual in prereservation times. Today a girl may look forward to a feast around the age of eleven or twelve years, at which time many members of her community will gather to honor her in the eight-day ceremony of 'Isánáklésh Gotal.

The first time that I observed this ceremony was when, at the age of nine, I was taken by my mother and aunt to Mescalero to attend the feast of a relative. The image of the girl dancing in the tipi at night stayed with me and became the impetus for my present research.[13] Although I was born in Las Cruces in Doña Ana county, New Mexico, I grew up in Barrio Logan neighborhood in San Diego. My first paying job was at El Porvenir, a tortilla factory that is still there today. As I listened to the older women talk about the realities of their lives, and they provided me with what I now know was an insightful critique of what they were experiencing. Our Lady of Guadalupe Catholic Church was the religious center for most of us. With both humility and religious authority the women created beautiful personal home altars when they felt the need for a more intimate form of prayer and reverence. Many of these altars honored the Virgin de Guadalupe, the principal religious figure in all of her different manifestations.

It was in the Barrio Logan years later that I first heard about Sarita Macias. Her Templo Espiritualista was across the street from the Chicano Cultural Center. Mexican and Chicana/o *espiritualismo*, as practiced today, encompasses a complexity of religious and cultural elements. It uses pre-Columbian medicinal traditions, sixteenth-century Spanish Catholicism, and messianic and shamanistic ritual beliefs and practices. The practice of *espiritualismo* involves trance, soul voyaging, and visionary traits, such as *videncia* (spiritual sight). For believers its teachings are legitimized by a divine charter that originates with an Ultimate Reality and other major Spirits who regularly speak through the spirit mediums (*guias*). The *guias* are, for the most part, women who act as spiritual guides, healers, and counselors. They have visionary experiences that become a source of power, according them respect and credibility in their congregations and the community at large.

Espiritualismo was first introduced into Mexico in the 1860s as a blend of native beliefs, Mexican folk Catholicism, and apocalyptic expectations that responded to the conflicts of church and state taking place in Mexico at that time. An exseminarian, Rogue Rojas, heralded the coming of the "Era de Elias," a messianic reign on earth that would bring salvation to the oppressed, called "espiritualistias Israelites." Rojas named his church "La Iglesia Mexicana Patriarcal Elias." Contemporary Mexican *espiritualismo* derives from this movement. My introduction to *espiritualismo* by Sarita in San Diego eventually led to my initiation by a *guia* in Mexico City. I did not myself seek to become a practitioner so much as to study the process of initiation, one that has deep ties to my Apache and Chicana heritages. Over time Sarita became a source of strength, and it was her guidance that saw me through my doctoral examinations and dissertation.

I don't presume to speak for the women whose voices I document in this essay. Yet I feel that their voices are also my voice, and I am in the process of understanding how to write the history that they speak about and how to describe their religious perspectives. I focus here on the voices of contemporary indigenous women. Too often we look to the old texts and feel comforted by the wisdom of those women who have now passed on. Yet there are indigenous women across this land whose religious and political perspectives can enrich us all today. The Chicano and American Indian Movement of the sixties produced writers who gave voice to our struggles and helped me to begin to find my own voice. Examining the warp and woof of a history whose tightly woven threads are not easily unraveled, I remember what a Dene weaver at the Hubbell Trading Post, Ganado, Arizona, once said to me as she sat before her loom. "Weaving," she said, "is about understanding power."

Notes

[1] Diane Bell, *Daughters of the Dreaming* (Minneapolis: Univ. of Minnesota Press, 1993).

[2] "San Juan Pueblo," *Handbook of North American Indians*, Vol. 9 (Washington, DC: Smithsonian Institution, 1979).

[3] Paula Gunn Allen, *Grandmothers of the Light: A Medicine Woman's Sourcebook* (Boston: Beacon Press, 1991).

[4] Vickie Downey, "Tewa-Tesuque Pueblo," in *Wisdom's Daughters: Conversations with Women Elders of Native America*, ed. Steven Wall (New York: HarperCollins, 1993), 2–21.

[5] Personal communication with Shirley Montoya.

[6] Personal communication with Shirley Montoya.

[7] Flora Jones is a Wintu religious leader and healer in northern California.

[8] *Jesuit Relations and Allied Documents: Travels and Explorations of the Jesuit Missionaries in New France, 1610–1791* (Cleveland: Burrows Brothers, 1896–1901).

[9] See Beatrice Medicine and Patricia Albers, eds., *The Hidden Half: Studies of Plains Indian Women* (New York: Univ. Press, 1983).

[10] Ella Cara Deloria, *Waterlily* (Omaha: Univ. of Nebraska Press, 1988).

[11] MALCS, *Mujeres Activas en Letras y Cambio Social* (Women Active in Letters and Social Change), is the major network for Latina women academics, writers, and social activists.

[12] Rigoberta Menchu, *I, Rigoberta Menchu: An Indian Woman in Guatemala*, ed. Elisabeth Burgos-Debray, trans. Ann Wright London: Verso Press, 1984).

[13] See forthcoming book by Ines Talamantez, *'Isánáklésh Gotal: Introducing Apache Girls to the World of Spiritual and Cultural Values.*

Evelyn Fox Keller (b. 1936), author of many books, is known as a feminist philosopher of science. Her work explores cultural stereotyping and its effects on the thoughts and actions of science. A Feeling for the Organism: The Life and Work of Barbara McClintock *(1983) and* Secrets of Life, Secrets of Death: Essays on Language, Gender and Science *(1992) are just two of her most important works.*

A Feeling for the Organism

Evelyn Fox Keller

There are two equally dangerous extremes—
to shut reason out and to let nothing else in.

Pascal

If Barbara McClintock's story illustrates the fallibility of science, it also bears witness to the underlying health of the scientific enterprise. Her eventual vindication demonstrates the capacity of science to overcome its own characteristic kinds of myopia, reminding us that its limitations do not reinforce themselves indefinitely. Their own methodology allows, even obliges, scientists to continually reencounter phenomena even their best theories cannot accommodate. Or—to look at it from the other side— however severely communication between science and nature may be impeded by the preconceptions of a particular time, some channels always remain open; and, through them, nature finds ways of reasserting itself.

But the story of McClintock's contributions to biology has another, less accessible, aspect. What is it in an individual scientist's relation to nature that facilitates the kind of seeing that eventually leads to productive discourse? What enabled McClintock to see further and deeper into the mysteries of genetics than her colleagues?

Her answer is simple. Over and over again, she tells us one must have the time to look, the patience to "hear what the material has to say to you," the openness to "let it come to you." Above all, one must have "a feeling for the organism."

One must understand "how it grows, understand its parts, understand when something is going wrong with it. [An organism] isn't just a piece of plastic, it's something that is constantly being affected by the environment, constantly showing attributes or disabilities in its growth. You have to be aware of all of that. . . . You need to know those plants well enough so that if anything changes, . . . you [can] look at the plant and right away you know what this damage you see is from—something that scraped across it or something that bit it or something that the wind did." You need to have a feeling for every individual plant.

"No two plants are exactly alike. They're all different, and as a consequence, you have to know that difference," she explains. "I start with the seedling, and I don't want to leave it. I don't feel I really know the story if I don't watch the plant all the way along. So I know every plant in the field. I know them intimately, and I find it a great pleasure to know them."

This intimate knowledge, made possible by years of close association with the organism she studies, is a prerequisite for her extraordinary perspicacity. "I have learned so much about the corn plant that when I see things, I can interpret [them] right away." Both literally and figuratively, her "feeling for the organism" has extended her vision. At the same time, it has sustained her through a lifetime of lonely endeavor, unrelieved by the solace of human intimacy or even by the embrace of her profession.

Good science cannot proceed without a deep emotional investment on the part of the scientist. It is that emotional investment that provides the motivating force for the endless hours of intense, often grueling, labor. Einstein wrote: " . . . what deep longing to understand even a faint reflexion of the reason revealed in this world had to be alive in Kepler and Newton so that they could in lonely work for many years disentangle the mechanism of celestial mechanics?"[1] But McClintock's feeling for the organism is not simply a longing to behold the "reason revealed in this world." It is a longing to embrace the world in its very being, through reason and beyond.

For McClintock, reason—at least in the conventional sense of the word— is not by itself adequate to describe the vast complexity—even mystery— of living forms. Organisms have a life and order of their own that scientists can only partially fathom. No models we invent can begin to do full justice to the prodigious capacity of organisms to devise means for guaranteeing their own survival. On the contrary, "anything you can think of you will find." In comparison with the ingenuity of nature, our scientific intelligence seems pallid.

For her, the discovery of transposition was above all a key to the complexity of genetic organization—an indicator to the subtlety with which cytoplasm, membranes, and DNA are integrated into a single structure. It is the overall organization, or orchestration, that enables the organism to meet its needs, whatever they might be, in ways that never cease to surprise us. That capacity for surprise gives McClintock immense pleasure. She recalls, for example, the early post-World War II studies of the effect of radiation on *Drosophila*: "It turned out that the flies that had been under constant radiation were more vigorous than those that were standard. Well, it was hilarious; it was absolutely against everything that had been thought about earlier. I thought it was terribly funny; I was utterly delighted. Our experience with DDT has been similar. It was thought that insects could be readily killed off with the spraying of DDT. But the insects began to thumb their noses at anything you tried to do to them."

Our surprise is a measure of our tendency to underestimate the flexibility of living organisms. The adaptability of plants tends to be especially unappreciated. "Animals can walk around, but plants have to stay still to do the same things, with ingenious mechanisms. . . . Plants are extraordinary. For instance, . . . if you pinch a leaf of a plant you set off electric pulses. You can't touch a plant without setting off an electric pulse. . . . There is no question that plants have [all] kinds of sensitivities. They do a lot of responding to their environment. They can do almost anything you can think of. But just because they sit there, anybody walking down the road considers them just a plastic area to look at, [as if] they're not really alive."

An attentive observer knows better. At any time, for any plant, one who has sufficient patience and interest can see the myriad signs of life that a casual eye misses: "In the summertime, when you walk down the road, you'll see that the tulip leaves, if it's a little warm, turn themselves around so their backs are toward the sun. You can just see where the sun hits them and where the sun doesn't hit. . . . [Actually], within the restricted areas in which they live, they move around a great deal." These organisms "are fantastically beyond our wildest expectations."

For all of us, it is need and interest above all that induce the growth of our abilities; a motivated observer develops faculties that a casual spectator may never be aware of. Over the years, a special kind of sympathetic understanding grew in McClintock, heightening her powers of discernment, until finally, the objects of her study have become subjects in their own right; they claim from her a kind of attention that most of us experience only in relation to other persons. "Organism" is for her a code word—not simply a plant or animal ("Every component of the organism is as much of an organism as every other part")—but the name of a living form, of object-as-subject. With an uncharacteristic lapse into hyperbole, she adds: "Every time I walk on grass I feel sorry because I know the grass is screaming at me."

A bit of poetic license, perhaps, but McClintock is not a poet; she is a scientist. What marks her as such is her unwavering confidence in the underlying order of living forms, her use of the apparatus of science to gain access to that order, and her commitment to bringing back her insights into the shared language of science—even if doing so might require that language to change. The irregularities or surprises molecular biologists are now uncovering in the organization and behavior of DNA are not indications of a breakdown of order, but only of the inadequacies of our models in the face of the complexity of nature's actual order. Cells, and organisms, have an organization of their own in which nothing is random.

In short, McClintock shares with all other natural scientists the credo that nature is lawful, and the dedication to the task of articulating those laws. And she shares, with at least some, the additional awareness that reason and experiment, generally claimed to be the principal means of this pursuit, do not suffice. To quote Einstein again, ". . . only intuition, resting on sympathetic understanding, can lead to [these laws]; . . . the daily effort comes from no deliberate intention or program, but straight from the heart."[2]

A deep reverence for nature, a capacity for union with that which is to be known—these reflect a different image of science from that of a purely rational enterprise. Yet the two images have coexisted throughout history. We are familiar with the idea that a form of mysticism—a commitment to the unity of experience, the oneness of nature, the fundamental mystery underlying the laws of nature—plays an essential role in the process of scientific discovery. Einstein called it "cosmic religiosity." In turn, the experience of creative insight reinforces these commitments, fostering a sense of the limitations of the scientific method, and an appreciation of other ways of knowing. In all of this, McClintock is no exception. What is exceptional is her forthrightness of expression—the pride she takes in holding, and voicing, attitudes that run counter to our more customary ideas about science. In her mind, what we call the scientific method cannot by itself give us "real understanding." "It gives us relationships which are useful, valid, and technically marvelous; however, they are not the truth." And it is by no means the only way of acquiring knowledge.

That there are valid ways of knowing other than those conventionally espoused by science is a conviction of long standing for McClintock. It derives from a lifetime of experiences that science tells us little about, experiences that she herself could no more set aside than she could discard the anomalous pattern on a single kernel of corn. Perhaps it is this fidelity to her own experience that allows her to be more open than most other scientists about her unconventional beliefs. Correspondingly, she is open to unorthodox views in others, whether she agrees with them or not. She recalls, for example, a lecture given in the late 1940s at Cold Spring Harbor by Dick Roberts, a physicist from the Carnegie Institution of Washington, on the subject of extrasensory perception. Although she herself was out of town at the time, when she heard about the hostile reaction of her colleagues, she was incensed: "If they were as ignorant of the subject as I was, they had no reason for complaining."

For years, she has maintained an interest in ways of learning other than those used in the West, and she made a particular effort to inform herself about the Tibetan Buddhists: "I was so startled by their method of training and by its results that I figured we were limiting ourselves by using what we call the scientific method."

Two kinds of Tibetan expertise interested her especially. One was the way the "running lamas" ran. These men were described as running for hours on end without sign of fatigue. It seemed to her exactly the same kind of effortless floating she had secretly learned as a child.

She was equally impressed by the ability that some Tibetans had developed to regulate body temperature: "We are scientists, and we know nothing basically about controlling our body temperature. [But] the Tibetans learn to live with nothing but a tiny cotton jacket. They're out there cold winters and hot summers, and when they have been through the learning process, they have to take certain tests. One of the tests is to take a wet blanket, put it over them, and dry that blanket in the coldest weather. And they dry it."

How were they able to do these things? What would one need to do to acquire this sort of "knowledge"? She began to look at related phenomena that were closer to home: "Hypnosis also had potentials that were quite extraordinary." She began to believe that not only one's temperature, but one's circulation, and many other bodily processes generally thought to be autonomous, could be brought under the influence of mind. She was convinced that the potential for mental control revealed in hypnosis experiments, and practiced by the Tibetans, was something that could be learned. "You can do it, it can be taught." And she set out to teach herself. Long before the word "biofeedback" was invented, McClintock experimented with ways to control her own temperature and blood flow, until, in time, she began to feel a sense of what it took.

But these interests were not popular. "I couldn't tell other people at the time because it was against the 'scientific method.' . . . We just hadn't touched on this kind of knowledge in our medical physiology, [and it is] very, very different from the knowledge we call the only way." What we label scientific knowledge is "lots of fun. You get lots of correlations, but you don't get the truth. . . . Things are much more marvelous than the scientific method allows us to conceive."

Our own method could tell us about some things, but not about others—for instance, she reflects, not about "the kinds of things that made it possible for me to be creative in an unknown way. *Why* do you know? Why were you so sure of something when you couldn't tell anyone else? You weren't sure in a boastful way; you were sure in what I call a completely internal way. . . . What you had to do was put it into their frame. Wherever it came in your frame, you had to work to put it into their frame. So you work with so-called scientific methods to put it into their frame *after* you know. Well, [the question is] *how* you know it. I had the idea that the Tibetans understood this *how* you know."

McClintock is not the only scientist who has looked to the East for correctives to the limitations of Western science. Her remarks on her relation to the phenomena she studies are especially reminiscent of the lessons many physicists have drawn from the discoveries of atomic physics. Erwin Schrödinger, for example, wrote: " . . . our science—Greek science—is based on objectification. . . . But I do believe that this is precisely the point where our present way of thinking does need to be amended, perhaps by a bit of blood-transfusion from Eastern thought."[3] Niels Bohr, the "father of quantum mechanics," was even more explicit on the subject. He wrote: "For a parallel to the lesson of atomic theory . . . [we must turn] to those kinds of epistemological problems with which already thinkers like the Buddha and Lao Tzu have been confronted, when trying to harmonize our position as spectators and actors in the great drama of existence."[4] Robert Oppenheimer held similar views: "The general notions about human understanding . . . which are illustrated by discoveries in atomic physics are not in the nature of being wholly unfamiliar, wholly unheard of, or new," he wrote. "Even in our culture they have a history, and in Buddhist and Hindu thought a more considerable and central place."[5] Indeed, as a result of a number of popular accounts published in the last decade, the correspondences between modern physics and Eastern thought have come to seem commonplace.[6] But among biologists, these interests are not common. McClintock is right to see them, and herself, as oddities. And, here, as elsewhere, she takes pride in being different. She is proud to call herself a "mystic."

Above all, she is proud of her ability to draw on these other ways of knowing in her work as a scientist. It is that which, to her, makes the life of science such a deeply satisfying one—even, at times, ecstatic. "What is ecstasy? I don't understand ecstasy, but I enjoy it. When I have it. Rare ecstasy."

Somehow, she doesn't know how, she has always had an "exceedingly strong feeling" for the oneness of things: "Basically, everything is one. There is no way in which you draw a line between things. What we [normally] do is to make these subdivisions, but they're not real. Our educational system is full of subdivisions that are artificial, that shouldn't be there. I think maybe poets—although I don't read poetry—have some understanding of this." The ultimate descriptive task, for both artists and scientists, is to "ensoul" what one sees, to attribute to it the life one shares with it; one learns by identification.[7]

Much has been written on this subject, but certain remarks of Phyllis Greenacre, a psychoanalyst who has devoted a lifetime to studying the dynamics of artistic creativity, come especially close to the crux of the issue that concerns us here. For Greenacre, the necessary condition for the flowering of great talent or genius is the development in the young child of what she calls a "love affair with the world."[8] Although she believes that a special range and intensity of sensory responsiveness may be innate in the potential artist, she also thinks that, under appropriate circumstances, this special sensitivity facilitates an early relationship with nature that resembles and may in fact substitute for the intimacy of a more conventional child's personal relationships. The forms and objects of nature provide what Greenacre calls "collective alternatives," drawing the child into a "collective love affair."

Greenacre's observations are intended to describe the childhood of the young artist, but they might just as readily depict McClintock's youth. By her own account, even as a child, McClintock neither had nor felt the need of emotional intimacy in any of her personal relationships. The world of nature provided for her the "collective alternatives" of Greenacre's artists; it became the principal focus of both her intellectual and her emotional energies. From reading the text of nature, McClintock reaps the kind of understanding and fulfillment that others acquire from personal intimacy. In short, her "feeling for the organism" is the mainspring of her creativity. It both promotes and is promoted by her access to the profound connectivity of all biological forms—of the cell, of the organism, of the ecosystem.

The flip side of the coin is her conviction that, without an awareness of the oneness of things, science can give us at most only nature-in-pieces; more often it gives us only pieces of nature. In McClintock's view, too restricted a reliance on scientific methodology invariably leads us into difficulty. "We've been spoiling the environment just dreadfully and thinking we were fine, because we were using the techniques of science. Then it turns into technology, and it's slapping us back because we didn't think it through. We were making assumptions we had no right to make. From the point of view of how the whole thing actually worked, we knew how part of it worked. . . . We didn't even inquire, didn't even see how the rest was going on. All these other things were happening and we didn't see it."

She cites the tragedy of Love Canal as one example, the acidification of the Adirondacks Lakes as another. "We didn't think [things] through. . . . If you take the train up to New Haven . . . and the wind is from the southeast, you find all of the smog from New York is going right up to New Haven. . . . We're not thinking it through, just spewing it out. . . . Technology is fine, but the scientists and engineers only partially think through their problems. They solve certain aspects, but not the total, and as a consequence it is slapping us back in the face very hard."

Barbara McClintock belongs to a rare genre of scientist; on a short-term view of the mood and tenor of modern biological laboratories, hers is an endangered species. Recently, after a public seminar McClintock gave in the Biology Department at Harvard University, she met informally with a group of graduate and postdoctoral students. They were responsive to her exhortation that they "take the time and look," but they were also troubled. Where does one get the time to look and to think? They argued that the new technology of molecular biology is self-propelling. It doesn't leave time. There's always the next experiment, the next sequencing to do. The pace of current research seems to preclude such a contemplative stance. McClintock was sympathetic, but reminded them, as they talked, of the "hidden complexity" that continues to lurk in the most straightforward-seeming systems. She herself had been fortunate; she had worked with a slow technology, a slow organism. Even in the old days, corn had not been popular because one could never grow more than two crops a year. But after a while, she'd found that as slow as it was, two crops a year was too fast. If she was really to analyze all that there was to see, one crop was all she could handle.

There remain, of course, always a few biologists who are able to sustain the kind of "feeling for the organism" that was so productive—both scientifically and personally—for McClintock, but to some of them the difficulties of doing so seem to grow exponentially. One contemporary, who says of her own involvement in research, "If you want to really understand about a tumor, you've got to *be* a tumor," put it this way: "Everywhere in science the talk is of winners, patents, pressures, money, no money, the rat race, the lot; things that are so completely alien . . . that I no longer know whether I can be classified as a modern scientist or as an example of a beast on the way to extinction."[9]

McClintock takes a longer view. She is confident that nature is on the side of scientists like herself. For evidence, she points to the revolution now occurring in biology. In her view, conventional science fails to illuminate not only "how" you know, but also, and equally, "what" you know. McClintock sees additional confirmation of the need to expand our conception of science in her own—and now others'—discoveries. The "molecular" revolution in biology was a triumph of the kind of science represented by classical physics. Now, the necessary next step seems to be the reincorporation of the naturalist's approach—an approach that does not press nature with leading questions but dwells patiently in the variety and complexity of organisms. The discovery of genetic liability and flexibility forces us to recognize the magnificent integration of cellular processes—kinds of integration that are "simply incredible to our old-style thinking." As she sees it, we are in the midst of a major revolution that "will reorganize the way we look at things, the way we do research." She adds, "And I can't wait. Because I think it's going to be marvelous, simply marvelous. We're going to have a completely new realization of the relationship of things to each other."

Notes

1. Quoted in E. Broda, "Boltzman, Einstein, Natural Law and Evolution," *Comparative Biochemical Physiology* 67B (1980): 376.

2. Quoted in Banesh Hoffmann and Helen Dukes, *Albert Einstein, Creator and Rebel* (New York: New American Library, 1973), p. 222.

3. Schrödinger, *What Is Life?*, op. cit., p. 140.

4. Neils Bohr, *Atomic Physics and Human Knowledge* (New York: John Wiley and Sons, 1958), p. 33.

5. Robert J. Oppenheimer, *Science and the Common Understanding* (New York: Simon and Schuster, 1954), pp. 8–9.

6. See, for example, Frtiz Capra, *The Tao of Physics* (Berkeley, Ca.: Shambhala, 1975), and Gary Zukov, *The Dancing Wu Li Masters* (New York: William Morrow, 1979).

7. The word "ensoul" is taken from Marion Milner, who wrote of her own endeavors as an artist: "I wanted to ensoul nature with what was really there." Marion Milner, *On Not Being Able to Paint* (New York: International Universities Press, 1957), p. 120.

8. Phyllis Greenacre, "The Childhood of the Artist: Libidinal Phase Development and Giftedness" (1957), reprinted in Phyllis Greenacre, *Emotional Growth: Psychoanalytic Studies of the Gifted and a Great Variety of Other Individuals* (New York: International Universities Press, 1971), p. 490.

9. June Goodfield, *An Imagined World: A Story of Scientific Discovery* (New York: Harper & Row, 1981), p. 213.

Feminist writer and lecturer, Gloria Steinem (b. 1934) is recognized as one of the foremost organizers of the modern women's movement. She is the co-founder and a past editor of Ms. *magazine and was inducted in the National Women's Hall of Fame in 1993.*

If Men Could Menstruate

Gloria Steinem

Living in India made me understand that a white minority of the world has spent centuries conning us into thinking a white skin makes people superior, even though the only thing it really does is make them more subject to ultraviolet rays and wrinkles.

Reading Freud made me just as skeptical about penis envy. The power of giving birth makes "womb envy" more logical, and an organ as external and unprotected as the penis makes men very vulnerable indeed.

But listening recently to a woman describe the unexpected arrival of her menstrual period (a red stain had spread on her dress as she argued heatedly on the public stage) still made me cringe with embarrassment. That is, until she explained that, when finally informed in whispers of the obvious event, she had said to the all-male audience, "and you should be *proud* to have a menstruating woman on your stage. It's probably the first real thing that's happened to this group in years!"

Laughter. Relief. She had turned a negative into a positive. Somehow her story merged with India and Freud to make me finally understand the power of positive thinking. Whatever a "superior" group has will be used to justify its superiority, and whatever an "inferior" group has will be used to justify its plight. Black men were given poorly paid jobs because they were said to be "stronger" than white men, while all women were relegated to poorly paid jobs because they were said to be "weaker." As the little boy said when asked if he wanted to be a lawyer like his mother, "Oh no, that's women's work." Logic has nothing to do with oppression.

So what would happen if suddenly, magically, men could menstruate and women could not?

Clearly, menstruation would become an enviable, boast-worthy, masculine event:

Men would brag about how long and how much.

Young boys would talk about it as the envied beginning of manhood. Gifts, religious ceremonies, family dinners, and stag parties would mark the day.

To prevent monthly work loss among the powerful, Congress would fund a National Institute on Dysmenorrhea. Doctors would research little about heart attacks, from which men were hormonally protected, but everything about cramps.

Sanitary supplies would be federally funded and free. Of course, some men would still pay for the prestige of such commercial brands as Paul Newman Tampons, Muhammad Ali's Rope-a-Dope Pads, John Wayne Maxi Pads, and Joe Namath Jock Shields—"For those Light Bachelor Days."

Statistical surveys would show that men did better in sports and won more Olympic medals during their periods.

Generals, right-wing politicians, and religious fundamentalists would cite menstruation ("*men*-struation") as proof that only men could serve God and country in combat ("You have to give blood to take blood"), occupy high political office ("Can women be properly fierce without a monthly cycle governed by the planet Mars?"), be priests, ministers, God Himself ("He gave this blood for our sins"), or rabbis ("Without a monthly purge of impurities, women are unclean").

Male liberals or radicals, however, would insist that women are equal, just different; and that any woman could join their ranks if only she were willing to recognize the primacy of menstrual rights ("Everything else is a single issue") or self-inflict a major wound every month ("You *must* give blood for the revolution").

Street guys would invent slang ("He's a three-pad man") and "give fives" on the corner with some exchange like, "Man, you lookin' *good*!"

"Yeah, man, I'm on the rag!"

TV shows would treat the subject openly. (*Happy Days*: Ritchie and Potsie would try to convince Fonzie that he is still "The Fonz," though he has missed two periods in a row. *Hill Street Blues*: The whole precinct hits the same cycle.) So would newspapers. (SUMMER SHARK SCARE THREATENS MENSTRUATING MEN. JUDGE CITES MONTHLIES IN PARDONING RAPIST.) And so would movies. (Newman and Redford in *Blood Brothers*!)

Men would convince women that sex was *more* pleasurable at "that time of the month." Lesbians would be said to fear blood and therefore life itself, though all they needed was a good menstruating man.

Medical schools would limit women's entry ("they might faint at the sight of blood.")

Of course, intellectuals would offer the most moral and logical arguments. Without that biological gift for measuring the cycles of the moon and planets, how could a woman master any discipline that demanded a sense of time, space, mathematics—or the ability to measure anything at all? In philosophy and religion, how could women compensate for being disconnected from the rhythm of the universe? Or for their lack of symbolic death and resurrection every month?

Menopause would be celebrated as a positive event, the symbol that men had accumulated enough years of cyclical wisdom to need no more.

Liberal males in every field would try to be kind. The fact that "these people" have no gift for measuring life, the liberals would explain, should be punishment enough.

And how would women be trained to react? One can imagine right-wing women agreeing to all these arguments with a staunch and smiling masochism. ("The ERA would force housewives to wound themselves every month": Phyllis Schlafly. "Your husband's blood is as sacred as that of Jesus—and so sexy, too!": Marabel Morgan). Reformers and Queen Bees would adjust their lives to the cycles of the men around them. Feminists would explain endlessly that men, too, needed to be liberated from the false idea of Martian aggressiveness, just as women needed to escape from the bonds of "menses-envy." Radical feminists would add that oppression of the nonmenstrual was the pattern for all other oppressions. ("Vampires were our first freedom fighters!") Cultural feminists would exalt a female bloodless imagery in art and literature. Socialist feminists would insist that, once capitalism and imperialism were overthrown, women would menstruate, too. ("If women aren't yet menstruating in Russia," they would explain, "it's only because true socialism can't exist within a capitalist encirclement.")

In short, we would discover, as we should already guess, that logic is in the eye of the logician. (For instance, here's an idea for theorists and logicians: If women are supposed to be less rational and more emotional at the beginning of our menstrual cycle when the female hormone is at its lowest level, then why isn't it logical to say that, in those few days, women behave the most like the way men behave all month long? I leave further improvisations up to you.)[1]

The truth is that, if men could menstruate, the power justifications would go on and on.

If we let them.

Note

[1] With thanks to Stan Potinger for many of the improvisations already here.

Anne Fadiman (b. 1953) is a recipient of a John D. Knight Fellowship in Journalism and a National Magazine Award for Reporting. Fadiman is an editor of American Scholar *and worked as an editor and writer for* Life *magazine and* Civilization, *the magazine of the Library of Congress. She is the author of* Ex Libris: Confessions of a Common Reader *(1998) and* When the Spirit Catches You and You Fall Down *(1997). Fadiman resides in New York City.*

Do Doctors Eat Brains?

Anne Fadiman

In 1982, Mao Thao, a Hmong woman from Laos who had resettled in St. Paul, Minnesota, visited Ban Vinai, the refugee camp in Thailand where she had lived for a year after her escape from Laos in 1975. She was the first Hmong-American ever to return there, and when an officer of the United Nations High Commissioner for Refugees, which administered the camp, asked her to speak about life in the United States, 15,000 Hmong, more than a third of the population of Ban Vinai, assembled in a soccer field and questioned her for nearly four hours. Some of the questions they asked her were: Is it forbidden to use a *txiv neebs* to heal an illness in the United States? Why do American doctors take so much blood from their patients? After you die, why do American doctors try to open up your head and take out your brains? Do American doctors eat the livers, kidneys, and brains of Hmong patients? When Hmong people die in the United States, is it true that they are cut into pieces and put in tin cans and sold as food?

The general drift of these questions suggests that the accounts of the American health care system that had filtered back to Asia were not exactly enthusiastic. The limited contact the Hmong had already had with Western medicine in the camp hospitals and clinics had done little to instill confidence, especially when compared to the experiences with shamanistic healing to which they were accustomed. A *txiv neeb* might spend as much as eight hours in a sick person's home; doctors forced their patients, no matter how weak they were, to come to the hospital, and then might spend only twenty minutes at their bedsides. *Txiv neebs* were polite and never needed to ask questions; doctors asked many rude and intimate questions about patients' lives, right down to their sexual and excretory habits, *Txiv neebs* could render an immediate diagnosis; doctors often demanded samples of blood (or even urine or feces, which they liked to keep in little bottles), took X rays, and waited for days for the results to come back from the laboratory—and then, after all that, sometimes they were unable to identify the cause of the problem. *Txiv neebs* never undressed their patients; doctors asked patients to take off all their clothes, and sometimes dared to put their fingers inside women's vaginas. *Txiv neebs* knew that to treat the body without treating the soul was an act of patent folly; doctors never even mentioned the soul. *Txiv neebs* could preserve unblemished reputations even if their patients didn't get well, since the blame was laid on the intransigence of the spirits rather than the competence of the negotiators, whose stock might even rise if they had had to do battle with particularly dangerous opponents; when doctors failed to heal, it was their own fault.

To add injury to insult, some of the doctors' procedures actually seemed more likely to threaten their patients' health than to restore it. Most Hmong believe that the body contains a finite amount of blood that it is unable to replenish, so repeated blood sampling, especially from small children, may be fatal. When people are unconscious, their souls are at large, so anesthesia may lead to illness or death. If the body is cut or disfigured, or if it loses any of its parts, it will remain in a condition of perpetual imbalance, and the damaged person not only will become frequently ill but may be physically incomplete during the next incarnation; so surgery is taboo. If people lose their vital organs after death, their souls cannot be reborn into new bodies and may take revenge on living relatives; so autopsies and embalming are also taboo. (Some of the questions on the Ban Vinai soccer field were obviously inspired by reports of the widespread practice of autopsy and embalming in the United States. To make the leap from hearing that doctors removed organs to believing that they ate them was probably no crazier than to assume, as did American doctors, that the Hmong ate human placentas—but it was certainly scarier.)

The only form of medical treatment that was gratefully accepted by at least some of the Hmong in the Thai camps was antibiotic therapy, either oral or by injection. Most Hmong have little fear of needles, perhaps because some of their own healers (not *txiv neebs*, who never touch their patients) attempt to release fevers and toxicity through acupuncture and other forms of dermal treatment, such as massage; pinching; scraping the skin with coins, spoons, silver jewelry, or pieces of bamboo; applying a heated cup to the skin; or burning the skin with a sheaf of grass or a wad of cotton wool. An antibiotic shot that could heal an infection almost overnight was welcomed. A shot to immunize someone against a disease he did not yet have was something else again. In his book *Les Naufragés de la Liberté*, the French physician Jean-Pierre Willem, who worked as a volunteer in the hospital at the Nam Yao camp, related how during a typhoid epidemic, the Hmong refugees refused to be vaccinated until they were told that only those who got shots would receive their usual allotments of rice—whereupon 14,000 people showed up at the hospital, including at least a thousand who came twice in order to get seconds.

When Foua Yang and Nao Kao Lee brought their three sick children to the hospital at Mae Jarim, they were engaging in behavior that many of the other camp inhabitants would have considered positively aberrant. Hospitals were regarded not as places of healing but as charnel houses. They were populated by the spirits of people who had died there, a lonesome and rapacious crew who were eager to swell their own ranks. Catherine Pake, a public health nurse who spent six months working at Phanat Nikhom (a camp where refugees from Laos, Vietnam, and Cambodia came for their final "processing" before they were sent to a country of permanent asylum), concluded from a study of the hospital log that "in comparison to refugees of other ethnic groups, the Hmong have the lowest per capita rate of visits." (Pake also discovered, not coincidentally, that the Hmong had an extremely "high utilization rate" of indigenous healing arts: shamanism, dermal treatments, herbalism. She published an article in the *Journal of Ethnobiology* identifying twenty medicinal plants she had collected under the tutelage of Hmong herbalists, which, in various forms—chopped, crushed, dried, shredded, powdered, decocted, infused with hot water, infused with cold water, mixed with ashes, mixed with sulphur, mixed with egg, mixed with chicken—were indicated for burns, fever, weakness, poor vision, broken bones, stomachaches, painful urination, prolapsed uterus, insufficient breast milk, arthritis, anemia, tuberculosis, rabies, scabies, gonorrhea, dysentery, constipation, impotence, and attacks by a *dab ntxaug*, a spirit who lives in the jungle and causes epidemics when he is disturbed. In this last case, the plant, *Jatropha curcas*, is crushed and its oil left in a cup, to be consumed not by the patient but by the *dab*.)

Wendy Walker-Moffat, an educational consultant who spent three years teaching and working on nutritional and agricultural projects in Phanat Nikhom and Ban Vinai, suggests that one reason the Hmong avoided the camp hospitals is that so many of the medical staff members were excessively zealous volunteers from Christian charitable organizations. "They were there to provide medical aid, but they were also there—though not overtly—to convert people," Walker-Moffat told me. "And part of becoming converted was believing in Western medicine. I'll never forget one conversation I overheard when I was working in the hospital area at Ban Vinai. A group of doctors and nurses were talking to a Hmong man whom they had converted and ordained as a Protestant minister. They had decided that in order to get the Hmong to come into the hospital they were going to allow a traditional healer, a shaman, to practice there. I knew they all thought shamanism was witch-doctoring. So I heard them tell this Hmong minister that if they let a shaman work in the medical center he could only give out herbs, and not perform any actual work with the spirits. At this point they asked the poor Hmong minister, 'Now *you* never go to a shaman, do you?' He was a Christian convert, he knew you cannot tell a lie, so he said, 'Well, yes, I do.' But then their reaction was so shocked that he said, 'No, no, no, I've never been. I've just heard that *other* people go.' What they didn't realize was that—to my knowledge, at least—no Hmong is ever fully converted."

In 1985, the International Rescue Committee assigned Dwight Conquergood, a young ethnographer with a special interest in shamanism and performance art, to design an environmental health program for Ban Vinai. He later wrote:

> I heard horror story after horror story from the refugees about people who went to the hospital for treatment, but before being admitted had their spirit-strings cut from their wrists by a nurse because "the strings were unsanitary and carried germs." Doctors confidently cut off neckrings that held the life-souls of babies intact. Instead of working in cooperation with the shamans, they did everything to disconfirm them and undermine their authority . . . . Is it any wonder that the Hmong community regarded the camp hospital as the last choice of available health care options? In the local hierarchy of values, consulting a shaman or herbalist, or purchasing medicine available in the Thai market just outside the entrance to the camp, was much preferred and more prestigious than going to the camp hospital. The refugees told me that only the very poorest people who had no relatives or resources whatsoever would subject themselves to the camp hospital treatment. To say that the camp hospital was underutilized would be an understatement.

Unlike the other camp volunteers, who commuted from an expatriate enclave an hour away, Conquergood insisted on living in Ban Vinai, sharing the corner of a thatched hut with seven chickens and a pig. His first day in the camp, Conquergood noticed a Hmong woman sitting on a bench, singing folk songs. Her face was decorated with little blue moons and golden suns, which he recognized as stickers the camp clinic placed on medication bottles to inform illiterate patients whether the pills should be taken morning or night. The fact that Conquergood considered this a delightful example of creative costume design rather than an act of medical noncompliance suggests some of the reasons why the program he designed turned out to be the most (indeed, possibly the only) completely successful attempt at health care delivery Ban Vinai had ever seen.

Conquergood's first challenge came after an outbreak of rabies among the camp dogs prompted a mass dog-vaccination campaign by the medical staff, during which the Ban Vinai inhabitants failed to bring in a single dog to be inoculated. Conquergood was asked to come up with a new campaign. He decided on a Rabies Parade, a procession led by three important characters from Hmong folktales—tiger, a chicken, and a *dab*—dressed in homemade costumes. The cast, like its audience, was one hundred percent Hmong. As the parade snaked through the camp, the tiger danced and played the *qeej*, the *dab* sang and banged a drum, and the chicken (chosen for this crucial role because of its traditional powers of augury) explained the etiology of rabies through a bullhorn. The next morning, the vaccination stations were so besieged by dogs—dogs carried in their owners' arms, dogs dragged on rope leashes, dogs rolled in on two-wheeled pushcarts—that the health workers could hardly inoculate them fast enough. Conquergood's next production, a sanitation campaign in which a parade of children led by Mother Clean (a huge, insanely grinning figure on a bamboo frame) and the Garbage Troll (dressed in ragged clothes plastered with trash) sang songs about latrine use and refuse disposal, was equally well received.

During Conquergood's five months in Ban Vinai, he himself was successfully treated with Hmong herbs for diarrhea and a gashed toe. When he contracted dengue fever (for which he also sought conventional medical treatment), a *txiv neeb* informed him that his homesick soul had wandered back to Chicago, and two chickens were sacrificed to expedite its return. Conquergood considered his relationship with the Hmong to be a form of barter, "a productive and mutually invigorating dialog, with neither side dominating or winning out." In his opinion, the physicians and nurses at Ban Vinai failed to win the cooperation of the camp inhabitants because they considered the relationship one-sided, with the Westerners holding all the knowledge. As long as they persisted in this view, Conquergood believed that what the medical establishment was offering would continue to be rejected, since the Hmong would view it not as a gift but as a form of coercion.

William A. Myers (b. 1944) received his Ph.D. in philosophy from the University of New Mexico in 1979. He has worked as a journalist, photographer, salesman, mechanic, hospital orderly, and teacher. Since 1980 he has taught philosophy at the College of St. Catherine. He is also an active book artist and printmaker on the faculty of Minnesota Center for Book Arts.

Individual Action and a Global Ethic

William A. Myers

Consider the idea that whatever we do, whatever action we deliberately take, is an expression of what we want the world to be. To help a stranger with car trouble is to say that we want to live in a world in which people with car trouble get helped, and also it is to create that kind of world. To stand by passively while people use violence in disputes is to say that we want a world in which violence is unchallenged, and it is to create that kind of world. The way we live and interact with people around us makes the world what we want it to be.

The day the Berlin Wall opened, November 10, 1989, I was in Warsaw participating in the founding of the International Society for Universalism, a worldwide group of scholars working on ways to create and foster dialogue across boundaries of culture, ideology, religion, philosophy, and language. As we academics from five continents began discussions about the bases for communication and understanding across borders, the geopolitical world began the upheaval which is redefining the borders themselves. At the first ISU meeting and the ones which followed in Berlin, London, and St. Catherine's, Ontario, the idealism of the participants was complemented by the belief that geopolitical changes were going to make it possible in a practical way to change the way the peoples of the earth relate to each other.

Five years later, the rich conversation among universalists which began at that 1989 meeting continues, through conferences and the ISU journal, Dialogue and Universalism. But we are more sober about the possibilities. The civil wars in Bosnia and Rwanda, the Gulf War, and worries about nuclear proliferation all point to continued willingness to use violent force for political ends and the failure of leaders to construct viable contexts for dialogue. Of course from the standpoint of the so-called realists in politics, dialogue can never replace violence as an instrument of national policy.

From a Universalist point of view, however, building the bridges which make dialogue the normal basis for relationships, rather than violence and the threat of force, is not mere ivory tower idealism: it is a practical mandate upon which depend our prospects for species survival. The conditions of human life have changed fundamentally during this century, with the result that a universalist ethics—a framework for assessing the rights, responsibilities, and consequences of human actions—must become the conceptual basis for large-scale human interactions.

It is commonplace to observe that we live in a different world than our parents and grandparents did. But it is not so often made clear what the momentous changes in human life in the twentieth century mean for humans as ethical agents. I think the human condition itself—the fundamentals of human living—have changed in ways that also change who we are in relation to the rest of creation. Think of just five areas of fundamental change:

First, we have seen since World War I the development of weapons of mass destruction and intellectual justifications for their use on civilian populations. Centuries of development of a theory intended to limit the means used in warfare, called Just War Theory, which had historically influenced politicians in forming international agreements to observe non-combatant immunity, seemed to have no effect on the planners who perfected aerial bombardment during World War II and its logical outgrowth, the intercontinental nuclear missiles. Every human being on earth has become a viable target in the eyes of strategists. The superpower arms race as ended; but nothing fundamental has changed, as long as the weapons and the strategic theories which would justify their use are accepted as givens of international relations.

Second, we have developed means of communication across borders that allow creation of a global culture in which information, and more important, systems of understanding, can be delivered to anyone with access to a television set. Whereas it took three days for news of President Lincoln's assassination to cross the continent in 1865, in 1981 three-fifths of the population of the earth watched a broadcast of the British royal wedding as it happened. Third, since the 1920s and the invention of effective antibiotics, we have made progress in medical technology which gives those with access to it greater life expectancy and higher quality of life than ever before possible. For members of intact developed societies, medicine gives average people an expectation of healthy longevity previous generations would not dream of.

Fourth, our various technologies, from industry, farming, and natural resource extraction to consumer waste habits, military testing, and energy production, have produced enormous and long lasting toxic pollution which will threaten human health and well-being for generations to come.

Fifth, the post World War II era has seen the spread of universal concepts of human rights. The United Nations Univérsal Declaration of Human Rights, produced in 1949 and as of 1976 part of international law, sets out a long list of specific rights that governments are bound to protect. These rights are said to pertain to people as such, not merely to persons as members of specific societies which happen to recognize certain rights. They are thus asserted to be universal possessions of all human beings regardless of whether their governments recognize them as rights or not.

These five areas of change, I contend, add up to changes in the basic circumstances of human life. The implication for our ethical responsibilities is that we must assess the consequences of actions and policies in a much larger context than before, because our ability to affect the lives of others is more vast than before. And because of the communicability of actions, it is not just direct consequences we should be aware of but the effects of modeling certain kinds of action as well that we should assess.

Those with positional power and those responsible for holding them accountable for their actions and policies need new norms of conduct based ·on a long-term, large scale idea of human flourishing. The idea of flourishing is a description of what it means for human beings to live well, to bring about their best potentials in a full life. To think this globally about the prospects for all humanity to achieve the maximum possible level of human flourishing is the work of universalist ethicists.

But ethical understanding develops in local settings, not universally. As Carol Bly has argued, for ethical character to develop, we need lots of discussion of ethical ideas around the dinner table. It is in face to face interaction that we become who we are and undertake the responsibilities that mark our moral characters. Without interconnection in a locality, universalism threatens to become hopelessly abstract and vague. Our actions can affect remote others as never before; but we still learn how to actin our own families, neighborhood, and workplaces.

In American life, many forces push us toward apathy, indifference and passivity. The very idea of the consumer is an idea of human life at a biological minimum. I can consume goods without being a citizen, without interacting much with others,without being a functioning member of a community. But if I am to act as a fully formed ethical person, I must be much more than a mere consumer.

Citizen politics is the idea that individuals control democratic process by engaging in myriad small processes of partnership and egalitarian decision making. It is primarily individuals taking responsibility for what happens in their neighborhoods, homes, and workplaces by insisting that leadership be shared, that hierarchical decision structures be leveled, that policies be developed through consultative processes rather than through executive fiat.

By expressing values of cooperation, egalitarian partnership, and shared power in organizations, we express locally and personally the world we want to live in; in fact, we create that world. We do the same thing negatively to the extent that we live in relationships constituted by dominance and allow those with positional power to act arbitrarily and without accountability. If dialogue is to become the norm in international relations rather than threats of violence, then we have to do the hard and time consuming work in our everyday lives of listening to others and building dialogue, especially with people whose ideas we disagree with.

If democratic process is universally viable, we create the potential for that universal by modeling it in everyday practical relationships, in homes, churches, classrooms, jobs, and local government. In the end, the long term well-being of the "global village" will depend on the quality of ethical interactions among individuals in the local settings we all live in.

Terry Tempest Williams (b. 1959), a Utah native, is author of Refuge, an Unnatural History of Family and Place *(1992) and other works of creative nonfiction. She has worked as a teacher at a Navajo reservation, a naturalist in residence at the Utah Museum of Natural History, and as an environmental activist with the Utah Wilderness Coalition.*

The Clan of One-Breasted Women

Terry Tempest Williams

Epilogue

I belong to a Clan of One-Breasted Women. My mother, my grandmothers, and six aunts have all had mastectomies. Seven are dead. The two who survive have just completed rounds of chemotherapy and radiation.

I've had my own problems: two biopsies for breast cancer and a small tumor between my ribs diagnosed as a "borderline malignancy."

This is my family history.

Most statistics tell us breast cancer is genetic, hereditary, with rising percentages attached to fatty diets, childlessness, or becoming pregnant after thirty. What they don't say is living in Utah may be the greatest hazard of all.

We are a Mormon family with roots in Utah since 1847. The "word of wisdom" in my family aligned us with good foods—no coffee, no tea, tobacco, or alcohol. For the most part, our women were finished having their babies by the time they were thirty. And only one faced breast cancer prior to 1960. Traditionally, as a group of people, Mormons have a low rate of cancer.

Is our family a cultural anomaly? The truth is, we didn't think about it. Those who did, usually the men, simply said, "bad genes." The women's attitude was stoic. Cancer was part of life. On February 16, 1971, the eve of my mother's surgery, I accidently picked up the telephone and overheard her ask my grandmother what she could expect.

"Diane, it is one of the most spiritual experiences you will ever encounter."

I quietly put down the receiver.

Two days later, my father took my brothers and me to the hospital to visit her. She met us in the lobby in a wheelchair. No bandages were visible.

I'll never forget her radiance, the way she held herself in a purple velvet robe, and how she gathered us around her.

"Children, I am fine. I want you to know I felt the arms of God around me."

We believed her. My father cried. Our mother, his wife, was thirty-eight years old.

A little over a year after Mother's death, Dad and I were having dinner together. He had just returned from St. George, where the Tempest Company was completing the gas lines that would service southern Utah. He spoke of his love for the country, the sandstoned landscape, bare-boned and beautiful. He had just finished hiking the Kolob trail in Zion National Park. We got caught up in reminiscing, recalling with fondness our walk up Angel's Landing on his fiftieth birthday and the years our family had vacationed there.

Over dessert, I shared a recurring dream of mine. I told my father that for years, as long as I could remember, I saw this flash of light in the night in the desert—that this image had so permeated my being that I could not venture south without seeing it again, on the horizon, illuminating buttes and mesas.

"You did see it," he said.

"Saw what?"

"The bomb. The cloud. We were driving home from Riverside, California. You were sitting on Diane's lap. She was pregnant. In fact, I remember the day, September 7, 1957. We had just gotten out of the Service. We were driving north, past Las Vegas. It was an hour or so before dawn, when this explosion went off. We not only heard it, but felt it. I thought the oil tanker in front of us had blown up. We pulled over and suddenly, rising from the desert floor, we saw it, clearly, this golden-stemmed cloud, the mushroom. The sky seemed to vibrate with an eerie pink glow. Within a few minutes, a light ash was raining on the car."

I stared at my father.

"I thought you knew that," he said. "It was a common occurrence in the fifties."

It was at this moment that I realized the deceit I had been living under. Children growing up in the American Southwest, drinking contaminated milk from contaminated cows, even from the contaminated breasts of their mothers, my mother—members, years later, of the Clan of One-Breasted Women.

It is a well-known story in the Desert West, "The Day We Bombed Utah," or more accurately, the years we bombed Utah: above ground atomic testing in Nevada took place from January 27, 1951 through July 11, 1962. Not only were the winds blowing north covering "low-use segments of the population" with fallout and leaving sheep dead in their tracks, but the climate was right. The United States of the 1950s was red, white, and blue. The Korean War was raging. McCarthyism was rampant. Ike was it, and the cold war was hot. If you were against nuclear testing, you were for a communist regime.

Much has been written about this "American nuclear tragedy." Public health was secondary to national security. The Atomic Energy Commissioner, Thomas Murray, said, "Gentlemen, we must not let anything interfere with this series of tests, nothing."

Again and again, the American public was told by its government, in spite of burns, blisters, and nausea, "It has been found that the tests may be conducted with adequate assurance of safety under conditions prevailing at the bombing reservations." Assuaging public fears was simply a matter of public relations. "Your best action," an Atomic Energy Commission booklet read, "is not to be worried about fallout." A news release typical of the times stated, "We find no basis for concluding that harm to any individual has resulted from radioactive fallout."

On August 30, 1979, during Jimmy Carter's presidency, a suit was filed, *Irene Allen v. The United States of America*. Mrs. Allen's case was the first on an alphabetical list of twenty-four test cases, representative of nearly twelve hundred plaintiffs seeking compensation from the United States government for cancers caused by nuclear testing in Nevada.

Irene Allen lived in Hurricane, Utah. She was the mother of five children and had been widowed twice. Her first husband, with their two oldest boys, had watched the tests from the roof of the local high school. He died of leukemia in 1956. Her second husband died of pancreatic cancer in 1978.

In a town meeting conducted by Utah Senator Orrin Hatch, shortly before the suit was filed, Mrs. Allen said, "I am not blaming the government, I want you to know that, Senator Hatch. But I thought if my testimony could help in any way so this wouldn't happen again to any of the generations coming up after us . . . I am happy to be here this day to bear testimony of this."

God-fearing people. This is just one story in an anthology of thousands.

On May 10, 1984, Judge Bruce S. Jenkins handed down his opinion. Ten of the plaintiffs were awarded damages. It was the first time a federal court had determined that nuclear tests had been the cause of cancers.

For the remaining fourteen test cases, the proof of causation was not sufficient. In spite of the split decision, it was considered a landmark ruling. It was not to remain so for long.

In April 1987, the Tenth Circuit Court of Appeals overturned Judge Jenkins's ruling on the ground that the United States was protected from suit by the legal doctrine of sovereign immunity, a centuries-old idea from England in the days of absolute monarchs.

In January 1988, the Supreme Court refused to review the Appeals Court decision. To our court system it does not matter whether the United States government was irresponsible, whether it lied to its citizens, or even that citizens died from the fallout of nuclear testing. What matters is that our government is immune: "The King can do no wrong."

In Mormon culture, authority is respected, obedience is revered, and independent thinking is not. I was taught as a young girl not to "make waves" or "rock the boat."

"Just let it go," Mother would say. "You know how you feel, that's what counts."

For many years I have done just that—listened, observed, and quietly formed my own opinions, in a culture that rarely asked questions because it has all the answers. But one by one, I have watched the women in my family die common, heroic deaths. We sat in waiting rooms hoping for good news, but always receiving the bad. I cared for them, bathed their scarred bodies, and kept their secrets. I watched beautiful women become bald as Cytoxan, cisplatin, and Adriamycin were injected into their veins. I held their foreheads as they vomited green-black bile, and I shot them with morphine when the pain became inhuman. In the end, I witnessed their last peaceful breaths, becoming a midwife to the rebirth of their souls.

The price of obedience has become too high.

The fear and inability to question authority that ultimately killed rural communities in Utah during atmospheric testing of atomic weapons is the same fear I saw in my mother's body. Sheep. Dead sheep. The evidence is buried.

I cannot prove that my mother, Diane Dixon Tempest, or my grandmothers, Lettie Romney Dixon and Kathryn Blackett Tempest, along with my aunts developed cancer from nuclear fallout in Utah. But I can't prove they didn't.

My father's memory was correct. The September blast we drove through in 1957 was part of Operation Plumbbob, one of the most intensive series of bomb tests to be initiated. The flash of light in the night in the desert, which I had always thought was a dream, developed into a family nightmare. It took fourteen years, from 1957 to 1971, for cancer to manifest in my mother—the same time, Howard L. Andrews, an authority in radioactive fallout at the National Institutes of Health, says radiation cancer requires to become evident. The more I learn about what it means to be a "downwinder," the more questions I drown in.

What I do know, however, is that as a Mormon woman of the fifth generation of Latter-day Saints, I must question everything, even if it means losing my faith, even if it means becoming a member of a border tribe among my own people. Tolerating blind obedience in the name of patriotism or religion ultimately takes our lives.

When the Atomic Energy Commission described the country north of the Nevada Test Site as "virtually uninhabited desert terrain," my family and the birds at Great Salt Lake were some of the "virtual uninhabitants."

One night, I dreamed women from all over the world circled a blazing fire in the desert. They spoke of change, how they hold the moon in their bellies and wax and wane with its phases. They mocked the presumption of even-tempered beings and made promises that they would never fear the witch inside themselves. The women danced wildly as sparks broke away from the flames and entered the night sky as stars.

And they sang a song given to them by Shoshone grandmothers:

Ah ne nah, nah	Consider the rabbits
nin nah nah—	How gently they walk on the earth—
ah ne nah, nah	Consider the rabbits
nin nah nah—	How gently they walk on the earth—
Nyaga mutzi	We remember them
oh ne nay—	We can walk gently also—
Nyaga mutzi	We remember them
oh ne nay—	We can walk gently also—

The women danced and drummed and sang for weeks, preparing themselves for what was to come. They would reclaim the desert for the sake of their children, for the sake of the land.

A few miles downwind from the fire circle, bombs were being tested. Rabbits felt the tremors. Their soft leather pads on paws and feet recognized the shaking sands, while the roots of mesquite and sage were smoldering. Rocks were hot from the inside out and dust devils hummed unnaturally. And each time there was another nuclear test, ravens watched the desert heave. Stretch marks appeared. The land was losing its muscle.

The women couldn't bear it any longer. They were mothers. They had suffered labor pains but always under the promise of birth. The red hot pains beneath the desert promised death only, as each bomb became a stillborn. A contract had been made and broken between human beings and the land. A new contract was being drawn by the women, who understood the fate of the earth as their own.

Under the cover of darkness, ten women slipped under a barbed-wire fence and entered the contaminated country. They were trespassing. They walked toward the town of Mercury, in moonlight, taking their cues from coyote, kit fox, antelope, squirrel, and quail. They moved quietly and deliberately through the maze of Joshua trees. When a hint of daylight appeared they rested, drinking tea and sharing their rations of food. The women closed their eyes. The time had come to protest with the heart, that to deny one's genealogy with the earth was to commit treason against one's soul.

At dawn, the women draped themselves in mylar, wrapping long streamers of silver plastic around their arms to blow in the breeze. They wore clear masks, that became the faces of humanity. And when they arrived at the edge of Mercury, they carried all the butterflies of a summer day in their wombs. They paused to allow their courage to settle.

The town that forbids pregnant women and children to enter because of radiation risks was asleep. The women moved through the streets as winged messengers, twirling around each other in slow motion, peeking inside homes and watching the easy sleep of men and women. They were astonished by such stillness and periodically would utter a shrill note or low cry just to verify life.

The residents finally awoke to these strange apparitions. Some simply stared. Others called authorities, and in time, the women were apprehended by wary soldiers dressed in desert fatigues. They were taken to a white, square building on the other edge of Mercury. When asked who they were and why they were there, the women replied, "We are mothers and we have come to reclaim the desert for our children."

The soldiers arrested them. As the ten women were blindfolded and handcuffed, they began singing:

> *You can't forbid us everything*
> *You can't forbid us to think—*
> *You can't forbid our tears to flow*
> *And you can't stop the songs that we sing.*

The women continued to sing louder and louder, until they heard the voices of their sisters moving across the mesa:

Ah ne nah, nah̲
nin nah nah—
Ah ne nah, nah
nin nah nah—
Nyaga mutzi
oh ne nay—
Nyaga mutzi
oh ne nay—

"Call for reinforcements," one soldier said.

"We have," interrupted one woman, "we have—and you have no idea of our numbers."

I crossed the line at the Nevada Test Site and was arrested with nine other Utahns for trespassing on military lands. They are still conducting nuclear tests in the desert. Ours was an act of civil disobedience. But as I walked toward the town of Mercury, it was more than a gesture of peace. It was a gesture on behalf of the Clan of One-Breasted Women.

As one officer cinched the handcuffs around my wrists, another frisked my body. She found a pen and a pad of paper tucked inside my left boot.

"And these?" she asked sternly.

"Weapons," I replied.

Our eyes met. I smiled. She pulled the leg of my trousers back over my boot.

"Step forward, please," she said as she took my arm.

We were booked under an afternoon sun and bused to Tonopah, Nevada. It was a two-hour ride. This was familiar country. The Joshua trees standing their ground had been named by my ancestors, who believed they looked like prophets pointing West to the Promised Land. These were the same trees that bloomed each spring, flowers appearing like white flames in the Mojave. And I recalled a full moon in May, when Mother and I had walked among them, flushing out mourning doves and owls.

The bus stopped short of town. We were released.

The officials thought it was a cruel joke to leave us stranded in the desert with no way to get home. What they didn't realize was that we were at home, soul-centered and strong, women who recognized the sweet smell of sage as fuel for our spirits.

Computer visionary, journalist and venture capitalist, Esther Dyson (b. 1951) is the founder, editor, and publisher of Release 1.0, *a daily electronic newsletter focused on the computer industry. She has been a columnist for* Forbes, *a commentator for National Public Radio, and serves on the boards and committees of several corporate and non-profit organizations. Her current book,* Release 2.0: A Design for Living in the Digital Age *(1997) discusses her latest predictions about the internet and its emerging culture.*

Communities

Esther Dyson

By 1997, "community" had become one of the trendiest words around, both on and off the Internet. In the context of this book and of the online world in general, a community is the unit in which people live, work, and play. Most individuals live in several communities online, just as they do in the physical world—family, church or temple, soccer club, professional society, workplace. Some communities are formal, with rules and duties, entrance requirements, and perhaps membership fees; others are less formal groupings with loose boundaries and revolving membership. As the world seems to get more complex and more overwhelming, and public life ever more scary, people look to communities for fellowship and security.

Used right, the Internet can be a powerful enabling technology fostering the development of communities because it supports the very thing that creates a community—human interaction. One benefit of the Internet is that it allows the formation of communities independent of geography. People need only share interests or goals and find one another. Conversely, people are not stuck in the communities they are born in—not entirely, at least. The programmer in India can argue with his peers in Silicon Valley or Budapest about the finer points of the Java programming language. Also, the Internet overcomes some of the barriers of time: both between time zones, and in the sense that it's quicker to send an e-mail than to drive to a community center—let alone cross the world. It's even quicker than finding an envelope and a stamp, and you can do it at your convenience, while the other person does it at *his* convenience.

There will be—there already is—a profusion of online communities. They are easy to find, and relatively easy to form. But what holds them together? Can a single person in fact be a member of twenty different communities, with each getting his attention fifteen minutes a day (for a total of five hours online)? Online communities may engage in conversations and other interaction through the medium of a particular Website or

Community vs. Culture

Communities often have a culture, but there is an important distinction between culture and community. Culture is a set of rules, perceptions, language, history, and the like. It is embodied in books and songs, people's minds, and Websites. Culture can be learned, even though there are some communities that believe you need to be born into them to be a member (as in Germany and many Asian countries, as well as certain Jewish groups).

By contrast, a community is a set of relationships. You could (in principle) take a culture and revive it: You could teach people the history, the manners, and the rules, and they could live by them. But you could never revive a particular community, because a community depends on the people in it. Just like education, a community is not a passive thing. Its members need to invest in it for it to exist. An individual can be familiar with any number of cultures simply by studying them. But to be a member of a community he has to be present in it, contribute to it, and be known to other members. Thus, a television channel or an Internet "channel" can create or reflect a culture, but in order for it to become a community its members have to communicate with one another—ideally in the context of some goal. That goal may be only to homage a star, but it could also be political action, a business plan, or a school.

A community is a shared asset, created by the investment of its members. The more you put in, the more you take out.

"The love you take is equal to the love you make."

—The Beatles

through mailing lists or newsgroups—people linked together by text messages and increasingly through multimedia virtual places that they enter from time to time. A newsgroup is a virtual bulletin board, which members post to or read on their own schedule. A mailing list (or listserv) is like an active newsgroup; it sends regular messages out to its members, but it also generally maintains archives for people to search.

Online virtual places can be anything from a virtual room where people describe in text what is happening—"Alice looks at her shoes and bites her lip"[1]—to full-scale multimedia locations where people are represented by "avatars"—cartoon figures, images of themselves, or any other symbol they choose. Some of these places support voice, or even video. Then there are "buddy lists," which enable you to see which of your friends or colleagues are currently online, and virtually tap them on the shoulder as if to say, "May I talk to you now?" (People can put up "do not disturb" signs, or say something like "Working on Berkman project; don't bother me otherwise.")

Online as offline, what you bring to a community determines what you get out of it. This ranges from a community of two, of which the canonical form is marriage, to a community of two thousand. People's primary communities will reflect their daily lives as more and more people go online: their extended families; their colleagues at work, including customers and suppliers and possibly competitors; their school friends; and so on. As people move around physically, from school to camp and college and from job to job, from chance meetings on holidays to various kinds of interest groups, they will join new communities and probably drop others.

The Great Net Hope

For me, the great hope of the Net is that it will lead people first to get involved on the Net and then to change their overall experience of life. Power in one sphere changes one's perception of one's capabilities in general. Right now, politically, the United States is in a sorry state. Only 49 percent of the potential voters bothered to vote in the most recent presidential elections. (Compare that to Russia, where more people voted, but there's even less feeling of involvement.) People are rational, and they know that one person's vote won't change the outcome. Others feel a certain social responsibility, and so they vote anyway. But voting does not make a real democracy, any more than taxes are an expression of philanthropy.

From Cyberspace to Real Space

I feel this intensely because it so happens that I have never voted, although I have certainly paid a lot of taxes.[2] For many years, I just ignored the government and it ignored me. Then I started spending a lot of time in Washington because of the Electronic Frontier Foundation and the National Information Infrastructure Advisory Council, and my attitudes changed. To be sure, even with the advent of the Net not everyone gets invited to Washington, but suddenly everyone *is* invited to contribute if he or she cares enough to go to any relevant Website or discussion group. Although I haven't yet voted formally, I feel that I have a meaningful voice and a meaningful stake in what our government does. I'm a far more active citizen than before I raised my voice, and I care about the consequences. This doesn't mean that the folks in Washington are rushing to follow my advice. But if my ideas are valid, other people will amplify them and they will be heard.

The Net will involve a growing portion of the population in this kind of governance, and their feeling of empowerment will spread to other parts of their lives. The secret is that the Internet doesn't actually *do* much; it's a powerful tool for people to use. It's not something worth having, but it's a powerful lever for people to use to accomplish their own goals in collaboration with other people. It's more than a source of information; it's a way for people to organize themselves.

Net Participation

How many times have you wanted to complain about something, but you gave up because it was just too difficult? I recently flew Delta to Moscow and back from Warsaw, and neither time did they have power outlets for my computer, as they had more or less promised in their ads. I complained to the flight attendant. The next morning I went to register my complaint on the Delta Website. An hour later, I got an automatic notification that my message had been received. And less than three weeks later, I actually got a nice e-mail from one D. E. Coberly that didn't look like a form letter; it specifically talked about the schedule for upgrading the aircraft with power outlets.

Sometimes, I'm in a better mood. I might even like to compliment a company on something in hopes that they'll keep doing it—Marriot's excellent in-room facilities for computers, for example—although in this case I'd rather do it in public so that other hotels will follow suit.

Sometimes I want to write a letter to the editor, but it's just too inconvenient; by the time I get to a computer, type a letter, print it out, and fax it (let alone mail it!), I've lost the urge.

People are not naturally lazy, but they avoid useless effort and are overwhelmed by competing demands. Though we're not quite there yet, in the future the Net *will* make it easier for people to participate in a variety of communities—and more effective. Smart businesses will encourage consumer feedback; smart politicians will solicit and even listen to comments from constituents; smart newspapers will welcome letters by e-mail and foster online discussions.

And individuals will rise to the occasion. The Net will foster activity instead of passivity.

Basic Principles

Here are a few basic principles for communities, based on my own experience both on and offline:

- Each participant should be clear about what he is giving and what he hopes to get. Overall, those desires should mesh, although they may well be different for each individual.

- There should be a way of determining who is in the community and who is outside it. Otherwise the community is meaningless.
- Community members should feel that they have invested in the community, and that therefore it is tough for them to leave. The ultimate punishment in a strong community is banishment, expulsion, excommunication, exile. . . . All those words signify the terror of being cast out of a community.
- The community's rules should be clear, and there should be recourse if they are broken.

Some of the saddest communities arise when these principles do not apply: for example, the marriage in which one person loves a partner who is deceiving him, as opposed to one where one partner gives sex in exchange for a life of ease. Some people might see the latter as a moral failure, but it is a valid community. The dance club where people are screened in or out by a bouncer may or may not be a valid community, depending on how well the bouncer knows the crowd and whether they know one another. On the other hand, a good bartender can create a wonderful community, as illustrated in countless plays and television shows, or by Rick in the movie *Casablanca*.

Vested Interest

What kinds of investment can one make in a community? There are two things people can give easily, especially over the Net: time and money. Money is often the easiest. Paying $19.95 a month for America Online doesn't really make you part of the community, nor does it make it hard for you to leave (it may actually encourage you to do so to save money), but it does signify a certain commitment. Emotionally, you will want to justify that spending because you value what you have paid for.

In the real world, community members often contribute (or own) real estate, which is why in the past voting rights were often restricted to landowners; they were considered the only ones with a true stake in the community (and they paid taxes for that privilege). Now, in many countries, language as well as birth is a gauge of membership. In the Baltics, for example, the old ethnic identities are reasserting themselves through language; Russian residents, who went to Soviet/Russian schools and never learned the local language are now being disenfranchised in their local geographic communities. In the United States, use of Spanish is a political issue in border states such as California, Texas, and Florida.

Sharing food is another mark of community, reflected in everything from statements about breaking bread together to customs such as potluck dinners. In many communities, people share their labor, building houses for one family after another. On the Net, they share their time, ideas, and experiences—food for thought or discussion, so to speak.

Community Rules

A community sets its rules for itself. Often, they're invisible until they're broken or questioned; then they're discussed and somehow issues get decided. The decision could be made by the community moderator; it could be a vote. As it happens, while I was writing this, the question of use of people's comments outside a community came up. It happened on the Online Europe list, started as an offshoot of last year's High-Tech Forum in Europe and run by Steve Carlson, a Net entrepreneur in Hungary. About half its members are people who were with us at the forum in Lisbon; the other half have joined through friends and referrals. One point to note: This community does not run itself; Steve is always haranguing us to contribute, to be interesting. Sometimes he poses questions to get the conversation flowing. Recently, Bill O'Neill inadvertently started a discussion that needed no coaxing. Bill, editor of the (U.K.) *Guardian* newspaper's technology coverage, asked if he could quote us freely . . . But here! Read for yourself:

Date: 09:14 PM 5/26/97 + 0200

http://pk4.com

To: online-europe@isys.hu

From: bill.oneill@guardian.co.uk (United Kingdom)

Subject: Re: [online-e] question for posting to list

Comments contributed to online-europe are likely to be of interest (and of relevance) to a wider (and less specialised) audience. How would contributors feel if journalists (like me) published the material elsewhere (in my case, in the paper and on an associated Web site)? I'd always assumed that comments to online-europe were not only non-attributable but also off-the-record; in effect, that they provided informed background material, and that's all. However, I now realize that the material is posted on a Web site, which puts that material in the public domain (so that comments are as attributable and on-the-record as the medium allows). In practical terms, it would be foolhardy of me to promise to let anyone and everyone know if their comments are likely to be published elsewhere. But is there any objection to the idea of comments to online-europe being published in another medium, or in a different section of the same medium?

>================

> Bill O'Neill

> Editor, Online

> The Guardian

From: edyson@edventure.com (Esther Dyson)

Subject: Re: [online-e] question for posting to list

Hey Bill!

Why not play a version of Tom Sawyer, and offer to republish our witty, insightful commentary for a small fee? Just kidding! (Seriously, I had no expectations of privacy, and of course I'd be flattered.)

Esther

After my flip answer, a number of more serious people weighed in. . . .

From: Steven Carlson<steve@pk4.com>

>===============

I feel a discussion coming on . . .

Bill O'Neill has asked whether your comments to Online Europe are publicly quotable. As a journalist, he (and perhaps others) might find it useful to gather material here.

Esther has stated she finds this okay. Alex begs to differ. He thinks the journalists should ask for permission before quoting.

This is a question of list policy, and I'd like to hear your opinions. As the list moderator, I will make the final decision (somebody has to, after all) but I want to base that decision on the general consensus of the list. Here are my thoughts . . .

Whether you are aware of it, or not, this list is automatically archived at <http://www.isys.hu/online-europe/>. Thus, in a very real way what you say on Online Europe is already on record publicly.

Many of us wouldn't mind a bit of publicity, either. Knowing that you might be published in the Guardian (Bill's paper) might raise the value of participating in the list. At least for some.

And finally, Bill's job will be much easier if he can simply grab a quote and tell you later. Journalists usually work with ridiculously tight deadlines. Having said that, online works a bit differently than print. It's more informal. Many of us dash off a quick opinion, perhaps regretting it later, but figure what the hell, it all disappears into the ether anyway.

The people on the WELL long ago developed a policy Alex refers to, known as "You Own Your Own Words." That means, among other things, that others have to ask permission before quoting you in print. It allows us to express ourselves without worrying that those words might come back to haunt us. My suggestion . . .

Perhaps Bill (and others) could ask the lists questions, stating that he intends to use the answers in print. That makes it clear that your opinion will be "on the record." If you wanted to answer informally, you would write "off the record" to let him know.

Finally, as a courtesy, I'd like to see Online Europe mentioned in the quote. After all, this list is a form of publication, and is the source of the quote. And now I'd like to hear your opinions . . .

From here on, it's just excerpts, to save you the e-mail "overhead."

From: "Scott McQuade" <smcquade@hotmail.com>(United States)

>Bill O'Neill has asked whether your comments to Online Europe are >publicly quotable.

Of course they are.

1. They are already 'published', i.e., transmitted between two or more people.

2. They are archived in a public place. Bill can make 'fair use' of any material on the Web or any other forum—listserv, Usenet or whatever. Fair use only requires him to avoid repeating the entire contents and to cite the source, i.e., "Steven Carlson said in the Online Europe forum that . . ."

It's nice of him to warn us that he's likely to quote from postings. He's certainly not obliged. However, the operators of the list might best protect themselves by warning participants (e.g., upon entry) that the list is archived on the Web—it seems at least one of us was unaware.

Bill might also make the courtesy of providing a hyperlink to the original. He's already indicated he would advise the list/contributor once a quote has been lifted—again, something he is not obliged to do.

From: Dale Amon as Operator<root@starbase1.gpl.net>(Ireland)

If you don't want to be quoted, you don't go out to the local with a journalist. . . . One can make different policies on closed groups like this, but again, if you invite a journalist to your pub, you had better be ready to hear the echo of your words.

From: Boris Basmadjiev<boris@bulnet.bg>(Bulgaria)

You know, I strongly feel that what we say and write here is private—in the sense that many people can have a conversation which is private. Many of our remarks can mean quite a lot of different things to laymen, or if quoted out of place and character, etc. So I would suggest that anybody wanting a quote just ask for one—as some have done—and then quote the list, the person who said so, etc.

I would suggest that since this list is for professionals, it deserves the same attitude as (for instance) the conversation of a couple of doctors behind the closed doors of their office, right? Need I say more—we had a writer asking what INET was, and I wouldn't want to have him quote ANYTHING I ever say without prior permission.

Anybody can quote anybody else—as long as they ask for direct permission, I think.

And it goes on and on; online discussions, like other conversations, can get pretty involved. . . . You can see the whole thing at the URL Steve Carlson mentioned: <http://www.isys.hu/online-europe/>. And finally, one more message, from me:

And of course now I have to send another message to all of you, with the quote above, asking each one individually to give permission.

Because my resolution of the discussion would be the following:

Yes, our comments here are public-domain, in that no one could sue for having them used. But if Bill O'Neill, or I, or anyone, wants to remain a member of the community, he has to show both politeness and discretion, and judgment. That is, he should ask to use our quotes and he should use them in context. Should he correct the misspellings of his own name? Now there's a question!

Okay guys! May I quote you?

Esther

The Role of Government vs. Self-help

Government can play a divisive role vis a vis communities. Often, the more government provides, the less community members themselves contribute.[3] For example, parents tend to identify less with a government-provided school than with a private school they raise money for and oversee themselves. Yet in many public schools parents can "invest," too, by taking an active role in school administration, coaching soccer teams, running school events, and participating in parent-teacher meetings. Often, families join neighborhood communities through their children; single people tend to identify with their jobs or their after-work activities. All these facets of human nature translate easily to the online world. It's harder to build houses, but people can get together to build virtual environments, discussion groups, even markets.

It is just as deadly for the government to take over communities as for commercial interests to do so. And in cyberspace the results are the same: The members fight and then flee. There's a community spirit that has more to do with influence than with voting, more to do with being heard than with ownership.

Commerce and Community

As a concept, community is contrasted mostly with commerce. But one of my favorite communities is Jerry Kaplan's Onsale, an online auction house that specializes in computer equipment but also handles jewelry, cameras, and other high-ticket goods. (Their motto: "Put your money where your mouse is.") The traditional notion of online shopping is sterile and lonely—the user and an array of goods and prices, perhaps with a salesperson on call at the click of a mouse. But think of where people really like to go shopping: they like Loehmann's where they can get an opinion on an outrageous dress from the lady one mirror over in the communal dressing room; they like Borders or Barnes & Noble, where they can sip cappuccino with a fellow literature lover; or they like auctions, where they can bid against other people, not against a computer.

. . . [T]he people at Onsale have personalities, even though they don't have those cute avatars (cartoon representations) that some online services offer. To the members of the Onsale community, SY of Cambridge, AW of Honolulu, and DT of Lafayette are real people: stingy or spendthrift, wise or foolish, earnest or witty. They look to one another to see what's a good deal and what is best left to a die-hard fan of elephant memorabilia.

Many markets are communities, not just mechanisms for setting prices. On Wall Street, traders like to drink together after work. These people have invested in their community. They know one another and each other's reputations. They have watched each person's behavior, perhaps swallowed a bad deal in hopes of getting a better one later. They share history, dialogue, and perhaps common enemies—the guy who never gave anyone an edge on any deal.

These communities are built on participation; their members act and interact.

For-profit Communities

So, communities can be commercial, or they can be not-for-profit. The notion of commercial communities often offends people, although most people spend time in commercial environments every day. There are commercial communities at work; there are athletic clubs and hairdressers, bars and bookstores. Someone has to pay the rent—although the rent is usually a lot lower in cyberspace than in the physical world.

Often it works the other way: The "owner"—a company or an individual leader—thinks it owns the community. But then that owner finds out that even though it may own the facilities, collect the membership fees and provide the towels, golf clubs, alcohol or online entertainment, hairdressing, or editorial services, the community owns whatever it is that keeps people from leaving. The "owner" may make and enforce the rules, but if he tries to change them without general consent, the community may well take over. Worse, it may just up and leave. Something like that is now facing San Francisco's WELL, where a tight-knit membership is rejecting new, financially oriented management.

There's no necessary conflict in an owner's making a profit. Conflict occurs when the members aren't happy. Running online communities will become a big market in the long run. Many will be local, closer to an extension of the local shopper paper than to an extension of, say, *Time* magazine. Some will be sponsored by advertisers or supported by transaction fees. Others will charge membership fees.[4]

Like terrestrial communities, good online communities require care and tending. Members need someone to resolve disputes, set the tone, find the sponsors. Someone needs to maintain the database or whatever software manages the conversations, deal with the vendors who are supporting the community or communicating with it, and define the rules or modify them in accordance with community interests.

Online communities will vary broadly, and some community operators will do a good job while others won't. The criterion of a "good job" is set by the members—both the critical mass who stay, and those who leave. In the end, if the community does not operate in the interests of its members, whoever they are, it will not survive. But the damage is not as great as in physical communities, where buildings deteriorate, criminals take over, and the most defenseless people have nowhere to go.

Not-for-profit Communities

One real benefit of the digital medium is its low cost, at least by developed-world standards. Just as the Net will foster a profusion of entrepreneurs who can now set up in business for themselves with little capital, so will it encourage philanthropic entrepreneurs. The Net lowers barriers to entry in all kinds of activities. Already there are a number of online museums, many online interest groups, and Websites and mailing lists supporting interests ranging from Native American culture to the worldwide fight against child labor. Such groups will proliferate.

It used to take market forces or huge amounts of charity to foster long-distance communications and the communities they support; now it's cheap. One of the organizations I'm involved in, the Eurasia Foundation, makes a tight budget go a long way in helping nonprofit organizations in the former Soviet Union keep their community together. They can bolster their resolve in difficult circumstances and band together to lobby for new laws or spread information about existing laws that are being ignored by local authorities. The Net provides a continuing lifeline as graduates of foundation-sponsored economics courses, journalism training, and other programs try to apply their new skills at home in local communities that often find their ideas strange and their enthusiasm suspect.

Community Questions

Many facets of online communities aren't yet clear. What is the right size for a community? The answer certainly will vary according to a number of factors, but over time we should have a better understanding, much as we do of cities and villages today. How do communities split up into smaller communities when they get too large, or when a group simply decides to go off on its own for other reasons? One intriguing point, from anthropologist George Gumerman at the Santa Fe Institute in New Mexico, is that homogeneous communities can be relatively indifferent to size, whereas communities with complex social roles need to have the right number of people to fill those roles: one medicine man, one trainer of youth, one village chief, one spiritual leader, and so forth. If the community grows, too many people may be vying for one role; if it shrinks, certain roles may go unfilled. Such communities tend to have strong rules about family size, and about members joining or leaving the community. It will be interesting to see how that translates into online communities: one social director, one head of member programs, one advertising manager. . . .

What Doesn't Work

Clearly, some things do not foster community. You do not need a real identity, but you need *some* identity. You need to have a voice, a reputation, a presence to be part of a community, because it is (at least) a two-way proposition. Thus, "lurkers," people who only read or listen, are not really part of the community. They may fancy themselves to be, but no one would miss them if they left. They are fans, not friends. Lurkers may latch on to a culture, but they do not contribute to it. (That's why fandom is so eerie: There's usually no real communication between the fans and the stars, just lurkers and fantasies on one side and a PR machine on the other.)

Thus, a community may contain pseudonymous members who are valued on the basis of what they contribute to a particular community. If someone's contribution is based on falsehood, then that individual may have a problem. But pseudonymity is more likely to be a mask that allows the person to reveal a true identity than to hide one, or to allow a true expression of one facet of that individual's character.

Thus, a self-help group of anonymous people is hard to define as a community unless the members have at least persistent (though pseudonymous) identities. A monologue explaining who you are does not bring you into a community, however good it feels and however cathartic or liberating it may be.

There are good experiences without community . . . and there are bad communities. Imagine, for example, a community built around shared hatred of Jews or Serbians or the U.S. government, working on ways to "cleanse" the neighborhood or destroy supposed enemies. It may be a good example of a community, with shared contributions and common interests—but a horrible example of humanity.

That illustrates the biggest danger of the ease of forming and enclosing communities—their ability to insulate themselves from the rest of society. People in most physical communities encounter reality from time to time, be it on the streets of a neighborhood, a network television broadcast, or the front page of a newspaper. Online communities can exist sealed away from reality. They can trade lies or illusions among themselves without fear of contradiction. (As I said, the Net is a great medium for conspiracy, while television is best for propaganda.)

Tricky Questions: Freedom of Speech

Many social norms differ from community to community. They include censorship/freedom of speech, religion, the inclusion of children, and the like. On many of these issues, communities will simply agree to disagree, and observe and enforce the rules they think appropriate internally.

Freedom of speech is one of those near-absolute freedoms that Americans cherish and many other countries think we honor too much. In other societies, where convention governs more than law anyway, the sorts of things we may legally say in the United States are considered appalling and uncultured, to say nothing of offensive or dangerous. Americans (including me) answer back that this is the price we pay for freedom of speech—and our related freedoms to think for ourselves, to criticize our government, to believe as we want.

Communities will set their own standards for what is appropriate. People who select or receive content from the Net can use filtering tools to determine what they see as individuals, but here I'm talking about content within a community—what people say to one another, what they post in public "online spaces," and so forth. What will your company allow you to say about the chairman on the corporate intranet, or even outside on the Internet at large? How rude can you be when you disagree with someone? How much informality or bad spelling is tolerated at work? What about in a community of poets? How commercial can you be in a sports discussion group? Is Juan allowed to promote his sporting goods store when Alice asks a question about fishing tackle? How loudly can either of them criticize the person who sold her the fishing rod she uses now?

The answers to these questions are norms, not laws. Usually a community can handle them for itself. People chide one another, others complain; leaders calm things down. Over time, people in a group learn how to live together—or they go off in search of more compatible (for them) communities.

Many terrestrial governments that feel strongly about—against—freedom of speech will probably try to prohibit their citizens from visiting (let alone speaking in) Net communities outside their own countries. In the long run, that makes no sense. Apart from protecting children, the best response to "offensive" speech, however defined, is not to bury it, but to answer it. (The best response to obscenity is to ignore it. And the best response to child pornography, which involves actual children, is to track down and prosecute the people involved.)

More troubling than "indecency" is what to do with genuinely dangerous information such as bomb-making instructions, maps of sensitive security installations, and the like. There is no perfect answer. The kind of bomb-making information available in chemistry textbooks is best left free precisely so that it doesn't acquire the lure of the forbidden. And I do know that most laws against content can't ultimately be effective; they will simply drive information underground, where only the worst people can get at it. Nonetheless, some stuff shouldn't be published by the people who have it. Such information is often classified and probably could be kept off the Net by law and secrecy agreements at the source, and by the local decisions of communities that don't want the responsibility on their own heads.[5] Freedom of speech does not mean "obligation to publish."

Government censorship is unlikely to be effective in the long run, even though governments will keep trying. France outlawed the printing of polling information in the prelude to its recent national elections; those who cared simply got the information from the Net, published by French-language news sources in nearby Switzerland. Germany has embroiled CompuServe in a lawsuit over porn and Nazi material, with no resolution in sight.

Nonetheless, we live in a world where governments—even democratic governments—still do things Americans and others find unconscionable. As long as governments control people physically, they can instill fear and keep all but the most determined dissidents under intellectual control, too—not just by cutting wires or employing technical filtering tools and tapping lines (with encryption outlawed), but by getting neighbor to spy on neighbor. They will be able to control the overall level of discourse in their countries if they are willing to lose many of the Net's benefits. But they will fail to keep their most dedicated dissident citizens from connecting with the rest of the world.

Changing Culture

Clearly, Net culture is changing. It is no longer dominated by upper-middle-class males who speak (only) English. The commercial community has found the Net, and it is increasingly a business medium. But grandparents and social workers have found it, too. Nonprofit organizations are big users, especially in far-flung locations where other means of communication are prohibitively expensive. In the United States and in wired regions such as Scandinavia, the Net is becoming a consumer medium. In most other countries, it's still too expensive and exotic for all but the most sophisticated home users . . . for now.

Eventually, there will be a global society of the connected, laid over more traditional local communities that are usually less well off—in terms of material things, education, connectivity, and even the sophistication to judge the merits of what's online. This global culture (it would be a stretch to call it a community) will probably offend the sensibilities of many "antiglobal" people, but it will grow as a proportion of the world's population.

Some parts of local culture can easily transfer to the Net; others are fundamentally hostile to it. I'm not comfortable saying that everyone in the world should be on the Net. But in the end, everyone will be, except for a few holdouts. The challenge is to make sure that those holdouts are there by choice, not for lack of it.

Children Allowed?

Some communities will exclude children, for a variety of reasons. Some will be "unsuitable" for children because of sexual content; some will simply be adult by default because most Byzantine-art experts or nuclear physicists are adults. But in many cases children may operate successfully and undetected in adults-only communities, showing more maturity than many adults. (Those Byzantine-art experts can get pretty nasty when they disagree!)

Privacy

Communities will also vary in the level of privacy their members expect. What will people be expected to reveal about themselves or other people? What kinds of "omissions" are permissible? What is okay within the group, but should not be revealed to outsiders? Privacy on a commercial basis ideally should be handled through decentralized market mechanisms. But privacy among people within a community will be decided community by community, just as in the Online Europe group. How these decisions are made and what they are is part of the identity of each community. Members will take their own norms into account when they decide what to say. Of course, there will be conflicts and broken trust, just as there are when people break confidences, rat on their former employers, or gossip in real fife. (The difference is that the impact can spread farther and faster online.)

Community members will also share opinions about everything from people to commercial products, schools, and of course acceptable content, both in unstructured postings and conversation, and in more formal rating systems and services using technology designed for the task. Indeed, some communities will form around people who electronically express common opinions and interests and are matched through such rating services, whether commercial or not-for-profit.

Trust Me!

One basic value of a community is trust among its members. In the end, informal disclosures rather than ones mandated by rules, and shared experiences and discussions, create real communities. People can't live by rules alone, and that's why they will inevitably congregate in the company of other people whose presence they enjoy. Cyberspace is just one more place where they can do that, unfettered by the strictures of time and place. But in the end, many are likely to seek one another out in the physical world as well. You just can't share a sunset, a hot tub, or a hot meal over the Net.

Notes

[1] This compelling snip of text is courtesy of Amy Bruckman, a grad student at MIT who runs the MediaMOO online community.

[2] The one time I tried to register to vote I was told I had to go to some office with my birth certificate and passport, because I was born in Switzerland, even though I've been a U.S. citizen since childhood. I don't *have* my birth certificate and it just seemed so complicated that I gave up. I feel a little embarrassed about it; my only lame excuse is that I have had other priorities. I now *have* sent in a form to register, but I haven't voted yet.

[3] Even in the physical world, the government doesn't entirely control the community. A city may think it "owns" the city streets, but at some point, if the government doesn't do its job, the citizens may take those streets back, with their own neighborhood associations or their own vigilante groups. But that process is much slower and more dangerous than what happens in cyberspace.

[4] What's the difference between a tax and a user/membership fee? Basically, one is required and the other is optional. Is the fee we pay to Microsoft for Windows really closer to a tax we pay for the sheer benefit of membership in a Microsoft-dominated world?

[5] But in fact, way too much information is classified, most of it probably "dangerous" only to the officials involved.

Appendix

Joanne Cavallaro is Director of Writing Programs and Assistant Professor of English at the College of St. Catherine where she teaches writing and linguistics courses. She has degrees from the University of California, Berkeley; San Francisco State University; and the University of Minnesota and has taught at San Francisco State University; Hunter College, NY; University of Minnesota; Marie Curie Slowkowska University, Lublin, Poland; and the College of St. Catherine. Her areas of specialization include sociolinguistics, pragmatics, gender linguistics and composition studies.

How Writing Works

Joanne Cavallaro

Writing is a complex process. Indeed, it often seems mysterious or magical to people who don't write much. Often, people assume that a good writer is somehow born that way. Well, some people may be born with a talent for putting words together in interesting and evocative ways, but most good writers, whether published novelists or good student writers, have learned how to write through practice and feedback. Writing is a skill anyone can learn. We may not all end up published writers, but we can all learn enough to handle well any writing task we may encounter in college or on the job.

"How do I know what I think until I see what I say?"—E. M. Forster

Writing is a process of discovery. Despite what you may have been told before, most writers, when they start a project, do not usually have a complete picture of what they will write. Generally, they discover what it is they want to say as they go through the process of writing. They gather ideas and facts, start writing, see where the writing leads them, get feedback, write some more, get more facts and ideas, write again, revise, rewrite, change, add, delete, edit.

This process may seem messy and meandering, but if you learn to trust it, it works. Writing helps us give form to thought. When we try to write something down, we soon discover whether we really understand it or not. When we write our ideas down, we can examine them from different angles; we can question them, see where they lead us. By writing, we not only discover what we have to say, we also learn to say it better.

Sometimes writing takes place far away from pen and paper, or computer and printer. As we drive to school, wait for the bus, stand in line for a sandwich at the Grill, we can continue to work on our writing by thinking about it. Many of the best introductions I have written have come to me as I've showered in the morning. They've just popped into my head, probably because I went to bed the night before thinking about what I was writing. I also constantly write down ideas for papers on napkins, receipts, anything I find handy when an idea appears. Good writers often continue to work at their writing even away from the desk.

Good writers also know that writing is hard work. Someone once said that writing a college essay is cognitively one of the hardest things most of us are ever asked to do. The hard work comes from thinking things out. And it's only when we've written down our ideas and tried to develop them that we can see if they make sense and are worth keeping.

> "I suffer always from fear of putting down that first line. It is amazing the terrors, the magics, the prayers, the straightening shyness that assails one."
> —John Steinbeck

Sometimes the hardest part about writing is just getting started, so many writers use "tricks" to get started and keep themselves going to produce a first draft. The following section includes a list of some of these tricks that might be useful to you. Most writers know that they will be able to work things out if they just get started and keep going. They know they will revise their first drafts, so they don't need to worry about getting it all perfect the first time. In fact, they know that the quest for perfection early in the process will stymie their creativity and thinking. They write freely for the first draft, not worrying about spelling and punctuation for now. And they know that if they hit a stumbling block, they can mark it on the draft and come back to it later when they revise.

Planning what you want to write before you begin your draft helps make the writing easier, so most writers have some sort of plan before they sit down to write their draft. It may be an outline, or it may be a list of ideas on a sheet of scratch paper. They use the information they have gathered before they started to write the draft to help them create their plan. And for most writers, whatever plan they produce is tentative. Since we usually discover more about our topic as we write, any plan needs to be flexible, able to be refined and revised during the process of writing.

> "I have never thought of myself as a good writer. Anyone who wants reassurance of that should read one of my first drafts. But I'm one of the world's great revisers."—James Michener

Writing is rewriting, as Donald Murray says. Good writing rarely appears full blown on a first draft. To produce strong writing, writers have to revise, often going through several drafts. Hemingway claimed he rewrote the ending to *A Farewell to Arms* 39 times. When asked why, he answered, "To get the words right." Revising is an opportunity to get the words right. It's also an opportunity to gain an entirely new perspective on your subject, an opportunity to delve more deeply into your ideas. It may mean adding lots of new material or cutting out lots of stuff you've already written (always a difficult thing to do!). It may mean moving things around or rewriting whole sections. It may mean starting all over. The following section contains some strategies that might be useful for you as you revise.

"Well, it's a beautiful feeling, even if it's hard work."—Anne Sexton

Writing the Draft

As you write your first draft, it is best to focus on what you want to say first and worry about how it looks later. Remember, this is a draft so you will have an opportunity to go back and change it later. If you find that you worry so much about spelling and mechanics that you sometimes forget what you were trying to say, it might be best to stop worrying about those things for now. Worry about spelling and punctuation and precise word choice and other sentence-level matters only after you're satisfied that you've said what you want to say. It's not very efficient to stop and carefully fix all the possible errors in a paragraph that you may well delete later when you revise. Leave the editing until later.

1. Focus on your ideas first. As you write your draft, keep rereading what you've written and ask yourself: What am I trying to tell my reader? What's my point, my story here? What else needs to be added? What's no longer necessary? If you're stuck for a word or a transition, leave a blank or a mark that will remind you to come back to that spot later.

2. Allow yourself time. If a paper is due next week, start it this week, even if you don't yet have all the data or ideas you want. Beginning to write, if only for 10 minutes, will start the incubation process in your own mind. You'll find that once you start it, you'll actually be working on the paper in your subconscious as you go through your day. Plan to do more than one draft; very few writers can create a good paper in their first draft.

3. Imagine a real audience as you write and revise. Think of your classmates or teacher as your audience unless you have a more specific audience you are writing to. Ask yourself what information they will need in order to follow what you're trying to say. You already know that information and probably take it for granted; does your audience know it? If not, put it in.

4. Play with titles, introductions, and conclusions. These are important, highly visible points in any paper. Provocative titles catch readers' attention; good introductions keep readers going; strong conclusions leave strong memories in readers' minds. But these same elements work on the writer as well as the reader, for a good title, introduction or conclusion

can suggest changes for what follows or precedes. Sometimes these elements come early in the process, as controlling ideas. Sometimes they come later. In any case, they can capture the essence of your paper, telling you what to keep and what to cut.

5. Use a word processor. Some people write out their first draft by hand and then type it on a computer. Others compose directly onto the computer. Use whatever way suits you best, but do use a computer. Computers make all the difference when it comes to making changes easy. You can move things around, add and delete easily. When writers go to revise their drafts, most find it more efficient to print the drafts out and read them on paper rather than on the screen. It is much easier to see the whole picture when you read it on paper. It's also easier on paper to find your mistakes when you come to the editing and proofreading stage.

Some General Strategies for Revision

Once you've written your draft, take some time away from it; let it rest for a few hours at least. If you can, leave it overnight or a few days before you look at it again. That way, you can approach it more objectively, the way your reader will, without already knowing exactly what it says.

You may already have some ideas about what you want to change in your draft. That's a good place to start. Even if you do know what you want to change, it's a good idea to sit down and reread the entire thing, making notes as you go along.

Re-Reading Your Draft

1. Read the whole thing first. Read it straight through to see what it says, to find its central point. You may be surprised to find that it doesn't say exactly what you thought you were saying. That's OK right now. At this point, it's helpful to first get an overall sense of what your draft actually says. One way to do this is to outline your draft. The outline needn't be too detailed, just one that summarizes the main point of each paragraph. In addition to an outline, try writing down what the purpose of your essay is, who the audience is, and what strategy you have used in each paragraph to achieve your purpose (in other words, what each paragraph does). Jot down problem areas or things to return to later. As you read, keep asking yourself, "What am I trying to say here?"

2. Try to read the draft as your reader would. Remember, your reader doesn't know everything that was in your head as you wrote the essay. As you read, you might know the background information necessary to fully understand your points, but will the reader know that information?

Ask yourself what information the reader needs to know that you take for granted.

3. It's difficult to be objective about one's own writing, so getting someone else to read your draft is very helpful. Give it to a friend, or even better take it to the Writing Center. Either way, ask your reader or tutor to tell you if there are any parts that are difficult to understand, that need more elaboration, more support. Are there any connections that are not clear? Start by asking about the clarity and development of your ideas; leave the grammar issues for later. Make notes on the paper as you listen to your readers' reactions. Most good writers ask others to read and react to their work before the final copy is due.

Revising Your Draft

When you sit down to revise, don't try to do it all at once. Break the process up into stages. Look at the whole first and then move on to parts.

1. Start with the big picture, the main points, your overall purpose. Think about what you want to say. Does the draft say what you want it to? Is your thesis clear? Can the reader tell easily what your main points are? Do you develop your ideas enough? Do you support your points rather than just state them? Do you need to add more information? Have you thought through your ideas thoroughly? What are you really trying to say? Have you said it? Have you said it all?

Writers often don't get to the point they really want to make until the end of the first draft. If that happens to you, if you find you've gotten to your main point at the end of the draft, then use that main point. Begin a new draft with that point as your thesis. Use ideas and information from your first draft if they're relevant, but don't be afraid to throw things out if they don't belong. Cutting our own words is often hard to do, but almost always necessary. If you find it difficult, create a file (on your computer or in a file folder) and put the sentences or phrases you cut into this file to be used in a later paper.

2. Check your writing for clarity and coherence. Can your reader easily follow what you are saying? Is the organization logical? Is it clear to the reader as well as to you? Are there transitions that show the connections among your ideas?

3. Move on to style only after you have made your major revisions. Look at your sentences. Do you like the way they sound? Is your tone appropriate to your content? Reading your essay out loud is helpful in really hearing what you have said. Try reading it aloud to a friend or to a tutor in the Writing Center; you'll be amazed at how much you notice about your own writing style.

4. Finally, proofread for grammatical errors. It's best to leave this stage until the end; after all, what's the use of correcting sentences that you may well change later? Also, too much attention to errors too early in the writing process can limit your ideas and creativity. As with revision, it's more effective if you leave some time after you've written the final draft to read it over for spelling, punctuation, mechanics, grammar.

Using Your Instructor's Comments

If you are lucky enough to have an instructor who will read and comment on your draft, use the comments wisely. They are an indication of what your instructor thinks is important. When you receive your draft back, read it and the comments over carefully. Start with the substantive comments, ones about your ideas, about how well you explain them, about how clearly you state them. If you do not understand any comment, ask your instructor for clarification. If you are still unsure or if you cannot ask your instructor, bring the draft to the Writing Center.

As with revision in general, work on the big things first, the content, organization and clarity. If there are questions in the comments, be sure you have answered them in your revision. This may mean adding more information, elaborating on the ideas you already have, or even doing more research.

Once you have revised your essay to your satisfaction and have addressed the comments of your instructor, go on to look at the errors corrected or comments about grammar and usage. You may well have changed the sentence the original correction was in, but look at the correction anyway and see if you understand why your instructor made it. What was the error? How can you correct it? How can you work to avoid that error next time you write?

Remember, you are not your draft. When other people comment on your work, especially when they criticize it, they are not attacking or criticizing you. They are merely commenting on a draft, on an unfinished product, not on you.

Helen Humeston has taught in the Information Management and Master of Library Science program at the College of St. Catherine since 1995. She holds a Ph.D. in History from the University of Minnesota and a MLIS degree from the University of Wisconsin. She is the author of several articles and writes mystery stories on the side. Dr. Humeston lives in St. Paul with Mac the Cat.

Thinking about Using the Library

Helen Humeston

Introduction

When you begin researching the structured controversy assignment, you may feel as if you are trying to harness an octopus. As soon as you grasp one part, the thing seems to move in seven other directions at once. The purpose of this article is to help you to take control of the research process. Remember, no one is born knowing how to do research. Most of us have learned through long, sometimes painful, experience. I hope that by offering you a few tips, your research will be both efficient and effective.

Three major issues will be addressed: choosing a topic, designing an effective research strategy, and evaluating sources. This is intended only as a general introduction to library research. For more detail, I recommend Thomas Mann's *The Oxford Guide to Library Research.* New York: Oxford University Press, 1998.

Choosing a Topic

It is, unfortunately, easy to write a bad paper on a good topic. It is much more difficult to write a good paper on a bad topic. Your choice of which controversial issue to present is crucial. There are three basic questions you should ask yourself about your topic. First, is this issue interesting? You will be working on this project for several weeks, so the topic should engage you at some level. If, moreover, the subject bores you, the chances are that your audience will respond to it in the same way.

Second, are there at least two clearly opposing views on the issue? If not, there is no controversy. In several of my TRW classes, teams discovered that there was overwhelming support for one side of a topic and virtually none on the other. The pros and cons of tribal fishing rights in Minnesota is a case in point. The team advocating tribal fishing rights had no difficulty in finding evidence to support their side, even though most of the articles were published in a newspaper designed for Native Americans. The opposing team was hard pressed to find any information about why tribal fishing rights should be abolished or curtailed. A little preliminary research should tell you whether there is enough information about both sides of the topic to constitute a controversy.

The third question is whether you can cover the major points of the issue in the time allotted. Students usually find that they must narrow their topics to fit the amount of class time used for presentations. Obviously it is more efficient to refine the topic before you have spent a great deal of time looking for information and taking notes.

The best way to determine whether the issue is interesting, controversial, and manageable is to look up a few articles about it in general encyclopedias such as *Encyclopedia Americana, Britannica,* or the *American Academic Encyclopedia.* Most encyclopedias give a brief overview of the topic, list the major issues involved, and include a few recommended readings. Even more importantly, encyclopedia articles will give you terms that you can use when researching the topic. If your subject is not included in the general encyclopedias, try looking in some of the specialized, or subject, encyclopedias. There are special encyclopedias on virtually every academic discipline, such as the *Encyclopedia of Religion, Encyclopedia of Philosophy, Encyclopedia of Psychology, Encyclopedia of Social Sciences* and many more. There are, however, no encyclopedias of abortion, gun control, assisted-suicide, or similar issues. You may find articles on these topics in the special encyclopedias listed above or in other special encyclopedias. Ask a reference librarian for help in locating a useful encyclopedia that may include information on your topic.

If encyclopedias are the best place to begin reading about your topic, the World Wide Web is the worst. The reason is that you will probably find too much information, which may or may not be accurate, and seldom provides the kind of overview of the topic that you need before you begin your research. There are, however, some Internet-based resources such as *FirstSearch* that you may wish to consult in the early stages of your work.

Diagramming the Research Strategy

You probably would not start driving across the country without a map. For the same reason, you should design a map or diagram to guide your research. The purpose of doing a diagram is to assure that you are connecting the research topic or thesis statement to the types of library materials that are likely to contain the information that you are seeking and to the access tools that you can use to locate this information. There are four basic steps to diagramming a research strategy as listed below.

Step 1

Write your topic or thesis statement in the center of a sheet of paper and draw a circle or oval around it. Underline the key terms. Leave space at the top of the page to write subject headings from *Library of Congress Subject Headings* and/or another thesauri such as *ERIC, The Thesaurus of Psy-*

chological Index Terms, etc. Getting the right subject headings is vital to the success of your search. Reference librarians will be happy to help you. Please see Figure 1. I am using homeschooling only as an example. Your topic and sources may be quite different, but the general approach should be applicable. Although I am illustrating how to diagram a research project in four steps, each builds upon the previous one. By the end of this exercise, you will have only one page that should look like Figure 4.

Figure 1

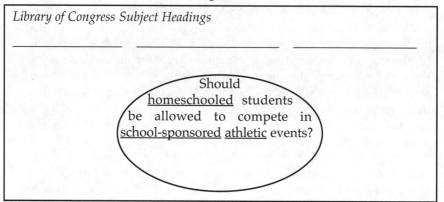

Library of Congress Subject Headings

Should homeschooled students be allowed to compete in school-sponsored athletic events?

Step 2

The next step is to think about all of the possible *types* of library materials that might offer information on your subject. Arrange these around the periphery of the oval in the center of the page. Background sources include encyclopedias, almanacs, and other general reference works that you might consult early in the research process.

I have not included Internet resources here because there are so many of them and they are so diverse. I found, for example, more than one hundred thousand Web sites on the topic or homeschooling alone. This is not good news for a harried TRW student who is trying to get the research finished in a reasonable amount of time.

Figure 2

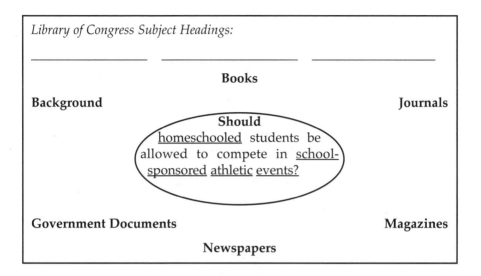

Library of Congress Subject Headings:

Books

Background

Journals

Should homeschooled students be allowed to compete in school-sponsored athletic events?

Government Documents

Magazines

Newspapers

Step 3

The third step is to jot down some titles of materials that you might examine. You might not know the exact title, particularly of books. That is fine, because you are merely trying to brainstorm about possible areas of inquiry. This task may seem rather difficult at first, but you can always add or delete titles later. "CSC Periodical and Subject Heading List" can be very helpful in locating periodicals. The first half of this source lists all of the journals and magazines in the CSC libraries in alphabetical order. The second half arranges them according to academic discipline.

Figure 3

Library of Congress Subject Headings:

_____ _____ _____

Other lists of subject headings:

ERIC

_____ _____ _____

Books

> **Should** homeschooled students be allowed to compete in school-sponsored athletic events?

Background
Encyclopedia Americana
Academic American Encyclopedia
International Encyclopedia of Education
West's Encyclopedia of Law

Journals
Journal of Education
Journal of Psychology

Government Documents
U.S. Department of Education
Congressional Information Service
Minnesota Legislative documents
Court cases

Magazines
Time
Newsweek
U.S. News & World Report

Newspapers
Education newsletters
New York Times
Los Angeles Times
Washington Post
Wall Street Journal
Christian Science Monitor

Step 4

The final step is the one that will save you the most time. This involves
thinking of indexes that will help you to find information quickly. Nearly
everything in a library is indexed somewhere if you know where to look.

Figure 4

Library of Congress Subject Headings:

_____ _____ _____

Other lists of subject headings:

ERIC

_____ _____ _____

Books
(Online catalog)
(Bibliography of Bibliographies)

> Should
> homeschooled students be
> allowed to compete in school-
> sponsored athletic events?

Background	**Journals**
Encyclopedia Americana	*Journal of Education*
Academic American Encyclopedia	*Journal of Psychology*
International Encyclopedia of Education	Homeschooling Journal?
West's Encyclopedia of Law	School Athletics Journal?
(Ask at the reference desk)	*(Ulrich's International Periodicals Directory)*
(*ERIC* on CD-ROM)	
(*First Stop: The Master Index to*	*(Social Science Index)*
Subject Encyclopedias)	*(Education Index/Abstracts)*
(ARBA Guide to Subject Encyclopedias)	
(Guide to Reference Books)	

Government Documents	**Magazines**
U.S. Department of Education	*Time*
Congressional Information Service	*Newsweek*
Minnesota Legislative documents	*U.S. News & World Report*
Court cases	
(Monthly Catalog of U.S.	On CD-ROM:
Government Publications)	*The Magazine Index;*

```
(CIS/Index)                                          Business Index:
(LEXIS on CD-ROM)                                    InfoTrac; General
                                                   Periodicals Index;
                                             Expanded Academic Index
                                                              NEXIS)
                          Newspapers
                     Education Newsletters
                       New York Times
                       Los Angeles Times
                       Washington Post
                       Wall Street Journal
                     Christian Science Monitor
       Many of the newspapers are indexed in the sources for
       magazines or see National Newspaper Index.
```

Once you have read a few background articles in reference books and have sketched a diagram to guide your research, you are ready to begin finding materials. A reference librarian is an invaluable ally as you begin looking for information on your topic. No one knows better than a librarian that libraries are not particularly easy to use. People become reference librarians because they want to help others to find the information they need. Librarians will not think that you are stupid if you ask a question. The worst way to use a library is to spend an inordinate amount of time looking for something when a librarian can put you on the right track in a few minutes.

Evaluating Sources

One of the most daunting questions in research is whether the information found is trustworthy. The fact is virtually everything that is written is biased, if only because of what the author chose to omit. Most writers, moreover, have a particular point of view and are trying to persuade readers to accept the author's position. There is nothing wrong with taking a stance. Using inaccurate or misleading information to support an argument is, of course, intellectually dishonest.

Most encyclopedias, scholarly journals, and books published by reputable publishing houses go through a thorough editorial review. Editors know that their publications must be accurate or they will not be in business very long. Please note, however, that the information contained in these sources is out of date by as much as a year by the time of publication. That means any kind of statistical data about a current topic will probably not be accurate.

Well-known magazines and newspapers are reasonably reliable, although many have an editorial slant. Larger problems occur with small newsletters directed to a targeted audience. Bubba Smith's *The Commies in Washington Are Trying to Take Our Guns Away*, for example, will not present an even-handed treatment of gun control.

There are no checks on what individuals post on the Web. You may, of course, use these sources but you should weigh them against what you have read in more conventional publications.

Government documents can be a cornucopia of excellent information. Finding the documents is not always easy. Please refer to the list in Figure 4 for sources that can help you to begin to search government publications.

Conclusion

I hope that this brief survey of how to research the structured controversy assignment has provided some useful tips on choosing a topic, designing a research strategy, and evaluating sources. You control the process. Now you know how to harness an octopus.

The O'Neill Center for Academic Development is the College of Saint Catherine's academic support department. The Writing Center's talented writing assistants have taken The Reflective Woman *and are available to assist you with questions about your TRW papers and about proper documentation.*

Avoiding Plagiarism

O'Neill Center for Academic Development

Plagiarism is the act of passing off someone else's work as your own. It includes such dishonest practices as buying, borrowing or stealing a paper to turn in as your own or simply copying someone else's words without putting them in quotation marks and identifying the author and source. Most students are not so dishonest as to buy or steal a paper. Many students, however, inadvertently plagiarize because they do not realize that what they are doing is, in fact, plagiarism and thus dishonest. Avoiding plagiarism is much more complicated than simply not copying other people's work.

In an attempt to avoid plagiarizing, students often paraphrase the passages they want to use. Basically, paraphrasing is stating something in different words. As such, it is a useful device. The problem is that it can lead you to unintentional plagiarism if it is not done properly. Changing a few words in a passage and then using it in your paper without documentation is plagiarism. Changing a few words and then using it in your paper even *with* proper documentation is also plagiarism. When you paraphrase other people's ideas, you have two choices: 1) you may quote the passage exactly, put it in quotation marks, and cite it; or 2) you may change the wording of the passage so that the ideas are explained substantially in your own words and cite it. Anything in between is plagiarism.

One reason some students inadvertently plagiarize is the pressure they feel to come up with new ideas, to be original, even with topics that they know little about. In academic settings such as college courses, it is difficult if not impossible to come up with totally original ideas, especially on topics with which you are unfamiliar. When an instructor asks for original thinking, she often means thinking through ideas to find your own perspective on them and then expressing those ideas in your own way. In doing so, you may and often should use other people and their ideas to add to or support your own. When you do so, however, you must give them credit.

Some examples might help at this point. Below are several paraphrases of some material. Two constitute plagiarism; the third shows one correct way of using other people's ideas.

The original material:

> It is not generally recognized that at the same time when women are making their way into every corner of our work-world, only one percent of the professional engineers in the nation are female. A generation ago this statistic would have raised no eyebrows, but today it is hard to believe. The engineering schools, reacting to social and governmental pressures, have opened wide their gates and are recruiting women with zeal. The major corporations, reacting to even more intense pressures, are offering attractive opportunities to practically all women engineering graduates.

> from Samual C. Florman, "Engineering and the Female Mind,"
> *Harper's Magazine* (1974)

Case 1: Overt Plagiarism

> Because women seem to be taking jobs of all kinds, few people realize that only 1 percent of the professional engineers in the nation are female. A generation ago this would have raised no eyebrows, but today it is hard to believe. The engineering schools, reacting to social and governmental pressures, have opened wide their gates and are recruiting women with zeal. The major corporations, reacting to even more intense pressures, are offering attractive opportunities to practically all women engineering graduates.

After adding a bit to the first sentence, the writer here merely copies the original source word for word, an obvious case of plagiarism. And she doesn't even cite her source! She could avoid plagiarism here by putting quotation marks around the borrowed passage and citing her source. The problem is that there is no pressing reason to quote this passage, and if she does this often, she will produce a paper full of quotations, a paper that has more of other people than of her. Not a good thing.

Case II: Plagiarism Caused by Improper Paraphrasing

> Few people realize, now that women are making inroads into every corner of the work-world, only a small percentage (1%) of professional engineers in the United States are female. A generation ago, this fact would not have surprised anyone, but today it is hard to believe. Engineering schools, reacting to pressure from the government and society, are recruiting women with zeal. And many major corporations, reacting to even more pressures, offer attractive employment opportunities to just about any women who is an engineering graduate.

Although this writer does not copy word for word, she only substitutes her own words in a few cases and does not substantially change the original. The ideas appear in the same order and are expressed in basically the same words. She also does not cite her source. Again, this is plagiarism. She could improve this by acknowledging and citing her source, something she must do to be academically honest. Even with that improvement, however, the charge of plagiarism would still stand because the expression is not substantially her own.

Case III: Proper Paraphrasing

> In the last twenty years, women certainly have made great gains in the world of employment. There are now more women working as doctors, lawyers, legislators, and janitors than probably ever before. In one area, however, they still lag far behind men, at least in terms of numbers in the field. That area is engineering. Samuel Florman (1974) points out that of all the professional engineers in the U.S., only one percent are women. He adds that engineering schools and major corporations alike have responded to social and governmental pressure to increase the number of female engineers from this surprisingly low rate. They are now actively recruiting women into both the schools and the corporations.

This writer weaves the information supplied by Florman into her own paragraph, paraphrases it and gives proper credit to him through her citation. She summarizes Florman's ideas so that they fit in with hers and then acknowledges that she has done so.

If you have any questions about how to use your sources without plagiarizing, talk to your instructor or go to the Writing Center (basement of the Chapel). The Writing Center has tutors to help you and additional handouts about citing your sources.

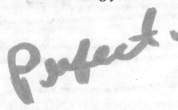

Perfect.

Acknowledgments

Acknowledgments

pp. 2–9: Presentation for the College of St. Catherine Faculty/Staff Workshop, August 30, 1994, by Joan Mitchell, CSJ.

pp. 10–28: From *More Than a Dream: Eighty-five Years at the College of St. Catherine* by Rosalie Ryan, CSJ and Joan Christine Wolkerstorfer. Copyright © 1992 by the College of St. Catherine, St. Paul, Minnesota.

pp. 29–32: From *On Lies, Secrets, and Silence: Selected Prose 1966–1978* by Adrienne Rich. Copyright © 1979 by W. W. Norton and Company. Reprinted by permission of the publisher.

pp. 40–45: From *Listen Up: Voices from the Next Feminist Generation* by Sonja D. Curry-Johnson. Copyright © 1995 by Seal Press.

pp. 46–51: Copyright © 1990 by Amy Tan. First appeared in *The Threepenny Review*. Reprinted by permission of the author and the Sandra Dijkstra Literary Agency.

pp. 52–55: "Being Poor: A Look Inside This Secret Society" by Alia Ganaposki appeared in *About Campus*, November/December 2001. Copyright © 2001 by John Wiley and Sons, Inc. Reprinted by permission of the publisher via The Copyright Clearance Center.

pp. 62–68: "You're Short Besides!" by Sucheng Chan, as appeared in *Making Waves: An Anthology of Writings by and about Asian American Women*, edited by Asian Women United. Copyright © 1989 by Sucheng Chan. Reprinted by permission of the author.

pp. 69–70: Copyright © 1980, 1987 by Lucille Clifton. First appeared in *Two-Headed Woman*, published by The University of Massachusetts Press, 1980. Now appears in *Good Woman: Poems and a Memoir 1969–1980*, published by BOA Editions, Ltd. Reprinted by permission of Curtis Brown, Ltd.

pp. 71–84: "Cathedral" reprinted by permission of International Creative Management, Inc. Copyright © 1981 by Raymond Carver.

pp. 93–97: Reprinted with permission of Simon & Schuster Adult Publishing Group from *Boundaries* by Maya Lin. Copyright © 2000 by Maya Lin Studio, Inc.

pp. 98–106: From *Language and Art in the Navajo Universe* by Gary Witherspoon. Copyright © 1977 by University of Michigan Press. Reprinted by permission of the publisher.

pp. 107–109: As appeared in *Public Art Review*, Spring/Summer 1995. Copyright © 1995 by Forecast Public Artworks. Reprinted by permission of the publisher via the Copyright Clearance Center.

Author Index

Author Index